D1095143

On Firm Foundation Grounded

On Firm Foundation Grounded

The First Century
of
Concordia College (1891–1991)

Carroll Engelhardt

Concordia College
901 South Eighth Street
Moorhead, Minnesota 56562

Printed in the United States of America

printing number
2 3 4 5 6 7 8 9 10

Library of Congress Cataloging in Publication Data

Engelhardt, Carroll
    On firm foundation grounded: the first century of
Concordia College/ Carroll Engelhardt.
    414 p.
    Includes index.
    ISBN 0–9630111–0–3
    1. Concordia College (Moorhead, Minn.)—History. 2.
Lutheran universities and colleges—Minnesota—History.
I. Concordia College (Moorhead, Minn.). II. Title.
LB1281.C30672E57 1991
378.776'86—dc20

DEDICATION

"It is ... a small college, and yet there are those that love it."

—Daniel Webster
Dartmouth College v. Woodward (1819)

To Family—
for all those Cobbers
and for the women in my life:

Ruby, Jo, Kristen and Rachel—

Mother, Spouse, Daughters

CONTENTS

PART I
From Academy to College, 1891–1925

PART II
President J.N. Brown, 1925–1951:
The College Established, Maintained and Expanded

PART III
President Joseph L. Knutson, 1951–1975:
Managing Growth and Maintaining Christian Integrity

PART IV
President Paul J. Dovre, 1975–
Continuing Mission, Enhancing Quality
and Maintaining Accessibility

FOREWORD

This Centennial history has its own story. The *Cobber Chronicle*, its precursor, was prepared in celebration of the college's 75th anniversary. It provided both context and inspiration for the current project and we acknowledge its author, Erling Nicolai Rolfsrud, with thanks. In 1981 a group of interested persons was invited to begin conversation about the task of preparing the college's Centennial history. It was agreed that the college's archives needed to be properly organized, expanded and maintained; that a systematic effort should be made to expand the college's oral history file; and, finally, that an early appointment should be made for the preparation of the official Centennial history. Dr. Carroll Engelhardt, professor of history at the college since 1970, accepted the assignment as principal researcher and author in 1985 and devoted most of the following summers as well as a sabbatical leave in 1989–90 to the preparation of this volume. This history is a testimony to Dr. Engelhardt's rigorous work ethic and his high professional standards.

In welcoming the reader to this volume, one is mindful of the many purposes and the multifaceted character of history. History may entertain, inform, and help us shape the future. In Israel the exiles sought a better life for themselves and their children. In response the prophet Isaiah told them that they should "look to the rock from which you were hewn, and to the quarry from which you were dug." (Isaiah 51:1) That imagery is appropriate for a college whose hymn and history both speak of "firm foundation." While being a Norwegian immigrant was not the same experience as being a Babylonian exile, Isaiah's words must have been a source of hope to the immigrants for whom the founding of Concordia was a way of endowing their tradition with permanence while providing for their children what they themselves lacked.

The book of Isaiah tells us something about the character of stories that are told about people called to be faithful to a sacred trust. First of all, the story of the Israelites was not ideal, it told of hard times and good times, it marked the internal divisions as well as the expressions of unity, it described the struggles with faith and purpose as well as moments of high resolve and achievement. All of this was part of the story of real people who struggled and sometimes triumphed and at other times failed. In similar vein this history of Concordia's first century includes the stories of triumph, tragedy and testing which make up our past.

The history is also like the story of the Israelites in that it is not so much an account of individuals and events as it is of larger purposes. So there will be untold stories behind each story that is included in this volume. And behind the major actors included in this story stand hundreds more including the students, faculty, staff and regents who exercised their vocations faithfully and often heroically; the parents whose sacrifices insured that their children would have an opportunity for a life fuller than their own; and the alumni and friends in the parishes, farms, communities and cities who would by word and act give witness to their confidence in the college.

The story of the Israelites also informs us about the purpose of this history: to prepare people for the future by recalling the lessons and the purpose of history itself. This Centennial history will enlighten and inspire as it tells the stories of commitment, sacrifice and steadfastness which mark this first century of Concordia's passage. This volume will instill pride as it details the college's transition from secondary academy to accredited college, from Depression survivor to one of the largest private under-graduate colleges in the Upper Midwest, from a local college to a college of regional, and in the case of some programs, national distinction.

But this Centennial history will serve its highest purpose and promise as it helps us see the rock on which the college is built, the rock of faith in the Gospel. Academic quality and Christian commitment are inseparable elements in the mission of Concor-dia. Concordia must always communicate the special truth of the Gospel within the academic community and do so with faithfulness, integrity and mutual respect. So as we look to the rock, to our *Soli Deo Gloria*, we find the theme of this story and the purpose for our future.

On behalf of the college, thanks are extended to those who guided and completed this volume, most especially Professor Engelhardt; to the cloud of witnesses living and triumphant to whom these pages bear witness; and to our firm foundation, Father, Son and Holy Spirit. "In strength and faith forever."

—Paul J. Dovre

PREFACE

A centennial history should be cause for celebration. After all, not many human institutions last a century. Concordia has not merely endured; it has prospered. If the founders could be brought back to life today, the physical appearance of the college would exceed their fondest dreams. Indeed, as we survey the parklike grounds and numerous buildings we assume that institutional survival and success were inevitable. This is an error. For much of its history, Concordia's survival has been problematic. Many other schools founded with similar high aspirations in the region and throughout the nation have long since vanished. That success was not assured, that Concordia's founders sometimes disagreed and often proceeded with little to sustain them except their faith and courage is an even greater cause for celebration. Of them it may be said as novelist Ole E. Rölvaag said of the Dakota pioneers, "They threw themselves blindly into the impossible and accomplished the unbelievable."[1]

Institutional histories are difficult to write. As Paul Conkin observed in his monumental work on Vanderbilt University, the historian cannot capture the unique experiences of everyone who has made up an institution throughout a century. Everyone has her or his experience embodied in favorite stories about the place. Whose stories does the historian tell? The thousands of Cobbers who have attended? The hundreds of faculty who have taught? The dozens of administrators who have led? The hundreds of regents who have governed? The thousands who have sustained the school through sending children or cash? As Conkin notes, images vary widely; what one knows may be only a fragment of the institution known by others.[2]

This history focuses on community, a point of convergence for millions of unique experiences at the school. Throughout its history, the college has defined itself as a community of God's people dedicated to Christian service through the vocation of education. The oft-heard phrases, "the Concordia family" and *Soli Deo Gloria*—"To God alone the glory"—express this concept of community. The former denotes that the church school is an extension of the Christian home. The latter enunciates the foundational belief of Christian faith and hope that have sustained the college through difficult and prosperous times. That this community is composed of humans who often fall short of their Christian aspirations makes their institutional achievements even more impressive.

This religiously defined educational community originated in the rural Norwegian communities of the Red River Valley. The history of Concordia therefore can highlight aspects of Norwegian ethnic experience, Norwegian assimilation into American society and the interaction of high and low culture. According to anthropologist Robert Redfield, all communities exhibit an interaction of the great tradition of the reflective few and the little tradition of the unreflective many. Concordia served as an intermediary for this interaction. As a private institution of higher learning owned by rural Norwegian Lutheran congregations, it reflected the unconscious folk traditions of those communities while it cultivated and transmitted the great traditions of civilization.[3]

As the foregoing suggests, I believe that a college history should reveal tendencies of the surrounding culture; I therefore have tried to set Concordia's development in the larger context of regional and national history. While pursuing this goal, I have attempted to write an honest account. Negative as well as positive features of Concordia's past are treated, because the most useful history is one which presents a full picture of the past, "warts and all." Neither students of American culture nor alumni and policy-makers can benefit from a sanitized, self-promotional narrative.

An historian accrues many debts, especially to librarians. My thanks to emeritae Anna Jordahl and the late Margaret Nordlie who began collecting materials long before the creation of a college archives. A special tribute is due Nordlie, who as the first archivist in 1980 began imposing order on the chaos of materials, and who contributed so much to the Concordia oral history project. Head librarian Verlyn Anderson and present archivist Sharon Hoverson have cheerfully assisted in countless ways. Archivists and librarians Joan Olson, Saint Olaf College, Charlotte Jacobson, Norwegian American Historical Association, Paul A. Daniels, Luther Northwestern Seminary, and Margaret Anderson, Augsburg College, generously provided aid and access to their holdings.

Non-librarians contributed much to the book. Jo Engelhardt patiently typed, photocopied, listened and in other ways shared the task. Intrepid student researcher William C. Block ('89), blessed with the critical awareness of a questioning mind, extended the breadth, depth and understanding of my research. Joseph Shaw, author of *History of St. Olaf College*, graciously discussed with me the problems of writing institutional histories. Erling Rolfsrud generously allowed use of his research materials for *Cobber Chronicle*; the materials and book both provided enormous assistance. Dr. Junald L. Rendahl, emeritus executive vice president, contributed not only his extensive knowledge of Concordia's history, but translated many documents from Norwegian and conducted numerous thoughtful interviews for the oral history project. President Paul Dovre early encouraged the collection of oral histories and other materials for the centennial history. My thanks to him also for his confidence in assigning me the project and his unstinting support. I am additionally indebted to Dovre, Rendahl, Anderson and Hoverson for reading and critiquing the manuscript; my thanks to many others for the same favor—Carl Bailey, David Danbom, Ray Farden, James Haney, James Hausmann, Harding Noblitt, Carl Lee, Walther Prausnitz, Richard Solberg and Olin Storvick. Jennifer Ristau ('93) searched the Concordia archives for the photographs in Parts I, II and III. John Borge, photo lab director, combed his files for the pictures in Part IV; I am also grateful for his permission to use so many of his own photographs in that section.

The good folks at Hetland Ltd. afforded immeassurable assistance. Doug Fliss designed the page layouts; Jennifer Nelson did the typography and compiled the index. Nancy Edmonds Hanson and Jennifer Nelson bore with patience the copy editor's burden of straightening out tangled prose and compelling a reluctant author to say what he meant. David Hetland created the cover, depicting the book's major themes.

This long list of acknowledgements cannot possibly repay my debts. It reveals that institutional histories are truly institutional projects. They are written only with considerable support and involvement. Appropriately therefore, this history of a community has been throughout a communal enterprise.

On Firm Foundation Grounded

Prologue

Toward 1891

Concordia College, founded by a small group of Norwegian Lutheran laity and pastors, opened in Moorhead on October 15, 1891. Seemingly a "local" occurrence, Concordia emerged from international and national events: trans-Atlantic Norwegian migration to America, settlement of the Red River Valley, creation of "little Norways" that began the process of assimilation into American life, synodical battles of Norwegian Lutheranism and national expansion of educational institutions.

Throughout most of the nineteenth century only the famine-stricken Irish exceeded the emigration rate of Norwegians who were pushed by overpopulation and economic crisis. Norway's population doubled from 883,440 in 1801 to 1,792,833 in 1875 due to peace, potatoes and smallpox vaccine as one bishop pithily explained. Infant and child mortality declined, as farmers increased areas of cultivation, productivity and dairy herds. Although the first group departed in 1825, modest economic growth delayed mass migration until forty years later when a combination of overpopulation, food shortages, mechanization and changing markets led to starvation, farm foreclosures, reduced demand for agricultural laborers and the decision to sell by small farmers who could not afford machinery. Industrialization and urbanization began relatively late; economic depressions occurred in the 1860s and 1880s, the decades of the largest emigration.[1]

In the period from 1825 to 1865, only 77,873 emigrated; of this number, slightly more than one-half left in the decade after 1856. This was followed by the even larger exodus of 110,896 between 1866 and 1873. Although the entire country was represented, most early migrants came from the inner fjord districts of West Norway and the eastern mountain valleys. Those in the 1860s originated primarily from East Norway where the economic crisis was most acute. Although a substantial number of independent landowners departed after 1865, most were landless renters, laborers and servants. From 1868 to 1875, for example, 22,000 out of 27,669 were from underprivileged classes. In general, patterns varied by region. Those that provided the greatest economic opportunity were least likely to experience large-scale internal or external emigration. Influenced by prospects at home and by access to information about opportunities elsewhere, some regions experienced internal migration to Norwegian cities or the coast; others pursued agricultural possibilities in the United States.[2]

If population increase and economic crisis pushed people from Norway, empty land and economic opportunity pulled them to the United States. Short of people and labor, midwestern states and railroads advertised for settlers in Europe. The "American letter," passed so often from hand to hand that a single missive might be copied one hundred times, stimulated "American fever" which became epidemic. Often letters were accompanied by prepaid tickets; in some years 40 percent received this aid. The reduction in fares brought on by the competition of steamship lines after the Civil War also facilitated movement.[3]

Ironically, the conservatism of Norwegian farmers may have prompted migration.

Their momentous decision to break with their homeland was predicated on a desire to perpetuate their rural life and cultural traditions. Their peopling of the rural Midwest in a process of three-stage chain migration demonstrates this conservatism and continuity of national customs. In the first stage, Norwegians moved to specific rural regions in colonies of kin and neighbors. Subsequent letters and remittances fostered further migration from their native region to the new Norway in America. Overcrowding prompted second-stage movement further west, where the process was repeated. The third stage occurred when others from the homeland were drawn directly to the recent settlement.[4]

Minnesota, the Red River Valley and Dakota Territory drew many Norwegians looking for land. Minnesota attracted more of the approximately 850,000 emigrants between 1825 and 1928 than any other state; it became a Norwegian-American population and cultural center and they became the state's third largest ethnic group. After 1851, different Norwegian parties moved into western Houston and eastern Fillmore Counties. From these core settlements they expanded west along the Iowa border, and only after 1865 did they move into districts north and northwest. With the arrival of the St. Paul and Pacific Railroad in the 1870s, the Red River Valley was the last major agricultural region in Minnesota to be developed, the third major area of Norwegian settlement and the most heavily settled by Norwegians.[5]

Norwegian interest in the valley began with trail-blazing journalist Paul Hjelm-Hansen, whose writings in 1869 about the ease of cultivating the rich, black, stoneless, stumpless prairie soil dispelled the myth of Great Plains as desert. The earliest settled first on the Minnesota side, then pushed across the river into North Dakota. These came not from Norway but from Norwegian settlements near St. Ansgar (Iowa), Coon Prairie (Wisconsin) and Fillmore and Goodhue Counties (Minnesota). The first European ethnic group in North Dakota, Norwegians initially settled the two eastern tiers of counties and then westward along the Great Northern Railroad. "Dakota Fever" of the 1880s, fostered by the rapid expansion of railroads, active publicity and a series of wet years, made North Dakota the most Norwegian state as they increased from ten (1870) to 73,744 (1900), nearly one-fourth of the total.[6]

Norwegians settled in the countryside and tended to remain there. Only slightly more than one-fourth lived in towns with more than 25,000 inhabitants in 1900, the lowest percentage among European immigrants. By 1920, 52 percent of the Norwegian-born and 65.4 percent of those with Norwegian ancestry were still rural. These communities centered on the church. Pastors frequently became undisputed leaders as congregations became tightly knit and all-encompassing institutions that provided—in addition to worship—opportunities for business and social life in the form of church suppers and picnics, youth societies, Ladies Aids and choirs. Under such circumstances, church membership promoted ethnic identity by segregating Norwegians from Yankees and other ethnic churches surrounded by their own national enclaves. Consequently, Norwegians retained their native cultural characteristics longer than other Scandinavians and remained theologically conservative by avoiding the social gospel and liberal theology evidenced by Yankee denominations. Temperance became their major social justice concern and sole concession to cooperation with other churches. Despite clerical opposition to the formation of an independent temperance society they feared might cause defections from Lutheranism, membership in the Norwegian Total Abstinence Society grew from 7,000 (1879) to 83,000 (1887).[7]

Although strongly attached to native traditions, Norwegian-American communities experienced cultural change and began the complex process of assimilation into American society. They participated in economic and political life, adopted standards of bourgeois respectability, entered the public schools, learned English, organized ecclesiastical synods and founded schools of their own.

In the economic sphere, where American environmental demands were great, change was rapid. As Norwegians succeeded economically and acquired more wealth, they accentuated bourgeois respectability. Greater emphasis was placed on moral propriety in courtship and on observing the two spheres in which men worked at tasks associated with the market and women managed the household. This concern should not be attributed solely to Americanization, however. In part it stemmed from emulating behavior patterns of gentlefolk in Norway. Observing that wealthy women did not work in the fields in Norway, Norwegian-American magazines urged that this pattern be observed in the United States as well. Similarly, American middle-class women in market centers, for whom many Norwegians worked as servants, offered another example of bourgeois domesticity.[8]

Norwegian-Americans were strongly committed to education and willingly became bilingual. They often adopted English as the language of commerce and politics but preserved Norwegian, language of the heart, for home and church. Because most had learned to read in Norway through public schools and required confirmation in the state church, illiteracy was almost unknown. Most willingly entered the common schools to learn skills for making their way in American life, despite resistance of some clerical leaders. They founded schools of their own for religious instruction. A North Dakota Lutheran leader was surprised by the readiness of Norwegian parents to sacrifice for the education of their children. He "actually saw large families living in sod shacks on the open prairie" who were sending children to Concordia College. This patronage was duly noted by a Moorhead paper which early complimented Norwegian youth on their "fixed purpose to acquire an education."[9]

Politics represented another area of change and assimilation. By the 1880s, Norwegian-Americans were deeply involved in local and state politics. In the 1850s they had joined the Republican Party which for them represented Protestantism, high moral ideals, antislavery and prohibition; the Democrats were associated with Catholicism, corrupt machine politics, slavery and the saloon. Then farm protest in the 1880s and 1890s undermined Republican allegiance. The one-crop farmers of the Red River Valley and North Dakota, dependent on world wheat prices and railroad rate abuses, were often attracted to a succession of third-party political causes: Farmer's Alliance, Populists, the Non-Partisan League and the Farmer-Labor Party. Even those who remained Republican often gave support to progressives during the first two decades of the twentieth century. Theodore Roosevelt, president from 1901 to 1909 and Progressive Party presidential candidate in 1912, was a particular favorite. Participation in American reform movements had Norwegian roots. Many immigrants brought socialist ideas with them to the new land. Often socialists and other reformers drew on a tradition of communalism that characterized rural communities in Norway and the United States.[10]

Church divisions in the New World reflected religious differences in the old, but Lutherans in the American environment modified and adapted their European inheritance from the beginning. Divided by national origin, social class, place and time of settlement, lifestyle and doctrine, Lutherans in the late nineteenth century represented twenty-four different language groups and formed sixty-six independent organizations. Norwegian Lutherans, their religious milieu shaped by the State Church of

Norway and the pietistic revival movement begun in the eighteenth century by Hans Nielsen Hauge, contributed to this multiplicity. To simplify, their proliferation in the free air of the United States can be summarized in terms of three major groupings.[11]

The Haugean wing, splintered and poorly organized, had a greater impact and following than statistics show; there were Haugean pietists in all Norwegian settlements. Eventually they formed Hauge's Norwegian Evangelical Lutheran Synod in America (Hauge Synod) which in 1879 established Red Wing Seminary as its chief educational institution. The Haugeans distrusted a learned clergy and seventeenth-century Lutheran Scholasticism, encouraged an affective Christianity, stressed personal conversion and condemned all worldliness. In North Dakota, Hauge pastors tended to come from the more revivalistic and reform-minded areas of western Norway and from the less-educated lower classes.[12]

The state church group in 1853 created the Synod of the Norwegian Evangelical Lutheran Church in America (Norwegian Synod) and in 1861 founded Luther College. Within the free church framework adopted in the United States they retained many characteristic features of the state church: the liturgy and ecclesiastical dress of the Church of Norway, the prerogatives of ordained clergy, the Augsburg Confession's ban on lay preaching, scholastic theology and confessional authority on doctrinal questions. In North Dakota, Norwegian Synod pastors were more often from higher social strata and the conservative areas of eastern Norway. Early in its history, the Norwegian Synod developed close ties with the German Lutheran Missouri Synod and for a time trained ministers at Concordia Seminary in St. Louis.[13]

Those bodies of the third grouping, which eventually comprised the United Norwegian Lutheran Church, combined Haugean zeal with use of ministerial dress and the state church liturgy. Dissatisfied with the clericalism and dogmatism of the Synod and the emotional extremes of the Haugeans, a Norwegian-Swedish element in 1860 fashioned the Scandinavian Augustana Synod. In 1870 the Norwegians withdrew from this union and formed the Norwegian Augustana Synod and the Conference for the Norwegian-Danish Evangelical Lutheran Church in America (the Conference) which assumed control of Augsburg Seminary, founded in 1869. Then in the late 1880s, a theological controversy over election to salvation and a mixture of other issues divided the Norwegian Synod. One-third of the pastors and congregations withdrew in 1887 and formed the Anti-Missouri Brotherhood. The Anti-Missourians joined with the Norwegian Augustana Synod and the Conference in 1890 to create the United Norwegian Lutheran Church, the largest Norwegian-American synod at that time. In North Dakota, United Church pastors numbered 160 among the 350 immigrant clergy who served in the state between 1870 and 1915; they tended to be solidly middle class and to come from the eastern and more conservative areas of Norway. The United Synod soon adopted Saint Olaf College, and an association of synod members founded Concordia College in 1891.[14]

Although each main division of Norwegian Lutheranism supported its own theological school and divisive tendencies remained strong, a unity of faith and practice existed beneath the multiplicity. Lutherans shared an understanding of faith rooted in Luther's Small Catechism and Augsburg Confession which kept more pietistic synods in communication with the liturgical traditionalists. In addition, the freedom inherent in the American environment induced a growing unity of religious practice. By the turn of the century, Norwegian Synod pastors modified their churchly heritage to identify more closely with their parishioners and to join the Haugeans in condemning worldly pleasures of alcohol, card-playing and dancing. All three groups felt a moral obligation to develop a more inclusive Lutheran fellowship, but the United Church in particular represented a center in church life and thought around which the Hauge, Norwegian and United Synods finally united in 1917 to form the Evangelical Norwegian Lutheran Church. An ethnic appeal aided the merger; all synods readily agreed that it was desirable to have only one Norwegian Lutheran Church in America. Even so, merger probably had much greater support among ordinary parishioners than among some doctrinaire church leaders.[15]

Many members of the Norwegian and other national Lutheran groups formed voluntary associations and established their own schools. In this they did what representatives of other American church bodies had done from the beginning of settlement. College-founding accelerated with westward expansion. There were nine colleges when the American Revolution began. At the time of the Civil War there were 250, of which approximately 180 still survive. Perhaps another 700 were attempted and failed before 1860. Nineteenth-century college building was undertaken with the same "booster" spirit as community, canal and railroad building. Denominational competition contributed as members translated their religious differences into educational institutions state by state. This produced a large number of small, weakly supported colleges, and a high rate of failure.[16]

College-founding early manifested itself in regional settlement. Methodists created Red River Valley University (Wahpeton) in 1881; the Presbyterians, Jamestown College (1883), and the Congregationalists, Fargo College (1887) soon followed. Catholic academies opened at Fargo (1882), Jamestown (1890), Bismarck (1878) and several other places. Lutherans established Hope Academy in Moorhead (1888), Bruflat Academy in Portland (1889), Grand Forks College (1891), Concordia College (1891) and Park Region Luther College in Fergus Falls (1892). By 1912 North Dakota had two dozen private schools. A similar proliferation occurred in Minnesota. Virtually all Minnesota private colleges began as academies. These were maintained until college work was well-established and public high schools made them less necessary to prepare students for college-level work. Beginning as an academy which trained students for college was a sound, conservative approach to college building.[17]

Thus Concordia began as another educational institution among many founded by religiously-motivated groups. More specifically, it originated from the Norwegian Lutheran "academy movement" which began in the 1870s and peaked in the early 1900s. Stimulated by synodical competition, the movement established more than seventy-five secondary and normal schools in the Midwest, Pacific Northwest and Canada. Several—including Concordia, Saint Olaf, Gustavus Adolphus, Bethany and Pacific Lutheran—became colleges. Academies differed from the classical schools Lutherans had founded to prepare men for the ministry, but they were equally grounded in Lutheran educational philosophy. These transplanted Norwegians hailed "the Lutheran, an educating church." They emphasized that the Reformation was born in German universities, that Lutheranism was the parent of the modern popular systems of education, and that Lutheran nations had the lowest illiteracy rates in the world.[18]

To justify their claim about popular education, they appealed to the ideas of Martin Luther. Luther's doctrine of vocation led him to formulate an inclusive concept of education for life and service. Because the temporal community required well-educated men and women to assure its well-being, Luther urged the establishment everywhere of schools for both boys and girls. Academy proponents, inspired by Lutheran educational beliefs, advocated secondary schools offering both religious and secular instruction to prepare students to fulfill their duties as Christians and citizens in whatever secular vocation they pursued. Although academies which did not become colleges had mostly disappeared by the 1930s, they had served the church well by educating laity and providing preparatory training for nearly all Norwegian-American pastors between 1850 and 1925.[19]

A midwestern tradition of coeducational higher education and common schools combined with the Lutheran commitment to inclusive education to make Norwegian-American academies coeducational. Admission of women to academies and eventually to most Lutheran and other colleges did not mean equality in education, however. For some, coeducation merely offered a convenient way of increasing enrollment which kept private schools in business. The courses leading to the baccalaureate therefore long remained under male domination. By 1900, universities which had welcomed women when they represented economic salvation now worried that they might suffer the worse fate of feminization. To avoid this fate, schools segregated women in the "female disciplines." Women educational leaders responded to this pressure by seeking to combine a college education with the domestic ideology that woman's place was the home. Women were urged to embrace the social service occupations as compatible with their natures. Hence most female faculty and collegians were attracted to normal, commercial, domestic science, social work, music and art departments.[20]

The founding of Concordia College as a coeducational academy by a voluntary association of United Norwegian Lutheran Church laity and pastors was thus neither accidental nor merely local. The founding resulted from a complex cultural process set in motion by Norwegian emigration to America. Immigrants settled in "little Norways" that gradually adapted to American society and yet were strongly communal and deeply conservative in their attachment to land, customs, language and religion. Concordia and other Norwegian Lutheran colleges were similarly communal, theologically conservative and dedicated to bourgeois respectability. They long reflected a devotion to the low culture tradition of rural Norwegian-American communities while teaching the high culture tradition embodied in the Christian liberal arts. Founded to perpetuate a Norwegian-American Lutheran identity, these institutions from the beginning inculcated an ethic of service in the world and fostered assimilation to American life by teaching English, citizenship and other practical skills needed to assume leadership roles in their local and state communities. Thus educated, graduates often did not return to the "little Norways" from which they originated. Socially and geographically mobile, they entered into the wider American society.

PART I

From Academy to College, 1891–1925

*"Reaching the vicinity of the Comstock residence on Eighth
Street, I caught sight of the ... [Bishop Whipple School] as it
loomed up in its loneliness of prairie across the coulee. ... A large
space then containing scarcely a house, intervened between me
and the building. Beyond the structure to the south was not a
house to be seen. ..."*

— I.F. Grose (1920 reminiscence)

*"That Christianity thrives at our school, and that our school
thrives and grows with Christendom, bodes well for the future .
... This is of no little significance when we remember that we are
living in the midst of a materialistic period. We will not forget
that the fear of the Lord is instructive in all things. Our wish
and hope is that all instruction be penetrated with the power of
Christianity since only that power is strong enough to carry our
school into the future—thus can we know it to be secure!"*

— J.M.O. Ness (1895)

*"[The Christian school is designed] to make intelligent Christian
men and women, whatever may be their position or occupation in
the world—to make them a greater power for good in the church. ..."*

— Valborg Nelson Bogstad (1900)

*"The history of Greece, Rome ... and other countries show how
empty, nay, even injurious, intellectual culture may become when
divorced from Christian faith. We therefore seek ... to build up a
school which is actively and aggressively Christian. We desire to
train men and women to fear God and keep His commandments,
to labor for upbuilding of all institutions which make for the coming of the kingdom of Christ, and to oppose all enterprises which
hinder the progress of His work."*

— Catalog (1902–1903)

*"Now is our golden opportunity to rid ourselves of the jargon of
the flapper and frequenter of pool halls, and to develop a type of
speech that is befitting of college bred men and women."*

— Concordian (1924)

"The credit for the work which I have been permitted to do among you is not due me, but to the loyal pioneers who laid the foundation for this work, to the farmers among the prairies of Minnesota and Dakota, to the fathers and mothers of the students who attended Concordia, to the businessmen and bankers of Moorhead and Fargo, and to the faculty who have worked with me, to my good wife and last but not least to the All Wise God who directs our humble efforts here below."

— J.A. Aasgaard (1925)

Chapter 1

The Founders, the Founding and the First Years

Founding Concordia College

During the 1880s about twenty Lutheran pastors, nearly all members of the Anti-Missouri Brotherhood, met biannually in the Red River Valley Lutheran Pastoral Conference. Prompted by an offer from the Swedish Lutherans to have Norwegian children attend Hope Academy in Moorhead, the September 1889 meeting at Perley, Minnesota first discussed the possibility of founding a Norwegian Lutheran school. Because Hope lacked facilities for all Lutheran children and more Norwegians than Swedes lived in the valley, the pastors decided to act. Perhaps they were also reacting against the patronizing tone adopted by Yankees at the dedication of Fargo College in 1887 and at state and county Sunday School conventions. According to one founder, when Yankees established schools "to evangelize and Americanize foreigners" they really intended to proselytize them away from the Lutheran church.[1]

Hope Academy, early Swedish Lutheran competition for Concordia.

Having determined that a Norwegian Lutheran school would save their youth from Swedish Lutheranism or Yankee Congregationalism, the pastors allowed the location to be determined by the highest bidder—the customary way for handling these matters in the nineteenth century. Immediately, rivalry developed among voluntary associations representing Fargo, Crookston and Grand Forks. Persuaded by Rev. G.H. Gerberding—an Easterner, a member of the Pittsburgh Synod and the English Lutheran pastor in Fargo—the Fargo Board of Trade offered eighteen acres and $10,000. Crookston and Grand Forks boosters combined to defeat Fargo's bid. The Norwegian Lutheran College Association then met in Crookston to hear overtures from Grand Forks and Crookston. After this gathering voted in favor of the host city, Grand Forks supporters cried "conspiracy." When more conservative Crookston promoters had second thoughts, Grand Forks proceeded with plans to establish the school.[2]

Meanwhile, Moorhead became a contender. Interested laity and clergy organized the Northwestern Lutheran College Association and negotiated the $10,000 purchase of six acres and the Bishop Whipple School building valued at $30,000. Established in 1882, Bishop Whipple Academy had been promoted and financed by local businessmen. Named for Henry W. Whipple, the first Episcopalian bishop of Minnesota, who was called "Straight Tongue" by Native Americans for his work among them, it had an Episcopalian clergyman for its president. Although church-related in these ways, the school was not sponsored by the Episcopal Church. Nor was it a financial success; lack of pupils compelled its closing in June 1887. From 1888 to 1891, the building became Normal Hall, housing students and faculty for the recently opened state normal school.[3]

Bishop Whipple Academy, a Norwegian-American real estate bargain.

Even when Moorhead citizens offered to raise one-third the purchase price, the city was an unlikely location for a church college. Moorhead earned a reputation as "the wickedest city in the world" shortly after its founding in 1871. Saloons, dance halls and brothels were initially established to serve the appetites of the Northern Pacific construction crews. After the railroad crews moved west, more respectable elements established businesses, schools and churches; but the saloons and associated enterprises remained. When North Dakota entered the Union as a dry state in 1889, Fargo saloon keepers promptly moved to Moorhead. They clustered around two drawbridges spanning the Red River. Taverns did a booming business serving "dry" North Dakotans who rode "jag" wagons free of charge from Fargo. At the turn of the century, the city had forty-eight saloons and a population of almost 4,000, which had more than doubled during the previous decade. The $1,000 liquor license fee proved an unexpected boon by financing such urban improvements as a water and sewer system, sidewalks and bridges. Booze, brawls and brothels nevertheless dissuaded many from becoming residents.[4]

A flourishing liquor trade made Moorhead into a Sodom for some.

Given Moorhead's unsavory reputation, how could pious Lutherans consider establishing a school there? Clearly, practicality triumphed over piety. As one of the founders, Lars Christianson, recalled many years later: "When we heard of the

From Academy to College, 1891-1925

opportunity to buy this place in Moorhead so cheap, we couldn't afford to turn down the offer." Besides a good bargain, the choice proved fortunate in ways Christianson could not have foreseen. Served by both the transcontinental Northern Pacific and Great Northern Railroads, Fargo-Moorhead was the gateway between the twin cities of Minneapolis-St. Paul, the twin ports of Duluth-Superior and the northern Great Plains. Fargo became the distribution point for almost all of North Dakota. By the 1920s, an industrial and wholesale district stretched along railroad tracks for almost ten miles from the stockyards and packing plants of West Fargo to the railyards and shops at Dilworth, Minnesota. Fargo-Moorhead population grew from 13,315 (1900) to 36,270 (1930); impressive Main Street facades were built; and an even more impressive electric street-car network established.[5] This expanding urban environment aided institutional survival by providing a rich potential source for students and financial support.

Moorhead (1879) was small but two railroads ensured growth.

Pastor J.M.O. Ness

Confronted with the news of the real estate coup, Grand Forks boosters consoled themselves with the belief that enough Norwegians lived in the valley to support two schools. They gave their blessing to the Moorhead project and proceeded with plans to establish a college in their own city. Fargoans comforted themselves with the thought that it would be virtually a Fargo institution. Thus encouraged and having secured the approval of valley congregations, the leaders in early July finalized the organization of the Northwestern Lutheran College Association. The association elected Perley Pastor J.M.O. Ness and Fargo druggist Lars Christianson president and secretary respectively. His long side whiskers and black skull cap gave Ness a patriarchal appearance; he played the role well, giving the college dignified leadership for thirty-seven years. A successful businessman, Christianson provided a business head and financial assistance in emergencies during his forty-three years as secretary. The dedication, leadership, sacrifice and long service of Ness and Christianson were instrumental in the school's survival. The name adopted for the school, suggested by Fargo Pastor John O. Hougen to commemorate the union of the three synods that in 1890 formed the United Norwegian Lutheran Church, refers to the goddess of harmony. It literally means "hearts together—working in unison."[6]

Association Secretary Lars Christianson

Unlike Luther, Augsburg and Dana, Concordia was not founded primarily as a school for prospective clergy, although decades later college officials sometimes suggested that it had been. Contrary to this belated assertion, its establishment as a coeducational institution suggests a broader social purpose than theological training. Specific goals of the founders can be found in the articles of incorporation and the *Kaldsbrev* (letter of call) issued in August 1891 to the first principal, Ingebrikt F. Grose. The articles state that the "general purpose of this Corporation is the establishment and maintenance of an institution of learning to be known as Concordia College." The type of institution can be surmised from the listing of the branches to be taught: "Christian religion as set forth by Luther's Catechism and the Augsburg Confession, ancient and modern languages, physical and exact sciences, music, and such other branches of learning as shall from time to time be introduced into the curriculum." By designating it a college and by providing for teaching religion and other liberal arts, the founders clearly intended that Concordia would eventually evolve into a church college. Religious purpose and Lutheran identity were further emphasized in the *Kaldsbrev*. Grose was called in the name of the Triune God and was bound by the Confessions founded in the Old and New Testaments, the Augsburg Confession and Luther's Small Catechism. His duties were to manage all internal affairs and "to direct and lead the school in a Christian spirit and in the interests of the Lutheran Church." Because it was coeducational, "there will be need for special care" in maintaining Christian discipline. For these tasks, Grose received an annual salary of $1,000 and free housing at the school.[7]

Principal I.F. Grose Opens the School

Ingebrikt F. Grose, born in Kenyon, Minnesota, in 1862, acquired his baccalaureate and master's degrees from Luther College. He became a professor of mathematics at Saint Olaf in 1886; he returned there in 1900—four years after he left Concordia—to teach English, elocution and religion until his death. As a Luther graduate, Grose firmly believed in the value of the classical course; he was an exacting scholar and teacher. Anticipating from the city's evil reputation that

Principal I.F. Grose

Moorhead was located in the western wilderness, he was pleasantly surprised to find many fine houses with lawns as beautifully kept as any in Northfield. He immediately discovered much to like. Concordia had young, energetic management; the people were enterprising and the country healthy. He promptly learned the region's rules for healthful living: Avoid bad whiskey and patent medicines, drink artesian well water and wear woolen underclothes to guard against weather whims. Not all of his impressions were favorable. Shocked to see Sunday threshing crews, Grose observed that Norwegians were as diligent as Yankees in their sabbath-breaking, but he assumed that church people did not work on Sunday because they would be liable for expulsion from their congregations. Besides sabbath-breaking, liquor consumption loomed as the area's favorite sin. Because of its saloons, Grose wrote, Moorhead "may be likened unto Sodom." He counted it a blessing to live in the respectable Second Ward undominated by "the liquor element."[8]

Years later, Grose described his first view of the school in words which convey something of its isolation from the city and the emptiness of the land. Standing near the

First twelve students and their teachers.

Comstock House on Eighth Street, Grose reported this scene: Bishop Whipple Academy "loomed up in its loneliness of prairie across the coulee. ... A large space then containing scarcely a house, intervened between me and the building. Beyond the structure to the south was not a house to be seen." Taking up residence on September 1 in Bishop Whipple, which was in the turmoil of remodeling, Grose was kept awake nights by mice in the walls which aroused his fears of the tramps who infested the valley each autumn.[9]

Meeting Moorhead businessmen and calling at the local newspaper soon after his arrival, Grose was described as "a young man of fine dress and agreeable manners [who] made a very favorable impression upon all whom he met." Grose informed the newspaper that he would proceed slowly and that initially the school would offer no more than preparatory work. Grose later wrote that he viewed the institution in terms of the educational task of the United Norwegian Lutheran Church. Therefore it would be an academy feeding Saint Olaf College. Reflecting an awareness of the rising controversy over biblical scholarship in Yankee denominations, Grose insisted that both Concordia and Saint Olaf were to be "depositories of Biblical truths untouched by scorching blasts of modern theology and higher criticism." At the Willmar Colloquy in 1892, United Church and Norwegian Synod representatives agreed to a statement on the inspiration and inerrancy of Scripture which indicated that others shared Grose's hostility to historical criticism.[10]

Concordia opened on October 15 with three professors and twelve students.

Concordia College,

MOORHEAD. MINN.,

OPENS OCTOBER 15.

A preparatory school for both sexes. Comprises a business, a practical, and a classical course. Teaches the principles of Christianity, also English, Norwegian, German, Latin, Arithmetic, Algebra, Geometry, Physiology, Physics, Botany, Geography, History, Civil Government, Book-keeping and Commercial Law.

HAS AN ACTUAL BUSINESS ROOM.

Instruction given on the Piano and Organ.
For tuition, room, board, and other particulars write
I. F. GROSE, Principal.

1891 newspaper advertisement announces the opening.

Grose taught English literature and religion. Elmer D. Busby, an eastern Lutheran and graduate of Thiel College hired upon the recommendation of his friend G.H. Gerberding, taught mathematics, natural sciences and religion. The prominent role played by Gerberding and Busby is noteworthy because it suggests that the founders were not so wedded to Norwegian Lutheran exclusiveness that they feared contamination by eastern Lutheranism. Busby's wife became preceptress, or dean of women. The third teacher, Caroline Finseth, taught piano.[11]

The number of students encouraged Grose. Moorhead Normal began its first year with only eight; in 1891 Hope Academy commenced with six and Fargo College with seven. As it would for many years, agricultural activity determined enrollments. Three weeks of rain delayed threshing; with hands scarce, farmers kept children at home until fall work was done. "When it freezes," Grose wrote, "we look for an influx." His expectations were more than fulfilled. By the Christmas holidays, more than sixty were in attendance. In January, there was a phenomenal rush; eventually more than 200 came, which created severe problems of overcrowding for a building that could only house sixty and seat 120 for meals. But it was also tangible evidence, if any were needed, that the school met an established demand. Two hundred was unhoped for, unexpected and unheard of; Luther and Saint Olaf considered 125 a big attendance. That same month, Fargo College and North Dakota Agricultural College each enrolled fifty and Hope Academy 110, a drop of twenty-five due to the loss of Norwegians to Concordia.[12]

As principal, Grose faced many problems. He had to travel, something he did not like because the region lacked good hotels. On one occasion when lighting a lamp to dress upon rising, Grose discovered a "museum of wide-awake insects" in such variety on the floor and walls that it "would have made an entomologist enthusiastic." In best professorial fashion, Grose became so preoccupied with observing insect life that he almost missed his train. Selection of teachers also gave Grose much trouble. Choosing a religion professor proved most difficult because it reawakened factional disputes within the recently created United Norwegian Lutheran Church. Apparently the consideration of a former Anti-Missourian prompted protests from the Conference for Norwegian-Danish Evangelical Lutheran Church. Some threatened not to send students or money to Concordia. This prompted Northwestern Lutheran College Association member Rev. John Hougen to complain: "Had this school's management been left to Conference people," he wrote, "there would not have been a school. They want only one school: Augsburg." Rasmus Bogstad, Anti-Missouri pastor of the Salem congregation, finally accepted the call in late October, thus becoming the first ordained professor.[13]

Rev. J.O. Hougen

Tensions with the Conference surfaced again during the dedication held on Reformation Day, October 31. Sven Oftedal, Augsburg representative, was upset because he was not on the program. When prevailed upon to speak he did not offer congratulations, but gave the impression that only his school served Christ. This incident revealed disagreements about theological and humanistic education that soon produced separation and formation of the Lutheran Free Church. Aside from this unpleasantness and disagreeable weather, the dedication went well. Led by a band, a large procession of men and women marched from the Grand Pacific Hotel to the college for a Saturday morning and afternoon of many addresses in both English and Norwegian. That evening the building was illuminated with Japanese lanterns, wax candles and colored lights. Messages of congratulation were read, including one from Saint Olaf: "St. Olaf sends his best wishes to sister Concordia. May heaven's blessings rest upon her until the end of time." Ceremonies concluded with a mass meeting of Lutherans in the Fargo Armory on Sunday evening.[14]

The Grand Pacific Hotel (1882) epitomized elegance.

By January, Grose faced the problem of Concordia's success. Bishop Whipple Hall only housed sixty; no decent accommodations could be found in Moorhead. To quiet complaints the association promised to erect a new building. "Too much success is also an evil," Grose wrote. "The Association is compelled to some such arrangements or Concordia College has seen its day." These pressures caused insomnia and anxiety about his health. "I have wrought myself up to such a pitch" he reported, "that I feel as if I can work night and day without ceasing."[15]

These worries were not the only things on Grose's mind; scholars pestered him "to hunt for lost rubbers and caps as well as to arrange their studies and classify them." One requested the establishment of a freshman college class, but Grose so eloquently encouraged him to attend Saint Olaf that the student asked: "What made you leave such a beautiful place?" Grose may have wondered as pressures mounted. Local papers were often quick to criticize his management. *Normanden*, a Grand Forks Farmers Alliance newspaper, accused the school of being an ally of the saloons, a remarkable accusation given the faculty's prohibitionist sentiments. Apparently the charge originated from the fact that Concordia notices were published in *Dakota*, a paper which also carried saloon advertisements. More serious were demoralizing press criticisms during a diphtheria outbreak in February. Without any rooms available for quarantining the sick, the principal could not refuse pupils permission to return home; consequently, the school closed for two weeks. No wonder Grose could report: "I find the principalship more interesting than pleasant." Complicating his task was what he perceived as a western spirit of independence which infected even students, who had to be handled very carefully. "I am about the only person," Grose complained, "that cannot afford to show people that I am independent."[16]

Life in a Christian Academy

Difficulties did not prevent Grose from doing his duty as principal. He asserted firm control, established detailed rules for conduct and advertised Concordia as a church school with Christian standards of discipline. Grose's emphasis on Christian discipline and the school's semi-rural setting south of the sinful city demonstrate that this Norwegian academy already conformed to the American tradition of the collegiate way of life. Imported from England in the seventeenth century, the collegiate way preferred quiet rural locations with collegians dependent on dining halls and dormitories permeated by paternalism. In such residential institutions, character development was as important as academic instruction. Even state-sponsored Moorhead Normal conformed to this pattern and did not differ significantly from Concordia in its moral expectations: rules regulated behavior, chapel started each day and regular Sunday worship at a church of choice was expected.[17]

Adherence to the collegiate way made physical expansion an absolute necessity. Bishop Whipple Hall, which housed the entire college under its roof, had overflowed. Obviously scholars could not be supervised properly if they were not housed or fed on campus. Accordingly, construction soon began on a dormitory and a basement addition. The new building (present Academy Hall), sided with steel brick, consisted of a basement, three stories and seventy-one rooms accommodating 142 boys. As the structure rapidly filled in January 1893, Moorhead Normal somewhat enviously noted that it had similar potential for growth, but only if it erected an adequate dormitory. The basement addition, built on the south side of Bishop Whipple for use as a kitchen and boiler room, allowed an enlarged dining room seating 140. Despite the new construction, students were still compelled to eat in two shifts during the crowded winter term and others were required to board and lodge with private families. Even the Dalen Hotel, established by a board member who expanded his home to house forty, filled quickly and turned others away. Limited campus housing curtailed further growth for Concordia in the winter months; nonetheless, no plans were made for adding a west wing to the new dormitory due to the lack of funds and the seasonal nature of attendance.[18]

Boys' dormitory as conceived by the architect.

This early pattern of off-campus living jeopardized the character goals of the collegiate way and therefore made Concordia officials extremely nervous. Christian disciplinary standards could not be left to chance, given parental expectations, pupils ranging in age from early adolescence to the late twenties, and the well-deserved "wild and woolly" reputation of Moorhead. Parents were genuinely frightened by the city, but thought of the school as an oasis for Christian living where their children would be safe. It is hardly surprising that the college attempted to inculcate Victorian standards of respectability by adopting the rules of the well-conducted Christian home. Students were forbidden to use tobacco on school property. They could not visit saloons; they could only visit those places of amusement and engage in those amusements approved by the faculty. With experience, prohibitions became more explicit. By 1894 students were not permitted to purchase or drink intoxicating liquor but they might use alcohol for medicinal purposes with the principal's permission. The rule on tobacco was clarified to prohibit tobacco spit. By 1901 dancing and card playing were also banned. Scholars were required to stay in their rooms during study hours, which began at 7:00 p.m., and to attend recitations unless excused. Promptly at 10:00 p.m., the wooden sidewalks were pulled in, the doors locked and kerosene lamps blown out. Those who did not comply might face expulsion and forfeiture of funds paid.[19]

Rules were not always obeyed. As one enrolled in 1891 later remembered, a fifth column let in those locked out. Each year the principal dealt with violators who attended improper concerts, frequented saloons or brought liquor on campus. "Hardened" types were expelled, but others were given a second chance. Those consuming liquor appeared before the school and acknowledged they had broken a rule. Seven who entered the Tivoli Theater without knowing it was a saloon signed a certificate of better behavior. Five others, who knew it was a saloon, were expelled but allowed to petition for readmission, which was granted. Leniency was shown because none of the twelve had consumed liquor.[20]

Besides mercy, officials reasonably provided alternative proper amusements. One-half hour of supervised play was scheduled each evening except Sunday; extra play was permitted on Saturday. Criticized as unbecoming a Christian institution, the play hours were dropped when Hans Aaker replaced Grose as principal. Consequently, scholars sought unacceptable entertainment off campus. The faculty soon reinstated "play time." As Rasmus Bogstad explained, youth wanted to socialize and needed training in manners; play hours kept them "from going to the cities where they might meet ... less desirable companions" and destroy their character. Some appreciated the discipline. An 1893 class member recalled that "us plow boys ... learned to have better manners."[21]

As a Christian school, Concordia early established religion requirements. By 1894, these included instruction for Lutherans in Norwegian or English, and attendance at daily chapel and church at least once every Sunday. With seven Lutheran churches in the two cities, scholars could enjoy services in their native language, whether Norwegian, Swedish, German or English. They might also attend the Sunday Bible class or

An early literary and debating society.

Luther League which studied Lutheran doctrines and aimed to improve "members spiritually, intellectually, morally, and socially."[22]

Besides religious observances, a few extracurricular activities were available. What became a strong choral tradition early made its appearance. By October 1892, the choral class directed by John Dahle numbered more than eighty and was practicing Haydn's *Creation*. It was performed with "great success" in March before a packed crowd in the Fargo Armory. By December 1899, the Concordia Echo Band had been organized by students who had solicited enough money to buy thirteen instruments. Monday evening public entertainments by the literary society regularly attracted the Moorhead elite. Debating societies, another favorite popular entertainment of the day, met Saturday evenings. Five special lectures were scheduled each year; in 1891–1892 lecturers addressed such edifying subjects as "Character," "Abraham," "Joseph," "Temperance" and "Temptations of Youth."[23]

Sometimes unplanned events provided additional excitement. Concordia's nickname originated from one of these occasions. According to Rasmus Bogstad, "Cobbers" comes from "Corn-cobs," applied in 1893 as term of derision by Swedish students of Hope Academy. The Swedes disrupted Concordia literary entertainments with the chant:

"Corncobs! Corncobs!
Hva' ska' De ha?
Lutefisk and Lefse —
Yah! Yah! Yah!"

The disruptions ended when the Norwegians ambushed the Swedes, who were left knee-deep in the mud of a ravine located near present-day Prexy's Pond. Why the Swedes picked "Corn cobs" is not clear. Bogstad thinks it was suggested by the initials C.C. in the school name. Or, according to student lore, it came from the cornfield located south of the recently erected boys' dormitory.[24]

To attract the pupils necessary for institutional survival, Concordia advertised itself as a Christian preparatory school for both sexes. It also publicized its location, facilities, low costs and special programs. The south Moorhead location—a half-mile from the principal businesses, the post office, the Norwegian Lutheran Church, and the Northern Pacific and Great Northern depots which were served by nineteen passenger trains daily—was close enough to be convenient for the necessities of railroad and religious services, but far enough to avoid contact with disreputable saloon elements.[25]

Committed to a residential scheme by the collegiate way, Concordia naturally proclaimed its comfortable accommodations. Both dormitories were steam-heated and supposedly kept comfortably warm in winter. Students might have questioned this claim because drinking water in the rooms froze when the school turned off the heat at night for the sake of economy. The catalog boasted that "standpipes in the halls, connected with the city water works, furnish abundant water for washing and protection against fire." Two fully equipped bathrooms soon were built in each dormitory and a separate laundry facility provided for the women. Electric lights were added to the bathrooms, kitchen and dining hall in October 1897. Concordia bragged about its drainage fa-

A typical dormitory room provided students with the essential amenities.

cilities which made the school sanitary and healthful. This boast attempted to offset the bad publicity of typhoid fever cases linked to earlier sewer problems. These modern conveniences must have made Concordia seem luxurious to many farm children for whom electricity was unknown, winter baths rare and keeping warm doubtful.[26]

Concordia's fully equipped facilities, publicity emphasized, were available at reasonable costs. Annual charges for room, board and tuition ranged from $114.75 (1891–1892) to $125.50 (1900–1901). At the turn of the century, Concordia discounted $8.50 if pupils paid in advance for an entire year. For these fees, the school supplied—in addition to room, board and instruction—bedsteads, bedsprings, washstands, chairs, tables and heat. Students furnished their own

From Academy to College, 1891-1925

First Graduation Class: Commercial students (back, L-R) Oscar Simonson, Wilhelm Rognlie, Peder Lyng, August Aanenson, Hans Widness, (seated) Nels Muus, Prof. Hans Aaker, Christian Johnson (Dosland).

mattresses, bedclothes, light, towels and wash bowl. Modest by today's standards, these expenses were difficult to meet in a cash-starved pioneer society. The Depression of 1893 lasted five years. Wheat prices reached new lows in 1894, and drought increased financial woes.[27]

For their money, pupils received a full schedule. Classes began at 8:00 a.m. with religion; chapel followed at 8:45, with three class periods scheduled from 9:05 to 12:20 and three more from 1:30 to 4:45. The day ended with vocal music (1891-1892) or gymnastics (1892-1893). Students might choose from three courses of study prescribed by Principal Grose: The commercial taught English and the business branches; the practical trained parochial and common school teachers in those subjects deemed necessary for intelligent citizenship; and the classical was comprised of Latin and other college preparatory classes. Despite his own classical education, Grose displayed an admirable ability to adapt to the circumstances of farm people. He defended the flexibility afforded by the three courses of study which avoided the rigid classical curriculum of public high schools and enabled Concordia to serve a variety of educational needs. An elective course added in 1893 further enhanced flexibility by allowing scholars to attend any term and take any subject they desired if sufficiently mature.[28]

Appealing to the utilitarian values of a frontier community, Concordia stressed the practicality of its offerings. For the commercial course, Professor Hans Aaker—who had studied business in college and subsequently operated a general store—taught pupils in "an actual business room" where they carried on trade and banking "as in actual life," according to the catalog. Practical training in parliamentary practice and the English language prepared Norwegians for American citizenship. An 1897 graduate later remembered that about one-half of the large winter enrollment were recent immigrants who came to learn English.[29]

Concordia's first class of eight men and one woman graduated in 1893. The program—beginning at 8:30 p.m. in a hall decorated in national colors, leaves and flowers—consisted of prayer, scripture reading, music, declamation, oratory and original addresses by six of the graduates. Principal Grose presented diplomas and reminded the class that they should work for the extension of God's Kingdom; if they did well, they would be a credit to their school. A banquet of ice cream, cake and lemonade followed and a long program of toasts ended the evening at midnight. Commencements and related exercises soon became annual community celebrations, generally attended by large audiences of appreciative townspeople who enjoyed the display of oratorical and musical talent.[30]

By 1898, seventy-six had graduated. In addition, many teachers had been trained; 133 were teaching in common schools and forty-four in parochial schools. For its aspiring pedagogues, Concordia gave the state-mandated teacher certification examinations. For others, the school administered tests in subjects required for admission to the state university.[31]

Principal Grose Resigns

In June 1893 the directors reluctantly accepted Grose's resignation from the principalship. He disliked travel, public criticism and other aspects of administration. The job had cost him sleep and had endangered his health. Having submitted his resignation in December, by May Grose reported that "I am well, happy, have a good appetite [and] sleep my allotted time." That summer Grose returned a call to the United Church Seminary in Minneapolis. He wanted to accept, but Concordia's management did not give him permission to leave. Grose graciously accepted this refusal as a sign that he was well-liked. Despite other offers, he remained as treasurer and as a teacher of Norse, literature, arithmetic and civics until 1896, when he departed for the seminary.[32]

Although his tenure was brief, Grose made significant contributions to Concordia which shaped future development. He recruited the first faculty who were predominantly but not exclusively of Norse ancestry and educated at Lutheran schools. Of the nine who served in 1891–1892, only Bogstad had been born in Norway. In ancestry, six were Norse, two German and one Italian. Two had attended Thiel College, and four Saint Olaf and Luther.[33] This pattern of pluralism within defined limits in faculty recruitment persists to the present.

Grose established other precedents which endured for decades. He conceived of the institution as an academy within the Anglo-American collegiate tradition, established what he considered Christian standards of discipline, articulated the original program of religious instruction and developed a curriculum that emphasized practical training in pedagogy and business. Religion and morality combined with practical subjects met the educational desires of Norwegian-American Lutherans in the region, as evidenced by the large numbers who enrolled. Due to the unanticipated attendance, Grose presided over the first physical expansion with the construction of the basement addition and the boys' dormitory. He then faced the problem of repaying the debt on the new building in a period of severe depression for the region and nation.

With so many pressures associated with beginning a school on a recently settled frontier, it is not surprising that Principal Grose resigned. It is perhaps more surprising that Hans Aaker willingly accepted the burdensome post.

Chapter 2

A Glorified Business College

Principal Aaker's Business School

Business teacher Hans Aaker did not feel qualified and accepted the principalship only as an experiment. He resigned in 1897 but the boards of directors and trustees, apparently pleased with his work, reappointed him. A student of the day and a future faculty member

Principal H.H. Aaker

J.P. Hertsgaard characterized Concordia in these years as "a glorified business college." According to Aaker's later opponent Rasmus Bogstad, the principal emphasized business training because he believed in the sufficiency of his own business education and thought it foolish to waste "time and money in studying dead languages and other subjects offered in classical and literary courses."[1]

Yet practical education had already been accentuated by Principal Grose. Indeed, the character and demands of an agricultural frontier largely determined this emphasis. Most students came from ungraded rural schools that provided only the beginnings of an education, as illustrated by Ole T. Berg. Berg emigrated as a child in 1882 from Norway to northwestern Otter Tail County. When he quit

school a decade later at age sixteen he had begun the fifth reader, which qualified him to register at Concordia. The Depression of 1893 similarly fostered a practical approach to education. Short of funds, rural residents were interested in the quickest return on their schooling. The commercial course, completed in only one or two years and promising a job, seemed most prudent.[2]

Principal Aaker's business orientation did not alter religious commitment. This combination of business and religion reflected Christian assumptions about calling and Lutheran assumptions about secular learning. Indeed, the willingness of Concordia and other midwestern colleges to offer practical education expressed a conviction that the chief aim of Christian higher education is vocational preparation; it should not be limited to the professions but should be extended

September 1899.

Practical education headlined in Concordian Banner.

to the callings of the common people as well. On ceremonial occasions the Lutheran origins of educational enterprise were often noted. At the tenth anniversary celebration, the main speaker argued that the Reformation, through the stimulation of Luther's life and work, had fostered education in Germany and England. By implication, Concordia was only the most recent expression of Luther's educational theory.[3]

As at Saint Olaf College, Christianity permeated the institution but did not dominate the curriculum. As Lutheran educators, Concordia officials combined instruction in Christian principles with all secular branches. By attending a school where

"Christian morality is fostered, where Christianity and culture are united, and where instruction is by Christian teachers," students became "intelligent Christian men and women who would be useful in every walk of life."[4] Already at this early date, the institutional mission of serving the world by sending forth educated men and women had been sounded.

Aaker's actual businessroom in boys' dormitory basement.

Destined to be repeated often throughout the succeeding century, this conception of mission notably extended education to include all subjects and Christian service to embrace all occupations.

The numbers enrolled and graduating during the first decade reflect the character of a business college. Although 1,789 had attended, only 105 graduated. (See Table I). Of these, ninety (85.7 percent) completed the commercial and shorthand-typewriting courses; only seven (6.7 percent) finished the classical and eight (7.6 percent) the practical. Enrollments reflect the needs of an agricultural society. The majority came during the winter term (January through March), leaving them free to help parents with the fall harvest and the spring planting. Accordingly, the school adapted to these needs and advertised the value of business training. Prospective pupils were told that success depends on the application of business principles and that such an education gave one a competitive edge. Moreover, commercial instruction benefited merchants, farmers, doctors, lawyers, ministers and others who had limited time for schooling and who must soon support themselves. To enhance its offerings, shorthand and typewriting were added in 1894, and publicized as great employment opportunities.[5]

Business was not the only practical preparation offered. A domestic science department instructed women in housekeeping, dressmaking, fancy needlework and painting, which prepared them for their es-

Sewing class, a practical offering of the Ladies Course.

sential family duties. By 1900 domestic science had been incorporated into the ladies' course, a three-year program offering home economics, music, religion and the common branches of elementary education. Elsewhere in the United States at this time, home economics had gained an academic place in most colleges. The field advanced rapidly due to the desire of some educators to develop a female collegiate curriculum that

From Academy to College, 1891--1925

prepared women for their future lives as wives, mothers and homemakers. In common with these educators, Concordia officials believed that women should have equal access to a practical education that would add to their prosperity, but they also affirmed that women should be prepared only for the traditional role of homemaker or the related maternal role of teaching.[6]

Women were attracted to teacher preparation. Of the forty-seven graduates from the normal course between 1893 and 1912, thirty-four (72.3 percent) were females who then taught in the common schools.

Enrollments**				
	Total	Fall	Winter	Spring
1893–1894				75
1894–1895		71	192	71
1895–1896		73	233	
1896–1897		86	210	79
1897–1898	250	75	223	83
1898–1899	261			
1899–1900	276	109	251	86
1900–1901	220	94	214	42
1901–1902	218	90	190	45

Graduates**				
	Total	Commercial	Practical	Classical
1893	9	8	1	
1894	19	12	5	2
1895	11	11		
1896	13	13*		
1897	13	11	2	
1898	3			3
1899	8	7		1
1900	19	19*		
1901	10	9*		1
1902	1	1		

* includes shorthand and typing graduates
** From Principal's Report in Northwestern Lutheran College Association, Annual Reports, 1894–1902; Catalog, 1911–1912, 45-54.

Table I: Enrollments and Graduates, 1893–1902

The 1897 addition of a parochial course, a two-year program designed to prepare for teaching in summer Norwegian religious schools sponsored by congregations, enhanced female opportunities for employment and for serving the church. Those who creditably completed the normal and parochial courses were assured they could easily secure employment or a first-grade certificate from county superintendents.[7]

The classical course, a four-year program with few enrolled and even fewer graduates, was a male domain; only seven men graduated between 1893 and 1901. It did not disappear entirely because it too

Cooking class, another practical subject for women.

An elocution class studied the practical art of public speaking.

offered practical training for those who would enter college and eventually the professions. As initially organized, the course consisted of three years of Latin, four terms of German and two terms of general history supplemented by the common branches. To cultivate a taste for wholesome literature, nine additional books were assigned from English and American classics by Bunyan, Scott, Dickens, Goldsmith, Longfellow and Whittier. The classical course was upgraded in 1901 so that graduates would be admitted to any college or to the University of Minnesota. The following year, it became identical to the course at Saint Olaf: four years of Latin, English and religion; three of history; two of German and Norwegian and one of algebra, geometry and botany. These changes signaled a growing disenchantment with Aaker's business emphasis that would soon divide the faculty.[8]

As another kind of practical instruction, the school pioneered in physical education. This was consistent with a Christian emphasis on educating whole persons by developing their physical, intellectual, and moral natures. Aware that the mind might consume the body if physical activity is neglected, the faculty planned daily exercise so that bodies might be made fit temples the Holy Spirit. To better attain this goal, Rose Evelene Knestrick came in 1896 as a new instructor in elocution and physical culture. Soon Knestrick offered a special class for the male and female residents of Fargo-Moorhead. It promised great results for "those of middle age, the stout, the nervous and the busy."[9]

Professor Rose Knestrick

Teaching physical culture reveals that Concordia's brand of Lutheran pietism did not reject the sensual pleasures of physical exercise, except for dancing and except on Sunday. In compliance with the Minnesota sabbath-keeping law, Principal Aaker in 1900 banned ice skating on the college pond. On other days, most activities might be enjoyed. Collegians participated in the bicycling craze of the 1890s; at one point ten "wheels" were reported and a club organized. Professor Bogstad complied with the fashion when he bicycled to preach at Comstock and Wolverton. A baseball game concluded a day of track and field events held on campus in May 1897. Other approved exercise included tending to the two college milch cows and bailing out the boiler room during the great spring flood of '97.[10]

Educating for Citizenship

Civic education afforded another kind of practical training that fostered the Americanization of Norwegian immigrants. Public education in the United States had been established to inculcate what Lawrence Cremin calls an American *paideia;* that is, those civic values necessary for participation in a democratic culture. The diverse immigration of the nineteenth century produced a variegated population and rendered problematic the issues of Americanization and attainment of citizenship. As a counterpoint to the ideals of the evangelical united front of Yankee denominations often embodied in public education, a variety of ethno-religious groups founded schools of their own which institutionalized alternative versions of Americanism. Concordia typifies this experience; through civic education and use of English the college aided assimilation. This process was eased by the openness of Norwegian Lutherans to particpating in United States culture, an openness not shared by all European pietists.[11]

Throughout a decade noted for patriotic observances in the public school, Concordia achieved local fame for its diligent celebration of Washington's birthday. Each February Commercial Hall was decorated with flags, bunting and Washington's portrait; the literary society presented the commemorative program to a large audience of appreciative local residents. This annual display of American patriotism did not preclude regular observance of Norwegian independence, however. Every May 17 was celebrated by the college and Norwegian flags were displayed on many public and private residences.[12]

Annual Washington Day Celebration in well-decorated Commercial Hall.

The founders' willingness to teach in English indicates an openness to assimilation. They agreed with Saint Olaf Principal T.N. Mohn who said he headed "an institution founded by Norsemen for the purpose of turning Norwegians into Americans." Norwegian immigrants, early embracing English as the language of politics and business, generally wanted their children educated in that tongue. Founder and English Lutheran Pastor G.H. Gerberding, went further in urging Norwegian-Americans to adopt English for worship. He feared that otherwise the Reformed Sunday School movement would win children away from Norwegian Lutheranism.[13]

Gerberding's views were too advanced for the time. Norwegian communities retained their native speech in home and church. Oscar Overby, who in 1906 completed eighth grade in a rural school in the Sheyenne Valley of Griggs County, recalled how his teachers encouraged pupils to speak English. One teacher offered a 50-cent prize if any student did not speak Norwegian for one week. No one collected the prize because everyone spoke Norwegian, except for class recitation or talking to the teacher.[14] Reflecting the cultural values of these communities from which students came, the college remained bilingual for more than four decades. Just as they observed the patriotic holidays of both Norway and the United States, scholars heard English in the classroom, spoke Norwegian in the dormitory and used both in daily chapel services.

By the 1880s Norwegian-Americans actively participated in local and state politics. Political interests were apparent at the school. The parliamentary practice class concluded with a mock convention to which the public was invited. Nominating specches were made, a president and vice-president elected, inaugural addresses given, cabinet members appointed and confirmed by the senate. The *Concordia Banner,* the bilingual eight-page quarterly begun in 1896 to advertise the school, advocated Henry George's single tax, a rather radical reform panacea of the late nineteenth century. Publicizing reform ideas might appear surprising for a business college and an institution that after the 1930s exuded rock-ribbed Republicanism, but it reflected Principal Aaker's ideas and was not out of place in the reformist Norwegian-Americanpolitical

Concordia Banner, an early bilingual school publication.

culture of the day. Faculty reform sympathies were evident in 1896 when a Republican student characterized them as "narrow-minded Popocrats," indicating that some were supporting William Jennings Bryan, Populist-Democrat fusion candidate for president.[15]

Aaker personified political participation for the pupils in 1900 when he ran successfully as a prohibitionist candidate for mayor against Jacob Keifer, a liquor dealer. Elected in 1898 on the issue of good government, Keifer had promised to end graft, stop gambling and reduce the city debt. Although Keifer had the support of most businessmen, who recognized that without the saloons the city would be bankrupt or that taxes would be raised, Aaker was the "surprising" victor according to the newspapers who had supported Keifer. As mayor, Aaker enforced the state law on night and Sunday closings of saloons, ordered the removal of gambling devices, closed houses of prostitution and established a curfew for children under age sixteen. In early June, the *Daily News* estimated that 1,000 men were turned out at the north bridge saloons at the 11:00 p.m. closing time. No wonder Aaker became known in the press as the chief "boogie man of the saloons of Moorhead." Shot at on several occasions, he hired armed protection.[16]

Meanwhile, Aaker sought Populist endorsement for his congressional candidacy on the Prohibitionist ticket. Failing in both, Aaker did not seek re-election because the office required more time than he could give as principal of Concordia. He stoutly defended his mayoral record from attack, however. His government had been clean and honest; he had attempted to suppress the evils that former administrations had openly permitted. Perhaps he felt vindicated by the election of Mayor William R. Tillotson, who carried on his policies of regulating vice in order to make Moorhead a finer residential city and a safer place for students. After Aaker left Concordia, he remained politically active until his death in 1929 but his Non-Partisan League views were not popular with the Republican businessmen with whom he associated as the head of a business college.[17]

Financial Struggles

Finances for the fledgling institution remained difficult throughout the depression decade. Compelled to borrow $10,000 to build the boys' dormitory, the Northwestern Lutheran College Association (NWLCA) struggled to escape the burden of this and other debts. Association President Ness constantly urged repayment because high interest imposed a constant strain on current operations. After much discussion at a succession of annual meetings and some unproductive summer solicitations, a drive was launched in 1897 to pay off the $12,000 indebtedness on the property. The times

Rasmus Bogstad

were favorable; prosperity was returning to the nation and the valley. The Moorhead *Daily News* boosted the college, calling it "one of the most beneficial institutions in this city ... from a business standpoint." The paper estimated that during its brief existence Concordia had generated $131,864 additional income for the city.[18]

Once again, master solicitor Pastor Bogstad with team and buggy traveled from farm to farm throughout the valley. Once again, druggist Lars Christianson offered a major gift as he would so often in the future; Christianson promised to pay $1,000 when $9,000 had been raised. On November 27 Bogstad reported to the trustees that $8,200 had been subscribed; he then resigned to accept a call from a Wisconsin congregation. A motion was passed unanimously requesting the professor to withdraw his resignation. Another motion passed instructing each member to raise part of the funds. Bogstad stayed and eventually subscriptions totaled $10,300.[19]

This successful drive improved finances, but only temporarily. The debt had been reduced. A fortunate decline in interest rates from 10 to 8 and even 6 percent on the balance reduced payments from $1,572 to $600, a considerable savings on the current budget. The treasurer reported in 1899 that the college had the financial resources to pay all but $3,900 of its debt. No wonder Ness, addressing the annual meeting, gave thanks for what God had enabled the association to accomplish and announced that the school was on more solid ground than previous years. That solid footing immediately shifted when the association again borrowed to install sewers, water closets, ventilating systems and new floors. Ness again urged action, saying "we must try to obliterate the indebtedness or it will obliterate us." Borrowing nevertheless continued as the college struggled to pay salaries and other pressing obligations. Despite Ness's alarmist urgings and the efforts of field workers to publicize the college, recruit students and raise funds, by 1902 the debt had increased to $14,000.[20]

Why these precarious finances? Without an endowment, the college depended almost entirely on student fees. Unfortunately, enrollments and the fee income derived from them were inherently unstable. Sharp declines in registrations, whether caused by poor crops, low farm prices or epidemic diseases, created immediate shortfalls. Because many expenses like salaries were fixed for the term, a sudden decline in income necessitated borrowing. Charged with financial management, Principal Aaker often undertook field work to solicit additional funds. The association appreciated these extra efforts and offered to pay traveling expenses for professors who undertook field work during summers. In addition to fundraising, Aaker looked for ways to reduce expenses. Scholars worked for room and board by cleaning the buildings, tending the boiler, milking the cows, chopping wood, and helping in the kitchen. Aaker did much work himself; in 1896 he painted most building interiors and assisted a student in hanging wallpaper.[21]

Contagious disease, a constant worry for authorities in the early years, often had immediate, disastrous effects on enrollment. A serious outbreak of typhoid fever occurred in Fargo-Moorhead and on campus during 1897 and 1898. Nine cases developed that fall followed by twenty-seven resulting in one death in the spring. Concordia closed a week early and awarded graduates diplomas even if exams had not been taken. The next spring, sixteen fever cases and two deaths were reported. Attendance dwindled to only twenty; the college again closed early. Although the cause of fever was unknown, Principal Aaker recommended repairing the basement sewer, disinfecting the ground and replacing the floor in both buildings. A smallpox scare followed the quarantine of Moorhead Normal in 1901. Attendance declined from 200 to seventy-five in one week. To avoid financial collapse, refunds were refused those who left without just cause. As a result of this scare, only forty-two attended that spring, a drop of more than 50 percent from the previous year. Diphtheria outbreaks in 1900 and 1902 also reduced attendance.[22]

Management of the boarding department, assigned in 1893 to Rasmus Bogstad, became another factor in attracting and retaining pupils. Bogstad believed that a well-managed boarding department generated institutional income and improved morale. If youth had good food they were happier and complained less. Bogstad had the good fortune to hire Helga Fjelstad as matron in 1895. She managed the kitchen until 1930, when she retired for the second and final time. Fjelstad, an excellent cook and competent manager, became a practical teacher in domestic science. More important, as a woman who quietly practiced her Christian principles, she became a mother to several generations of scholars.[23]

An Academic Rebellion

Enrollment and financial worries contributed to an internal dispute about proper academic policy resulting in Principal Aaker's resignation in 1902. Already in 1899, NWLCA Association President Ness indicated some dissatisfaction with Aaker's business emphasis when he called attention to the need for encouraging more pupils to enroll for fall and spring terms in the longer classical and normal courses. Ness recognized that having students attend for three terms and return for three or four years would stabilize income. To accomplish this change, Ness suggested drawing the outlying circuits of the United Norwegian Lutheran Church into closer relations and working through congregations to reach youth. Believing that the benefits of Christian education could not be attained in two short terms, Ness successfully urged the association to adopt in 1901 a report from a committee on courses. Two consequences followed. First, the classical course was strengthened to fulfill entrance requirements for the state university. Second, pupils were encouraged to enter the fall term, enroll in either the classical, normal or ladies courses, and remain throughout the year.[24]

Rasmus Bogstad and Elmer D. Busby, the only faculty to have completed a classical course and received the baccalaureate, were the chief supporters of these new academic policies. In the *Concordia Banner*, published in late 1901, Professor Busby defended the new direction.

Busby insisted that the founders had established Concordia College as a "higher institution of learning for the Christian culture of young men and women." He maintained that the school must uphold the lofty standard of general education and furnish students with well-rounded development of powers that make them useful leaders in community, public affairs and church. Busby worried that few spent sufficient time to obtain a well-rounded development of their powers. He expressed concern that the list of graduates did not differ from that of an ordinary business school, which he found "diametrically opposed to the Lutheran conception of an educational institution." He deplored the emphasis on "getting through," the substitution of the diploma for knowledge and the American rush for worldly wealth which threatened to materialize education. Against materialism, church colleges should offer the elevated vision of Christian culture. It was appropriate, therefore, that the association now emphasized advanced courses of study.[25]

Professor E.D. Busby

In Spring 1902 the smoldering conflict between educational philosophies burst into flame. Aaker, leading faculty advocate of business training, submitted his resignation as principal in March. He referred to recent attacks by Bogstad which implied that his work as principal had hindered the progress of the college. Apparently stung by a charge that while mayor he had not devoted sufficient time to his duties, Aaker asserted that he had served the school "in the morning, during the day, in the evening, and often during nights, seven days a week and for practically twelve months in the year." No wonder he concluded by writing, "I am tired and feel that I need a change." Within days, Bogstad, not to be outdone by his competitor, also resigned. Bogstad somewhat peevishly suggested that this gave the association an opportunity to hire someone more competent because he had been unable to achieve the higher standards desired by the management and general public. This action triggered Aaker's resignation as a teacher because the Busby and Bogstad attacks "indicated that we three could hardly work advantageously together."[26]

At its meeting on April 23, the board of directors—responsible for the institution's academic affairs—took steps to end the crisis. Disliking harmful dissension and composed primarily of clergy who favored higher standards, the directors backed Bogstad and Busby. They recommended that the trustees accept Aaker's resignation, reject Bogstad's and call Pastor H.B. Kildahl of Chicago as principal. The board of trustees, which managed finances and had final authority in decision-making, adopted these recommendations on the same day.[27]

Aaker's opposition to the new academic policies did not end with the acceptance of his resignation. In his report to the association at its June meeting, Aaker pointedly noted that fixed courses had not achieved their hoped-for advantages and suggested that "more time and experience might be necessary to prove their impracticality at an institution of this kind." Because spring attendance had declined to one-half of the previous year, Aaker hinted that it had been caused by the experiment with fixed courses, although diphtheria was a factor. He also complained that the commercial course had been practically destroyed by the new policy. In two years its enrollment had dropped from ninety-six to forty-six.[28]

Aaker thanked the association for its kindnesses, but noted that "I am not in sympathy with the new plan of the school and am glad that I am in position to withdraw so as to leave the field clear for those who hold different views." Even his best wishes for the future contained a last blow at his opponents: "Concordia, even though hampered now, I hope will, in her more limited sphere, be able to succeed and succeed beyond your fondest hopes." In describing the new program, Aaker's very choice of words—"impractical," "hampered," "limited sphere"—indicates his displeasure. Truly committed to his educational ideas, he founded Aaker's Business College in Fargo. His institution offered new competition for Concordia, and his relations with his old school were further soured by a petty dispute over the ownership of two typewriters.[29]

Aaker did not have the last word. The committee on his report disagreed with his conclusions, which is not surprising because the committee was comprised of Busby and Ness, both sympathetic to classical training. Busby and Ness found attendance encouraging. Despite poor crops in many areas and competition from other Lutheran schools, numbers totaled 218, a decline of only two from the previous year. Although commercial courses had declined, institutional registrations had not; they therefore concluded that "the students who did not enter the commercial courses must have certainly enrolled in the other longer and higher courses offered by the institution." Like Aaker, they concluded the new policy had not yet been given a fair test, but unlike Aaker they expected it would succeed in time. Also like Aaker, they threw barbs at their opponent. The new policy would not be given a fair test "until all members of the faculty are in harmony and give it their fair support."[30]

Although the dispute over the future direction of the former business school had been settled, the college still had no principal because Rev. Kildahl had rejected the call. Discouraged, the directors gave Bogstad the opportunity to operate Concordia as his own property. Shocked, he refused on the grounds that people would not donate to an institution owned by one man. The board countered with an offer of the principalship beginning July 1, 1902, at no increase in Bogstad's $1,100 salary. Lars Christianson's terse comment accompanying the association's letter of call indicates his impatience with recent academic difficulties: "Now, for God's, our, and everyone's sakes, accept it."[31]

Bogstad did accept and thereby opened a new chapter for Concordia. It had an auspicious debut when more students than ever before returned for the fall term. According to supporters of the Bogstad-Busby academic policy, this demonstrated the wisdom of establishing regular and higher courses of study.[32]

Chapter 3

The Liberal Arts Dream Revived

President Bogstad

Rasmus Bogstad became Concordia's first president in 1906, an indication of the intention to move toward college status. After all, real colleges are not led by principals! He headed the institution at an opportune time, which contributed to his success.

The opening decade of the new century was generally prosperous for the nation and for many Americans; industrialism continued apace, big businesses grew rapidly and agriculture entered its "golden age." Many "evils" existed but reformers promised cures. Progressivism—a reform movement that aimed at greater democracy, good government, business regulation, social justice and public service—affected politics at local, state and federal levels. Urban business and professional leaders advocated businesslike, efficient solutions. Humanitarians crusaded for women's rights, the urban poor, workers, peace, prohibition and other causes. Progressivism affected higher education as well. Vocational training for practical efficiency, scientific intelligence that fostered the common good, and social service to society at large were emphasized. Enrollments expanded at a host of new private institutions—academies, normals, junior colleges, business schools—and many upgraded into colleges and universities.[1] These developments affected Concordia in a variety of ways, directly and indirectly.

Rasmus and Valborg Nelson Bogstad, the college's first presidential couple, pictured in later years.

President Bogstad had attained substantial upward mobility since his Norwegian birth in 1861, poor boyhood, rudimentary education and emigration in 1880. Bogstad worked as a farm hand while he attended and graduated from Luther College and the Northfield Seminary, established by the Anti-Missouri Brotherhood. Ordained in 1890, he accepted a call from the Kindred congregation before coming to Concordia the next year. Offered the presidency of Grand Forks College in May 1892, Bogstad chose to remain in Moorhead.[2]

Valborg Nelson Bogstad often taught at the academy and later became a lecturer, novelist and short story writer. Her account of the family trip to Norway in 1904 describes her husband's triumphant homecoming. The first from his village to be ordained, a professor and a principal, Bogstad was treated with great respect. Invited to preach in his home church, he gave two Sunday sermons and conducted several meetings at a time of religious awakening. One, held outdoors with people seated on the hillside, lasted for several hours until the setting sun forced his attentive audience reluctantly to depart. Bogstad's lengthy sermonizing in fluent Norwegian had surprised his listeners. In keeping with their religious convictions, the Bogstads made a pilgrimage to the home of Hans Nielsen Hauge.[3]

As the Norwegian trip demonstrates, Bogstad was a man of deep religious feeling who respected the traditions of Haugean pietism. An intense, fervent speaker, Bogstad had an exciting vision of expansion for a Lutheran school in the Northwest. A practical visionary, Bogstad firmly believed that his successful fundraising could both save the school and finance its expansion.

Bogstad's Vision

Bogstad envisioned Concordia as a Christian school of liberal learning. His vision emerged from the English collegiate tradition, Lutheran educational ideals and current discussions about American higher education. The collegiate way blended character training with intellectual instruction in the Western humanistic tradition. Luther College, Bogstad's alma mater, similarly combined the classics of the Norwegian Latin School with religious instruction. This Lutheran version of Christian humanism regarded the classics as important in themselves, secondary only to the Word of God. Norwegian Lutherans educated in this tradition were thus open to the study of secular subjects complemented by instruction in Christianity. Bogstad's vision was also informed by debates about higher education at the turn of the century which appealed to the fundamental ideals of religious piety, liberal culture and utility.[4]

Skilled at public relations, Bogstad expanded the advertising efforts of his predecessors to publicize his educational vision. He had printed 10,000 brochures, despite trustee objections to spending $150 on a frivolity. Bogstad believed the expense justified and himself vindicated when Concordia became the first Lutheran school to enroll 500. Bogstad combined mass advertising with individual consideration. In a 1907 recruiting letter he wrote, "should you come here, I would be glad to give you my personal attention and would try to make your stay a very pleasant and profitable one." With Concordia's wide choice of courses and moderate expenses, Bogstad promised the prospective collegian, "you can get more for your money here than at any other school. ..."[5]

The phrase, "Christian school," entered prominently into publicity efforts. It became the letterhead on new stationery. The catalog edition of *The Record*—a new quarterly published by the college to advertise itself—reprinted for many years a long statement on "the Christian school," which deplored the materialistic and secularizing tendencies of the age. These tendencies were evidenced in "dancing, card playing, drunkenness, profanity, impurity, secret association," and—in contrast to Norwegian practice—the lack of formal religious instruction in United States public schools. The history of Greece and Rome demonstrated how "injurious intellectual culture may become when divorced from Christian faith." Because it resisted secularism, Concordia deserved support. "Actively and aggressively Christian," Concordia promised to teach "men and women to fear God," to "keep his commandments" and to work "for the coming of the kingdom of Christ." A college education informed by the gospel message "shall make men and women pure, cultured, and strong" and is "the best preparation for any profession of life that a young man or woman may wish to choose."[6]

Both Bogstad and Ness echoed these themes in their reports to the association.

In 1906 Bogstad maintained that a religious school, which gave students an idea of the truest and the best, stimulated the idealism needed to develop them mentally, morally and physically. Ness agreed in 1909 when he attacked secular higher education for rejecting moral absolutes and adopting moral relativism. In the face of this secular challenge, Christian youth required a school like Concordia that stood "for God, Christian morality, righteousness, truth and light."[7]

As these Lutheran educators implied, Christianity complemented liberal learning. Asserting that "Concordia College aims at placing a liberal education within reach of as many as possible," Bogstad called the school "a department store of education." It is ironic that the man who ardently criticized Aaker's business college should use a business metaphor to describe his own conception of liberal education. His metaphor suggests that he did not think liberal education incompatible with practical training. Indeed, Bogstad envisioned Concordia as a hybrid of the European university, with its ideal of culture, and the United States business school, with its ideal of efficiency. He believed that the best education lay between these extremes, and therefore he established several departments which instilled both efficiency and culture. These departments strengthened each other, and their coexistence reminded students and faculty that each subject is not the only one to learn. To thus foster breadth in scholars is vital, according to Bogstad, because it ensured success. Breadth showed pupils the way to develop and increased their capacity for growth. Successful people were those who viewed their professions in the broadest light, advanced to the highest points and never stopped growing.[8]

The ideals of liberal learning and Christian education, articulated by Bogstad and Ness, were not mere rhetorical decorations brought out only for ceremonial occasions. Indeed, the association and its boards of directors and trustees charged the principal/president with governing the institution according to these precepts. These ideals therefore markedly influenced discipline, extracurricular activities and the curriculum.

Training Character

Following the collegiate pattern, Concordia authorities managed all aspects of the school environment to train character. Their rules were based on a Victorian and Christian moral code, paralleled those of other institutions and were perpetuated as well by progressive educators. In the face of youthful demands for more freedom, public institutions compromised first on the issues of dancing and automobiles. Many religious colleges modified codes after World War I; Lutheran schools more successfully resisted changes until after World War II.[9]

At Concordia, discipline remained parental with pupils governed by the rules of every well-ordered Christian home. Liquor, tobacco, cards and dancing were banned. The change from kerosene lamps to electric lights did not alter the dormitory lights-out policy. Complaining about the low moral standards and bad habits of many, Bogstad devoted much time to Christian discipline. Wrongdoers were lectured, admonished both publicly and privately, and given opportunity to correct behavior. If they did not repent and persisted in disobedience of the rules, then they were expelled. Disciplinary problems led the trustees in 1908 to strengthen the president by empowering him to dismiss without consulting the faculty. The trustees also ruled that any student or teacher who refused to give evidence when requested could be terminated. Thus empowered, Bogstad expelled several in 1909 including two from the "bloody eight," one for detrimental influence and one for stealing. A female was suspended for breaking most of the rules: going to entertainments and keeping gentlemen company without permission, using improper language in Ladies Hall and coming in through

A dormitory clique, 1906.

windows after hours. Given the steady traffic through dormitory windows, later recalled by alumni, it is remarkable that only one was expelled. Either the authorities were not very vigilant, or the number of violators have increased proportionally with the years. Although Bogstad disliked discipline, he viewed it as necessary. "Christian schools that insist on good discipline," he said, "are having a great influence for good upon the young people of the present day."[10]

Responding to a conflict between President Bogstad and Professor J.P. Hertsgaard, the trustees modified the rules in 1908. A native of Kindred, a member of Bogstad's former congregation, an 1898 academy graduate and Saint Olaf alumnus, Hertsgaard had been personally recruited by the president in 1904 to teach history and science. By 1908, Hertsgaard sympathized openly with students, criticized other faculty and complained to visitors about Bogstad's autocratic ways and failure to understand discipline. According to Bogstad, Hertsgaard had called the president "stubborn, morose, incompetent and not up-to-date"; Mr. Hjelmstad "too much of a stick"; and Miss Sunne "unreasonable, strict and dry." He further reportedly stated "that the old war horses ought to go" for the school to progress. While these comments were perhaps heard sympathetically by some students, others almost certainly reported them to the president. As one of the "war horses," Bogstad neither chose to depart nor tolerate open insubordination. He asked Hertsgaard to resign. At this point, the directors intervened to rectify the strained relationship that the board believed had hurt the school. Holding it supremely important "that reverence for authority be maintained," the board upheld the president. After meeting with the directors, Hertsgaard assured them he would work to improve his relations with Bogstad.[11] Neither man remained long enough to test this agreement. Bogstad resigned in 1910; Hertsgaard left the following year.

Because of Bogstad's devotion to discipline it is perhaps not surprising that an alumnus remembered him as "an austere figure" given to commenting on what was right

Professor J.P. Hertsgaard

and proper. The pupil "was left with the feeling that nothing that was right and nothing that was proper could ever, ever be any fun." Certainly the president did not intend to give this impression. Like the father in the well-regulated Christian home, he enforced necessary but not harsh rules and he promoted supervised daily play hours. Some graduates recalled these activities as fun. Besides games, songs included "Pig in the Parlor," "The Needle's Eye," and "Skip, Come My Lou." The finale was always the grand march of partners around the room in time to music. In addition, the Bogstads entertained pupils in their new house, constructed on campus in 1903. At an early entertainment, seniors played progressive anagrams and Santa Claus paid a visit. Constituents were assured that these activities did not interfere with learning; the school still inculcated industry, punctuality and Christian principles.[12]

Bogstad House, the first presidential home.

As Concordia became more established, extracurricular activities expanded. These were either begun by the college, or if organized by collegians, closely supervised to perpetuate Christian morality. Lectures devoted to edifying subjects continued. During the 1905–1906 year, students heard three addresses on "The Reformation" and others on "The Value of Character," "Character in Education," "Christian Character," "The Christian College," and "Ideals in Education." In 1904 a new religious organization, *Norsk Laererforening*, appeared for the purpose of furthering the cause of the congregational Norwegian school. On Wednesday evenings, pupils conducted in Norwegian a prayer meeting with Bible readings. Religious earnestness is also evidenced by those who worshiped both Sunday mornings and evenings. Trinity Lutheran, located within six blocks on the same street, already afforded a church home for most scholars and faculty. Trinity conducted morning services in Norwegian and evening in English; therefore everyone had the opportunity to worship in "the language of his heart."[13]

Trinity Lutheran early became the college church.

That religious services were conducted in Norwegian demonstrates a continued strong Norse influence. As Bogstad informed a prospective speaker, "we have a few Americans but you can use the Norwegian if you prefer." For many years the library reading room stocked leading papers, periodicals and magazines in both English and Norwegian. Dual loyalties are indicated by the annual observance of Washington's birthday and Norwegian Independence Day. Indeed, a 1904 class night oration delivered in Norse argued that retaining Norwegian language and culture was compatible with American loyalty.[14]

Student-initiated athletic activities troubled officials. Authorities wanted to encourage physical culture because they believed it promoted health and welfare. They even appealed to the classical tradition for justification: "The ancients emphasized ... to have a sound mind, a person must have a sound body." Yet they worried when enthusiasm for the baseball club, organized in 1903, led some to neglect their studies. Consequently, baseball was placed under faculty control; students whose average fell below 75 (later 85) percent were banned from participation. J.P. Hertsgaard, "an old college player of considerable repute," became the coach; an athletic director was appointed in 1908 and that spring monograms were awarded participants in an appropriate ceremony.[15]

Drama was also questionable. A temperance play, *Out in the Streets,* played in 1903 before a packed house of 500 in Commercial Hall. Dramas in Norwegian were performed, sometimes for independence day celebrations, and by 1906 senior class plays were staged annually. That comedies were now presented may have aroused the ire of those pietists opposed to worldly pleasures. The association in 1909 heard a recommendation to abandon drama. The following

Out In The Streets (1903), the first dramatic production.

year, the directors let the faculty decide. As pietists who were devoted to the humanistic tradition, the professors permitted plays. Other activities like music and debate, popular Norwegian-American entertainments, were considered edifying and therefore less worrisome. By 1904 the school had a band, an orchestra, four singing groups, three debating societies using both English and Norwegian, and a literary society which continued Monday evening programs. The Boosters' Club—formed in 1909 "to boost for Concordia, to make it known to the people ... and to foster a spirit of loyalty and cooperation among the teachers and students at the school"—proposed the *Corn Cob*, a new monthly publication. This first student newspaper soon appeared as the *Crescent*, a name thought more appropriate.[16]

A Practical Curriculum

Under Bogstad's leadership Concordia built its curriculum on the ideals of piety, culture and utility. Because piety pervaded the entire institution, officials promised that each class would be taught in a Christian spirit. By fostering breadth, academic subjects and the different courses of study served culture. Utility clearly informed the school's stated aims: to be "the greatest service to the greatest number possible" and to give "the student a thorough and useful training for the duties of life." Through its diversity of offerings, the school attempted to meet every educational need by providing something for everyone; it thereby insti-

A newspaper appeared in 1909, a sign of an emerging college.

Parochial course students (1907) pictured in New Main Auditorium.

tutionalized Bogstad's department store metaphor. Initially it offered five courses of study: classical, normal, ladies, commerce and stenography. Music, manual training, elocution and physical culture had been added by 1907. Special Bible and English classes were still given for those interested. In 1907 and 1908, summer work was scheduled in business and music respectively.[17]

As could be expected after his victory over Aaker, Bogstad encouraged pupils to enroll in the classical course. He appealed to both culture and utility in defending the value of classical education. Because it required thoroughness of preparation, such training promoted the full development of an individual's faculties and thereby the capacity for further growth. Promoting individual culture gave the classical course its utility; it was useful both to the individual, who became well-trained, and the community, which acquired educated leadership. The course thus had broader application than merely college preparation. Bogstad insisted that classical graduates were assured of becoming leaders in the new communities of the Northwest which needed well-educated farmers, businessmen, ministers, teachers, lawyers, doctors and politicians.[18]

His love for the classics did not lead Bogstad to neglect practical subjects. Partly a matter of survival, because such courses attracted the necessary registrations, it was also a matter of intellectual commitment. Besides establishing close ties with the local community, this training equipped Christians to serve the world in even the humblest occupation. Thus manual training and domestic science developed practical skills useful in the workplace and the home; by "training to do things" and by increasing individual efficiency both enhanced the welfare and happiness of families. The parochial course reflected a similar utilitarian emphasis directed toward a religious purpose. Students were given specific training for a specific Lutheran occupation: "the constantly increasing demand for parochial school teachers." Because the public schools could not give religious instruction, the church was "compelled to lay great stress on the religious training in the home and parochial school."[19]

Clearly Bogstad did not oppose practical training, but he did not want the school limited to business or the preparatory level. Bogstad believed that the founders had intended a college, if only in anticipation. He therefore worked diligently to realize that dream. He found a willing ally in Rev. Ness, president of the association. At the 1905 annual meeting both men recommended an extension of the classical course by adding two years of college-level work. The association concurred and authorized the faculty to prepare a course of study. That year the catalog listed college subjects for the first time. The curriculum included much language study: two years of Greek, one of Latin and four terms (out of six) of German. Students took no mathematics, only one term of zoology and two of botany.[20]

As generations of collegians know, there is often a discrepancy between listings and offerings. Longtime faculty member Herman Nordlie later recalled, "adding the college department ... was a slow process." Few academy graduates continued and none finished the junior college. Apparently, only electives were taken by a few individuals. Then in 1908, chemistry was added because schools were now placing more emphasis on modern science; the addition also reflected Concordia's aspirations to higher status. The first freshman class of twenty-seven was organized in 1909. Despite opposition by some Saint Olaf professors and others who believed "there should only be one college within the church," Bogstad and Ness pushed ahead. Academy graduates had requested college work. Increased revenues from higher college tuitions were needed to maintain the recently constructed New Main. Only forward-looking institutions survived, Bogstad insisted. Ness agreed that creating the college course would be advantageous.[21]

Were Bogstad and Ness correct? Was their strategy of emphasizing the classical, college and other fixed courses advantageous? Fortunately, their innovations were well-timed. The return of agricultural and business prosperity in 1897 produced an upswing in students throughout the Midwest and nation. Enrollment in colleges and universities increased at a rate four times faster than the population at large. Favorable circumstances thus vindicated their policies by producing a 219 percent increase in total graduates and enrollments between 1902 and 1908 (See Table II).

Success did not come without anxiety or effort, however. Competition, disease and agricultural conditions continued to affect adversely Concordia's enrollments. When Aaker opened his business college in 1902, Concordia feared the new competition. The fears proved groundless; with great relief Bogstad reported that fifty had regis-

Table II: *Enrollments and graduates, 1902–1908**

	Enrollments*			
	Total	Fall	Winter	Spring
1902–1903	230	108	223	85
1903–1904	311	155	310	100
1904–1905		125	320	125
1905–1906	380			
1906–1907				
1907–1908	503			

			Graduates*			
	Total	Commercial**	Classical	Ladies	Teachers***	Music
1903	16	7		3	6	
1904	25	15	3	5	2	
1905	29	14	4	6	5	
1906	29	15	4	5	4	1
1907	35	12	5	3	13	2
1908	35	13	8		13	1

*Compiled from President's Report in Northwestern Lutheran College Association, Annual Reports, 1903–1908; Catalog, 1908–1909, 48-50.
**includes shorthand graduates.   ***includes parochial course

tered on the first day and that the number had increased to 108 by term's end. The prevalence of disease—measles, smallpox, diphtheria, pneumonia—and occasional deaths were a more serious deterrent. Because the public believed the school plagued with sickness, NWLCA President Ness in 1904 reassured patrons through the Norwegian press that good health prevailed. The next year, poor crops in the valley led many to cancel their room reservations. Bogstad responded to these crises with increased advertising and personal recruiting. He sent out a circular letter to more than one hundred in 1905 which sustained enrollment. Besides carrying on an extensive correspondence with past and prospective students, Bogstad addressed many congregations on the subject of Christian education.[22]

These efforts to market the new academic policies, combined with growing popular interest at the time in higher education, enabled Concordia to grow during the Bogstad presidency.

Growing Pains

Increased enrollment proved a mixed blessing. More students generated more revenue, but also led to overcrowding and additional expenditures for buildings and faculty. Annually, officials published an urgent plea in the local newspaper for community assistance in providing board and room for the winter influx. As dormitories and classrooms became cramped, physical expansion could not be avoided. A new basement kitchen was added between the dormitory and the heating plant; Commercial Hall became the dining hall as it had earlier become the chapel. Crowding and his growing family made it impossible for Bogstad to live in the dormitory as had previous principals. He therefore built an administrator's residence on the grounds in 1903 at a personal cost of $3,800. Approved by the executive committee, the trustees were instructed to repay Bogstad as soon as possible. Even an

The dining room (1901) set family-style.

increase in annual fees from $131 (1904) to $167 (1909) could not cover these rising costs.[23]

Meanwhile plans were being discussed for the construction of a new main building. The association agreed in 1904 to build at a cost not to exceed $25,000 when funds were assured. Bogstad, the practical visionary, held out for a $50,000 building as more adequate to the needs of the growing school. He privately purchased the present site and by summer of 1905 had raised $20,000. He then boldly requested funds from philanthropists John D. Rockefeller, James J. Hill and Andrew Carnegie. Surprisingly, the non-Christian Carnegie responded favorably and promised $12,500 when the association had paid $37,500 on the structure, which they did by March 1907. The Moorhead Commercial Club had been enlisted to raise the balance and eventually contributed one-fifth of the total cost.[24]

The cornerstone was laid in an impressive ceremony during June commencement. Severe crowding compelled construction before all monies were gathered and instruction in January 1907 before all work was done. A student later remembered surveying piles of lumber and pipes in the halls as she sat on a nail keg waiting for her classes. Building was complicated by a "corner" on local brick, which led to the substitution of granite for the foundation. The San Francisco earthquake created a shortage of bricklayers which delayed work into cold weather. Stoves used to keep the plaster from freezing ignited the floor, but Bogstad, following a premonition, appeared in time to extinguish the blaze with wet plaster.[25]

Even loyal supporters complained about the pretentious size; how could it ever be paid for or filled? The edifice was paid for promptly without increasing indebtedness and filled more quickly than even the most sanguine supporters hoped; annual enrollment for 1907-1908 topped 500 for the first time. Besides relieving over-crowding and enabling expansion, New Main served an important public relations purpose. The handsome neo-classical granite and brick structure more impressively represented Concordia and the cause of Christian education. Indeed, New Main was an imposing structure for Fargo-Moorhead of that day. It contained classrooms for 500, a library, a science laboratory, a gymnasium, an auditorium seating 800 and offices for the president, treasurer and registrar.[26]

It was indeed fortunate that New Main was built. For almost four decades it would be Concordia College; virtually all academic and administrative activity occurred there.

There were other campus improvements. Freshly planted shade trees and new walks beautified the grounds. As part of an extensive program of urban betterment, the city in 1906 installed an arc light in front of the buildings, erected a bridge across the coulee on Seventh Street and laid a cement walk from the college to the nearest street car line. A fountain and lily pond were installed on the newly landscaped New Main lawn. No wonder the Moorhead *Independent* called the grounds "the prettiest in the city." Renamed Ladies Hall, Old Main (Bishop Whipple) was remodeled to house one hundred women. Alumni contributions financed a new campus hospital, erected in 1910.[27]

These additions neither ended financial strains nor overcrowding. Indeed, New Main added to administrative costs. Charged with superintending the construction in addition to his other duties, Bogstad first engaged a parttime stenographer. Then Professor Busby managed the school during the winter and spring terms of 1907 while Bogstad concentrated on completing construction. Liking this division of responsibilities, Bogstad proposed that it become permanent. The president should take charge of fundraising and finances; a dean should be appointed to supervise instruction.

Impressive New Main added substantially to the campus.

Expense notwithstanding, the boards attempted to act on this recommendation in 1909 when they offered the deanship to Pastor C.O. Solberg, a Saint Olaf professor. Unfortunately for Bogstad, Solberg did not accept. Besides demands for expanding administration and paying for campus improvements already underway, the boards faced pressures for even more construction. In 1908 Pastor Ness reminded the association of the need for new buildings to house music, commerce and the hospital. Yet the debt, and fears of increasing indebtedness, constrained further expansion except for the hospital.[28]

Henry Shurson

Board concern did prevent the debt from climbing steadily. In 1906 Concordia paid $1,200 in annual interest; by 1909 this had increased to $2,000 on a debt of $30,000. As early as 1903, Ness recommended hiring a field secretary to gather funds for reducing indebtedness and for financing new buildings. In lieu of a permanent secretary, Bogstad successfully solicited most of the cost for New Main, but he did not succeed in reducing indebtedness. Hired as field secretary in 1906, Henry O. Shurson helped Bogstad solicit funds, but equipment for manual training and the new science laboratory quickly absorbed the $9,000 he raised.[29]

To meet its financial needs, Concordia launched several new initiatives. It successfully established a closer relationship with the United Norwegian Lutheran Church. At the annual church convention in June 1902, the church adopted the school as a part of its educational system. The next year, the synod granted an annual appropriation of $250. That small amount marked the beginning of an almost constant lobbying effort. For the next several decades, Concordia sought increased church funding to relieve its own financial burdens. Also in 1903, the association sold "dormitory shares" to its members; they purchased only $3,700 of an authorized $20,000. Bogstad struggled to attract more scholars in the fall and spring terms because he realized that an even enrollment throughout the year used plant more efficiently and improved cash flow. When advertising fixed courses failed to attract sufficient numbers, discounts of 6.5 percent (1904) and 10.2 percent (1909) were offered those who paid the entire annual fee in advance. As another income source to finance the recently instituted col-

The faculty, 1906.

lege course, Bogstad and Ness in 1909 proposed a $100,000 endowment.[30] Of course, to produce income an endowment must first be raised. That would not be accomplished for another decade.

The need for paying the higher salaries of more qualified college professors was yet in the future; in the meantime, the institution survived by saving money where it could. Employing women offered a convenient savings. The faculty in 1906 numbered eighteen; in keeping with the social standards of the day, the ten women were paid 40 to 60 percent less. President Bogstad received $1,200 and a free house; Professors Busby and Rognlie were paid $900 and $1,000 respectively. The women earned $600 to $750 annually. Parttime instructors were paid at the rate of $1.00 per hour for men and $.40 to $.50 an hour for women. More savings flowed from not insisting on faculty specialization and having them teach many subjects. O.I. Hertsgaard, called as director of music in 1909, also taught penmanship, debate, oratory, Shakespeare, English, and newcomer English.[31]

In addition to his many other duties, Bogstad recruited faculty. It was expected that professors would be moral and Lutheran. J.P. Bohlin, a Baptist hired in 1907 as director of music, was the exception that proves this rule. By special action, the trustees approved this contract subject to the condition that Bohlin "does no proselytizing." Bohlin resigned after one year. Presumably other non-Lutherans were not hired because there is no record of board dispensation. To find suitable teachers, Bogstad relied on the Lutheran college network and simply corresponded with other presidents. He wrote Saint Olaf's J.N. Kildahl in late 1903 to recruit one or possibly two instructors. Apparently the woman teaching classics suffered from consumption and might be unable to continue. For the definite opening, Bogstad wanted to hire someone he knew, Concordia alumnus J.P. Hertsgaard. Reliance on personal contacts did not always produce perfect results. Hertsgaard soon became a severe critic of the president.[32]

Director of Music
O.I. Hertsgaard

Conflict with the trustees darkened President Bogstad's last years. By 1909, Bogstad and Ness both complained about disruptive factionalism. The cause of this divisiveness is not known but most likely it ensued from the unresolved differences of the Aaker-Bogstad dispute. As practical men of affairs, some trustees may have been more sympathetic to Aaker. Their resentment probably increased when Bogstad demanded a $1,500 bonus for the extra work he had performed from 1905 to 1907. Indignation intensified as they listened to Bogstad's ambitious and expensive plans for a greater Concordia: New Main, a college course, an endowment and division of the president's duties. Frustrated by growing trustee opposition, both Ness and Bogstad threatened to resign in Summer 1909. Worn out from his herculean fundraising and construction efforts, Bogstad had suffered from nervousness and insomnia for several months. As a cure for his neurasthenia, a common middle-class affliction of the time, doctors recommended the standard rest cure. Hence Bogstad requested a year's leave and the division of his administrative duties. A committee recommended granting both requests, but the trustee board referred the report back to committee. Bogstad responded by declaring his willingness to resign as soon as a suitable replacement could be found. As he explained to Ness, this simplified "matters for the committee," brought "matters to focus" and satisfied those who had wanted him to leave for the past five years. But Bogstad urged Ness to remain in his post and prevent that faction from governing the institution. The association apparently agreed; they unanimously rejected Ness's resignation.[33]

Although apparently willing, Bogstad did not actually resign. At an August meeting of the boards, the directors recommended a year's leave for Bogstad and appointment of Henry O. Shurson as acting president. The trustees adopted these recommendations; they also elected Professor H.S. Hilleboe as permanent president (effective July 1, 1910) and named Bogstad the business manager. Ness, Bogstad and the directors protested and sought legal advice. A lawyer declared the action illegal for two reasons. First, it violated the by-laws; the trustees could not make appointments without recommendation or concurrence of the directors. Second, Bogstad was permanent president and could only be removed for cause or by resignation. Since no cause had been given and no hearing granted, the trustee action was a "flagrant violation of rights and injurious of his reputation." In short, Bogstad had a case.[34]

Thus advised, Bogstad informed the trustees that unless they revoked their action the directors planned legal proceedings. Meanwhile, Bogstad responded to a letter from H.S. Hilleboe, who had read in a newspaper that he had been called to Concordia. Bogstad informed Hilleboe that the call was illegal; there was no vacancy because he had not resigned. Furthermore he "had no attention of resigning until matters were settled." On September 17 the trustees revoked their call to Hilleboe and expressed regret for any "injury to the character and reputation of Bogstad." The board also noted that the president had been with the institution eighteen years and that its successes were "due more to his efficient work and untiring efforts than to any other individual."[35]

Victorious, Bogstad prepared to enjoy his leave. He had inquired earlier about pursuing a master's degree at Capital University, but financial reverses prevented graduate study. To pay his creditors, he worked as a fundraiser for Saint Luke's Hospital in Fargo. At the same time, he solicited funds for the Concordia library and endowment by calling on Andrew Carnegie, the Rockefeller Foundation, Dr. Pearson of Chicago—who had financed Fargo College—and James J. Hill. These efforts were unsuccessful. When it proved financially impossible in 1910 for Concordia to hire both a president and dean, Bogstad, not wanting permanently to impair his health, resigned. At first the association was reluctant to accept. Finally, after Bogstad explained his reasons, they agreed on the third vote. Elected to the board of trustees, Bogstad served until 1912, when he moved west and again assumed presidencies of Lutheran colleges: Spokane (1913–1914), Columbia (1914–1918) and Pacific (1918–1919). He later served as a director of a home for the elderly.[36]

Bogstad's Contributions

President Bogstad's leadership did much to shape Concordia. He overcame substantial opposition and built the impressive New Main; this essential building housed most college activities for almost four decades. He set the institution on the road to becoming a liberal arts college without entirely abandoning Aaker's commitment to business education. He thus combined liberal arts and practical training in a way that has characterized Concordia since his time. Bogstad's successor, President Henry O. Shurson (1909–1911) served only with the understanding that his appointment be temporary. He kept urging the association "to find a man worthy of the position." That man, J.A. Aasgaard, was called to the presidency in April 1911. He would carry to fruition Bogstad's attempts to establish college work and to raise funds for a library and an endowment.

Chapter 4

A College At Last!

The Coming of J.A. Aasgaard

Approaching its twentieth anniversary, Concordia faced an uncertain future. Recent discord had raised doubts and hindered fundraising. Henry Shurson had been forced to abandon his promising work as field secretary and temporarily to assume the presidency. Without additional financial support, the management reluctantly postponed needed improvements. Clearly it was not a propitious time to search for a permanent president.

Yet the association found a capable man in Johan Arnd Aasgaard, a well-known preacher and editor of religious periodicals. Given the recent well-publicized disharmony, it is not surprising that Pastor Ness wrote to assure Aasgaard that his election had not provoked any dissent and had been unanimous by both boards. As an additional sign of harmony and continued interest in the enterprise, board members had assumed $6,000 of the school debt. Thus assured of harmonious support and offered an annual salary of $1,500 plus a free residence, Aasgaard accepted the call.[1]

A dynamic, forceful personality, Aasgaard had been born in 1876 to Norwegian immigrant parents in Albert

President J.A. Aasgaard

Lea, Minnesota. His family soon moved to Lake Mills, Iowa, where his father kept a hardware store and Johan left school at age twelve to work as a "printer's devil." Five years later, he enrolled in the Saint Olaf preparatory department; he achieved his baccalaureate at Northfield in 1898 and became a candidate in theology at United Church Seminary in Minneapolis, followed by ordination in 1901. While serving as pastor from 1901 to 1910 at DeForest, Wisconsin, Aasgaard earned a B.D. from Princeton Theological Seminary, served as secretary of the church educational board and edited two religious newspapers.[2]

Concordia colleagues remembered Aasgaard as a man generous in his praise who worked hard and delegated work well to the faculty. He expected teachers to be thorough and to assume authority over their pupils who were to do as commanded. Collegians recalled his forceful chapel talks in which they were ordered to clean up the campus, urged to write their parents often and frequently reminded they owed service to the church after the privilege of attending Concordia. Despite a vigorous, almost brusque, manner, Aasgaard had a remarkable facility for reprimanding without causing anger; students greatly admired him as an excellent teacher and a very capable president. His extensive community activities—numerous speaking engagements, Kiwanis, Red Cross and the library commission—earned him the respect of Moorhead and the gift of a Studebaker Brougham from townspeople and alumni on his forty-ninth birthday in 1925.[3]

Norwegian Ethnicity

Concordia scheduled Aasgaard's inauguration ceremony on October 31, the same day that the school celebrated its twentieth anniversary. Both religious and political dignitaries spoke, including the leading local citizen, Solomon Comstock, and the district congressman. The ceremonies evidenced a Norwegian-American identity. Morning exercises conducted in Norwegian and afternoon observances in English were held in an auditorium decorated in the colors of Norway and the United States. As president, Aasgaard showed continued interest in Norwegian culture. He welcomed the erection on campus of the Hauge and Aasen monuments in 1912 and 1913 respectively because these events were "the best advertising that Concordia has ever received." The Hauge memorial dedication attracted an estimated 15,000, "the largest crowd ever gathered in Moorhead."[4]

Norwegian ethnic consciousness seems to have peaked in these years before the Great War. This heightened Norse consciousness revealed itself in many ways: the monuments to the Norwegian folk-heroes Aasen and Hauge; association minutes and reports suddenly written almost entirely in Norwegian; the demand of some pastors that "Yankee fever" for American customs must be cured by church colleges teaching Norwegian culture; and, the 1914 centennial celebration of the constitution that signaled Norwegian independence. Reflecting these ethnic concerns, Aasgaard in 1915 recommended that several hundred dollars be expended for Norwegian library books. Students of the day used Norse in conversation; Herman Nordlie recalled that when he walked through the hallways after his arrival in 1917 it was difficult to find a group speaking English. As late as 1920, alternate chapel services were conducted in Norse.[5]

The college thus mirrored the linguistic loyalty of Norwegian-Americans which

The Hauge Monument Dedication (1912) publicized the college.

The Ivar Aasen Memorial evidenced loyalty to the Norwegian language.

remained strong until after World War II. This loyalty was rooted in the high proportion of Norwegians living in numerous rural enclaves that existed well into the twentieth century. As late as 1940, one half of all midwestern Norwegians lived on farms or in villages of less than 2,500.[6]

The Burden of Debt

The debt, the most critical issue confronting Aasgaard, became immediately apparent to him shortly after he assumed office at midyear. A new president, local businessmen decided, offered an excellent opportunity to collect on overdue bills; Aasgaard soon moved to the basement to avoid the numerous collectors descending on his office. By March 1911, the debt had increased to more than $49,000 with an intolerable annual interest payment of $3,000. Many current bills—including groceries and one-half the salaries—had not been paid because the trustees used revenues to cover interest and repair costs. To pay creditors, the trustees were again forced to borrow, increasing the debt to $63,000 on September 1. A year later, the amount had climbed to $67,550, requiring a $4,000 annual interest payment. As Aasgaard pointed out, this equaled the salary of four more teachers. Although the institution could be operated on revenue from student fees alone, this meager income did not permit making interest payments or expensive repairs in addition. Clearly the debt required quick repayment. But how?[7]

As the United Norwegian Lutheran Church prepared the Jubilee Fund Campaign to celebrate its twenty-fifth anniversary in 1915, it requested that academies and colleges refrain from fundraising. Ness therefore recommended that each member of the association raise a share toward repayment of the debt. Fortunately for members, the United Church decided that money collected in the Concordia territory of North Dakota, western Minnesota and northern South Dakota should be applied toward debt repayment. By 1915, it had been substantially reduced with hopes that it would be completely repaid by the next annual association meeting. Of course, Concordia had earned this favor by allowing Aasgaard to devote much of his time for two years to the campaign. Although the instructional program suffered, Ness and the association encouraged Aasgaard to continue because the school benefited economically.[8]

Of great significance for Concordia, debt reduction opened the way for construction of a new heating plant and gymnasium, closer relations with the United Church and adoption of a four-year college course. Excavation of the gymnasium basement to house the heating plant and manual training department began in July 1914. The following year, financed in part by student fundraising efforts and finished by the manual training class, the "largest gymnasium in this section of the country" was erected on the foundation. A capacity crowd of four hundred for the first basketball game in January 1916 watched Fargo College overwhelm the Concordia "Lutefiskers" by the score of 25 to 15.

Completion of the new gymnasium meant that the floor in the east basement of Main eventually would be raised to the present level and the old gym would serve successively the commercial, domestic science, chemistry, physics, sociology and education departments.[9]

A new gymnasium, largest in the region, opened in 1915.

A constitutional amendment proposed by NWLCA President Ness in 1913 pointed the way toward closer church ties. The association agreed that United Church congregations should replace individuals as members of the association. When Ness said this change provided the most secure defense and guaranty for Concordia, he had in mind more than financial obligation. Indeed, as Aasgaard pointed out, debt reduction was a precondition for the change; it inspired the confidence of congregations which were naturally suspicious of assuming large financial responsibilities. Although Ness did not minimize the advantage of wider financial support, he emphasized that the greater benefit of congregational ownership would be a spiritual defense of the school as a Christian institution in a materialistic age. Despite the advantages of the proposed change, legal complications in part prevented it from being implemented until 1925. Under then-existing Minnesota law, corporations (i.e. congregations) could not own another corporation (i.e. the Northwestern Lutheran College Association). As attorney and trustee C.G. Dosland explained in 1914, it would take time to work out the legal problems.[10] He certainly did not expect it would take another decade for ownership of the college to be transferred to congregations, but other factors intervened.

Creating the College Program

Debt reduction also cleared the way for Concordia to adopt a four-year college program. This had been considered before. By 1911, twelve collegians were fulltime and several others parttime. They wanted a full college course and protested when the directors, fearful of worsening an already precarious financial situation, did not implement this change. Apparently they had been aroused by some unwarranted statements made by Professors Martin Tonning and J.P. Hertsgaard. Ness deplored the uprising; administrators, not students, should manage the school. The crisis ended with Hertsgaard's resignation and the readmission of the protesters, who had been expelled for their impertinence, after they asked pardon of the board.[11]

When finances had improved in 1913, Ness urged the immediate addition of a third year, with a fourth to begin the following fall. The association agreed, if it could be

Park Region Luther College in 1917 surrendered its college program.

done without increasing indebtedness. Insufficient numbers apparently delayed implementation for two years. Uncertain enrollments rendered it difficult but necessary to adopt college work, as Aasgaard clearly perceived. Already in 1913 he complained of the steady canvassing and advertising required to meet the competition from the growing number of public high schools. Despite poor crops and bad financial conditions, the president's mailing of 2,000 catalogs and 4,000 letters produced for 1914–1915 an enrollment of 345, an increase over the previous year. Noting that a higher number had registered for more than a single term and that forty-nine, the largest class ever, had graduated from the academic department, Aasgaard hoped these numbers would make it possible to offer the full college course. But he warned there were still many single-termers who came only in the winter when expenses were highest.[12]

Nonetheless, Aasgaard and Ness persisted because they believed that survival depended upon adopting a full college program and recruiting public high school alumni. They recognized that the junior college alternative had not been popular. They warned that the Minnesota legislature was considering a bill to require college work for a school to bear the college name. They feared that further delay might doom Concordia to academy status forever. With the pending merger of three synods that produced the Norwegian Lutheran Church in 1917, Park Region College in Fergus Falls, which graduated its first college class in 1912, had the advantage in joining Luther and Saint Olaf as the colleges of the new church.[13]

Adopting the view "now or never," Concordia delayed no longer. With the debt almost paid, the $4,000 formerly used for interest funded the new college program. In 1915 the school described a four-year course in its catalog and implemented senior college work. The general distribution of required courses, which remained basically unchanged for many years, included sixteen units of Bible, twelve each of English and foreign language, and six each of history, math, science, mental science and physical

From Academy to College, 1891--1925

education. A major and a minor of twenty-four and twelve junior-senior units respectively rounded out the curriculum that was oriented toward traditional humanistic disciplines. Approximately seventy units out of 128 required for graduation were general distribution. In declaring their major, collegians consulted with the president before the end of their sophomore year. Once decided, it could not be easily changed except by faculty vote or by departmental recommendation.[14]

The first class of five men and one woman who completed this curriculum graduated in 1917. Their commencement could not have been more timely. It established Concordia's credentials as a college in the same year that the Norwegian, Hauge and United Synods merged to form the Norwegian Lutheran Church in America. As had been anticipated, the merger raised the question of the futures of Park Region, a Norwegian Synod institution, and Concordia.

The new synod decided that it should not continue two colleges located in such close proximity. The church formed an educational committee empowered to visit each site as part of the process for determining the location of a merged college program. Aasgaard organized community support in both Fargo and Moorhead for situating it at Concordia. Speaking to 150 members of the Moorhead Commercial Club in January, the president outlined a plan for boosting the local school. Stirred by Aasgaard's eloquence, the club unanimously instructed him to inform the church that the community was willing to help raise $30,000 for paying the institution's debt. *The Forum* urged Fargo businessmen to back this Moorhead effort.[15]

A week later the educational committee, after a visit to Fergus Falls, arrived for its

Park Region Faculty, 1910-1911.

inspection of Concordia and Moorhead. The committee was impressed with the promised financial support which removed one of the strongest objections to Concordia. In addition, Aasgaard presented population charts based on the 1910 census which showed that several thousand more Scandinavians lived within fifty and one hundred miles of Moorhead than lived within a similar radius of Fergus Falls. This demographic advantage combined with superior rail service, Aasgaard argued, gave Moorhead a greater potential for growth and therefore a greater opportunity to develop the church in northern Minnesota and North Dakota. Persuaded by Aasgaard's eloquent case and the better rail connections, the committee recommended locating the merged college programs in Moorhead.[16]

On April 10 Concordia's boards of trustees and directors adopted the committee report on union and articles of agreement. The agreement was complicated, as could be expected from delicate diplomatic negotiations between formerly warring parties. Park Region dropped its college program; collegians and seven faculty were transferred to its rival. Concordia discontinued the normal department, parochial course and special English for newcomers; when average college attendance reached 200 the academy program would cease. Both schools could offer music and business if desired. The boards of both in the future should have representatives from the three former synods. Both corporations were to cooperate in developing both institutions. And the

Northwestern Lutheran College Association would transfer full control and ownership of the college to the church whenever demanded.[17]

The church merger and the amalgamation with Park Region were decisive for the emergence of Concordia College. Both contributed in substantial ways to the future success of the fledgling program, but in 1917 that prospect was not immediately apparent to observers. Although the settlement provided that Park Region collegians would attend Concordia, most did not. Apart from the hard feelings which existed for a long time, many attended Saint Olaf because they feared the recently established college might soon collapse. Those who did come felt a bit superior because they moved from a college to an academy; they also appeared worldly to one native who knelt outside their rooms and prayed for their salvation.[18]

Historian Herman Nordlie

Professor Christian Bale

Nonetheless, Concordia did benefit materially and immediately from the six professors who came from Park Region: Christian E. Bale (English), Herman Nordlie (history), I. Dorrum (education and Norwegian), T.C. Wollan (mathematics), A.O. Utne (chemistry) and Jacob A.O. Larson (Greek and Latin). Several were outstanding teachers. Five had master's degrees and were therefore qualified to teach college subjects. Three—Bale, Nordlie and Wollan—remained until the end of their careers. J.L. Rendahl, an academy graduate and 1923 college alumnus, suggests that the original Park Region and Concordia teachers engaged in scholarly competition. As a result, higher academic standards were set that enhanced the school's scholastic reputation.[19]

Rules, Religion and Student Life

Concordia's goals did not change with the emergence of the college. In his report to the association in 1914, Pastor Ness clearly stated the school's purpose: "To be able to give our youth a sound and all-around preparation for life with Christianity as a foundation."[20]

This task may have been rendered more difficult by the institution's Moorhead location. A town with forty-one saloons in 1910 was not perceived as an ideal site for a church college. Indeed, many believed that Moorhead's notoriety as "a saloon town" discouraged frightened parents from sending their children to Concordia. Because excessive drinking often took a heavy toll on isolated rural people, Norwegian pastors and laity by the 1880s had formed temperance groups in most valley communities. From the beginning, school officials shared this dry sentiment. Therefore when Clay County voted for prohibition in 1915 both President Aasgaard and the college rejoiced. Immediate results encouraged respectable citizens. Drunks now became a curiosity, whereas in past years "hundreds of them could be seen on the main street at almost any time of the day." Arrests for the period from July to September declined from 2,145 in 1914 to only ninety in 1915. This celebration of a clean, orderly city was short-lived; "the liquor element" soon staged a comeback.[21]

Because of Aasgaard's prohibitionist beliefs and prominence in community affairs, several citizen delegations called on him to run for mayor in 1916. He declined due to the time demands of his educational and religious work. Despite ongoing efforts by the "drys," the "blind pigs" continued to operate; throughout the period of National Prohibition (1919–1933) one could always buy a drink and "the liquor element" remained strong in Moorhead.[22]

The paternalistic supervision of behavior that characterized all denominational and state colleges of the day continued under President Aasgaard. As new personal vices appeared and popular entertainments changed, the school lengthened its list of prohibitions. Smoking cigarettes and visiting pool rooms, bowling alleys and theatres were first banned in 1912. As more collegians enrolled, officials supervised more closely the relations between sexes; men and women could not board at the same house and could not visit others of the opposite sex in a private room except by special permission in case of illness. Those who did not live at home or with relatives were required to live in the dormitories, which enhanced surveillance. Residents were supposed to be in their rooms when study hours began at 7:00 p.m.; lights were turned out at 10:15. A preceptress supervised the women; they needed her permission to be absent from rooms and to ride, walk or attend social events off campus.[23]

Regulations were not all negative. Authorities stressed the benefits of dormitory living, especially on blizzard days, and attempted to provide wholesome entertainments. The experience of those who remained in the residence halls during Christmas vacations demonstrates the truth of the Norwegian Lutheran adage that "one need not drink or smoke to have fun." Rules were relaxed. Invariably, all reported they had enjoyed themselves. According to one account, "even the 'iron-bound' doors of the ladies' hall were thrown open, so the young men could call upon the fair 'coeds' as often as they desired." Special foods offered by "Mother" Fjelstad and "royal entertainment" provided by President and Mrs. Aasgaard were additional pleasures. As academy seniors and collegians increased in number, play hours were replaced in 1916 by popular class entertainments—always suitably chaperoned, of course. These activities included the senior men giving their female classmates a boat ride on the Red River; the women later reciprocated with a picnic at Gooseberry Mound. Class adviser Emma Norbryhn supplied fudge on the first occasion and joined in the activity of being thrown off Tarpeian Rock on the second.[24]

Sigurd Mundhjeld 20's

(Keep for Future Reference)

Rules and Regulations
GOVERNING THOSE ROOMING
IN MEN'S DORMITORY

To make your stay in the dormitory agreeable, safe, and profitable, the following rules and regulations have been drawn up and must be strictly observed and lived up to. The fact that you are enrolled as a student implies that you will cheerfully abide by the rules and regulations and will lend your assistance in their administration.

I.—Calls.
 6:30 a. m.—Rising bell.
 6:55 a. m.—Formation for roll call in first floor hall.
  Sunday at 7:55.
 7:00 a. m.—Breakfast.
  Sunday at 8:00.
 7:50 a. m.—Study hours and recitations begin.
 12:00 a. m.—Chapel devotion.
 12:35 p. m.—Dinner.
  Sunday at 1:00.
 1:15 p. m.—Room inspection on Saturdays.
 1:30 p. m.—Study hours and recitations begin.
 4:30 p. m.—Study hours and recitations end.
 6:00 p. m.—Supper.
  Sunday at 5:45.
 6:55 p. m.—First call for study hours.
 7:00 p. m.—Study hours begin.
 9:30 p. m.—Study hours end.
 9:50 p. m.—Warning to retire.
 10:00 p. m.—Lights out.
II.—No recitations or study hours on Sunday.

Specific rules and regulations kept students on schedule and informed them of proper dormitory behavior.

A College At Last!

Students reacted variously to *in loco parentis*. Some rebelled and were eventually expelled if they refused to conform. Others responded with gentle humor when restrictions and dormitory conditions proved troublesome. Although the college advertised the benefits of steam heat and warm water, residents found both uncertain. Indeed, constant cold water led to a threatened shaving strike in 1915. Organizers believed "that the daily appearance of our stall-fed Corncobs with their unharvested facial foliage" should move officials "to give us warm water." If it did not, with the coming of spring "nature will solve the problem of the conservation of steamless heating plant heat."[25]

Afholds Forening (1905-1906), student temperance society.

When play hours ended the following year, the *Crescent* reported much inward rejoicing among many Corncobs who would not miss "the rigors of the grand march in lockstep unison over barren wastes of the gym floor." Others, who had internalized the moral code of their rural and college communities, vocally supported the regulations and joined their elders in condemning the evils of the saloon and ragtime. The American pietist moral imagination associated drink, dance halls and sexual license. These young Lutherans were much alarmed therefore by ragtime, a popular musical craze. "The lustful dance hall" depended on ragtime and its "luring rhythm and filthy story" which conveyed "foul thoughts." To end these evils, the students supported prohibition. With the abolition of alcohol, the saloon and dance hall would disappear, the city's moral climate would improve and collegians would be saved from temptations of the flesh.[26]

Their shocked reaction was similar to that of other middle-class moralists in the period. Ragtime was only the beginning of a dancing and jazz craze that swept the nation after 1912. Most of these dances originated in African-American culture, encouraged more intimacy between partners and featured heightened bodily expressions. Their very names—bunny hug, monkey glide, grizzly bear and lame duck—suggested a surrender to animality and rebellion against older sexual mores. To many of the respectable middle class, these popular entertainments represented the collapse of civilization.[27]

As the college emerged, extracurricular activities increased in number. This early appearance of college life hardly yet constituted an undergraduate culture with its own values and rewards. This culture had become so pervasive at some institutions that Woodrow Wilson, then president of Princeton, could say in 1909 that "the side shows are so numerous, so diverting . . . they have swallowed up the circus."[28]

These dangers were scarcely apparent at a fledgling college. To the contrary, the administration encouraged activities as a means for fostering its goals of intellectual and moral training. Student objectives were not incompatible. Collegians viewed activities as an antidote to regimented schoolwork which reduced them to "mere machines for acquiring knowledge," as well as an opportunity to apply their book learning and an occasion for developing character.[29]

Among the extracurricular opportunities, the administration favored religious organizations as most compatible with its goals. Widespread participation demonstrated that pupils shared institutional objectives. The Young People's Luther League undertook in 1914 to support at least one foreign missionary. Wednesday night Bible study supplemented formal religious instruction, chapel and Sunday worship at local churches. When Billy Sunday came to Fargo in 1912, many attended. An ex-baseball player turned revivalist, Sunday was a popular if somewhat controversial speaker. Some were filled with enthusiasm and could not wait to return; others were satisfied with one trip; and a few doubted the wisdom of attending at all. Despite the concern of many Norwegian-American Lutherans for doctrinal purity at the time, the *Crescent* urged a surprisingly broad-minded view: "Hear all; cleave unto that which is good."[30]

Athletics expanded. As interest grew, the administration extended its control, if not its financial support. A director of athletics supervised track, tennis, baseball and basketball teams.

Students first attempted to introduce football in 1909. By 1912 they were actually learning the game. Two society teams competed against each other in 1913. Three years later, Concordia's initial interscholastic gridiron appearance ended disastrously. Controversial because of its excessive roughness, which caused eighteen deaths in 1905 and prompted Teddy Roosevelt to call a White House meeting on the subject, the game had been regulated and reformed in keeping with the progressive ethos. At Concordia, collegians defended football; they minimized injuries and upheld the game's virtues: It drew the student body together, promoted physical development and trained future coaches. By 1918, the Lutheran presidents were seeking a uniform position on the question of intercollegiate football. It had been forbidden at Luther but both the Luther and Saint Olaf presidents thought it questionable to fight something collegians demanded when they had no moral or theological grounds for opposition. Football survived at Lutheran schools for the same reasons it endured elsewhere; it was compatible with the collegiate goal of training character. As President Aasgaard said in his muscular Christian defense of

The Concordia College Band made its first concert tour to Wolverton in 1910.

A College At Last!

athletics, competition prepared young men to face life's challenges. Like faculty everywhere, Aasgaard nonetheless insisted on regulation.[31]

Additional controls had been established in 1911 when Concordia joined Moorhead and several North Dakota normals in the Interstate School Conference. According to conference regulations, collegians must be enrolled two weeks before an event, carry full loads and pass 75 percent of their work. Faculty, professionals and those playing on outside teams were ineligible. At Concordia, students formed an athletic association to manage teams and finance them with a membership fee of $1.50. Supplemented by ticket sales and occasional basket socials, these funds were inadequate. Collegians deplored lack of money and urged imposing a general fee for everyone. If unwilling to support activities, no one should be permitted to enroll.[32]

Other activities competed for time and attention. Music remained important and the band continued as the strongest organization. Directed by Oscar I. Hertsgaard, a Saint Olaf alumnus who had been assistant director of that band when it toured Norway in 1906, the Concordia Band made its first tour to Comstock and Wolverton in May 1910. President Shurson accompanied the group and preached at each church. After graduation that year, the band and the octette traveled to the little Norways of North Dakota performing at Mayville, Hatton, Northwood, Grand Forks, Reynolds and Hillsboro. From this humble beginning, concert tours soon provided important publicity for the college and, by stimulating members, an occasion for further developing the band.[33]

Besides music, debate and literary work retained popularity. The two literary and three debating societies were excused from classes to meet regularly during the last two periods on Saturday afternoons, the final class day of a week that began on Tuesday at the time. To further stimulate interest, Dr. O.J. Hagen and Attorney C.G. Dosland in 1909 presented the Chrysostom and Pereclesian Literary Societies with a cup and medals and requested that they compete annually for these prizes. As part of the effort to improve the literary quality of their work, the societies in 1916 were organized by gender. Evidently mixing the sexes made the weekly meetings a social rather than scholarly time. Apparently this reform did not correct all problems because programs were still criticized for being too musical and for giving too little attention to literature.[34]

Following developments at other schools, collegians in 1916 called for the creation of student government. If a proper committee were established, they argued, then they could solve many problems by themselves without involving faculty. This suggestion would not be acted upon until after the Great War and then only with close faculty supervision.[35]

The *Crescent* stimulated much writing on a wide range of significant social issues that reflected the ferment of the progressive era in the United States. Besides publishing prize compositions from society competition, the editors selected the best from essays submitted by students on topics of their choice. Their writing exhibits traits of the campus rebels which historian Helen Horowitz has identified at more established institutions. The rebels demanded that college not be a place of withdrawal from politics but a forum for addressing the hard issues of the day. Accordingly, they insisted that undergraduates debate questions of war and peace, capitalism and socialism, and other controversial topics.[36]

Concordia collegians debated these and other subjects including the nature of education. According to one essayist, a private college like Concordia should work in the area of "general culture" by focusing on literary, philosophical and social studies.

Such education trained "the whole man, with all his latent powers and energy, into a complete individual," and therefore prepared "pastors, teachers, literary men and social workers" in a way that the "state universities offering science and specialized training for experts" could not. Although manual training in the academy might be defended on vocational and cultural grounds, the narrowness of vocational training was not appropriate at the higher level. At college, scholars should acquire breadth of culture and should also "get in touch with the social, economic, political and religious problems of the day."[37] The *Crescent* provided the principal vehicle for "getting in touch" during the first decade of Aasgaard's presidency.

As could be expected at a Christian school, *Crescent* articles addressing cultural, political and social topics were permeated with evangelical Christianity. This tendency was not confined to schools like Concordia; American culture was fervently evangelical during the progressive era. Evangelicals committed to preserving the absolute moral values of Victorian culture were troubled by the popularity of vaudeville and the movies. Essayists mirrored this concern by distinguishing between good and bad art: "Good theatre aims to offer the public something of real literary value, while the degenerated forms aim only to please and fascinate." Bad theatre did not raise the moral quality of society but good theatre did. Thus movies, which too often seemed "to pander to a sickly sort of craving in their patrons for the sensational and sentimental," qualified as bad theatre. Of course, collegians should avoid movies and other

George Brekke

forms of bad theatre. Defenders of Victorian culture were ambivalent about the role of movies in American life, however. Essayists reflected this ambivalence by recognizing that films educated as well as entertained. They conveyed information about current events, world leaders and foreign peoples. Movies which thus met Victorian standards were a beneficial new art form that edified the masses. These films joined the novel and the theater as forms of good art and could be shown at Concordia. Accordingly, *The Pilgrim's Progress* was viewed on campus in 1915.[38]

Similar religious and moral themes pervaded discussions of politics. Many essays reflected the reformism of both progressivism and Norwegian-American political culture at the time. One essayist defended Theodore Roosevelt for his support of progressive insurgents against the old guard Republicans on the grounds "it is simply an application of old-time moralities to new conditions." Another argued that more politicians of the Woodrow Wilson type were needed: "more honest and more able men must come to the front—men who make it a point to enter the political arena for the sake of duty and necessity and not for the purpose of gratifying selfish motives."[39]

A similar moralism imbued discussions of socialism. In 1911 the senior class play, *Out in the Street*, dramatized the immoral "cruelty of capitalists toward those in distress and poverty." Similarly, an essayist made a plea for universal peace on moral grounds and linked that prospect to the triumph of socialism. The author rejected the militaristic interpretation of United States history usually taught in public schools, one that exalted a narrow nationalism and glorified leaders and wars. Instead the United States should work for peace by creating "a socialistic feeling of brotherliness towards other peoples." This could be easily achieved through the schools because they "gathered pupils from several nationalities." Another wrote about the claim on the young to work for social justice. He urged them to prepare by carefully cultivating the mind, developing an upright character, fostering a public spirit and practicing personal religion. George Brekke, known as a socialist by his fellows, advocated organization to further the moral progress of modern society. He defended the Non-Partisan League because it organized farmers to protect their interests and achieve justice for themselves. A North Dakota native, Brekke graduated from the academy in 1915 and the college in 1918. His advocacy of socialism and the Non-Partisan League did not hinder his campus popularity. Elected president of his class, president of Luther League and *Crescent* business manager, he also participated in the athletic association and the Mondamin Literary Society. Brekke later practiced law in Minot, an early center of socialism in North Dakota.[40]

The Great War Comes to Concordia

The outbreak in August 1914 of the Great War in Europe, an event seemingly far removed from the concerns of a struggling Norwegian-American academy and possible college, eventually had a major impact on Concordia. Initially the war generated much discussion. Indeed, it provoked so much discussion that one student expressed disgust with "certain people who have uncovered secrets of European diplomacy and will talk you deaf, dumb, and blind to prove their case on the causes of the war." Informed by socialist and Non-Partisan League principles, *Crescent* essays reflected the antiwar, neutralist attitudes prevalent in North Dakota and parts of Minnesota and took a detached, critical view of the war. One short story told of Fritz, a good German patriot, who died as a consequence of his dream of one world serving humanity. Presented in human terms, the character of Fritz revealed the author's

Concordia flag-raising ceremonies (1917) marked the United States' declaration of war.

sympathetic understanding of the human plight of the German soldier. Another essayist criticized the American patriots waging the preparedness campaign in 1915 and insisted that "enlarging our army and navy does not necessarily answer the problem of national defense." To the contrary, "preparation for war as a means of ensuring peace and security has been proven a failure" by the European events which culminated in the war. Other essays mirrored the socialist and Non-Partisan League adage that "it was a rich man's war and a poor man's fight." War only created millionaires by enriching industrialists, bankers and grain speculators. Farmers and other common folk should not be misled by war-related prosperity and should not be duped into fighting for the profits of a few capitalists.[41]

Criticisms of American capitalism and sympathy for German soldiers disappeared from the *Crescent* once the United States entered the war on April 6, 1917. College support for American participation, like that of most North Dakota and Minnesota citizens, was immediate and wholehearted.

On the day Congress declared war, the band paraded down the main streets of Fargo and Moorhead playing national songs. At 10:00 a.m., the entire student body and many townspeople assembled in the auditorium for patriotic addresses by President Aasgaard and former North Dakota Governor L.B. Hanna. The American flag was raised over New Main where, officials promised, "it will remain until the war with Germany is over." On April 29 everyone assembled in the gym to bid farewell to two academy pupils, Luther Ersland and Gilbert Olson, who had enlisted in the marines. More than eighty others would eventually serve. Students were given other opportunities for aiding the war effort. On May 10, Dr. Hagen spoke about Red Cross work and urged the girls to help in their home communities. The band gave a Red Cross benefit concert on May 12 and made several additional appearances for the Red Cross during that spring.[42]

Displays of patriotic unity, sacrifice and service were cultivated consciously and extensively by the Woodrow Wilson administration. Reluctant to rely on the power of the federal government for mobilizing the country and alarmed by the divisions of opinion revealed by the "preparedness" controversy of the neutral years, President Wilson resorted to a policy of superheated patriotic appeals in liberty loan, food conservation and selective service campaigns. The voluntary self-sacrifice of bond purchases, "wheatless-meatless" days and service to country was preferable to compulsory heavy taxation, rationing and conscription.[43]

These patriotic appeals brought the military virtues of service and discipline to the fore on campus. The college opened late that fall to allow male students to finish farm work in compliance with the national food conservation movement. When classes resumed, President Aasgaard at opening exercises emphasized that "this is not a time for intellectual loafing. ... [W]e are living in a time of war and it is therefore more important than ever that the student ... apply himself with the utmost diligence." Collegians were similarly concerned with the issue of slacking during national emergency. They assured themselves that it was not unpatriotic to attend college since men could not be called into service faster than need or training facilities allowed. While awaiting the call, college men "may best serve their country by so training themselves that they will be able to render greater service at some future time." Because they were "in an intellectual training camp that develops future leaders of national thought and action," they were not slackers. The *Lutheran Church Herald* concurred with this analysis and cited President Wilson in support of college training as patriotic duty.[44]

The college enlisted in the war effort in other ways as well. At the 400th anniversary celebration of the Reformation in 1917, an offering of $175 was taken for support of the ministers and religious work in military camps. Men attended Thursday night drills in the manual of arms, and women knitted and engaged in other Red Cross work. By January 1918, collegians were selling war savings stamps as part of the national thrift campaign. Using the slogan "for the country and my college," the campaign generated 300 pledges from 90 percent of the students and $1,700 for the library fund when the government repaid the loan. A united war work campaign, begun on Victory Day (November 11, 1918), quickly raised $1,000. The students had clearly heeded the chapel speaker, who had pleaded for more unity of thought and action in support of the war on the part of the Lutherans.[45]

As members of a foreign church and an ethnic group suspected by Yankees of being against the war and sympathetic to Germany, Norwegian-Americans were anxious to prove themselves patriots. When the Norwegian Lutheran Church opened its national convention in Fargo in 1918, only American flags were displayed and "the stars and stripes" formed the background to the main platform set with an improvised altar and a great white cross. While sessions were still conducted in Norwegian, the *Forum* assured readers that "every feature of the convention was thoroughly American in spirit." The church made other concessions to Americanism. The national organization actively supported the liberty fund drives and the proportion of Norwegian language services dropped from 73.1 percent to 61.2 percent between 1917 and 1918.[46]

A Student Army Training Corps detachment, some of whom attended Concordia.

Early in 1918 Concordia had applied to the United States War Department for a Student Army Training Corps (SATC) unit. The aim of the War Department in establishing SATC was to use colleges and universities for selecting and training officer candidates and technical experts for military service. Colleges were attracted to the program because it promised to relieve their critical financial situation. It offset declining numbers; guaranteed tuition, room and board for every student-soldier enrolled, and reimbursed schools for administrative expenses and use of facilities. No one objected to the militarization of academe because they viewed SATC as fulfilling the service ideal of American higher education. Besides, it generated badly needed income.[47]

On October 1, 140,000 men at 516 institutions became student-soldiers. Concordia did not participate initially because it did not receive authorization until after the fall term had started, and sixty men had already transferred to schools which had SATC. Nonetheless Concordia belatedly began the program and by October 30 twenty-one had enrolled. Disbanded December 14, the unit was honored with a banquet and praised for having "the best and cleanest barracks in the two cities." The commander had disciplined by having

From Academy to College, 1891--1925

men on their hands and knees scrub the entire gymnasium floor. For participation in SATC, Concordia received its first federal money—$1,265.[48]

During Fall 1918, Fargo-Moorhead and Concordia suffered through the Spanish influenza epidemic that had spread from the western front throughout the world. Schools, churches and theatres were closed; collegians were quarantined to campus from October 9 until November 7. Classes, chapel and social activities continued, but only those confined to the dormitories were permitted to attend. Although seventy-eight died in Moorhead, no one became ill at the college. The only fatality was a young woman who broke quarantine to return home, where she contracted the disease. Soon after the quarantine was lifted, city fire whistles and church bells at 4:00 a.m. on November 11 joyfully announced Victory Day. Boys rushed from the dormitory to shout about the campus. An expedition visited the president to request a holiday. When granted, students joined street celebrations in both cities and thanksgiving services in the churches that evening.[49]

Carl J. Aardal

Although the war had ended, war-induced hatreds and emotions endured. Patriotic appeals by the Wilson administration fostered anti-German feelings on campus and throughout the nation. Carl Aardal left for the military promising "to squeeze Kaiser Bill's adam's apple until he spits cider." Emil G. Bagley wrote from France that "we are determined to conquer the beast that is preying upon the weaker nations of Europe, ravaging innocent children and defenseless women, and doing everything possible to crush our free democracy." Another soldier warned: "I hope our pro-German citizens will be very careful when I come home because I have comrades that lie asleep in Belleau Woods and their memory does not grow old or die." Minnesota Commission of Public Safety cartoons, published in the *Crescent*, stressed the negative image of the brutal, hob-nailed boot-wearing hun.[50]

This anti-German cartoon appeared in the Crescent.

In general the college seemed to accept the Wilson administration's view of the war. Collegians adopted Wilson's idea that the United States was fighting to "make the world safe for democracy." Support for the war was not viewed as being incompatible with the function of the college. Indeed, the school took pride in the enthusiasm of the college man for the war. According to a *Crescent* essayist, it showed "that our American educational system has been able to inculcate that spirit of loyalty and love of justice which is to dedicate the future of our country to the cause of humanity and democracy." Furthermore, such enthusiasm was sound because "it is based on a keen understanding of the great principles at stake." It was not following blindly the gods of war. Widely shared by other professors and students throughout the nation, this enthusiasm for the American cause led the *New Republic* to label it a thinking man's war. To the editors of this progressive magazine, the war effort appeared to be a disinterested crusade in support of ideals rather than interests.[51]

The excesses of wartime crusading zeal at times belied thought, however. This zeal expressed itself in the campaign for 100 percent Americanism that persisted after the Armistice. The baccalaureate sermon in 1919 self-righteously proclaimed that German ideals derived from Satan and American ideals originated from God. American Legionnaires visited campus and explained their commitment to Americanism and their opposition to all reds—Bolsheviks, International Workers of the World and Anarchists. *Crescent* essayists mirrored these ideals when they attacked those "mild traitors" who "incessantly cavil at our government" and who should either "shut-up or pack-up." Others challenged this chauvinism. They labeled red-baiting a form of idol worship. They complained that the patriotism of conservatives focused only on workers and the foreign-born who were largely responsible for building industrial America.[52]

Doubts about patriotic excesses did not diminish institutional pride in its record of service. During the Great War, Concordia served the nation in many ways. Like other educational institutions, it cooperated with SATC and assumed the initiative in mobilizing its resources for national defense. Similarly, Concordia viewed its war effort as an extension of its commitment to the ideal of serving society. The association "commended the splendid patriotic spirit shown by the student body" and did not worry that the wartime crusade might compromise the school's integrity. Like progressive intellectuals generally, Concordia collegians expected many benefits to flow from United States participation. By teaching Americans to Hooverize, American wastefulness would be curbed and thriftiness improved. The war would also "mold the heterogeneous mixture of races that constitute the population of the United States into a composite race" and "put a stamp of Americanism on them." Moreover, wartime idealism would overthrow the materialistic conception of life, encourage people to work for the benefit of humanity and foster better class relations between the workers and the wealthy.[53]

These hopes were not fulfilled. Nevertheless by participation, as President Aasgaard no doubt intended, Concordia demonstrated that it was indeed an American institution and that Norwegian-Americans were fully assimilated into American society. Moreover, the college appealed to patriotism in its 1919 endowment fund drive by publicizing the endowment as a memorial to the men of the Northwest who had fought in the Great War.

Aasgaard's Achievements

By 1918 President Aasgaard had accomplished much. He had worked closely with Pastor Ness and with the United Church Jubilee Fund Campaign to reduce a burdensome debt which, so long as it existed, hindered future expansion. Debt reduction opened the door to a closer relationship with the church and to the establishment of a four-year college program. In proposing that congregations replace individuals as members of the association, Aasgaard and Ness wanted to guarantee the financial and spiritual integrity of the institution. In proposing a senior college, they wanted to ensure survival. Aasgaard perceived that the competition from public high schools rendered precarious the future of a private academy at the same time it increased the pool of potential applicants for a private college. He also knew that Concordia had to act quickly or it might lose permanently the prospect of college status to Park Region after the church merger which occurred in 1917.

As president, Aasgaard maintained Christian discipline. Extracurricular activities expanded in response to student demand, but these were carefully directed to serve the school's educational goals of intellectual and character development. During the Great War, Aasgaard led the college in supporting the war effort; he demonstrated thereby that Concordia was a patriotic institution in service of American society. These successes laid the foundation for Aasgaard's more substantial achievements of the 1920s.

Chapter 5

Into the Collegiate Mainstream

Seeking Accreditation

When Concordia instituted senior college work President Aasgaard pointed to the importance of being accredited by the North Central Association. Accreditation would require an endowment fund, a library and a more qualified faculty.

Before his resignation, President Bogstad had proposed a $100,000 endowment. Aasgaard sympathized with this goal; but the United Church Jubilee Campaign Fund, his work in reducing the school debt, the beginning of the senior college and the Great War postponed the campaign until 1919. Entitled Lutheran Soldiers and Sailors Memorial Endowment Fund—"In Memory of Those Who Died, In Gratitude for Those Who Returned"—the drive set a goal of $200,000, appealed in the name of congregations comprising the Northwestern Lutheran College Association and was endorsed by the presidents of the North Dakota and Northern Minnesota Districts of the Norwegian Lutheran Church.[1]

Lutheran Soldiers and Sailors Memorial Endowment Fund

A 1919 brochure appealed to Lutheranism and patriotism.

The Rev. O.H. Pannkoke, a prominent New York Lutheran fundraiser employed in the campaigns of more than twenty eastern and midwestern Lutheran institutions, assisted in planning and prepared the publicity. Announcements conveyed the message that 6,000 had enjoyed the blessings of Christian education since the founding and that Concordia advanced God's Kingdom by training ministers, missionaries, teachers and the Christian men and women who would provide community leadership. The literature also appealed to denominational self-preservation; Concordia deserved support "to keep a Lutheran territory Lutheran." Too many Lutherans were not members of the church, according to Luther professor O.M. Norlie, who estimated that 70 percent of the Norwegian-American immigrants had not affiliated with any Norwegian Lutheran synod in America. Unless strong counter measures were taken, church leaders feared continued defections to other denominations like the Congregationalists, who hoped to raise $400,000 in 1919 for Fargo College. As evidence of competition, Aasgaard cited a booklet from the Congregational Education Society that called on North

Dakotans to support Fargo College or "people will turn to the Lutheran Church with its dogmatic and anti-American tendencies." The memorial campaign for Lutheran veterans effectively countered this anti-American smear by a Yankee church.[2]

The campaign began well. Aasgaard reported that $75,000 had been quickly pledged. Unfortunately, crop shortages and the postwar decline in farm prices forced abandonment of the drive in many congregations. Although $100,000 was raised, this proved insufficient when the North Central Association in 1923 increased the endowment fund requirement to $500,000 above indebtedness. Another drive would be necessary to qualify for accreditation.

Undeterred, Aasgaard proceeded with efforts to build a library. The trustees in 1921 approved construction on the existing foundation connected to Ladies Hall (present Bishop Whipple) for the cost of $30,000. The board later authorized Aasgaard to borrow and spend $10,000 for library books and laboratory equipment. Instructed to take the matter before the Ministerial Association of Northern Minnesota and North Dakota, Aasgaard persuaded the ministers to arrange for church organizations to reimburse the college. Herman Nordlie later remembered how Aasgaard boldly borrowed the money and "gave the department heads virtually carte blanche to order books."[3]

The new library (now Grose Hall) opened in February 1922 after volunteers earlier had moved books and equipment from Main 17 and 18. By June, 3,000 books had been acquired and were being cataloged by the librarian and a newly hired assistant. The purchases by Professors Bale, Nordlie, Fossum and others had started a quality library; with some justification the institution claimed "one of the finest collections of books in the Northwest for college work." Both president and students agreed that the "new library had raised the standard of study." The library occupied only the first floor for the next two decades; the second was used as storage and the third as a women's dormitory. Plans were soon made to set aside part of the space for a museum. By 1925, Professors Holvik and Nordlie were collecting relics, mementos and documents of the early pioneers and churches in the Northwest.[4] The remnants of this collection are presently stored in the basement of Park Region Hall.

Professor Jacob Tanner

President Aasgaard attempted to improve faculty qualifications and, as a consequence, raise salaries. The American Council on Education in 1921 suggested these minimum standards: For department heads, the equivalent of a Ph.D.; for instructors, two years' graduate training in field of teaching at a recognized graduate school. At that time only classics professor Andrew Fossum, who came from Park Region in 1918, had a doctorate. Aasgaard expected four others—Bale, Nordlie, Tanner and Wickey —to soon complete their degrees. If professors were required to attain more graduate training, Aasgaard said, then institutions must pay higher salaries. He recommended $2,400 for department heads in 1920. He justified these large raises of $700 in some cases by pointing to faculty qualifications and to the high cost of living. "We can be well satisfied with the training and scholarship of our faculty," Aasgaard proclaimed. "It is well above the faculty average in this part of the country." The high cost of living, the principal economic concern after the Armistice, was constantly in the headlines. By 1919 the cost of living had risen 77 percent above 1914; it jumped another 25 percent in 1920. For professors and others tied to salaries, postwar inflation was a nightmare. Moved by their plight, the boards approved Aasgaard's requests with two conditions: First, teachers earning more than $2,000 should not assume permanent work for pay without consulting the president and without joint permission of the president and the board chairman; second, such professors should be at the disposal of the college for the entire year except for one month's vacation.[5]

The demands of accrediting agencies and the increasingly secularized society evidenced in the 1920s Jazz Age made the distinctive character of church-related liberal arts colleges a major issue. The Lutheran Educational Conference, organized in 1910, and the Association of American Colleges for the Advancement of Liberal Arts Education, formed in 1915, became national forums for presidents to wrestle with the concept of the modern church-related college. Dr. N.J. Gould Wickey, professor of psychology and philosophy, addressed the Lutheran Educational Conference on this issue in 1923. To develop a wholesome Lutheran denominational consciousness, Wickey said, Lutheran colleges must have Lutheran faculties. To achieve this goal in a time of higher accreditation standards, more Lutherans must undertake study at recognized graduate schools. They would have employment opportunities at Lutheran colleges because one-sixth of the positions were filled with non-Lutherans. A more highly trained Lutheran faculty

Dr. N.J. Gould Wickey

would enable the colleges to better serve the church. As a consequence, the church would contribute more to learned discussion and produce more literature for the general public. This would increase church prestige, develop greater loyalty and assist laity in knowing what to believe.[6]

To recruit the Lutherans Wickey advocated, President Aasgaard corresponded with other Lutheran presidents. In 1923 he wrote Saint Olaf's Lars Boe seeking a man to teach English in the academy and to college freshmen. For qualifications, the candidate must be seriously interested in "the freshman problem," have "a good Christian personality" and be academically talented. Boe needed "men of the same type" and therefore could not recommend anyone. Unfortunately, "few men major in English, and fewer still ... take the master's degree."[7]

Despite difficulties, Lutherans were recruited. By the mid-1920s, the faculty numbered thirty-five; 77 percent were of Norse ancestry and 65 percent had studied at Lutheran colleges. The staff included five doctorates, six master's degrees, four ministers and fifteen women. The women tended to concentrate in certain departments; nine were distributed equally among home economics, music and languages.[8]

Salaries approached the levels recommended by Aasgaard. The president received $2,500 and a free house. Fulltime men and women averaged $2,327 and $1,570 respectively. The institution rationalized this inequity as follows: Men had graduate degrees, were department heads and headed families, in contrast to single women who had only themselves to support. Aasgaard had hoped that higher salaries would help Concordia retain its best teachers and encourage faculty to acquire degrees. Unfortunately, those who completed doctorates often left. In 1924 Jacob Tanner departed for Luther Theological Seminary and in 1926 Gould Wickey accepted the presidency of Carthage College before enjoying a distinguished career as executive director of the National Lutheran Educational Conference. A graduate of Gettysburg College—

the hotbed of Lutheran radicalism in America, according to Tanner—Wickey greatly enlivened the college. He was a great preacher; to hear him speak, many students walked to St. Mark's in Fargo.[9]

Secular Learning in a Church-College Curriculum

Concordia's curriculum reflected its mission as a Christian liberal arts college. The relationship of Christianity to secular knowledge was greatly agitated during the 1920s as fundamentalists sponsored anti-evolution bills in many states; this campaign culminated in 1925 with the famous Scopes Trial in Tennessee. The Norwegian Lutheran Church shared the fundamentalist antipathy to evolution, declaring it to be "a philosophy of religion" and an "anti-Christian theory" that ought not be taught in public schools. Nevertheless, Concordia as a Christian college asserted the compatibility of science and religion. In arguing this position in 1922, a *Concordian* editorialist distinguished between science and scientists, between facts and theories. Scientists might err in their interpretation of the facts and thus come into conflict with Scripture. It was thus the inferences and theories of scientists that conflicted with Scripture, not the facts of science. "If scientists would wait for more light there would be less criticism of scripture," the editor maintained. This argument represented a traditional Baconian view of science long held compatible with religion by American Protestants. This Baconian view was made even more clear in a subsequent article. Science merely collects facts and groups them according to time, space and similarity. From this objective collection of facts, untainted by inference of the scientist, a correct explanation compatible with Scripture emerged. Thereby science explained how something happens, but could not explain why it happened.[10]

This distinction between theory and fact allowed biology professor A.M. Sattre to discuss evolution in his science classes at Concordia. He carefully labeled evolution a theory and then answered questions about it. By treating evolution as a theory, Sattre gave it lesser status than scientific fact. Moreover, conflict with Scripture could be attributed to the mistaken inference of scientists in constructing the theory and therefore need not lead to a reexamination of assumptions about the Bible. Sattre did oppose teaching evolution in the elementary schools. When his daughter came home from the Moorhead State campus school with a book showing the evolution of the horse, the professor visited the principal and the book disappeared. Sattre's views were shared by other Lutherans of his day; evolution should not be taught to immature minds in the public schools but it ought to be discussed in Christian colleges that are engaged in scien-

Professor A.M. Sattre

tific inquiry. Ironically, this openness to natural science by the colleges eventually undermined the church's opposition to evolution and the related historical-critical approach to Scripture.[11]

Despite sensitivity on the issue of evolution, Concordia did not exhibit hostility to secular learning, as revealed by the diversity of its science, philosophy and social science offerings. Although geology—linked closely to evolutionary theory—was notable by its absence, physics, chemistry and biology—including comparative anatomy, embryology, genetics and eugenics—were studied. History of philosophy examined ancient, medieval and the modern philosophers Descartes, Hume, Kant, Hegel and Royce. A course in present philosophical tendencies surveyed pragmatism, materialism, neo-realism and idealism. To be sure, collegians were protected from contamination by secular ideas; they (and their parents) were assured that the course "will aim to develop for the student a constructive Christian view of the universe and life." After 1920, psychology was listed with philosophy; general, applied and social psychology courses were taught.[12]

Chemistry lab students experiment in the 1920s.

As in most denominational colleges of the day, social science offerings developed in fits and starts depending on the interests of professors who had been hired. Nevertheless, a number of economics courses—principles, money and banking, labor problems, business organization and public finance—were offered regularly from the introduction of the college program. Similarly, sociology was taught until 1920, when instructor D.A. Leonard left; thereafter it might be combined with courses in education and religion, depending on the inclinations of instructors. American government appeared annually after 1923.

Professor J.H. Hjelmstad

Languages occupied a prominent place; required to take twelve units in each of two languages, pupils chose from among French, German, Greek, Hebrew, Latin and Norse. Education, English, history, home economics, mathematics, music, physical education, public speaking and religion comprised the remainder of the curriculum.[13]

Although Concordia adopted a traditional liberal arts course of study dominated by the arts and sciences, the early commitment to practical subjects did not disappear. Aasgaard suggested to the board in 1919 that the college should organize a department of business and commerce. Aasgaard argued that the sons of merchants, businessmen and farmers wanted advanced business courses that only universities offered; he believed "we should not let the universities get these men who will be leading and prominent men of the Northwest during the next twenty-five years. ..."[14] The department was not then established. Economics professor J.H. Hjelmstad taught some business subjects, and a commercial department for training secretaries and business teachers was added in 1941. Thus for many years most graduates became teachers rather than pursuing business careers.

A Growing College

By demonstrating the potential of higher education for service and by creating incentives for attendance, the Great War accelerated the postwar growth of American higher education. At the time, most institutions were small; more than half enrolled fewer than 300 students. Then an unprecedented boom boosted registrations an estimated 25 percent nationwide between 1917 and 1920.[15]

Swept away by an optimism induced by growth, Aasgaard in 1919 predicted an enrollment of 500 or even 600 from the beginning of the next year. "Concordia College has come into its own," he exulted. "There is no longer any question about the standing of our college. We have today the largest attendance of any of the educational institutions in the two cities." Yet failure of the grain crop in the Northwest yielded 118 fewer students that fall. The unexpectedly low enrollment of 362 made "this the hardest financial year since coming to the institution," Aasgaard reported. Combined with the large salary increase and the high inflation which raised the price of coal and other commodities, the decline created a $10,000 deficit.[16]

The slump in total attendance stemmed from diminished numbers in the academy. Registrants in the college program expanded steadily from 1917 to 1925 (See Table III) while those in the academy decreased. By 1924, when 325 registered, the academy accounted for only one-third. Aasgaard attributed this decline to hard times and the growth of public high schools. Nevertheless, the president hesitated to close the academy. He thought that it should be kept open for North Dakota parents who probably would not send their children to Park Region. Shrinking numbers settled the matter. In 1923 the directors decided to phase it out one class at a time, starting in 1924; the academy closed in 1927.[17]

Postwar inflation dramatically increased operating expenses. To offset spiraling costs, Concordia raised fees and engaged in more intensive recruiting. In 1917 annual fees of $240 were guaranteed for those who paid in advance, but the institution reserved the right to raise fees for the winter and spring terms if required by conditions. By 1921, fees had increased 25 percent to $300; within three years they had jumped another 11 percent to $332. These increases, combined with the depressed agricultural economy occasionally worsened by poor crops, triggered innovation. The Concordia College Women's League, organized in 1921 by women teachers and professors' wives, established a student loan fund. From 1921 to 1926 this organization raised $4,000 that was mostly loaned to seniors. Sixty-two benefited and graduated who might not have otherwise. Similarly, President Aasgaard's correspondence includes many letters requesting assistance in finding work to help pay college expenses. Accordingly, the institution advertised for jobs in the local newspapers.[18]

Concordia responded to financial difficulties by adopting new recruiting techniques. Collegians were told they could do a valuable service by reporting their activities to hometown newspapers, recruiting during vacations and boosting the college at all

Table III: *Growth of College Enrollments, 1917–1925**

	17-18	18-19	19-20	20-21	21-22	22-23	23-24	24-25
Seniors	9	10	17	18	29	41	22	49
Juniors	10	13	16	28	36	25	46	66
Sophomores	21	12	27	44	26	44	68	74
Freshmen	40	47	62	46	64	83	82	101
Total	80	82	122	136	155	193	218	290

*From President's Report in Board of Directors, Minutes, 25 June 1925, Governing Bodies Papers.

times. The *Crescent,* which solicited opinion on a wide range of issues, would not publish criticisms of the school because that would convey the wrong impression to the public. The Mondamin Literary Society promoted *"one hundred percent Corncobism"* which, they maintained, "has appealed to the real student and discouraged the knocker." Promotion also was assigned to new publications like the *Scout,* a college triannual first published in 1920, and the *Concordian,* a semimonthly newspaper which replaced the *Crescent* in 1920. In addition, students assisted in spring clean-up, another form of

Mondamin Literary Society promoted one hundred percent Corncobism.

good public relations. Usually in early April, men were dismissed from class at 2:00 p.m. for an afternoon; when the campus had been cleaned, the women fulfilled their gender role by serving lunch.[19]

The men and women attracted by these techniques came from the Red River Valley. Distinctively local, the institution had few from any distance. Those who came were encouraged by parental interest in education. Next to land acquisition, schooling was the most favored means of upward mobility in Norwegian-American culture. Coming from a cash-starved, depressed rural economy and lacking access to financial aid, students took all kinds of jobs to finance their education. As meals were served family-style, several waited tables in the dining hall, the most preferred campus job. Many worked off campus; women cooked and cleaned, and men joined the National Guard. One sold honey and silk stockings throughout the valley. Working on farms and teaching parochial school provided summer employment.[20]

First year men and women rake leaves for 1928 homecoming bonfire.

Despite intensified recruiting and increased fees, the college debt had increased to $100,000 by the end of Aasgaard's presidency. He defended this amount as a wise investment because "it represents land, buildings and improvements ... and not money that had been used up for running expenses." Besides the library, other new buildings had been acquired. The Darrow Hospital (former North Hall) was purchased in 1919 for use as a women's dormitory. The next year, a private residence was secured for the president's home (present Aasgaard House). This freed the Bogstad house to become the music conservatory, soon named "Agony Hall" by collegians. A garage—converted in 1921 and 1922 into a bookstore, post office and lunch room—became a popular gathering place. Two more large homes near North Hall were bought to house women.[21]

New presidential home, purchased in 1920.

Aasgaard also spent several thousand dollars annually "to repair and maintain buildings." He wanted to keep the grounds in "first-class shape" because it attracted students. Accordingly, the men's dormitory was coated with cement stucco in 1918 to improve its appearance; the dormitories were subsequently remodeled and furnished in a modern manner so that collegians would want to live there. These improvements were financed in part by two bequests totalling $30,000. If necessary for expansion, Aasgaard bravely borrowed, as he did in 1923 to purchase the Lamb property for $19,500. Acquired "for the eventual growth and expansion of the college," this sixty-five acre tract was expected eventually to contain all new buildings and an athletic field. This dream was only partially fulfilled when it became the site of present-day athletic fields and Hallet-Erickson Halls. For more than two decades, however, it remained undeveloped and a matter of controversy. The college rented the ground for planting potatoes, other vegetables and small grains.[22]

To cover the costs of the debt, operation and expansion, money needed to be raised. This remained primarily the president's responsibilty, but he repeatedly asked for help. Aasgaard believed that as the institution grew it should have a man in the field constantly collecting money. The college called a field secretary in 1922 but he soon left for another position and was not replaced. By 1925, the school publicized

The Bookstore housed a lunchroom where students gathered.

its financial needs through the catalog issue of *The Record*: "The work at Concordia College has greatly outgrown its present equipment and there are urgent needs for additional endowment funds, scholarships, buildings, and support for needy students." Once the needs had been clearly stated, an appeal followed: "Persons interested in extending the work of God's Kingdom through Christian education can make no better use of funds than by donations to Concordia College."[23]

With the exception of three major fundraising campaigns, this remained the extent of development activity until the Knutson administration in the 1950s. Like most American colleges and universities, Concordia lacked a sustained and systematic approach to raising money. Without a development program, the college relied chiefly on an occasional bequest, student fees and an annual grant from the church.

The Church Ownership Issue

The need for a broader financial base propelled Concordia toward a closer relationship with the Norwegian Lutheran Church. In May 1919 the church board of education recommended transferring ownership of Concordia to the Norwegian Lutheran Church on the same basis as Luther and Saint Olaf. Then in April 1920, the board decided to defer. It appointed a committee to study details and report by April 1, 1923; the board intended to submit its recommendation that summer to the triennial church convention for final action. Aasgaard expected the board to recommend transfer of title to the church. If done, the church would maintain the corporation which would be identical to the church body, meet at the same time and elect a board of trustees to govern the college. Aasgaard warned the Concordia trustees not to oppose this move because "we will not be in the same position as other institutions in regard to receiving money until we are owned and controlled by the church." And, Aasgaard emphasized, "the money question is very serious."[24]

Aasgaard met with the church board of education in February 1923. He reported that the college corporation had changed its articles of incorporation in order to be placed in a legal relationship to the church similar to that of Luther College. In April the board recommended that the church accept Concordia on this legal basis. Aasgaard's report to the church convention in 1923 noted that the last general convention had voted to accept the transfer of Concordia. He informed the body that the college was ready to complete this action when final instructions were received. The convention again voted to extend Concordia the same legal status as Luther and Saint Olaf. Lawyers began work on the legal details which delayed transfer for a year.[25]

Meanwhile the board of education, forced to readjust the church educational program to cut costs, reversed its position. In January 1924 the board resolved "that Concordia College be continued as heretofore drawing its maintenance chiefly from its territorial constituency but that the church give it an annual grant of $15,000." Nonetheless the Concordia trustees recommended, and the corporation approved, transfer to the church. Despite Concordia's willingness, the 1925 church convention adopted the board of education recommendation. It approved the $15,000 annual appropriation and assigned North Dakota and the adjoining counties in Minnesota as Concordia's territory where it would be allowed to canvass exclusively for students and financial support. Henceforth Concordia would be owned by an incorporation of churches in its territory. Making the best of what the college had been given, Aasgaard suggested that this arrangement would be worth more in the long run than a larger appropriation because it will "fix in the mind of our constituency that Concordia College is their school."[26]

Although Aasgaard's assessment proved correct, the benefits were less clearly obvious in the short term as the college faced the exigencies of depression and war. After the area was canvassed successfully for the 1926 endowment fund campaign, Concordia battled to keep its territory free of the recruiters and financial agents of the other church colleges. At the same time, it demanded a larger appropriation from the church to meet pressing financial needs.

Student Personnel Begins

Changes in administrative structure followed from the decision to become a college. Creation of deans of men and women reflected the influence of the emerging student personnel movement that urged using professionally trained staff to supervise more closely the growing number of extracurricular activities. President Aasgaard recommended hiring a dean of women in 1919. Because there were a large number of college women in attendance with more to come, Concordia should secure a "first-class, well-educated woman who shall have complete charge of girls." German instructor Gina Wangsness in 1919 became the first to be named dean of women. She was better liked by her charges than her preceptress predecessor, who had feared popular music and did not fit the changing times. Two years later, Professor Gould Wickey was selected dean of men. He introduced the "Character Card" which summarized information about students, supervised men's life and counseled them on personal, social and school problems. Collegians responded positively to these innovations, in part because the deans gave them a new avenue to faculty.[27]

**Dean of Women
Gina Wangsness**

Forms of student government had been present in American colleges since the post-Civil War era; stimulated by the ethos of progressivism, it spread widely in the early twentieth century. Under the tutelage of the recently hired deans, it even emerged at Concordia. In 1919 a Women's Self-Government Board began as an experiment and was permanently established two years later. The board, comprised of the dormitory chaperon and officers, had no power of jurisdiction but met when necessary to discuss problems, welfare of girls and material needs. Male dormitory residents seem to have had more autonomy; they drew up a system of regulations for conduct, selected a committee to supervise and appointed five proctors to maintain order during study hours. Ten seven-member boards—five each for academy and college—consisting of three faculty and four students were created in 1920 to supervise literary, athletic, musical, religious and social activities.[28]

Although willing to submit to "invisible guiding influence," students wanted still more self-government. They proposed an institution-wide structure of governance in October 1923. Adopted that same year, this proposal created the Student Forum composed of the four student body officers, class presidents, representatives from the five existing boards and two academy representatives. The Student Forum had several duties: promote "school spirit that will express the ideals of Concordia College," consider disciplinary problems, appoint committees and nominate delegates to conventions.[29]

As constituted, student government became part of the administrative structure of the institution. It assumed some functions formerly performed solely by the president but, carefully supervised by the deans of men and women, it served the Christian goals of the college. It assisted with maintaining discipline and gave youth an opportunity to develop leadership skills.

Maintaining Christian Discipline in the Concordia Family

Although President Aasgaard relinquished some administrative functions to collegians, his concern for Christian discipline did not diminish. Traditional evangelical Christian values faced a strong challenge from secular society during the Roaring '20s. As interpreted by Frederick Lewis Allen in his seminal *Only Yesterday,* the decade witnessed a "revolution in manners and morals." Many men and women of every age and from every region drank, danced and adopted liberated views of sexual morality.[30]

Early in the decade Aasgaard responded to these hedonistic tendencies by giving a series of talks on "the amusement problem." Describing the "conservation of the child—physically, mentally and morally"—as "the greatest problem facing this or any other country," Aasgaard noted that the country had gone wild in search of amusements, which he attributed to lack of supervision and obedience in home and school. He urged parents and school officials to perform their duty by providing children with the kind of amusements that will make for the highest citizenship. This is precisely what Concordia attempted in the uncertain moral environment of Moorhead, which supported twenty-eight "speakeasies" during the 1920s.[31] College administrators clearly believed they must protect youth from the moral evils of dancing and drink.

Concordia continued to advertise itself as a Christian college run on Christian principles. The role of clergy in governing the institution helped maintain these standards. In 1917 the six directors, five of fifteen trustees, the corporation president and the college president were ministers. Aasgaard functioned as a principal; he closely supervised discipline and all other aspects of college life. The institutional moral code remained that of a well-regulated Christian home as determined by the standards of Norwegian-American Lutheranism. Liquor, tobacco, dancing, cards, pool, billiards and dormitory visitation were prohibited. Efforts were made to keep collegians on campus. For this reason, the remodeled men's dormitory and the new bookstore and post office pleased Aasgaard because "it keeps students on campus more"; fortunately, the numbers going down town declined. Dormitory doors were still locked and lights turned out at 10:15 p.m.[32]

Many collegians upheld the moral code and sharply criticized those who broke the rules. One resident complained in 1918 that the dormitory had become "a rendezvous for cigarette fiends ... to judge from the smoke clouds that occasionally creep through the transoms." Another welcomed college life as a "golden opportunity to rid ourselves of the jargon of the flapper and frequenter of pool halls and develop a type of speech that is befitting college bred men and women." An editorial in 1925 emphasized that regulations were law and must be obeyed regardless of personal beliefs. When these appeals to moral principle proved ineffective, as they often did, students might resort to vigilante action. Two noisy women in 1919 were tied to their beds with ropes, had mustard smeared on their faces and were "left ... to have sweet dreams for the remainder of the night."[33]

As the vigilante episode demonstrates, one should not imagine Concordia as a cloister populated by humorless prigs. Some rules were simply unenforceable. Then as now, the library reading room was a social gathering place for the two sexes. Then as now, their more serious-minded comrades complained: "Are you one of those unprincipled persons who talk, flirt, and giggle in the reading room, where silence should reign?" Other regulations were softened by leniency. Carl Narveson recalls sneaking out of the dormitory frequently for late lunch downtown with resident head and football coach Rudolph Lavik. Once Narveson returned alone after hours and rang the bell. Coach Lavik bawled him out loudly, and then whispered, "You darn fool, why didn't you go through the window?" Faculty of the day took turns policing the Crystal Ballroom near Island Park in Fargo. An alumna remembers that when her father's turn came he would phone ahead to warn Cobbers.[34]

These episodes contributed to the emerging ideology of "the Concordia family" that viewed the church college as an extension of the Christian home. Like other midwestern denominational colleges of the day, Concordia attempted to make itself a home and family for students. To a remarkable degree it succeeded.[35]

"Mother" Fjelstad is a case in point. Hired in 1895, Helga Fjelstad was the popular matron of the college until her first retirement in 1920. She fed a large number on a very small budget. She superintended everything in the dining hall including teaching table manners to those who did not know how to eat with a fork. The *Crescent* in 1920

Matron Helga Fjelstad

estimated that she had been "mother ... to more than 6,000 sturdy boys and girls of the Northwest, creator of more than 6,000,000 meals or 18 billion calories of food value, to be thoroughly modern and scientific. From the standpoint of motherhood, that is quite a record." Fjelstad called troubled students into the kitchen for coffee and a chat; they recalled how she "always gave us kindly advice and comfort when it was most needed and did it in a way ... that reminded us of mother." Creation of a big sister program in 1922 enlarged the family to include siblings. New collegians were assigned to junior and senior women who met them at the station, brought them to the dorm, introduced them to new friends and assisted them in registering. Big sisters were responsible for one year; they were expected to put forth their best effort in creating a contented and loyal collegian who would be a credit to the institution.[36]

Appropriately, the official college ring of ruby and gold was created by alumnus and Moorhead jeweler Oscar Martinson in 1920. It eventually became an important symbol and a ready means of recognition for family members worldwide.[37]

The spirit of the Concordia family manifested itself especially at Christmas. Before classes ended at the holidays, professors and collegians gathered in the gymnasium to light the Christmas tree, sing carols, eat and exchange gifts. Many carols were sung in Norwegian in accordance with the Norse custom of forming concentric circles and singing to the measured pace of their marching feet. For the many who remained in the dormitories through vacation, a tree was set

The college ring, designed in 1920.

up and decorated in the dining hall on Christmas eve; the evening was spent with President Aasgaard, several professors and their families. Mother Fjelstad made special treats; gifts were distributed, carols sung and games played. On other evenings the president and professors entertained residents at their homes. As Alfreda Sattre Torgerson ('31) recalled these years: "It was such a family."[38]

A shared religious outlook and activity provided the basis for the ideology of the Concordia family and for Christian discipline. President Aasgaard worked hard to foster campus spiritual life. His efforts were spurred by the shocking spread of Jazz Age immorality, evolutionary science and religious modernism, all of which threatened to undermine traditional morality and Scriptural authority. Besides daily chapel, Sunday worship and Young People's Luther League, Tuesday evening Bible study, taught by Professor Samuel Miller from the Lutheran Bible Institute in Saint Paul, was arranged by Aasgaard. In 1924 the president proudly reported that more than one hundred come regularly "though they are not required to attend." He urged continuing this activity because "no greater blessing can come to our students than the knowledge of the word of God." Once they heard the word, they acted on it; in 1919 collegians donated $144 to Armenian-Syrian Relief Fund. A mission society, organized in 1924 to study missions in China and Madagascar, presented plays—*Broken China, The Pill Bottle, Two Masters*—dramatizing problems of the work, the medical ignorance of the heathen and the need for medical missionaries.[39]

In addition, the school encouraged those with talent to enter the ministry. In 1922 Aasgaard proudly announced that fifteen alumni were attending seminary. With equal pride the *Scout* reported in 1926 that 24 percent of the male graduates had entered the ministry. No other Lutheran institution could match that record.[40]

Expanded Extracurricular Activities

As they conceived religious organizations, the faculty similarly considered all other extracurricular activities to be a vital part of a Christian liberal arts education. Yet they urged a proper balance because in small schools students were tempted to overload. To regulate participation, the Women's Self-Government Association in 1921 adopted a point system popularized by Smith College. Under the system, women were limited to fifty points distributed as follows: debate—twenty-five, choir and *Concordian*—twenty each, class officer—ten, temporary committees—five each.[41] It is not known if this system was then extended to men or ever rigorously enforced; in any case, it allowed considerable latitude for students to choose from a wide variety of activities.

Musical organizations expanded and occupied many. Most important were the band and the new a cappella choir, founded in Fall 1919 by Agnes Skartvedt. The band of forty pieces gave a number of concerts in the city and annually toured the region.

Expanded from sixteen to fifty voices by Paul Ensrud, the choir first toured outside Fargo-Moorhead in 1921, traveling "an entire week in Northern Minnesota" and singing at Perley, Hendrum, Ada, Fertile, Hitterdal, Ulen and Hawley. Director Herman W. Monson returned to the college in 1923 and during the next fourteen years brought the choir a national reputation. The chorus made a 1,000 mile tour of central North Dakota in 1924 and a memorable 800 mile trip over the muddy

Model T choir buses logged many miles on choir tour.

roads of northern Minnesota in 1925. Traveling in Model T buses, the choristers became Volga boatmen and road contracters to reach their concerts; they pulled the machines out of mudholes with ropes and even built a fifty yard stretch of roadway out of logs. In March 1927, the choir made its first tour of the Pacific Northwest.[42]

With the shift in ownership to the congregations of North Dakota and northern Minnesota, the band and choir trips became a vitally important way of making the college known to its constituency. As the tours became longer, the aging vehicles added to the frustration. Chartering commercial buses began in 1935.

Throughout the United States during the 1920s, athletics became a major campus activity and assumed most of the professional attributes associated with college sports today. Concordia mirrored this national trend, joining the Minnesota Intercollegiate Athletic Conference (MIAC) in December 1920. The football team, founded by Professor A.M. "Hooks" Sattre in 1916 and playing on a field where Brown and

Livedalen Halls are now located, opened conference play disastrously the next fall. They held Carleton and Saint Olaf to 74 and 97 points on successive Saturdays while scoring their customary zero. Beaten but not defeated, the team overcame Jamestown for its first victory and managed to tie Fargo College. Despite lack

The 1922 football team strikes a determined pose.

of victories, teams were recognized by the school. On athletic day, a special feature of closing chapel exercises, letters were awarded to football and basketball men. President Aasgaard spoke, emphasizing the need for cleaner athletics and the importance of sports in the curriculum. Coach Fenwick Watkins (1922–1926), Concordia's first African-American faculty member, stressed the high scholarship that went hand-in-hand with cleaner athletics.[43]

Organized women's sports appeared in 1920 with the establishment of intramural basketball. Games were scheduled with other schools the following year; the academy team won the championship of North Dakota and western Minnesota in 1922. By 1923 women hoped to organize interscholastic tennis competition. Through athletic competition, women departed from their conventional gender role and learned masculine routes to power. They engaged in team play, developed strength and endurance, tested themselves in physical contests and wore unconventional attire.[44]

Athletics brought the problem of a team name to the fore. Obviously, one ought to select a title connoting dignity, courage and even fear. The *Concordian* in 1923 suggested Vikings, but it did not not capture the fancy of their descendants. Because it implied hayseed, "Corncob" was no longer acceptable to these citified Norwegians captivated by the bright lights of Fargo-Moorhead. At this time, *Forum*

Coach Fenwick Watkins

sportswriters adopted a shortened version of the rejected term and used Cobbers consistently. By 1928, the *Concordian* had embraced this usage; when the school annual changed its name from *Scout* to *Cobber* in 1932, acceptance was complete.[45]

For students lacking in musical talent or physical ability, Concordia offered activities of a more intellectual nature. Organized in 1921, the artist-lecture series has continued to the present. Five lecturers and seven artists were scheduled the first year. Featured were a slide presentation, a novelist and lectures on "Russian Women," "China As A World Factor" and "Prisons." Two pianists, a violinist, a cellist and four vocalists presented the artistic programs.[46]

With the increase in number of collegians, clubs appeared. Founded in 1918 at the instigation of Professor Herman Nordlie, the historical society sponsored a mock

The Historical Society (1918–1919) advised by Herman Nordlie (center).

peace conference and met monthly for reports, addresses and discussions. The science club in 1922 pioneered campus radio; they installed an aerial above New Main and the boys' dormitory and purchased a wireless set. When later properly equipped, their premier broadcast was a debate between Jamestown and Concordia. Created in 1923, the Edda Norse Society studied Norwegian literature, music and early social conditions. Under the direction of Professor J.A. Holvik, cuttings of Norse dramas were occasionally presented. In 1925 they staged an outdoor pageant by Prexy's Pond on the history of Norsemen in North America. Apparently it was less than well received; a newspaper described it "as one of the most pretentious affairs ... ever staged in this part of the country."[47]

Intercollegiate debate premiered March 7, 1921 when Concordia debated Fargo College on the question: "Resolved that the Chinese immigration restrictions should be applied to the Japanese." The student newspaper proudly publicized the event, reported that both sides were evenly matched in their well-researched presentations and called for more activities. Both the *Crescent* and its successor in 1920, the *Concordian*, provided an outlet for aspiring journalists and served as an institutional public relations organ by informing alumni, high schools and the constituency.[48]

1927 debating team, negative (top) and affirmative.

A lively intellectual life ensued. Through their publications, collegians addressed a wide variety of cultural, political and social issues. Vocation and the value of a college education were favorite topics. Aptitude and service, not wealth, were criteria stressed in choosing a vocation. Because all occupations and rural communities needed intelligent men and women, college should not dictate choosing an intellectual profession. This democratic rejection of elitist education was combined with a traditional defense of liberal learning, however. As liberal arts preparation, classics and humanistic studies still found defenders. Classical authors were important in philosophy; the classical foundations of political and social science helped to understand present day problems;

and classical language developed a thorough understanding of English. From a practical view, classical studies therefore deserved a place in the modern curriculum. These arguments reflect the humanistic orientation of these early collegians. In 1923 when forty-two graduated, twelve majored in history, fourteen in English and only seven in the sciences and math.[49]

Social issues attracted considerable attention, which many thought appropriate. According to one editor, "as graduates of a Christian institution we are especially fitted for useful service due to our training in Christian principles." Because "there is work to do for the Christian citizen," social problems should not be shirked by college graduates. Although compelled by their Christian commitment to address social issues, students often reached conservative conclusions about those issues. In the case of industrial labor, some opposed government action to improve working conditions. To secure justice for both workers and owners, industrial intelligence should be promoted. Applied intelligence would guide workers "along the lines of pure and unselfish service to God and man"; presumably owners would be similarly guided but that was not specified. Another argued that women's suffrage was unnecessary because "the modern woman" through her power as a consumer can control the economic world without the right to vote. As the chief purchasers for the home, women could create a demand for good quality goods and thereby benefit the laboring class and alleviate urban poverty.[50]

Stimulated by the 1917 Russian Revolution, widespread strikes and several bombings, the Red Scare afflicted American society in 1919–1920. Collegiate discussions reflected these anxieties. One described the Russian Revolution as a movement that could not control itself; a morally disciplined people like United States citizens would never attempt to establish a utopian government like communism. Speaking on "Bolshevism" at the Mondamin Public Program in December 1919, academy senior Benjamin Duckstad argued that Bolshevism had replaced the Kaiser as the new enemy of democracy. Despite some democratic elements, Bolshevism was built on autocracy—rule by an elite. If communism were not checked, Duckstad warned, "our very civilization will hang in the balance."[51]

Crescent Editor
Benjamin Duckstad

Not everyone shared these conservative views of the dangers of radicalism, women's suffrage and labor. Rural North Dakotans openly sympathized with the Non-Partisan League, which more conservative urban Norwegians equated with socialism, and League speakers appeared on campus. Others called for government action to end child labor and, as early as 1912, demanded the vote for women. A *Concordian* editorial in 1922 complained about the difficulty of breaking with established traditions which prolonged the struggle for female emancipation. The remarks were occasioned by the refusal of another college to debate because Concordia's team had a woman member. This smacked of the dark ages; the editorialist hoped these medieval attitudes would soon change.[52] They changed, but perhaps not as the writer envisioned. For many years the college would be represented by male and female debate teams.

By the mid-1920s Concordia had become a full-fledged college, exhibiting traits of other denominational schools. Intercollegiate competition occurred in football, basketball and debate. The band and choir publicized the college with annual tours into Concordia's territory. Debate, clubs, *Concordian* and artist-lecture series fostered intellectual growth. The emergence of college life did not alter commitment to Christian spiritual life or moral code; indeed, Jazz Age immorality increased determination to maintain Christian standards. Religious activities remained popular and even expanded. More attention was given to recruiting ministers; LBI Bible Study and the Mission Society afforded new opportunities for religious expression.

Aasgaard Assumes the Church Presidency

On June 25, 1925, J.A. Aasgaard resigned to assume the presidency of the Norwegian Lutheran Church of America. During his last years he had traveled extensively for the college and the church. He had toured the West Coast in 1920 for the foreign relief segment of the Lutheran World Service Campaign to raise $1.8 million. Aasgaard's schedule for 1924 reveals a dynamic personality widely engaged. He traveled 25,000 miles on the railroad, delivered ninety-two sermons and addresses (many on the subject of Christian education), attended committee meetings twenty full days, district conventions twenty-two days and conducted 124 chapel devotions. In addition he taught three religion classes. This was not a bad year's work.[53]

During his presidency, Aasgaard significantly improved the campus. In 1911 he came to a sleepy school which fenced the baseball diamond as a temporary pasture for the college horse, had a hen house behind the president's house and had recently removed a hogpen. When he left in 1925, he had built a library (Grose Hall), a gymnasium (Berg Maintenance) and a bookstore-post office; purchased North Hall and the Aasgaard House; and acquired the sixty-five acre Lamb property.[54]

For his successor, Aasgaard recommended a six-year term, a $3,000 annual salary and a free house, including utilities. He justified the $500 increase because of demands made for subscriptions, gifts and personal entertainment. He submitted the names of four men qualified for the position. The Rev. Martin Anderson, a former Trinity Church pastor, was rumored to be the likely successor. Nonetheless the Rev. J.N. Brown, president of Canton Normal in South Dakota, was elected. Brown accepted and pledged himself to continue the "policy so successfully begun and carried on for ten years by my beloved friend and predecessor, Dr. J.A. Aasgaard." He requested the prayers of the boards on his behalf for "only as we build on ... Jesus Christ will our work be blessed and the mission of Concordia College be accomplished."[55]

On August 8, 2,500 people attended the farewell service held in Moorhead City Park for this highly regarded and much beloved contributor to civic affairs. A longtime trustee, Mayor C.G. Dosland, praised Aasgaard for his community service as a member of the Commercial Club and as the organizer and first president of Kiwanis. The Rt. Rev. Johan Peter Lunde, Bishop of Oslo, placed Aasgaard's presidency in the context of immigration and Americanization: "God did not call the Norse to establish a Norse province here, but to be good Americans."[56] Conducted in the English language under the leadership of a civic-minded president, Concordia had contributed to Americanization by preparing its graduates to serve as Christian citizens who performed many different tasks in the world.

PART II

President J.N. Brown, 1925–1951:

The College Established, Maintained and Expanded

"We are living in a restless, impatient and unsatisfied age. ... The atmosphere is charged with new social, economic, political and religious ideas and hypotheses. You will be taught to deal frankly and fearlessly with knowledge in every sphere of human experience and accomplishment at Concordia College, but you will be taught that Truth is eternal and unchangeable because God, the Author of Truth, is unchangeable."
— *J.N. Brown (1925)*

"May then Concordia College ... remain a torch-bearer of true, evangelical, historical Lutheranism. May there go forth from these halls of learning an ever increasing army of men and women, marked by breadth of scholarship, fineness of culture, soundness of character, and uncompromising devotion to truth, and loyalty to their Christian faith."
— *J.N. Brown (1925)*

"Four short years—and in them some souls must be helped to be stabilized, some to grow, some to be born for the first time. Yes, in Jesus' name it must be done; without His name the work cannot even be begun. It must come through regular instructions, through definite religious classes, through extra-curricular activities, through social contacts, through campus conversation— it [the Holy Spirit] must drip constantly so the atmosphere is charged with Great Light."
— *Frida R. Nilsen (1937)*

"Concordia aspires to send out saved and sanctified men and women to serve the Holy Christian Church, the Communion of Saints and to reflect Christ in all relations with their fellowmen. "
— *Carl B. Ylvisaker (1937)*

"It would have been a pleasure to attend [homecoming], but circumstances intervene. ... In spite of all that is done for the comfort and the welfare out here [in the Pacific], one still misses the fellowship and the pervading pleasant spirit that permeates the atmosphere of Concordia."

— Lt. Norman Lorentzsen (1945)

"Do not lose sight ... of the tremendous possibilities of Concordia College in its service to the Northwest, the church and the entire Kingdom. ... Keep the college in the old paths. Shun compromises of those time-tested practices and policies which have made Concordia a truly Christian college and you may be assured of God's continued blessings upon your work in making Concordia an even greater instrument in the Hands of God. ... "

— J.N. Brown (1951)

Chapter 6

Accreditation Achieved

President J.N. Brown and His Times

Shortly after becoming president, J.N. Brown wrote that the call to Concordia had come unsolicited. Although the call may have been unsolicited, it was not without the prior planning of two powerful movers and shakers in the church—Brown's predecessor, J.A. Aasgaard, and Saint Olaf President Lars Boe. Two years earlier, Boe had congratulated Aasgaard on his selection as church vice-president, pointed out that he would eventually become church president, and urged him to "plan on getting Brown as your successor when you quit" because "it is going to mean everything that we have men of our type up there." Boe did not explain what he meant by "men of our type," but it probably referred to their former membership in the United Norwegian Lutheran Church. Brown's United Church background thus helped him become president; but former Norwegian Synod faculty from Park Region, pastors and congregations felt betrayed. They believed that one of their own in due recognition of the 1917 merger should have succeeded Aasgaard. Synodical differences may have been bridged at the national level, but local conflicts were common, persisted for decades and caused Brown serious problems in the future.[1]

President J.N. Brown

Aside from this cloud on the horizon, the new president possessed solid qualifications which ensured his initial acceptance by the community. Iowa-born in 1883 to Norwegian immigrant parents, Brown had graduated from Saint Olaf (1906) and United Church Seminary in St. Paul (1909) before serving parishes in Beloit, Wisconsin (1909–1916) and Austin, Minnesota (1916–1921). Vice president of the Young People's Luther League of the United Church, Brown became first president of the International Luther League in 1917 with formation of the Norwegian Lutheran Church of America. In 1921 he was called to South Dakota to reorganize and reopen Canton Lutheran Normal. By this time, his earlier ambitions for further graduate study had been displaced by growing family and church responsibilities.[2]

These qualities—interest in graduate study, parish experience, youth work and educational administration—well suited Brown for a college presidency. His qualifications were enhanced when Carthage College, at the request of its new president N.J. Gould Wickey, bestowed an honorary doctor of divinity degree in 1927. Dr. Brown's stature in church and educational circles brought him additional national responsibilities that indicate his commitments to the causes of Lutheran cooperation and church-related higher education. Between 1928 and 1930, he served as vice-president and president of both the National Lutheran Educational Conference and the American Association of Colleges.[3]

President Brown's spiritual leadership of Concordia reflected the tensions that sharply divided American culture during the Roaring '20s. Change on many fronts challenged the traditional moral values of American Protestantism. The carnage of the Great War; postwar disillusionment, strikes, bombings, red scare and race riots; and the revolt of manners and morals first evidenced among flaming college youth seemed about to overwhelm long-accepted religious and moral truths. Protestantism militantly defended itself from modernism and its associated evils of higher criticism and evolution. The Ku Klux Klan—relying on promotional techniques honed by war and business, appealing to the anxieties of the age and promising to uphold traditional moral values—mushroomed to a membership estimated variously at between three and eight million. Ironically, flaming college youth were more myth than fact. Despite the popular stereotypes of fiction and film, most led less exciting lives than critics feared. Certainly Cobbers were shocked when they heard the designation for the decade; as Erling Rolfsrud ('36) reported, Tranquil '20s more aptly described the life and times of the rural communities from which he and others came.[4]

Nonetheless, Minnesota and the Norwegian Lutheran Church of America (NLCA) were stirred by controversy in 1922 when William Jennings Bryan visited the state as part of his national anti-evolution crusade. That same year, the NLCA declared evolution an "anti-Christian theory" and "a philosophy of religion" that ought not be propagated in the public schools. Baptist fundamentalist William Bell Riley of Minneapolis agreed; in 1927 he secured the introduction of an anti-evolution bill in the Minnesota legislature. Although Lutheran college presidents and church leaders opposed this legislation as unenforceable, the NLCA continued to attack evolution and responded more directly than other Lutheran synods to the religious controversies of the decade. Norwegian Lutherans especially feared scientific modernism, a theological movement emphasizing a socio-historical approach to Scripture that had established itself at the University of Chicago Divinity School and some other theological seminaries. Modernism was widely discussed in church theological journals and before his retirement in 1925 President H.G. Stub called the synod to Christian faithfulness against this rival creed. Stub listed inspiration of Scripture, divinity of Christ and the other fundamentals to be defended at all costs. Yet he sought to maintain Lutheran exclusiveness by warning that this doctrinal solidarity with fundamentalists did not abrogate the church prohibition against unionism.[5]

The NLCA stand against evolution and modernism echoed the fundamentalist crusade and reveals another way that an ethnic church was becoming Americanized. In the nineteenth century the Church of Norway had responded to the challenges of modern science with "Repristination Theology," which emphasized verbal inspiration of the scriptures and legalistic use of confessions. In 1925 these theological premises were re-stated in the fundamentalist-influenced "Minneapolis Theses." The Theses accepted "without exception all the canonical books of the Old and New Testaments ... as the divinely inspired, revealed and inerrant words of God." Believers were to submit to Scripture "as the only infallible authority in all matters of faith and life." Thus Norwegian Lutherans, as did fundamentalists in the older American denominations, reaffirmed the traditional values of evangelical Christianity.[6]

President Brown shared the cultural attitudes of his church. In the face of challenges posed by what he called "a restless, impatient and unsatisfied age," he upheld the Bible as the only trustworthy guide for life. He asserted that Christian students had nothing to fear from knowledge acquired at college. Because Concordia was loyal to the church, it is a "safe ... place to educate a young boy or girl." Students need not fear exposure to the anti-churchly tendencies of modernism and evolution which "at the present time [make] our universities ... largely anti-Christian in their influence."[7]

The president attempted to ensure that science at Concordia would be interpreted in light of Christianity. Thanking Rev. Byron C. Nelson for his anti-evolution book, Brown promised to order a copy for the library, and hoped it would be widely circulated among students. A few years later, Brown assured Nelson that many faculty spoke favorably of his books and he expressed a desire to have Nelson join the staff when economic conditions improved. In recruiting faculty, Brown refused to consider "a crass evolutionist." He believed that when theories of science did not conform to biblical truths the Bible should take preeminence. Indeed, Brown years later memorialized longtime biology professor A.M. Sattre for exactly this quality; in Sattre's instruction the theories of science were always explained in light of God's word.[8]

President Brown's equivocal position on the Ku Klux Klan also reveals his sensitivity to the cultural issues that divided America in the decade. Minnesota had ten Klan organizations by 1923; that same year in North Dakota the Klan was especially strong in Grand Forks, claiming 500 members. A Klan paper, the *North Dakota American*, was published in Fargo, and a Klan rally held in September 1925 at the Cass County fairgrounds—for which approximately 800 paraded in regalia—attracted 8,000 spectators. Brown was forced to take a public stand in February 1926 when Dean Samuel Miller of the Lutheran Bible Institute in St. Paul criticized the Klan during a radio-broadcast Bible study lecture at Concordia. The *North Dakota American* headlined the attack and questioned the potential success of Concordia's impending endowment fund drive in Fargo-Moorhead.[9]

LBI Dean Samuel Miller

As a first-year president, and with an endowment and North Central accreditation both hanging in the balance, Brown nervously treated the issue "with utmost caution," claiming "there is at least a 50-50 division of opinion among our pastors regarding the Klan." He wrote to the *North Dakota American* assuring the Klan that "Dean Miller's criticism came without my knowledge or sanction," that Concordia was entirely neutral toward the Klan, and that Concordia "faculty have no restrictions placed upon them by the administration regarding your organization." Brown also wrote Miller about the incident. He did not question Miller's right to speak as conscience dictates under guidance of the Holy Spirit, *but* preferred that he "speak regarding secret societies and Klan organizations at the first hour" and make the broadcast devotional. This would eliminate those "questions which are mooted questions among the pastors of the church." Brown assured Miller that the lectures would continue and did not mandate omitting all references to the Klan.[10]

It is surprising that Norwegian-American Lutherans were attracted to the Klan in the numbers Brown estimated. After all, their church officially opposed membership in secret societies and many Norwegian-Americans were foreign-born themselves. Perhaps the Klan's anti-Catholicism appealed; this accounts for its strength in Grand Forks. More than religious bigotry or Aryan superiority were involved, however. The Klan defended American ideals, the Bible and Christian morality. It opposed bootlegging, jazz age immorality, modernism and evolution. These were all positions that Norwegian-American Lutherans supported and that would attract their sympathy, if not outright membership in the Klan, until well-publicized scandals in Indiana and elsewhere contributed to a rapid decline of the organization.

The cultural issues of modernism, evolution and the Klan indicate how Brown and other Norwegian Lutherans were becoming Americanized and adopting stands similar to the evangelical Christians of Yankee denominations. At the same time, Norwegians clung to their ethnic identity. The 1925 centennial celebration of Norse immigration prompted new outpourings of ethnic pride at Concordia and elsewhere. Over 500 participated in Professor Holvik's pageant, "Norsemen in America," which depicted Norwegian contributions to American development from the arrival of Leif Erickson to the first graduation class of Concordia College. Presi-

Norse Professor J.A. Holvik

dent Calvin Coolidge's address, delivered to an estimated crowd of 100,000 and praising Norwegians for becoming good American citizens, highlighted the main celebration, held June 6–9 at the Minnesota State Fairgrounds. Concordia participated in several ways: The choir performed; President Aasgaard delivered the festival sermon; and Holvik served as secretary of the centennial committee, program director of the exposition and editor of the centennial book containing all speeches delivered. The festival inspired new efforts of historical study and preservation; in October a Norwegian-American Historical Society was established at Saint Olaf and professors Holvik and Nordlie began a Norwegian-American museum collection at Concordia.[11]

President Brown sympathized with efforts to make Concordia a regional center of Norwegian culture. During the 1926 endowment fund campaign, he encouraged speakers to use Norwegian when demanded by audiences and he attempted to arrange weekly broadcasts of Norwegian services. Ibsen plays were frequently presented in translation and occasionally there were Norwegian productions: Bjornson's *Geografi og Kjaerlighed* (1927) and *En Fallit* (1931). Small groups still used idiomatic Norse expressions; one student recalled writing a religion placement test in Norwegian because that had been the language of instruction in her home congregation. Professor Carl B. Ylvisaker accepted her answers and placed her in the top Bible class.[12]

These expressions of a flourishing Norwegian-American subculture were doomed by the end of immigration, however. The centennial celebration itself reflected this change. The program had been in English and had emphasized the adjustment and material progress of Norwegians in America. Similarly, each new student generation was progressively more American than Norwegian. The Norse Society disappeared. *En Fallit* was the last Norwegian play. The museum project developed slowly due to poor funding. Already by the late 1920s many students did not understand Norwegian; it was spoken less frequently on campus. Brown himself preferred to preach in English because Norwegian sermons required lengthy preparation.[13]

These on-campus changes reflected the decline of the Norwegian ethnic subculture in the United States despite preservation efforts by Ole Rölvaag and other Norwegian-American intellectuals. Ethnic identity was tied to language; as the use of English increased more rapidly with cessation of immigration, the separate Norwegian culture faded. The 100 percent Americanism stimulated by United States entry into World War I hastened the trend toward English as evidenced in the church. Norwegian services declined from over 70 percent in 1917 to 40 percent in 1928; English increased proportionately to about 90 percent by 1943. Norwegian religious instruction of youth ceased during the 1930s. Church leaders like President Aasgaard supported these changes because they regarded English as necessary for effective church work in an American setting. Although the language and an ethnic subculture persisted in isolated rural communities, geographical and social mobility of the young—fostered in part by college education at places like Concordia—increasingly limited Norse culture to an older generation.[14]

Presidential Visions and Innovations

In most respects, the college remained the lengthened shadow of the president. Granted substantial powers by the board and expected to act authoritatively, the president set the institutional course by articulating a vision for the future. Brown's vision contained traditional and innovative elements.

In his first public address, delivered at the formal opening of school in September 1925, the new president presented a traditional American argument for the values of Christian education. Since the nineteenth century, denominational college presidents and other educators had stressed their devotion to the ideal of educating the whole man and woman. Preaching on the text, "Jesus increased in wisdom and stature and in favor with God and man," Brown argued that Concordia—a Christian college based on the precepts of Jesus—similarly trained body, mind and soul. Brown's address focused on mind and soul. A thorough liberal education best developed mind if students diligently applied themselves. Chapel, religious organizations and religious instruction increased student knowledge of the Word and the way to salvation. Brown returned to these themes in his installation address, "Why the Church College?", given on Reformation Sunday during homecoming. He asserted that the Christian college is the only avenue through which Christianity can be taught effectively, and that such teaching trained Christian leadership for church and state. Concordia graduates would qualify only if they were "marked by breadth of scholarship, fineness of culture, soundness of character, ... uncompromising devotion to truth, and loyalty to their Christian faith."[15]

Although traditional in his conception of a denominational college, President Brown innovated by being more aggressively Lutheran than his predecessors; this reflected the formal relationship with the Norwegian Lutheran Church of America, finally confirmed in 1925. Consequently, Brown worked to enhance ties both with the Lutheran congregations in the territory and with the seminaries. When he preached in surrounding communities, Brown insisted on giving "Lutheran sermons." As he explained to someone who tried to arrange something less denominational: "I do not make my sermons offensive to those of other denominations, but I feel that we should stress our Lutheran doctrines on every possible occasion since we believe that they are the true interpretations of the Word of God." Such sermons, moreover, established rapport with those congregations that owned the college. Brown also encouraged efforts to send more men to seminary. To this end, he supported Saint Olaf President Boe's proposal to open discussion with seminary faculty. If seminaries improved instruction and sent representatives to college campuses to interview and inform, Brown maintained, their attendance might increase.[16]

The president worked to make the institution Lutheran in other ways as well. He believed it desirable to have textbooks that were "orthodox from our Lutheran point of view," but unfortunately these were "practically impossible to find." Therefore textbooks were adapted and teachers trusted to use them in conformity to Lutheran faith. This made recruiting Lutheran faculty essential, however difficult. Higher qualifications set by accrediting agencies, "ridiculously low" salaries and synodical politics complicated Brown's task. Being Lutheran, as required by the church board of education, was not enough. Concordia faculty had to be the right kind of Lutheran. Because the college was a product of the merger of Park Region and Concordia, Brown tried "to keep an equal balance between the members of the former Norwegian Synod and the United Church on the faculty." The Lutheran network facilitated recruiting as Brown requested nominations from presidents, pastors and professors.[17]

The president's stated criteria for a chemistry teacher suggest that religion ranked as the most important qualification: 1) a strong Christian personality; 2) a capable scholar and instructor; 3) an interpreter of scientific truths in light of the Word of God (which meant that no evolutionists need apply). For a religion professor, Brown wanted a serious-minded man, experienced in congregational work, who stood for evangelical Lutheranism and for personal Christianity. He obtained Carl B. Ylvisaker, a saintly man from a well-known church family, whom Brown believed more than met these criteria. Besides, Ylvisaker was unmarried and thus could afford an additional year of graduate study.[18]

Spurred by the ever-higher standards being imposed for accreditation, President Brown quickly took several steps to improve conditions for faculty. He secured board approval for electing permanent teachers for a period not to exceed six years. This replaced the procedure of electing the entire faculty each year. Upon the president's recommendation, the boards in 1927 adopted a group insurance plan for employees with one-half the premium paid by the college. At Brown's urging, the institution granted $500 to $1,000 stipends to selected faculty for graduate study. Brown also warned that accrediting agencies demanded smaller classes, which necessitated hiring more teachers, and higher salaries. At the time, Concordia's salaries were "woefully below ... other arts and science colleges." As a result of Brown's pleas, dictated in part by his desire for North Central accreditation, the budgeted amount for salaries increased from $47,775 in 1925–1926 to $72,210 in 1928–1929.[19]

President Brown envisioned future greatness for Concordia, desired to become a "builder president" and quickly acted to fulfill these ambitions. Expecting enrollment to surpass 500, he hoped to erect two new buildings. To have room, the college purchased five blocks immediately south of the men's dormitory (present Academy Hall). Brown considered this a wise investment; rent from five houses on this property paid loan interest and Moorhead's growth would soon make adjacent land too expensive. By December 1928, Brown presided over a ten-acre campus and its buildings, a sixty-five-acre future campus, eleven Moorhead houses, and 1,346 acres of improved farmland. In addition, the board had granted his request for a committee to select an architect to plan future campus development.[20]

Other Brown innovations stemmed from the student personnel movement that emerged at universities early in the century as an effort to recreate the denominational college's concern for non-intellectual training. The new behavioral sciences shaped programs; mental testing and counseling used by the army in World War I gave impetus to the movement. During the following decade, specialists emerged and student personnel became a distinct profession. Many colleges and universities established testing, counseling, housing, health and placement services; implemented intramurals and freshmen orientation; built unions; and expanded student government.[21]

Within the limits of its resources, Concordia under Brown's leadership readily adopted some of these innovations because the movement clearly served the Christian college goal of educating the whole person. Standardized mental testing and freshmen orientation began in 1926. On the intelligence test, Cobber freshmen scored above the national average. Orientation week greeted newcomers with social mixers, campus and community tours, instruction in library use, examinations, registration and lectures by faculty on institutional purpose, Christian responsibilities, good manners, the practical value of the liberal arts and vocational guidance.[22]

Professor Peter "Pa" Anderson

The placement service headed by Peter (Pa) Anderson began shortly after he joined the education department in 1925. One consequence of this change is that the college published its first placement statistics in 1929. Out of 416 graduates by January of that year, high and grade school teachers numbered 248 (68 percent) and religious workers forty-six (11 percent). Thirty-two married homemakers (7.6 percent) comprised the next largest group. Although Cobbers resided in twenty-one states and four foreign countries, the school's regional character is revealed by the fact that most remained in their home states of Minnesota (41.6 percent) and North Dakota (39 percent).[23]

Liberal education reform, another major trend of the decade in higher education, also affected Concordia, but in less visible ways. The criticism raised by the antics of flaming college youth facilitated reform. Stung by the charge that the colleges and universities were not educating properly, educators widely debated the meaning of liberal arts education. Many innovations attempted to make better use of traditional subject matter: preceptoral work at Princeton, general examinations at Harvard, Frank Aydelotte's honors program at Swarthmore and programs of independent study elsewhere. Prestigious institutions—Harvard, Yale, Princeton and Chicago—adopted more rigorous admissions standards, enhancing the value placed on the liberal arts. Evidently what becomes more exclusive automatically becomes more desirable.[24]

Although Concordia benefited from this prestige and Brown even suggested that enrollment might be restricted to 500, the college could not afford the luxury of limiting numbers; it merely coped with those who came. President Brown enthusiastically supported the liberal arts college movement begun in 1930 by the American Association of Colleges. This movement publicized the service of liberal arts colleges in hope of enhancing financial support. Hard times of the Great Depression doomed this campaign, just as they prohibited adopting any of the widely publicized educational reforms of the previous decade.[25]

Administrative Changes and Practice

When Brown arrived in 1925 Concordia's administrative structure was still quite simple, consisting of the president, assisted by a superintendent of grounds and buildings, parttime deans of men and women, and a registrar. Following higher educational trends toward administrative specialization and enacting what President Bogstad had proposed twenty years before, Brown brought H.M. Dale, who had succeeded him as president of Canton Normal, to Concordia as business manager in 1927. Meanwhile the work of the registrar had expanded and could no longer be handled by a fulltime teacher. When history professor Herman Nordlie resigned as registrar in 1927 he was replaced for one year by a non-teacher, Henrietta Burgess. Subsequently, Martha Brennun served while teaching parttime in mathematics and Norse.[26]

**Business Manager
H.M. Dale**

The student personnel movement inspired another of Brown's administrative innovations. He early attempted to involve collegians in decision-making, a move unusual for a period in which the divine right of college presidents was still an article of faith. Brown submitted twenty questions concerning institutional problems to the Student Forum for their consideration. A few years later, he created faculty committees with collegian representatives to share in the administrative burdens. Brown instituted these changes because "it helps to promote a healthy atmosphere when the students have an opportunity to voice their sentiments regarding the administration of the college."[27]

President Brown presided over implementing the ownership arrangement approved at the Norwegian Lutheran Church Convention in 1925. The articles of incorporation, as finally revised and approved in 1928 by 150 pastors and lay convention delegates from the territory, assigned ownership to the Concordia College Corporation formed

**Registrar Martha
Brennun**

from the 812 congregations in the Districts of Northern Minnesota and North Dakota. The pastors and delegates to the national church convention became the governing body of the corporation; they elected a single board of directors to govern the college. The North Central Association required that the former two boards of directors and trustees be replaced by this single ruling body. Although this common form of higher education administration was similar to the hierarchal structure of business corporations, it did contain democratic elements. The non-resident directors and corporate delegates broadly represented the sustaining congregations and fostered community ties. The president's extensive powers were diluted somewhat by a check and balance system of directors, president's council, faculty and collegians.[28]

Despite administrative changes which broadened decision-making and community support, the president still deeply involved himself in all aspects of college life and retained final authority on all internal matters. Brown's correspondence reveals this close personal supervision of daily details. He ordered potatoes for the dining hall; corresponded with troubled parents about their offspring; and tended to farm management—mortgages, rents, taxes, planting and harvesting. Parental letters include one to a pastor informing him that his son's work had been unsatisfactory. As a remedy best suiting the boy's talents, Brown suggested that he take music courses second semester, and then transfer to a conservatory. Another letter to a mother concerned her boy who had reserved a room in the men's dorm "on east side with sun, alone" and was now missing classes without excuse. In addition, a bottle of brandy had been found during a routine inspection by the dean of men. Brown was relieved to have the mother confirm that it was indeed for medicinal purposes.[29]

The president also involved himself in institutional publicity and recruiting. The college publicized itself through one-page newspaper advertisements, faculty speakers to churches and church meetings, annual choir and band tours and *The Record*. Published several times each year, the last carried articles on Christian education, academic programs and extracurricular organizations. As late as 1926 several issues were still written in Norwegian. In addition to these techniques which had been employed by the college for some time, President Brown quickly seized upon commercial radio, which had expanded rapidly since the first regular programs broadcast by KDKA in Pittsburgh in November 1920. On a November Sunday in 1925, WDAY carried Concordia's first musical program by the band, choir and men's quartets. On January 1, 1926, WDAY began broadcasting college chapel and LBI Bible Hours. Many letters of appreciation convinced Brown that using the radio made the college better known and justified the expense.[30]

Annually during June and July, before leaving for his August fishing vacation at Blackduck, Minnesota, Brown devoted himself almost entirely to recruiting. He solicited names, answered questions, sent catalogs and awarded scholarships. Brown early introduced two recruiting techniques. Special postcards, included in college advertising, made it easier for prospects to respond and secure more information. Blanks, distributed at chapel, solicited names of interested high school seniors. Consequently 1,000 received mailings in January 1927. Through correspondence, Brown advised students against taking overly heavy academic loads and encouraged their active participation in the extracurricular activities he considered essential for a well-rounded education. In this Brown reflected the desire of many middle-class parents who expected college to develop their children's social skills.[31]

If complaints surfaced, Brown responded. A pastor complained about the large number of "heathen" (i.e. non-Lutherans). Brown objected to the term but assured him that Concordia made no special effort to recruit non-Lutherans and therefore had fewer than any other church college. Occasionally the process produced undesirable recruits. Brown informed one such case "that Concordia was not the dumping ground for flunks from other institutions." Brown told this particular "flunk" to enroll at Mayville Normal or the North Dakota Agricultural College.[32] The incident reveals Brown's often superior attitude toward neighboring non-liberal arts institutions and his effort to enhance his school's scholarly reputation.

Concern for quality underlay Brown's stated intention of limiting Concordia's enrollment to 500 until endowment, buildings and equipment warranted an increase. He quickly found that his major problem would be enough rather than too many. College enrollment climbed from 353 (1925–1926) to 405 (1926–1927) and reached 461 in Spring 1929. Brown still expressed concern for quality; at a time when most schools lacked admission standards and formal selection procedures, he pioneered by having candidates obtain two unqualified recommendations regarding their moral character and academic ability. Yet Concordia could not afford to become unduly selective because enrollment remained problematic due to agricultural depression and uncertain crops. When poor conditions in northern Minnesota slowed registrations in 1927, the president put four solicitors into the field in mid-August. Through this extra effort the school maintained its enrollment.[33]

Securing an Endowment and Accreditation

Uncertain enrollments translated into uncertain finances. This placed Brown in the role described by Upton Sinclair when he said "the college president spends his time running back and forth between mammon and God." To ease financial strain, Brown attempted to rent the empty buildings during summers. In 1926 a Bible Institute was planned; the gym and chapel rented to *Gudbrandsdalslaget;* and the boarding club and dormitories promised to Moorhead State Teachers for its large summer enrollment.[34]

President Brown also lobbied to increase annual appropriations from the church and to protect the territory from intrusions by sister institutions. Church appropriations increased from $19,146 (1926–1927) to $27,718 (1928–1929) which covered 17.8 percent of budgeted expenses. Brown requested an increase to $30,000. By agreement, no other Lutheran school could solicit funds or students in a church-assigned territory. Accordingly, Brown protested Park Region Academy's planned fund drive and the summer scheduling of the Saint Olaf Quartet. Both intruded on Concordia's territory and, Brown feared, might detract from its own scheduled endowment campaign in 1926.[35]

Brown correctly perceived that accreditation and hence institutional well-being hinged on a successful endowment fund drive. It was not a propitious time. Agricultural depression and bank closings gripped the territory. "I do not understand where $500,000 is to come from," Brown confessed, but he placed his trust in God and the power of prayer: "The silver and gold belong to the Lord and He knows where it is to come from, if He wants us to have it. I have therefore, prayed Him earnestly to point the way."[36]

Successful fundraising in hard times required careful planning. An executive committee including Moorhead Mayor S.G. Dosland and President Brown was formed in December 1925. The next month Professors Herman Nordlie and John Nystul were released from teaching to work on the drive. Following the plans of Luther and Saint Olaf, designed with the advice of professional Lutheran fundraiser Dr. Otto H. Pannkoke, campaign and publicity committees spent four months preparing for two weeks of soliciting. They adopted the slogan, "Ask God and tell the people." They prepared a *Campaign Handbook for Speakers and Workers* containing sermons, addresses and other essential information. They targeted large donors capable of giving $500 to $5,000, but appealed to everyone with mailings sent at two week intervals to every family in the corporate territory. Under the leadership of the North Dakota and Northern Minnesota District presidents, a meeting of chairmen from twenty-five ministerial circuits was held in Fargo. In turn the chairs met twice with the field organizers of their circuits. Then fund rallies were held in each circuit. Church President Aasgaard, President Brown, former North Dakota Governors A.G. Sorlie, L.B. Hanna and R.B. Nestos, and Professors Nordlie, Nystul and Holvik addressed these meetings. After months of careful preparation on May 16, 4,000 workers opened a personal canvass in 812 congregations, inviting everyone to invest in Christian education.[37]

A professional fundraiser, Gettysburg College graduate Dan Weigle, assisted by his advance man Seth Gordon, conducted the Fargo-Moorhead campaign. Weigle expressed the religious and commercial boosterism of 1920s business culture when he promised Brown, "there is no man in America that can sell your college to business as I can, for I talk both languages." Indeed, his campaign literature and speeches exhibited a blend of religion and commerce. Weigle emphasized the themes of "education, religion, business—the great triumvirate of temporal progress, happiness and success." These must be balanced "for religion alone leads to fanaticism, education only to agnosticism and atheism, and business to materialism." The religious foundations of the United States, according to Weigle, made it the wealthiest, most powerful and progressive country in the world. Therefore a denominational school— the best agency for teaching religion to youth—deserved support for the essential role it played in national success. As a clincher, Weigle pointed out that it was in everyone's interest to support Concordia. The college annually spent $250,000 in Fargo-Moorhead and its commitment to Christian education benefited all denominations. Although it was a Lutheran institution, it did not enroll Lutherans exclusively.[38]

The Fargo-Moorhead campaign produced mixed results. Moorhead responded enthusiastically, which should not surprise, given local boosterism that advertised the city as "an educational center." More than seventy men and women, led by Solomon Comstock, systematically canvassed and raised more than $40,000 from 6,000 people including a $75 contribution from Teachers College President R.B. MacLean. In contrast, several Fargo merchants publicly opposed the effort. This angered Brown,

who privately threatened a student boycott if these merchants did not change their tactics. Threats were of no avail. Brown could not explain the Fargo failure. He thought the campaign support of a former North Dakota governor and conservative Republican banker L.B. Hanna, which had caused criticism, was perhaps a factor. Nonetheless Brown believed that Hanna, who had capitalized politically because of his connection with the drive, could be pressured to save the campaign. Brown hoped, with Hanna raising $25,000, to reach $40,000 in a city more than four times Moorhead's size. If this effort had succeeded, Fargo's per capita giving would have been only one-fourth that of Moorhead. The effort failed. Excluding the $10,000 gift from longtime board secretary Lars Christiansen, the city gave less than $15,000.[39] Fargo

Louis B. Hanna

apparently did not claim Concordia. As President Joseph Knutson would say after a similar frustrating fundraising effort twenty-five years later, "That Red River is mighty wide and mighty deep."

To reach its goal, the drive had to overcome many other obstacles. One was the opposition of Saint Olaf President Lars Boe. Writing to J.A. Aasgaard, Boe lobbied for delay and for allowing Saint Olaf and Luther to experiment with a high-pressure campaign. Boe feared that Concordia and Augustana might prevent Saint Olaf and Luther from retaining the accreditation necessary for their existence. On the other hand, he thought Concordia and Augustana would survive many years without North Central approval. To the extent that territorial pastors who were Luther and Saint Olaf alumni shared Boe's beliefs, they too were obstacles. Others may not have participated because they believed reducing church indebtedness should have priority over funding education. Still others balked because of unfounded rumors. One farmer opposed aiding a college that permitted dancing. Another regretted his gift because Concordia had paid $4 a plate for a campaign banquet. Brown wrote both, attempting to quash rumors that might hurt local campaigns and assuring the latter that not more than 75 cents per meal had been spent. A final obstacle was the rural character of the constituency. At the time the church had 538 congregations but only 162 pastors in North Dakota. It had more churches in open country than any other denomination. These rural congregations struggled to support a minister; little surplus remained to support a college.[40]

Despite these enormous difficulties, the campaign more than attained its goal. When President Brown announced during the final chapel on May 29 that $500,000 had been pledged, jubilant applause followed. By the end of 1926, subscriptions totaled $758,596 and collections $280,000. Donations came in cash, pledges, farmland, city property, government bonds and even an automobile. Expenses of $32,169 (4.2 percent) had been modest. Two follow-up efforts secured $450,000 by November 1928. Eventually, collections reached between $500,000 and $600,000, depending on the valuation of real estate.[41]

Board President David Stoeve

North Central accreditation followed on March 17, 1927, thanks to board president David Stoeve and other trustees who signed the $30,000 note needed to meet the $500,000 endowment requirement. With characteristic humility, Brown credited these achievements to the cumulative efforts of many persons working over many years. He correctly assessed the importance of the endowment fund and accreditation when he called them the greatest events in the history of the college.[42]

Formed in 1895, the North Central Association early set standards for high schools and by 1912 had established them for colleges. By meeting the twelve North Central criteria—including faculty with graduate study equivalent to an M.A. at reputable institutions, adequate library and laboratory equipment, and at least eight full-time liberal arts departments, each with one full-time professor—Concordia established itself as a reputable academic institution. Officials expected that annual interest from the endowment and appropriations from the church would provide adequate income for maintaining a quality college. By early 1928 North Dakota and Minnesota had granted Concordia full recognition for its college work, and Brown expected soon to be fully recognized in every state. Besides assuring acceptance at graduate and professional schools throughout the nation, North Central approval meant that Cobbers could obtain jobs at midwestern high schools that were required to hire at least three-fourths of their faculties from North Central-approved institutions if they wanted to maintain their own accreditation.[43]

President Brown's Achievements

The record speaks for itself. Brown's first years were a great success. He had asserted firm control of the institution by stressing the social value of Christian education and by taking a strong stand against what he perceived as the anti-Christian influences of modernism and evolution. He had clearly established criteria for hiring Lutheran faculty and had plans for upgrading salary and professional standards. He envisioned expanding the college physical plant and had already secured the necessary land for that expansion.

Most important, an endowment fund had been established and North Central accreditation had been secured. Brown believed the former gave the college a solid financial base that would make it possible to raise salaries; the latter secured the academic future by giving Concordia the necessary recognition from the secondary schools, which hired most Concordia graduates, and from the graduate schools, which provided opportunities for further training.

Unfortunately for Brown, the Great Depression of the 1930s would shatter his dreams of physical expansion. Nonetheless, the successes of Brown's first years gave Concordia the strength to survive the economic blows of that depression decade.

Chapter 7

Surviving the Great Depression

The Depression, President Brown and Norwegian Lutheranism

Triggered by the stock market crash of October 1929, which aggravated the weaknesses of a deceptively prosperous economy, the Great Depression ranks next to the Civil War as the most severe crisis yet faced by the American republic. The economy spiraled continuously and disastrously downward. Operating banks declined from 25,568 (1929) to 14,771 (1933) with the consequent loss of 9 million savings accounts and $2.5 billion in savings. Many businesses closed and unemployment rose from 1.5 million (1929) to over 12.8 million (1933). Farm income fell 60 percent between 1929 and 1933; one out of eight farmers lost his property. As living standards declined with income, the Depression affected almost everyone and everything.[1]

Although higher education fared better than most institutions, the Depression did create anxiety, as many schools were plagued by the constant fear of impending financial disaster. Only a few closed, however. Of 1,700 colleges and universities, thirty-one shut down and twenty-two others merged between 1934 and 1936. Only three were four-year colleges, and nearly all were private. Among Lutherans, most of the remaining academies and normal schools disappeared. Park Region, which had absorbed these Concordia programs after the 1917 merger, closed in 1932. Several junior colleges either failed or were merged with other collegiate institutions.[2]

To ease its own financial stress, the Norwegian Lutheran Church discussed various plans for reducing the number of its senior colleges from four to two. Following the principle of preferential treatment for Luther and Saint Olaf, all plans involved closing

Main at night, adorned for the fortieth anniversary.

Concordia or downgrading it to a junior college. Fortunately for Concordia, financial conditions improved after 1934 and the church abandoned these designs. It did not cease the pattern of preferential treatment that Brown struggled vainly to change; not until the 1950s would Concordia be accepted on equal footing as a legitimate child of the church. Severely tested in the meantime, the college struggled from year to year to survive the depression decade.[3]

Despite hard times, Concordia celebrated its fortieth anniversary at Homecoming 1931. Four pioneers were honored for extended, dedicated service: two original members of the corporation, President Emeritus J.M.O. Ness and Secretary Lars Christianson; longtime board member Rev. S.G. Hauge; and college matron Helga Fjelstad. "Hymn to Concordia," composed by Herman W. Monson with words by Borghild Torvik and Mrs. Paul Rasmussen, was dedicated to Fjelstad. Indeed, the love and hope that the hymn attributed to these pioneers were emulated by President Brown and a new generation of Cobbers; this firm foundation contributed strongly to institutional survival. J.N. Brown drew on his Christian faith and refused to become discouraged in the face of trying times. As he stated in a letter to Luther professor O.M. Norlie: "If the Lord has a place for our institution, I am confident He will also supply the needs."[4]

Music Instructor
Borghild Torvik

The financial crisis did not alter President Brown's commitment to local civic affairs, regional and national associations and close supervision of college life. Brown regularly attended meetings of the National Lutheran Educational Conference and the American Association of Colleges, as well as the annual pastoral conference and biennial convention of the Northern Minnesota District. He occasionally addressed the latter and often gave speeches at commencements and other special occasions in neighboring communities. During late February and early March 1938, he went on a three-week West Coast speaking tour for the Norwegian Lutheran Church Centennial Campaign. He was elected president in 1931 of the newly formed Association of Lutheran Institutions of North Dakota and Minnesota and reelected in 1939 as Minnesota vice president of the Norwegian American Historical Association. In 1941 he and J. Edgar Hoover contended for the national presidency of Zeta Sigma Pi, a social science honorary society. In June 1940 King Haakon of Norway, his country recently occupied by Nazi Germany, bestowed upon Brown the Order of the Knight of St. Olaf, First Class; the knighting ceremony took place on campus at Fjelstad Hall in October.[5]

Activities and honors did not prevent Brown from writing many personal letters of encouragement and closely supervising the *Concordian*, the *Cobber*, recruitment and discipline. He assured a troubled pastor that the literary board had prohibited any further theatre advertisements in the newspaper. He warned Pelican Rapids officials that the college band would not appear at the 17th of May festival if a community dance were held. He complimented a mother on her son's "good scholastic record" and participation in extracurricular activities. Many other letters encouraged and recommended students for seminary. A Native American who had attended Canton Normal and Concordia received from the president a seminary recommendation and several additional letters seeking economic assistance.[6] This man was only one of many to benefit from Brown's kindness and lifelong commitment to helping former students.

The Depression did not weaken Brown's devotion to the cause of Norwegian Lutheranism. He often congratulated Lutherans who had been elected or appointed to public positions because he believed they ought to participate actively in public affairs. While Brown wanted Norwegian Lutheranism to uplift American culture, he protected it from negative cultural influences. He deplored modernism and "creedless Americanism." To maintain a pure Norwegian Lutheranism, Brown asserted, "our Lutheran seminaries and colleges need Lutheran textbooks written by men of our own church, and, if possible, men of our own country." Here Brown speaks the language of a narrow midwestern religious outlook and ethnic insularity. At the time, the Norwegian Lutheran Church feared contamination by the "unorthodox" United Lutheran Church in America and new currents in European theology.[7]

The Board of Directors balanced the budget despite the Depression.

As an orthodox midwestern Norwegian Lutheran, Brown shared some cultural assumptions with fundamentalists of the day. Brown believed in the unchanging truth of the gospel message and in evangelism. Yet he warned against the dangerous tendencies of the "Pietistic Party" within Lutheranism because "we cannot afford to develop a little Church group inside of the Church with a 'holier than thou' attitude." Although Brown supported the Lutheran Bible Institute, he "feared a dangerous [pietist] tendency ... in this institution" just as he had seen "some evidence of it ... in our own student body." Similarly, Brown warned Lutherans that they could not cooperate with Reformed churches in modern revivalism because revivalists disregarded the Lutheran conception of the church's role in bringing salvation.[8]

By cautioning against the excesses of Lutheran and Reformed pietism, Brown worked to overcome Norwegian insularity. He urged Lutherans to cooperate with Reformed Christians in promoting "civic righteousness and improvement." Even in his early years as a pastor in Beloit, he had advocated more fellowship among the town's five Lutheran churches. With greater fraternal spirit Lutherans had the potential to become one of the leading denominations in the United States.[9]

Brown attended the organizing convention of the American Lutheran Conference in October 1930. The conference, consisting of five midwestern Lutheran Synods— the newly formed American Lutheran Church, the Augustana Synod, the Norwegian Lutheran Church of America, the Lutheran Free Church, and the United Danish Evangelical Lutheran Church—considered matters of mutual interest, formed several study commissions and devoted much discussion to the issue of church-related higher education. Brown believed the Holy Spirit was leading these Lutherans to closer fellowship and he correctly predicted an eventual union by the next generation.[10]

While it is possible to see the American Lutheran Conference as a positive step toward eventual Lutheran union, it was also a defensive alliance of midwestern Lutherans against the eastern United Lutheran Church in America (ULCA). The American Lutheran Conference emerged from the 1925 meeting that produced the Minneapolis Theses. The Theses specified points of opposition to the ULCA on the inspiration and inerrancy of the Bible, unionism (the degree of cooperation with other churches) and membership in secret lodges. Throughout the 1940s, Norwegian Lutherans opposed fellowship with ULCA until it demonstrated doctrinal soundness. The Norwegians remained suspicious of the ULCA because they believed it had been misled by its European-inspired Erlangen Theology and had developed a false view of Scripture.[11]

Although Brown shared these misgivings about eastern Lutheranism, he worked to turn this midwestern union to the practical benefit of Concordia. Quite apart from his own commitment to unity, Brown clearly perceived the demographic and financial implications. Formation of the American Lutheran Conference greatly increased the college's potential constituency; in addition to 315,000 Norwegian Lutherans in the three closest districts, there were 253,654 from other synods located within 150 miles. The board of directors agreed; at their January 1932 meeting they authorized negotiations. Accordingly, the president sought support from the Swedish Augustana Synod, the American Lutheran Church, the Icelandic Synod and the Free Church. Discussion continued throughout the decade. In 1935 Brown described his goal to the National Lutheran Educational Conference in an address, "Lutheran Unity Through Education." Admitting it would take time, Brown believed the effort worthwhile "because the cooperating synods have no schools in the territory."[12]

The Depression prescribed other political activities on other fronts; Brown responded with a spirited defense of institutional interests. Church politics were especially important. Throughout the decade he lobbied the denominational board of education for larger appropriations, demanded enforcement of agreed-upon territorial limits and protested the privileged status accorded Saint Olaf and Luther. They not only received more funds but constantly intruded into Concordia's territory. By 1937 Brown expressed a bit more optimism. He hoped new board of education member Rev. A.E. Hanson, a Concordia friend, might effect a fairer division of the budget. Meanwhile Augustana and Luther cooperated in respecting boundaries even though Saint Olaf was still "over-running the territory." Apparently permissible under a new arrangement, which Brown wished the church had not made, the invasion violated a gentleman's agreement among the four presidents to respect old boundaries. In self-defense Brown threatened to enter Saint Olaf's area in canvassing for students.[13]

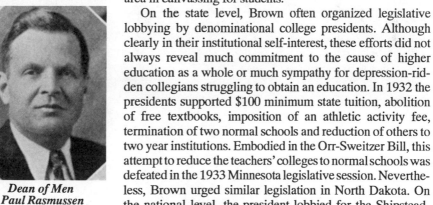

Dean of Men
Paul Rasmussen

On the state level, Brown often organized legislative lobbying by denominational college presidents. Although clearly in their institutional self-interest, these efforts did not always reveal much commitment to the cause of higher education as a whole or much sympathy for depression-ridden collegians struggling to obtain an education. In 1932 the presidents supported $100 minimum state tuition, abolition of free textbooks, imposition of an athletic activity fee, termination of two normal schools and reduction of others to two year institutions. Embodied in the Orr-Sweitzer Bill, this attempt to reduce the teachers' colleges to normal schools was defeated in the 1933 Minnesota legislative session. Nevertheless, Brown urged similar legislation in North Dakota. On the national level, the president lobbied for the Shipstead-Guyer bill that would have authorized federal government funding of private college loans to students.[14]

Discretion is the better part of valor, especially for college presidents. Brown's political opinions and lobbying were always expressed privately. Moreover, his political stance often reflected his audience. Although a Republican, his sympathies were "liberal and progressive" when writing Farmer-Laborite Minnesota Governor Floyd B. Olson and conservative when assuring a pastor that Concordia was not "a hot bed of Bolshevism." The latter charge stemmed from Dean of Men Paul Rasmussen's efforts for the Farmer-Labor Party during the 1934 campaign. The criticism, expressed in "a flood of letters," led Rasmussen to cancel some speeches and Brown to recommend to the board "that no member of the Concordia College faculty shall hereafter take part in political campaigns."[15] Although President Brown later relaxed this restriction, he did alter his public nonpartisan stance. His successor as president created a very different political climate. Joseph Knutson expressed his own opinions openly and actively encouraged faculty political participation.

A College Financial Crisis

Depression-era college finance is a story of shrinking numbers (see Table IV). The college faced financial crisis, as church funding declined from $24,000 (1929–1930) to a low of $12,060 (1933–1934), and endowment income plummeted from $19,512 (1930) to $2,471 (1936). Invested almost entirely in farm mortgages, the endowment mirrored the fate of the farm economy, buffeted first by depressed prices, then by drought and finally by grasshoppers. President Brown fought desperately for increased church appropriations, but often failed to secure them because the church trimmed its own budget and because the board of education gave preference to institutions owned by the church—the seminary, Saint Olaf and Luther. This preference is expressed in the proposed distribution for 1932: Saint Olaf, $60,000; Luther, $30,000; Concordia and Augustana, $25,000 each. Even cuts were inequitable—$2,500 from Luther and $5,000 from each of the others. Actually reductions were greater. Concordia saw its $18,000 allocation halved in January 1933. This created salary payment problems, forcing the board to shift $3,000 from Saint Olaf to Concordia. While annual

Table IV: College Income, Expenses, Enrollments, Salaries, 1929–1943**

	1929	1930	1933	1935	1936	1940	1943
Endowment Income		19,512	5,747	5,621	2,471	2,676	35,170
Church Income	24,000	24,000	16,933	14,774	15,000	19,800	21,967
Tuition/Fee Income		54,822	60,153	61,821	69,731	96,187	117,474
Notes-Receivable							
Students			38,598		48,356		8,744
Enrollment	450	458	413	420	450	534	519
General College Income			90,233		103,773		287,181
General College Expenses			88,949		102,828		275,374
Excess			1,284		945		11,806
Faculty Salary	72,210*		50,642		51,061		66,354
Number of Faculty	39*	30	29	30	30	32	34
Average Salary	1,852		1,746		1,702		1,952

* Includes administrators, library, music.
**From Annual Treasurer's Reports, 1932–1933, 1935–1936, 1942–1943, and Miscellaneous Financial Statements, 1926–1947, in Business Office Papers, Concordia College Archives; Catalog, 1928–1943.

President J.N. Brown, 1925–1951

allotments slowly increased, by 1943 they had not yet attained the pre-depression level, as Table IV indicates.[16]

In attempting to limit church indebtedness, the board of education repeatedly frustrated Concordia by rejecting requests for special funding. It did not assume financial responsibility for the 1935 Norway band tour; it refused to pay for the annual audit required by the church; it did not subsidize radio broadcasts (as it did for Luther and Saint Olaf); it declined a request for the Park Region Endowment when that school closed in 1932; and it vetoed a congregational fundraising campaign to construct a women's dormitory. Once more, dire need led the board to relent; it allowed using the endowment if room rent paid repairs, insurance and 4 percent interest, and repaid the principal in a reasonable period.[17]

Tuition/fees provided the largest share of college income (see Table IV)—66 percent (1933) and 69 percent (1936)—which made enrollment crucial to institutional survival. Despite recruiting efforts, hard times sent enrollment down 9.8 percent from 458 (1930) to a low of 413 in 1933, the worst depression year. After that, numbers slowly climbed until World War II sent them tumbling again. Because students were the largest income source, Brown labored mightily not only to recruit, but to keep other recruiters out of the territory. At this time Saint Olaf and Luther apparently wanted the territorial rule changed and, according to Brown, continually infringed in a "desperate competition for students." These protective efforts often were not appreciated. One pastor complained about Brown's constant criticism of other church colleges and warned that Concordia required the friendship of the majority of North Dakota pastors who were Saint Olaf and Luther alumni. Undaunted, Brown reiterated territorial rights and demanded pastoral support through sending their children and congregational youth to Concordia.[18]

Fundraising afforded an alternate source of income. As the Depression deepened, the president attempted to revive the Greater Concordia Association, formed in 1929 to tap alumni and constituency support. In 1930 Brown hoped to raise $5,000 to $10,000 through annual one-dollar dues, using the funds for current expenses and seed money on the new gymnasium desired by alumni and students. Although the board of directors in 1931 discussed a $40,000 gymnasium campaign as a fortieth anniversary gift and $21,000 was pledged by the 1929 and 1930 senior classes, construction was delayed for two decades by depression, war and the post-war enrollment surge. President Brown did not abandon the idea of the Greater Concordia Association, however. Another drive in 1933 aimed to enroll a scaled-down goal of 2,000 members. Despite planning, organization of ministerial circuits and the efforts of Professor Herman Nordlie, only 650 members enrolled. The association never produced the hoped-for income. Gifts totaled only $273 for the 1935–1936 school year. In 1938 association dues were only sufficient to pay the WDAY broadcasting costs.[19]

Another effort aimed at securing a building fund. In the midst of this difficult work, Brown at times displayed a healthy sense of humor. As he wrote privately to a friend in 1936: "Next week I start out with a six-shooter in each hand to hold up the natives for enough money to build ladies hall." L.B. Hanna, a wealthy friend of the college who had been counted on to save the endowment campaign in Fargo and who was known for being tightfisted, again became the focus of attention. The college wanted Hanna both to contribute and to solicit gifts from wealthy Fargo and eastern friends. In January 1937 the finance committee decided to seek contributions totaling $75,000, one-half the anticipated cost of a new women's dormitory. The balance was to be borrowed from the endowment and repaid from dormitory rent. A meeting at the

Gardner Hotel formally launched the drive with public announcement of $5,000 gifts from Hanna and Lars Christianson. Soliciting from territorial congregations was prohibited by the synodical boards of education and trustees because of the church's poor financial condition. Congregational canvassing was postponed until the Golden Jubilee Fund Drive scheduled in 1942.[20]

Almost-constant fundraising in hard times created a troublesome legacy for Brown's presidency. It alienated alumni and generated personal dislike of Brown. Particularly vexing were the 1929 and 1930 class pledges totaling $21,000 for the new

gymnasium. If the pledge had not been paid, alumni resented the continued obligation. If the pledge had been paid, alumni resented that it had not been used for the designated purpose. To heal this rift, Alumni Association President Carl Narveson secured a resolution during his term (1939–1941) which asked the college to excuse all class pledges. This action improved relations.[21]

Relatively unsuccessful in securing additional funding, the college economized. Salaries were reduced on several occasions by a total of at least 21 percent or more between 1931 and 1934. Monthly checks were always issued on schedule, but severe cash flow problems often necessitated short-term borrowing to meet payroll.

Alumni President Carl Narveson

During the bank closings of March 1933, the board sold $7,000 in *Forum* bonds on the condition that the Fargo newspaper bought them at par and resold them in the fall after students made their deposits. Again in November and December, $5,000 loans were taken to pay salaries.[22]

Pay cuts were not accepted willingly by everyone. Some protested the first decrease on the grounds that the board could not legally reduce the amounts on signed contracts. Brown agreed, but insisted that the board had a moral obligation to balance the budget. In February 1933, when the president asked staff for signatures on statements voluntarily accepting another salary reduction, only 62 percent signed. This did not prevent the cut; subsequent contracts contained the proviso that the agreed-upon amount could be reduced at the board's discretion.[23]

Additional economies came from a variety of measures. When Professor T.C. Wollan died in 1932, his classes were taught by existing staff. Three other positions were eliminated for the next academic year. Meanwhile department budgets were trimmed from $2,417 to $1,440, library expenses cut to $206, and class sizes increased. Electric costs were closely monitored. Based on one standard 40- to 60-watt bulb per room of two students, charges were increased 75 cents per month for an extra light, a radio or an electric appliance. By 1934 Brown feared the college had reached its limits of economy; it could not continue without risking its North Central accreditation.[24]

Despite hard times, the college balanced its budget throughout the decade. Many attribute this amazing feat to the skills and long hours of business manager H.M. Dale. He supervised the farms, managed the economizing and annually balanced the books, occasionally surprising even the president. Several farms, acquired through land endowment gifts and investments in farm mortgages, produced badly needed income. During 1933, the worst depression year, a number were sold and the mortgages on others refinanced through the Reconstruction Finance Corporation. That same year the college received its largest gift to date, a productive, well-equipped 1,383 acre farm from O.L. Jensen of Harvey, North Dakota. Exigency fostered self-sufficiency. Emulating the Saint Olaf farm project, in 1929 the school purchased a local dairy and produce farm, expanded it from 240 to 713 acres and developed a prize-winning dairy herd. The operation made economic sense: Farm produce supplied the campus kitchen and usually generated a boarding department surplus that covered other general college deficits; collegians found parttime employment; and the rural constituency appreciated the frugal household management.[25]

The Concordia dairy farm helped Concordia survive the Depression.

Notwithstanding this significant economic contribution, in the early 1940s the board voted to sell the endowment farm property as quickly as possible. Apparently the farms were a public relations curse. Many had been acquired through investing in farm mortgages, which then had been foreclosed if payments could not be made. No wonder every neighbor became a critical observer, who quickly detected any sign of mismanagement. The difficulty of securing dependable farm help, especially with the wartime manpower shortage, compounded the problems of management. Given these difficulties, the decision to sell is understandable but it appeared an economic mistake when land values rose after World War II.[26]

Fortunately, conditions improved after 1934. Favorable sales after that date indicated that no losses would be sustained on investments in real estate and mortgages, representing 54 and 18 percent respectively of the endowment fund. The board approved the Norway band tour and allowed Brown a three-month vacation to accompany the band. Tour losses of $3,500 were absorbed by individual gifts and by the general budget. For the 1937 spring term, the faculty were awarded a 5 percent increase, their first since the Depression began. By 1938 President Brown could report to the directors that Concordia was "in the best enrollment and financial condition in its history." This statement suggests not only that economic conditions had somewhat improved, but that the college had always faced difficult times financially.[27]

Maintaining Enrollment

To survive the Depression, Concordia had to maintain its enrollment. As it had previously, the college relied on institutional advertising to attract students. As before, corporate self-image formed the core of all publicity; at this time, Concordia viewed itself as a pioneer institution patterned after the traditional American college. It had grown in response to the changing needs of the rural region it served. It had been built from a combination of elements: the Norwegian university and classical traditions brought by faculty from Saint Olaf and Luther, the ideals of graduate schools where professors had trained and borrowings from other liberal arts colleges. Its Norwegian Lutheran heritage had produced a homogeneous student body devoted to the ideals of spiritual growth and community service.[28]

Dr. Thomas Burgess

During the 1930s, these elements were combined into a new institutional self-image; more clearly than earlier, Concordia identified itself as a Christian liberal arts college. Faculty were annually assigned the task of explaining the "Christian liberal arts" to prospective students and the constituency. All agreed that Christianity and the liberal arts were compatible because both stressed spiritual values. According to Professor Peter Anderson, the Christian liberal arts made a twofold spiritual contribution: to society by preserving and promoting culture, and to individuals by establishing a Christian world view. For this to be accomplished, as Thomas Burgess pointed out, the college must "combine the highest ideals and standards in the field of higher education with a clear and uncompromising Christian testimony." Thus students were trained to acquire and to use broad and specific knowledge (i.e. general education and major field), and to develop "open, critical, and cultural attitudes of mind." This was done confidently; no truth was covered up because "truth rightly understood always supports the Christian faith." Professors Frida Nilsen and Carl B. Ylvisaker concurred with emphasizing the centrality of spiritual values. Nilsen

envisaged the church school as a "Christian Power Station" where "light-filled teachers" remade lives through the influence of the Holy Spirit. Ylvisaker imagined the school's spiritual life as a ship on a "straight course between the Scylla of Pharisaic bigotry and the Charybdis of arid liberalism." By providing a healthy spiritual environment with many opportunities for expressing the Christian life, Ylvisaker said, Concordia aspired "to send out saved and sanctified men and women to serve the church and reflect Christ in relations to fellow man."[29]

Professor Frida Nilsen

Radio, print and speakers carried the Christian liberal arts message throughout the corporate territory. Daily chapel broadcasts continued on WDAY, joined in 1935 by the annual Christmas Radio Party that united Concordia parties in more than 200 towns. By early 1938, WDAY also carried a Concordia Music Hour, featuring performances and explanations by the band, choir and other college groups. Initially twenty-one half-hour programs, it later increased to thirty. During the 1938–1939 school year, Professor G.L. Schoberg began broadcasting his weekly Cobbercast, "Concordially Yours." Prepared from copies of the *Concordian*, Shakespeare and a book of quotations, Schoberg's program highlighted college activities.[30]

Formed in 1934, the Concordia Service Bureau directed all groups and individuals who represented the college. It sent announcements to pastors, school officials and alumni; it supplied speakers for churches, service clubs, PTAs, women's clubs and patriotic organizations; and it provided musical and dramatic programs for schools.

The publicity board (or news bureau)—comprised of one collegian and four professors —compiled and distributed all college news dispatches and bulletins. It sent articles about students to their hometown papers, informed regional newspapers about campus events, edited *The Record*—a bimonthly publication distributed to prospective collegians—and planned recruiting publicity.

A special issue of the *Concordian* publicizing campus activities was mailed each spring to 3,500 high school seniors. In 1941 another mailing was sent to alumni, pastors and friends for use in counseling prospective Cobbers. It consisted of "Facts for Freshmen," answering questions about attending a Christian liberal arts college; "Faculty People in the News," and "Cobber Mothers Mobilize for Semi-Centennial."[31]

G.L. Schoberg's "Cobbercast" began in 1938.

The 1939 Royal Commencement, a dramatic news event, produced a publicity windfall. The Norwegian Royal Tour of Crown Prince Olav and Princess Martha, an effort to strengthen ties with Norwegian-Americans as Europe drifted toward war, drew large crowds during a three-day visit to Fargo-Moorhead but probably did not alter the strong isolationism of the valley. President Brown chaired the twin city reception committee; at Concordia loudspeakers were installed, Seventh and Eighth Streets closed and three miles of planking used to construct seating for 2,000 people. On graduation day, Prince Olav received the first honorary doctorate bestowed by the college and delivered an address to a crowd of 15,000 gathered on the lawn in front of Main.[32]

Crown Prince Olav receives the school's first honorary degree.

Speakers advertised the school as well. Ordained faculty, numbering usually four throughout the decade, preached regularly; collegiate groups often visited neighboring congregations. President Brown frequently appeared at special events. Besides serving the church, these speakers—as did all other institutional advertising—served the utilitarian purpose of attracting students. Personal contacts supplemented publicity. The college relied on alumni, friends, high school teachers and pastors to generate prospect lists. Usually two recruiters then traveled the territory visiting high schools in the spring and interviewing graduates during the summer. Depression conditions called forth innovations and produced variations in this pattern. The college in 1931 invited pastors to campus from twelve neighboring circuits to discuss recruiting and Concordia's educational problems. Due to poor North Dakota conditions that summer, three solicitors and the male quartet canvassed. For recruiters, the college usually relied on outstanding students or graduates. Faculty were sometimes used. The president thought Carl B. Ylvisaker and Paul Rasmussen especially effective; they did much recruiting. If sent, teachers received additional pay.[33]

Payment of fees complicated recruitment. Given the depressed economy, how could individuals pay? Semester charges were not increased over the previous decade and averaged about $185 in the early 1930s; by 1938 these had increased to approximately $200. Books were $20 annually and social expenses minimal. Four free all-college social events were scheduled and the social committee limited charges for all society and class entertainments. Spending for clothes and railroad fares varied with individuals.[34]

However minimal these costs seem, $400 was a substantial sum for almost all collegians and their families. They relied on a variety of methods in their struggle to pay their fees. Throughout the decade, scholarships were awarded to the highest ranking boy and girl in each high school graduation class. In theory granted without regard to religious affiliation, Brown admitted confidentially that exceptions were made for "our purpose is to obtain Lutheran students." These awards varied from $50 to $100, depending on college grades, and were payable second semester. Although private colleges discussed eliminating freshmen scholarships as an economy measure, lack of unanimity dictated continuing the practice. The Norwegian Lutheran Church Women's Missionary Federation established $75 scholarships for worthy students.

The Concordia Women's League provided much-appreciated loans to needy Cobbers.

Four were awarded in 1938. Loans were available to juniors and seniors. They could borrow up to $150 from the school; given a high demand, often less was loaned to ensure an equitable distribution. Concordia College Women's League loans, not to exceed $100, were to be repaid with interest within one year of graduation. Seminarians were allowed a longer period. The league loaned $3,210 to thirty-eight students in 1930; in 1941 they loaned $5,781 to fifty-seven. Repayment was excellent with only a few bad debts. Another (unadvertised) source for loans, longtime janitor Nels Mugaas, helped several men complete their education.[35]

The extent and repayment of institutional loans is less clear. As did many other colleges, Concordia increased financial assistance even though this drained its budget. It really had no choice; it could not operate without students and they could not attend without help.

Borrowing increased as the Depression deepened. Student debts totaled $33,000 in 1931, up from $5,000 only three years earlier. Alarmed, Brown wrote that these notes "must be collected this year if the college is to maintain its credit." Throughout the decade, the president attempted to collect by encouraging debtors to begin monthly payment plans. Despite his efforts, the amounts owed climbed to $38,598 in 1933 and then to $48,356 in 1936 (see Table IV, p. 110). These figures reflect the region's poor economy. To help collegians meet expenses during the first months of 1933, probably the worst depression year, the college made individual arrangements with almost everyone. They were permitted to enroll if they could pay all expenses except tuition (which could be paid over the summer). Reliable persons were extended credit for a second year.[36]

Evidently these debts were not soon paid. This created cash flow problems, but the college maintained its credit and apparently stayed afloat by securing short-term loans. To read Brown's correspondence concerning these obligations is to read the personal economic difficulties of the Depression. Loans went unpaid as working children aided destitute parents. Teachers, paid in warrants by school boards without funds, applied the warrants toward their Concordia debts. Unemployed graduates had their interest excused if they paid the principal. A Paynesville teacher, who had taught four years without pay cuts, in May 1933 completed payment on his $700 note dating from 1929. That had been the largest individual loan made at the time.[37]

Many worked to pay their expenses. Directed by a head janitor, collegians performed most of the janitorial and maintenance tasks. Others labored as secretaries, librarians and dining hall waiters. The exceptionally talented received the rare laboratory assistantship, especially prized because it paid tuition and all fees for the term. Because on-campus jobs were limited and quickly taken, most took off-campus positions although these were also hard to find. A number of men worked at the Moorhead Creamery; others toiled in restaurants, cafeterias and even beer halls. Women commonly did housekeeping; three hours were required daily for board and an additional hour daily for room. The number working increased from 25 percent (1931) to 50 percent (1938). The percentage would have been higher if employment had been available.[38]

Even this increase required funding from the National Youth Administration (NYA), a New Deal work-study program that assisted more than 600,000 collegians during its decade of existence. Facing bankruptcy if they did not for the first time find substantial amounts of financial aid, many institutions were anxious to participate in any program of federal assistance. President Brown was no exception; he recognized the institutional value of NYA and supported it wholeheartedly. Well he should. In

1938, NYA assistance was given to ninety-eight Cobbers—19 percent of those enrolled and 45 percent of those employed.[39]

Summer jobs were similarly scarce. Teaching in church summer schools earlier had been a favorite occupation, annually attracting fifty or more Cobbers who earned $60 per month for one or two months work; now it declined to almost nothing as congregations economized. Although opportunities increased by 1939 with improving conditions, the numbers employed were only one-half the previous decade. If all else failed, the president looked for "angels" to aid worthy Cobbers. By these means, Concordia helped many graduate. The hard times did not prevent and probably even contributed to a short-lived work stoppage by student waiters in March 1930. To obtain higher wages, they refused to serve one meal. When they were called before Farm-Labor activist and Dean of Men Paul Rasmussen, he jokingly opened with the remark—"you bunch of communists." The wages of waiters and waitresses were raised to 17 cents per meal for the balance of the term, but President Brown warned that the arrangement was not binding for the next academic year, when contracts would be signed.[40]

Through its recruiting efforts and innovations in financial aid, Concordia managed to keep its enrollment above 410 during the worst depression years; graduation classes averaged eighty-five for the decade. After 1934, following a national trend, numbers edged upward until by 1938, with economic conditions slightly improved, 513 enrolled. Enrollment remained above 500 until the onset of World War II (see Table IV, p. 110). During the Depression, female college enrollment nationally continued its interwar decline from a peak of 47.3 percent (1920) to 43.7 percent (1929–1930) and 40.3 percent (1939–1940). Although the percentage dropped, absolute numbers increased as the proportions of youth attending more than tripled. To some degree, Concordia followed the direction of these trends but exceeded the national average. The percentage decreased from 49.5 (1929–1930) to 46.8 (1939–1940) while the numbers increased from 227 to 245. For the decade, female enrollment annually averaged 223 (47.6 percent). A higher percentage of women graduated, however. For the decade, female graduates annually averaged forty-five and comprised 51.3 percent of the total.[41]

Sons and daughters of farmers, ministers and merchants, most Cobbers still originated in the little Norways of the Red River Valley. The student body numbered 534 in 1939; of the 293 (54.9 percent) who reported parental occupations, 143 (25.1 percent of those enrolled and 48.8 percent of those reporting) were farm offspring. Fifty (9.5 percent and 17 percent) and forty (7.5 percent and 13.6 percent) were children of ministers and merchants respectively. Most originated in the valley; in 1935, 92.6 percent came from within a radius of 100 miles; in 1941 Minnesotans (47.5 percent) and North Dakotans (42.5 percent) comprised 90 percent of the students. Eighty (15 percent) were Fargo-Moorhead natives. That same year 91.9 percent (489) were Lutherans distributed among ten synods. Although most were Norwegian Lutheran, President Brown's efforts at Lutheran cooperation had at least attracted eighty-four from other synods.[42]

During hard times the college toiled to recruit, collegians labored to pay, and both struggled with placement upon graduation. The prospect of unemployment or low-paying teaching positions complicated the repayment of institutional loans, further straining college finances. Peter "Pa" Anderson directed the placement bureau efficiently, using shirt boxes as files for recommendations and information. In the worst depression years the percentage placed declined to 67 (1932), 60 (1933) and 70 (1934).

Poor as these numbers were, they were better than the national average or the records of other Minnesota colleges. Figures improved markedly to 90 percent in 1935 and 100 percent from 1936 through 1938. Of these, between 70 and 80 percent took teaching positions in small high schools where they had ample opportunity to use their four recommended teaching fields and more besides.[43]

The experience of Cornelia (Coya) Gjesdal ('34) was probably typical. She took her first job in Penn, North Dakota, a German community of ninety people located forty miles from her family in Edmore. A bank, blacksmith shop, general store, drug store, pool hall, meat market and railroad depot lined the block-long main street. There

Coya Gjesdal Knutson

were three churches. She did not join the Missouri Synod Lutheran because it differed from her Norwegian Lutheran upbringing. At the high school, with four to ten graduates annually, two teachers instructed four grades. Gjesdal taught music, American literature, English literature, history, psychology and grammar (second semester), and directed all school music programs. For this she received $85 per month; she was fortunate because at the time 67 percent of North Dakota teachers received less than $500 per year.[44]

Gjesdal's experience is typical in another way. Nationally, from the 1920s through the 1940s, most female graduates worked fulltime at some point after commencement, but the majority did not work for long after marriage. Similarly, Coya Gjesdal Knutson and other Cobbers ceased employment with matrimony. In 1942, 38.4 percent of the female graduates were teaching while 35.9 percent were homemakers, a dramatic increase from the 9.3 percent so occupied in 1930.[45] Yet in another sense Coya Knutson was untypical; she returned to work during World War II, subsequently became involved in DFL politics, served as a state legislator, and from 1954 to 1958 represented the Minnesota Ninth District in Congress.

Administrators and Faculty

The Depression imposed some hardships on college administration and faculty. Despite the added burden of farm management, administrative structure remained simple and did not change much during the decade. All administrative offices were located in one large connecting room in Main; unless President Brown had a meeting, his door always stayed open. When the temperature topped 114 degrees during the torrid summer of 1936 a tub, a block of ice and a fan served as air conditioning. Mattie Ostby Dale still handled all the bookkeeping, working nights to dispatch her duties which expanded with the growing number of institutional loans to students. Due to lack of funds, administrative duties were either concentrated in the hands of the president and business manager or else parceled out to faculty on a parttime basis. Consequently, H.M. Dale had extremely wide and varied responsibilities—he managed the college farms, business affairs, and buildings and grounds. Dale lacked the time to perform all these tasks and was frequently criticized when jobs were not completed. To assist Dale, Sigurd Mundhjeld came in 1938 as treasurer and parttime mathematics instructor. At the same time, Dr. O.A. Tingelstad, president of Pacific

Lutheran, was called to be dean of instruction. This office was created for the man; after Tingelstad's rejection the title did not reappear for a decade although Peter Anderson increasingly assumed these duties. In managing the college, the president was assisted by an administrative council comprised of Dale, Vice-President J.H. Hjelmstad, the dean of men, and (after 1938) Treasurer Mundhjeld. It is worth noting that Dean of Women Frida Nilsen was excluded. She disliked the situation but was unable to correct it during her tenure as dean.[46]

Mattie Ostby Dale

Athletics, music, social discipline, publications and other aspects of college life were governed by sixteen or more faculty committees, many with a single student representative. This arrangement supported the president's claim that he was guided by a democratic ideal of administration which gave both collegians and professors unusual freedom in shaping policy. This framework also enabled Concordia and other American colleges to channel extracurricular activities in directions compatible with administrative goals.

President Brown closely supervised and exercised final authority over this structure; in turn he reported to the board of directors, elected by the corporation which represented the congregations of the territory. Throughout the decade, the directors were often clergymen; in 1930 and 1935, eleven of twenty-one members were pastors.[47] A clerical president supported by clerical directors ensured that Concordia would remain true to the Norwegian Lutheran Church.

Following the student personnel trend in higher education, the personnel council was created in 1939 to supervise student services. Membership included the deans of men and women, the college pastor (often Carl Ylvisaker), registrar, director of the health program, director of the placement bureau and the personnel secretary. The council met to consider student problems; it kept detailed records which were available to teachers and advisers for counseling. Beginning in 1936, all collegians were assigned faculty advisers. After they declared a major at the end of their sophomore year, that department head became their adviser.[48]

During the 1930s Concordia faculty endured several salary reductions, totaling perhaps more than 21 percent, leaving them with a paycheck that Brown said "could not be justified before God or man." Families struggled to balance household accounts; several had large unpaid bills with local grocers. To further economize, three teachers were released in 1933. Whatever the strain for individuals, college faculty as a group survived the Depression as well as or better than all other professions and most blue collar workers. Stable employment, security of positions and regular paychecks for most account for their comparative advantage. At Concordia, most retained their jobs; and the college regularly paid cash, for which President Brown was much praised.[49]

Even with reductions, department heads were not poorly paid by the standards of depression America. Senior faculty in 1935 received $2,160 and junior instructors about $1,320. This is lower than the national professorial average of $2,403 in 1934, but higher for senior professors than the $1,920 set by the North Dakota Legislature in 1933 for all university, college and normal school teachers. A salary of $2,500 in 1939 marked one as well-to-do; only 4.2 percent of the labor force received that much, while factory workers earned about $1,250.[50]

Despite depression-induced adjustments, the faculty profile changed little in the decade. Between 1925 and 1931, faculty increased from thirty-five to forty, doctorates declined from five to three, and the percentage of women remained at about 43 percent. Of the men with faculty rank in 1931, 68.4 percent were professors. Reflecting the gender discrimination prevalent in higher education of that day, all the department heads with the exception of home economics were men. No women held the rank of professor, 76.5 percent were instructors, and most of the seventeen females were concentrated in four departments—music (five), language (four), home economics (three) and English (two). By 1940, the faculty of forty-five included twenty women (44.4 percent). Mae Anderson, a Ph.D. in mathematics from the University of Chicago, held the rank of professor; she joined Florence Kruger, home economics, as the only female department heads. Among women, 56.2 percent still were instructors while 66.6 percent of the men were professors. Women were less concentrated in traditional female fields and taught in nine different departments. Five faculty (11 percent) held doctorates.[51]

Dr. Mae Anderson

Besides working for what they regarded as low pay, faculty served without a sabbatical leave program, a retirement plan or tenure. After an initial year they might receive a six-year contract, annually renewed, that the board could terminate at any time for valid reasons. These "permanent" employees were required to be Lutheran church members, although a higher percentage were now drawn from other synods than previously, and non-Lutherans might fill temporary and parttime positions. Without a written constitution faculty had no formal role in governance, but did serve on standing or special committees as has been noted. They performed many duties discharged by specialists today. A few devoted summers to recruiting. Some instructed at Bible camps. Others handled college publicity. In 1932 those who were not ordained were even asked to speak in chapel. They met semimonthly for an hour on Friday afternoons to conduct college business or, in the mid-1930s, to discuss educational policy. In 1937 they joined with the student body in passing separate resolutions urging citizens to vote against legalization of hard liquor in Clay County. In addition, they met monthly, usually to socialize but occasionally for study. Professor J.H. Hjelmstad in 1931 spoke on "Business Cycles"; a 1936 book discussion series opened with

Florence Kruger

W. F. Schmidt's review of *The Social Sources of Denominationalism* by H. Richard Niebuhr.[52]

Given their many activities, the heavy teaching loads of at least eighteen hours (six courses) per week, the lack of offices and the institutional mission of a Christian liberal arts college, they were not expected to publish; it is not surprising that they rarely did. Yet when Thomas Burgess's article appeared in the *Journal of Educational Sociology* in 1931, President Brown called it an honor for Burgess and the college; he also inserted an announcement in the *Concordian*. These remarkable people even found time and money to make a fortieth anniversary gift, perhaps under pressure and certainly belatedly. In 1932, each donated $5 to a building fund, constructed bleachers seating 800 and formally presented the gift at homecoming.[53] For little reward and without the security of a tenure system, faculty thus did much. Their sacrifices contributed greatly to institutional survival during the Depression.

The Church College Curriculum

Despite financial limitations imposed by the Depression, significant curricular developments occurred in the decade. *Studies in Lutheran Higher Education*, the 1933 report of a committee representing the higher educational institutions of the American Lutheran Conference, prompted an extensive institutional self-study. This faculty effort expressed a serious concern for religious and educational mission, and anticipated the *Blueprint* series, begun in 1960 and continued every decade since.

The report was a pioneer effort to develop solutions for common problems in Lutheran higher education. Recognizing that the rise of modern secular culture based on the dominance of science and moral relativism had called into question the centrality of home, church and higher education, the report reaffirmed the fundamental authority of the evangelical Christian message. It defined the three-fold task of Christian education: train pastors, educate laity and propagate a Christian world view. For Lutheran institutions the last meant disseminating these distinctively Lutheran beliefs: a positive attitude toward human culture and an emphasis on personality, fellowship and nurture.[54]

Traditional in its Christian suspicion of scientific naturalism, the report nevertheless incorporated modern progressive and scientific educational theory. It represented the impact of progressive education by its implementation of curriculum revision through the democratic process of faculty self-study groups. Lutherans thus adopted what progressive educators acknowledged; the techniques of group dynamics must be used to engineer consent for philosophy and programs. The report embraced science by adopting psychology, testing and measurement, and by its analysis of societal and educational trends. Yet because scientific naturalism neglected religious values, the church college curriculum of secular learning must be built around a Christian center. To that end, the following were emphasized: religion courses as the core for integrating learning; general education requirements to overcome the evils of the elective system; mastery of the natural and social sciences; appreciation for global integration and the fine arts; and limited vocational offerings.[55]

The report envisioned a great future for Lutheran higher education; the colleges must cooperate in pursuing "their supreme task of educating Christian men and women for conscious, competent Christian leadership" and they must "guide Lutheranism while it is being welded into unity and while it is finding its place in the new secular order so that it does not lose its character, identity and sense of divine mission." The implication is clear: Lutherans must be prepared to enter fully into the life of American civilization; the isolation and separation which characterized their past in the United States would no longer serve; and the colleges would show the way to Christian service in society.[56]

During the year preceding publication (1932–1933), Concordia staff met alternate Fridays to hear presentations and to discuss ten topics including "A Changing Social Order," "The Curriculum," "Selection of Students" and "The Future of Lutheran Higher Education." In the academic year following publication (1933–1934), five study groups considered institutional objectives and clientele, curriculum, student personnel practices and faculty organization. These discussions produced significant institutional and curricular changes. Administrative changes regarding student personnel practices have already been discussed. The new statement of institutional goals more clearly articulated the self-image of a Christian liberal arts college. This statement emphasized that the founders had established a Christian school to preserve the cultural ideals and religious heritage of Norwegian Lutheran immigrants. Their Christian perspective had been formulated in the school motto, *Soli Deo Gloria*— "To God Alone the Glory." As a liberal arts institution its aims were to develop the student's spiritual, intellectual, physical, civic and social life according to the ideals of the Lutheran church; to train character; to achieve scholarship in fields of knowledge essential for a broad cultural education; to provide a foundation for further professional training; to develop special talents through extracurricular activities; and to acquire and maintain health. These goals, the institution maintained, embodied the Lutheran philosophy of education which aimed at training the body, mind and spirit. Actually such training was not peculiarly Lutheran; it had long been the stated goal of most denominational American colleges.[57]

Curricular changes were also made. Distribution requirements, religious emphasis, the social and behavioral sciences and the fine arts were strengthened. To ensure that collegians took a distribution of courses from among the traditional liberal arts disciplines, offerings were placed in six groups—religion and philosophy, languages and literature, sciences and mathematics, social sciences, personal hygiene and physical education, and everything else (education, home economics, music, psychology and speech). Students were required to take something from each group. The foreign language requirement was reduced from four to two years. Graduation requirements, earlier set at 128 plus six credits of physical education designed to develop physical abilities and proper habits of living, remained unchanged.[58]

Personal hygiene, after 1927 listed separately for men and women under physical education, could be elected to learn "hygiene of the body and sanitation in daily living." As in other institutions, hygiene may have been introduced as a mild form of sex education to warn against the dangers of venereal disease. In addition to six religion courses (14 credits), students took two years of English (12 credits) and two years of foreign language (12 credits). Electives (12 to 20 credits) were selected from all departments by freshmen and sophomores. The limited number of introductory courses ensured distribution among several disciplines. A major (18 credits) and a minor (12 credits) were completed in the junior and senior year. This curricular design, widely adopted in the 1920s and retained in the next decade, distinguished between general and professional education by separating the undergraduate experience into a division of junior and senior colleges. Freshmen and sophomores were required to take a breadth of courses; as juniors and seniors, Cobbers could pursue areas of special interest.[59]

Freshmen-sophomore courses in English Bible and church history were taken by everyone because Concordia aimed to combine instruction in religious with secular education. Non-Lutherans were excused from the upper-class courses in Lutheran doctrine. No major was offered in religion, but otherwise it was placed on the same academic level as other subjects; students were informed they would need to study religion the same amount of time. According to the Lutheran philosophy of education, secular subjects should also serve a religious purpose. To this end, six departments— biology, chemistry, home economics, Norse, philosophy and religion—identified spiritual development as one of their goals. Philosophy best illustrates this integration.

Courses in ethics, aesthetics, history and currents of modern thought aimed "to encourage an adequate integration of the values of all fields of learning, thereby assisting [students] to construct a Christian philosophy of [their] own."[60]

Sanctioned by *Studies in Lutheran Higher Education*, social and behavioral science offerings expanded in the decade. Laboratory work in psychology first had been given in April 1928 when several collegians conducted trial-and-error learning with white rats. A tests and measurements course was added to others in general, applied and social psychology. To foster an understanding of global integration, international relations (1934), Latin America (1939) and the Far East (1939) were added to comparative government, first given in 1928. In addition to principles of sociology, which had been taught only infrequently between 1920 and 1935, the social order, the family and sociology of rural life were now offered. Introduction to social work and a sociology minor were introduced in 1940 and 1941 respectively; a separate department and major were not implemented until after World War II.[61]

Art, introduced in 1938, became a major in 1940 upon the arrival of Cyrus Running. To strengthen its music program, the college in 1929 purchased the Fargo-based Dakota Conservatory of Music. A 1938 reorganization brought the Fargo Conservatory under direct supervision of the music department. The requirements of the National Association of Schools of Music were met; for the first time the college offered a fully accredited Bachelor of Music degree in public school music. Before, only a public school music certificate had been granted. Musical training, deeply rooted in the Lutheran religious tradition, also had utility; as President Brown noted, high schools often hired Lutheran college graduates as band and choir directors.[62]

Adding art and improving music strengthened the liberal arts. At the same time, vocationalism was increasingly emphasized. When the academy became a college and the last high school class graduated in 1927, the commercial, manual and normal departments disappeared but vocational training did not. Even as a denominational arts and science college, most Cobbers enrolled in teacher education and 70 percent or more were placed as teachers. The remainder were prepared for admission to graduate and professional schools of medicine, dentistry and law; and for service to the church as ministers and missionaries. President Brown suggested in 1934 that programs in commerce and journalism should be established when finances permitted. He thought more vocational work could be offered without sacrificing a liberal arts identity. By that time, the economics department offered several courses in business administration—accounting, money and banking, business organization, public finance, marketing and business law. Library science and physical education courses, added in 1937, certified high school librarians and physical education teachers. At the same time, classes were added in journalism and radio. Four years later, commercial and nurses training programs appeared. Vocationalism reflected a national trend among liberal arts colleges and was strongly approved by Cobbers.[63]

As the curriculum expanded, library holdings grew. Financial exigency slowed but did not prevent the development of either. In 1932 the library consisted of 20,000 books and 8,000 pamphlets, a small increase over the 19,000 and 6,000 owned in 1927. Current issues of the 135 periodicals received were kept on file. The library had been augmented by the purchase of 500 volumes and the book stacks from recently closed Fargo College. Although annual library expenditures had declined from $967 (1930–1931) to a low of $280 (1933–1934), they rose thereafter and by decade's end holdings had increased to 26,879 books and 26,700 pamphlets. During 1940–1941, 660 volumes had been added.[64]

The library was cramped and its hours were limited. The main reading room seated only eighty. It opened from 1:00 to 8:00 p.m. daily except Sundays, Saturdays and evenings when college activities were scheduled. When a student in 1938 protested the library not opening on Saturdays and closing at 7:45 three times in a single week, a respondent pointed out that only a single person had been in the building on two of the evenings mentioned. Thus lack of student use justified early closings and limited hours. Despite its limitations, Brown reported proudly in 1932 that University of Minnesota inspectors called it "the finest selection of any small college library in the state."[65]

Library reading room, facing west in present Grose Hall.

Other program changes were considered and sometimes made in the 1930s. Summer school was discussed but not implemented. The faculty had been given permission in 1928 to conduct a summer session if it did not obligate the corporation to additional expense. In 1932 summer courses on demand were announced to aid students in completing certification. Apparently this was accomplished through correspondence. By 1933, the faculty council had assumed supervision and uniform standards had been established for correspondence work.[66]

Preserving Accreditation

The college struggled to maintain North Central accreditation during the Depression. North Central inspections in 1934 and 1936 were a trial for Brown, who bore the brunt of preparation and worried that a negative report might sink the institution. His worries were justified. After the first visit, the college was given two years to correct the major institutional deficiencies: low non-student income, insufficient graduate education for several key faculty and a crowded, antiquated physical plant. Association percentile rankings illustrate these weaknesses: sources of income, 10; stability of income, 19; faculty salaries, 17; load, 66; doctor's degrees, 24; master's degrees, 2; library book expenditures, 17.[67] The unfavorable North Central report shaped institutional priorities for the remainder of the decade.

With North Central accreditation at stake, the college insisted that several faculty return for graduate study. Most went, perhaps reluctantly because of the added expense, with the notable exception of Herman W. Monson. Monson—composer of "Hymn to Concordia," popular choral director and builder of the choir—refused unless remunerated. Poor financial conditions rendered this impossible. Unfortunately for Monson, his lack of a master's degree from an accredited institution was the major cause for his dismissal in March 1937. In addition to Monson's tendency to be uncooperative, there apparently were other reasons. At that time, the college decided to move the Fargo Conservatory to campus and appoint a new director of the combined music programs. The president did not think Monson would make a good director of the school of music. Whatever his possible deficiencies as an administrator, his lack of degree made him unacceptable by North Central standards.[68]

Embittered, Monson retained lawyers and publicly campaigned for retention. He appealed, unsuccessfully, to the educational and executive committees and finally to the board itself. He then circulated among students, faculty, alumni and the constituency a document castigating the college. This created a potentially damaging situation. An institution that relies on public goodwill fears bad publicity. President Brown responded in May 1938 by having Trinity Church Pastor F.A. Schiotz, Professor Carl B. Ylvisaker and Professor Christian Bale dissuade Monson. If necessary, Brown was prepared to bring suit for malicious slander. The board prepared a letter for use by its members when approached by others for an explanation. The directors also decided that Rev. Schiotz should meet with the faculty and the alumni at commencement. He would explain the steps that led to Monson's dismissal and the board's justification.[69]

Director Herman Monson

At the time of the initial decision, Brown had recognized that Monson's ties to the Norwegian Synod posed special difficulties. Indeed, the matter spilled over into a Northern Minnesota District meeting where Norwegian Synod pastors rallied to support their fellow Luther alumnus. Many had never accepted Brown because he came out of the United Norwegian Lutheran Church and because Park Region, a Norwegian Synod school, lost its college department to Concordia and eventually closed in 1932. Brown took much criticism at this meeting until Ylvisaker, a Luther graduate from Norwegian Synod background, rose to his defense. The pastors respected Ylvisaker and were silenced.[70]

This is only one of the many times that Ylvisaker smoothed things over for Brown with students, alumni and pastors. Ylvisaker's public relations skill and strong support for Brown's policies contributed greatly to his success as president and to institutional survival in the depression decade. For this, and his contributions to the church, the college named the new library for Ylvisaker when it was built in 1954.

A rumor of the day had Monson fired in order to secure a famous name by hiring Paul J. Christiansen, son of F. Melius who had established the Saint Olaf Choir and earned an international reputation in choral music. This is not true. Plans to move the conservatory and to call a new director of music preceded any consideration of Christiansen. After he applied, Christiansen was appointed over

Professor Carl B. Ylvisaker

others because he would soon complete his master's degree, required by the North Central Association to be academically qualified for the directorship. That is not to say that fame did not influence the decision. As Brown admitted, the directors believed "that the name would be worth a good deal to the college." By July 1938 the controversy had subsided. At the commencement meeting of alumni, the board-inspired explanation by Rev. Schiotz "squelched the movement so thoroughly" that it disappeared.[71]

Although overshadowed by Paul Christiansen, Herman Monson is remembered as a fine musician who built the choir and who received critical praise for his choral work. After sixteen years and 35,000 miles touring over bad roads, Monson for the last time counseled his singers: "The purpose of this choir is to spread the Word of God through song. We make this trip not merely to have a good time but to publish the Gospel."[72]

Understandably, choristers much regretted Monson's departure and Christiansen had to overcome that loyalty. In addition to choral directing, during his first year Christiansen set out to gain accreditation from the National Association of the Schools of Music; conducted the orchestra; taught classes in harmony, counterpoint, ear training and conducting; gave private lessons; and kept the pianos tuned. He soon concentrated on the choir in order, as President Brown said, to achieve "for Concordia what your father did for Saint Olaf." He built on Monson's solid foundation and more than lived up to his famous family name in choral music. He took the choir to a higher level of artistic accomplishment and earned an international reputation during his half century at Concordia (1937–1987).[73]

Paul J. Christiansen

However painful to individuals and difficult for the institution, the faculty strengthened itself through graduate study. Upon North Central reinspection in 1936, the school made a good showing academically and retained accreditation.[74] Finances and physical plant still rated low, and correcting these deficiencies formed the president's agenda for the remainder of his tenure. Unfortunately, the exigencies of depression and war were not conducive to either fundraising or construction.

Motivated by obvious institutional necessity and a personal dream of becoming "a builder president," Brown pressed plans for physical plant improvements. Immediate needs were a library, a women's dormitory and a gymnasium. Hopes early in the decade for the gymnasium had been dashed by the worst years of the Depression. Discussions of the project continued intermittently until 1939, when the alumni set a new field house as their "loyalty gift" for the fiftieth anniversary.[75]

This was not realized, but progress occurred in other areas. As a step toward beautifying the grounds, Federal Emergency Relief Administration student workers cut down many trees, trimmed others and planted 2,000 more. Arthur Nichols of Minneapolis and William Ingemann of St. Paul were appointed landscape and building architects respectively. Nichols' preliminary drawings featured development of the Lamb property (present football stadium) because the new site would allow a more aesthetic arrangement of buildings and adjoining athletic fields. This talk of moving the campus even induced an invitation from the Grand Forks Commercial Club to relocate there. After reviewing finances, the directors in 1936 rejected relocation and adopted a design for the existing campus which the president hoped "will give us one of the most beautiful and serviceable college plans in the Northwest." Although the Grand Forks invitation had not been accepted, Brown believed it would make Moorhead more cooperative in the future.[76]

Meanwhile, arrangements went forward for a new women's dormitory designed in Tudor Gothic style by William Ingemann and constructed out of Kasota stone to convey a sense of permanence and beauty. Ingemann persuaded the board to adopt Tudor Gothic, a traditional architecture long associated with cloistered college life, as the pattern for all future buildings. Modern forms and traditional Scandinavian styles were rejected as either too transitory or too strange. The red tile roof and stone exterior were intended to render the

Fjelstad Hall, a significant Depression-era achievement.

building hospitable even on cold, gray winter days. Two lounges with open roofs, large fireplaces, wood-block floors and light-filled bays suggested gracious living. Similarly, the paneled alcoves of the entrances and the ample windows of natural wood in the rooms added a homelike effect. Completed in 1938 and appropriately named for longtime matron and cook Helga ("Mother") Fjelstad, the residence hall generated tremendous pride when completed and is still the most beautiful campus building. Called "Brown's Folly" for its expensive design and construction during the Depression, the $225,000 edifice was financed by an unrestricted donation of land holdings from O.L. Jensen, other gifts, $100,000 in bonds and church-authorized borrowing from the endowment.[77]

Other significant construction occurred in Summer 1938; the school erected a home economics building and remodeled North Hall into a conservatory. Intended as temporary structures, they served for a half- and quarter-century respectively. As a visionary builder Brown did not like temporaries, but he realized that the institution could not consider another permanent building until it paid the Fjelstad debt. Built to relieve congestion in Main, Home Economics housed a fully equipped kitchen, a serving room, the bookstore and a lunchroom. It became the student center. With completion of Fjelstad, North could be remodeled from residence into music hall. Although these modest physical improvements did not fulfill Brown's dreams as a builder, they did represent substantial progress in hard times.[78]

Home Economics Building, a "temporary" structure.

Bad luck continudd to plague President Brown as he attempted to improve financing, another area of need revealed by the North Central report. When depression conditions improved slightly, Concordia finally received permission from the church for a major fundraising effort. Yet the United States had already entered World War II as the Golden Jubilee Year Drive started in 1942. Besides problems posed by the international crisis, the drive came on the heels of the Church Centennial Campaign which had canvassed the territory; Saint Olaf and Luther, despite the usual admonitions from Brown, recently had raised funds in the area. After a decade of crop failure and depressed agricultural

President J.N. Brown, 1925–1951

conditions, the president asked, what chance will Concordia have of securing contributions?[79]

The Golden Jubilee Drive began with "The One Thousand ... $100 Club" which sought $100,000 from non-alumni toward the final goal of $350,000. This attempt did not succeed, but the idea foreshadowed the fruitful C-400 Club of the 1950s. Major

Professor G.L. Schoberg

campaign objectives were to pay the Fjelstad bond issue and to secure monies for a library and an auditorium-field house. Five fulltime workers and a dozen parttime helpers sent news releases to 320 newspapers and publicity to 60,000 people. The Concordia Music Hour, Cobbercast and other radio broadcasts publicized the campaign. Planning and publicity were necessary because, as Brown wrote Lars Boe, "putting on a campaign in wartime is no picnic." Nonetheless the president confidently predicted, "we will at least get our Fjelstad Hall bonds paid, with a reasonable chance at getting one building."[80]

Brown's hopes were not realized. By January 1944, only $212,000 had been raised; from that the dormitory bonds were paid. In 1945 the Jubilee Campaign was merged with the Memorial Gift Appeal, headed by Professor G.L. Schoberg, which aimed to raise $1,000,000 for post-war construction of a $300,000 men's dormitory and the long-dreamed-of library and gymnasium. The drive designated the latter as a memorial to war veterans and the former as a memorial to the pioneer founders of the Norwegian Lutheran Church in the Northwest. By October 1945, the ingathering totaled $425,000. This allowed construction of the residence hall to begin as soon as the government eased wartime restrictions on building materials.[81]

Concordia College Turns Fifty

As the 1940s opened, President Brown and the college looked back on the very difficult depression decade. Brown's administrative burdens were compounded by personal worries. Ada Johnson Brown, who had been very active in the Women's Missionary Federation and very visible through attending chapel and eating in the dining hall during the early years, was hospitalized for mental illness in 1938. She remained institutionalized until her death twenty-four years later. Her illness was a great worry for her husband, who developed an ulcer at this time.[82]

Moreover, Brown's dreams of physical expansion had been largely frustrated by the exigencies of the 1930s. Despite the significant additions of Fjelstad, Home Economics and remodeled North Hall, the physical plant remained inadequate. Classrooms were too few and the library, gymnasium and auditorium were too small.

Yet the school had survived the Depression and, as it celebrated its fiftieth anniversary in 1941, its physical expansion had been impressive. Concordia began in 1891 with one building and two blocks; by 1941 it consisted of eleven buildings, eleven city blocks, and sixty-five acres for an athletic park. The faculty had grown from three to thirty-seven and the student body from twelve to 525. The curriculum had developed from that of an academy to that of a college awarding B.A. and B.M. degrees. There were fifteen departments and a conservatory of music; new programs in art (1938), nursing education (1941) and business education (1941) had recently been added. Moreover, the college could assert with some confidence that it remained true to the great aims of its founders. Even though major social changes had occurred since 1891, the college still taught the great fundamentals of the Christian faith which, Brown believed, "offer the only sure foundation during these perilous times of world crisis."[83]

The Golden Jubilee and Memorial Fund Drives indicated that better days were coming. After surviving the Great Depression, President Brown had renewed hope that his dreams for physical expansion might be fulfilled. But once again a national crisis delayed their realization. Before the Jubilee drive could be completed successfully and before construction could begin, World War II had to be fought and won. This national emergency, like that of the Great Depression, threatened the very survival of Concordia.

President J.N. Brown, 1925–1951

Chapter 8

College Life in Hard Times

Despite the hard times brought first by the agricultural crisis and then by the Great Depression, college life governed by the institutional ideology of Christian education flourished at Concordia in these decades. By permitting and encouraging the activities prevalent at other colleges and yet insisting on the school's traditional religious mission, President Brown and the faculty presided over the transformation of Concordia into a modern church college. Given the financial constraints of the time, this is a remarkable achievement.

Community as Family

At the opening of school in 1933, the *Concordian* urged students to make "a homelike, congenial and stimulating atmosphere for everyone in our Cobber family."[1] Carl Tiller ('35) thus clearly articulated the institutional ideology of Christian education which sees the church school as an extension of the Christian home. Just as they viewed the home as a total environment for training character, administrators conceived of the Lutheran college as "a seven day educational experience." Thus student life did not exist independently of official purpose. It was not only the classroom and curriculum that instructed; dormitory, dining hall, stage, playing field and extracurriculum also trained for a future life of Christian service.

Concordian editor Carl Tiller

Many activities bonded newcomers to "the Concordia family." Freshmen orientation week, instituted by President Brown in 1926, introduced fledgling Cobbers to the social life desired by the college. Before arrival, freshmen women received letters from Dean Nilsen assuring them that she was eager to see them comfortably settled "as full-fledged members of our Cobber family." Big sisters also corresponded, welcoming their little sisters and offering real friendship. Upon arrival, new collegians were oriented through mixers, tours and lectures on library use, institutional purpose, Christian responsibilities, good manners, study techniques, liberal arts and vocational guidance. Soon after school began, newcomers ran the gauntlet of the annual "shakathon," shaking hands with every professor and fellow Cobber. These activities were considered sufficiently important to award one college credit starting in 1936.[2]

Green beanies, first imposed on the freshmen of 1922, and hazing by resolute sophomores were unofficial orientation rituals but important for bonding nevertheless. As *Concordian* editor Lucile Oehlke ('37) emphasized, it is the duty of freshmen to wear beanies because thereby they reflected respect and loyalty to Concordia. Frosh wore them until homecoming, when they could be freed if they defeated the sophomores in two out of three contests: a tug-of-war, a men's foot race and a women's foot race. Defeat dictated two more weeks of wearing green. Because these activities were largely student-inspired, the faculty struggled to bring them under official control and prevent abuses. In 1933 they outlawed green caps in the spring and stipulated that hazing could only be enforced according to written rules adopted by the Student Forum. In 1939 faculty made cap wearing optional and absolutely forbade hazing. A shortage of green dye for commercial use during World War II compelled the adoption of gold caps. Returning veterans temporarily ended the custom, but "the golden domes" reappeared in the mid–1950s and are still worn each fall.[3]

Other activities similarly nurtured the Concordia family. Parents' Day was an annual observance begun in 1935, continued until 1944 and resumed in 1962. It symbolized the close tie between Concordia and the Christian home. Homecoming— with a torchlight parade, coronation, literary society reunions, alumni business meeting, football game and Foundation Day program—united Cobbers of many student generations. Annual fall and spring "campus clean-ups" fostered identification with the college and its values. During President Brown's early years, male frosh— supervised by the dean of men or by zealous sophomores—were dismissed from class to clean the campus; female frosh served a lunch provided by the college. By the 1940s all students were dismissed for the ritual.[4]

Homogeneity facilitated creation of the Cobber family. The vast majority were white, Lutheran, recent high school graduates from Minnesota and North Dakota. Only occasionally were other cultures repre-

sented. An African-American singer appeared in 1937, contralto Marian Anderson in 1938 and a debate team in 1941. At times Native Americans enrolled. Imogene Baker, a Mandan descendant and daughter of a farmer, was elected homecoming queen in 1938. She majored in home economics; participated in Alpha Zeta Phi, Omicron Tau Delta, Girl Scouts, German Club and Speaking Choir; and served as president of the Fjelstad Hall House Council and Women's Athletic Association. After graduation, she worked for the Bureau of Indian Affairs. Ernie Bighorn from Montana lettered in basketball in 1940, but did not return. Perhaps he did not appreciate the *Concordian* running his picture with a caption in language common for the day: "Cobbers' Indian athlete who is ...

Imogene Baker, 1938 homecoming queen.

making heap lots of trouble for the enemy."[5]

Because they perceived the college as a family, Concordia officials upheld an extensive moral code derived from their view of the parental rules that ought to prevail in a well-regulated Christian home. Students were prohibited from dancing, using tobacco and intoxicating liquors, visiting bowling alleys and poolrooms, and leaving the city without permission. They were expected to attend classes, daily chapel and

Sunday worship at a local church. By the late 1930s, the tobacco ban was eased to permit a smoking room in the basement of the men's dormitory; by 1943, only women were not permitted to smoke. Similar restrictions were imposed by other denominational and even state colleges of the day. Yet Norwegian Lutherans differed from many institutions and some other Lutheran synods in their preoccupation with off-campus dancing and use of liquor. These concerns indicate a persistence of pietism that led the relative of an Episcopalian attending Concordia to observe, "Oh those Norwegians! They are so narrow, their ears touch!"[6] This ethnic slur reveals two points of historical significance: it suggests a narrowness in outlook that sometimes characterized Norwegian-American Lutheranism in the 1930s and the anger this attitude occasionally aroused in observers.

President Brown, Professor Carl B. Ylvisaker and other faculty often upheld the ethical standards of Norwegian-American pietism. Although President Brown did not consider dancing a sin, he deplored lack of parental and congregational concern for this "worldly amusement that has caused the downfall of a half-million women in our country." Because they believed dancing fostered sexual excesses that undermined Christian morality, Brown and the faculty organized opposition to the licensing of a Red River recreation park and dance hall north of Moorhead. In addition, the college invariably expelled or suspended students who violated the rule. Parents, feeling keenly the disgrace associated with expulsion, appealed to the president, who displayed firmness tempered by mercy. While Brown did not reverse the decision, he assured them of his kind feelings for their children and his prayers "that the Lord may use this incident for their true welfare."[7]

Both Concordia and the Norwegian Lutheran Church took a strong stand against liquor. Faculty campaigned to keep Moorhead dry. In 1929 Professor Herman Nordlie was elected mayor on the prohibition ticket. President Brown worked actively for the election of Nordlie and other dry candidates for county sheriff, county attorney and Moorhead chief of police. In January 1931 the college celebrated the eleventh year of prohibition in chapel. It was a sad day when the ban on alcohol ended in April 1933. As Brown commented, "it is too bad ... that intoxicating liquors were legalized as the women and children of the nation will have to pay for it." Undaunted by defeat in his attempt to prevent the sale of beer in Moorhead on Sunday, President Brown led faculty and students to adopt resolutions against the legalization of hard liquor in Clay County.[8]

In 1938 Carl B. Ylvisaker, a widely respected professor of religion, penned a *Concordian* series on "problems confronting the modern college student." The problems Ylvisaker picked—dancing, card playing, secret societies—are indicative of the pietistic strain among Norwegian-American Lutherans. To develop criteria for judging behavior, Ylvisaker derived three fundamental principles from the Bible and the Augsburg Confession: Can it be observed without sin? Is it profitable? Will it cause offense? Christians were obligated by God to be good stewards of their time, talents, personalities and possessions. On these grounds, he maintained that dancing, card playing and membership in secret societies were all sins to be shunned. Because dancing represented "the early, unnatural and abnormal stimulation of the sex instinct," it could not be practiced without sin. Police, pastors and social workers all testified that dance had led thousands to sacrifice their virtue. Card playing was renounced for emphasizing chance, in which Christians did not believe; chance made card games addictive, anti-spiritual and time-wasting. Secret societies were rejected because their secrecy was contrary to the spirit of Christ who held nothing in secret, their oaths contradicted Scripture which forbids oaths and they created rival, mock religions.[9]

Modern readers guided by less strict standards of personal behavior may smile at Ylvisaker's earnest, soul-saving discussion. Yet his solemn arguments were weighed seriously by his readers. He had a devoted following among the student body, who in 1941 dedicated the *Cobber* to him. Many came with moral convictions similar to those Ylvisaker expressed. At a Christian school in contrast to secular state universities, they expected to reject a worldly existence for "a Christian life through faith in Jesus Christ."[10]

Despite the strong strain of Norwegian-American pietism which shaped college life at Concordia, these Lutherans were not puritanical killjoys opposed to all amusement. To the contrary, they perceived entertainment as a legitimate need; but it should be wholesome ("One need not drink, smoke or dance to have a good time!") and it should be attractive enough to keep Cobbers out of dives and dance halls. In addition to athletic, dramatic and musical events, all-college parties were frequently planned. As technology made available new amusements, these were readily adopted. The men purchased in 1930 a new Majestic radio for their dormitory parlor. Like all pleasurable activity, school officials believed that radio was best enjoyed in moderation; listening hours were therefore limited to Saturday afternoon, all day Sunday except the church hour and weekdays from 4:00 to 6:00 p.m. and 10:00 to 11:00 p.m. The women inherited the men's phonograph while they raised money to purchase their own radio.[11]

College officials believed that well-regulated Christian families ought to inculcate manners as well as morals. Accordingly, Concordia consciously taught etiquette. Cobbers were addressed as Mr. and Miss in classes. Women wore dresses and men, coats and ties, to gain admission to the dining hall, where they dined family-style until 1943. Cobbers appreciated this effort to train young ladies and gentleman and sometimes requested more. An editorial in 1934 suggested an annual basket social and fortnightly teas to give students poise and social knowledge. Dean of Women Frida Nilsen worked to comply. In 1935 Ladies Hall held its first-ever open house. That year Dean Nilsen scheduled the first annual Dean's Dinner for senior women; it was served by home economics majors under the supervision of department head Florence Kruger. Teas, scheduled regularly, gave all Cobbers an opportunity for social training. Nilsen viewed the dormitory itself as an "opportunity to learn gracious living" because it was a laboratory housing every personality type. Therefore its friendly camaraderie taught democracy, tolerance and consideration of others.[12]

Of course, socialization did not always succeed; rules were violated, and bonding to the Concordia family and its values could never be complete when a substantial number spent much of their time off campus. Due to limited dormitory space, 40 percent of the women and 50 percent of the men in 1934 lived in private homes; 35 percent of all Cobbers did not board at the college. Others fled for studious and financial reasons; Erling Rolfsrud recalls seeking the solitude of an off campus room after only one week in the noisy men's dormitory. When he could no longer afford the luxury of college board at semester's end, he and a Montana friend bought a hot plate, waffle iron and dime store dishes; they subsisted on rice porridge and waffles.[13]

Although many Cobbers shared the school's Christ-centered vision and most went along with the regulations, not all were angels. There were some "fast-moving pleasure seekers" in attendance. Others came for the knowledge and enjoyable social life available at any college. Nor could religious piety, moral training or good intentions inoculate every exuberant Cobber against the virus of pranks or hazing. Perhaps the most famous caper occurred in 1934 when Cobbers torched, rebuilt (after being caught in the act) and then burned again the Moorhead State homecoming bonfire. Freshmen and society initiation, a mild form of student rebellion, persisted despite institutional efforts at control.[14]

Religious Life

Acting on their conception of the proper Christian home, school officials made religious devotions and conduct central to the Concordia family. For many Cobbers, campus religious life allowed them to continue the church involvement of their childhoods. They attended daily chapel, worshiped on Sunday and participated in a range of religious activities which reflected a national upsurge among Lutherans in ministry to students.

The administration required chapel, just as did 91 percent of the other church colleges on the eve of World War II. Speakers included the president, religion professors, local pastors and board members. Collegians did not speak in the late 1920s because few were thought to have the necessary ability. During the Depression, the college discontinued for a time the practice of inviting local pastors. Cobbers complained when chapel failed to meet their religious expectations. They condemned discourteous whispering, talking and passing notes. Many desired more inspirational services. A few criticized non-attendance by students and faculty. Although some missed, most came; an educational psychology class survey in 1941 found that 88 percent attended chapel daily.[15]

Alumni from the 1920s recall they could not avoid mandatory Sunday worship because resident heads rousted the entire dormitory. Most attended Trinity in Moorhead, the closest Norwegian Lutheran congregation and long considered "the college church." Although faculty admonished Cobbers not to study on the Sabbath, their admonitions were ignored by the studious. They prepared Monday's lessons on Sunday afternoon, the only time available. When classes ended at noon on Saturday, that afternoon became a recess and books were laid away.[16]

College religious life centered on three organizations—Luther League (later the Lutheran Students Association), Lutheran Daughters of the Reformation (LDR) and Mission Crusaders. Luther League subscribed to the motto "Word Alone, Grace Alone, Faith Alone." It met Sunday evenings for devotions and discussions, and conducted programs for local church Luther Leagues. Guided by the inspirational leadership of Frida Nilsen, LDR met Wednesday evenings for programs, often supported overseas missions and frequently presented devotional programs to various Fargo-Moorhead institutions. Mission Crusaders, the most pietistic group, numbered about sixty. It met Sunday mornings for devotions and the study of mission fields. Members also formed gospel teams to present mission programs to outlying congregations.[17]

League, LDR and Crusader activities were complemented by weekly fellowship hours, dormitory devotions, prayer groups, the Pocket Testament Movement and local church work. In 1937 ninety-five Cobbers were active in the churches of Fargo-Moorhead. Trinity led with forty-nine participating in Luther League, choir, Sunday School and weekday religious instruction. Summer Bible teaching in congregations resumed its popularity when the Depression ended. The college provided orientation classes and placement. Through multifarious activities Cobbers served others and became active lay persons.[18] As a Christian college, Concordia therefore succeeded in attaining its goal of training laity for active congregational leadership.

Bible study and spiritual emphasis week offered other opportunities for religious reflection and expression. Both demonstrated the importance of evangelism in the Norwegian Lutheran Church and indicated a continuation of the Haugean emphasis on "living Christianity" and "edifying meetings." The Lutheran Bible Institute (LBI) Tuesday evening Bible study, ten weekly lectures given each fall on a biblical book, continued until 1940, when it was suspended due to a shortage of LBI instructors. Collegians and city residents packed Main auditorium for the series. Students from the decade recall it as "marvelous"; *Concordian* editor Engebret Kvikstad in 1931 called it "an hour set apart" that "brings true spiritual satisfaction." Spiritual emphasis week, begun by the administration in 1934 "to provide some opportunity for a mountain top experience" brought in outside speakers for chapel, evening devotions and private conferences. Organizations suspended activities and the *Concordian* urged Cobbers to attend all sessions in order to gain "the benefit of the inspiration." At the same time, they were cautioned to emphasize spirituality every day and not just this week.[19]

Extensive activity did not ensure harmony. Indeed, the campus seems to have been divided between "religious haves" and "have nots." This division stemmed partly from whether collegians lived in dormitories or not, and partly from two religious styles existing within Lutheranism. Alumni from the 1930s remember great peer pressure to join the organizations. Members worried about the "have nots" who did not participate and encouraged more to join. Yet those off-campus, comprising between one-third and one-half the enrollment, felt excluded, viewed the associations as elitist and perceived the "haves" as morally self-righteous. These resentments suggest that more than residence was involved. They were also rooted in the existence of two religious styles which complemented but also conflicted with each other throughout Concordia's history. On the one hand, the level-headed, practical Lutheran disliked religious

Rev. Dr. J.W. Johnshoy

exhibitionism or sentimentality; on the other, the warm-hearted Lutheran emphasized the conversion experience and a life of notable piety. It is probable that the latter controlled organizational life, which the former resented.[20]

At other times, these differences in style surfaced in open conflict. On one occasion, a professor—probably J. Walter Johnshoy—questioned the need for a spiritual emphasis week and challenged several points made in the addresses. This criticism provoked a sharp editorial from Baptist Carl Tiller who charged that the critic could hardly have had a Christian experience himself or else did not understand the speakers. The incident was apparently part of an ongoing argument between student followers of the scholarly, level-headed Johnshoy and the warm-hearted Ylvisaker. Their disciples often became more indignant about these subtle differences in Lutheranism than the men themselves. When this indignation was expressed publicly in the *Concordian*, President Brown intervened. Because he did not want religious disagreements broadcast to the constituency, Brown met with the newspaper staff. In the next issue they expressed regret, apologized and recanted the editorial.[21]

Another episode revelatory of religious beliefs occurred with Dr. Toyohiko Kagawa's scheduled appearance at the Moorhead Armory in February 1936. Kagawa's Kingdom of God movement in Japan was anti-communist, attempted to clean up the slums and was devoted to saving society by nonviolent means. His doctrines and books were discussed by the Mission Crusaders; in leading these discussions, Professor Ylvisaker concluded that Kagawa was not a Christian because he taught that Christ was not divine. President Brown was also troubled by Kagawa's contradictory belief in atonement and his rhetoric of evolutionary modernism. Nonetheless, after carefully inoculating Cobbers against possible modernist infection, the president planned to dismiss classes. He urged Cobbers to hear Kagawa calmly and kindly. The precautions were not necessary; Kagawa's Moorhead appearance was canceled.[22]

Cobber religious attitudes toward social problems reflected those of the Norwegian Lutheran Church, the least socially concerned of National Lutheran Council members, and were not much altered by the Depression. Suspicious of social gospel attempts to Christianize society as wrong-headed "salvation by works," Norwegian Lutherans insisted that the church's primary responsibility should be proclamation of the gospel which alone saves men from sin, death and the devil. Hence, Christian welfare should be directed toward saving individuals. Accordingly, their social concerns traditionally had been expressed through an institutional ministry, a powerful movement in the nineteenth century churches of Germany and Scandinavia that had established charitable hospitals, orphanages and homes for the aged.[23]

Campus religion mirrored these beliefs by focusing on personal religion and charitable activity. Beginning in 1929 and continuing for several years thereafter under sponsorship of the National Lutheran Student Association, Cobbers collected money for support of the Lutheran Seminary in Russia. Led by Dean of Men Paul Rasmussen, a Farmer-Labor activist, Cobbers in 1931 joined in an effort planned by the local Chamber of Commerce and the American Legion to pick up and pack potatoes for relief of the poor. When students discussed depression-era social issues, they focused on individual religion. In 1935 editor Edmonde Evanson ('36) warned that government alone could not accomplish economic recovery; individuals must apply their religious convictions in every aspect of their lives. Similarly, a 1938 editorial—"Church Can Supply Guidance in Social Problems"—argued that "the cure of economic ills is in the gospel of redemptive forgiveness through Jesus Christ." The problems between capital and labor could only be solved by changing "self-centered and self-seeking individuals into individuals who love God." After the church enlightened its members through the gospel, the will of God would be done on social issues.[24]

Extracurricular Activities

Extracurricular activities made up a large part of college life and persisted despite hard times. Collegians demanded activities as an opportunity to assert their independence, an occasion to express their youthful vigor and a staging ground for adulthood. Faculty generally agreed, but often worried about excessive activity detracting from studies. On the one hand, they encouraged Cobbers to partake widely as essential to their liberal arts education; on the other, they adopted a point system in 1929 which attempted to limit activity, equalize participation and ensure sufficient time for study.[25]

This effort apparently did not alter traditional patterns of collegiate behavior. A poll taken by Dr. Burgess's educational psychology class in 1940 revealed that most Cobbers distributed their time between extracurricular and curricular at a three-to-one ratio. This commitment and their high degree of participation—90 and 98 percent respectively in religious or some other activity—suggests that students closely identified with the college community. Besides religion, opportunities beckoned in student government, interest clubs, literary societies, forensics, drama, debate, publications, music and athletics. Five activity boards—usually comprised of three professors, one student and the deans of men and women—were appointed by the president. That students were represented reflected President Brown's belief that they ought to be consulted. Of course, this looked less democratic to collegians than it did to the president. Even in the 1930s, some Cobbers desired more control over "their" activities. To ensure that institutional goals were served, however, the administration retained dominance.[26]

In addition to the boards, student government consisted of residence hall councils and the Student Forum. The dormitory bodies planned parties, promoted neatness and maintained Christian conduct.

The student forum conducted student government.

The twelve-member forum, comprised of three elected officers plus activity and class representatives, functioned as a link between collegians and the administration, a clearinghouse for collegiate problems and a nominating body for selecting committee members and delegates to conventions.[27]

During the mid-1930s, Cobbers joined the National Student Federation (NSF). This liberal organization set forth an extensive rights agenda including the right to disagree with teachers, have representation in faculty meetings and criticize the institution and its personnel. Collegian indifference and administrative resistance ensured that this agenda would not soon be achieved at Concordia.[28]

A significant change before World War II involved off-campus men and women; they were organized and granted meeting rooms of their own. This marked official recognition that these students were not fully integrated into the community. Hence the administration attempted to overcome their alienation, as revealed by the tension generated over religious organizations, and involve them more deeply in the "seven-day educational experience."[29]

Literary societies remained important but their character changed. Starting in the 1920s, they became more exclusive, and hazing rituals more elaborate. By the next decade, they were more social, less literary and more secret. An alumna recalls that societies were almost too important; it was a traumatic experience for those who were turned away. Societies enjoyed a paradoxical relationship with the Cobber family. On the one hand, their exclusive quality—as had been the case with religious organizations—contradicted the inclusive family. On the other, they were an important source of campus entertainment and education. Advocates emphasized that societies provided an outlet for talent; developed literary, oratorical and musical skills; met the need for friendship; required assumption of responsibility; and trained executive ability. Accordingly, the administration harnessed these associations to serve institutional goals. Following the philosophy of a week-long educational program, the clubs met after classes on Saturday morning. The eight societies had 255 members in 1932; this comprised 56.5 percent of those enrolled. A higher percentage of women (60 percent) than men (53 percent) belonged. An intersociety council, formed in 1929, established rules for rushing and governed society activities. All freshmen were encouraged to apply for membership in the second semester. Public programs in December and open house programs in February allowed frosh to assess the talent and personnel of each organization.[30]

Lambda Delta Society, costumed for an entertainment.

As societies became more social, they were criticized in the late 1930s for abandoning their original scholarly purpose, for becoming a modified fraternity-sorority system and for developing into hotbeds of ill-feeling. The *Concordian* even discontinued reports of literary programs in 1938 because they were so hastily and poorly done. Two societies apparently agreed; they dropped literary from their title. Many supported the change, arguing that the campus needed more social life. Others were not so sure; they looked for ways to combine the traditional literary functions with the desire for social life. Intersociety Council, under its energetic president Alan Hopeman, breathed new life into the organizations during the 1940–1941 school year. Consequently, they published a quarterly literary magazine, *The Cobber Classic*; resumed public programs; continued one-act play and oratorical contests; and established a sweepstakes to determine the leading association based on points accumulated from winning competitions.[31]

The growth of interest clubs and honor societies indicates how seriously faculty and collegians fostered academic development. By scheduling special programs which gave additional opportunities for developing collegiate talents, these organizations contributed significantly to the week-long educational experience. The

Intersociety president Alan Hopeman

science club met semimonthly to discuss scientific problems, inventions and lives of great scientists. Organized in 1933, the international relations club promoted greater understanding of world problems at its fortnightly meetings. Mu Phi Epsilon, a national music honor society established on campus in 1935, sponsored visiting artists and semimonthly programs on musical skills. A press club, formed that same year, encouraged work on the *Concordian*. The creation of other interest clubs and honor societies in journalism, dramatics, forensics and social science similarly functioned to complement academics.[32]

Debate, drama and forensics afforded other educational opportunities. Intercollegiate debate revived in 1926–1927 when two male and two female teams competed under the direction of Paul Rasmussen. That same year Sock and Buskin organized to study drama, an all-college play was given, the first freshman-sophomore oratorical contest was held and Alpha Psi Omega, a dramatic honorary, appeared. The following year, Concordia hosted its first intercollegiate oratorical contest. Due to enlarged forensics work under Rasmussen's leadership, the college gained a chapter of Pi Kappa Delta, a national forensics fraternity. The energetic Rasmussen in 1933 organized the first Red River Valley Debate Tournament. Four years later, the event had grown from an initial nine colleges and thirty-six debaters to 162 participants from thirty-one institutions. Work in drama similarly expanded from a single all-college play to three all-college plays plus one-acts, religious dramas and pageants staged by other organizations. The Norwegian Lutheran Church did not regard drama as inherently sinful but did insist that plays be moral. This moral emphasis complemented a college commitment to educational theater which aimed at the cultural enrichment of the student body. These objectives dictated the presentation of many classics: Ibsen, *A Doll House* in 1928; Ibsen, *The Feast of Solhaug*, Shakespeare, *The Taming of the Shrew*, Sheridan, *The Rivals* and Wilde, *The Importance of Being Earnest* in 1933; Zangwill, *The Melting Pot*, in 1934, and Shakespeare, *Merchant of Venice* in 1936.[33]

The *Concordian* offered an outlet for aspiring journalists. Throughout this period, editors generally aimed to reflect student life and opinion, and to uphold institutional ideals. This similarity of editorial stance and institutional goals suggests that Cobbers often shared administrative values. It is well that the editors were compliant because the president insisted that the paper present a harmonious view of college life. He watched it closely and quickly intervened

The International Relations Club discussed world issues.

to delete material he regarded as controversial. This presidential oversight did not prevent a spirited examination of domestic and international issues, as will be discussed elsewhere.

Editors carried on the perennial debate of whether their paper should address itself to campus or to world events. After three years of editorial emphasis on domestic and international politics, new editor Lucile Oehlke in 1936 bravely announced a change: Hereafter *Concordian* editorials would concern themselves almost wholly with campus topics of interest to everyone. Regardless of its editorial orientation, the *Concordian* was judged to be a high quality newspaper. As a biweekly from 1929 to 1934, it won five consecutive "superior" (All-American) ratings from the Associated College Press, a remarkable achievement for a poor college in hard times. After it became a weekly in 1934 it maintained an "excellent" rating annually until 1939 when it won its first All-American rating in the new category. Two new honorary societies— Alpha Phi Gamma (1937) and Inkwell (1940)—added journalistic distinction.[34]

Directed by "Duke" Holvik, the Concordia College Concert Band achieved renown with its appearance at the Chicago Exposition in 1933 and its tour to Norway in 1935. National and international recognition of the band's quality were a significant success for a struggling college and indicated a potential for even greater accomplishments in the future. Chosen as the official Norway Day band at the World's Fair, the troupe— equipped with two buses, one car, one truck, three tents and an efficient military organization—made a three-week combined concert tour-camping trip to Chicago.

The bank played before large crowds on the *Soerlandet,* a full-rigged sailing vessel which was the Norwegian exhibit at the Century of Progress Exposition. This appearance led to an invitation from *Nordmanns-Forbundet* (Norsemen's Federation)

The Concordia Band marches in Gjovik, Norway.

for a thirty-concert, three-week tour of Norway. Rev. S.G. Hauge of the board of directors and President Brown accompanied the band as official representatives. To finance the trip, friends of the college raised $2,000 and members each contributed $150 for the return voyage; their parents were cautioned that this expense should not prevent payment of future tuition or repayment of institutional notes. Female members were excluded, perhaps because of a strenuous month-long concert tour as the band camped its way to New York City, or perhaps Holvik thought that women would not be accepted because of Norway's tradition of military bands. One alumna recalls she did not protest too much; she lacked the necessary money.[35]

Before sailing, the band gave two concerts in New York City and appeared in a thirty-minute broadcast on national radio. In Norway it played before large, enthusiastic crowds, enjoyed critical acclaim and watched with pride the day that Holvik, only the second American honored, received the Frederikstad Music Society's Gold Medal, only the fifth awarded. President Brown—dressed in an immaculate white morning suit, white gloves, top hat and cane—and Professor Holvik, attired in a spotless uniform, appeared for an audience with King Haakon VII. Upon the band's return to the United States, a car caravan, a parade, large crowds and banquet welcomed the musicians home to Moorhead.[36]

Besides the band, other musical organizations in 1932 included the choir, directed by Herman Monson; an orchestra; a pep band; a Concordia chorus, directed by Clara B. Duea; male quartets and ladies sextets. The WDAY Concordia Music Hour provided a showcase for musical accomplishment and soon necessitated an expanded band repertoire. Therefore Holvik began daily rehearsals during 1938–1939 which required more rehearsal space. The North Hall annex soon provided a practice room for both band and choir. Musicals like Gilbert and Sullivan's *H.M.S. Pinafore,* directed by Clara Duea, were also popular. The range of musical activities available and the institution's reputation for excellent training helped to

Professor Clara B. Duea

attract the students who enabled Concordia to survive the Great Depression.[37]

The 1920s were "a golden age of college sports." With surging popularity came a professionalism that belied the amateur standing of student-athletes. This change provoked much criticism, some of which echoed in the *Concordian.* Editor Leif Dahl ('26) criticized athletics for having no educational value and deplored the intense cultivation of the least academic extracurricular activity. President Brown did not agree. As had President Aasgaard earlier, Brown defended sports from the viewpoint of muscular Christianity. Coach Frank Cleve therefore had succeeded, despite losing records in football and basketball, because "the manly virtues of honesty, loyalty, and high Christian idealism have been instilled into the minds and hearts of our boys."[38]

Believing that athletics fostered character and that a complete education included physical development, Concordia advertised its program as one that provided good health instruction and sports for all. A physician gave newcomers a thorough physical examination. Two hours of weekly supervised activities during the first three years were required along with instruction in personal hygiene from the college nurse. Intercollegiate sports, an intramural program and the Women's Athletic Association also served institutional goals by training mind, body and spirit.[39]

Coach Frank Cleve

Intercollegiate men's sports before World War II consisted primarily of football and basketball with occasional offerings in baseball, hockey, golf, tennis and track. Organized by students in February 1928, a hockey team played several contests and then disappeared until 1947. Track first appeared in the spring of 1930. Coached by Dr. Burgess, it began with intersociety competition and gradually evolved into an intercollegiate sport. A Cobber baseball team competed in the Minnesota Intercollegiate Athletic Conference (MIAC) in 1929 and 1930, then disappeared. An attempt to revive

The Ninepins, a freshmen pep squad.

baseball in 1932 and 1933 foundered in the Depression; it reappeared in 1939 with hopes, unfulfilled, of re-entering the MIAC in 1940. Tennis, coached at times by Professor Ylvisaker, occasionally played conference competition. The sport was handicapped by lack of adequate courts. In 1941 asphalt courts were constructed using mostly student labor to cut costs. Even football could be hampered by lack of facilities. Concordia home games in 1934 were played at Moorhead State Teachers College because the Cobber field was rendered unplayable when the city refused a watering permit and the drought killed the newly seeded grass.[40]

Despite occasional setbacks from national and economic disasters, athletics flourished. A lettermen's club, organized to foster firmer fellowship, sponsored the lettermen's banquet each spring. Cobber teams were cheered on by an active cheering section led by Rooter King and two female assistants; in 1930–1931 nine freshmen women—each wearing the appropriate letter to spell out C-O-N-C-O-R-D-I-A—organized a pep squad to aid cheerleaders and to entertain at intermissions.[41]

Rooter King Carl Westberg assisted by Jan Broten and Phyllis Stuvland.

These innovations must have helped, because athletics enjoyed a banner year in 1931 when both the football and basketball teams captured their first MIAC championships. These league crowns won by a fledgling school against the competition of older, better established Minnesota colleges did much for Cobber pride. As *Concordian* editor Engebret Kvikstad ('32) stated, "It makes Concordia known to scores of people who knew nothing about it before and it adds to Concordia's ever-widening circle of influence." It is well Cobbers enjoyed the moment because titles would be few. Cobbers did not win another basketball title for a half century and achieved only two football championships in the next two decades. Frank Cleve's "Clevemen" won in 1934, and Cobbers led by the legendary Jake Christiansen in his first season shared the championship in 1942.[42]

MIAC Champions (1931).

Spurred by the student personnel movement and concerns about the lack of exercise for unskilled undergraduates, intramural sports won the support of athletic departments and established themselves in American colleges and universities during the 1920s. After 1925, Concordia joined this trend. In the early years most of the activity came from a winter basketball league. By 1936, tournaments were held to determine champions in a number of other sports: tennis, golf, horseshoes, softball and touch football. In 1938 the program expanded to include ping pong, badminton, volleyball, boxing and wrestling.[43]

Women were not omitted from competition but were excluded from intercollegiate athletics after 1922–1923. In 1927 women organized an athletic club and became members in the national Women's Athletic Association (WAA). Women's sports included kittenball, basketball, volleyball, tennis, hiking and soccer. In 1931 lessons at the YWCA were added for seniors who wanted to learn to swim or to earn lifesaving badges.

Women's Athletic Association Executive Committee (1939).

Through these activities, the WAA sought to increase interest in athletics and provided awards for active participants. A WAA pin could be earned with 400 points; a monogram with 700; and a sweater with 1,000.[44]

The Depression notwithstanding, Concordia under President Brown's leadership by decade's end had progressed considerably toward becoming a modern church college. It offered more religious activities than many institutions but its religious orientation did not preclude providing many of the extracurricular activities available at most other colleges—athletics, music, drama, debate, forensics, journalism, societies, government or whatever attracted student interest. Both faculty and collegians, moreover, considered these activities as integral to the goals and curriculum of a Christian liberal arts college. As did academic preparation, extracurricular participation trained Cobbers in the many skills they would need for a future life of Christian service and success in their chosen vocations.

Intellectual Life

Many elements, ranging from the informal dormitory bull session to the formal curriculum, comprise the intellectual life of any college. Carl Bailey, a 1940 graduate and later a physics professor and dean, remembers Concordia as "a lively place" with "lots of things to argue about." Although academically not at the level it later attained, the school opened aspects of the world for the North Dakota native that he had never before suspected. His awakening often occurred in residence hall conversations which took place in any one of a dozen rooms, almost any night on almost any subject. Hence it is understandable that Bailey as a sophomore enthusiastically proclaimed, "The bull session is the most important part of our existence. Long may it prosper!"[45]

Bailey's experience suggests something important about the institution. For serious-minded Cobbers there were always opportunities for thoughtful discussions and for an adequate academic training. Despite strained finances, inadequate physical plant, overextended faculty and the strong Lutheran pietism epitomized by the 1936 senior class motto, "Faith Before Intellect," Concordia was more lively intellectually than one might expect.

Of course, the earnestness associated with Lutheran pietism may have helped more than hindered academic endeavor. Viola Eid, a 1932 graduate memorialized by Frida Nilsen's biography, personified this relationship between piety and scholarship. Although Eid lost her vision as a child, she maintained a cheerful disposition and "radiated happiness in Christ." As a senior, she ranked first in her class, received the Dr. O.J. Hagen Award for the highest grade average, was elected salutatorian and won a scholarship to the Perkins Institution for the Blind at Harvard University.[46]

Viola Eid, an honor student.

Scholarly effort was promoted in various ways. For many years, the *Concordian* each semester listed the top ten academically by class and the grade averages for each class, society and organization. Debaters often compiled the highest average, trailed usually by the *Concordian* staff. The Athenians were first among male societies in 1935, but finished a close second to the Delta Rhos in 1940. The Alpha Zeta Phis led women societies in 1935 and 1940. The seniors had the highest class averages during the same years.[47]

In an attempt to de-emphasize competitive grade-seeking which undermined the educational values of the community, the registrar and the faculty in 1940 ceased publicizing the top ten. Membership in Alpha Society, special class honors and selection of a valedictorian and salutatorian were thought sufficient rewards for academic achievement. Martha Brennun had been valedictorian of the first collegiate class, but shortly thereafter it became customary for seniors to express traditional gender attitudes in annually electing a male valedictorian and female salutatorian from among the five highest ranking men and women. This custom persisted until 1949, when seniors finally disregarded gender and voted that the two highest ranking students scholastically should be named valedictorian and salutatorian.[48]

What and how collegians learned from the formal curriculum is hard to determine. Alumni recall that Herman Nordlie and Charles Skalet, longtime professors of history and classics respectively, stressed memorization of facts. *Concordian* editor Kermit Overby ('32) in 1930 articulated a similarly passive conception of education. It should enable scholars to absorb, assimilate and catalog knowledge for future reference. By this method, the individual is trained "so that in his maturity he shall be able to make contributions—to do something for himself and for society." On the other hand, Thomas Burgess's educational psychology students found in 1941 that 80 percent of those polled preferred discussion classes.[49] One cannot be sure whether these results reflect experience with more active learning or a wistful desire for something not available.

The curriculum did allow for expression of unpopular cultural ideas. A science major who graduated in 1940 does not recall administrative repression of evolutionary theory in biology and geology; he did not feel in any way restricted in his scientific studies. To be sure, relations between science and Norwegian Lutheranism were no easier in the 1930s than previously. Church authorities sharply criticized Dr. Burgess, a well-known pioneer in medical hypnosis, for engaging in the work of the devil. Burgess survived by suspending for a time his practice on campus and on students. His demonstrations for doctors were held in other locations such as St. John's Episcopal Church. Similarly, the Norwegian Lutheran Church remained hostile to evolutionary theory; Lutheran clergyman Byron Nelson's anti-evolutionary books were much discussed and faculty like Brown and Ylvisaker staunchly opposed evolution. Nevertheless, the administration displayed a remarkable facility for treading a fine line between disapproval and tolerance. It never took an official stand against either hypnosis or evolution and thereby avoided rigid provincial positions on these controversial issues.[50]

Although women's issues were not dealt with systematically in the curriculum, the college displayed some gender awareness within the limits of prevailing Norwegian Lutheran attitudes. The church did not take an official position on women's suffrage. Women were active in the denomination but pastors were male and regarded biblical scholarship as men's work. Role models for women occasionally appeared in chapel. In 1925 Mrs. E.C. Cronk, superintendent of children's work in the United Lutheran Church and assistant editor of the *Missionary Review of the World,* gave an "inspiring chapel address entitled 'I Can Do Anything.'" Six elements were necessary: decision, determination, enthusiasm, elimination of non-essentials, perseverance and Christ.[51]

Marie Malmin

At least one alumna followed Mrs. Cronk's example, as the *Concordian* noted with pride in 1929 when Marie Malmin ('21) became the first Cobber female to earn a doctorate. Armed with her degree in English from the University of Minnesota, Malmin taught at Saint Olaf. Women's debating teams first appeared in 1926–1927. The *Concordian* approved because experience in political analysis would make them better voters. Other collegians occasionally raised issues of female equality. A few suggested in 1927 that the freshman-sophomore declamation and oratorical contest should be coeducational and not divided by sex. Another in 1928 protested the 10:30 Saturday night curfew for women only. Why, the writer asked, in an age of equality when women attained a higher scholastic average than men, shouldn't women have the same hours as men? The question went unanswered; the double standard persisted at most colleges and universities into the 1960s.[52]

Alumnae recall there were only three professions open to women—teaching, nursing and home economics. Most taught but were forced to quit when they married. This derived from a traditional but depression-reinforced belief that only male heads of households should be employed. Most Cobbers agreed, as suggested by their responses to a Luther League questionnaire sent to Lutheran collegians in 1936. Of the 199 responding from all institutions, 90.5 percent definitely planned for home and children of their own. Only 19.3 percent of eighty-eight women said they would choose a career in preference to early marriage. The seventeen Cobbers who responded answered similarly.[53]

These attitudes persisted into the 1940s. The results of a 1942 National College Student Survey, reported in the *Concordian*, revealed the following: Only 38 percent thought women should be educated like men, 82 percent believed it a bad idea to combine career and marriage, and 57 percent thought more equality would result in more divorces. That Cobbers shared these widespread American beliefs is implied in *Concordian* editorials. A writer in 1936 urged Cobbers to uphold the sanctity of the home in the face of rising divorce rates and suggested three reasons for this social problem: the freedom and equality granted women to pursue careers outside the home; growth of individualism; and the tendency to view divorce as a cure for evil rather than an evil to be shunned. Another editorialist defended the new nursing program on the grounds that "nursing, like teaching and home making, is one of the noblest professions for women."[54] Seemingly progressive in permitting female employment, this argument rested on the traditional view that the maternal qualities of women uniquely prepared them to perform certain social roles. Hence women were restricted to nursing or similar occupations which suited their nurturing female natures.

Special institutional programs promoted the discussion of educational issues and the experience of high culture. As recommended by the North Central Association, the faculty continued the study series on college policies and higher education trends at semimonthly meetings. Devoted to such topics as scholarship, the humanities and the contribution of secular learning to a secure Christian faith, the sessions were intended to cultivate alert, self-critical and thoughtful professors true to the traditions of Lutheran higher education. An artist series, which had been sponsored by the college for many years, offered high culture to Cobbers and city residents. In 1937 Concordia began a cooperative arrangement with Moorhead State Teachers and the Amphion Chorus that lasted until the early 1950s. It brought nationally recognized artists like Jascha Heifetz to Moorhead. Although the quality of the program could not be faulted, some professors criticized the exclusive emphasis on music. They suggested that the series be supplemented with lectures, art exhibitions and readings.[55]

Undergraduates also participated in the discussion of cultural issues outside the classroom. Reflecting the ferment of those dormitory bull sessions prized by some Cobbers, the *Concordian* of these years reveals a lively interest in several topics including the Christian liberal arts, domestic politics and international relations. That collegians discussed the Christian liberal arts should not surprise, given the school's publicizing of institutional goals and their own decision to attend. Many chose Concordia as a place to be educated and still preserve their faith in God. They viewed religion as a necessary component of a complete education and welcomed the emphasis on moral values and eternal truths which trained them for service to society. They asserted that a liberal arts college ought to give "a well-rounded education," and they endlessly debated the proper balance between academics and activities in order to achieve optimum well-roundedness. A few insisted on a scholastic emphasis. Others stressed extracurriculars because of their value in developing personal skills, obtaining teaching positions and training community leadership. Most called for both, and recognized a proper balance as the key.[56]

Reflecting the general trend at American colleges and universities, the *Concordian* exhibited a much greater interest in domestic and international politics during the decade. The Depression and its related international crises raised the consciousness of an entire generation to a wide range of social, economic and political problems. While Concordia did not share in the spirit of protest and radicalism that characterized some campuses, the college did display heightened political awareness.

Cobbers took great interest in national political campaigns. They formed a Republican Hoover-Curtis Club in 1928 and cast 159 votes for Hoover and 83 for Roosevelt in a campus straw poll for the 1932 election. The 1936 election attracted even more attention. The *Concordian* reported on North Dakota Congressman William Lemke's Union Party campaign and on an address in Fargo by Socialist candidate Norman Thomas, attended by "the more progressive members of the student body." The straw poll produced the largest turn-out in its history. Despite strong support for third party candidates, Republicans maintained their two-to-one margin over Democrats: Landon, 209; Roosevelt, 100; Thomas, 39; Lemke, 14. For the 1940 election, students organized political clubs; the *Concordian* and international relations club sponsored a "get out the vote" effort and the campus poll. With 396 votes cast, the poll produced the usual two-to-one advantage for the Republican Willkie over the Democrat Roosevelt. This contrasted with the National Student Opinion Survey in which 50.5 percent of those surveyed favored Willkie and with the result of the national election that produced another substantial Roosevelt victory.[57]

Although the Concordia community was Republican, when President Roosevelt visited Fargo in October 1937 Cobbers were excused from classes and joined the large crowds at the Great Northern Depot. Regardless of their political affiliation, most united with President Brown in welcoming the New Deal program of student aid dispensed initially through the Federal Emergency Relief Administration and later the National Youth Administration.[58]

At times Cobbers attached themselves to liberal causes and expressed liberal opinions on certain issues. The Concordia student body affiliated with the NSF—National Student Federation of the USA—which represented 150 colleges and universities. Along with many proposals for enhancing the student role in college governance, the NSF strongly supported freedom of speech.[59] Free speech became an important issue prior to World War II due to witch hunts for campus radicals which were part of "the little red scare" stimulated in part by domestic politics and in part by European events—the rise of Russian Communism, Italian Fascism and German Nazism.

The NSF connection and the witch-hunting climate account for the several *Concordian* articles that defended free speech from patriotic intolerance. A 1935 editorial—"Repression Threatens American Education"—called the efforts of super-patriots to root out communism a fascist threat to fundamental constitutional rights. The "patrioters" were on the wrong track; free expression on social issues must be permitted in classrooms. An editorial by Lloyd W. Sveen ('40) in 1938 responded to constituent complaints that *Concordian* editors were "communists, reds, radicals." These charges were generated by articles predicting a victory by Farmer-Labor candidate Elmer Benson and describing a day for Farmer-Laborite Paul Rasmussen who had left Concordia to take a state government position. To defend himself, Sveen simply affirmed that freedom of speech protected the right of collegians to express honest opinions. Besides, as Sveen pointed out in subsequent issues, opinion polls indicated there was little danger of ideological brainwashing on campuses. Nationally only one in ten believed they had been victims of indoctrination. At Concordia, all of the forty-six Cobbers polled denied any ideological influences. Sveen thought this evidence should allay fears of constituents who believed that Concordia had communists and fascists lurking on its faculty.[60]

Cobbers devoted considerable attention to international affairs during the decade. Beginning in 1931 under the leadership of Herman Nordlie, they attended model assemblies of the League of Nations which discussed topics like "The World Economic Dilemma" and "Disarmament." Rolf Daehlin ('35) delivered a speech in Chinese in representing that country in the assembly hosted by Moorhead State Teachers College in April 1933. An international relations club met fortnightly and debated such important issues as recognition of Russia and United States membership in the League. In 1934 the club hosted a model assembly; obtained 300 Cobber signatures in a national petition campaign which asked the United States president to take steps toward League membership; and participated in a tri-college conference at North Dakota Agricultural College devoted to the discussion of Henry A. Wallace's *American Must Choose*, a book which argued for a middle course between internationalism and economic nationalism. That same year the club also sponsored the appearance of Saint Olaf President Lars Boe who spoke on his recent trip to Germany. Boe praised Hitler for uniting Germany and asserted that the chancellor had not been treated fairly in the American press, a point of view he later regretted.[61]

The campus peace movement of the mid-1930s also stirred interest at Concordia. In 1935 the student government sent a supportive letter to North Dakota Senator Gerald P. Nye, chairman of the Senate committee investigating the causes of United States entry into World War I. That same year 275 Cobbers participated in the famous *Literary Digest* peace poll. A *Concordian* editorial defended peace polls on the grounds that they provoked discussion about international problems among those who must fight the next war. Although many Cobbers sympathized with peace movement objectives, most refused in 1936 to participate in "the strike for peace." They objected to the concept of "strike," equating it with labor violence. The next year the *Concordian* urged Cobbers to think seriously about international relations and to participate in the meeting scheduled in lieu of the strike. That same year the *Concordian* enlisted in the Emergency Peace Campaign which sought to prevent American participation in future wars by molding public opinion against war.[62]

The desire for peace translated into isolationism as the world drifted toward military conflict in the late 1930s. Reflecting the isolationist political culture of the Upper Midwest and ignoring the efforts of Governor Harold E. Stassen after 1938 to lead Minnesota Republicans toward an internationalist position, several *Concordian* articles warned against actions and ideas that might lead to United States intervention. Thus the paper opposed an economic boycott of Japan as punishment for its aggression against China; certain Japanese retaliation would assist those jingoists who wanted war. The paper warned against listening to war propaganda about atrocities in Spain,

Italy, Germany and Asia; similar propaganda had involved the United States in the last struggle.[63]

To be sure, the paper published a series of articles by John Anker ('40) criticizing British Prime Minister Neville Chamberlain for his "appeasement policy" during the Czechoslovakian crisis of 1938. That same year an article expressed mild criticism of President Roosevelt for not opening the United States to Jews who faced increased Nazi economic persecution. Yet in neither instance did the authors suggest any action that might lead to United States involvement in a future war. Indeed, the *Concordian* maintained an isolationist stance from the beginning of war in Europe on September 1, 1939, until the Japanese attack on Pearl Harbor more than two years later. This mirrored the silence of the Norwegian Lutheran Church on the developing international crisis. Not until the invasion of Norway in April 1940 did Norwegian-American Lutherans exhibit hostility toward the German invader. After Pearl Harbor, campus, church and nation rallied to the colors and supported the United States military effort.[64]

Concordia may have been isolationist but it was not isolated from the pressing political and cultural issues of the day. Cobbers had occasion to discuss many subjects. Apparently a sufficient number took advantage of the opportunity to make the campus a rather lively place intellectually.

Memorable Professors

Faculty, whose antics entered into Cobber legend and folklore, played a significant and memorable part in college life. Many of these remarkable men and women devoted their entire lives to the institution and its collegians. Without their dedication and sacrifice, the school could not have survived. The following few are illustrative of others too numerous to discuss.

Emma Norbryhn, a native of Norway and a graduate of Concordia Academy and Saint Olaf College, taught Latin, German, French and Norse at the same desk in Main 19 from 1908 until her retirement in 1948—the longest tenure of service at that time. She was a charter member of Concordia Women's League, an expert horticulturist, avid fisherwoman and proficient cook. Martha Brennun, the daughter of Norwegian immigrants and a Norbryhn student, began teaching mathematics after her commencement in 1917. During thirty-eight years at the college, she served for twenty-five as registrar and occasionally instructed in Norse and religion as well as mathematics. Brennun had many firsts to her credit: the

Emma Norbryhn

first woman to receive a baccalaureate from Concordia and the first to become president of the first senior class, the alumni association and the literary society for college women—Alpha Kappa Chi. Brennun's activities away from Concordia reveal that combination of religious piety, Christian service and scholarly endeavor so characteristic of Lutheran faculty of the day. She taught grade school at an Eskimo mission in Alaska for two years and took other leaves for study at the University of Minnesota and Lutheran Bible Institute. She attended summer school at various places, went to Europe three times, and instructed in Sunday and Thursday School at Trinity Church.[65]

Frida Nilsen, former China missionary and future author, served in the 1930s as "temporary" dean of women and from 1929 until 1962 as an inspirational English professor who had her students memorize poetry. Political turmoil in China prevented her return and made her interim position at Concordia permanent. Very strict in her demands, Professor Nilsen challenged Cobbers to make something of themselves. She took intellectual life seriously and provided a role model of varied experience and wide interests. This was especially important for her female students at a time when many considered college wasted on women. Carrie Braaten, the librarian from 1924 to 1937, is remembered as a fierce individual who objected to a collegian who smiled when entering the library because it disturbed everyone. Yet on her ninetieth birthday she sent a $300 check for the library to purchase books it could not otherwise buy; she and her entire family became major financial contributors to the institution.[66]

Librarian Carrie Braaten

Dr. Mae Anderson, head of the department of mathematics at the time of her death from leukemia in 1948, was a student of the remarkable T.C. Wollan, who came to Concordia with the Park Region merger in 1917 and taught until his death in 1932. As a University of Chicago graduate student, Anderson greatly impressed her professors, who marvelled at her remarkable undergraduate training. Sigurd Mundhjeld, another Wollan student, replaced Anderson upon her death; he taught Gerald and Charles Heuer, current department members, and many other college and university mathematics professors. Wollan, an unusual and successful teacher, thus established an institutional academic strength in mathematics that has been perpetuated by his students and their disciples.[67]

Given the college emphasis on religion, it is appropriate that many alumni of the 1930s recalled most fondly professors Ylvisaker and Johnshoy. As religion department head and college pastor (1927–1945), Carl B. Ylvisaker preached a religion of the heart. For him, having an open heart was more important than having a trained mind. Collegians should therefore pray to God to save them from becoming sophisticated and worldly. A fine tennis and ping pong player, Ylvisaker coached the tennis team. A good pianist and organist, he played the organ in chapel. An excellent speaker with a good sense of humor, Ylvisaker spoke often to Luther Leagues and taught Bible camps each summer. He always visited and brought flowers to hospitalized students. He had a great capacity for remembering names and details about those he met. No wonder Cobbers have canonized him. Mostly they recall his sincerity, humility and saintly behavior; they were especially thankful for the spiritual guidance they received which, for many, continued to be offered long after graduation. At Ylvisaker's death the church lost a distinguished servant who had reached a large number in a special way.[68]

Of course, not all Cobbers shared Ylvisaker's pietistic version of Lutheranism and some were even repelled by its anti-intellectual implications. "Quite to the contrary," as J. Walter Johnshoy often intoned, many preferred that professor's more scholarly Lutheranism. Head of philosophy and teacher of religion, Greek, Hebrew and social work (1925–1947), Johnshoy was serving three congregations when he died. "The good doctor's" apparent interest and knowledge in all fields constantly amazed Cobbers. A published poet and author of three devotional books, Johnshoy fearlessly denounced violations of God's teachings and critiqued "religion of the heart" in his chapel addresses. This did not endear him to Ylvisaker's followers. Very patient with questions, Johnshoy extended help and friendship to all who came to him. His philosophy course helped at least one alumna preserve her faith when she encountered anti-religious graduate school professors.[69]

Perhaps Concordia's greatest faculty "character" was Christian Bale, who came to Concordia from Park Region in 1917 and taught English until his retirement in 1952. A Democrat who liked to talk politics, Bale seldom looked up in class; it made him the target of many pranks. One year students registered a fictitious "Anna Jacobson"; Bale did not catch on until Christmas, when he received several cards from this non-existent coed. The class thereupon held a funeral, draping an empty chair in black. On another occasion, when Bale's suit-coat hung in the hall, they replaced his pocket handkerchief with lefse. Putting on his jacket for class, he did not discover the switch during the period. Bale was not always oblivious to misbehavior because, when irritated, he would look up and say, "you should be out pulling weeds." Unappreciated by most undergraduates, Bale is remembered as an excellent teacher by those seriously interested in literature.[70]

While eccentricity made Bale unforgettable, fear made memorable Charles Skalet, a classics professor (1923–1962). Very strict in his demands, Skalet expected thorough preparation regardless of what went on at the college or in collegian lives. Consequently Cobbers always first prepared their Greek. The consequences could be devastating

Classicist Charles Skalet

if they did not. Skalet might sarcastically remark: "Man alive! This is Mr. Johnson! His parents are paying me to make a pastor out of him. But how is he ever going to be able to preach the gospel when he can't even read it?" Because Skalet had often taught their fathers, more than one student found the marginal note appended to their examination—"Your father was no Greek scholar *either.*"[71]

Herman C. Nordlie, professor of history (1917–1954) and Bale's former Park Region colleague, is recalled for giving "write all you know" final exams and for his dry sense of humor that he used to deflate "know it alls" and to make his annual talks to freshman a landmark in an otherwise stilted orientation program. A Luther graduate, Nordlie had a master's and "all but dissertation" for a doctorate at the University of Wisconsin. During his thirty-seven year career, he taught all five political science and thirteen of the fifteen history courses offered. At the forefront of all campus discussions, Nordlie was a committed internationalist, an avid traveler and a dedicated public servant. Sometimes students accompanied him on his frequent summer travels: a three-month tour of western states (1927), a one-month visit to eastern historical sites (1928) and a forty-one day "Educational Tour Through Historic Europe" (1935). He was also active in civic affairs: president of Kiwanis (1927), a one-term "dry" mayor of Moorhead (1929–1931) who was defeated in his re-election bid, and twice president of the Clay County Historical Society (1934 and 1935). As mayor, prohibitionist Nordlie attempted to cleanup the city and create an ideal college town by honestly enforcing the law. He therefore assured parents "that Moorhead is morally clean, and is a perfectly safe place for ... sons and daughters." Nordlie felt privileged to work at Concordia because, he said, "church colleges help build character and give a person a correct view of life."[72]

J.A. Holvik, professor of Norse (1923–1952), is recollected most as band director (1927–1949), a "temporary" position he acquired when Herman Monson led the choir on its first extended tour to the West Coast. Knighted by the Norwegian government for his work as officer of the Norwegian-American centennial and for his authorship of two Norwegian textbooks, Holvik was thereupon called "Duke" by Cobbers. An excellent, businesslike conductor who genuinely loved music, Holvik had played in the Saint Olaf band that toured Norway in 1906 and had led instrumental groups at Waldorf. Only paid $100 for directing, Holvik nonetheless did not charge for private lessons to those who could not play an instrument; by giving free lessons he built up the band. A pipe-smoker who lit up as soon as he reached the edge of campus, Holvik levied fines of one cigar for glaring concert errors. The Norway band tour of 1935 meant much to Holvik personally; it was the first European invitation to a Concordia group and it was a critical success. At one of the many receptions and parties Mrs. Holvik tasted champagne for the first time and said simply, "it tickles." Besides music, Holvik's other passion was the Kensington rune stone. He carried on an extensive correspondence to disprove its authenticity because he feared that people would laugh at Norwegians for believing a hoax.[73]

"Doc" H.N. Grunfor

Not all professors were faculty. "Doc" Hegland Nikolai Grunfor was known for his boiler-room discourses; Cobbers claimed to have learned philosophy listening to him. Officially designated as a steam engineer, the Norwegian-born Grunfor performed many tasks, possessed a particular talent for avoiding the inquiries of building inspectors and probably suffered more for Concordia during his thirty years than any other person in the school's history: He sawed off one finger serving as a carpenter; lost sight of one eye sanding floors; broke both legs painting and shingling; and gassed himself into unconsciousness fumigating North Hall. One day President Brown left his 1939 Plymouth with a sign: "Grunfor, wash my car. J.N. Brown." The president returned to find his muddy car with a new sign: "Brown, wash your own ____ car. H.N. Grunfor." Amazingly, they remained on speaking terms. The Grunfor home was always open to students; each homecoming he received a flock of visitors.[74]

Given such memorable, dedicated and talented professors as those recounted here, no wonder Cobbers enjoyed a college life that enriched itself during hard times. If faculty failed to amuse, entertain or enlighten, then collegians could divert themselves with the many extracurricular activities that, when combined with a reformed curriculum and Lutheran religious emphasis, were transforming Concordia into a modern church college.

Chapter 9

Concordia Goes to War

Adapting to Wartime Demands

Prior to Pearl Harbor, higher education in the United States was largely unaffected by World War II. Selective Service, enacted in September 1940, did not decrease attendance because nobody under age twenty-one was liable for conscription. After December 7, 1941, when it became apparent that the draft age eventually would be lowered to eighteen, many institutions confronted the likelihood of financial hardship brought on by drastically diminished enrollments. To prepare for this crisis, the American Council on Education met on January 3 in Baltimore. This meeting, attended by 1,000 educators including President Brown, pledged colleges and universities to winning military victory. Committed to making higher education an integral part of the war machine, educators called for specialized training programs that would minimize disruption of academic life.[1] This strategy neatly combined principle with self-interest; it maintained collegiate numbers through specialized training as a patriotic contribution to the war.

This message Brown brought back from Baltimore; these ideas formed the basis of his wartime administrative policies. Addressing chapel and Kiwanis upon his return, Brown emphasized that the government needed specialized personnel during and after the war and that this was a war of ideas. "On one side is the philosophy of war . . . plunder and totalitarianism," Brown said, "on the other is the philosophy of freedom." As a church college, Concordia contributed directly to freedom because it preserved American ideals and fostered "the culture, intelligence and welfare of our community." He knew the struggle would be difficult for academe. As he expressed privately to Saint Olaf President Boe, "we are going to face the most trying period in the history of our institutions." Noting "an unrest among the students, many of them wishing to enlist ... [or] go into nursing," Brown hoped the numbers would be limited but would not discourage anyone. He urged the faculty to greater economy and to the development of military-related programs to sustain enrollments. As compensation to schools for their military contributions and their student losses, the president desired federal subsidies.[2]

United States entry and subsequent accelerated military build-up simultaneously diminished collegiate numbers and increased the proportion of females. Approximately 1,200,000—63 percent men—entered higher education in Autumn 1941; a 38 percent decline over two years reduced the count to 740,000—67 percent women. Similarly, Concordia's enrollment (see Table V) dropped 33 percent from a previous high of 545 (1941–1942) to the wartime low of 365—more than 80 percent female—in Spring 1944.[3]

Several factors mitigated the impact of this precipitous drop. It occurred over six semesters which permitted necessary reductions in costs. Female enrollment, which had been higher than the national average prior to the war, increased 45 percent from 275 (1941–1942) to 398 (1943–1944), slowing the rate of decline. Summer school,

	Enrollments							
	Total	Men		Women		1st Sem	2nd Sem	Summer
		#	%	#	%	Total	Total	Total
1941--1942	545	270	49.5	275	50.5		475	
1942--1943	519	207	39.9	312	60.1		441	71
1943--1944	489	91	18.6	398	81.4	441	365	70
1944--1945*	428	66	15.4	362	84.6	449	387	65
1945--1946*	660	175	26.5	485	73.4	616	635	102

*does not include summer school, music or cadet nurse enrollments.

	Graduates				
	Total	Men		Women	
		#	%	#	%
1941	102	47	46.1	55	53.9
1942	85	47	55.3	38	44.7
1943	86	38	44.2	48	55.8
1944	85	31	36.5	54	63.5
1945	45	5	11.1	40	88.9
1946	54	11	20.4	43	79.6

Compiled from Catalog, 1942–1946 and 1953; Moorhead Daily News, 3 February 1942 and 11 February 1943.

Table V: Enrollments and Graduates, 1941–1946

begun in 1943, and sixty-three cadet nurses (1944–1945) bolstered annual totals. As in the earlier crisis of the 1930s, the institution again successfully maintained its numbers. Although the average graduating class declined from eight-seven (1929–1940) to eighty-one (1941–1945), average total enrollment actually increased from 471 (1929–1940) to 528 (1941–1946). A dramatic 49 percent rise in the average female enrollment from an earlier 225 to a later 336 rendered this possible. Despite worry about numbers, the faculty in November 1942 refused to admit students from among the 120,000 Japanese-Americans who had been forcibly evacuated from California to internment camps in Great Plains states. That the proposal was considered may evidence Christian concern for the oppressed; that it was rejected reflects the racial hysteria and the growing popular thirst for revenge which gripped the United States at this time.[4]

The administration cooperated wholeheartedly with the war effort. The president early appointed three faculty committees to handle war-related matters. The committee on academic plans for wartime service developed an accelerated program with a summer school that enabled students to receive their degrees in three years; it also reviewed new courses and course revisions helpful in meeting wartime and postwar military and civilian needs. The student health service in wartime committee supervised health and physical education activities in cooperation with government authorities. Another committee, induction of students into wartime service, advised on federal regulations for the draft. Peter Anderson, the key faculty adviser on military matters, corresponded with Cobbers and patiently relayed detailed information about their options for enlisting in various forms of naval service or the Army Enlisted Reserve Corps. From a collegiate perspective these programs were initially attractive because, as originally structured, they allowed collegians to complete school before reporting to active duty. This feature soon disappeared as manpower needs quickly increased. Nonetheless, Anderson still recommended that Cobbers enlist in the reserves. If called, they could at least complete the semester and be considered for officer candidate school.[5]

Concordian editor Harold Poier ('42) commended the creation of these committees to counsel students on the best way to serve their country. Remaining in school, he urged, was the superior service because scientific warfare required educated men and women. Established after large numbers had departed campus, the committee on relations to the armed forces operated as a clearinghouse of information and communication to the 796 Cobbers who were serving by July 1945.[6] It thereby enabled the now far-flung global family to maintain contact with one another and with the college.

Increased church appropriations and tuition charges eased the financial strain of war. Allocations rose from $21,996 (8 percent of Concordia's expenses, 1942–1943) to $30,000 (11.1 percent of expenses, 1944–1945). General fees were raised from $95 (1943–1944) to $110 (1944–1945). These increases, combined with a reduction in expenditure of almost $40,000, again produced balanced budgets. Despite larger church assistance, Brown remained sensitive to any possible unfairness. He therefore remonstrated when the board of education made a special appropriation to Pacific Lutheran to relieve its indebtedness. Brown's objections were twofold; the board had unfairly favored Pacific Lutheran and had appropriated without consulting the college presidents who were responsible for raising almost the entire educational budget. After all, Concordia had long carried an indebtedness of over $100,000, had paid $4,000 interest annually and still lived within its means.[7] On this issue, Brown displayed the same protectiveness of institutional rights that he had demonstrated repeatedly throughout the depression decade.

The global conflict postponed for the duration hoped-for policy initiatives and new building construction. Most serious for faculty security was the delay in creating a retirement program. Study had begun in 1940 on a Teacher's Insurance Annuity Association plan; it would not be implemented until 1947. A new library, music hall and gymnasium were not built, but planning proceeded for a library and an auditorium-gymnasium.

Planning a new library proceeded despite the war.

According to a colleague, Librarian Oivind Hovde and Athletic Director Jake Christiansen drew pictures daily. Already in 1944 it appeared that Christiansen's dreams would be realized first. His early plans called for Tudor Gothic architecture, swimming pool, large stage, regulation playing floor, two handball courts, roller skating rink, and seating capacity of 2,500 for basketball and 3,500 for stage events.[8]

New construction ceased, but remodeling did not. Renovating the dining hall and the old library relieved pressing physical plant needs. In 1943 eight modern classrooms were made available in the refurbished library. Installation of a cafeteria—accommodating 300 at one sitting and conveniently accessible from the men's dormitory (Academy) and Grose (Bishop Whipple)—had been discussed for some time. Work began in Summer 1942, but military-related shortages of plumbers and electricians disrupted progress. When students complained about long lines and higher food prices, the president responded in the *Concordian*. He thanked editor Gerald Brekke ('43) for his dignified editorials and students for their opinions which the administration highly valued. Complaints were not justified, however. These were not normal times; resulting inconveniences must be endured. Higher food fees stemmed from inflation and not from remodeling costs. Brown closed by chiding Cobbers for not praising improvements in the men's dormitory showers and parlors.[9]

Important changes were made in the corporation at this time. Previously, the annual corporation meeting had been comprised of church convention delegates from the territory and had been held in conjunction with that gathering; limited time and unrepresentative attendance rendered this arrangement unsatisfactory. In 1943 President Brown therefore proposed changing the constitution and bylaws to permit the meeting on campus by delegates especially chosen for the corporation; he believed these alterations would promote a more thorough understanding of the actual accomplishments and needs of the college. The board approved these proposals in March 1944 and they were ratified at the corporation meeting. Under the new plan, each ministerial circuit sent three lay and two clerical delegates to an annual assemblage at the college. Another change enlarged the corporation; the assembly in November 1945 admitted the Montana circuit east of the continental divide, increasing the number of owning congregations from the 893 to 1,025. The corporation also attempted to enlarge its constituency within the territory. They authorized the directors in 1945 to enter into agreements with other Lutheran synods. In exchange for financial support, these synods would be given representation on the board. Ownership would not be affected; it remained with the congregations of the Norwegian Lutheran Church.[10]

Changes in Academic Life

The war deeply affected faculty and the curriculum. Declining enrollment usually translates into staff contraction. With seventy-five fewer collegians in Autumn 1942, the president looked to cut three positions. Fortunately from Brown's viewpoint, reductions seemed possible from professors who entered war work. Dean of Men Rudolph L. Lokensgard became an instructor for the army. Thomas Burgess, ready to leave in a minute, expected an army commission and an imminent call to duty. The call never came. Nevertheless, Burgess later worked nine weeks during the Summer of 1943 as a journeyman electrician at Portland Kaiser Ship Yards and then as a research analyst for California Shipbuilding Corporation.[11]

Physicist Konrad Lee gave ground instruction for pilots.

As a longterm policy, Treasurer Sigurd Mundhjeld preferred not to balance the budget by relying on military induction to reduce the number of professors.[12] Hence Concordia attempted to maintain enrollment, remain solvent and avoid the pain of staff cuts by altering its curriculum to meet military-related demands. These curricular initiatives preceded United States entry and continued for the duration.

Training pilots and nurses were new war-related programs. Ten Cobbers began pilot training under a Civil Aeronautics Administration plan in September 1940. This project was part of the Roosevelt Administration's initiative for strengthening American defenses in response to the European war. Physics professor Konrad Lee gave ground instruction at Concordia; the students then took flight instruction at Hector Airport. Those completing this elementary phase were eligible for Army Air Corps pilot training. The 1/10 quota on female enrollment was first filled by freshman Gail Gandrud in March 1941. The program ended in Autumn 1942 with ten who had completed the initial phase on campus now training at Hector under a new Army Air Corps glider program. Then in September 1943, forty-five nurses from St. Luke's Hospital in Fargo first registered for a semester of psychology and science at Concordia. Part of the United States Nurses Cadet Corps program, this work continued until war's end in 1945.[13]

The war produced other changes in the content and structure of academic life. Inducted seniors with 120 credits graduated with their class in the spring; those with fewer credits were decided as special cases. The war offered men additional opportunities. The college in 1942 had eight openings for training Marine Corps officers. That same semester, five Cobbers planned to enter medical school under a deferred enlistment program. A year later the college administered a naval screening test to enlisted freshmen and sophomores. Women were not omitted from mobilization. Pre-induction courses recommended for them included: nutrition, consumer education, home nursing and child care followed the subsequent semester by institutional management, guidance and personnel work, experimental cookery and quantity cookery.[14]

U. S. Army Announcement

To College Women in their Senior Year

1943 Concordian advertisement called women to the colors.

New courses originated from the crisis: Economics 114, "America at War," became an elective in lieu of required freshmen work in economics-history and History 380, "Historical Geography," focused on the geography of the conflict. Business offered "Army Office Training," and physics taught "Meteorology." As part of its wartime community service, the college in 1944 offered an evening course in Spanish that was open to the public. The new business education department advertised the military relevance of its one-year stenographic and two-year secretarial courses in meeting the growing wartime demand for stenographic and clerical workers. Physical education requirements were altered in 1942 in response to a defense-related emphasis on physical fitness. In addition to regular physical education classes, all men were now required to participate in intramurals at least two hours weekly for freshmen and sophomores, and three hours for juniors and seniors.[15]

Several structural changes were made in accordance with military-requested acceleration of education. The first summer session ever was held in 1942, was directed by Herman Nordlie and enrolled fifty-six. It offered defense training in specific war skills through completing any of these subjects: contemporary economic problems, civil servicetraining,worldpolitics,nutrition,homenursing,trigonometry,solidgeometry, mechanical drawing, recreational leadership, health education, first aid, electrical measurements, meteorology and elementary radio. Summer sessions enabled students to graduate in three years. Similarly mid-year graduations, held in 1943 and 1944, were designed to alleviate teacher shortages and to provide commencement for those leaving immediately for armed service. Another attempt at acceleration, begun in 1943, involved early admission of exceptionally talented high school juniors.[16]

In another defense-related attempt to stabilize enrollment, the college requested and received permission to establish a training school for a unit of 250 Army Air Corps cadets. Even before 125 arrived in March 1943, President Brown had anxiously written Saint Olaf requesting information about possible problems: How are salaries determined for faculty teaching armed forces? Who pays for new equipment? What problems arise from the presence of military personnel? Assured that the army would pay for equipment and that the commander would vigilantly segregate his unit from all Cobber females, the president worried most about salary. He finally decided to place all salaries on the same scale and hoped that the directors would fund this pay increase. To prepare Cobbers for any inconveniences, Brown wrote a *Concordian* guest editorial appealing to their patriotism. As a matter of civic duty, he was sure they would "accept cheerfully ... any transformations that may be necessary." To make space, the women vacated Grose Hall (present Bishop Whipple), the library was moved to the Fjelstad Hall recreation room, and the old building (present Grose Hall) was remodeled into classrooms.[17]

Despite these accommodations, the marriage was not happy. After only a month, Cadet Commander First Lieutenant Richard F. Burke suddenly announced that the unit would move to Moorhead State Teachers College because it had better facilities and its administrators were willing to clear two women's dormitories by finding rooms in private homes. President Brown's rejection of Burke's request for Fjelstad Hall prompted the abrupt departure. Brown did not comply because he did not want 163 women living off campus, and he did not think that the college could operate its civilian program without the dormitory. In self-defense, Brown wrapped himself in the mantle of patriotism. Concordia was preparing students for wartime duty; to discontinue would be unfair to them and would end a significant national service. He also prudently negotiated a financial settlement from the Army for the campus improvements made for the now nonexistent program. The move was a terrible blow to Cobber pride. Army airman George Howell ('41) was relieved that he had not been transferred to Moorhead "because it would break my heart to have to go to MSTC" and because an almost certain conflict with "Burke the jerk" would result in his being busted to ground crew. Institutional advertising soon made a virtue of necessity, however, when it proclaimed that the "entire college and plant [are] devoted to education of civilian students."[18]

Mobilizing for War

Once Japan attacked Pearl Harbor and the United States declared war, Cobbers rallied to the colors. Isolationism, which had been vigorously expressed during the considerable collegian discussion of international issues during the 1930s, abruptly disappeared. Encouraged by a variety of methods, the student body mobilized for war. Long silent on the European crisis, the Norwegian Lutheran Church in 1942 adopted

President J.N. Brown, 1925--1951

a strong resolution urging members to support the military effort because it upheld principles essential to human welfare and freedom of conscience and worship. The 1943 commencement address, "Education and Democracy" by Dr. Richard Beck of the University of North Dakota, similarly emphasized the tenets at stake. In light of the crisis, Dr. Beck said, "there can be no 'business as usual' on the educational front for the duration of the war. ... Service to the war effort of our nation such as the training of men and women for our armed forces and industries must come first." Portraying the war as a struggle in which "the ideals of democracy ... hang in the balance," Dr. Beck assigned education—especially the liberal arts that preserve cultural tradition—a

crucial role because it was "both the breeding ground and the safeguard for such ideals."[19]

Similar ideas were communicated to Cobbers in other ways. Throughout the crisis, freshmen orientation included a faculty lecture on the topic, "Going to School in Wartime." A student war committee, formed in October 1942 and chaired successively by Rebecca Johnson ('44), Corrine Johnson ('45) and Adelaide Bjertness ('46), pursued three objectives in compliance with the national policy sponsored by the Office of Civilian Defense: to further the sale of war bonds and stamps on campus; to sponsor extension programs for neighboring Army and Navy camps; and to enlist students for special courses and duties.[20]

A Concordian cartoon promoted war bond sales.

Apathy toward the war, evidenced by the purchase of only $50 worth of stamps and bonds between January and October, was the major reason for creating the committee. An editorial by Gerald Brekke attributed this poor record to apathy, selfishness and ignorance which the war committee was expected to cure. To a large extent it did. Campus organizations were assigned to sell war bonds and stamps. Using slogans—"Bonds and Stamps Lick Axis Tramps" and "More Bombs for Berlin"—sales increased dramatically to $2,870 (May 1943) and to $2,290 (December 1943). The committee encouraged students and the cafeteria to cooperate in the nationwide "clean plate campaign" of 1944. To avoid waste, pledge cards—a clean plate after each meal—were issued to every Cobber.[21]

Many campus organiza-

The Servicemen's Bureau kept Cobbers in touch.

tions involved themselves directly in war work. The music club in April 1942 presented a program and a tea to raise funds for the purchase of sheet music and a musical instrument for a military camp. The second annual winter carnival was held in February 1943 as a war benefit. Zeta Sigma Pi, the social science honorary, in Fall

1943 established the Cobber Serviceman's Bureau. It compiled the names and addresses of those serving and invited others to use the bureau in sending information. The society also contributed a service flag—with a star for each Cobber serving since 1939—to hang in chapel.[22]

The international relations club expanded to 113 members and its programs took on a wartime flavor as faculty addressed timely topics—"Evaluating Japan's Strategy" by Professor Nordlie and "War Propaganda" by Professor Burgess. To encourage campus-wide patriotic service, the club sponsored a national defense week culminating with a defense musicale in March 1942. A ten-cent war stamp secured admission to a special program of music written by Garland Lockrem ('48), William Jones ('44) and Karl Holvik ('43). The societies also exhibited a patriotic spirit that spring. Many substituted defense stamps for corsages, and all conducted their parties as inexpensively as possible. The junior-senior banquet adopted the theme, "Wings Triumphant," and decorated in red, white and blue. Cobbers canceled the homecoming window decoration competition and donated the savings to the war fund.[23]

Cobbers participated in off-campus defense work as well. Coeds knit mittens for Norway and folded surgical dressings for the Red Cross each Tuesday and Thursday evening at City Hall. Others volunteered three hours weekly to assist the Clay County Price and Rationing Board. Still others presented plays in March 1944 as a fundraiser for China relief. These sacrifices probably were not painful because, as historian Richard Polenberg has pointed out, Americans frequently derived great satisfaction from contributing to the common good during World War II. The Office of Civilian Defense preached that people through discipline and self-denial could contribute to an American victory. Cobbers heard the message and made their contribution.[24]

Patriotic participation in war work colored student opinions on other issues. War-induced labor shortages altered attitudes toward working women. An estimate made in December 1943, that five million women not presently working would be placed in war industries, led Dean of Women Theresa Holt to articulate the new work responsibilities of coeds. They must train scientifically and thoroughly for jobs. Their training must include life and social sciences. They must abandon that "fetish of the coddled mind" which maintained that women could not learn certain subjects. By calling for scientific instruction and training for jobs, Holt thus questioned the conventional image of woman as wife and mother.[25]

Dean Theresa Holt

Besides assigning new social roles to women the war generally led to a new emphasis on the importance of scientific training. In "An Open Letter to Seniors," a new recruiting technique utilizing the *Concordian*, Sterling Kuhlmey ('47) asserted that science is the foundation of the modern world; therefore collegiate education should combine scientific with liberal training. The war-induced accentuation of science did not diminish the traditional commitment to Christian values, however. A 1943 Lutheran Student Union resolution urged students to engage their Christian principles in postwar planning. Collegians were obligated as Christians to be informed and to work for a better world. On the basis of these principles, Cobbers were told in 1945 to support the United Nations charter as a significant instrument for global improvement.[26]

Whatever their hopes for the postwar world, Cobbers generally did not dispute the ends for which the United States fought or the necessity for fighting. Only rarely were questions raised which indicated that traditional isolationism had not died in North Dakota. A former Cobber objected in February 1945 to a college news release that referred to World War II as a "holy cause." How could a Christian college, presumably founded on a New Testament ethic of love and brotherhood, teach that war is holy? How could the proposed gymnasium be made a "war memorial"? What could be commemorated? After all, common people were compelled to fight by governments and wars were planned by those who profited financially.[27] This protest was not heeded; that it was not indicates the high degree of popular support for World War II.

The *Concordian* also went to war. Almost immediately a war-related decline in advertisements reduced the paper to a tabloid. Sent to alumni and former students in the service, the *Concordian* ran military features: "Cobbers in the Service," "Cobbers and the Colors" and "Dear Joe"—letters from coeds to lonely GIs. The paper reported inductions and casualties, including Harris Christiansen ('40), the first alumnus killed on active duty; ran advertisements for war bonds and stamps; editorialized about lack of patriotism when a scrap metal drive failed in 1944; and proudly related special assignments and decorations earned by Cobbers.[28]

Jean Ahlness

Lieutenant Grace Berg (ex '42) of the Army Nurse Corps was an "angel of mercy" evacuating the wounded in the Mediterranean Theatre. Jean Ahlness ('43), assigned to a legation at Cairo, Egypt, by the State Department Foreign Service, could not reveal the nature of her work due to wartime secrecy. Captain Paul G. Johnshoy ('43), pilot of a B-24 Liberator Bomber named the "Minnesota Mauler," won the Distinguished Flying Cross for action in Central Europe. Captain Harold Thysell ('44), a P-38 Lightning pilot flying from a Russian base, was awarded the Distinguished Flying Cross for a strafing mission in occupied Poland. Lieutenant Verner F. Hanson ('38) received the Silver Star for navigating while wounded an alternative bombing mission over Germany for his B-17 Flying Fortress.[29]

The Cobber family extended to enfold these recent collegians now dispersed around the globe. As Navy Lieutenant Norman Jeglum ('42) observed, "It seems funny ... [that] the people with whom you've walked in and out of classes ... are so far away now." Professor Mae Anderson, secretary to the committee on relations to the Armed Forces, faithfully corresponded and collected information on those who served. The letters home to Anderson, all duly stamped by the naval censor or army examiner, reveal a strong

Pilot Paul Johnshoy won the Distinguished Flying Cross.

attachment to the college, much interest in other Cobbers and heartfelt appreciation for her "newsy letters." She must have spent hundreds of hours on this correspondence and must have appeared as a model of motherly devotion to these servicemen.[30]

Navy Lieutenant Milton Lindell ('43) expressed his gratitude: "Today I received your most welcome letter with more news from Cobberdom than I have received for a long time. I surely appreciate your spending your busy hours writing to me." Lindell also praised his alma mater: "I guess we all have to give credit to Concordia for any good that comes out of us." Lieutenant Waldo Lyden ('41) wrote from "Somewhere off the coast of France" in June 1944. He looked forward to the *Concordian* and enjoyed immensely Anderson's letters filled with college news.[31]

Norman Lorentzsen

Lyden, an eyewitness of the historic cross-channel D-Day invasion, recorded his impressions: "We had ringside seats to the big show here on June 6 and it really was a sight to behold. Not that I am asking for a repeat performance! But I am glad I didn't miss it. One feels he is doing more, the closer he gets to the actual making of history." From the Pacific Theatre, Navy pilot and Lieutenant Norman Lorentzsen ('41) wrote to thank Anderson for the announcement of homecoming and dryly commented: "It would have been a pleasure to attend, but circumstances intervene. Somehow too, the invitation took three and a half months finding its way out here." Noting that regular church and midweek prayer services were provided, Lorentzsen added, "In spite of all that is done for the comfort and welfare ... one still misses the fellowship and the pervading pleasant spirit that permeates the atmosphere of Concordia."[32]

College Life

College life, however altered to serve the war, persisted in familiar ways despite the crisis. President Brown was re-elected in June 1942 for another six-year term. At the annual faculty reception that fall, president, faculty and students again lined up to shake hands with incoming freshmen. Spiritual emphasis week, all-college parties and other familiar extracurricular activities all continued. Before the war ended, however, the band resembled a women's orchestra; the mixed chorus became a female choir; and the theatre put on its shows with coeds playing male parts. "Whole men" who were not 4-Fs were a novelty on campus and had little competition in being chosen for collegiate activities; some played in the band, sang in the choir and practiced football all in the same day. These few did so much that in 1945 a solicitous faculty would restrict students to traveling with only one organization and would again revive the point system for regulating participation. The football squad of twenty-two players, almost pre-war numbers, curtailed its schedule to four games as the Minnesota Intercollegiate Athletic Conference stopped competition for the duration.[33]

Debate and forensics endured with the well-attended Red River Tournament as a major event. Debate topics—"Resolved: That a permanent American program of compulsory military training should be established" and "That the United States should cooperate in establishing and maintaining an international police force on the defeat of the Axis"—accurately reflected the wartime and postwar preoccupations of the nation. As usual, traditional senior tree-planting ceremonies, cap and gown day exercises and commencement observances concluded college life for another year. Of course, the war altered the immediate future for most of the thirty-eight male graduates in 1943 who would soon enter the service of their country.[34]

Campus sprite Nels Mugaas—nattily attired in pinstripe suit with vest, gold watch and chain, spats and a slender cane—could still be seen occasionally strutting across the grounds with a coed on each arm. South Hall men, echoing the advice they had received about proper dating behavior, would yell from their windows—"Don't let them touch your skin!" College custodian and resident of the men's dormitory, Mugaas fancied himself as something of a ladies' man. He did have the gift for keeping spinsters' hopes alive and often had invitations to Sunday dinner. In March 1944, the *Concordian* paid tribute to the "Master of the Keys" by printing a charcoal portrait done by Elmer Halvorson. The paper praised Mugaas for his "long record of valuable service" and for his kindness, humor, "old country charm and hospitality." They might have added generosity, because Mugaas often aided needy collegians; many alumni owed their education to the benevolence of this remarkable janitor.[35]

Custodian Nels Mugaas financially helped many Cobbers.

Despite the war, college Christmas customs were still observed. For many years, the institution had served students a formal dinner with President Brown and the dean of women presiding at the head table and with chamber music between courses. Although the new cafeteria could no longer accommodate everyone at one sitting, the Christmas dinner tradition persisted. The faculty annually feasted on lutefisk in the Fjelstad Hall recreation room and afterward enjoyed a program and social hour in the Fjelstad North Lounge. In 1942 the fifteenth annual Christmas concert shifted from local Lutheran churches to the Moorhead Armory to accommodate crowds larger than the more than 2,000 who had attended the previous year. This move created the need for erecting a shell to project sound. The practice of decorating this shell with murals, designed by art professor Cyrus Running, evolved almost accidently. The Cy Running and Paul J. Christiansen partnership of using murals and music to illustrate Biblical texts would continue for thirty-two years until ill health forced Running to relinquish this labor of love.[36]

World War II Endured

Perceived by President Brown as a threat to the very survival of the institution, World War II turned out to be less of a strain than feared. As we have seen, the war altered college life and slowed institutional growth but did not permanently damage the school. Average enrollment actually increased over that of the depression decade, facilitating balanced budgets. The college even embarked on two major capital fund projects—the Golden Jubilee and Memorial Campaigns. These efforts raised monies for badly needed, but long-delayed, buildings—library, gymnasium-auditorium and men's dormitory. The need became even more pressing when enrollment increased a dramatic 44 percent to 616 in Fall 1945. The college, having maintained itself through

The 1945 student body was mostly female.

the crisis of depression and war, stood on the brink of its greatest growth. Rapid postwar increases in student numbers—requiring more faculty, more building, more *money*—posed new challenges for the institution that were as grave as those faced during the critical period just ended.

Chapter 10

Rapid Postwar Growth

The Crisis of Growth

Even before the surrender of Germany in May and Japan in August 1945, the United States began the process of reconversion to peace. Reconversion brought inflation and other economic dislocations, but not the major depression that everyone feared. The public demanded, bring the boys home; hence demobilization was rapid. By mid-1946, the armed forces already had been reduced from the wartime high of almost 12 million to just under 3 million; additional cuts quickly followed. To prevent joblessness and economic distress, the Servicemen's Readjustment Act of 1944—popularly known as the GI Bill of Rights—offered 16 million veterans a federal subsidy to continue schooling or training. The GI Bill democratized higher education by dramatically expanding educational opportunity. More than 2.2 million veterans attended colleges and universities, probably four times the number who would have otherwise.[1]

Faced with expanded numbers, the American Council on Education requested that President Truman appoint a commission on higher education. The commission reports, *Higher Education for American Democracy (1947–1948)*, argued that scientific and technological changes would generate even larger enrollments. Institutions should therefore welcome expansion, remove barriers and adjust to meet the needs of a more diverse student body. Due to these social trends, Concordia would now face a new crisis of growth that replaced the previous crisis of maintenance. From 1946 to 1951, all Lutheran colleges were strained to the limit of their resources to expand plant, personnel and services. Then the Korean War (1950–1953) again diminished collegian numbers while inflation drove costs upward.[2]

TESTIMONIAL DINNER

HONORING

Dr. J. N. Brown

in appreciation of

Twenty Years of Service

as

President of Concordia College

§

September 14, 1945

Program for dinner honoring President Brown.

At war's end President Brown had served Concordia for two decades. The community and the Norwegian Lutheran Church honored him with special banquets in September and then again at homecoming. Church dignitaries appeared at both events; Dr. H.O. Shurson, church treasurer and former Concordia president, spoke at the first gathering; Dr. J.C.K. Preus, executive secretary of the board of education, addressed the second. Friends solicited contributions for a new automobile. Recently ended wartime production rendered that gift impossible, but at homecoming they presented an $1,800 check in appreciation for his faithful service. Brown promised to purchase the car as soon as peacetime production made one available. Another honor soon followed when Brown was awarded the Danish Medal of Liberation for his services to the relief of Denmark during Nazi occupation.[3]

An experienced and honored executive, President Brown would need both his acquired knowledge and prestige in handling complex postwar challenges of rising enrollments and costs. Brown developed valid insights into the crisis of growth. He vigorously alerted the directors and the corporation about the implications and bravely offered a strategy of institutional expansion in response to the crisis. "The increase in college enrollment is not temporary," he warned; "according to recent government reports the enrollment in American colleges will be double the prewar figure by 1956." This did not exaggerate Concordia's prospects; indeed, it was insufficiently sanguine, as the college doubled by 1947. Brown stated the options bluntly for the corporation: "Either the enrollment must be dramatically curtailed, which will mean that the college must deny the privilege of a Christian education to many young people from homes that have supported the college for years, or the corporation must provide additional facilities and funds to care for more students."[4]

Faced with this stark choice and a growing market demand for its product, the corporation followed Brown's lead and attempted to supply more Christian education. This decision to grow ensured future well-being and therefore was one of the most significant events in the history of Concordia, as Emeritus Executive Vice President and former Director of Admissions J.L. Rendahl has pointed out. According to Rendahl, "we were careful to keep the college as crowded as possible. We walked the line between a good enrollment and student revolt." Because so many were veterans and all had grown up in depression-straitened homes, the poor facilities were acceptable.[5]

Director of Admissions
J.L. Rendahl

At the same time that Brown successfully spurred the corporation and directors to expand, he lobbied legislators to curtail potential state competition for collegians. These activities reveal that Brown's educational vision was limited to a spirited defense of private college self-interest; he did not conceive of the need to expand public institutions in order to offer educational opportunities for those unable to attend schools like Concordia. In particular, he opposed legislation in 1951 to change the teachers colleges into liberal arts institutions and to establish tuition-free junior colleges in every county. Brown urged the association of private colleges to demonstrate what their existence saved the state in annual educational expenditures; he hoped this would be sufficient to defeat the pending obnoxious legislation.[6]

Brown and the private schools eventually lost this battle. As it turned out there were students enough for both, but it continued to rankle President Brown and his successor that state institutions expanded much more rapidly than private.

To cope with the new demands of growth, Concordia revamped its administrative structure. For two decades the administration had been Brown and H.M. Dale assisted by others who also taught. Location of the president's secretary suggests simplicity and informality. Not until 1945 did Christina Fjelstad move into a room outside the president's office. No longer could all callers march in at once; the secretary now made appointments. Similarly, expansion dictated other specialization. For many years business management had been understaffed with H.M. Dale solely responsible for multifarious tasks. In addition, departments did not have budgets and all purchases required presidential approval, which entailed many trips and sometimes many battles. To remedy some of these problems, duties were now divided among three people: Dale, manager of endowment; Sigurd Mundhjeld, director of finance and treasurer; and John A. Olson, business manager.[7]

Appointed in 1945, Olson served as purchasing agent and general supervisor of the campus and facilities. By December 1946 a new superintendent of buildings and grounds had been appointed, a plan of organization adopted and regulations published. The president hoped these innovations would make possible more careful financial planning. J.L. Rendahl, beginning as director of public relations and admissions in April 1945, assumed duties as vice-president by 1947. That same year the directors named Peter Anderson—longtime professor of education—as dean of instruction, another new post. The faculty had long resisted creating this position because they did not want anyone coming between department heads and the president. They finally accepted the office, but without the powers normally possessed by a dean. The registrar and deans of men and women, all previously existing titles, completed the administrative structure.[8]

Growth changed other procedures, including registration. When Carl Narveson, a former Lake Park superintendent of schools, became registrar in 1947 he was horrified at the slow process. His threat to resign brought him authority to change the system. For the second semester he instituted the three-step procedure still used: 1) advisement (completed before); 2) registration (completed in the gym); 3) fee payment (completed later). Students praised Narveson's reforms, which eliminated tedious line-standing; they also enjoyed the two additional vacation days previously wasted on registration.[9]

As the college strained to cope with the crisis of growth, President Brown faced and survived a direct challenge to his authority. Near the end of Brown's fourth term, criticisms of his leadership surfaced among alumni, faculty, students and the board. Several issues fostered opposition. Many alumni were disgruntled with the president's constant fundraising and the decision to build two dormitories before constructing the auditorium-field house they desired. The faculty had divided into pro- and anti-Brown factions. Several former Norwegian Synod members had long opposed the former United Churchman and some new professors desired more youthful, progressive leadership. Veterans chafed under the restraints of *in loco parentis*; covertly encouraged by professorial opponents, they joined with others to demand enhanced powers for student government.[10]

President Brown evidently did not handle very well this "postwar rebellion." Cast in the traditional mold of the patriarchal college president and at times stubborn and insensitive, Brown "dug in his heels" and initially refused to listen sympathetically to demands for change. This resistance convinced critics that the president had served too long and should be replaced. Hence the timing of public opposition; it appeared to block Brown's re-election in Fall 1948 and to force the election of someone new.[11]

Whatever their grievance, opponents coalesced in the Concordia Volunteer Committee (CVC). Chaired by Howard G. Johnshoy ('40), class valedictorian and son of the philosophy professor J. Walter Johnshoy, the CVC claimed support of alumni, faculty, directors and prominent Fargo-Moorhead businessmen and on September 15,

1948 published *The Concordia Volunteer Committee Review* for distribution to alumni. The paper criticized Brown for ignoring efforts to improve the college; for being "undemocratic" in repressing a critical alumni questionnaire in 1938, rejecting the student plan for improved government in 1946 and appointing committees which excluded senior faculty; and for employing "Hollywood public relations" to suggest a non-existent harmony. The directors were criticized for not taking seriously these complaints. Apparently they had been beguiled by false publicity.[12]

The dispute divided the board, producing many bitter meetings. Director of Public Relations Rendahl, responsible for keeping directors happy, brought boxes of 25-cent cigars to their sessions. If such time-tested political techniques did not end conflict, they perhaps attracted some support. In any case, board and corporation backed the president. A series of board resolutions, adopted in November 1947, deplored the agitation of "self-appointed pressure groups which create dissension and suspicion." Care should be exercised to prevent any further detrimental publicity. In the interest of harmony, grievances should be channeled properly through agencies agreed upon by the directors and administration. Most important, the board expressed confidence in Brown and assured him of continued support. At the corporation meeting held October 26, 1948, the Concordia Volunteer Committee's campaign failed when the corporation, acting upon a board recommendation, reelected Brown for two years. The president rejected a full term because he planned to retire in 1951 at the age set by the college retirement plan. The directors recommended reelection because the institution had progressed, Christian principles had been upheld and Brown's experience was especially prized at this critical time. The *Concordian* extended congratulations, pledged support and reported that the spirit of unity, though still imperfect, was returning.[13]

The terms of this settlement suggest an artful compromise aimed at reconciling the deep divisions of warring factions. The president saved face by being reelected and by publicly declaring when he would retire. Moreover, he was allowed to leave office at the standard age set forth in the college retirement plan and to preside over the sixtieth anniversary celebration of the college. Opponents were assured of a definite date for Brown's departure and that the institution would have new leadership in 1951. This delicate arrangement sufficiently reconciled differences for the school to avoid paralysis and to carry on its work. Nevertheless, the incident left a residue of hostility and damaged public support; fears of a recurrence haunted administrators for a long time.

Although criticized for resisting change, President Brown actually initiated and accepted (sometimes grudgingly) many innovations. He requested information from Saint Olaf in 1947 before proceeding with plans to reorganize the board of directors. He wanted a procedure for obtaining more competent and active members. The board was restructured in 1949 with the creation of three new committees—finance, building and education. Membership expanded to twenty-seven with inclusion in 1951 of three women, the District Women's Missionary Federation presidents. Ministerial influence remained strong, with nine members (33 percent).[14]

Meanwhile the president reluctantly accepted the first faculty constitution, characterized by Dean Peter Anderson as "democratic to the point of being unworkable"; it created a faculty senate and provided that the faculty should establish institutional rules and regulations. By 1949 a student-faculty forum, comprised of the twelve student cabinet members and twelve elected faculty, had been created. One of the most important structural changes to emerge from Brown's administrative crisis, the forum institutionalized the legitimate expression of grievances; it discussed campus activities and made recommendations to the administration.[15]

Buildings and Finances

Expecting its postwar enrollment to exceed 1,000, Concordia needed desperately to build. Long hampered by an inadequate physical plant, the college in 1945 announced a million-dollar building program that included a gymnasium, library and men's dormitory. Enrollment dictated that the dormitory be built first. Women had taken over the three existing residence halls during the war; with demobilization the number of men attending under provisions of the GI Bill was expected to increase dramatically. Accordingly, the corporation in November 1945 authorized use of endowment funds to construct a $300,000 building, housing 191 men when it opened in 1947. Designed by architect William Ingemann in the English Gothic style and built of Kasota stone, the structure followed the plan for campus construction he had begun with Fjelstad Hall.[16]

Meanwhile, officials took other steps to relieve the housing crunch. In 1945 the college had purchased the G.L. Gosslee residence at 709 Eighth Street South. Intended to be the president's home, it became a women's dormitory and then a home management house before it was occupied by President Joseph Knutson in 1951. When 940 enrolled in Fall 1946 civic clubs helped find rooms in private homes for 350 Cobbers. The college rented a large house near campus as quarters for twenty-five women. Double bunks were set up in the gymnasium for sixty veterans; they lived in what they called "Paradise Hall" until the men's dormitory was completed. That same fall, the Federal Housing Authority provided ten trailers which were parked by North Hall and fifteen two-family barracks units which were located on the southwest corner of campus. Another barracks erected at the same time housed seventy-two veterans;

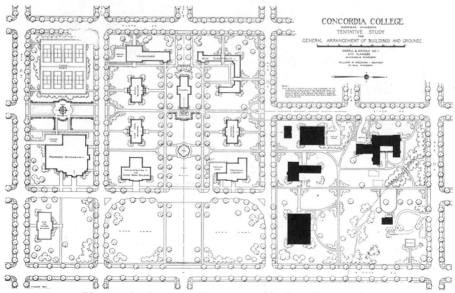

Plans projecting expansion appeared in the college catalog.

Boe's Bunkhouse/Cobber Hall housed veterans before it became a classroom and office unit.

initially named "Boe's Bunkhouse" in honor of Dean of Men Victor Boe, it later became Cobber Hall, a classroom and office unit.[17]

Additional construction followed. An expanded campus required a larger heating capacity. Fortunately the Federal Works Agency (FWA), as part of the veterans training program, donated a four-boiler heating plant and building which was installed at its present location in 1947. That same year the FWA made available four hospital units from a Sioux Falls air base; when joined together these provided a science building with badly needed space for biology and chemistry. Because the men's residence hall occupied the former football field, a new one was prepared. Supervised and built by the personal labor of Athletic Director Jake Christiansen and his crew over the course of two summers, a tiled gridiron, a cinder track and graded playing areas were dedicated at homecoming in 1947. Thus more than two decades after President Aasgaard had purchased the sixty-five acre Lamb property, the college finally took its initial step toward translating an old dream of a large athletic grounds into reality.[18]

Construction of a new music hall and library were delayed in order first to build an auditorium-field house. This decision was severely criticized at the time. Many maintained that the proposed structure was too large and expensive. Others objected to placing athletics, which had no cultural and educational value, above a library—the center

A new heating plant, required by an expanded campus.

of education and culture. Although the faculty agreed that for these reasons a library should be the next project, they believed the gymnasium should have priority. By combining an auditorium, gymnasium and field house under one roof, its versatility promoted community and met a number of other pressing institutional needs. The large auditorium seated the entire student body at chapel; athletic and music events could be returned to campus instead of being scheduled in the Moorhead Armory or the junior high school; and church conventions could be hosted during the summers.[19]

Approved in January 1950, construction began in August on a facility capable of seating 6,500. Jake Christiansen is credited with insisting on the large size which proved extremely fortunate in the long run. Almost four decades passed before the institution outgrew the building. Brown hoped it would crown his presidency and Concordia's sixtieth anniversary. Collapse of the steel superstructure during an April windstorm doomed him to disappointment. Arguments over insurance claims and liability delayed completion until December 1952.

Amidst the flurry of planned and actual construction, Cobbers in 1947 proposed a student union to provide badly needed recreational facilities on campus. The alumni adopted a resolution urging construction and created a planning committee. This effort went nowhere. Nonetheless, the desire did not disappear. Students suggested in May 1951 that the old gymnasium be converted into a union. The administration rejected their proposal and made plans to remodel the building for the art department.[20] This would be the fate of all Cobber requests for a central union in the next quarter century; they lost out to other priorities as Concordia strained its financial resources to construct classroom, dormitory, library and administration buildings to keep pace with surging enrollment. Instead of a centralized structure, dispersed recreational facilities were located in several newly constructed dormitories.

Funding rapid postwar expansion proved difficult. Just how difficult is revealed by the fact that in addition to capital improvements undertaken in a period of high inflation, current expenditures more than doubled in three years from $349,698 (1946) to $832,000 (1949). This necessitated additional income from several sources: private gifts, the church, tuition and, unexpectedly, the federal government. Indeed, federal assistance enabled the private higher education alternative to survive these hard times. Even with increased income the college ran a deficit in Brown's last year, breaking his remarkable record of successfully balanced budgets under perilous financial circumstances.[21]

Initially, Concordia attempted to obtain needed monies through general appeals. The Golden Jubilee Campaign paid the $120,000 Fjelstad Hall bond and raised an additional $70,000. Another drive, begun in 1945 with a goal of $1,000,000, yielded only $456,214 for the Memorial Fund. Private gifts supplemented these dollars. In the most generous received, the Alfred Hvidsten family gave $60,000 toward completion of a $100,000 music hall. Given the many needs created by post-war expansion, these terms could not be met until 1963 when Hvidsten Music Hall was constructed. As he had done previously, President Brown again offered ideas for increasing private giving. He suggested reviving the Greater Concordia Association with substantially increased annual contributions ranging from $25 to $500, and he urged congregations to hold Concordia Sundays. The association was revived, but at the level of $5 to $10 annual fees; only a limited number of congregations responded to the request for annual gifts. By 1947 there were signs that too many fund appeals were alienating the constituency. Brown nevertheless proposed another general college campaign for building funds; in 1949 the directors approved but later postponed this drive to avoid conflicting with the Evangelical Lutheran Church Christian Education Appeal.[22]

Although frustrated by this delay, Concordia's relations with the church generally improved with the better economic climate. A longstanding minor irritant had been removed by the board of education assuming the expense of auditing college accounts. Annual appropriations continued but their percentage value of total college expenses declined. For 1945–1946 the church appropriated $30,000 which covered 8.6 percent of institutional expenses. The appropriation increased to $44,583 for the next year but this comprised only 7.9 percent of expenses. For 1947–1948 the estimated appropriation of $30,000 made up only 4.7 percent of expenses. The church supplemented annual appropriations with additional gifts. Its Christian Education Appeal raised more than $1,500,000 in 1949, and in 1951 it distributed to college staff an additional $300,000 cost-of-living bonus.[23]

Tuition hikes provided yet another way to increase institutional income. Fearful that higher costs might diminish attendance, President Brown resisted raising rates.

Initially J.L. Rendahl, later joined by Carl Narveson, argued for sharp increases on the basis of rising costs and what other schools were doing. Higher fees in an inflationary period, they insisted, would not decrease enrollment. Their view eventually prevailed and proved correct. A modest $10 annual tuition increase for 1946–1947 was followed by a 43 percent enrollment jump from 660 to 945. The following year's large $70 hike did not prevent a 28 percent gain. Another $20 jump accompanied yet another 9.2 percent advance. There were no further hikes during Brown's tenure; as veterans graduated and others were drafted for the Korean War, enrollment dropped from its postwar high of 1,316 (1948–1949) to 973 (1950–1951).[24]

Although collegians kept coming, they did suggest that the institution offset rising costs by awarding more scholarships and raising campus wages. Of course, this could not be done unless the college found new funding sources and more funds. Despite strenuous efforts and substantial income growth from private gifts, church appropriations and tuition, the college needed even more funds for construction. Fortunately for the institution, the federal government was forthcoming in meeting some of these physical plant and equipment needs.

Federal assistance for a private college administered by officials suspicious of federal aid to education is doubly ironic. As Dean Peter Anderson warned a congressman, funds distributed by federal agencies might lead to national totalitarianism in education. Federal aid to individuals as provided by the GI Bill averted such dangers, however. Well might Anderson make an exception for the GI Bill. The college benefited substantially from this legislation. From 1946 through 1949, federally subsidized veterans comprised approximately 31 percent of the student body. Their proportion declined to 18.5 percent (1949) and then to 10.1 percent (1950). In addition to ample student aid, the college received large federal grants in the form of buildings and equipment. The heating plant and science hall came as war surplus gifts under the Federal Works Agency program to assist veterans training. Wary administrators could thus comfort themselves by viewing these gifts as another form of aid to individuals. Valued at $500,000, the donations

The new Science Hall made possible by timely federal aid.

were indeed considerable. To cover moving and erection costs Concordia raised $150,000 from private sources. Cobber Hall and individual family units, valued at $135,000, were additional war surplus given to house veterans. The physics and other science departments also shared with other Minnesota colleges and industrial high schools in the distribution of $600,000 worth of specialized war surplus electronics equipment.[25]

Federal gifts, valued at more than $630,000, almost equaled funds raised from private sources in the postwar period (1945–1951). The buildings given, moreover, were desperately needed and were utilized by the institution for many years. The heating plant is still used; the "temporary" science hall served more than three decades. The housing units survived through the 1950s as homes for faculty and Cobber Hall lasted as a classroom and faculty office building until 1969. It is not unfair to say that aid from the federal government enabled Concordia to cope with and substantially eased strains of the postwar crisis of growth.

The postwar crisis of growth generated considerable excitement on the campus. As Sigurd Mundhjeld noted in Summer 1947, the place hummed with activity. He did not recall a time when the college had been involved in so many projects. The men's dormitory, science hall and heating plant were almost completed. The hospital and football field had been moved. Moreover, many faculty were personally involved in these physical changes. Jake Christiansen and students constructed the athletic field. Al Eliason headed a student paint and repair crew who worked on all the old buildings. Dr. Skalet painted the windows of Fjelstad Hall. Kon Lee and Art Sanden did the concrete work for extending the cafeteria into the basement of Grose Hall (present Bishop Whipple).[26]

Even with savings from using faculty-student crews for minor repairs, major remodeling and construction generated costs higher than income. Consequently the college ran an $18,554 deficit in President Brown's last year, ruining his perfect record of balanced budgets; it faced even more red ink for 1951–1952. These deficits stemmed partly from shrinking enrollments brought on by the Korean War and partly from extra remodeling expenses. The Gosslee home was altered from home management house to president's residence and Cobber Hall was changed into classrooms and faculty offices. The administration did not consider this shortfall a matter of undue concern. To cover it, they requested the directors to find individuals willing to loan money for two years at 3 percent. Eventually, they planned to appeal to congregations for funds to eliminate the deficit.[27]

Academic Life

A loyal faculty, willing to work long hours for little pay and to make extra sacrifices, contributed greatly to balancing budgets and to meeting the crisis of growth. After the war salaries were low, a heritage of the financial exigencies of the Great Depression. As Brown explained to a county treasurer seeking employment: "I am sure you realize that salaries in our church colleges are considerably lower than they are in political or commercial fields." If salary did not attract people to church colleges, what did? Brown explicitly stated the religious motive: "One needs to have a great deal of interest in the work of the Kingdom to accept positions in church colleges." This religious commitment enabled Concordia to survive the difficult economic times of depression and war. Thus faculty salaries in 1946–1947 were at about the same level that they had been twenty years earlier. At $3,600 plus house, Brown was highest paid. Amy Erickson, cafeteria manager, received $3,535 plus board. Department heads earned $2,700. The average monthly salary for males was $290; females were paid $218.[28]

A housing shortage and inflation aggravated the problem of low salaries. Moorhead experienced a postwar boom; its population reached 14,870 in 1950, a 56.7 percent gain in the decade. With most of the increase coming after the war, a housing shortage developed, making it very difficult for newly hired teachers. Concordia coped by renting college-owned houses and the recently vacated Quonsets of graduated veterans. Monthly rents of $30 to $35, about one-third the commercial rate, made this appealing for newcomers, however unattractive they found the housing when they arrived. Carl Narveson, one of the fortunate in 1947–1948, paid $35 monthly rent for a college house and $170 and $175 annually for utilities and coal respectively. A large garden enabled the Narvesons to can many fruits and vegetables. High inflation rates necessitated such economies. President Brown complained in 1947 that the cost of living had risen 60 percent since 1939. Thus to maintain their real income, department heads should be paid $800 more than they were. Inflation did not disappear, as the outbreak of the Korean War in June 1950 triggered a 20 percent jump in cost of living by year's end. Living costs were twice as high in 1951 as they had been in 1940.[29]

To offset inflation the college and the church attempted to give cost-of-living increases, budgets permitting. The directors, apparently not believing that two can live as cheaply as one, awarded monthly raises of $10 for marrieds and $5 for singles at the end of 1942. As salary bonuses to be distributed in December and April, the board appropriated an additional $14,000 in 1946 and another $28,000 in 1948. In 1951 the Evangelical Lutheran Church distributed to its colleges an extra $300,000 earmarked for salaries. Even with these raises and economies similar to those practiced by the Narvesons, many professors sought summer employment. Some worked for the institution, an additional sacrifice and inconvenience according to H.M. Dale, but he was pleased to have faculty paint and repair "because they can be depended on to do the right thing, having the interest of the college at heart."[30]

Fringe benefits were undeveloped in 1945. Sick leave and disability did not exist. If teachers became ill, department colleagues took their classes. For any prolonged absence, the professor secured and paid a substitute. Adoption of the Teachers Insurance Annuity Association (TIAA) Insurance and Pension Plan in 1947 was a major step forward and part of a national trend in higher education stimulated by the psychological and economic insecurities of the Great Depression. Initially, faculty and the college each contributed 6 percent. Due to earlier fears that the federal government might dominate colleges and universities, social security coverage for professors did not begin until January 1, 1951; at that time, Concordia reduced TIAA to 4½ percent to allow for a 1½ percent payment to social security. Some faculty had requested increasing the contribution to 7½ percent but President Brown balked; he did not think the institution could carry the added cost.[31]

Faculty worked hard for limited pay and benefits. They did not have individual offices or telephones. Some departments had their own room as an office for the entire staff; several professors had their own desks in a classroom where they counseled Cobbers. Others were compelled to use a conference room in the academic dean's office. Teaching loads remained heavy, varying from twelve to twenty hours. The standard was fifteen, but some teachers voluntarily assumed additional sections to accommodate rapidly climbing enrollments. Coaching, administrative and other supervisory duties reduced teaching assignments. Most departments were staffed by one or two people. The head selected textbooks for all sections and usually taught all advanced work; an assistant might teach the introductory classes. Teaching assignments could be varied as well as heavy. J. Walter Johnshoy and Herman Nordlie, longtime heads of philosophy and history respectively, perhaps hold the records for variety. Johnshoy listed twelve courses in five departments: Greek, Hebrew, philosophy, religion, and sociology. Nordlie offered eighteen in three: history, geography and political science.[32]

Despite limited pay for extensive work, professors found other ways to serve. "Faculty Fantasmagoria," a comedy program, was offered as an annual college benefit. Several loaned their personal savings at 3 percent to Concordia. Less expensive for the school than bank loans, these helped meet short-term institutional obligations and paid individuals a higher return than passbook savings. Those with substantial notes from the institution in 1946 included Mae Anderson, $1,600; H.M. Dale, $1,700; J.N. Brown, $2,050; and the Brennun sisters, $10,800.[33]

Busy faculty also found time for research, additional education, community service and even socializing. Norse Professor J.A. Holvik upset regional Viking enthusiasts when he questioned the authenticity of the Kensington rune stone found near Alexandria. Holvik argued that the stone had been "discovered" twice in a single year, the first time with no inscription, and that a preliminary draft existed for what had later been inscribed on the stone by its "discoverers." Other faculty carried on less controversial research which gained recognition outside the campus. In 1948 Reidar Thomte, recently hired as professor of philosophy and soon to become an internationally recognized authority on the Danish theologian and philosopher Sören Kierkegaard, published his first book, *Kierkegaard's Philosophy of Religion*. That

Coach Jake Christiansen, 1949 Clay County Man of the Year.

same year, physics professor Carl Bailey published an article in *Physical Review* and the following year was featured in the *American Journal of Physics* for using high-speed motion pictures to portray experiments considered too dangerous for classroom use. Those gaining recognition in 1950 included Dr. Allen L. Hanson, professor of chemistry, awarded a grant for metal plating study and Ruth Berge, assistant professor of organ, granted a scholarship for study in Norway. Others engaged in political and community activity. Economics instructor Roy Tollefson in 1948 became the Ninth District chairman of the Progressive Party, organized to support presidential candidate Henry Wallace. Jake Christiansen in 1949 was named Clay County Man of the Year for his accomplishments in youth work, developing a new athletic field and planning a field house.[34]

Amid these diverse faculty activities, the administration nurtured community through regular meetings. At the opening of school each fall, the staff assembled in the North Lounge of Fjelstad Hall for devotions, words from the president and an address by a guest speaker; the president's reception and dinner followed in the cafeteria that evening. Throughout the year, they met semimonthly to discuss faculty papers on academic issues and to act on committee reports. And they gathered monthly just for socializing. Events included fall and spring picnics; a congressional speaker; the annual Christmas dinner; art, literature and music nights; and a costume party.[35]

Where did the college find people willing to do so much for so little? The task was complicated by rapidly rising attendance that dictated quickly hiring relatively large numbers. At the same time, replacements were needed for several valued staff lost to death. Carl B. Ylvisaker passed away in 1945 after a lingering illness. Dr. Johnshoy died of a heart attack in a dentist's chair at the beginning of the academic year in 1947.

The following spring, Dr. Mae Anderson expired from leukemia. A heart attack in April 1950 claimed A.M. Sattre, head of biology.[36]

To replace these dedicated individuals and to find needed new teachers, the institution—as in the past—relied on the Lutheran network and insisted on religious criteria. The dean of instruction and the president interviewed candidates and sometimes consulted department heads. Because so many were needed, standards were simplified: Applicants must be professed Christians and must be academically qualified. The first was more important than the second. Although the president recognized that "no amount of piety will atone for a weak academic," he justified religious and moral requirements for employees because "the Christian College should be different." After all, the primary purpose of a Christian College "is to win and hold souls," to produce "full time workers for the Kingdom and an enlightened lay leadership for our congregations."[37]

Lutherans were still preferred, but if unavailable the college quietly ignored an earlier requirement that faculty be Lutheran and hired professing Christians with good character references. Yet times were changing. On the one hand, administrators could be deceived. An economics instructor with excellent papers assured the dean and president, "I am a true believer." He turned out to be "a true believer in nothing." On the other hand, even good Lutherans now questioned moral requirements. An alumnus bluntly stated that as a student he had not agreed with college prohibitions against dancing and card playing. He now drank occasionally, considered being able to play bridge a social asset and might spend Sunday mornings in a duck blind or trout stream. The administration appreciated the candidate's "fine frankness," insisted on maintaining moral standards and offered a contract. The candidate signed with an understanding that he would support college policy if made democratically and if allowed to maintain his intellectual integrity when he did not agree.[38]

This episode is significant for what it suggests about future disharmony; it reveals a growing generational difference in Lutheran moral beliefs that increased existing tensions on the staff. Despite the president's efforts at community building, longtime professors were often bitterly at odds. The new generation added to these tensions by challenging what they regarded as the obstructionist tactics of the administration and by objecting to a moral sensibility that distinguished between "square games," which were permitted, and "square dancing," which was not.[39]

The faculty expanded from thirty-nine to seventy-two members. The proportion of women increased from 30.8 percent (1945) to 41.7 percent (1950). In the latter year, one-half were concentrated in three departments: music (six); English (five); language (four). Sixty percent were instructors, up from 33 percent in 1945; 30 percent were assistant professors, down from 41.6 percent. Among male faculty, 52.4 percent held the rank of professor, 26.2 percent were assistant professors and 14.3 percent were instructors. The percentage of Ph.D.s had increased slightly from 10.3 percent (four faculty including one female) to 12.5 percent (nine males).[40]

The status of faculty women reflected widely held social attitudes. Traditional beliefs about women's social role were often expressed on campus. Throughout these years, the *Concordian* regularly published pictures and announcements of engagements. This headline—"Cupid Plays Santa ... And No Exchanges Reported"—announced ten Cobber betrothals in January 1951. Even when the *Concordian* urged women to enter the nontraditional field of chemistry it employed traditional arguments in justification: Women should study biochemistry because they are particularly interested in the chemistry of life; women should study chemistry because they are in demand as technical research assistants, chemical technicians, laboratory workers, stenographers and scientific writers.[41]

This discussion about openings in science proved symptomatic as women's opportunities and interests declined in the first postwar decade. From all sides came pressures for American college women to prove themselves as wives and mothers. Nationally, the number of female academics and medical doctors decreased. Of those educated women who worked outside the home, most remained employed in the traditional female occupations of teaching, nursing and social work. Smaller percentages of women relative to men enrolled in graduate and undergraduate schools but they did gain in absolute numbers. The pattern at Concordia is somewhat similar. The average female enrollment increased dramatically from 223 in the 1930s to 521 for the postwar period while the percentage relative to men rose slightly from 47.6 to 48.9. Meanwhile the average number of female graduates grew from forty-five to seventy-four while the percentage dropped from 51.3 to 47. Other small signs of changes in women's status mingled with expressions of traditionalism; at the February 1951 directors meeting, women board members participated for the first time.[42]

As the student body grew and became more diverse, new demands were placed on the library and the curriculum. Although the library collection expanded from 30,083 volumes in 1945 to 36,337 in 1950, the facility itself could not grow. The main reading room in Fjelstad Hall basement seated only 125, a small fraction of the 1,316 enrolled in 1948–1949. Clearly the school needed a larger library, but other projects delayed construction until 1954. The academic program in 1951 consisted of twenty-two departments offering thirty-one majors and minors. Most departments listed both except for majors only in home economics and business education, and minors only in education and physical education.[43] Curricular trends continued those begun in the 1930s: expansion of community service, the social sciences and vocational programs.

Service is evident in the hosting of conferences and in the attempt to obtain a ROTC (Reserve Officer Training Corps) program. Both expressed a traditional Christian commitment to service which fostered a desire for practical training and vocationalism in the curriculum. Business education head Ivan Larson hosted the first commerce teachers workshop in 1948; these are still held annually. Concordia also hosted two annual Lutheran Rural Life Institutes that emphasized the role of the church in changing rural communities. Besides attempting to serve its region, the college expressed an interest in national service with its application for a ROTC unit in Fall 1950. Desire to provide Christian leadership and to perform patriotic duty were given as reasons for this application. Worry about maintaining enrollment during the Korean War draft and an opportunity for obtaining this form of federal aid to offset a possible decline also played a role. When the Air Force rejected the application, Cobbers were informed that they need not be in ROTC to remain in college.[44]

Community service and vocationalism combined to continue an earlier trend of expanding social science offerings. "Historical Geography" had been added as a war-related course in 1943; by 1947 geography was listed as a separate department. Taught for many years, sociology finally attained separate departmental status in 1945, first offered a major in 1946 and listed an interdepartmental socio-psychology major in 1948. The emergence of sociology as a separate department coincided with the church giving more attention to Christian social work. Already in 1945 a Social Welfare Conference held at Concordia emphasized job opportunities in the field and urged students to think seriously of social work as a profession. That same year, recognizing the growing demand for full-time Christian workers, the school outlined a four-year course with double majors in sociology and religion. A social work minor developed more slowly. By 1948 "Fields of Social Work" and "Public Welfare," which addressed general problems of society, were taken the first year. The second year focused on problems of the individual. "Introduction to Casework" featured on-the-job training with local welfare agencies in helping the poor.[45]

Vocationalism—training Cobbers for a particular service to society—is also evidenced in programs for nursing, elementary and parish education. Proposed in 1941, nursing had finally been established by 1945. A five-year course leading to a bachelor of science, it combined liberal arts work given at Concordia with professional courses taken at Minneapolis Fairview Hospital. In 1950 the program was discontinued indefinitely by Fairview because enrollments from Concordia and Saint Olaf had been too small to warrant special courses. Concordia remained interested in nursing education and by 1951 had resurrected a four-year program with half completed on campus and the remainder at an accredited hospital training school. A numerically more important vocational opportunity became available to Cobbers when the institution inaugurated its elementary education program in 1951. Due to the significant rise in birthrate that followed World War II and the emergence of the baby boomers, a shortage of elementary teachers had developed. To relieve this shortage, Minnesota in 1949 authorized elementary training at private colleges. Although regarded as "a friendly rival" by Moorhead State and cautioned by the Minnesota Division of Teacher Personnel not to prepare teachers with less than a baccalaureate, Concordia instituted two and four year courses. The shorter program provided teachers for North Dakota and Montana, areas that had long supported the college. Concordia provided another vocational opportunity by combining longstanding professional commitments to religion and education when Carl Narveson originated the courses, "Curriculum in Parish Education" and "Methods of Teaching in Parish Education." Narveson innovated in yet another way by creating a six-week non-credit course in the use of audio-visual materials for public and church school teachers.[46]

Cobbers welcomed these curricular steps toward vocationalism. Thus they viewed elementary education as "a long-awaited and much needed advancement" which not only increased their opportunities for jobs but, echoing the official justification for Christian education, gave area communities the "benefits of Christ-centered elementary teachers." Students even demanded more vocational training such as a journalism minor. As with other programs offered at a church school, the argument for journalism combined vocationalism with a religious rationale: Christian colleges should supply talented and trained writers for church periodicals.[47]

Besides applauding steps toward expanding student choices for vocational education, Cobbers attempted to influence the academic program by instituting a system for rating teachers at the end of each semester. Students believed there were too many faculty who did not teach; they hoped that ratings would promote better understanding between professors and collegians and improve instruction. Although this idea made faculty nervous, eventually the student-faculty forum in January 1951 endorsed the system and urged that faculty make greater use of it. Results from an instrument recommended by the dean of instruction were collected by professors and known only to them.[48]

Public Relations/Attracting Students

The faculty-rating episode demonstrated a new institutional sensitivity to student opinion. Another indication occurred in Autumn 1950 when thirty-one professors and collegians discussed student-faculty relationships at Paul's Resort near Battle Lake.[49] Well should the institution be sensitive to students because it remained heavily dependent on tuition income to finance its operations. Advertising played a crucial role in helping Concordia attract necessary numbers.

With the appointment of J.L. Rendahl as director of public relations, publicity became more professional. *The Record* added new features, furnished regular information about campus activities, and for a time devoted some issues to an *Alumni Magazine* that reported alumni news and views. In 1950 a new sign—designed and painted by Professor Cy Running—was erected on Highway 75, Moorhead's north-south artery running adjacent to the campus. Gold-lettered on maroon background and lighted so it could be viewed at night, the six-by-four-foot construction had a detachable part for announcing special events like homecoming. Newspaper advertisements and the catalog explained the college's need to restrict enrollment in 1946 and its plans for physical expansion in order to accommodate the many who wanted to attend. From 1946 onward, the catalog included sketches of the proposed field house and library and a tentative plan for the general arrangement of buildings and grounds (see p. 169). Developed by site planners Morell and Nichols and architect William Ingemann, this scheme showed a tract of twelve city blocks with the proposed gymnasium and library located on their present sites; another half dozen buildings were indicated—music, chapel, fine arts, administration-classroom, and two undesignated. Such emphasis on the physical did not exclude the spiritual themes of a Christian liberal arts education: "In an age of confusion Concordia proclaims the Christian as the only sustaining philosophy of life."[50]

As it had done before World War II made it impossible to obtain broadcast time, the institution relied heavily on the radio to make itself known. Responding to popular demand in 1946, Concordia resumed broadcasting chapel, G.L. Schoberg's Cobbercasts and the Christmas Radio Party over WDAY. That same year on the first and third Thursday monthly, KVOX broadcast half-hour Concordia band programs of classical pieces, novelty numbers and military marches. These were carried by stations in Fergus Falls, Aberdeen, Valley City, Jamestown, Devils Lake, Mandan, Bismarck, Minot, Williston and Sidney. KVOX continued these broadcasts for the next four years. Then in 1947 the Cobbercasts became a regular Saturday feature and the Concordia Radio Hour could be heard daily on Fargo FM Station KVNJ. By 1949, immediately following chapel broadcasts, KVNJ featured a daily five-minute newscast direct from the public relations office. Hundreds of cards and letters indicated considerable popular interest in these programs.[51]

Cobbers and their activities were utilized for publicity. Viewed as public relations agents to their home towns, students were urged to expound on the advantages of attending Concordia and to stress the school's most important aspect: "the firm foundation on which we stand—the Christian principles that underlie and influence campus activities." The *Concordian* asserted that "it is the policy of putting God first that makes Concordia different from other schools." Musical events offered another potent promotional device. The annual Christmas concert grew steadily in popularity. In 1947 an estimated 5,500 people attended three evening performances. By 1949 more than 7,000 packed the four concerts, which were called "outstanding" and

The 1950 Christmas Concert closed with massed choirs singing in front of the Cyrus Running mural.

"[high] caliber fine arts entertainment." Given the quality of musical organizations, it is understandable that the annual band and choir tours were viewed as an effective way of informing prospective collegians about the work of the school. This form of advertising soon extended beyond the region Concordia served. The board of directors proudly accepted an invitation in 1947 from *Nordmanns-Forbundet* (Norsemen's Federation) for the choir to tour Norway in Spring 1949. The directors accepted because they viewed it as a great opportunity for establishing an international reputation for the choir and the college.[52]

Postwar social trends rendered effective Concordia's extensive publicity efforts. Economic prosperity and the GI Bill made it possible for larger numbers to respond positively to institutional advertising. Consequently, Concordia's enrollment jumped 257 percent, from 513 (1944–1945) to 1,316 (1948–1949). At this time veterans comprised approximately 31 percent of those attending. Yet veterans were only part of this dramatic growth; even when their numbers declined to ninety-seven in 1950, the student body remained at 960, substantially above that of the Depression and World War II. This suggests that postwar prosperity enabled a higher percentage of the region's youth to attend college.[53]

Elsewhere expansion made Lutheran colleges more diverse, leading some to question whether less homogeneous campuses would still perform the traditional tasks of preparing clergy, training lay leadership for congregations and buttressing youthful faith. Indeed, the Evangelical Lutheran Church requested in 1948 that the board of education appoint a commission to visit and ascertain whether these tasks were still performed properly. In Concordia's case there seemed little cause for concern. The administration believed firmly that the institution should serve the church. Besides, growth did not produce much diversity; 91 percent were Lutheran and 75 percent were Evangelical Lutheran. Minnesotans and North Dakotans comprised 42.4 percent and 44.5 percent respectively. Of those responding to a questionnaire in 1948–1949, 40 percent came from farm homes, 5.9 percent were children of clergy and 17.9 percent originated from business families. That those from farm background had increased 8 percent since 1946 perhaps suggests that an improved farm economy and the trend toward larger farms both enabled and necessitated the attendance of more rural children. Thus Concordia played its role in the migration from farm to city. This fact, as well as returning veterans, helps account for the rapid postwar enrollment increase.[54]

A rapid increase in Concordia's fees evidently did not prevent growth. To keep pace with inflation, finance necessary physical expansion and cover its own rising expenses, Concordia raised its fees 26.8 percent. In 1945 the charges for room, board and tuition ranged from $410 to $460. By 1950 costs were $520 to $580. Apart from the significant financial assistance provided by the GI Bill, other forms of financial aid remained distinctly limited. Freshmen scholarships were awarded until 1950 when they were dropped. Juniors and seniors were eligible for loans from the college to help them complete their education. Conventional wisdom considered it too risky to make student loans before the last two years.[55]

Graduating classes increased from fifty-four (1946), a war-related low, to 250 (1950), a postwar high. Graduates of the postwar years from 1945 to 1951 represented 29 percent of the total Cobber baccalaureates. Among the alumni in 1946, 28.6 percent were educators; homemakers comprised 24.3 percent; religious work occupied 8.8 percent and the armed forces still claimed 12.9 percent. Although many came from the farm, only 1 percent of the graduates returned to agriculture. A number attended professional and graduate school: Twenty seniors (13.1 percent) in 1948 planned to enroll in Luther Theological Seminary; four in 1950 obtained graduate assistantships; and nine others in 1950 were admitted to medical school.[56]

Student Life

After the war, student life continued in the familiar channels of extracurricular activities and social life. Despite persistence of these traditional collegiate concerns, Cobbers became more assertive due to the presence of worldly veterans who chafed at the numerous restrictions imposed by a conservative church college. Although veterans shared the religious, regional and occupational backgrounds of the majority, their age and military experiences made the them less timid and more willing to question authority.

In student government, assertiveness took the form of new demands which essentially restated part of the liberal National Student Federation agenda: representation of student affairs in the administration, a collegian disciplinary board, voice in determining schedules and vacations and voice at faculty meetings. Despite assurances that they did not disagree with the Christian principles of the institution, had not suggested amending disciplinary rules and did not intend to take over the school, the administration delayed approving any changes. Cobbers complained about this peculiar form of democracy; the administration did as it pleased regardless of what students thought. Nonetheless, by April 1949 a new constitution was approved which adopted the new name of Concordia College Student Association, introduced a senate-commission system and provided for an executive council of president, vice-president, secretary, and treasurer. The president reported on senate business at a monthly student body meeting. Although the new constitution was hailed as an important step forward, apathy hindered its operation. *Concordian* editor Lloyd Svendsbye ('51) complained in March 1950 that the senate had not met since November 1949 for lack of a quorum. As a result, government through the executive council had reverted to the old student forum under a different name.[57]

Veterans enjoyed more immediate success with other changes they initiated. At their request in March 1946, cafeteria manager Amy Erickson instituted an evening lunch at the cafeteria that quickly became popular with other groups. Now a study break no longer needed to be the nightly trip downtown. Instead a light lunch—sandwiches, hot fudge sundaes, cake and coffee—could be obtained on campus. An electric phonograph furnished background music. A veterans' petition, ratified by a poll of the student body, resulted in an extended Thanksgiving vacation from Wednesday noon to Monday morning.[58]

Lloyd Svendsbye

Emulating veterans, others questioned restrictive policies. The special hours required for women created anomalies. Myrtle Rendahl recalled her first year on campus in 1945 when her six-year-old daughter went alone to the Dairy Queen after 7:00. The dean of women soon informed her about the serious difficulties this caused; coeds complained because a six-year-old could go out after 7:00 but they could not. Questioning the lights out policy for women, *Concordian* coeditors Helen Narveson ('50) and Peter Teisberg ('50) asked in 1949: How many rules are necessary for regulating human behavior? What is the best way to train Cobbers in standards of self discipline? They urged that the usual pattern of bullheaded students and authoritarian deans be avoided and that the issue be settled by frank, open and rational discussion. It was not; they were called to account for their opinion by the president and the policy did not change while Brown remained in office.[59]

An earlier concern about non-participation in religious organizations persisted into the post-war period. Enrollment doubled but attendance at religious functions did not. Raymond Farden ('47) assured readers of the *Concordian* that participation need not be limited to preachers' kids or pre-seminarians. All were urged to take part because everyone needed stimulation to advance spiritually; organized activity provided an opportunity for that advancement. Broader participation would help all Cobbers walk in the difficult way of Christ and end the undue friction between the "religious haves" and "have nots."[60]

In the aftermath of World War II, the Evangelical Lutheran Church demonstrated greater social concern that was reflected on campus in various ways. In 1945 Lutheran Welfare Days were observed at Concordia. The four-day program was designed to interest students in the field of social work. The following year another program was held to acquaint students with the activities of Lutheran World Action; this was part of a campaign to publicize the need for relief in European countries. Cobbers subsequently made collections of clothing for European relief.[61]

The choir and band resumed their normal concert tours at war's end. The 1949 Norway choir tour led by Paul J. Christiansen was a musical highlight, a critical success and a major boost for institutional pride. In its first international trip, the choir played to packed houses and warm receptions in thirty Norwegian cities. Upon its return, the organization enjoyed other major successes. During its eastern trip in 1951, a New York critic hailed the choir's Carnegie Hall Concert, crediting it with attaining "the ideal of perfect execution." Leif Christianson replaced Holvik as band director in 1949; because the 1933 uniforms were well worn, raising money for replacements became his first task. The Student Association made the band uniform drive an official project. The faculty and students held benefit carnivals in April and November 1950, helping raise $5,000. Faculty pledges included a waffle supper for eight by Anna Jordahl and Christina Fjelstad, a date with Roy Stahl and a Thanksgiving dinner for two at the Narvesons.[62]

1949 Norway choir tour aboard ship.

That year marked the beginning of extensive participation by supplementary instrumental groups. The brass ensemble became important in the annual Christmas program. The Cobber Band marched in parades and at homecoming half-times and it played at home basketball games. A student swing band, dedicated to appreciating the modern trend in music, appeared in 1945. Andy Van and His Band, "five brass, five saxes and three rhythms," played for college parties.[63] Cobbers were not allowed to dance, but were permitted to listen. Apparently the standards of Garrison Keillor's Leftfooted Brethren did not prevail; Cobbers were permitted to move and walk rhythmically.

The Women's Athletic Association continued to occupy a key position in the recreational life of females after the war. Roller skating and bowling were new activities. Another addition, the Cobberettes—a women's basketball team—played a total of six games with NDAC, MSTC and UND in 1949. By that time swimming had moved to the Fargo High pool; beginning, intermediate, advanced, and life saving classes were taught.[64]

Although football and basketball remained the major sports for men, postwar intercollegiate competition expanded significantly. In 1946 baseball returned after a two-year hiatus and in 1947 student Bob Bain ('50) reintroduced hockey after an absence of almost two decades. Golf and tennis teams were formed and track, having lapsed during the war, returned in 1948. Athletics occupied a central place in student life. Varsity letters were awarded in the last chapel of the year as they had been for many years. The prospect of losing seasons led some to demand even more emphasis on athletics. A 1948 editorial quoted Jake Christiansen: "We are have nots in a conference of haves." The editorialist urged increased financial support on the grounds that participation had educational value. Christiansen returned to this theme in 1950 as the plans for a new field house were finalized. The new facility would not solve Concordia's athletic problems, he warned. Better athletes were necessary to have winning teams. He urged students, the administration and the board of directors to cooperate in creating a modern athletic policy. The entire constituency should work to encourage outstanding Christian athletes to enroll.[65]

Coach Christiansen's plea brought several interesting responses. A Montana pastor warned that athletic success should not be defined by winning. A student complained that basketball practice was scheduled at the same hour as Bible study; the basketball time should be changed because a proper Christian education would put Christ first. On the other hand, Howard Wagner ('51) appealed to religion in justifying an increased athletic emphasis. He resorted to the familiar institutional rationale that it was the business of Concordia to train Christian leaders. There is need for Christian leadership in athletics, Wagner wrote, and the college is not filling that need with losing teams. Losing records would prevent communities from hiring Cobbers as coaches.[66]

In addition to attending or participating in athletics or music, other activities rounded out campus social life. The social commission in 1950 scheduled a Friday evening program of roller skating, movies and music. These all-campus activities were

The Phi Kappa Chi-Beta Tau Omega radio orchestra for a society program.

especially appreciated by Cobbers with flat pocketbooks. Societies declined during the war but rebounded strongly after victory. Four new societies were created in 1946 to accommodate additional students. Open houses, public programs and society competition all resumed. If these activities failed to entertain, there was always the communal ritual of work. By the 1940s, all Cobbers were dismissed to participate in the campus clean-up. Work crews headed by professors in 1948 did preliminary landscaping around new buildings, removed rubbish and raked lawns. Coeds now took another small step toward campus equality; they were issued rakes and allowed to participate in the physical labor of cleaning. Students regarded the clean-up as a fair trade: The college had the grounds cleaned at minimum expense and students had an afternoon free from class, the fun of working together and an opportunity to demonstrate pride in a well-kept campus. Complaints soon surfaced about lack of participation, however. Only 100 of 960 Cobbers took part in Spring 1950, leading editor Lloyd Svendsbye to assert, "Something is wrong with student body spirit if that's the kind of cooperation that we display toward student body activities." Perhaps the criticism helped; almost 40 percent worked the following year.[67]

A number of events stimulated campus intellectual life. Coffee conferences were scheduled each Monday afternoon during the early 1940s. These were generally popular although some freshmen and sophomores objected to an almost exclusive focus on national affairs;

Alpha Kappa Chi-Mondamin performed sections from the newspaper.

they requested more discussion of campus issues. In 1945 Concordia also joined with North Dakota Agricultural College to sponsor five "Talk of the Month" lectures.[68]

During World War II, the *Concordian* devoted little space to the discussion of domestic and international politics. Once victory was won and veterans flooded the campus, the paper resumed a lively discussion of these issues. As during the depression decade, the views of newspaper editors and writers probably were not representative of the student body as a whole. The *Concordian* frequently lamented "provincial Cobbers" who were interested almost exclusively in campus events. Returning veterans were acutely aware of this provincialism; it was their presence that largely explains the paper's considerable postwar interest in national and international politics. Imbued with a new global perspective, in 1946 *Concordian* editor Vee Thorkelson ('46) reminded "provincial Cobbers" of their responsibilities as world citizens. They should be informed; they should combat intolerance and prejudice; and they should support organizations like the international relations club that aimed to promote friendly relationships with humans everywhere.[69]

Besides the substantial influence of veterans, campus discussion of current events reflected new political forces revealed in the election of 1944. North Dakota isolationist Gerald P. Nye was defeated. Although isolationism remained a force in North Dakota politics, it was less evident at Concordia. Other political trends that surfaced were bipartisan accord on major aspects of Roosevelt's programs, the power of organized labor and greater reliance on public opinion polls.[70]

The Cobber Poll—conducted during 1946–1947 by David Brown ('48)—embodied the new trends. Brown surveyed student opinion on a number of domestic and international issues. Domestically, labor union power preoccupied the American public as strikes increased proportionally with postwar inflation. Accordingly, 82.4 percent of the 200 polled answered yes to the question—"Have the labor unions in general gained too much power in the United States?" On other labor-related issues, 64.3 percent opposed outlawing strikes; yet 57.4 percent wanted stronger labor legislation; and—partly due to unhappiness over strikes, high taxes and inflation—62.3 percent wanted a Republican majority elected in Congress.[71]

Most of the polls surveyed opinion on the foreign policy issues that absorbed the country and the Truman administration as the nation entered the Cold War. Only 13.6 percent agreed with Henry Wallace's famous foreign policy speech calling for a more cooperative policy toward the Soviet Union. That 40.8 percent did not know about the speech indicated that many Cobbers were not reading newspapers regularly. On the Nuremberg Trials, 64.9 percent did not think they had set a bad precedent. Many of Brown's questions focused on the United Nations: 86.3 percent agreed that the United Nations should be made stronger in order to keep world peace. Yet it apparently was not clear to Cobbers exactly how the United Nations should promote peace—63.1 percent did not think the organization should initiate a disarmament program at the present time; 58.7 believed that some plan of universal military training should be put into effect in the United States; only 47.1 percent thought it would improve relations with other nations if the United States stopped production of atomic bombs; and only 40.9 percent thought the veto of the five major powers should be abolished.[72]

Not surprisingly, many editorials reflected attitudes revealed in the Cobber polls and in the nation. A few advocated anti-strike legislation as a necessary step to curb the excessive power of labor. Others disagreed. Another argued that industrial strife would not cease until both sides recognized the Christian principle of loving your neighbor as yourself. Civil liberties also received attention: A few appealed to the constitutional principle of free speech in opposing a proposal to outlaw the Communist party; another supported the 1947 civil rights report calling for racial equality in the United States. In this struggle Cobbers were warned not to overlook prejudice and discrimination at home; on campus one often heard slighting references toward "niggers" and "Jews." On foreign policy, one editorialist supported Truman's "get tough" policies because the Soviets could not be trusted. On the other hand, a few recognized that the pursuit of self-interest by both major powers undermined the United Nations and perpetuated the Cold War; by retaining military control of Pacific islands for reasons of national security, the United States did not practice what it preached about supporting the United Nations.[73]

As noted by the *Concordian*, campus interest in domestic and international issues began to wane by 1950. Lloyd Svendsbye attributed this decline to the disappearance of veterans from campus. Former GIs, keenly interested in world problems, had been replaced by Cobbers characterized "by a kindly, apathetic attitude of quiet contentment [and] concern for the trivial." Even the Korean War did not end this "quiet contentment." Coeditors Clarice Foss ('51) and Howard Wagner did observe that the war had brought global problems into a private, little college world. Carl Zander ('50), serving in Korea, wrote a letter urging Americans to support the "Care for Korea" drive.[74]

But the last months of Brown's presidency did not exhibit any marked reawakening of Cobber interest in political issues. Apparently the complacent 1950s had already begun at Concordia.

President Brown Retires

The search for President Brown's successor began almost immediately after his election to a two-year term in 1948. There was a strong sense of urgency and opportunity. It had long been expressed that with the right kind of leadership the college could move forward into a bright future; hence the early start in the search for a new president.

It was not easy to find Brown's successor. The faculty elected a committee to confer with the directors and representatives from the board of directors met with the church board of education to discuss the process of selection. By May 1950 the directors had nominated Dr. George Aus, a professor of systematic theology at Luther Theological Seminary since 1939. When Aus declined, the corporation in October unanimously elected Dr. Alvin M. Rogness, a Mason City pastor, who was described as "one of the profoundest minds of contemporary Lutheranism, a capable writer and a speaker with a unique gift, and a man equipped by God to deal with young people and to make a lasting impression on the thinking of youth." After a campus visit in late November Rogness also returned the call.[75]

Why these rejections? Perhaps the bitterness produced by the attempt of the Concordia Volunteer Committee to remove President Brown still lingered. Perhaps the widespread rumors of factionalism made the job appear undesirable. Perhaps too the candidates were discouraged by the obviously great physical needs and equally limited financial resources of the institution. After two major disappointments, Concordia was indeed fortunate that the third choice, Rev. Joseph Knutson, accepted in May 1951. A forty-five year-old Saint Olaf and Luther Theological Seminary graduate, Knutson's background as a college pastor in Minneapolis and Ames and his popularity as a Bible camp lecturer and speaker qualified him for the presidency.

President Brown left office in Summer 1951. That year's *Cobber*, dedicated to Brown, praised "his leadership, his patience, and above all his humbleness." The faculty conferred an honorary Doctor of Laws and the directors named the new men's dormitory John Nikolai Brown Hall. Board President Selmer Berge praised Brown for his strong spiritual leadership, for maintaining "an unusually deep, pious, conservative, Lutheran Christian spiritual tone" and for keeping Concordia a safe place to send youth. Brown, in his turn, reminded the board of its responsibilities to the school's spiritual mission. If the directors kept the college in "those time-tested practices and policies which have made Concordia a truly Christian College," then "you may be assured of God's continued blessings upon your work."[76]

To help the former president qualify for social security, the college in 1951 employed him to solicit funds at a single-year salary of $4,800. Provided with living quarters in Brown Hall, he elected instead to live in a Quonset. He did not want to retire in Moorhead, and he wanted employment to occupy his time. During his last year at the college, Brown considered his possibilities. He sought unsuccessfully a position with Saint Olaf as an administrator of its Oslo Summer Session. He spent several weeks in California visiting his oldest son and a sister. He considered taking charge in April 1952 of an All-Lutheran Bible Camp on a five-month trial basis. Upon leaving Concordia in July 1952, he was paid a $200 monthly annuity for life. By September he had settled in Minneapolis where he promised to "loaf for awhile" and accept only a reasonable number of speaking engagements. He soon began working as an independent "Consultant and Director of Fund-Raising Projects."[77]

When President Brown retired he had many critics. Moorhead businessmen complained that the college did not do enough business on Main Street. New faculty charged that the president had made promises he did not keep about housing and research money.[78] These faults notwithstanding, Brown had given the institution twenty-six years of distinguished service. During his tenure, he had maintained the school's spiritual tone and Concordia had experienced considerable material expansion in spite of most unfavorable economic conditions. The student body increased from 275 to 960; $2 million was raised for endowment and buildings; several buildings—Fjelstad (1937), Home Economics (1938), Brown (1946), Science (1947), Heating Plant (1947)—were erected. Until it was delayed by an "ill wind," he hoped the Memorial Gymnasium-Auditorium would crown his presidency. By securing an endowment and North Central accreditation, by maintaining enrollment in the hard times of depression and war and by obtaining the necessary buildings quickly after 1945, Brown could rightly claim that he had laid the economic foundation for Concordia's subsequent expansion.

PART III

President Joseph L. Knutson, 1951–1975:

Managing Growth and
Maintaining Christian Integrity

"The superscription of the cross is over Concordia and every Christian college. I can think of no better delineation of the place, purpose, and program of Concordia than the Christ of the Cross, with the superscription proclaiming that He is King in every area of life."
— *Joseph L. Knutson (1951)*

"No matter what curriculum we offer, we must never permit it to be merely vocational. To do so would be a betrayal of the mission of the college and a betrayal of the best interests of those who look to us for education. To those who argue that we haven't time to broaden a course of study, we ought to answer that we can't afford not to broaden it; for technical training, no matter how thorough, and no matter in what field, is not enough."
— *Carl Bailey (1957)*

"The purpose of Concordia College is to influence the affairs of the world by sending into society thoughtful and informed men and women dedicated to the Christian life."
— *Blueprint (1962)*

"Just what is a Christian liberal arts education? Christian education is God's hand through Christ reaching into every subject and area of life to bring completeness, His fullness and love to mind, body, and spirit and to give life the wholeness it craves."
— *Cobber, 1963*

"If the Concordia family and constituency had not been so wonderful, we would never have been permitted to serve for twenty-four years. We have had to face crises, opposition, disappointments, unrest and rebellion, just as other college administrators have. Yet, under God, Concordia had a faculty, student body, and constituency that never let the college veer from the course her charters had mapped out. There was always a majority who insisted that Concordia be true to her motto, 'Soli Deo Gloria.'"
— *Joseph and Beatrice Knutson, Christmas 1974*

Chapter 11

"Prexy Joe" Takes Charge

The New President

Joseph L. Knutson, the man who became "Prexy Joe," never intended to be anything other than a parish pastor. Consequently, when Rev. Jacob Stolee invited him to dinner at the Curtis Hotel in Minneapolis, Knutson suspected nothing. Upon arrival, he was surprised to find Rev. Erling Jacobson of Moorhead's Trinity Lutheran Church and Arthur P. Diercks, executive director of the Moorhead Chamber of Commerce. He was even more surprised when these representatives of the board of directors informed him that he had been nominated for the presidency of Concordia College. Subsequently, the corporation at its April 17 meeting unanimously voted to call Knutson for a six-year term, beginning July 1, at a salary of $5,000 with a free house and utilities. Knutson was floored by this opportunity. As he recalled many years later, "When the call came I concluded that it must have been the work of the Holy Spirit; never in my wildest dreams or most unbridled ambition had I ever given thought to such a post."[1]

President Joseph L. Knutson

The post was not particularly desirable, as Knutson quickly discovered. Not having seen Moorhead or Concordia College, he wisely visited before accepting. Although it was a lovely day, the lack of beauty disappointed him. It had been a wet spring. An unpaved Seventh Street ran south from the campus through a desolate residential area where streets, sidewalks and houses were being

A small Concordia and an empty south Moorhead greeted Knutson.

constructed. Knutson had never seen so much mud. He was so discouraged that he wanted to leave immediately but did not because he had promised to meet the board. At that meeting, he was offered complete authority to name administrative staff and faculty. Knutson recognized that Concordia had a natural constituency in the strongly Lutheran Red River Valley, a strong faculty with many talented people and institutional vitality. After all, many enrolled despite meager facilities. Fortunately for Concordia, Knutson accepted. After rejections by two previous candidates, the institution breathed a collective sigh of relief. As Dean Peter Anderson reported reaction to the news: "Everyone ... is very happy, as he seems to have qualities desired in a president."[2]

The new president had roots in the valley. Born the son of a Hauge Synod minister in Grafton, North Dakota, in 1906, his family moved in 1908 to Radcliffe, Iowa, for a decade before resettling in Jackson, Minnesota. After graduation from Jackson High School, Knutson attended Saint Olaf College, graduating in 1927. In 1930 he received a bachelor of divinity degree from Luther Theological Seminary, married Beatrice Olson, and took a mission church in DeKalb, Illinois—a town hard-hit by the Depression. After two years, the Knutsons moved to a rural parish in Fillmore County, Minnesota and served five years before relocating in Lake Mills, Iowa. This particularly happy period was followed by a reluctant move in 1943 to Ames where Knutson became pastor of a college church, Bethesda Lutheran, and director of the Lutheran Student Association at Iowa State College. In 1948 he relocated in Minneapolis as pastor of University Lutheran Church of Hope. In addition, he served on the board of the University Lutheran Student Association and taught occasional courses at Luther Theological Seminary. Knutson's performance of these tasks attracted the attention of the Concordia board.[3]

The Knutson family pictured in their 1951 Christmas greeting.

When the corporation called Knutson it obtained more than a president; it secured a team. Beatrice, his spouse, became the gracious hostess for all official functions and guests of the college. She also provided important psychological support during difficult and discouraging times. As Knutson wrote during one such trial, "Beatrice has to give me a pep talk every once in a while, telling me to have faith and to believe that the Lord will vindicate the confidence put in Him."[4]

To prepare for his new vocation, Knutson visited other campuses and read their histories. Besides this willingness to learn and an intellectual curiosity evidenced by his wide reading in theology, history, philosophy and literature, he possessed other assets. His personality blended dynamic forcefulness with an unassuming, folksy charm. The charm was immediately displayed in his first letter to the faculty. "I am not used to giving orders to such an august body," he wrote. He then expressed hope that all would show up for the opening meeting of the academic year in order to assure him "that my being President of Concordia is not just a dream."[5]

This charm combined with personal magnetism and energy were essential for the successful exercise of his perceived role as president. As he explained to the faculty, "I was not called to Concordia because I'm a scholar or because I am an expert in education. ... I know I was called to be a promoter and that is what I'll try to do." As a promoter, Knutson believed that "a small college moves through its business office." He therefore cultivated the constituency by frequently addressing churches, service clubs and commencements in Fargo-Moorhead and the corporate territory. If small towns or congregations could not pay expenses or a fee, he willingly went for nothing. His speeches were delivered extemporaneously and did not hide his strong opinions and religious views. His energy, charm, speaking style and beliefs represented Concordia in a way that generated confidence in him and in the institution.[6]

Knutson always clearly expressed over and over throughout his presidency his conception of what a church college ought to be. He viewed himself as a pastor to the college family; and the pietism of his Haugean background led him to emphasize Concordia as a distinctive Christian community. As he wrote to Lutheran clergy in the territory when he assumed office, "My chief concern shall always be to keep Christ and His church preeminent in the policy and life of Concordia College."[7]

President Knutson's evangelical theology and his conservative ideology became the most important elements in his leadership style. Knutson's ideas were part of the tradition of cultural conservatism descended from the eighteenth century philosopher Edmund Burke. According to historian Ronald Lora, cultural conservatives adhere to several basic principles.They believe that humanity is dependent on God, religion provides the sole philosophical justification for morality and a providential plan governs society. This reliance on suprarational standards of conduct is necessitated by the inadequacy of human reason, social progress and the egalitarian emphasis of modern mass society. Although conservatives value freedom, it is viewed as a consequence of order and is subordinated to the ultimate ideal of social harmony. Property rights and laissez faire are similarly valued, but are limited by the principles of community and Christian virtue.[8]

These beliefs informed Knutson's conception of a Christian college. Again and again throughout his long tenure, he warned against the dangers of worldliness, affirmed an evangelical Lutheranism as the source for the standards of a distinctive Christian community and asserted that the gospel promoted true learning. Similarly, Knutson sounded the alarm against creeping statism and articulated a laissez-faire, free-market Republicanism limited by Christian principles. Knutson's conservative ideology gave Concordia a distinctive public image, easily identifiable in marshalling potential constituency support. But it was not so rigid that it hindered institutional development, as his flexibility on federal aid would demonstrate. By this ideology he built the constituency and shaped the college.

The new president's ideas emerged clearly in his inaugural address, "The Superscription of Concordia," delivered during homecoming in the Moorhead Armory on the Saturday morning of October 13. Knutson affirmed that the superscription of the cross is over Concordia and every Christian college because they proclaim that Christ is King in every area of life.Knutson articulated the implications of Christ's supremacy in the areas of religion, morality, politics and culture. Christ is the "basis for true religion ... not ... natural law and graduated ethical concepts." Indeed, Christianity claims that the redemptive work of Christ is the sole adequate motivation for right conduct. Moreover, only as the "light of Christ comes into individual lives is the social order transformed for the better." Knutson maintained that this had been demonstrated historically by the great social advances—women's rights, abolition of slavery, foreign missions, education and the rise of democracy.[9]

In politics, Knutson argued that modern democracy is the fruit of Christianity because Christianity had brought into life the conviction of the dignity and worth of all individuals. For present society, the gravest problem was how to preserve freedom of the individual in the midst of increasing complexity. The popular solution, much feared by conservative Republicans like Knutson, was more state control. Citing Arnold Toynbee, Knutson warned that the rise of super-states had destroyed civilizations in the past and would again by stifling creative minorities. Therefore, Christian colleges like Concordia must resist state pressures and seek to solve social complexities by educating more citizens motivated by the love of Christ.[10]

Culturally, "a Christian college believes that education, to be effective, must be connected with the Cross of Christ. In education alone there is no redemptive power." Affirming the centrality of Christ did not imply the rejection of secular learning, however. Using the Renaissance and Reformation as symbols for secular learning and Christianity respectively, Knutson argued that "the Renaissance ... needs the redemptive element of the Reformation and the Reformation needs the intellectual endowments of the Renaissance" because the "Renaissance by itself leaves man to be its own savior" and the Reformation without scholarship "makes life a fog of subjectivism."[11]

President Knutson's conservative ideology and leadership skills were immediately tested by the critical situation Concordia faced in 1951. Conditions seemed so poor that many advised him not to accept the presidency. Other Minneapolis pastors thought him crazy when he did and a friend wrote simply—"I admire your courage and offer my prayers." Indeed, Knutson recalls his acceptance as his most courageous act. The physical plant was inadequate. Many teachers did not have campus offices and the college did not have a library building. Music professors taught in North Hall, a wood-frame converted hospital built in 1893. And the steel superstructure for the new gym had collapsed April 14, completely stopping construction for several months as tangled legal issues were sorted out. An enrollment decline of 10 percent to 890 students, caused by a combination of the low depression birth rate and the draft for the Korean War, translated into a $60,000 loss of income at the same time the college faced a rising rate of war-induced inflation. Several key professors in English,

A collapsed field house posed Knutson's first problem.

history, Norse, economics and education who had served more than twenty-five years were due to retire. Low salaries needed to be raised to attract new faculty with Ph.D.s. That only 12 percent possessed doctorates threatened Concordia's North Central accreditation. Endowment remained at less than $600,000, the amount raised by the 1926 campaign, and gift income had been often negligible and always unstable.[12]

As a further complication, Howard Johnshoy resurfaced. President Brown's former nemesis had earned a Ph.D. in university administration, campaigned for the nomination as president and now expressed interest in the deanship when septuagenarian Peter Anderson retired. Moreover, he criticized the decision to create an elementary teacher's education program and to include Women's Missionary Federation district presidents as members of the board. Assured by Brown that this old problem was not serious, Knutson bluntly informed Johnshoy that some of his suggestions were "unsympathetic" and "unrealistic." This sufficed; Johnshoy vanished from Concordia annals to become a professor and eventually dean of academic affairs at Gustavus Adolphus College. After his death in a plane crash in South Vietnam, the Johnshoy family in 1968 endowed two annual memorial scholarships for father J. Walter and son Howard.[13]

However committed the family to the welfare of the college, the memory of the turmoil generated by Howard Johnshoy's Concordia Volunteer Committee, which complicated the search for President Brown's successor, haunted Concordia for many years. The Knutson administration long worried that any disagreement might develop into a similar public conflict harmful to institutional interests. Meanwhile, the problems of finances and physical plant required the new president's immediate attention.

Financial and Physical Plant Woes

The gymnasium was Knutson's first big problem. He was surprised to find that everyone had walked away from the collapse and that the insurance company had done nothing. After a series of meetings with college attorney G.L. Dosland, the architect, steel erector, contractor and college agreed to assume mutual liability for the damages and to bring suit against the insurance company for the costs. This removed one obstacle to renewed construction, but another quickly appeared. National rearmament, brought on by the Korean War, made it difficult to obtain steel. Intervention by North Dakota Senator William Langer, a good friend of President Harry Truman, secured the necessary government authorization; after a delay of one year, construction resumed in April 1952 when the new steel arrived. The field house caused financial

Memorial Auditorium-Gymnasium significantly boosted Concordia.

headaches as well. After the superstructure collapsed, the board postponed a $200,000 Fargo-Moorhead fund drive to cover the balance of the cost. Years later, Knutson remembered the resumption of this effort as his hardest task. When no chairman could be found, he headed the campaign himself. The drive raised only $65,000; Knutson became painfully aware that he faced the delicate task of improving community relations so that Fargo-Moorhead in the future would more generously support its local Lutheran college. This was essential if Concordia were to grow.[14]

Despite all difficulties, the building was completed and was dedicated on homecoming Sunday, October 19, 1952. It produced immediate benefits. Concordia finally had a common meeting place. The opening basketball game on December 2 attracted 4,500; 12,000 attended the annual Christmas concert. District and regional high school basketball tournaments were soon scheduled. Professor Irvin Christenson's fine work in managing these events helped build rapport with local high schools. As Knutson noted at the time, "already the building has demonstrated its possibilities." He later said that the gymnasium gave Concordia a new image and developed badly needed community goodwill.[15]

In his first report to the corporation, Knutson called attention to other pressing physical plant needs. Two old dormitories—Grose (now Bishop Whipple) and South (now Academy) Halls—required mod-
ernization. Old Main needed refurbishing to become an adequate classroom build-ing. The exteriors of Science and Cobber Halls should be faced with materials to make them more permanent and attrac-tive. Most critical of all, he said, "a music hall and library are so much needed that it has come to a point where it is hamper-ing our efficient operation as a liberal arts college." Knutson also suggested that it would be better stewardship to construct functional buildings that cost less. This is the first hint of abandoning the Gothic

South Hall required repair.

style and Kasota stone favored by President Brown and adopting the buff brick construction utilized during the rapid expansion of the 1950s and 1960s. Most of what the president proposed would not be completed for several years. He did obtain permission to modernize Grose and South Halls, however. Even this modest physical plant improvement required $75,000.[16] Where would the new president acquire the necessary funds?

Financially, Knutson's first years were very difficult. The sudden enrollment drop produced an $18,554 deficit for fiscal year 1950–1951. In May 1952 it appeared that

Grose Hall also needed modernization.

the college might run $47,800 in the red. Through special fundraising and extra economies, income unexpectedly exceeded ex-penditures. But these economies, Knutson warned the corporation, curtailed the efficiency of the institution. As one of the faculty noted, "Concordia balances its budget at the expense of buildings and equipment." Professor R.E. Fuglestad even suggested a 10 percent salary reduction, which Knutson refused since salaries were already so low.[17]

The tight budget meant that no funds existed for extras and sometimes not even for essentials. Knutson later recalled a cold winter day when Art Sanden, superintendent of buildings and grounds, came into the president's office with a broken chain from the elevator that boosted coal from the bin to the boiler. He had overspent his budget and the treasurer would not authorize expenditure for a new chain. Faced with an unheated campus, Knutson ordered the chain. During that financially constrained first year, Knutson saved funds by not attending the North Central meeting in Chicago or

196   President Joseph L. Knutson, 1951–1975

the Association of American Colleges meeting in Washington, although he knew he should attend and felt compelled to explain to the Gustavus dean why he had not. Under these strained circumstances, Knutson greatly appreciated Fjelstad Hall women when they painted their own rooms during the 1954 semester break. Their volunteer effort saved scarce dollars at the same time it taught them the problems of maintaining buildings.[18]

Faced with a desperate financial situation, the president somehow had to raise money. But how? Concordia had no development office and no organized stewardship program. Knutson was reduced to the piecemeal approach of soliciting the constituency for every exigency. Within weeks of taking office, he was writing personal friends for gifts to pay for routine painting and repair because the $4,500 appropriated had already been spent. The next year, he appealed to pastors and congregations for $75,000 to modernize Grose and South Halls. That same year, he pleaded with Concordia staff to include gifts to the college as part of their regular church stewardship because only 38 percent had contributed to the field house fund drive. In 1952 Knutson beseeched 2,800 friends of Concordia for funds to cover the apparent shortfall of $47,800. After one month, sixty-five people had contributed $1,592, arousing his hopes that the books might be balanced. Two years later, he again wrote the congregations to complete the dormitory appeal because only $42,542 of the needed $75,000 had been raised.[19]

In the meantime, he requested pastors in the corporate territory to submit names of ten potential donors who could afford annual gifts to the school. This was part of an effort to revive the Greater Concordia Association, first proposed during the even harder times of the early 1930s. No wonder Knutson became discouraged about being successful and required pep talks from Beatrice. As he explained to a friend, he recovered his happiness by "claiming the New Testament truth that God did not ask us to be a success, but only to be faithful." Two events did reward Knutson's faithfulness and afforded some relief for institutional financial woes. The budget did balance in 1952 and the Evangelical Lutheran Church Cost-of-Living Special yielded a 9 percent Christmas bonus for employees in 1951, with the promise of a similar reward for the next holiday season.[20]

To aid in recruiting students, President Knutson stressed new buildings, refurbishing old structures and keeping the campus clean. "If we only had a little more in the way of buildings," Knutson stated to a pastor at the time, "we would have the banner enrollment of all the colleges." Concordia has a good faculty, he wrote, "all we need is a new dress." Meanwhile, the institution made do with the old wardrobe, however often mended. Collegians, like money, were solicited through Lutheran pastors and congregations. Directed by J.L. Rendahl, the admissions office secured names and addresses of seniors from pastors and other friends of Concordia. These friends were encouraged to call on at least one senior and to encourage that person to send an application immediately. Once students had returned applications, they and their parents were invited to visit the campus.[21]

The president similarly appealed to congregations, asking them to arrange special programs for seniors at which a professor or a delegation of Cobbers might speak. Pastors and their youth groups were invited to campus for the annual Luther League Day and for other special musical and athletic events. Besides delivering many commencement addresses annually for area high schools, Knutson also wrote directly to graduates telling them of Concordia's Christian atmosphere, new facilities and faculty. As an added inducement, the college offered parttime employment; the president contacted local employers seeking jobs and expressing gratitude for positions provided. He assured them that since most Cobbers came from farms and small towns, they knew how to work. As a final contribution, Knutson urged faculty to show more personal interest in collegians. This could boost enrollment by retaining those who might otherwise drop out.[22]

The Administrative Council

When the directors called Knutson, they gave him the extensive authority common for the day. Modeling himself after such dynamic leaders as Evangelical Lutheran Church President J.A. Aasgaard and former Saint Olaf President Lars Boe, Knutson embraced the traditional belief in the divine right of college presidents, absolute monarchs of their domains. He subscribed to Carlyle's theory that an institution is an extension of one or a few people. Besides, Christian colleges required commanding leaders to keep them true to the church. Although he believed in a strong presidency, Knutson learned to live with the democratic faculty constitution he had inherited however much he disliked the implication that professors should involve themselves in issues of management, planning and personnel selection.[23]

He also used his authority to build a talented administrative team with which he shared power. At the suggestion of Carl Bailey, longtime dean of the college, Knutson formed an administrative council consisting of the business manager, director of admissions, dean of instruction, personnel deans of men and women, superintendent

Some Administrative Council and faculty members pictured in late 1960s.

of buildings and grounds, registrar and food service director. This body met weekly throughout Knutson's long tenure. He called it a marvelous instrument because it built up positive feelings among administrators and it could respond effectively to criticism. Bailey remembered the council as an intelligent and dedicated group who complemented one another very well. Knutson expressed his ideas forcefully, but decisions were made by the body and not by the president alone. His recommendations to the board were consistent with those of the council. Knutson willingly shared power with these trusted associates whom he had appointed; most remained part of his administrative team until near the end of his presidency when a few of the principals retired. This council made the important decision that the college should grow, and it coordinated the complex blend of bodies, bricks and bucks that made growth possible.[24]

Talented individuals comprised the administrative council. One of the most important was William Smaby, Knutson's choice for business manager. After he assumed the presidency, Knutson discovered a business office run by two men who did not get along and who had not cultivated the business and professional people of Fargo-Moorhead. The president soon decided to replace both with Smaby, a Rushford, Minnesota, banker, an excellent choice for many reasons. The two had been friends since they were freshmen at Saint Olaf. As a friend, Smaby had the president's trust, enabling them to discuss freely the many problems facing the college. As a banker, Smaby understood that the school could borrow money for productive purposes; his personal contacts soon enabled him to secure $500,000 in building loans from the Minneapolis Farmers and Mechanics Bank. Smaby also worked hard to improve ties with the local business community. That relations improved greatly during the next two decades owed much to his efforts and the credibility of his banking background. Finally, his experience as a banker for a farming community gave him a good understanding of Cobbers.[25]

William A. Smaby

It is characteristic of this modest, dedicated man that working with students gave him the greatest satisfaction. He extended credit to many deserving collegians because he wanted to help them get an education and make their way in the world. Apparently an excellent judge of character, Smaby wrote off only 2 percent in bad debts in twenty-three years. Diligent preparation enabled Smaby quickly to overcome his only shortcoming, an admitted ignorance of college finance. He visited Saint Olaf, met with Orville Dahl of the church board of education and with the church auditor for the colleges, and attended a week-long conference for college business managers. Fortunately, he inherited a good staff who had kept records competently. This helped him through his first months while he learned his position.[26]

The president wisely retained J.L. Rendahl, director of admissions and public relations since 1945. Credited by Knutson for knowing more than most chief executives, Rendahl in fact had headed Waldorf College during the Depression. Blessed with sharp intelligence, Rendahl had a passion for numbers. His statistical records on high school graduates revealed the size of the available student pool. Aided by automated addressing equipment, he sent mailings to a list of 50,000 names based on Lutheran church membership and test scores.[27]

Admissions played a key role in the policy of growth. For expansion to proceed, collegians first had to be on campus. Then federal loans could be secured for the construction of dormitories. Government use of a student-space ratio to determine allocation of funds dictated a similar strategy for academic facilities. Because Concordia had many students and lacked instructional space, its disadvantage became an advantage in the competition for federal largess. Successful implementation of this plan involved risks. Inadequate facilities made it difficult to recruit. A sudden drop in enrollment in the middle of the process invited financial disaster. Despite these hazards, the administrative team successfully maintained the delicate balance between numbers and facilities and achieved remarkable physical expansion during the next two decades.[28]

This achievement is a credit to the abilities and cooperation of Smaby, Rendahl and the other members of the council. They also benefited from the good fortune of implementing their policies in a time of national stability, economic prosperity and federal aid to education. Favorable circumstances made it difficult for them to fail.

Carl Bailey—a gentle, fair-minded professor of physics who had been an atomic scientist at Los Alamos, New Mexico during World War II—unexpectedly became dean of the college in 1954. Another wise Knutson appointment, Bailey's intellectual stature commanded faculty respect, which translated into both higher academic standards and support for the president. Bailey pushed to improve the faculty, recruit better students who would make the most of college, eliminate easy courses and strengthen the liberal arts. He worked cooperatively with the president to move

Carl Bailey

Concordia in the direction of what the Danforth Commission would call a "free Christian college"—free because the college did not restrict thought and Christian because its religious commitments were vigorously maintained. Asserting that he could not have been a successful president without Bailey, Knutson praised the dean "as our Leonardo da Vinci" who "lives the liberal arts ideal" and who "has given Concordia Christian leadership and scholastic glamour." Bailey had returned to his alma mater because he believed that teachers, by multiplying themselves many times, can make greater contributions than researchers. Ironically, this would-be professor was drafted as an administrator. He loyally set aside personal preferences to serve the institution effectively as dean until 1971.[29]

Two popular personnel deans worked well together at the difficult task of meeting collegiate needs and maintaining the Concordia family during the crowded conditions of rapid growth. Both regarded discipline as secondary to their primary function of helping Cobbers. Both willingly performed in comic skits for incoming freshmen. This annual nonsense taught newcomers that it was all right to have fun at college.[30]

Former teacher, school superintendent and Montana pastor, Rev. Victor Boe came as dean of men in 1946 and remained in that position until he retired in 1973. In a

Victor Boe

remarkable display of affection by collegians for the dean, a special issue of the *Concordian* paid tribute to Boe: "The wit of Will Rogers, a touch of the philosopher, the warmth of a loving grandfather, a man of strong faith, a sense of fairness, a love of life." The dean earned these accolades by taking pleasure in Cobbers and their antics. He enjoyed his nine years as resident head of Brown Hall—which Hilda Groberg Boe described as "sort of like living in the middle of a bus station"—because it gave him more intimate contact with students and an appreciation for the problems of dormitory living. He even delighted in his nicknames assigned by veterans—"Dim Bulb" and "Bean Doe"—and, in a response to his knock on a dormitory door—"Friend or Boe?"[31]

Dr. Dorothy Olsen came as dean of women in 1953. She almost rejected the offer because "I didn't want to be one of those things." Initially planning to serve two years and then return to the University of Wisconsin, "Dean Dot" fell in love with Concordia and stayed until she retired in 1972. In 1960 she bought a house near campus where she entertained freshmen women each fall and individual housing units throughout both semesters. Indeed, she held so many gatherings that upon her retirement, Dean Boe asked, "Does she have enough? She has fed everyone on campus!" Olsen taught counseling courses in the psychology department for sixteen years; she appreciated this opportunity to know Cobbers better. Earlier she had changed her field from history to guidance and counseling because "I found I liked

Dorothy Olsen

the students better than the subject." Thus it should not surprise that she took greatest pride in those women she encouraged to remain in school, graduate and make something of themselves.[32]

Olsen brought Dorothy Johnson with her as resident head; the two were given a free hand to develop a guidance program based on student need. Soon Johnson assumed a fulltime position in the English department where she developed reading. The counseling project nevertheless went forward under the leadership of Deans Olsen and Boe. They even formed a church school association of deans and college counselors because they believed their problems differed from those of state institutions.[33]

Registrar Don Dale, Food Service Director Amy Erickson, Buildings and Grounds Superintendent Arthur Sanden and the director of stewardship were the other council members.

The desperate need for facilities, intensified by growing numbers, dictated that the development office be expanded during the 1950s. Edward N. Larson, who succeeded T.C. Hanson as director of stewardship in 1953, initially presided over this often difficult process. The program grew by fits and starts as the president labored to cultivate the constituency and the administrative team worked to improve local community relations. This took several years, the direction of outside consultants and the leadership of Paul Thorson (1962–1965) and especially Roger Swenson (1966–1973) before development began to yield a significant amount of gift income required to finance physical expansion. The successful program that finally emerged after painful

Roger Swenson

experimentation rested on a long-term soft-sell approach to fundraising. That way it could be perpetual. This philosophy sharply contrasted with that of Knutson's early years when he was repeatedly forced to raise funds for immediate, specific needs.[34]

Student Life at a Christian College

From its origins, Concordia had openly proclaimed itself a Christian college. Historian William Ringenberg has defined such institutions as communities of believers that recruit only Christian scholars, require Bible courses for everyone, maintain a campus-wide program of religious worship and offer an education integrated by the Christian world view, in contrast to the fragmented knowledge of secular universities. Thus President Knutson's conception of a Christ-centered education was in keeping with the heritage of American church colleges, the Concordia tradition and the attitudes that the predominantly Lutheran student body brought from their homes and congregations.[35]

In officially welcoming the new president, *Concordian* editors Sally Ann Warner ('52) and Donald Sponheim ('53) asserted that although the institution might be financially poor, it was spiritually rich in having a Christ-centered leader like Knutson. This welcome reflected the religious orientation of that year's staff, who aimed to keep

Christ alive in the pages of the newspaper. Lyle Rich ('54) even noted that the Latin inscriptions on Brown Hall—*Soli Deo Gloria* ("To God alone the glory") and *Vincet Omnia Vientas* ("Truth conquers all")—were inseparable in collegian Christian lives; Christ as the way to salvation is the truth that conquers all. Of course, not all Cobbers were so pious. Indeed, a 1952 poll revealed that only 32 percent regularly read *"Soli Deo Gloria,"* the weekly religious column. Nonetheless, subsequent editors reaffirmed that the newspaper ought to be a voice for a Christian environment; to that end, editor James Narveson ('55) pledged that the *Concordian* would reflect the various shades of opinion within the Christian community. On several other occasions during Knutson's first term, Cobbers affirmed the centrality of Christ in campus life. Fargo radio station KFGO broadcast a student-produced and funded program, "Crusading for Christ." *Concordian* and *Cobber* editors understood the first line of the college hymn to mean that Concordia was grounded on the firm foundation of faith in Christ. They praised the institution for helping "each student establish a firm foundation for life in a troubled age."[36]

Cobbers expressed their Christ-centered conceptions in a variety of ways. These included their perceptions of the Christian liberal arts, their responses to institutional rules and their campus religious activities. *Concordian* and *Cobber* editors, nominated by the respective staffs and approved by the literary board and the president, took the lead in articulating observations about the Christian liberal arts. Because Christianity's spiritual truths answered the "why" questions and gave significance to all study, it was impossible to have genuine education without Christianity. That Christianity had been omitted accounted for the disoriented and fragmented learning offered by state universities. Editors were so committed to these goals that they often chastised faculty and Cobbers for failing to take full advantage of a Christian liberal arts environment. One article complained that some professors forget the breadth entailed in liberal arts education and teach as though their subject was the only one worth mention. Another charged that student apathy, evidenced in vandalism and poor attendance at lyceum programs, conferences, government and society meetings, was akin to ungratefulness and could not be tolerated. As *Cobber* editor Omar Kaste ('53) sternly warned, "We cannot expect to convince our people of Concordia's worth if we are not ourselves convinced, and if we do not *live* our concern for its existence and continued growth."[37]

Cobbers usually accepted with minimal resistance the institutional regulations. These were extensive, common to most midwestern Lutheran and many other denominational colleges, and vindicated by reason of developing habits of Christian conduct. Class attendance was required. Unexcused class absences counted as failure and, if excessive, compelled the offender to petition for readmission to the course through the deans of men and women and, subsequently, the scholastic regulations committee. Drinking liquor, dancing, cardplaying, gambling, visiting taverns and (for women) smoking were banned. Social functions were properly chaperoned. Special permission was required in order to leave the city, to have a car and to live off campus. To be sure, rules were broken as disciplinary action against violators make clear. Interestingly, a change in discipline was introduced during the Korean War enrollment slump. Whether this was due to expediency, humanitarianism or both is uncertain. In any case, a system of fines for violations replaced the earlier policy of automatic suspension. As explained by the administration, suspension hindered progress in school and embarrassed the parents and student. The new policy avoided these evils, yet held the guilty responsible for their misdeeds. They promised not to break rules, paid a fine and were warned that any further violations would result in suspension.[38]

Occasionally Cobbers complained—sometimes about restrictive regulations, more often about other issues. The perennial complaint against the lights-out-at-10:30-p.m. rule for women surfaced again during President Knutson's first weeks. Students recommended a careful consideration of the issue; the new president complied—for several months. Tired of waiting, the student senate passed "a lights-on-all-night" resolution. Urged by Dean Dorothy Olsen and Dorothy Johnson to relax strict hours, Knutson yielded. Lights-out was dropped; curfews were raised from 7:30 p.m. on weeknights and 10:00 p.m. on weekends to 10:00 p.m. and 11:00 p.m. for first-year women, and to 11:00 p.m. and 12:00 p.m. for upperclasswomen. Dismayed by these changes, former Dean Frida Nilsen told Knutson that he knew nothing of female physiology and that abolition of the curfew would ruin the health of Cobber coeds.[39]

Other complaints were less momentous. Cobbers grumbled about standing in line and about congestion in the cafeteria and the field house during a sold-out basketball game in 1953 between the Minneapolis Lakers and the Baltimore Bullets. They griped about the poor quality of cafeteria meat and the high price of cafeteria coffee, a Scandinavian staple. And they lamented icy sidewalks that produced many falls and some broken bones.[40]

Significantly, more complained about chapel than about repressive regulations. Although President Knutson ended required chapel in January 1953, he still regarded worship as the center of daily life, providing the "unifying factor that makes for a feeling of family solidarity at Concordia." Interestingly, the *Concordian* was as likely to complain as the president about poor attendance of collegians and professors. Complaints were followed by administrative notices that attendance would again be checked. This prompted a student poll which asked, "Do you favor compulsory chapel?" Only 33 percent answered "yes." Upon completion of the field house, a mild debate ensued over whether chapel should be moved to the new facility. Another poll revealed that 75 percent favored keeping it in the Old Main auditorium even though that required two sessions. The majority preferred the convenient central location that made lunch easier, thereby demonstrating the truth of the adage that "a light lunch is the way to a Norwegian's soul." They also wondered why it should be transplanted after several thousand dollars had been spent the previous year for remodeling Old Main stage and auditorium. Nonetheless, worship relocated because the administra-

Chapel services in field house were initially resisted.

tion believed that the entire community should gather at the same time. Cobbers still objected. They disliked having their lunch inconvenienced and they disapproved having the preacher at the "bottom of the hill." They claimed that the wide-open space of the gym floor behind speakers made it difficult to concentrate. Despite these grievances, chapel remained in the field house.[41]

Extensive religious activities fostered a Christ-centered conception of education. The spiritual life conference met four days each January, as it had for many years. Outside speakers addressed chapel and special evening services, conducted discussions at regular dormitory devotions and were available for private counseling. An all-college communion service closed the week. Lutheran Student Association, the largest organization, met Sunday evenings in the auditorium. It subdivided into twenty twelve-member teams who presented programs on campus and for neighboring Luther Leagues. Mission Crusaders strengthened students in Christian faith and life, studied home and foreign missions and supported mission work. Lutheran Daughters of the Reformation met on Wednesday evenings to study and support missions and charities. Cobber Brotherhood, Prayer Fellowship, dormitory devotions and Lutheran Bible Institute Bible Study held weekly or monthly meetings. During the summer of 1952, the Concordia Couriers traveled under the theme, "Onward Christian Soldiers," and presented the gospel in word and song on a special 100-concert Pacific Coast tour.[42]

The quality of religious life much impressed President Knutson upon his arrival. He attended a voluntary Saturday night prayer meeting of 105 students, found the message inspirational and noted an absence of censoriousness often present at such gatherings. Religious life was not confined to pious observances, as piety often expressed itself in certain kinds of Christian and community service. At Christmas, Cobbers collected money and toys to be distributed among the needy. The Lutheran Student Association sold Christmas cards to raise funds for Lutheran Student World Relief. And Cobbers volunteered to sandbag during the 1952 flood and to donate blood for the armed forces in 1953.[43] All these activities were thought central to the mission of a church college. All contributed to a Christian liberal arts education. All trained Lutheran laity and clergy for future service to congregation and community.

Student government absorbed the energies of many. Despite frequent complaints about apathy, a voter turnout of more than 75 percent indicates considerable interest. Similarly, an annual fund drive to raise money for campus organizations netted 95 percent of its $2,000 goal in 1952–1953, suggesting respectable support. Often disagreeing with the administration about issues, Cobbers perceived that the Student Association enabled them to work constructively with administrators in solving problems. A student-faculty retreat, held at the beginning of school each fall, provided a forum for discussing many topics ranging from counseling to women's hours. Collegians were thankful for this cooperation and urged its continuation.[44]

Their governmental concerns were not confined to campus. Cobber leaders affiliated with the National Student Association (NSA). This federation, organized in 1948, soon enrolled approximately two-thirds of United States collegians on some 300 campuses. The NSA attempted to articulate a national student stand on such issues as academic freedom, universal military training, the McCarran immigration bill, tax deductions for educational expenses, international student cooperation, the desegregation of higher education and improved student government. Registered as a Washington lobby, the NSA was accused of being pro-left and communist in the McCarthyite atmosphere of the day. Cobbers were assured that leftist groups had failed to seize control and that the FBI and the House Un-American Activities Committee had approved the NSA. Nonetheless, the faculty worried about communistic and Catholic influence and never officially recognized the organization.[45]

Nationally, McCarthyism and loyalty investigations undoubtedly dampened collegian and professorial interest in politics and social reform compared to the 1930s. Consequently, college students of the 1950s were labeled "the silent generation." Silence did not mean complete inaction, however. Besides their NSA membership, Cobbers found other ways to express themselves politically. In 1952, as in previous national elections, they formed political candidate clubs which sponsored campus activities. The *Concordian*, as usual, editorialized about voting as a civic duty. And the straw poll revealed the normal two-to-one majority for the Republican candidate, Eisenhower, over the Democrat, Stevenson. The very next year, Young Republican and Democrat Clubs were organized. A speech by Senator Hubert Humphrey at the field house in February 1954 greatly fanned political talk. Because of the ongoing Korean War, the *Concordian* informed male Cobbers that they must take the College Qualification Test as the first step in obtaining deferments. Cobbers in Korea reported on the wartime damage and the resulting severe malnutrition.[46]

Perhaps this war, like its predecessor, fostered a greater international awareness. The *Concordian* carried several stories about international students in which they usually discussed differences in customs and always expressed their enjoyment of American life. Sometimes they addressed significant questions. A three-part series by Iranian Iraj Niroomand ('52) defended Iran's nationalization of oil, condemned Britain's imperialistic exploitation of Iran and assured Americans that nationalization did not mean a triumph of communism. Although it is unlikely that conservatives among the Republican majority believed this assertion, at least they had been exposed to the idea.[47]

Campus and community speakers, all duly reported in the *Concordian*, enhanced awareness of other domestic and international issues. In 1953 at the North Dakota Agricultural College, Eleanor Roosevelt lectured on the topic, "The United Nations and World Peace." The next year the Norwegian director of the United Nations Department of Public Information spoke in chapel. This was followed by a visit of the Norwegian ambassador to campus in May. That fall Roger Baldwin, founder of the American Civil Liberties Union, addressed the Fargo-Moorhead Open Forum. Speaking on "The Status of Our Civil Liberties," Baldwin charged that the current anti-communist crusade in the United States, which had been inspired by Wisconsin Senator Joseph McCarthy, did more to hurt civil liberties than it did to halt communism. He was followed in the series by Dr. Charles Mayo, who addressed the topic, "The United Nations, Its Problems and Ours." Mayo informed his audience that the UN was not a world federation but only an instrument for maintaining peace and preventing aggression. He advised that Americans should not be discouraged with the UN's failures because it was still the best instrument for peace-keeping now available to the world. Paul Dovre ('58) remembers a good student response to visiting speakers, who often stimulated a lively political dialogue.[48]

The annual lecture and artist series similarly broadened the horizons of many Cobbers. As in the past, the series consisted of a varied program of classical music and academic speakers. And, as they had done before and since, many Cobbers resisted these well-intentioned efforts of a liberal arts institution. They demanded a program more appealing to their interests. Expression of such provincialism prompted an angry letter from former music professor Gertrude Szaroletta. She pointed out that the series was meant to enhance a liberal arts education by exposing Cobbers to culture. Hence it was not supposed to be generally appealing. No matter how painful, Szaroletta implied, Cobbers should attend because it was good for them.[49] This perennial debate indicates some awakening collegiate cultural interests and commitment to this form of liberal arts education.

Roller-skating was a popular entertainment.

Although some were enthusiastic about culture, for most students physical vitality dictated an interest in social life. To that end, they continued their longstanding agitation for a student union. Completion of the field house offered the possibility of a basement room for this purpose; the board of directors approved it in October 1952. Having secured this concession, students then requested inclusion of a lunch counter. The administration complied but decided to relocate in Brown Hall both for convenience and to open the gym for roller skating, a popular recreation of the day. Volunteers reduced costs by painting and doing carpentry. The new lunch room and lounge opened for use in April 1953. The suggested name, "Brown Jug," provoked campus and alumni protest on the grounds that it connoted "a gin and rum tavern" and did not belong in a Christian environment. A poll revealed that 56 percent favored the title. That the controversy subsided and the name disappeared suggests that the administration quietly resolved the issue. The next year, the senate purchased a television for the lunch room and a hi-fidelity record player for the lounge. Unfortunately these modest improvements did not satisfy Cobber longing for more entertainment. They even suggested establishing a five dollar fee per student per semester to be placed in a special construction fund. Only when an adequate union was built, many maintained, would their meager social life improve.[50] The same argument would be repeated for the next four decades.

Cobber Capers committee plans an all-society variety show.

In the meantime, Cobbers made do with the traditional Scandinavian "light lunch" each evening. A roller-skating club provided beginning and advanced instruction. Television viewing offered a new diversion for some, but others lamented the "TV craze." These high-minded malcontents refused to contribute to the purchase of a set for Brown Hall on the grounds that it was an unnecessary novelty which would detract from their studies. When not eating, skating or viewing, some would-be bronzed but often burned Cobbers sunbathed each spring, however fleeting the season.[51]

If these activities proved insufficient, the twelve non-literary literary societies afforded the major share of campus social life. Early in the decade, sweaters and jackets identifying societies by colors and insignia became popular. LDS-AES won the largest share of prizes in public programs and homecoming float awards. Comprised of many athletes, AES obliged their sister society to adjust their joint activities to the athletic schedule. Athenians continued to lead in scholarship until overtaken by the Alpha Zetes. Besides pledging, initiation rites, parties, dinners and perennial debates over the appropriate forms of hazing, societies amused by instituting in 1953 a new all-society variety show called "Cobber Capers." Not wishing to be deprived of this fun by their exclusion from society membership, freshmen in 1954 produced their own one-act musical.[52]

Much social life focused on homecoming. Each class and society prepared for the festive weekend. They decorated buildings, constructed floats, built and burned a bonfire and, in 1954, initiated a variety show displaying talent from all classes. The president's annual message, printed in the *Concordian*, greeted returning alumni. In

First homecoming service in field house (1954) attracted 3,000.

his first, Knutson expressed hope that they would always remember how their Concordia liberal arts education had prepared them for life, and that they would always return with thankful memories to their alma mater. Despite the vitality evidenced, Knutson was dissatisfied that activity did not extend beyond the campus. He was particularly disappointed that only 150 outside the college attended his inaugural.[53]

Knutson envisioned a larger Concordia community and he seized on homecoming as one way to realize that vision. The administrative council took up the problem and worked on making this annual event into a fall festival for the region. In this, they were assisted by the recently completed Memorial Auditorium-Gymnasium and the newly appointed alumni director Alice Midgarden Polikowsky ('30). Polikowsky had been appointed by Knutson to improve relations with the inactive, uninterested alumni he had inherited from the Brown administration. In addition to editing the Concordia *Alumnus*, which first appeared in March 1954, Polikowsky helped plan homecoming. Alumni headquarters and a continuous coffee hour, complete with ash trays, were established in the north gym. Amy Erickson made Cobbers welcome with lots of food. One hundred and ten lettermen returned for their reunion. A Montana alumnus strolling the campus was thrilled to be personally greeted by Knutson. He joyfully reported, "Just think ... the president visited with me!" The new facility enabled everyone to gather in a single place. When 3,000 attended the worship first held in the gymnasium that year, Knutson called that "the first homecoming." By using the new facility for worship, the coronation and alumni coffees and banquets, the administration was rewarded with larger and larger crowds.[54]

By this means, President Knutson enlarged the constituency and enhanced its commitment to the institution. Both were necessary to sustain Concordia's remarkable growth under his leadership in the years ahead.

Chapter 12

Bodies, Bucks and Bricks

The Decision to Grow

Immediately following World War II, Concordia authorities made the decision to grow. The college reached beyond the valley, drawing from all of North Dakota, eastern Montana, northern and central Minnesota and the Twin Cities. It expanded its physical plant in an attempt to enroll those who wanted to come. After the slump caused by a combination of the Korean War draft and the low Depression birth rate, growth resumed during the Knutson presidency. As Knutson explained the administration's view: "It is always dangerous to put a ceiling on development. ... Even in the area of enrollment one must be constantly reaching out; after all, the educational ideal is to teach, influence and serve as many people as possible."[1]

Demographic and economic circumstances enabled this outreach to bear fruit. Although the birth rate declined during the Depression, a higher percentage of these attended college when they came of age. This rate had climbed to 20 percent by 1950; it continued rising to 35 percent in 1964. The GI Bill and the Truman Commission Report on Higher Education furthered this democratization of higher education by fostering equality of access through ideological commitment and financial assistance. Then, beginning in 1958, the college benefited from the wartime increase in birth rate and, commencing in 1964, the postwar baby boom.[2]

These demographic changes combined with altered agricultural conditions to boost enrollment. Good rains, bumper crops and global demand stimulated by World War II brought farmers a new era of prosperity. Government price supports and a strong world market sustained these high prices for a decade after the war. Several trends—the increased size of farms, mechanization, crop specialization and a shift of agriculture from a labor- to a capital-intensive industry—limited opportunities for rural children and encouraged their pursuit of higher education.[3]

To reach these potential collegians, the president played a key part. He wrote parents directly and often addressed commencements. Knutson's role as spokesman for Christian education was enhanced by the greater public visibility attained when he was elected president of the Association of Minnesota Colleges in 1956 and when he delivered the concluding address at the Minneapolis meeting of the Republican State Central Committee in 1959. Although Knutson limited his political activities to avoid giving the impression he was only a parttime president, his occasional partisan speeches, which were well received and well publicized in the media, enlarged his reputation as a spokesman for private education. Knutson conceived his role as one of persuading the public "that this type of college is really needed, that here a student gets an orientation and an attitude toward life which will be both a boon to him and to the society in which one makes his particular contribution." Concerned that Lutheran colleges were not getting their share of the growing college-age population when the percentage of Evangelical Lutheran youth attending church schools had declined to only 15 percent, Knutson asked Lutheran families to be loyal to their institutions. He added an economic argument to this emotional appeal to traditional loyalties. Because graduates earned more than those who did not attend, "parents should realize that college really does not cost a cent" and that "students are well paid for going to college."[4]

Besides using the president to disseminate the message of Christian education, the college employed a variety of new as well as previously used public relations techniques to attract enrollees. Chapel services were broadcast daily on a local radio station. Two other radio programs, the student-produced "Thy Kingdom Come" and the annual "Radio Christmas Party," lasted until 1956 and 1961 respectively. "Cobber Campus," a weekly television program, was produced by collegians and broadcast over WDAY in 1953–1954 and KXJB in 1954–1955. In addition, new efforts were

made to reach parents and alumni. Homecoming expanded its activities to attract ever-larger numbers. Innovations included a faculty-parent tea, first scheduled in 1958, and in 1960 a WDAY telecast of the "colorful 50-unit Cobber parade." Longtime faculty were excited to see this growth. One professor attributed it to "the inspiring Christian leadership you [Knutson] have brought to Concordia." The *Alumnus* was succeeded in 1962 by *Concordia Alumni News*. That same year the annual parents' day resumed after an eighteen-year hiatus. Activities included parent-group discussions, a panel on "The Influence of Christianity in the Classroom" moderated by Dean Carl Bailey, the all-college musical—"The Pirates of Penzance," breakfast and dinner in the Commons, and Sunday worship at area churches.[5]

Myrtle Rendahl

A small, efficiently managed admissions office capitalized on enhanced institutional publicity and accomplished an enrollment miracle. J.L. Rendahl, the ace demographer and affectionately known as "the Philadelphia lawyer" to his administrative colleagues, watched birth rates closely and planned carefully. Myrtle Rendahl worked as receptionist, office manager, counselor, tour guide and unofficially as a second mother to international students. Active in church and community leadership positions in addition to her admissions duties, she kept a Christmas card list of 1,000 friends made throughout the years. Only one fulltime admissions counselor was employed. Ed Ellenson, who assumed that position after his graduation in 1958, recalls that he traveled about 40,000 miles annually from early September through March. To reduce the number of cancellations, several collegians were hired each summer to visit high school students who had already applied for admission.[6]

The admissions office contacted potential collegians directly by techniques long used. Cobbers were urged to spread the good word about Christian education to high school seniors in their home communities. Pastors, re-

Admissions Counselor Ed Ellenson

warded only with complimentary athletic passes, supplied names and local contacts. Congregations scheduled Concordia Day programs and annual Luther League Days attracted large numbers to campus. Rendahl's direct mail program was designed to draw students from a larger area than admissions counselors could cover. Seizing the opportunity afforded by demographic trends, he kept the college as full as possible. As he described the institutional strategy years later, Concordia "walked the line between good enrollment and student revolt." By recruiting more collegians than spaces available and finding them housing off-campus, the college after 1954 could take advantage of government loans for dormitory construction. Armed with statistics, Rendahl always looked ahead. In 1955 he estimated that by 1970 enrollment would double to 2,400, a remarkably accurate prediction. In 1963 he noted that the population of 18-year-olds would increase more than 30 percent in the next two years; therefore to harvest its fair share of this collegiate crop, Concordia must continue expanding its physical plant.[7]

The abundance provided by the wartime and postwar baby boom made it possible for numbers to rise steadily after Fall 1951, when 890 enrolled. A 52 percent increase produced 1,354 Cobbers by Autumn 1955. At that time second generation Cobbers were becoming a factor, as 132 alumni children registered in September 1957. The 1,685 attending in 1960 represented an 89.3 percent growth during Knutson's first decade. By 1965 enrollment had climbed another 24.6 percent to 2,101, including a record 815 freshmen.[8]

The 19.6 percent jump between 1955 and 1960, however, was exceeded by the national increase of 35 percent for higher education in the same period. This differential indicates that public institutions were growing faster than private due to government decisions that state schools ought to expand and to the more rapidly rising costs of private education. In 1956–1957 the ratio of private to public college tuition stood at 3.5:1; by 1974–1975 it would be 5:1. Consequently, the percentage attending private schools declined from 50 in 1950 to slightly more than 40 in 1960. It dropped to 25 percent during the next decade.[9]

This decline bothered Knutson greatly. Yet this concern was secondary to his major challenge of finding more dollars to erect more buildings and to hire more professors to serve the growth in absolute numbers attending Concordia.

Although the quantity of Cobbers increased greatly between 1951 and 1965, their character did not much change. Like its sister institutions, Concordia remained a solid church college. More than 90 percent of the student body annually was Lutheran. Often encouraged by local pastors and teachers who were enthusiastic alumni, they mostly came from the small towns and farms of the region where Norwegian Lutherans had settled. Growth altered some characteristics. As the recruiting area expanded beyond the valley, the percentage coming from North Dakota declined to 28.7 while the percentage originating in Minnesota increased to 52.9 by 1959. Historically, these figures had been approximately equal. While the absolute number of North Dakotans remained unchanged, the institution grew by attracting more students from the larger population of Minnesota, especially the metropolitan area of the Twin Cities.[10]

The dormitory building program advanced the institution toward the collegiate ideal of a residential campus. The percentage living outside residence halls declined from 40.9 in October 1960 to 26.9 in 1965. Meanwhile, academic quality improved. By 1965 most incoming freshmen were in the top half of their high school classes; their median test score was in the top 15 percent of all secondary graduates. Nonetheless, because many came from small schools which did not offer a complete curriculum, the college continued a remedial program begun in 1952. It was apparently effective; scores on the Princeton achievement tests for sophomores revealed that Cobbers scored above the national mean in everything except the fine arts.[11]

Registrations rose despite rising costs. During Knutson's first year, the comprehensive fee totalled $770. By 1960, this had increased 72.7 percent to $1,330. In 1965 the comprehensive fee totalled $1,800, another 35.3 percent jump. Cobbers were excited about expanding enrollments, despite complaining about longer lines in the cafeteria, in the bookstore and at registration. They were understandably less happy about constant price hikes. Their discontent was apparently confined to grousing until 1963, when complaints became serious enough for discussion by the student-faculty forum. They were particularly distressed by their exclusion from the fee-making process and by substitution of a set food fee for the item-pricing of the cafeteria plan. In response, the administration argued that item-pricing was inefficient and would soon disappear from campuses, but agreed to have undergraduates on the committee deciding details of the board plan. Elizabeth Hassenstab of the food service worked with student representatives to resolve these issues. Concessions included a plan with choices on food items that represented "all you can eat for a fixed price" and the option of eating several meals at the Normandy snack bar. Collegians were happy to have choices; administrators were pleased with the possibility of a healthier collegiate diet.[12]

Elizabeth Hassenstab

Cobbers complained, but consoled themselves with the thought that an excellent private school education justified the added costs. They would have been less sanguine had these expenses not been offset by increased financial aid made possible by federal assistance. That students wanted to come, and were able to find the means to pay, was critical to growth. Federal monies provided the means which fueled expansion of higher education in these decades. Aid figures for Concordia demonstrate how much the college benefited from these national policies.

For the 1950–1951 academic year, Concordia awarded only $9,900 in scholarships and $26,682 in loans. An estimated 10 percent earned one-fourth of their expenses during the term and another 50 percent earned that amount during the summer. In 1963 the institution loaned $750,000, an expansion enabled by the National Defense Education Act (1958) and USA Funds, a private nonprofit service corporation which endorsed low-cost long-term loans by hometown banks. While other colleges hesitated, J.L. Rendahl applied for the $500,000 maximum allowed, received $250,000 and secured an early recruiting advantage. Others soon followed. By 1959, Concordia was only one among the more than 1,400 of the nation's 2,000 colleges which participated. Although many Christian schools feared assistance as a step toward federal control, they preferred aid to individuals rather than institutions, as demonstrated by their earlier acceptance of the GI Bill. For the 1964–1965 academic year the financial aids program at Concordia for the first time exceeded $1 million. This represented a twenty-seven-fold increase over the minuscule funds available in 1950–1951. In addition, the college through Deans Boe and Olsen continued to assist in finding parttime jobs. A $19,440 federal grant, received in February 1965 at the onset of the federal work study program, helped expand campus employment.[13]

Expanding and Enhancing the Faculty

More bodies necessitated more professors. Recruiting teachers who were both academically qualified and religiously committed was not easy during the years of growth, either for Concordia or its sister institutions. The faculty expanded 67 percent from seventy-five in 1954 to 125 by 1965. At that time, when almost one-half had been at the institution less than five years, a two-faculty problem surfaced. As a more professionalized new staff was recruited through an emphasis on hiring those with advanced degrees, it alarmed older professors who feared that "the character of the college will soon be secularized."[14]

The president shared this concern. Although Knutson recognized that piety cannot replace academic ability and no longer expected all teachers to be Lutherans, he was "very anxious that they be committed Christians who are in sympathy with the church college." That meant they should teach their academic subjects within a Christian orientation by making "all knowledge relevant to God's redemptive purpose in Jesus Christ," maintain a Christian lifestyle and seek "to strengthen the ideal of Christian community." Such people were most likely to be found in colleges of the church. Consequently, Knutson minimized Cobber complaints in 1958 when approximately 30 percent of the faculty were alumni. He maintained "that a church college is something like hybrid corn. There has to be enough inbreeding to set the strain." Despite the president's theory, in practice inbreeding was reduced and a more academically and intellectually diverse faculty was deliberately recruited.[15] Earnest discussions have continued, however, about the degree of permissible diversity while preserving the Christian community believed necessary to sustain the religious mission.

These religious and communal concerns led to a presidential emphasis on chapel. To achieve institutional Christian objectives, President Knutson expected all teachers to attend voluntarily. That not everyone did is evidenced by his many letters on the subject. The executive committee concurred with the president in 1957; instead of pursuing the material pleasures of the coffee room, professors ought to worship regularly as a good example for collegians and for their own spiritual benefit. Actually, most did, although they usually sat in the north section of the gymnasium in order to escape more quickly to morning coffee.[16]

Hiring was generally a three-way partnership between president, dean and chairperson. If department heads were trusted, they initiated their own search; if not, the dean and president assumed major responsibility and consulted departmental members. In either case, President Knutson generally interviewed all candidates before they were employed. Dean Bailey remembers the process as informal and congenial. The informality is best illustrated by the experiences of English professor Walther Prausnitz and history professor Martin Lutter. The German-born and Chicago-educated Prausnitz arrived for his interview on the train "one fine spring morning—in a blizzard." President Knutson, upon meeting him at the station, compassionately surrendered his own overshoes. Thus protected against the elements, Prausnitz took the job. Quickly recognized by undergraduates as a great teacher, who led them in singing "Home on

Professor Walther Prausnitz

the Range" and proclaimed himself "king of the buffaloes," Prausnitz has made numerous contributions in curriculum development and assessment.[17]

Lutter, an Augustana alumnus, was teaching summer school at Eastern New Mexico State in 1953. One day he received an unexpected Concordia contract; he had not met Knutson, had not seen Concordia College and was not asked to interview. He decided that if the college had the faith to make an offer sight unseen then he should have the faith to accept. Lutter never regretted his decision[18] nor did the administration. He succeeded Christian Bale as leading faculty character, developed a devoted student following and for many years dedicated himself to fostering the extensive activities of Pi Gamma Mu, a national social science honorary chartered locally in 1957.

Concordia seemingly had little to offer that might attract teachers. Salaries were low even for private colleges, but administration effort improved them an average of $1,200 or 32.4 percent between 1952 and 1956. In 1956 the scale ranged from $3,500 for the lowest-paid instructor to $5,300 for the highest-paid professor. The academic dean received $6,500 and the president $7,000 plus a house. By academic year 1960–1961, salaries had improved again. They now ranged from a low of $4,400 to a high of $7,500. The median for thirty-two professors was $6,900; that for twenty-five instructors was $5,050. Among administrators, the president received $12,000 and the academic dean and business manager $10,000 each. At that time Sidney Rand, executive director of the church board of higher education, complimented the administration for its great improvement in salaries.[19]

In addition to this effort, the availability of college-owned houses made a difference for some. Political science professor Harding Noblitt recalls that instead of leaving, he stayed at Concordia and finished his degree because he could rent a house from 1954 to 1961. To further augment low pay, Dean Bailey in 1959 proposed a plan of summer employment other than teaching. Besides supplementing salaries and relieving faculty from seeking work elsewhere, the scheme promised additional benefits of enlarging summer programs, completing valuable committee work and attracting new faculty. Once the plan was implemented, then funding would be sought.[20] Evidently this proposal had no immediate impact, but subsequently the institution has secured financing for many summer institutional and faculty development projects.

Fringe benefits and faculty policies were rather undeveloped at the beginning of Knutson's tenure; due to presidential leadership, and occasionally in spite of the president's desires, these became more extensive and sophisticated. After a prolonged debate about insurance that lasted more than a year, the president decisively broke the deadlock. In July 1957 the college assumed 50 percent of the cost for a group insurance plan with life, medical and disability coverage. The addition of CREF in 1953 strengthened the TIAA retirement plan. Then in September 1965 the matching individual-institutional deduction was increased from 4.5 to 5 percent, the life insurance coverage increased and tax-sheltered TIAA annuities made available. At this time, Dean Carl Bailey instituted a travel fund to encourage attendance at regional or national meetings recognized by the North Central; subject to approval by academic dean, each person received $25 annually, not to exceed $75 cumulative over three years.[21]

A more precisely defined appointments policy and a formal tenure system were other Bailey innovations that he developed despite the president's misgivings. Knutson feared the inflexibility of such legal formalities. To the contrary, Bailey argued, an established tenure plan would be more flexible than the then followed unwritten "three-year rule," which had considerable moral force and which made it very difficult to dismiss anyone, even of questionable quality. Faculty representatives began discussing Bailey's proposals in January 1959 and the regents approved new appointment policies in April 1962. Tenure decisions were now made by the president with the advice of department heads and the dean of the college. A positive decision was based on teaching competence, professional improvements and accomplishments, and evidence of sympathy to basic aims of the college. The policy was retroactive. With advice of the dean and heads, the president assigned existing faculty to one of three categories: tenured, ineligible for tenure and eligible for tenure after successful completion of a trial period.[22]

Appointment policies were also formalized in ways that curtailed the president's powers. Under the changed policy, all chairpersons now took the initiative in securing candidates with the help of other department members and the dean. Appointments were made by the president upon recommendation of the department head and the dean. The president still appointed chairs, but now with the advice of the dean and with consultation of the department.[23]

Four Supreme Court decisions between 1952 and 1959 recognizing academic freedom as both a substantive and procedural right compelled Concordia to make a public declaration on this important subject. Dean Bailey drafted a statement in February 1961 and the board approved it in April 1962. As defined by Bailey, "academic freedom means the right of the individual to hold whatever opinion he considers reasonable on any subject, and the right to discuss any subject from any point of view, under proper circumstances with due respect for common decency." In permitting professors to express themselves freely so long as they were temperate and dignified, this statement was consistent with standards of the American Association of University Professors (AAUP), the major defender of academic liberty on American campuses.[24]

Freedom posed problems for an avowedly Christian college, however. From a secular perspective, most Christian institutions had a double standard of truth: They permitted free inquiry into natural phenomena, but revealed truth limited their questioning of the supernatural. From a Christian perspective, on the other hand, secular education is limited because it does not expose students to religious knowledge and truth. According to this religious view, Christian colleges should be poised between the demands of free academic inquiry and theological loyalty. Without the former, intellectual viability is impossible; without the latter, Christian identity is lost. Concordia, one representative of what the Danforth Commission has characterized as the "free Christian college," wanted it both ways. It attempted to broaden academic pursuits at the same time it enhanced theological commitment. It expected sympathy for religious mission but it did not prescribe beliefs or restrict expression.[25]

Strongly committed to improving academic quality, Dean Bailey recruited staff with doctorates and developed a leaves program to help others complete their degrees. Discussions began in 1956. For the 1958–1959 budget he requested $18,000, an amount sufficient to fund three full-year leaves and some summer subsidies. He finally secured funding in 1960–1961. An urgent need to increase the low percentage of earned doctorates necessitated this effort. Besides, Bailey believed that a leaves plan would establish Concordia as a progressive institution and thereby cement the loyalty of younger teachers. To further assist degree completion, the administration battled the Internal Revenue Service so professors might obtain tax deductions for educational expenses. As they informed the IRS, "any college wishing to maintain its academic standards has to aim for 40 percent of its faculty holding doctorates." With only 20.5 percent possessing these degrees in 1959, Concordia faced a sizable task to achieve its goal.[26]

Other efforts included the "great teacher program" established by the development office in 1960. It sought funds for keeping great teachers in the classroom and recruiting others by enhancing their professional status and growth. This effort did not achieve the hoped-for dollars but Concordia's first endowed professorship—the Alma and Reuel Wije Distinguished Professor—was launched in September 1962. Many sought and successfully obtained outside funding. Kenneth Bailey (1957), Olin Storvick (1961) and David Green (1964) were awarded Danforth Teacher Study Grants. Several received Martin Luther Fellowships from the National Lutheran Educational Conference, or Faculty Growth Awards from the board of education of the American Lutheran Church. Philosophy professor Reidar Thomte won the most prestigious awards of anyone: a Guggenheim in 1954 for study in Copenhagen and a Fulbright in 1959 for continuing his research on the Danish theologian Sören Kierkegaard.[27]

Professor Reidar Thomte

Faculty development did not depend solely on outside funding, further education or research. On-campus organizations fostered growth as well. Efforts ranged from the formal Pi Alpha Alpha, a society to improve teaching skills established in 1963, to the informal "Brain Pickers Academic Fraternity," founded in the mid-1960s. Pi Alpha Alpha arranged for class visits by two or three members followed by discussions with the teacher of what had been observed. The "Brain Pickers," a group of relatively new faculty, had no requirements for membership other than a willingness to talk to each other about their respective academic disciplines. The rules were: "Thou shalt talk shop!" "Thy soul shall be required of thee!" "Thou shalt love thy colleague as thyself!"[28]

Faculty Fantasmogoria featured professors at play.

Faculty were not always serious, however. They continued the tradition of Faculty Fantasmagoria. In 1956 "Flunkers Frolic" offered a spoof on course evaluations and featured Walt Prausnitz as an opera singer, Cy Running as Liberace, the Reverends Grimstad, Larsen, Halvorson and Brevik riding motorcycles, Geneva Mauseth and Martha Silseth as heroines of a melodrama, and Martha Brennun arriving on stage in her little green Ford. Fourteen women piled out, including Ruth Berge and Elizabeth Strand from the trunk.[29]

Administrative Services

More students and faculty dictated an enlarged administration. Growth was not excessive because Knutson took pride in keeping administrative costs low; he loved to cite comparative statistics showing the college among the lowest. More sophisticated administrative procedures were adopted. It was news in January 1952 when the registrar's office obtained a photographic copying machine to speed its work. In January 1954 Registrar Don Dale adopted personal identification and class cards which used the McBee Keysort System for the purpose of speeding reports to students, parents and faculty. In February 1960 the college distributed a questionnaire about its policies to seniors. Developed by the administration and the student development commission, this questionnaire was perceived by collegians as a significant means of giving them a say in future policies.[30]

The health service gave required X-ray examinations to students and faculty, administered annual Mantoux tuberculin tests, and in October 1957 began distributing the recently developed Salk polio vaccine. A major change in the 1957–1958 academic year involved a Fargo Clinic physician spending time on campus each day. He joined school nurse Cordelia Skeim in staffing the health service.[31]

Another change included the creation of an office of special services in 1957 headed by Carl Narveson. The new office arranged the artist and lecture series,

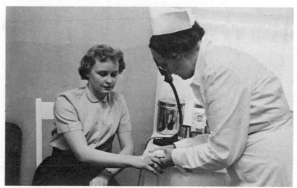

The Health Service administered medical tests and treatment.

furnished free films on weekends, supervised the new audiovisual aids program and directed the placement bureau. Placement helped graduates find jobs, a task eased somewhat by the fact that approximately 20 percent of each graduating class attended graduate and professional schools. In the early 1950s, twelve to fifteen annually entered theological training, six to ten began graduate study, ten entered medical school and others studied law. Most graduates taught. Between 1954 and 1959 the average number of graduates, who were 54.6 percent male, increased to 227. From 1960 to 1965 the number graduating climbed to 329 and the percentage of females rose to 51.1 percent.[32]

Church Mergers and College Relations

The American Lutheran Church (ALC) and the Lutheran Church of America (LCA) were formed in 1960 and 1962, respectively. These mergers evolved from the experience of World War II which had stimulated Lutheran cooperation to serve members of the armed forces and to provide relief for European churches and refugees. The ALC combined three synods and ethnic groups: the Evangelical Lutheran Church (Norwegian), the American Lutheran Church (German) and the United Evangelical

Lutheran Church (Danish). The Lutheran Free Church (Norwegian) joined in 1963, giving football coach Jake Christiansen the opportunity to inspire his men prior to the Augsburg football game, "This is your last chance to be mean to those people!" Beside depriving the coach of a motivational tool and not altering Concordia's administrative structure, the merger enlarged the college constituency and brought new channels of cooperation between ALC and LCA colleges and boards of education.[33]

Earlier Dr. Orville Dahl, executive secretary of the Evangelical Lutheran Church board of education, circulated a plan for a transcontinental Lutheran University of America inspired by the 1933 *Studies in Lutheran Higher Education.* Dahl's proposal to federate all educational institutions of the church was rejected by individualistic institutions which feared centralization. Thus Concordia continued to see itself as a regional college serving a strong Norwegian Lutheran area. To serve this region effectively, necessitated institutional autonomy at the same time that the church assisted with students, dollars, advice and other services. The college preferred to see this relationship as one of mutual helpfulness.[34]

Planning and Fundraising

It troubled President Knutson that Concordia needed so many things. At times he became discouraged by his inability to raise funds quickly for the rapid expansion necessary to capitalize on the opportunities he perceived. He occasionally pondered returning to the parish in order to vacate the presidency for someone with "a real Midas touch." Despite these frustrations, Knutson remained in office and, in retrospect, appears to have been the Midas required.[35]

Needs were catalogued and costs estimated in a bold twenty-year development program announced in 1955. Produced by the combined efforts of administrators, faculty, consultants and architects, the program set these objectives: to build an excellent faculty; to attract highly motivated students from many backgrounds and places; to provide the facilities for learning; and to create surroundings for intellectual and spiritual development. An estimated cost of $11.4 million was set as the price tag for improving faculty, enhancing endowment and constructing thirteen buildings by 1975. Traditional religious loyalties were set aside as Catholics, Jews and other Protestants were enlisted for the Concordia Development Council, chaired by businessman Eugene T. Paulson, and the Concordia Associates, headed by J. Luther Jacobson ('34).[36]

Luther Jacobson and Gene Paulson founded C-400.

Where would Concordia acquire the dollars to meet its pressing needs and to achieve its ambitious goals? Possible sources included the church, private contributors and the federal government. As a church college led by a rock-ribbed Republican who feared creeping statism, Concordia naturally preferred private funding. Prospects seemed promising.

A new era of development started in 1957 when Harvard launched its campaign to raise $82 million. Then in September 1960 the Ford Foundation committed $252 million to sixty-nine institutions if they could raise $654 million from non-government sources. Concordia had benefited earlier from a Ford Foundation grant of $289,000 paid in two installments in 1956 and 1957. The largest award received to date, it doubled the gift income of the previous year. The National Science Foundation, the Hill Foundation and Fund for the Advancement of Adult Education came of age and were of great assistance to Minnesota colleges. But these agencies alone could not meet all financial needs. Nor had business contributed much to higher education's current budgets for all its talk of the wealth created by the free enterprise system. Of the dollars needed to pay for the expansion of the 1960s, only 58 percent therefore would come from private sources—churches, foundations, alumni, business, friends; the balance came from government grants and loans. This dependence of private colleges on government support blurred one former distinction between private and public.[37]

To finance its physical plant expansion, the Knutson administration initially borrowed from bankers and soon from the federal government. The president credits Arthur Hanson, church district president and chair of the board, with this idea. He recalls Hanson coming into his office and saying, "Joe, we're going to get a couple of buildings up at Concordia and we're going to borrow the money. These Norwegians will pay for them, but never will they pay for something they can't see. They weren't born with enough imagination for that." Consequently, Business Manager William Smaby used his banking contacts successfully in 1952 to obtain a $150,000 loan from the Minneapolis

Board Chair Rev. A.E. Hanson joined Knutson in boosting growth.

Farmers and Mechanics Bank for completing the field house. An additional loan soon followed to finance a new library. By January 1960, a new request to borrow $150,000 for a music hall—combined with old debt of $310,000 with the Farmers and Mechanics Bank and $622,000 in dormitory bonds with the Federal Housing and Home Finance Agency—threatened to push indebtedness beyond the church-imposed $1 million limit. That fall Concordia asked permission to borrow an additional $1 million from the government for a new dormitory. These low-cost federal loans were repaid through dormitory rents. This capacity to borrow was enhanced by institutional skill in balancing annual budgets, which established a reputation for good stewardship and fostered good relations with the church hierarchy.[38]

As had President Brown, Knutson fought for Concordia to be treated as a legitimate child of the church and to achieve funding equal to that of Luther and Saint Olaf.

Despite heated resistance, Knutson won this battle. For fiscal year 1955–1956 his school received $117,000, seemingly not a large amount but significant because the appropriation and contributions from the Evangelical Lutheran Church were the chief gift income. Knutson thereafter lobbied to increase the church educational budget and the right to borrow for new construction. He maintained that church security should be used to underwrite a housing program so that the colleges might assume a rightful share of the growing student population. He complained about the borrowing limits imposed during the negotiations that culminated in the 1960 merger. Knutson enthusiastically supported Congregations for Concordia—established in 1958—and eagerly accepted their annual contributions, arguing that the college deserved support because it was an integral part of the church and that congregational interest and enrollees increased proportionately with their gifts.[39]

Meanwhile, private donations increased through growth of the development office. A priority of the president, development was enhanced by employing educational consultants after 1956. Knutson did not like expending more than $8,000 annually until 1962 but saw no alternative. This effort eventually paid for itself. Gift income totalled $658,611 in 1956–1957, a record, and the college hoped to increase this to $1 million annually by 1963. Knutson credited the consultants with needling Concordia into better administration, more consistent fundraising and a long-range program for cultivation of bequests and special donations. To achieve the latter, they emphasized that the development staff must get out of the office, spend time with people and engage in soft sell.[40]

The consultants encouraged new tactics and targets for solicitation. The Concordia Alumni Fund was established in 1954 because their support attracted other contributors. During its first year, 922 alumni gave $21,620. These numbers increased; for 1962–1963, 1,506 donated $83,207, 14.2 percent of total gift income. That year, alumni began a "three spring phonorama" to enlist 2,200 and thereby increase donors to the endowment and the proposed science hall. In 1959 and 1960, the college approached a list of 200 prospects, including foundations, for contributions to a new music hall. In 1961, the president wrote potential donors asking that they consider the tax advantages offered by educational gifts. An enclosed brochure, "The Economy of Giving," explained these benefits. Naming new buildings for major benefactors was also adopted as a device for attracting large donations.[41]

Significantly, the consultants urged fundraising by marketing the educational program. This effort was supposed to interest faculty in fundraising and publicize the many institutional opportunities available for people's investment. As a first step, an academic blueprint was constructed in 1960. *A Blueprint for Concordia College* (1962) adopted what would become the Danforth Commission definition of a "free Christian college" in articulating three foundation policies for academic and religious mission. First, "strengthen the Christian commitment of the college" in ways appropriate to a community of scholars. Faculty must do their best scholarly work. They should not impose religious restrictions on academic discourse, but should "explore and discuss ... the interplay between the Christian message and the academic disciplines." Foundation policies two and three further affirmed the compatibility of scholarship and Christianity: "to emphasize and strengthen our commitment to liberal studies ... [and] the quality of our academic work." Liberal studies were characterized as that "knowledge and understanding which distinguishes the truly educated person from the person who is merely trained for a job." These studies cultivate knowledge of human nature and world, tools for further learning and desire for service. That

The annual C-400 Founders' Day dinner (1963) was addressed by Walter Judd.

Concordia could not influence the world "by producing incompetent students indifferently trained" necessitated academic quality.[42]

To be effective, the blueprint planning required broad participation before the final document was edited by Carl Bailey, a man gifted in careful thinking and the capacity for writing clear prose. Approved by the board, administration and faculty, the document contained what has since become the familiar mission statement: "The purpose of Concordia College is to influence the affairs of the world by sending into society thoughtful and informed men and women dedicated to the Christian life." An excellent encapsulation of the college tradition of Christian service to society, this did not capture the imagination of the consultant. He complained that it was not exciting and did not create a satisfactory image. His response incurred the wrath of President Knutson, who expounded on the merits of a church college and informed him that this document should not be a gimmick. Although insubstantial compared to later efforts, the finished document was a significant first effort and the beginning of an important planning process for the institution.[43] Thus Blueprint was born; it has been visited upon all members of the Concordia family every decade since.

The C-400 Club was the earliest and greatest success of development. Created by local businessmen Luther Jacobson and Gene Paulson in 1955 to pay for the new Ylvisaker Library, C-400 recruited 400 persons to pledge $1,000 over a four-year period. The idea itself was not new. Similar efforts had been made in earlier fund drives, but this was the first to establish itself as a permanent organization and to raise substantial sums. C-400 contributions were very important; they covered down payments on new buildings and subsequently repaid construction loans. By January 1960, 280 members had been enlisted. At that time, Knutson reported a mortgaged indebtedness of $310,000. He expected the club to liquidate indebtedness within the next three years and thus avoid any depletion of current operating funds. Knutson's hopes were fulfilled. The C-400 Day drive on November 8, 1961, brought in forty-seven new members, the highest number ever obtained in a one-day recruitment. The new memberships exceeded the original goal. Fortunately for Concordia, the organization did not stop once it had paid for the library. It immediately pushed on to other projects. In March 1962, "Operation Gold Shovel" began an enlistment to build a new administration building and renovate Old Main. By the summer of 1965 nearly 800 persons were members.[44]

Collegians were enlisted for the development cause as well. A student development commission, formed in 1960, brought "the Concordia story" to prospective students and promoted the college on campus. Apparently the response was much less than desired, leading *Concordian* editors Sheila Mickelson ('62) and Jim Wagner ('61) to ask, "Will ... students respond willingly and sincerely ... or will they continue to display their passive and often antagonistic attitude toward the college?" Efforts continued, however. In April 1963, a contingent C-400 committee offered seniors an opportunity to become members. By joining the contingent group, they assumed some membership responsibilities: recruiting new members, maintaining contact with the college and being a public relations person for the institution. Upon completion of an initial pledge of $60 a year for ten years, they became full members with another $600 commitment. That year sixty-one enlisted, approximately 17.5 percent of the graduates.[45]

Despite Concordia's notable success in maintaining growth through private funding, federal money played a significant part as well. Due to the impact of the Cold War on domestic and international politics, large sums were made available. After the surprising Russian triumph in launching Sputnik the previous year, Congress in 1958 passed the National Defense Education Act. An active federal aid lobby, often defeated in the past, was pleased to seize national security as a vehicle to establish the legitimacy of government assistance. As the act's title suggested, higher education was to be used by the federal government as an instrument for furthering national manpower needs, defense objectives and foreign policy goals. Billions of dollars were allocated for · student grants and loans, university research in science and technology, foreign-language study, teacher training and, especially after 1963, construction of academic facilities.[46]

Government aid posed dilemmas for church-related liberal arts colleges. Gould Wickey, executive director of the National Lutheran Educational Conference, warned that federal aid "may make the definition of the purpose of the institution more difficult" and that project-oriented federal grants within single disciplines "tend to intensify the already serious fragmentation of the intellectual life on campus." President Knutson similarly worried about the consequences of federal assistance. To be sure, he was politically astute and had always been mindful of the implications of public policy for private education. To that end, he lobbied when necessary with Minnesota congressmen as President Brown had done. In 1952 he urged Congressman Harold Hagen to vote for the Springer Amendment to the Veterans Readjustment Assistance Act of 1952, which provided for separate tuition and subsistence allowances instead of a lump-sum payment. Knutson objected to the original bill because it discriminated against veterans who chose to attend private schools. On other occasions, Knutson lobbied congressional representatives to secure loans for buildings and science equipment; he also sought tax legislation that encouraged educational gifts. In all cases, his efforts were directed toward preserving the independence of private colleges. He only reluctantly accepted government bounty. As he wrote to Congressman Odin Langen, "I'm sorry that we ever had to have federal aid to education, but it's now with us. ... If this is the system that people want, even those of us who had our questions have to conform." Knutson admitted sadly that the survival of private education required public support.[47]

Figures reveal the truth of Knutson's judgment. Until the early 1960s, federal aid had been negligible for Concordia. Student fees accounted for 85 percent of the operating budget and gifts the rest. Individuals gave 43 percent and the church 39 percent of gift income. Less than 3 percent of the current budget came from federal and state grants. Yet an increasing share of student tuition income was now funded by government loans. In Minnesota, loans to private college undergraduates rose from $740,000 in 1960–1961 to $2,170,000 in 1969–1970. The Higher Education Facilities Act (1963), which provided grants and loans for the construction of academic facilities, financed twenty-five projects at private Minnesota institutions. Concordia shared this largess. National Defense Loans increased from $63,550 in 1959 to $357,455 in 1962. Cobbers received these funds enthusiastically; this is not surprising given spiraling costs and the growing tuition differential with state schools. In addition, the college received government housing loans for two dormitories. Later, an inadequate physical plant combined with burgeoning numbers placed Concordia in a favorable position to secure federal aid for academic buildings because government criteria emphasized growth and the fewest square feet per student. This worked well until the government refused funding for a proposed art building in the early 1970s. By that time, construction had caught up with the enrollment and the college no longer qualified for federal aid.[48]

Institutional growth and financial needs dictated a change in the composition of the board of regents. In contrast to a past preference for clergy, an attempt was now made to emulate what universities had done at the turn of the century and secure businessmen in order to better manage a multi-million dollar plant and budget. In part, this endeavor attempted to avoid what Knutson perceived as past financial mismanagement. He was particularly upset by the board's sale of college-owned farms in the 1940s. Sold before land values increased markedly, the farms brought only a fraction of the income they would have later and, Knutson insisted, "crippled the college for many, many years." When he inquired why they had been sold, a board member told him: "I don't want you to mention those farms again. If you had been on the board you would have sold them too. All they did was cause dissension and bitterness."[49]

Perhaps Knutson did not mention them again, but he did work with his newly established development office to elect business-minded regents. Development proposed nominees who were prosperous and prominent. The nominating committee generally accepted these suggestions; that way a financially skilled and well-

The Board of Regents sought members with proven business skills as the college grew.

connected board was built. In 1953, the board counted twelve clergy among its twenty-six members. By 1960, the twenty-four member board included only eight ministers. At the same time, the regents had organized a development council, reflecting the Knutson administration emphasis on a more organized approach to fundraising. The council was comprised of twelve committee chairs: special gifts, communications, church, C-400, parents, estate planning, corporations, alumni fund, individuals, faculty commission, students and foundations.[50]

New Buildings At Last!

The dollars obtained from public and private sources by the better organized development program were invested in new buildings designed by the Northfield, Minnesota, architectural firm of Edward Sövik and Associates. Between 1954 and 1965, major projects included a library, three dormitories, a commons, a music hall and an administration building. Expansion posed potential friction with the neighborhood and the city government. In general, the Knutson administration quietly purchased adjoining property

Architect Edward A. Sövik

when it came on the market, thereby obtaining room for growth without conflict. Desiring an enclosed campus space for aesthetic reasons and arguing that planned construction constituted a traffic hazard, the college requested in November 1954 that the city close parts of Ninth Avenue and Seventh Street. Concordia made arrangements to purchase four homes affected by this request, and eventually a longer segment of Seventh Street was closed. On other issues, the college avoided discord by remaining neutral; it withdrew from a petition for the installation of storm sewers in south Moorhead and did not oppose an ice-cream stand on Eighth Street.[51]

For Concordia to be truly a college, President Knutson insisted, a library must be built. The president's case was strengthened by the reluctant Minnesota Department of

Education approval of the elementary education major due to poor facilities and by fears that the North Central Association might soon withdraw accreditation. Brick replaced stone in the campus architectural plan because high costs prohibited duplicating the lovely Fjelstad and Brown Halls. Nevertheless, Sövik's modern design for the library—using vertical thermoglass and red enameled ceramic panels between buff brick columns—harmonized beautifully in materials, scale, line and color with the Gothic Kasota stone buildings favored by President Brown. Sövik believes that architecture ought to represent Christian ideas; hence his modern designs are coherent, authentic, hospitable and beautiful, reflecting belief in a coherent universe, the realities of modern life, the ethic of love and the beauty of the transcendent.[52]

Marie Ylvisaker, widow of Carl B., turned the first shovel of dirt in March 1955 for the $400,000 Ylvisaker Library that would seat 530, shelve 125,000 books and win an Award of Merit from the American Institute of Architects. Volunteers moved the 45,000 volume collection in January 1956 when the new facility opened for proud Cobbers who claimed that it made studying a pleasure.[53]

Begun in Summer 1955 and named Park Region Hall in honor of the school that merged with Concordia in 1917, a dormitory housing 228 women opened in Fall

1956. It was dedicated at homecoming by Dr. A.E. Hanson, a Park Region alumnus, district church president and chair of the board of directors. The college paid down

the first year's interest and principal on the $650,000 government loan payable in forty years at 3.5 percent. Room rents from a perpetually full residence hall, due to limited housing in Moorhead, financed the remainder.[54]

With the exception of the small atom smasher building erected in 1958, new construction halted pending completion of the ALC merger. The next project was student initiated. Cobbers had long agitated for a union. In April 1955, after a semester-long discussion of

Books are moved into Ylvisaker Library by Don Dale, E.T. Paulson, Marie Ylvisaker, J.L. Knutson and W.A. Smaby.

the issue, they voted for a five dollar per semester union fee. They began planning that fall, but the church-imposed limit on indebtedness delayed construction. After three years of talk, building finally began in April 1959 on the first phase of a scaled down $325,000 structure to house an enlarged cafeteria, student offices, a game room, an off-campus room and a student lounge. Instructed by the president to provide "a terrific amount of space for very little money," architect Sövik designed a building of buff brick with enameled metal panels and glass. The union fund contributed $50,000; the college

used funds from the church to pay the balance, avoided borrowing and thus stayed below the $1 million debt limit. Named the Commons, it opened in February 1960. Subsequent phases of the union projected the destruction of Academy, Grose and Bishop Whipple. These were not constructed as then planned.[55]

New construction, here of the Cobber Commons, would be a familiar sight throughout the 1960s.

Although some believed other facilities were more needed, the administration decided to construct another dormitory when 300 men overflowed Brown Hall. The ground-breaking occurred in October 1961 for a structure which accommodated 231 men, a bookstore, cafeteria and post office. Financed by a $1 million loan from the Federal Housing and Home Finance Agency, it was named Livedalen Hall in honor of a Hatton, North Dakota, farmer who had willed to Concordia its then largest single gift of $324,198. The dormitory opened in Fall 1962 and the connected wing in January 1963. Hoyum Hall, an adjacent women's dormitory housing 230, opened in September 1965.[56]

Meanwhile, other structures were refurbished. South Hall—home for 120 freshmen—had its gloomy grey stucco exterior covered with wood siding. It was renamed Academy to honor the institution's origins. New entries into Academy, Grose and Bishop Whipple Halls and the Regents Room in the basement of Bishop Whipple were

Alfred Hvidsten waited many years for this 1962 groundbreaking of the Music Hall.

also built. In 1963 the former bookstore—constructed in 1954—and Cobber Hall were remodeled into additional offices and classrooms.[57]

In May 1962, ground was finally broken by Alfred Hvidsten for the much-delayed music hall. Dedicated at homecoming in 1963, the building was named for Hvidsten, who had given $60,000 for the project in 1946 when he was a board member. Beginning in late 1959, officials approached major foundations in an attempt at last to bring Hvidsten's dream to fruition. Although results did not match hopes, the campaign received a $25,000 Kresge Foundation grant and a smaller amount from the Charles A. Frueauff Foundation. When the $700,000 facility opened in Fall 1963, it received rave reviews from music professors Stahl, Christiansen and Childs: "Almost like a palace!" "There isn't a college of our size with anything like it!" "We have absolutely the tops in facilities!"[58]

The administration building (present Lorentzsen Hall) opened in Fall 1964. Funded by C-400, this project not only provided administrators with new offices but allowed for converting Old Main into badly needed classroom space.[59]

Material Success Not Enough

President Knutson enjoyed remarkable success in managing growth from 1951 to 1965. Enrollment had grown from 890 to 2,100, assisted by federally funded student loans. Gifts from private sources had more than tripled, private bankers had been tapped and large government loans had been obtained to construct seven major buildings and remodel others. Concordia could rightfully take great pride in its remarkable record of material success. On the other hand, the president reminded the community that material success by itself is not enough. Ever mindful of the institutional motto, *Soli Deo Gloria*—"To God alone the glory"—President Knutson knew that Christian integrity must also be maintained.

Chapter 13

A Christian College
In Quiet Years

Defining the Christian College

President Knutson and the Concordia community took great care in describing the character of a Christian college and in defining the goals of the Christian liberal arts. They were not alone in these preoccupations. During the 1950s, a decade of a renewed interest by American society in religion, many conferences were organized in response to Harvard President Nathan Pusey's call for church-related institutions to reclaim their heritage. Meanwhile Lutheran higher education engaged in extensive self-assessment. As did Concordia, most schools published five-or ten-year master plans, often with the help of professional consultants. As at Concordia, faculty committees elsewhere debated these subjects endlessly.[1]

Several factors fostered reassessment. The GI Bill, an important first step in making higher education accessible to all, contributed to the decline of homogeneity in Lutheran institutions. Like the GIs, many of the postwar enrollees selected colleges less for religious than for geographical, financial and educational reasons. Part of the "silent generation" noted for its social conformity and desire for financial security, these collegians appeared to Lutheran educators as the possible forerunners of a secular, self-oriented society. New faculty with freshly minted doctoral degrees and a religious outlook different from the faithful old guard similarly aroused anxieties about secularization.[2]

President Knutson spoke often in chapel, articulating his vision of a Christian college.

Through chapel talks—delivered between six and ten times a semester, public addresses and short publications, President Knutson defined what it is to be a Christian institution. He noted that Lutheran schools possessed the three essential components—a faculty committed to Christ, a community organized around Christian activities and a Christ-centered ideology. Given these criteria for measuring faithfulness to mission, it was imperative to recruit Christian professors. With a committed faculty, the ideological and communal elements could be achieved more easily. Staunchly evangelical, Knutson explained mission in terms of the gospel to collegians and constituents. As an institution of the gospel, Concordia taught the grand truth of redemption in Christ, "the Truth that can make all knowledge meaningful and redemptive in human personality." Although Knutson as a Lutheran emphasized faith, he also asserted that faith expressed itself in daily life as a well-defined code of Christian conduct. Therefore Christians had always abstained from certain worldly activities in order "to grow unto the stature of the fullness of Christ." For this reason, a Christian college must be a community with a distinctive atmosphere conducive to righteous living. If it were not, it would no longer be a Christian college.[3]

President Knutson often said that his biggest worry was that Concordia would become "a sophisticated, worldly institution." In an appealing, folksy manner, Knutson's chapel talks bluntly addressed such topics as "The Prodigal Cobber" and "The World, the Flesh and Concordia College." He equated worldliness with secularism and defined it as life without spiritual motivation or goal. He repeatedly scolded Cobbers for their shortcomings and warned that worldliness was the primary threat which historically had destroyed many formerly Christian institutions. "Prodigal Cobbers" were fascinated by the world and guided by instincts and momentary passions. Their inherent sinfulness manifested itself in "a nightclub atmosphere," "shocking language" in college productions, off-color jokes in Cobber Capers and newspaper editors whose "main purpose seems to be embarrassing the administration and the church."[4]

Combating worldliness was a major presidential preoccupation; he repeatedly requested church support for enforcing those standards he considered essential. In 1951, Knutson buttressed his stance as presidential enforcer by appealing to the 1950 report of the commission on higher education to the general church convention which reiterated the denomination's stand against "worldly amusements of colleges." By 1957, changing societal standards were already making Knutson's position more difficult. In that year, he suggested a discussion of social trends that affect campus Christian living as an agenda for a meeting of Lutheran personnel deans, religion department chairpersons and college pastors. Asserting that it was not fair to expect the academy to maintain moral standards most congregations ignored, Knutson constantly sought ways to strengthen the commitment of Lutherans to their colleges.[5]

Rules and regulations embodied the institutional conception of the Christian life. By 1955, rules had been modified slightly, reflecting changing social mores; card-playing was no longer banned and students were now expected, but no longer required, "to attend daily chapel services and public worship every Sunday." As regulations eased, their rationale was rewritten. Standards were necessary for developing Christian community and were therefore good for individuals and groups. For this reason, collegians were "asked to refrain from doing these things not because they are sinful in themselves or part of the fundamental moral law, but because in the life and tradition of our people their practice has not been conducive to vital Christian living and devotion." By the 1960s, the college retreated slightly on the issue of social dancing in the face of changing moral attitudes among its Lutheran constituency. It now simply said that social dancing is not part of its organized social program. Previously it banned attendance at any private and public dances. To the dismay of some constituents, Knutson permitted square dancing. In his defense, he said it had existed when he arrived. Besides, he had watched it carefully and found nothing wrong. "It is very vigorous exercise and there isn't much chance for anything sultry or suggestive," he reported. "It is like a lot of games we used to play in Luther League."[6]

Most Cobbers seem to have accepted most regulations. A psychology class survey of 100 coeds in 1961 found that 83 percent did not drink liquor; 83 percent did not smoke; 80 percent attended church and chapel at least once a week. To be sure, 76 percent of the women had attended dances while at Concordia. Official student spokespersons often upheld standards and chastised violators. When Concordia's first panty raid made the *Forum* front page in 1963, for example, *Concordian* editor Marc Borg ('64) worried about the adverse effect of negative publicity on institutional image: "To many people, all they know of Concordia is what they read on the front page. They never hear of our real accomplishments. But a panty raid? They hear of that, and this becomes Concordia to them."[7]

Not all Cobbers were supportive. Even in the 1950s, which Knutson later remembered as wonderful, some tried to change the institution. A mimeographed manifesto called "the blue paper" appeared in December 1960. Authored by Jim Hoxeng ('61), Don Burton ('61), Bob Alexander ('61) and others, the document indicted the college for not fulfilling its self-proclaimed goals of the Christian liberal arts. The application of Christianity to life had not occurred. Unrevised courses, dully taught did not achieve liberal arts habits of mind. Academic dishonesty was too often tolerated. Faculty committees and the Student Association did not work together. Rules governing relations between the sexes were too repressive. And fear of reprisals prevented everyone from speaking frankly.[8]

It is noteworthy that these authors were not inhibited by the stifling atmosphere they portrayed. Indeed, the administration's response to unrest often exhibited a flexibility belied by Knutson's public rhetoric. Administrators met extensively with unhappy groups, let them criticize freely and then made changes that would not compromise academic program, Christian integrity or public image.[9]

Similarly, the student-faculty forum, dormitory councils and other committees worked to settle disputes over women's dormitory lounge hours and a dress code. By 1962, lounge hours had been extended from 7:30 until 9:55 on weeknights. The dress code proved more problematic. In January 1962, the student senate recommended that women be permitted to wear slacks in classrooms, library and cafeteria on days when the temperature was below freezing. The administration vetoed the proposal on grounds it would adversely affect institutional image. Finally, in 1964 a student committee submitted a code acceptable to an administrative committee and it went into effect immediately. Rollers, short shorts and bare feet were blacklisted. In the library, cafeteria and classrooms, classroom dress—skirts, sweaters, slacks (men) but no bermudas, blue jeans or sloppy sweatshirts—was required at all times Sunday through Friday. In the Normandy, casual dress—sports clothes, slacks (women) and bermudas—was always acceptable. On Saturdays, casual dress was permitted in the cafeteria. Women might wear slacks on extremely cold days and in the library on Saturdays or to pick up books the remainder of the week. Within a year, complaints surfaced. Apparently the code was not obeyed. *Concordian* editor Tom Pierce urged revisions to secure compliance. Interestingly, the concept of a code itself was not rejected.[10]

As the communal element in Knutson's conception of the Christian college shaped institutional expectation of a Christian lifestyle, the ideological element informed the articulation of the Christian liberal arts. In the mid-1950s, the catalog statement of purpose was revised. The new description pointed out that the Latin root of liberal, *liber*, means free; it was therefore appropriate that "a liberal arts education seeks to *give* free man the knowledge, methods, attitudes, and discipline that should control his life and make him an effective servant of God and man." In addition, this education should be Christ-centered. In what were Knutson's words, "The integrating factor in the life and curriculum of a Christian liberal arts college is the revelation of God in

Jesus Christ. ... [S]uch a college is something far greater and more significant than an institution with a few courses of religion and a daily chapel service. ... Every responsible vocation is a spiritual ministry. The natural sciences ... as well as courses in religion reflect God's purpose and handiwork, witnessing to the declaration of Christ and the apostles that all things are to become complete in Him." Significantly, this statement emerged when many colleges were abandoning their religious ties. By articulating the centrality of Christ in the educational mission, Knutson made explicit what had always been implicit and signaled his intention that Concordia would resist secularization and hold fast to its Christian identity.[11]

The president's ideas mirrored institutional commitments and discussions of the decade. Concordia joined the North Central Association Committee on the Liberal Arts in 1954 and sent delegates to a summer workshop. Carl Bailey, Allan Hanson, Reidar Thomte, Sigurd Mundhjeld and Olin Storvick represented the college in the Christian Liberal Arts Project carried on for ten years by a committee comprised of members from Augustana (Sioux Falls), Luther, Luther Theological Seminary, Saint Olaf and Waldorf in addition to Concordia.[12]

The project began with consideration of the question, "Is there a Lutheran philosophy of education?" The published rejoinder, *Christian Faith and the Liberal Arts* (1960), did not claim to be distinctively Lutheran; rather the essays were representative of the classical intellectual tradition of the Western church qualified by Reformation concerns. Carl Bailey's contribution, "Natural Sciences," affirmed the essential compatibility of the natural sciences, liberal arts and Christianity. The natural sciences imparted knowledge, analytical skill, methodological tools and aesthetic appreciation. Because of epistemological limitations, modern science can not disprove essential Christian beliefs. At the same time, the Bible should not be read as though it were a textbook in science and scientific findings should not be bent to fit religious doctrine. Nonetheless, Bailey concluded, if science teaching emphasized humility, wonder before God's creation and the limitations of human capacity, then it had been taught liberally and had contributed to religious understanding.[13]

The Christian liberal arts were publicized by Knutson and Bailey articles in *The Record*, a Bailey interview in the *Forum*, *A Blueprint for Concordia College* (1962) and the college catalog. According to a more elaborate statement of goals for the 1960 edition of the catalog, a liberally educated person possessed these characteristics: responsibility for perpetuating the best in the cultural heritage, particularly the Christian faith; appreciation of knowledge for its own sake; clear and precise speech and mastery of the use of numbers; skills in critical thinking; aesthetic appreciation; understanding of the scientific method and the physical and biological worlds; knowledge of human nature and society; and the desire to be a useful and productive citizen. Admittedly too much to accomplish in only four years, these goals were thought central to the institutional mission. To avoid betraying that mission, increased pressures for more technical training must therefore be resisted.[14]

Academic Life and Programs

The Christian liberal arts neatly expressed institutional commitment to both religious and academic mission. President Knutson's forceful explication of Christianity did not imply any lack of concern for academics. He wanted Concordia to become a first-rate college and he supported wholeheartedly Dean Bailey's efforts in raising the intellectual level. Dean and president did not work alone. They were assisted by a number of strong departments headed by able professors, including Cyrus Running, art; Ed Fuglestad, biology; Charles Skalet, classics; Pearl Bjork, elementary education; Walther Prausnitz, English; Sigurd Mundhjeld, mathematics; Reidar Thomte, philosophy, and Lloyd Svendsbye, religion. These people made the institution an interesting place intellectually and attracted others similarly inclined; their efforts in the classroom put Concordia on the road to becoming a better academic institution.[15]

To be sure, the school lacked many things and experienced many frustrations. Initially, professors did without private offices, typewriters, filing cabinets, telephones and secretarial assistance. Teaching loads remained heavy; despite a reduction from fifteen to twelve hours during the 1950s, enrollments of 150 to 200 were not unusual for some teachers. Utilizing the enhanced financial resources made available by a successful development program, administrators overcame many of these shortcomings.[16]

Concordia possessed a standard liberal arts curriculum organized in five groups: philosophy and religion, languages and literature, sciences and mathematics, social sciences, fine and applied arts. General education credits from each group except the arts were distributed as follows: fourteen in religion, six in English, twelve in foreign language, six to eight in science and mathematics, and six in social science. Lutherans took religion in each of seven semesters but non-Lutherans in only four. In addition, orientation, two years of physical education, a major and a minor were required. Majors consisted of eighteen senior credits and minors twelve. A concession to vocationalism is evident in a long section entitled "Courses Recommended in Preparation for Professional Study." This was tempered somewhat by the admonition that the best preparation for the professions listed, ranging from agriculture to vocational counseling and guidance, is a broad background of general knowledge; therefore completion of the four-year liberal arts curriculum was recommended.[17]

As part of the ongoing discussion of the Christian liberal arts, the faculty curriculum committee and senate between 1955 and 1958 reviewed the academic program and made small changes. Majors and minors were lengthened and varied in size according to department. A sophomore literature course and an elective from mathematics or philosophy were added to the general education requirements, which were set at sixty-four credits. More important, in January 1958 the college began publishing *Discourse: A Review of the Liberal Arts*. The quarterly encouraged creative work by collegians and professors. Walther Prausnitz chaired the editorial board comprised of four faculty and three students. In October 1962 Prausnitz relinquished and Carl Bailey assumed the editorship. By that time, *Discourse* was distributed to over forty states and several foreign countries. To further publicize

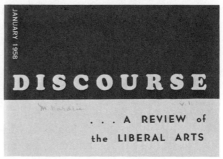

Discourse, a Concordia publication, expressed commitment to the liberal arts.

liberal education, Concordia sponsored a Liberal Arts Institute each summer between 1962 and 1966. The institutes were designed for anyone with an interest in the arts and sciences. Through a program of reading, discussion and lecture, enrollees were informed about the basic ideas and recent developments in several academic disciplines.[18]

An examination of department programs in this period reveals a mixture of commitments to Christian, liberal arts and vocational aims. The continuing conversation about institutional mission stimulated articulation of catalog goal statements. Some were more explicitly religious than others. The history department affirmed "the belief that the pattern of history reveals God's working through the affairs of men to the fulfillment of His plan for the world." Philosophy aimed "to stimulate students to an appreciation of the personal and cultural values of philosophic thought, ... and to aid the student in arriving at a personal and Christian view of life." Another declared its primary purpose to be developing insight into the facts and principles of psychology from a Christian perspective. Religion emphasized its commitment to the same high academic standards as other departments. Physics, on the other hand, stressed liberal arts goals "by acquainting the student with the nature of the physical world and the merits and limitations of the scientific method of investigation, by inculcating habits of critical reasoning, and by laying the foundation for professional work or advanced study."[19]

Some departments were more directly oriented toward vocation than others. A bachelor of science degree, approved by the faculty senate in 1952, replaced foreign language with electives from any curricular group for graduates in elementary education, business education, business administration, home economics, physical education, social work and medical technology. Convinced that the foreign language requirement deterred some from enrolling, President Knutson had requested this change to boost registrations at a critical time. This action reflected the president's concern for maintaining a balance between the theoretical and practical arts so that graduates could obtain jobs.[20]

Directed by Pearl Bjork, the elementary education program began in Fall 1951 with fifty enrolled. Approved by the Minnesota State Board of Education in February 1953,

it expanded to more than two hundred within two years, becoming the fastest growing major at the college. With Minnesota state certification, graduates of the four-year course were eligible for teaching licenses in Montana, North Dakota and Minnesota. The issue of national accreditation soon surfaced. President Knutson, ever the individualist, intensely disliked control by outside agencies. Private colleges discussed resisting oversight by the National Council for Accreditation of Teacher Education (NCATE). Unfortunately, states passed laws requiring this accreditation and Concordia had no choice but to comply. It secured NCATE approval for both elementary and secondary education on its first try in 1961.[21]

Professor Pearl Bjork

During the 1950s, home economics attempted to enhance vocational opportunities for its majors by meeting federal Smith-Hughes requirements. President Knutson again complained about the burden of federal rules, especially when the first effort failed in 1952. He consoled himself with the thought that graduates were not hurt because only one-third of the Minnesota high schools were in the Smith-Hughes program. Nonetheless, he promised to apply again when enrollments justified adding another teacher and when the post office and bookstore moved out of the basement of the home economics building. That move soon occurred and the space was renovated in May 1955. Alice Polikowsky and Margaret Tabbut joined the department in 1958. Minnesota State Board of Education approval came the next year; employment opportunities improved for 1960 graduates,

President Joseph L. Knutson, 1951--1975

who were certified as vocational home economics teachers for federally subsidized high school programs.[22]

The economics department pioneered in cooperative education when it began a five-year major in Fall l956. Seven semesters were spent in traditional study and three on the job with such firms as Delendrecie's, Penney's, Sears, Red Owl, General Mills, Lutheran Brotherhood, Otter Tail Power and Remington Rand. Selected on the basis of scholarship and attitude, four students participated annually. Cobbers thought the program appropriate for a church school because the world needed businessmen with a sense of Christian vocation. Besides placing collegians in business, the department annually brought sixteen outstanding regional businessmen to campus for a "tutorial lecture program." This afforded opportunity to an even larger number of majors for contact with practical business.[23]

*Home Economics Chair
Alice Polikowsky*

After the Sputnik-induced passage of the National Defense Education Act in 1958, mathematics and the natural sciences benefited from the enhanced role of the National Science Foundation (NSF) and shared in the federal largess distributed in the effort to improve science education in the United States. As part of the NSF-encouraged activities, science faculty lectured in area high schools, sponsored an annual science fair, scheduled in-service institutes for area high school science and mathematics teachers, and received grants for equipment purchases.[24]

Other equipment acquired independently of the foundation enabled the college to better prepare its graduates for teaching and research. Thanks to a timely tip provided by graduate student John Gjevre ('56), the physics department in 1957 procured for $75 an ion accelerator then valued at $100,000 from Iowa State University. Now professors could involve undergraduates in atomic energy experiments. In 1963, the college acquired an IBM 1620 computer at a 60 percent reduced price under the company allowance program.[25]

An ion accelerator involved collegians in atomic collision experiments.

The natural science departments enhanced vocational opportunities by successfully placing students in graduate or professional schools. By the mid-1960s, more than 100 Cobbers had become medical doctors. Approximately one-half of the 200 chemistry alumni since 1918 had obtained graduate degrees. Fifty of the eighty physics majors between 1954 and 1965 had continued study. Applied science programs are additional evidence of vocational concern. Although nursing disappeared in 1953, a medical technology major was established with the fourth year taken at St. Luke's Hospital.[26]

Service to nation represented another vocational opportunity. In 1962 military training options were again listed in the catalog. By taking the Marine Corps Platoon Leaders Class, qualified male Cobbers could enter and qualify for commissioning in the Marine Corps at commencement. Students were also informed that National Guard, Air National Guard and Reserve organizations are found in Fargo and Moorhead. Then in 1965, they were advised that Army and Air Force ROTC programs based at North Dakota State University were open to all Cobber men.[27]

Humanities departments also shared in the academic improvements of the decade. The old gymnasium, remodeled in 1953 and dubbed the Art Barn, allowed for more art exhibits and better served departmental needs. The music department adopted the view that pupils must hear performances to grow musically and must perform to experience great composers. They hired performance-oriented teachers, stressed their performances as models and increased the number of student recitals. The English department, rebuilt with new personnel in the 1950s because of complaints from high school superintendents about the poor quality of English graduates, demonstrated new life with new programs. Honors work gave talented majors an opportunity to do independent research in addition to their regular courses. Dorothy Johnson soon left counseling for teaching; funded in part by the Student Association, using magazines for materials and equipped with a stopwatch borrowed from the athletic department, she first taught reading in the foyer of Fjelstad Lounge in Fall 1954. The annual summer reading conference, still a highly successful event,

THE FOURTH ANNUAL CONFERENCE ON READING

JUNE 16 - 20, 1958

Theme:

HELPING STUDENTS READ BETTER

sponsored by The English Department *in cooperation with* Science Research Associates
CONCORDIA COLLEGE
Moorhead, Minnesota
57 W. Grand Avenue
Chicago 10, Illinois

The annual reading conference is still well-attended.

began in 1956 under the direction of Walther Prausnitz assisted by Johnson. Johnson soon assumed responsibility for the conference, which became one of the nation's very best; in 1978 she received the International Reading Association's Award for Distinguished Service.[28]

As did the natural sciences, foreign language study benefited from the Sputnik-aroused public interest in raising academic standards. Concordia made the most of this opportunity. In response to student demand, Russian had been first offered in Fall 1953. A second year, added in 1959, was taught by Mrs. J.J. Spier, who donated her salary to the new language laboratory which opened in January 1960. A Bremer Foundation gift had funded construction of a laboratory equipped with individual booths, head sets and a delayed recording system. To further stimulate interest in language study, the departments gave demonstration classes in local grade schools. The language camps, another innovative and remarkably successful program, were initiated in 1961 by Gerhard Haukebo, associate professor of education, and Erhard Friedrichsmeyer, professor of German. Advertised as the "next best thing to being there," the camps capitalized on the ability of children to learn languages more easily than adults. By 1963, Spanish

Russian professor Fira Spier in the new language laboratory.

and Norwegian had been added to the French and German offered previously. The next year, the Hill Foundation funded a comprehensive report assessing the achievements of the young program.[29]

The library, essential for a quality academic program, benefited from the spacious new building and improved greatly. It held 37,658 volumes and expended $2,975 on new books in 1951. The library committee, chaired by Walther Prausnitz, worked out a five-year plan for expanding and upgrading the collection. By 1960, holdings and expenditures had increased to 59,542 and $12,467 respectively. Microfilmed periodical files, a photocopy machine and long-playing records were acquired. Growing collegiate use of the library is evidenced by their demand for Sunday opening. In March 1956 an experiment began with a seven-day week to determine need. A decade later, some still called for longer weekend hours. These demands and expanded services reflected changes in teaching that enhanced the library's role in undergraduate education. Professors shifted from the lecture-textbook method to reliance on many books found in the library. No wonder theft increased and Cobbers requested more hours.[30]

Collegian attempts to influence academic policies expanded. Whether or not to use course evaluation forms persisted as an almost annual topic for the student-faculty forum. Assessment of subject matter was acceptable but appraisals of professorial performance remained controversial. Hence evaluations were dropped in 1956, reappeared in 1962, then disappeared in 1964 only to return in 1965. The creation of a student-faculty curriculum committee in 1958 formalized undergraduate participation in curricular issues. Cobbers also praised the new "voluntary" attendance policy instituted in 1955. They no longer needed a formal excuse for a missed class, but poor attenders might have grades lowered and might be reported to the personnel deans.[31]

Important instructional innovations benefited students. Arranged in 1958 with the department of government and public administration of American University, the highly successful Washington Semester program enabled two Cobbers to study for one semester in the national capital. Roger A. Matson, the first returnee, recommended the program highly as a unique supplement to the standard curriculum. Several departments, after many years of intermittent discussion dating back to the 1930s, instituted honors programs in 1956, giving the academically talented opportunities for independent research in preparation for graduate school. As designed by English, history and political science, mathematics, philosophy, physics, psychology and speech, the program called for heavier assignments, independent investigation, a senior thesis, and a comprehensive written and oral examination. The student tutor society, implemented in October 1962, sought to improve the academic environment, stimulate enthusiasm for teaching, provide an extracurricular activity for scholars and aid the scholastically troubled.[32]

The benefits of other innovations were more problematic. Television instruction and large lecture sections are not generally associated with quality. Nonetheless the school moved in this direction to solve problems of too few teachers and classrooms. The English, religion and sociology departments began experimenting in 1960 with university-style lecture classes held in Old Main auditorium. At the same time, Dean Bailey envisioned the possibility of TV as a medium joining Concordia to the outside world and called for an extended study of instructional TV. Harding Noblitt pioneered in 1961 when he taught American Government for credit over WDAY-TV on NBC's "Continental Classroom." In 1965 the English department began a four-year experiment with instructional television funded by a $49,120 Hill Foundation grant. Sixty

Prausnitz lectures were recorded for use in freshmen and sophomore English classes. Tests were administered to determine instructional effectiveness. Neither the lecture nor television experiment achieved the hoped-for results; after a few years' trial, both were abandoned.[33]

Another innovation prompted by enrollment pressures proved more enduring. In January 1962, Dean Bailey announced consideration of a trimester plan that would enable graduation in three years and allow enrollment to increase 30 percent without expanding staff or facilities. After careful study, a committee chaired by Prausnitz concluded that this plan would bankrupt the college. The committee did recommend adoption of an altered academic calendar comprised of two six-week summer sessions and two fifteen-week semesters which began September 1 and ended May 1. Introduced in Fall 1964 and persisting to the present, the new calendar had at least three advantages noted by Bailey at the time: It permitted quicker graduation, gave Cobbers a summer employment edge and allowed faculty longer summers for research. At the end of the new calendar's first year, a *Concordian* editorialist agreed that it was an improvement; the accelerated pace required better study habits and thereby enhanced efficiency.[34]

American Association of University Women (AAUW) membership, finally attained in 1961, meant much to women faculty who worked for it and for alumnae who benefited. It had not been easy to secure. The college first applied in 1955. The AAUW, under investigation by the Gustafson Committee, suspended its consideration of new applicants. Concordia's second application was rejected for two reasons: no registered campus physician and few, poorly paid faculty women. The former was corrected in 1957 by retaining a Fargo Clinic doctor for a brief period daily. A new salary schedule lessened salary discrimination. An AAUW representative visited in 1960; membership soon followed.[35]

The coaching clinic annually attracted several hundred.

This small step forward for womankind was unusual given the traditional attitudes toward gender existing at the time on campus and in the church. The *Concordian* reported engagements and in other ways displayed the assumption that women would soon become wives and mothers. This reflected attitudes then prevalent in American society and in the church. Women were not yet ordained and the 1960 American Lutheran Church document, *The Christian and His Social Living*, emphasized that a wife's work should not detract from her special responsibility for the home. She should be fulfilled in home, family and church.[36]

AAUW membership, *Discourse* and other innovations all testified to the liveliness of Concordia's academic life. The many summer programs offered annually throughout the 1950s and later were another sign of institutional vigor. In addition to the Reading Conference, workshops were regularly scheduled in music and band, speech and drama, art and coaching. Of these, the coaching clinic was one of the most successful and enduring. Headed by Jake Christiansen and Sonny Gulsvig, the clinic for almost two decades attracted several hundred annually to a program featuring big-name coaches, banquets and all-star games. The workshops enabled teachers, coaches and directors to learn new techniques and hone old skills. They were in keeping with the institutional ethic of service and allowed the college to build its reputation.[37]

Achieving Liberal Arts Goals

Campus intellectual life demonstrates that some collegians internalized at least some of the Christian liberal arts goals. An all-college poll, taken in February 1957, revealed that 74 percent believed that Concordia prepared them adequately. Cobbers disagreed when specifying how they benefited from their liberal arts education, however. Perhaps many concurred with *Concordian* writer Bill Naylor ('57) who asserted that liberally educated persons had better leadership qualities which allowed them to think and reason outside their chosen fields.[38]

But how were these leadership qualities developed? In answering this question, Cobbers reflected some criticisms of American education then current. Several editorials in 1959 and 1960 sustained Admiral Hyman Rickover's contention that learning in American schools had been downgraded and his proposed solution of hard work and a return to the basics. Collegians should therefore emphasize studies more and extracurriculars less. Others thought institutional size contributed to quality. Concordia's smallness made possible individual attention, rendering liberal arts schools far superior to impersonal state universities.[39]

Others accentuated Christianity. As Daniel Holm ('64) and Mervin Thompson ('63), editors of the 1963 *Cobber*, intoned, "Christian education is God's hand through Christ reaching into every subject and area of life to bring completeness, His fullness and love to mind, body, and spirit and to give life the wholeness it craves." That year's annual was dedicated appropriately to Frida Nilsen, who exemplified the Christian liberal arts because "hers was a responsible vocation, a spiritual ministry."[40]

Concordian editor Bruce Gronbeck ('63) argued in 1962 that contemporary intellectual disorder necessitated the Christian liberal arts as a solution. In the face of fragmentation produced by Freudian psychology, existentialism and modern physics, the Christian college sought to realize the harmony of body and soul, mind and matter, God and man, the worldly and unworldly. A religious viewpoint could be integrated with secular study through the common denominators of humility and a compulsion for social reordering. Both recognized the imperfections of the world and both called for rebuilding. Christianity recognized Christ as the only cornerstone for reconstruction and, consequently, the Christian liberal arts emphasized the essential unity of personality.[41]

Christian liberal arts habits of mind were inculcated in ways other than academic program. Entering its fourth decade of providing cultural enrichment, the artist course and lecture series of six to eight annual events exhibited new energy and quality after Walther Prausnitz became director in 1953. At times

Historian Henry Steele Commager commemorated the Civil War Centenary.

lectures focused on a single issue, as in the commemoration of the American Civil War centennial. Henry Steele Commager, a nationally known historian, initiated the observance in September 1960; Wyoming Senator Gale W. McGee followed with a lecture on "Lincoln and the War" in March 1961. This series generated some controversy. In light of the current sectional division over civil rights, *Concordian* guest editorialist JoelWatne ('61) asked, "Does it make sense to ... glorify a war that is not yet over?" Correspondent David H. Nelson ('61) pointed out that the Civil War centennial is a commemoration, not a celebration; therefore it did not glorify war but simply memorialized the losses, gains and experiences of the Civil War which were a common national possession.[42]

Many other prominent speakers appeared: John Dos Passos (1955), George Forell (1956), Norman Vincent Peale (1958), Werner Von Braun (1959), Carl Sandburg (1959), Krister Stendahl (1961), Richard Niebuhr (1962), and Gerald Brauer (1963). The artist course featured classical music and some theatrical productions. The Minneapolis Symphony appeared annually; other notable bookings included "The Caine Mutiny Court Martial" (1955), Robert Shaw Chorale and the Juilliard Quartet

(1956), "Mikado" by Fujiwara Opera Company of Japan (1957), and pianist Glenn Gould (1962). Despite its evident quality, the program was not popular with all Cobbers. The *Concordian* wrote annual editorials urging attendance. And collegians wrote their annual letters of complaint. Although not

Bard, Book and Canto stimulated interest in English.

unsympathetic to collegiate desire for popular music, defenders insisted on continued classical programming to ensure exposure to high culture. At least one alumnus appreciated this emphasis; he remembers this as a golden period culturally in which

238   President Joseph L. Knutson, 1951--1975

student attendance was very good. Indeed, performances often attracted audiences of 2,500 from the college and the city to the Memorial Auditorium.[43]

Clubs, conferences and exhibits provided other means for achieving institutional goals. Among the more active, the art club sponsored speakers, exhibits and art appreciation projects. Bard, Book and Canto, a club of junior-senior English majors and minors, heard speakers and discussed literature, departmental issues and job placement. The international relations club, devoted to "creating better understanding among the peoples of various nations," remained active; in 1963 the organization collected books for Asian students. A chapter of Pi Gamma Mu, a national social science honor society organized on campus in 1957, and the social work club, founded in March 1959, nurtured students in those disciplines.[44]

Sometimes associations sponsored conferences that brought others to campus. In April 1962, the Minnesota Student Philosophy Conference met at Concordia for the discussion of student papers. The Berg Art Center displayed exhibits frequently; in February 1959 the department invited Lutheran art students to submit work for the first annual Lutheran Brotherhood Fine Arts Festival. Occasionally more informal groups gathered. In February 1955 Pi Kappa Delta, the national forensic society, began "table talk" which discussed a variety of topics weekly at specially marked cafeteria tables during meals. At times, a few collegians even requested faculty panels and discussions, citing student interest in hearing professorial views.[45]

As they had in the past, discussions of domestic and international politics enlivened intellectual life. To be sure, the usual complaints surfaced about student indifference, often characterized as "Cobberism." On the other hand, President Knutson believed there was considerable political activity and controversy. He noted there were liberals at the college—Professors Farden, Grubb and Noblitt—but there were also outspoken conservatives—himself and Professors Larsen, Drache and Mundhjeld. This was good, the president maintained, because it demonstrated that the campus was politically conversant. As a cultural conservative, Knutson believed that ideas shaped societies; therefore ideologies must be studied at church colleges or collegians would not be educated properly.[46]

The record bears out Knutson's contention of considerable political interest and activity. The creation of political emphasis week in 1959 enhanced awareness. Presidential hopeful Hubert Humphrey delivered the main address and met informally with 250 Cobbers at a coffee hour following. Congressman Odin Langen, the North Dakota president of the AFL-CIO, an NAACP leader and local political figures also appeared.

Senator Hubert Humphrey initiated political emphasis week in 1959.

A mock senate heatedly debated bills related to labor, armed services, agriculture and foreign relations; these had been prepared after several weeks investigation by student committees.[47]

National elections still attracted Cobbers' attention. In 1956, they were treated to the appearance of three nationally prominent politicians in Fargo-Moorhead. Adlai

Stevenson, again seeking the Democratic presidential nomination, spoke on farm policy at the Memorial Auditorium in March as part of Greater Moorhead Days. In September, Vice President Richard Nixon held a press conference and spoke at a Fargo high school. Then in November, with the help of Clay County Republican Committeeman Hiram Drache, Secretary of Agriculture Ezra Taft Benson addressed Concordia and Moorhead State students in the Moorhead Armory. Otherwise the campaign on campus ran its normal course. A *Concordian* editorial urged Cobbers to vote. A mock national election, sponsored by the Young Republicans and Democrats, resulted in the usual Republican landslide—469 votes (73.8 percent) for Eisenhower to 160 (26.2 percent) for Stevenson. The Republican margin was slightly greater in 1960—Richard Nixon received 728 Cobber votes (77 percent) to John Kennedy's 217 (23 percent). Prior to the election, the Catholic issue attracted some attention. The *Concordian* reported that Lutheran church editors in Michigan had decided not to oppose a candidate solely because he was Catholic. A Cobber agreed; Kennedy had been moderate on church-state issues in the past and therefore Americans should vote for the best qualified nominee and forget Kennedy's Catholicism. This Lutheran openness on the religious issue did not change the basic Republican allegiance of the campus, however. Only in 1964 did Cobbers abandon their preference for the GOP; a poll of 100 revealed that 55 percent favored Democrat Lyndon Johnson and only 39 percent supported right-wing Republican Barry Goldwater.[48]

On international issues, Cobbers manifested some traditional commitments. Various proposals for relief still attracted support. They sent aid to Hungarian youth after the failed uprising of 1956, winter clothing to Korean orphans and clothing for Japanese typhoon victims. The Student Association continued support for foreign students. In 1955 they funded a Norwegian woman and a Japanese man. International scholars enriched collegiate intellectual life by commenting on global issues from the perspective of their national cultures. At times they criticized their hosts for not being more helpful in acculturating them to America or for not making sufficient use of their potential contribution to a liberal arts education. Perhaps this criticism led the foreign student committee in 1959 to establish a big brother-sister program to integrate foreign students more quickly into the Concordia family.[49]

The cold war tensions prevalent in American culture affected the college. Phone calls and letters to the dean named various professors as communists. The FBI investigated a "subversive" chemist whose crime was subscribing to a chess magazine and a chemical journal from the Soviet Union. *Concordian* editorials assumed that the United States was locked in struggle for world supremacy with the Soviets. The Soviet-launched Sputnik in 1957 therefore prompted fears that the United States was falling behind in weaponry, technology and science. Editors criticized peace proposals, warning that freedom must be the prerequisite to any lasting world peace. They censured Khrushchev for his bluster and the Berlin wall for denying freedom to millions. Participation in civil defense efforts enhanced campus awareness of possible nuclear war. A college unit worked with the Minnesota Civil Defense Organization and offered training courses in defense against atomic weapons. Students apparently learned mostly how to monitor radiation. Attitudes of this era are still evidenced in civil defense signs designating basements as air raid shelters.[50]

At the beginning of the 1960s, campus criticism of conservative anti-communism evidenced the disintegretion of cold war consensus. *Concordian* columnist Paul Peterson ('62) found it ironic that conservatives like Barry Goldwater who "cry for freedom are the first to suppress it" by jailing all those suspected of Red tendencies by the FBI. Similarly, editor Marc Borg criticized the proposed House Un-American Activities Committee (HUAC) investigation of the highly popular folksingers and their music. Borg feared an American tendency to suppress everything "that even hints of uncommon belief" because it could destroy freedom in the United States. Associate editor Tom Pierce and coeditor Dan Lee ('67) pointed out the dangers represented by the ultra-conservative John Birch Society which attracted a following in North Dakota, Minnesota and the nation. Its charges against Earl Warren, Dwight Eisenhower and Lyndon Johnson were unsupported and therefore abused freedom of speech. At the same time, liberal political editor Roger Hanson's proposal for a young socialist club generated much heated discussion. Hanson ('64) perceived the club as a center of information about socialism and as a sponsor for socialist and communist speakers. His critics, mostly North Dakota State students writing in the pages of the *Concordian*, disagreed with Hanson's major assumption. They already had adequate information about communism provided by HUAC and J. Edgar Hoover.[51]

Paul Peterson

The emerging civil rights movement indicated a more liberal attitude toward social reform. In 1957, 562 Cobbers signed petitions opposing forced segregation of South Africa's two remaining unsegregated public colleges. In April 1960, a *Concordian* guest editorial by Student Association President Jim Danielson ('60), who had attended a National Student Association conference in Washington D.C. on the sit-in movement, urged Cobbers to write their congressmen and start fundraisers to support Southern sit-ins for black constitutional rights. As a further indication of sympathy, the Student Association funded a scholarship for a southern African-American, Richard Green of Kentucky, who graduated from Concordia in 1961, earned a Ph.D. in chemistry and returned to teach for several years. In 1964, the student senate passed a resolution urging Congressman Odin Langen to vote for the pending civil rights bill. In 1965, collegians staged a campus demonstration in support of the voting rights bill and, due to the initiative of Professor Eleanor Haney, the college arranged a one-semester exchange program with Virginia Union University in Richmond.[52]

Richard Green

President Knutson was not unsympathetic to these efforts. He reported in 1964 that the college had cancelled concerts in two segregated halls on the southern choir tour and that Langen had voted for the Civil Rights Act. Knutson believed that the act was necessary but warned that "unless the Gospel and Christian love enter in, there won't be much brotherhood among races." Of course, presidential sympathy and student activism did not eliminate racism and prejudice. As late as 1964, minstrels in black face appeared in the homecoming variety show and a phone survey of off-campus housing revealed that eighteen of forty-three polled would not rent rooms to blacks. Nor did the Native Americans, victims of racism much closer to home, attract much institutional attention. A lone voice in 1958 asked why Concordia did not offer scholarships to area Indians.[53]

Religious Activities

Campus religious life remained central to the mission of Concordia as a Christian liberal arts college. Mission Crusaders, Lutheran Daughters of the Reformation and LBI Bible Study disappeared but the Lutheran Student Association (LSA) continued to direct Cobber stewardship, Christian life and community service. The spiritual life conference, held each November, and the mission conference scheduled in the spring were important expressions of campus piety. The prayer fellowship still met Saturday evenings; often other prayer and Bible study groups were informally constituted. Indeed, a request to establish quiet places for personal meditation triggered construction in 1961 of a small prayer chapel in Fjelstad Hall's attic. In addition, collegians met Sunday evenings for fellowship, Bible study and discussion of current issues—religion, politics, church life and mission, the ecumenical movement, social concerns and student needs. Many worship opportunities existed: daily chapel, midweek vespers, monthly all-college and weekly congregational worship and late evening dormitory devotions. The many activities sometimes created scheduling conflicts. President Knutson stated clearly the priorities of a Christian institution. In 1959 he informed Dean Bailey that the LSA ought to have Old Main Auditorium for its Sunday evening meetings; the speech department should be told that play practices on the Sabbath were unnecessary.[54]

In 1961, Rev. Carl Lee was called to the new position of campus pastor. Some authors of "the blue paper" were behind this initiative because they perceived a "student need" for more personal counseling. Lee's duties were extensive. He organized daily chapel services,

Campus pastor Carl Lee combined preaching and counseling.

served as spiritual counselor and father for Cobbers, coordinated all religious activities and programs, met with all religious organizations and directed the social program. Students were to pay part of his salary. To help meet this responsibility, they advocated a campus congregation. Knutson resisted because it would be divisive; most Fargo-Moorhead Cobbers belonged to local congregations that recently had begun to support Concordia handsomely outside synodical budgets. Eventually the matter was dropped without any action. In retrospect, Pastor Lee is glad that Concordia did not follow this trend among the other Lutheran colleges.[55]

Despite uncertain collegian financing, Lee thrived in his new job and developed a strong following. In a 1965 *Concordian* interview, he described his ministry. He attempted to make worship "meaningful to the student in whatever situation he may encounter, to bring the wholeness of the gospel to bear on his entire life." Whether as a preacher or a counselor, Lee defined his task as ministering "to these focal points of life and reality, in terms of the gospel of healing and wholeness, grace and forgiveness, acceptance and reconciliation ... on a horizontal level first, with self, others, parents ... and then the vertical with God."[56]

The LSA, guided by Pastor Lee and other spiritual advisers, fostered many expressions of Christian service. In addition to the usual collections for worthy projects and visitations to neighboring congregations, Indian missions were a significant innovation. Cobbers worked with Indians at Bethel Lutheran Chapel at White Earth and at Big Elbow Lake for several years. The LSA helped build a church at the Jack Pine Indian Mission east of Mahnomen. The church served twenty-six Indian and eleven white families. Each week, a carload traveled to these sites to assist with worship and Sunday School. Twice monthly they went for the entire weekend. They gave youth parties, visited homes and distributed food and clothing.[57]

Stimulated by the Vatican Council, the ecumenical movement affected campus religious life. In chapel during December 1964, Fargo Bishop Leo F. Dworschak, who had attended all three Vatican sessions, addressed the topic "Religious Liberty and the Vatican Council." This marked the first time that a Roman Catholic prelate had spoken at Concordia. It would not be the last. Ecumenism became the keynote of Luther League Day in 1965. Speakers were Father Coleman Barry, St. John's president, and Dr. Kent Knutson, Luther Seminary professor of systematic theology.[58]

Luther League Day brought many to the college.

Catholic speakers prompted criticism from constituents who were unwilling to surrender easily a traditional anti-Catholicism. The president defended the movement; he urged critics to thank God and to pray that He "will guide the ecumenical movement for the renewal of His church." Anti-Catholic attitudes were not confined to the constituency. A sociology course survey of a random student sample in 1967 discovered that two-thirds of the respondents would not marry a Catholic and over one-third would not tolerate a sibling marriage to a Catholic. *Concordian* editor Jim Nestingen ('67) urged learning more about Roman Catholic beliefs and teachings in order to dispel this prejudice.[59]

The Extracurriculum

Cobbers engaged in many extracurricular activities that were not obviously religious. As with the academic program, the institution hoped these would be infused with a religious spirit because they issued from a Christian community. Indeed, inactivity and apathy toward student government were deemed unchristian by one Cobber who would one day be president. All are stewards of God; therefore all have the responsibility to use their gifts to the fullest. Not to use them betrayed Christian principles. Another recognized the educational value of political participation. It contributed to a liberal arts education and it prepared for citizenship.[60]

The Student Association (SA) afforded Cobbers many opportunities for involvement. In 1960 it was organized as follows: a twenty-four member senate that served as legislative body; five commissions—intersociety, publications, social, religion and National Student Association (NSA); an executive branch—a cabinet comprised of the five commissioners and the four elected officers—which met biweekly; a student-faculty forum with fifteen student and twelve faculty members. Major SA activities included the social program, freshmen orientation, homecoming, political emphasis week, Friday chapel, publishing the *Student Directory* and *Who's New*, producing a musical and acting as liason between the student body and the administration.[61]

Student Association carried out the tasks of government.

Cobbers participated in administrative decision-making. An annual student-faculty retreat at an area resort addressed many issues of collegiate concern. Many of these were subsequently discussed by the student-faculty forum and were often implemented by the administration. Cobbers generally appreciated their opportunities and often praised the administration for its cooperative spirit. The prevailing good will is perhaps best symbolized by the student birthday gift in 1958 to President Knutson of an aluminum boat and trailer. At the presentation, SA President Gary Glomstad praised Knutson for his "leadership and understanding." This public display of affection, the *Fargo Forum* suggested, shattered the myth that the president is the natural enemy of the collegian. Several years later, the president cheerfully posed for a photograph by donning a hat and serenely fishing from his boat on Prexy's Pond.[62]

Many changes came from student participation. The present system of freshmen orientation clubs, introduced in 1954, was retained when the newcomers registered their approval. The next year, collegians assumed leadership of almost the entire program. Despite the perennial discussion of whether or not to wear beanies, the tradition persisted with the exception of Fall 1965 when freshmen resistance and upper-class compulsion led to temporary termination. Summer orientation, introduced by the administration in 1960, found popularity with Cobbers. It relieved fall registration pressures and has fostered the summer camp atmosphere so characteristic of fall orientation.[63]

Other student-initiated programs included an honor system, designed in 1961 to stop cheating on examinations by having all Cobbers sign a pledge of academic honesty. Despite periodic alterations and charges of indifference, a responsibility code

Golden domes enjoy a fall orientation event.

continues to the present. During the 1950s, Cobbers established more cooperative relations with Moorhead and North Dakota State. They attempted to coordinate and publicize events; and they formulated a tri-college responsibility code. Free intra-campus telephone service began in 1954. Under this system, Cobbers received incoming calls but used pay telephones to phone outside. In 1956 the system was changed to allow local service. Phones were now available by dormitory floors but lengthy conversations often tied up the system. This problem generated many complaints; cooperation, honor, fair play and a five-minute limit were suggested as solutions. The answer finally came in August 1968 with the installation of Centrex; each room received a phone with in-out dialing and direct-line service throughout campus.[64]

Continued affiliation with the NSA engendered controversy. Critics doubted whether membership justified the $500 fee. Defenders maintained that through the NSA Cobbers obtained an effective voice in society. Moreover, the NSA International and National Affairs Division created awareness of significant international and national problems by funneling information to international relations clubs, Young Republicans and Young Democrats. In 1960 the NSA participated in a national protest against discrimination practices by Woolworth stores. SA ended its membership the next year. In 1964 the SA rejoined, citing two membership benefits: free information from the student government information service and discount cards for overseas travel from Educational Travel Inc.[65]

Student government apparently operated effectively. It addressed and secured solutions to many issues of concern to Cobbers, yet the percentage voting in campus elections declined from 72 (1956) to 50 (1960). This touched off the usual charges about student apathy as a cause.[66] Other factors may have contributed. Perhaps Cobbers were satisfied with the success of their representatives or perhaps they were preoccupied with their involvement in the many other extracurricular activities available.

Many Cobbers contributed to the campus media—the *Concordian*, *Cobber* and radio. The *Concordian* took considerable pride in being an independent student voice. Again and again, editors expressed thanks for the absence of prior administrative censorship. Cobbers were so appreciative of their freedom that they dedicated the paper's fiftieth anniversary issue at homecoming 1959 to President Knutson for "his belief in the free press." What they described as a "smooth, congenial relationship with faculty and administration" at times resulted in their voluntarily removing offensive material "for the betterment of the college." Because editors were solicitous of institutional image, administrators used the *Concordian* as a public relations instrument, sending the paper's weekly circulation of 5,100 to a large number of homes and schools throughout the Upper Midwest. Meanwhile, the paper improved its technical quality. In 1955 a new office, print shop and printing process all combined to produce a bigger and better product. A darkroom, added in 1960, developed all *Concordian* and *Cobber* pictures. As a consequence, its improved quality was recognized nationally in 1957 when the paper won its first all-American rating in eight years. By 1961, the *Concordian* had captured college journalism's highest award eighteen times in its forty-year history. This high number made it one of the top college newspapers in the nation.[67]

The *Cobber* chronicled the yearly activities of the Christian community. Its quality was recognized by all-American ratings in 1956 and 1959. Other media included "Thy Kingdom Come," a radio program broadcast weekly for five years, and "Cobber Campus," a weekly television show that appeared for two years. Programs for one season of the former included a panel discussion on dating, an interview with the

Norwegian ambassador; sermonettes; a Lenten series featuring students in roles of Mark, Paul and others; musical selections; and special vocal and instrumental music for Thanksgiving and Christmas. Broadcast in its second year over KXJB (which provided free airtime), "Cobber Campus" examined the departments of remedial reading, physics, biology and art; broadcast musical shows featuring the band and choir; and presented two programs from Cobber Capers. After mid-decade both disappeared and were replaced by KOBB, a campus radio station. Often attacked for its expense and poor service, KOBB survived beyond 1965 broadcasting news, weather, music and play-by-plays of occasional basketball games.[68]

Many other Cobbers participated in forensics, debate and theatre. Theatre embraced a full range of representative classical and modern plays. In 1955 the college offered the first summer theatre in Moorhead. Although it reappeared for several summers and has been attempted at different times since, Concordia has not enjoyed the popular success of the Moorhead State Straw Hat Players. Debate trained quickness, accuracy, analytical thinking and public expression. The team traveled to several tournaments annually. Under new coach Paul Dovre, who joined the staff in 1963, the team enjoyed its greatest success to date. They journeyed to their first district tournament in March 1965 and to their first nationals in 1967.[69]

Ted Bey reports the latest news on Radio Station KOBB.

Even more Cobbers participated in the many music organizations: the sixty member choir, the seventy piece concert band, the Cobber band, the freshman choir, the chapel choir, the fifty-member women's chorus, the orchestra and numerous ensemble groups. Several of these were training grounds for the premier musical organizations, the band and choir. The Cobber band—initially a marching band but by the mid-1960s a non-marching pep band—provided experience for those who had not made the first team. The concert band went on extended annual tours and gave public performances in Fargo-Moorhead. In 1958 it made a record for RCA.[70]

The choir also toured, adding to its and Paul J. Christiansen's national and international reputation. In 1955 it was featured in a half-hour program broadcast nationally on the Mutual Network from New York City, and in 1959 it cut its first stereo recording at Allentown, Pennsylvania. In 1958 the choristers made their second European tour. Designated as Minnesota Centennial Ambassadors, the choir sang before large audiences in Norway and received critical acclaim in its appearance at the world-famous Vienna Music Festival. Funded in part by a Bremer Foundation grant, this trip for the first time did not require a college subsidy, which pleased President Knutson. It eased his struggles to maintain institutional solvency and it marked a victory in his battle to win institutional recognition and support. That same year, the choir broadcast nationally a twenty-five minute Christmas concert over the Mutual Broadcasting System. As it had been since its inception in 1927, the annual Christmas concert was a significant musical expression of the religious beliefs of a

Christian college. The new field house allowed expansion of the event and enabled even larger crowds to enjoy it. In 1954 it was broadcast on public television and in 1955 capacity crowds enjoyed all three evenings. By 1959, a record 15,000 people attended.[71]

1958 choir tour members are ready to embark.

Concordia provided a balanced athletic program to meet each Cobber's needs. Besides recreation, the program aimed at developing skills useful in later life. To this end, the institution supplied a variety of intercollegiate sports for men, intramurals for men and recreation for women. Concordia prided itself on its amateur athletes. Indeed, President Knutson exhibited so much pride that he drew fire in 1956 from Minneapolis sports writer Dick Cullum and Minnesota football coach Murray Warmath for his Concordia *Alumnus* editorial, "For Sale, An Outstanding Athlete." Knutson asked alumni to send athletic sons to Concordia rather than permitting their purchase by major football powers. He asserted that big schools ruined the characters of high school football and basketball heroes by offering gifts like Cadillacs and houses.[72]

Supervised by a faculty committee, intercollegiate sports observed the eligibility requirements of the Minnesota Intercollegiate Athletic Conference (MIAC). In the 1950s, football and basketball were central to college life and school spirit mattered greatly to many Cobbers. *Concordian* editorials praised and offered suggestions for improving school spirit. Editors encouraged more varied halftime shows, noted approvingly the organization of a rooter club and applauded the pep band when it "played with sincere feeling and spirit." Led by Jake Christiansen, the football team's many victories probably generated more spirit than the basketball team's losing records. Indeed, Cobber cagers suffered a forty-six-conference-game losing streak that stretched through three years. When the team finished at 1 and 15 in the MIAC and 4 and 22 for the 1955–1956 season under enthusiastic first-year coach Sonny Gulsvig, long-suffering fans rejoiced at the improvement. By 1959, Gulsvig's cagers were conference runners-up.[73]

Despite his football successes, even Jake endured frustrations. A rare Cobber victory over Gustavus in 1955—the first in twenty-one years—prompted an extra *Concordian* edition to commemorate the happy event. In 1964, Jake and the Cobbers enjoyed their greatest gridiron success to date. The team, Jake and the proposed new stadium appeared in *The Sporting News*, a national magazine. Jake was elected to the National Association of Intercollegiate Athletics Hall of Fame. Then in his twenty-fourth season of coaching the Cobbers, the "grey fox" had posted a 118 and 60 won-lost record with 9 ties and won conference championships in 1942, 1952, 1957 and 1964. The 1964 champions were ranked first in the final NAIA poll and played Sam Houston

1964 NAIA co-champions, the first of three national title teams.

State in the championship bowl at Augusta Georgia. That game, televised over WDAY, ended in a tie which earned the Cobbers their first of three national titles.[74]

Athletics came of age at this time. The program developed a larger budget that supported MIAC competition in several sports. Handicaps of poor facilities and parttime coaching did not prevent the creation of new athletic teams if a sufficient number of interested Cobbers could be found. A wrestling squad, added in 1954 and coached by Finn Grinaker for more than thirty years, finished second in the conference in 1956, 1957 and 1962 and first in 1964. Student interest maintained hockey throughout the 1950s despite lack of facilities and coach. They played on an outdoor rink that shifted locations from behind Cobber Hall to beside the field house. Baseball also existed for a long time without permanent coach or home. The team even competed at Moorhead Junior High until Cobber Field was re-vamped in 1958 for intercollegiate play.

Nonetheless in 1955 under a new coach, French instructor Dave Green, the Cobbers tied for first in the Steve Gorman League. When that league disbanded in 1959, baseball entered the MIAC. The Irv Christenson coached track team in 1955 won an MIAC title in its third year of conference competition. Tennis was another sport that suffered from inadequate facilities and lack of a permanent mentor. Allwin Monson, professor of speech, coached the team in 1956. In

MIAC track champions present trophy to President Knutson.

1955, for the first time in three years, a ski team entered intercollegiate competion. Then in 1958, after a few previous attempts at organizing, gymnastics was declared a new minor sport.[75]

The Women's Athletic Association, changed to the Women's Recreation Association (WRA) in 1956, remained the focus of female athletics. The WRA met weekly in the Memorial Auditorium for individual and team sports—basketball, volleyball, badminton, tennis, shuffleboard, golf and archery—and swam semimonthly at Fargo High School. Intercollegiate events began when the WRA sponsored basketball, volleyball, tennis and track competition against Moorhead State, North Dakota State and other colleges. Coached by Professor of Physical Education Joan Hult, these teams gradually expanded their schedules. In 1960 golfer Jane Farnum, who ranked fourth in Minnesota, competed with men in non-conference play, although she was ruled ineligible by the MIAC. Besides its activities on the playing fields, the WRA entertained the lettermen's club at the fall Sadie Hawkins Day and contributed women for dunking and baked goods to the spring lettermen's carnival. [76]

Professor Joan Hult

In keeping with its athletic philosophy, Concordia offered an extensive intramural program. To broaden participation, the program shifted from an intersociety to a club system in 1951; every man enrolled in one of eight clubs. The club managers and Intramural Director Irv Christenson organized and supervised competition in many sports—touch football, baseball, softball, basketball, volleyball, archery, golf, tennis, badminton, table tennis, shuffleboard, wrestling and horseshoes. The expanded recreational facilities of the new field house—basketball and volleyball courts, shuffleboard, badminton and a trampoline—enhanced intramurals. Despite the new facility and the recent reorganization, the program was criticized for not reaching many Cobbers. Another restructuring was suggested but not acted on at this time. [77]

In the 1960s, the fourteen brother and sister societies were the heart of campus social life and enjoyed their golden age. Participation was extensive; by the time Cobbers were seniors, 78 percent of the men and 68 percent of the women had joined. Joint brother-sister meetings became common, a return to the practice of their early days. The organizations no longer pretended to their original literary purpose; they now simply offered opportunities for individual development in small groups. This was often not enough for campus critics. They suggested that societies "should go beyond a purpose grounded in pure pleasure to one which better serves Concordia's ideals." Worthwhile projects should be added to their

Alpha Epsilon Sigma cheerleaders support their sisters' basketball team.

parties and weekly meetings. As usual, initiation prompted the most criticism. In response, societies attempted to mollify the administration by better policing of initiation and tried to justify their existence. For some, service activities ought to be expanded; for others, socializing was sufficient. Indeed, social life was so important that several proposed initiating freshmen before May. These pleas were rejected and spring initiation retained on the grounds that freshmen needed the first semester to adjust and another to look for a suitable association.[78]

Pranks provided other entertainment. Fastening a bag of Paris Green to the inflow pipe and turning Prexy's Pond bright blue-green for an entire day was a good joke, but the

Lambda Delta Sigma-Alpha Epsilon Sigma entertain an all-school Roaring '20s party.

"great silverware caper" in 1961 by the "Concordia Eight" ranks as the most famous in college history. During the night, the group transferred silverware and dishes from the cafeteria to the library. In the morning, food service workers were shocked to discover the theft and librarians amazed to find 120 banquet-style place settings on long study tables. Outside the library lay Dostoevsky's *Crime and Punishment* on a cart. Via campus mail, Elizabeth Hassenstab of the food service soon received this note: "Sorry to have inconvenienced you. We of the itinerant home economics department are proud to see the way you have been able to bear, laugh and enjoy the silverware shortage. The remainder of the silverware is located on third floor of the library. Good Hunting! P.S. The reserve reading room of the library shall henceforth be known as Amy's Nook." Twenty years later at homecoming, this best-kept secret was revealed and the perpetrators absolved by now-retired President Knutson. Of course, they still faced the charge imposed by emeritus Dean of Men Boe: "If we don't get sixty more C-400 memberships in two years, we'll reopen the case."[79]

Despite a plethora of activities, the cry was often heard, "But there is nothing to do!" Lack of social life was a perennial complaint. At times collegians even bestirred themselves to suggest solutions. Although a bowling alley was not built, a men's bowling league was formed. That eating was a traditional collegiate indoor sport was evidenced in 1957 when 119 attended the grand opening of the Park Region snack bar. That same year, inexpensive Friday night movies were offered. Indifferent attendance soon ran the program into debt. The annual winter

The Four Freshmen perform at the 1959 Winter Carnival.

carnival featured the Four Freshmen in 1959 and Henny Youngman's Gay Nineties Show in 1960. And at year's end one could attend the annual junior-senior banquet which in 1963 offered a Japanese theme on Norwegian Independence Day. Ethnic identity had indeed faded![80]

Dormitory living itself could be an adventure. As one female frosh noted, "You can't beat the piped-in music in Academy. Morning, noon or night, and usually in the middle of the latter, the steam pipes bang away." Academy Hall women also used their unique study lounge in an unfinished portion of the east attic because their rooms offered too many interruptions and the library required wearing a skirt. Fjelstad Hall women delighted in their private sinks, an attic prayer chapel and the luxury of rearranging room furniture. Bishop Whipple Hall housed sixty-eight upperclass-women who believed "its smaller size makes it friendlier, cozier and creates a more intimate group." Besides, Whipple women had the only color TV on campus in 1958 and therefore enjoyed packing their lounge with men during the World Series.[81]

Pressures for Change

By 1965, Concordia had done exceedingly well under President Knutson's leadership. Physical plant had enlarged extensively to accommodate the doubled enrollment. It had maintained successfully a conservative behaviorial code in order to preserve the moral atmosphere Knutson considered essential to a Christian college.

Nonetheless, pressures for change were building. A large freshmen class in 1964 forced many upperclassmen into off-campus living. Growing enrollment thus continued to generate pressures for physical expansion throughout the 1960s. That decade also witnessed campus upheavals that reached even traditional Concordia and made these years troubled for the nation and for President Knutson and his vision of a Christian college. Outwardly the college evidenced physical success, but the conservative president worried about its soul.

Chapter 14

Continued Growth

Administrative Changes

The administration managed growth and President Knutson managed the administration. His ideas directed the institution and defined its image in the public mind.

Knutson was the model of the good steward of scarce resources; his request for verification of room rates at the Minneapolis Athletic Club typified this concern: "I do not want expensive rooms as we are working for the college and the college pays the bill." He forcefully articulated his conception of the religious mission and sustained Concordia as a strong Lutheran college. At the same time, he recognized the claims of academic program and the obligation to serve society. Someone once asked him, "Surely you don't have Charles Darwin's book in the library?" He replied, "I hope so." Although Knutson feared that demands for social justice during the turbulent 1960s would destroy the church, he often attempted to direct the social concerns of the Lutheran Church. In a 1967 article, he urged the church to help farmers organize and protect their markets so they could live with dignity. "If we are sincere in praying for daily bread," Knutson wrote, "we dare not forget the farmer any longer." He received several requests to reprint his article in local newspapers and in the monthly National Farmer's Organization newsletter. He readily agreed.[1]

As enrollment grew, the administration expanded and adopted a more elaborate structure. Administrators and staff were added in admissions, business, student personnel, development and academic affairs. Despite additions, President Knutson still delighted in announcing annually that Concordia ranked last in general administrative costs among ALC colleges. Besides dealing with the increased work load, new positions sometimes addressed other strains caused by rapid expansion. When the position of associate academic dean was created in April 1967, for example, Dean Bailey appointed a youthful Paul Dovre—chairperson of speech and director of forensics—to overcome the "two-faculty problem" created by division of the professorate along generational lines. Dovre was destined to ascend quickly to academic dean in 1971 and president in 1975.[2]

Following a higher education trend already evident at other Lutheran colleges, the regents approved a restructured administration in November 1968. The reform created five vice presidents and thereby enhanced efficiency by greatly reducing the number of other officials reporting directly to the president. The vice presidents were Carl Bailey, academic affairs; J.L. Rendahl, admissions and financial aid; Roger Swenson, development; William Smaby, financial affairs; and Victor Boe, student affairs. They formed an executive council that met weekly with the president to make policy decisions. A much larger administrative council still met monthly to share information and to foster a sense of community.[3]

During 1968–1969 Paul Dovre replaced Bailey, who enjoyed a leave for physics research. Dovre presided over a year-long debate on a revised faculty constitution. The new document created a representative governance system; restructured committees were made responsible to an expanded senate, now the faculty deliberative body. When Bailey returned, H. Robert Homann became assistant dean and Dovre became executive vice president; he assisted the president by coordinating administrative planning, doing institutional and budget planning, chairing the president's executive committee, representing the president at all other meetings in his absence and coordinating presidential fundraising. Dovre also presided over the all-college council, newly formed in April 1969 to provide a forum for the three collegiate estates. Comprised of the president's executive council, the executive committee of the faculty senate and the Student Association executive council, it replaced the student-faculty forum.[4]

Paul J. Dovre

After Dovre became vice president for academic affairs, he brought Dr. Loren Anderson to the newly created position of director of institutional research. As director, Anderson assumed some of the duties Dovre had performed as executive vice president; he worked with federal programs on higher education and reported to all outside agencies to which Concordia was responsible. His research assisted institutional, budget and curricular planning. Anderson, one of Dovre's outstanding student debaters, had been recruited by his mentor while he pursued graduate study. An excellent appointment, Anderson soon became a highly successful vice president for development at Concordia.[5]

Changes in administrative practice accompanied expansion and restructuring. Following a national trend toward greater professionalization, student personnel services became more sophisticated. Terminology changed from extracurricular to co-curricular on the grounds that activities outside the classroom have educational value. Recognizing this potential, the college added personnel staff in order to involve more and more collegians in meaningful activities. Counseling assistance expanded, marking a growth that has continued to the present. Orientation clubs, student advisers, head residents, academic advisers, personnel deans, psychological and career counselors and the campus pastor were all available to aid Cobbers with all kinds of problems, ranging from the dormitory to the classroom, the trivial to the significant and course selection to career planning. In addition, two ombudsmen were established in 1969 to improve lines of communication between Cobbers and the Student Association on one hand and the administration on the other.[6]

Although the growth of "the student personnel empire" provoked criticism for a potentially dangerous blurring of the distinction between academic and non-academic learning and an excessive coddling that sapped self-reliance, its evolution was consistent with the institutional ideology of the Concordia family. "The whole person" has been a constant concern of the Christian college. Indeed, pastoral presidents, deans and professors were the first personnel officers.[7]

Affirmative action procedures were developed. These included a commission of equal opportunity, an equity salary adjustment program, a system to fill vacancies and a committee to study personnel policies for non-faculty employees. Search committees comprised of students, faculty and administrators were instituted to advise the president in filling administrative posts. In December 1970 the senate authorized the cabinet to consult with the president in choosing an academic dean. Formal search committees were selected in January 1973 when Dean Boe announced his retirement, and in 1974 and 1975 for the selection of a president and academic vice president respectively. These delegations publicized the vacancies, reviewed applications, conducted campus interviews in which candidates were subjected to public hearings before faculty and students, and then submitted a list of nominees to the president or to the board for action.[8]

Although the new procedure broadened community participation in decision-making, the process is often accompanied by suspicion and recrimination. On the one hand, some believed their contribution was meaningless because the president would do as he pleased; on the other hand, some resented being bothered by administrative business.

The practice of self-study and planning continued. In the mid-1960s, a joint administration-faculty planning group was created. At the same time, faculty groups discussed at length the Danforth Report on church-related higher education. Topics included social trends, secularization, enrollments, resources and costs, and status of the liberal arts. Other discussions followed in 1970–1972 in preparation for *Blueprint II*, published in 1974. The document provided direction by reaffirming the guiding principles and basic loyalties of Concordia as a church-related institution of liberal studies and offered a framework for developing specific plans and quantitative projections.[9]

Participation in the Tri-College University (TCU)—a consortium of Concordia, Moorhead State and North Dakota State—represented a significant innovation for the administration. Planning began in 1968. It had been preceded by a variety of cooperative efforts between the three institutions. To promote better understanding of educational programs, MSTC President Snarr in 1953 suggested an annual joint faculty meeting of Moorhead State and Concordia. Students had cooperated in various tri-college radio broadcasting efforts. A deans' committee had worked out a "common market" for course work in 1962, and the first annual tri-college art show had been staged in January 1967.[10]

The Tri-College University committee—formed in February 1968 as the brainchild of Casselton farmer and later North Dakota Governor George Sinner and consisting of the presidents, academic deans, board members and state legislators of the surrounding districts—explored the potential for cooperation. In April 1969 the Hill Foundation awarded $70,000 for hiring a fulltime director—Dr. Albert Anderson, Concordia philosophy professor. That fall, 125 students were enrolled in TCU classes with seventy-four at MSC, thirty-eight at NDSU and thirteen at Concordia. The most popular courses were business administration and special education at MSC, ROTC at NDSU and hospital administration at Concordia. A common calendar and tuition reciprocity were obtained between MSC and NDSU, a daily TCU bus service established and several other grants secured. Perhaps the greatest success came with the libraries coordinating their resources and services. This effort was initially funded in November 1970 by $94,000 from the Bush Foundation.[11]

Institutional Advertising and Recruiting

As it had in the past to attract students, Concordia advertised the values of Christian education through all available media. The message was modernized to fit the times. In November 1967, "A Legacy for a Son"—a half-hour color film broadcast over six North Dakota television stations—used homecoming events to tell the college story.

Alone, an admissions brochure prepared in the late sixties, mirrored the troubled decade in portraying tension, darkness and solitude. Yet potential Cobbers were assured that the institution's traditional religious message still addressed their needs: "Go with me, Lord. I need you. I simply cannot make it alone." And "Concordia ... Where 'the means' is always questioned, the 'end' never in doubt." Instead of walls, constructed to keep out heresies and the evils of life, windows and bridges were being built to serve the world. That Jesus controlled the institution made Concordia unique; collegians were told, "In pursuit of the sheepskin, keep the Shepherd in sight." By 1971, Cobbers were invited "to participate in the Concordia idea—an idea born of hope, nourished by knowledge, and expressed in living."[12]

Even a college history, commissioned for the seventy-fifth anniversary celebration in 1966, served public relations. Erling Rolfsrud agreed to undertake the project if given freedom to write a book that would appeal to the average alumnus and friend of the college. He envisioned an informal, photo-filled anecdotal history which he maintained would be as scholarly as a "stuffed shirt piece (annotated, footnoted, bibliography-laden—and dust-collecting)." Despite the obvious publicity value of Rolfsrud's intentions, some members of the development office objected to the negative image suggested by the description of student protests in his supplement to the 1975 edition of *Cobber Chronicle*. Because the institutional history was intended in part to introduce the college "to people who are potential donors ... [the work] should reflect the true picture of Concordia." Unfortunately, the critics charged, the section on student life did not. It left the impression that the institution was like any secular college in manifesting the decade's spirit of protest. On the other hand, the recently created Christian outreach teams demonstrated that Concordia had remained true to its Christian purpose and that "God is doing wonderful things here." Although Rolfsrud did not omit the offensive material, he did include an account of the spiritual renewal in part because the gospel teams had "turned out to be great tools of public relations and recruitment as they travel."[13]

Publicity helped boost enrollment. Numbers climbed 14.5 percent from 2,101 in 1965 to 2,405 by 1969. When the total declined the next year to 2,360—the first decrease in almost two decades—the downturn deflated an existing "boomer" mentality. The pessimism caused by this slump lingered even though registrations once more increased to 2,482 in 1973. Most Cobbers (55 percent) still came from farms and small towns. Indices of their academic ability rose gradually but steadily during the 1960s and remained stable thereafter. By 1970, the typical student's national test scores placed her above the 75th percentile among college freshmen and near the 90th percentile among high school seniors. More women than men now enrolled, reaching 52.2 percent in 1969 and increasing thereafter. Concordia's growing reputation as a strong academic institution attracted more non-Lutherans, contributing to a smaller percentage of Lutherans—whose absolute numbers nonetheless increased.[14]

Continuing to the present, this percentage decline has been cause for concern. Even the slight shift from 90 (1966) to 87 percent (1969) upset President Knutson who equated it with losing a natural constituency and thus endangering identity. Similarly, the president agonized when the ratio of Minnesotans increased to 63 percent while that of North Dakotans declined to 16.5 percent. In order to reverse the tide and serve the many Lutherans of North Dakota, Knutson repeatedly urged pastors to redouble recruiting efforts for the college.[15] These pleas were to no avail. Demography and exigencies of the farm economy offset the pull of Lutheran loyalty.

Spurred by spiraling inflation, comprehensive fees rose steadily from $1,800 in 1966–1967 to $2,990 in 1974–1975, a 66 percent increase. The administration attempted to ease this burden by keeping its costs lower than other regional private colleges and by freezing fees for two years from 1970 to 1972. The energy crisis of 1973 soon ended the freeze strategy, but not the practice of underpricing. Cobbers fatalistically accepted these hikes as an inevitable necessity not unlike death and taxes. Their compliance was more readily secured by steadily increasing financial aid. By 1966, assistance from private donors and the federal government totalled more than $1 million. That year 500 students worked, including those on federal work study, and 793 held national defense student loans. Federally guaranteed loans and federal opportunity grants were other important government-sponsored programs.[16]

New Construction

As enrollment continued upward, the college sought more dollars to construct more buildings. Fortunately, the development office was now well-established. Gift income increased from $874,425 (1965–1966) to $2.3 million (1972–1973), a record high. That year government funds—mostly for student aid and construction—accounted for 20.2 percent of the total, down from 32 percent in 1967. Believed to be one of the most successful money-raising groups in the United States, the C-400 Club enhanced private giving and spawned imitators around the nation. When the club recruited its 2,500th member in 1971, it was already engaged in Project 4 which sought dollars for library expansion, Norse Village construction and Old Main remodeling. Within fifteen months, the club had grown to 3,000 members. Although support from the Minnesota Private College Fund amounted to a seemingly insignificant 1.4 percent of the budget, this sum equaled the interest on an endowment of $1.25 million, a larger sum than most private Minnesota colleges then possessed. Lutheran support remained crucial. Although the annual ALC grant was less than 2 percent of the operating budget, Concordia's share of the Lutheran Ingathering for Education (LIFE) campaign boosted gift income. Between 1965 and 1975 LIFE distributed $10.4 million to the twelve ALC colleges, largely for capital construction. Tuition provided about 80 percent of operating funds. As most Cobbers were Lutheran, a high percentage of the institutional income thus came from Lutheran homes.[17]

Despite the fruitfulness of private giving, Concordia required federal assistance in what became a time of financial woe for American higher education. During the 1970s, enrollments leveled off as doubts developed about the value of a college degree in a depressed economy. Rising tuition priced some out of the market. Operating costs soared in a period of runaway inflation worsened in 1973 by the Arab oil embargo. Private institutions were hardest hit. While enrollments in Lutheran colleges increased 54 percent between 1960 and 1970, costs rose 223 percent. Deficits appeared in 1965; by 1970, sixteen of twenty-eight institutions were in the red. Timely expansion of state programs of student aid and the beginning of Basic Educational Opportunity Grants (later called Pell Grants) by the federal government in 1972 shored up enrollments and generated institutional income from tuition.[18]

Recognizing the growing importance of federal dollars, Concordia joined with sister schools in attempting to influence directly the development of public policy at both the state and national levels. Lutheran institutions maintained membership in college associations with permanent staff in Washington: the National Association for

Independent Colleges and Universities, the Council of Independent Colleges and the American Council on Education. The secretary of the Lutheran Educational Conference of North America served as the voice and ear for Lutheran higher education

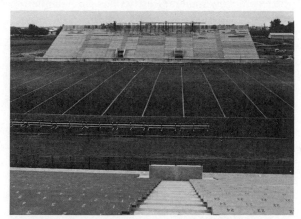

Jake Christiansen Stadium, a project of Moorhead businessmen.

in Washington. Nonetheless, expanding state and federal action by 1970 had not given the nation's colleges a solid financial base. This was reflected in annual deficits, growth of long-term indebtedness and belt-tightening.[19]

Although Concordia experienced the belt-tightening, it avoided large deficits while expanding significantly its physical plant. In the second half of the 1960s, the college completed four major projects and began

another. Community leaders in a sense forced Jake Christiansen Stadium on a reluctant administration. Despite the desperate need for a science hall, administrators decided after consulting with science faculty that they could not graciously reject a proferred substantial gift. Led by Carrol E. Malvey and Arthur P. Diercks, Moorhead businessmen raised $265,000 in Fargo-Moorhead. Their success contrasts sharply to the poor giving for the field house in 1951 and testifies to an achievement of the Knutson administration; what had been very weak community support had become notably strong. Moreover, the stadium project led to Fargo-Moorhead gifts for other institutional needs so the decision to build was wise in the long run. Approved by the regents in October 1964, construction of the 6,000 seat facility began in May 1966. An October dedication honored Jake Christiansen, "the fox of the MIAC," who had coached Cobbers for a quarter century.[20]

The new Science Hall substantially expanded classroom space.

Plans for a new science hall, announced in March 1963, called for a $1.25 million structure housing the departments of physics, biology, math, chemistry and psychology. When the $1.8 million edifice opened in September 1967, its 60,000 square feet increased the institution's classroom space by 40 percent and made it the largest campus building; nevertheless, biology had been omitted. That department agreed to remain in the old war surplus hospital where it had more space; otherwise what was eventually named Ivers Hall could not have been built. A federal grant of $595,697 and a federal loan of $750,000, obtained under the

Higher Education Facilities Act of 1963, contributed significantly to the construction. Much thought and soul searching preceded the decision to seek federal aid. Faced with a choice of inadequate science facilities or accepting government money, Concordia decided to take its chances with the federal government. Restrictions proved minimal and Concordia's Christian orientation was not affected.[21]

Dedication services, held in Memorial Auditorium on October 28, 1967, after a week of science lectures and seminars, were attended by delegates from forty-seven colleges and universities, Concordia faculty, students and friends. The three-story building included a two-story, 140-seat auditorium built by a $25,000 gift from Lutheran Brotherhood, eleven large classrooms wired for television, four seminar rooms and sixteen laboratories. The polished concrete floors and minimal decoration kept down cost and gave the center the masculine feeling desired by the architect.[22] Thus did traditional gender assumptions about male predominance in the disciplines of natural science enter even into the design of campus space.

In October 1965 the corporation authorized construction of men's and women's dormitories with attached food service on part of the sixty-five acre tract that previously had included only athletic fields. This action confirmed the departure from traditional campus design signaled by the location of Hoyum Hall. Previously, Concordia—like most American colleges—had divided the grounds into male and female areas. No longer. Male and female Cobbers would now occupy different wings of the same structure. Bids were submitted in February 1967 and the complex finished in

East Complex housed men's and women's dormitories and a cafeteria.

Fall 1968. The largest campus construction project to date, East Complex cost $2.6 million and was financed largely by a long-term $2.4 million federal loan from the Housing and Home Finance Agency. Eventually named for generous donors, the four-story Hallett and Erickson Halls were connected by Grant Commons; the facility housed and fed 462. Each dormitory had a large lounge, recreation room, small chapel, television and stereo rooms, laundry and separate study rooms on each floor. The Moe Lounge was named in honor of Rev. J. Melvin Moe, a member of the religion department from 1955 to 1969 and pastor of Fargo's Olivet Lutheran Church for twenty-five years.[23]

In November 1966, C-400 scheduled Project 3, the Humanities Center. It included a combination auditorium-theatre, audio center and art gallery. Contracts for this $850,000 project were let in October 1967; in addition to C-400 contributions it was financed by a $283,000 grant and a $354,000 loan secured under the federal Higher Education Facilities Act. The completed structure was dedicated on September 27, 1969. The exhibition space in 1974 was named the C.M. Running Art Gallery in honor of the artist who developed the department and taught there for thirty-five years. In 1980 the center was renamed the Frances Frazier Comstock Theatre in recognition of a major benefactor of the college.[24]

The center was only the first phase of a projected humanities-social science complex that included a six-story tower housing the departments of art, modern languages, English, speech and drama, religion, history, economics, political science and sociology. A combination of high inflation, uncertain enrollments and inability to secure additional federal funding prevented fruition of these plans and compelled the college to choose the alternative of remodeling Old Main. These unfavorable circumstances slowed other construction as well. The four-story, $950,000 library tower, dedicated at homecoming 1971, marked the end of major building for several years. It was financed by the last federal grant and loan under the Higher Education Facilities Act; by $195,000 in grants from the Bremer, Bush and Kresge Foundations; and by C-400 Project 4. The first two floors doubled

The Frances Frazier Comstock Theatre under contruction.

the space for books and increased seating capacity 50 percent. The top two floors were used as classrooms and offices until Summer 1989.[25]

Although construction slackened due to unfavorable financial conditions, it did not stop entirely. Concordia continued to improve its physical facilities within the means at its disposal. During Summer 1972 as part of a $150,000 undertaking, the field house received new bleachers, track and floor over the basketball court and the dirt football practice area; this doubled the playing space for intramurals. In March 1974, C-400 announced Old Main restoration as its Project 6. This $500,000 proposal called for remodeling the auditorium into faculty offices along with new windows, new heating and air conditioning system, new wiring and redecorating. It marked another project undertaken by Sandie Brothers Construction. Headed by foreman Kelly Sandie, a knowledgeable Norwegian carpenter noted for unvarnished speech, this firm earned the confidence of the administration and completed much work on campus for more than a decade.[26]

Kelly Sandie

Another phase in the ongoing collegian effort to secure a student union initiated the last construction of the Knutson era. Early in 1969, Cobbers founded SUN—Students for a Union Now. They organized a fundraising campaign complete with red, white and yellow campaign buttons which pointedly referred to their lack of a facility: "We're #1—the only one without one." In 1970 they raised $20,000 toward their goal. The C-400 Club boosted this effort in 1972 by making the union its Project 5.[27]

In September that year the regents approved the addition of an Olympic size swimming pool to the field house. When the facility opened in April 1975, it was dedicated with a presidential swim. The soon-to-retire Knutson swam the length of the pool, performing what one wag called "the Norwegian crawl." In his remarks, Knutson not only spoke of the pool but summed up what his administration had achieved for the entire campus: "This is a beautiful pool. When we do something here, we try to do it better and more artistically than any other place. We've got the finest college architecturally in the Upper Midwest." The other phase of the project—named the Joseph L. Knutson Student Life Center in honor of the president who, according to Rev. Lowell Almen, had led Concordia with such vision

President Knutson dedicates the swimming pool.

and skill for more than two decades—was appropriately attached to the Commons, an earlier structure erected due to student initiative. Besides two meeting rooms, offices for the college pastors, a large lounge area, campus information and the Korn Krib, the Knutson Center consisted mostly of the Centrum, a large multi-purpose room for chapel, concerts, lectures and other gatherings. These two structures, built at a cost of $1.3 million, provided Cobbers with places for worship, fellowship and recreation.[28]

A Changing Faculty

During the 1960s, Lutheran colleges successfully met the recruiting challenge. Faculties expanded and improved academically as the proportion of earned doctorates climbed to more than 37 percent by 1970. At Concordia 39 percent held the highest degree. This professional improvement did not comfort President Knutson, however. Hiring only those with the best academic credentials, he warned, led to a staff more and more unsympathetic to institutional goals. In a 1966 letter to a colleague suggesting this problem as a topic for discussion among Lutheran college presidents, Knutson pointedly posed the question: "Just how long shall we remain colleges of the church if our faculties become less and less Lutheran and less and less committedly Christian?" Religiously committed professors—preferably Lutheran—were necessary, Knutson maintained, to mold a Christian community marked by a distinctive life style.[29]

Growth, combined with retirements, complicated recruiting. The number of fulltime faculty grew from 132 in 1965 to 159 in 1975, while many giants retired. The few discussed are illustrative of others similarly dedicated. In 1968 football coach

Jacobi Melius "Jake" Christiansen, "the magician of the MIAC," ended one of the most colorful coaching careers in Minnesota sports. His shrewd offensive schemes helped win five conference championships and several second place finishes due to

his nemesis, Gustavus Adolphus. His 197 victories ranked first among active coaches. His endless fund of funny stories made him a popular high school banquet speaker who sold many athletes on Concordia. Through his efforts, Memorial Auditorium and the football field were built. The coaching clinic he started in 1953 developed into one of the best in the region, attracting several hundred annually. When hired in 1941 Christiansen had said, "I want to build my program and then live here the rest of my life and see it operate." That he did, with outstanding success.[30]

Colorful Jake Christiansen, a successful coach.

Born in Norway, Sigurd Mundhjeld migrated to North Dakota as a boy, graduated from Concordia in 1925, served as treasurer from 1938 to 1947, and chaired the mathematics department from 1947 to 1963. Before he retired in 1968, this humble, impeccably dressed teacher became the first to hold the Wije Distinguished Professorship (1962–1965) and produced a large number of mathematicians who earned graduate degrees and became college and university teachers. When his widow Pauline Prestegaard Mundhjeld died in 1987, she bequeathed $910,000 to the college, creating an endowed professorship. Their devoted service to the institution thus continues.[31]

R.E. "Ed" Fuglestad came to Concordia from a military academy in 1927 as instructor in biology and chemistry to teach the overflow in two one-person departments. All the professors knew virtually all the students and hung their coats in a single Old Main closet. True to his recent military experience, the new professor marched to the front of the room, executing perfect right-angle turns,

Sigurd Mundhjeld educated many professors of mathematics.

and terrified Cobbers by putting them on the spot with his pointer and rapid-fire questions. Pointers broke frequently because he had partially sawed them through for effect. A man who loved to entertain but who did not cook, Fuglestad is also remembered for his "dead fish" parties where he served a menu of fish and raw vegetables to alumni and retired teachers. When he retired in 1970, the professor had distinguished himself for instructing 187 Cobbers, two of them sons, who became medical doctors. Together with Olaf Torstveit, Howard Osborn and others, Fuglestad insured that students were well-drilled for the rigors of professional school. To support his growing family of seven children on often meager Concordia salaries was not easy. The Fuglestad family saved rent during the 1930s by spending summers at his parents' farm near Cooperstown, North Dakota; he earned additional income by working as a hail adjuster. In the 1950s, Clara Sigdestad Fuglestad operated a small grocery which "didn't make much money but the family got groceries wholesale!" She too exemplified the Concordia ideal of service to the community by working with the PTA, helping displaced persons and housing Concordia veterans.[32]

Cyrus Running began teaching art in North Hall in 1940 with four tables, a few chairs, some drawing boards and no sinks. The department moved around campus until the Berg Art Center was renovated in 1954. There he, Elizabeth Strand and Dean Bowman at last had enough space. Despite Moorhead's distance from a large art gallery and a limited slide collection of major works, Running believed he had the necessary tools an art teacher needed—talented students and the freedom to design cour-

Biologist R.E. Fuglestad prepared many future medical doctors.

ses. One of five sons of a Lutheran pastor who pursued artistic careers, Running studied with painter Grant Wood at the University of Iowa and explored religious themes in his work. According to his architect friend Ed Sövik, Running's love of the created world grew from his sense of life in the presence of God. This energized him and nourished his enormous production despite the heavy responsibilities of teaching and family.[33]

Cyrus Running, a well-known regional artist.

Like most professors in the lean early years, Running found outside employment; he worked for a commercial sign company. By the mid-1950s, salaries had improved and he now had funds for a sabbatical and time for his own work. He piled his family of six into a Studebaker Champion and went to Mexico for one year. He was able to paint all day, every day; in the evening he visited other artists and discussed painting. Upon his return, he taught by day and created by night. His paintings, murals, mosaics and several students made him one of the best known regional artists. His work with Paul Christiansen on the annual Christmas concert left behind a fund of stories illustrating his whimsy, joy and humor. All-night sessions were punctuated by Eldrid Running's Christmas cookies, strong coffee and Cy's impromptu piano concerts featuring an assortment of Mozart, Lutheran hymns and boogie woogie. One evening ended with an early morning breakfast at Wood's All-Night Restaurant with Running standing on the seat of a booth directing a chorus of sleepy, somber-faced truckers in singing "On the Wings of the Snow-white Dove."[34]

Sigvald and Isabelle Thompson retired in 1974 after a combined sixty-five years of devoted service to the music department and the Fargo-Moorhead Symphony. A cellist, Sigvald first came to the Concordia Conservatory of Music in 1929; after study at Juilliard he became conductor of the symphony when he joined the department in 1937. A violinist, Isabelle became concertmaster of the orchestra and a faculty member in 1948. Through their work with the symphony and their lessons which knew no time limit, both trained hundreds of musicians, many of whom performed with other orchestras or taught at schools and universities throughout the country. Under their influence the symphony survived and even flourished, growing from a small civic group to a fine regional orchestra. Thompson assiduously expanded repertoire and made the organization a national asset by choosing young performers as soloists and commissioning works by young composers. Thompson's placid face masked a fine wit; he once told a petulant pianist who insisted for the third time that he must have more clarinets, "I can't give you anything but love, baby." A professor recalled his impressions as a teen-ager upon first seeing Thompson perform: "He was too solid, too unemotional, too dry, too humorless to be a *real* artist." When he later shared this with the conductor, Thompson laconically replied: "That must have been in my unromantic period."[35]

Faced with the retirement of many master teachers and the coming of many novices, Dean Dovre in 1972 pioneered an experimental faculty development project assisted by the Hill Foundation. A seminar of ten professors and two collegians tested a new mode of faculty development by exploring jointly issues related to college teaching.[36] Thus began what has since become an annual summer opportunity for professional growth and development. Seminars deal with pedagogy, educational issues, the liberal arts and theology. They foster a sense of community among the faculty and thereby enhance commitment to educational and religious mission.

Given Knutson's conception of a Christian college, the teaching of religion became a sensitive issue. The president wanted the department to have a balance of religious perspectives and to assume pastoral care for collegiate spiritual life and welfare. This traditional pastoral expectation had prevailed in Lutheran colleges until the 1940s. Then, institutions attempted to make religion departments academically respectable by hiring instructors with advanced degrees. At the same time, schools sought to identify religion with the entire campus and not only the ordained or a single department. Inevitably, the pastoral function of religion faculty declined in this climate. Moreover, the presentation of a broader range of intellectual perspectives including the historical-critical study of the Bible created tensions at Concordia and other Lutheran schools.[37]

By the mid-1950s, Concordia joined the search for theologians with doctorates. Dean Bailey's vision of a free Christian college perhaps committed him to this more than Knutson; but the president went along, if sometimes reluctantly. In part he was forced to comply because accrediting agencies counted the number of advanced degrees. Although Knutson agreed that religion professors should be more qualified academically, he always had a certain type in mind. He wanted "smart evangelicals"; he did not want "a certain brand of sophisticated preacher" because "an institution cannot take too many of that kind." Apparently about this time, Lloyd Svendsbye—a staff member from 1957 to 1966—sold the president on an enlarged department. Svendsbye argued this expansion would reduce the size of excessively large religion classes, maintain loyalty to the church and create the right kind of spiritual atmosphere on campus.[38]

President Knutson later said he regretted this decision for several reasons. First, academic qualifications had been emphasized at the expense of pastoral experience and care. Second, because the majority came directly from graduate school they were immature, manifested a "whippersnapper attitude" and taught by the shock method. Third, "the social action side" had been overloaded. Fourth, a uniformity of thought had developed which belied a vocal commitment to academic freedom. As a consequence, Knutson maintained, the department had become overly sophisticated and had organized itself like a theological seminary. This contradicted Knutson's views of undergraduate education. He objected to bringing graduate school issues into a liberal arts college. He did not understand "why a freshman from Bearcreek, Montana, should be introduced to the critical problems of the Bible without first knowing what's in the Bible." Here Knutson's traditional pastoral conception shaped his criticisms of the department and its curriculum. Commending a young professor for seeking ordination, Knutson wrote, the "teacher has to show a definite commitment to the Christ and to the Church, and in his work with students he should always have the pastor's heart." And as he stated to another churchman: "I'm still Haugean enough to believe that somewhere in this business of operating a church college the Gospel should be sounded so that a poor sinner has a chance to commit his life to Jesus Christ."[39]

Paul Sponheim argued for academic integrity and Christian commitment.

Presidential scrutiny at times demoralized religion professors, but it did not prevent the gathering of scholarly and talented teachers committed to the concept of a free Christian college. Chair Paul Sponheim used a christological analogy in articulating the twofold human and divine aims of the department for the board of regents in 1969. As part of the liberal arts, religious studies sought to understand the human condition, an approach open to people of many faiths. At the same time, courses in the Lutheran tradition and the religion requirement fostered self-understanding for believers. Rejecting the argument that knowledge undermines faith, the department affirmed that academic integrity and Christian commitment could cohere. They believed that scholarly understanding helped people grow in faith and enabled them to worship God with mind as well as heart.[40]

Academic Innovations

The board of regents in 1968 chartered a complete study of the curriculum "with a view to updating requirements, courses and instructional techniques consistent with the best traditions and purposes of a church-related liberal arts college." This decision emerged from concerns being expressed widely in American society about the irrelevance and rising costs of higher education, and from local worries about the proliferation of courses and the low student-faculty ratio in several departments. Published two years later, *Curriculum Reform for Concordia College* was authored by a commission chaired by Walther Prausnitz and staffed by Carl Bailey, Tom Christenson, Paul Dovre, Robert Homann, Harding Noblitt and Omar Olson, a student. The final report proposed substituting a course plan for the existing credit system in hopes that the consolidation of a high number of low credit offerings into a fewer number of full courses would overcome fragmentation in student schedules. Equally important, fewer courses translated into fewer teachers, which lowered instructional costs. Other recommendations included the elimination of the B.S. degree, a reduction of credits required for graduation to 122 (thirty courses plus one-half course in physical education), a new system of core requirements, an increased number of pass-fail options, retention of the calendar, extension of library hours, a study of advisement procedures, increased student participation in academic planning and support for minority programs. After the faculty senate adopted the proposed core curriculum by a vote of 41 to 7 in April 1970, Prausnitz was named director of liberal arts studies; this new office helped guide the transition to the new curriculum in Fall 1972, administered the new core requirements and conducted academic research.[41]

As revised, core requirements now included two courses in skills (composition, argument and inference, research and reporting) and five courses in distribution from approved courses selected from at least three areas outside a student's major. Core areas were science and mathematics, social sciences, foreign languages, foundations and premises of civilization, and literature and the fine arts. Distribution courses were intended to introduce collegians to the fundamental assumptions and methods of disciplines. The religion requirement was reduced to two courses, one elected the freshman-sophomore year from Bible, Christian tradition and non-Christian religion and one elected in the junior-senior year from belief, ethics and spirituality. In their junior-senior years Cobbers chose an integration course from an approved list. These capstone courses were designed to relate disciplines to personal and societal life and to demonstrate the relations between disciplines. Besides the core, students completed a major for graduation.[42]

The curriculum commission report thus retained the traditional liberal arts emphasis on breadth and specialization. The core offered breadth through introducing students to a variety of disciplinary perspectives; the major offered specialization in a single discipline. The remaining third of a student's academic program either could be devoted to electives, to producing more breadth, or to specialization in a second major. By emphasizing skills rather than mere knowledge, the plan reflected the pervasive influence of progressive education in America. Similarly, its abandonment of the foreign language requirement and its adoption of core distribution selected from many course options mirrored the national collapse of general education based on common bodies of knowledge and the trend toward greater student autonomy. Given the knowledge explosion, not everything could be taught. The best liberal arts preparation therefore equipped graduates with tools and the desire to become lifelong learners.[43]

Theodore Heimarck (left) developed the hospital administration major.

Other curricular innovations included hospital administration, Norwegian and the self-teacher actualization program (S-TAP). Added in 1966 and directed by Theodore Heimarck, hospital administration was one of only four undergraduate programs in the nation. Revived interest in ethnic origins sparked the resurrection in Fall 1972 of a beginning Norwegian class taught by Elwin Rogers. From this came eventually a minor, and then a major, in Scandinavian studies. Designed by elementary education professors Linda Stoen, Loren Winch and Shelby Niebergall under the leadership of department chair Clark Tufte, S-TAP featured learning modules, clinical experiences and competency-based instruction. This highly innovative program aimed at providing prospective teachers "with a more relevant, more realistic and more effective" training. Although much revised in detail, S-TAP and its emphasis on self-actualized learning endures to the present.[44]

Following a nationwide development, non-resident study opportunities expanded greatly. In February 1965, Concordia completed an agreement with Schiller College that allowed twelve to study abroad for a year in Germany or Switzerland. Then in December the student senate approved a travel seminar proposal. Perhaps stimulated by this suggestion and the initial enthusiasm generated by the Schiller experience, Odell Bjerkness served as the catalyst for the May Seminar Program. The fledgling seminars took flight in 1968 when modern language professors Willard Hiebert, Thorpe Running and Bjerkness—after an on-campus pre-seminar course gave background and preparation for the European experience—led twenty-six Cobbers on tours of Germany, Spain and France respectively. This month of cultural immersion ac-

Odell Bjerkness (beret) leads first French May Seminar.

celerated language learning and enriched cultural understanding. The program soon expanded to include non-language offerings. When religion and drama joined in 1969 enrollment increased to eighty. By 1975, eleven seminars studied art and art history, archeology, drama, education, English, history, political science, religion and languages; nearly 1,500 had traveled with the May Seminars Abroad since its beginning. That year, 345 Cobbers, including the Concordia Band, left Fargo's Hector International on a chartered DC-10 for a month in Europe, Africa and Asia Minor.[45]

For those unable to journey abroad, other opportunities beckoned. The Washington Semester, arranged by the political science department with American University in Washington, D.C., permitted selected Cobbers to study one semester in the nation's capital. A twelve-day urban church seminar to New York City allowed others to "gain appreciation for the role of Christians in public life." The Monterrey Tec Program, administered by the Spanish department, enabled Cobbers to earn six credits in Spanish and English in the Spanish cultural environment of Monterrey, Mexico. A short-lived exchange stimulated by the social consciousness of the 1960s permitted enrollment for a semester at Fort Lewis College (Durango, Colorado), which specialized in southwest and Indian studies, or Virginia Union University (Richmond, Virginia), which offered immersion in the urban and black experience. It also featured special emphasis seminars—Indian, urban and rural (Concordia)—conducted on each campus during summer sessions. Students studied four weeks on their home campus, then traveled to the others for two weeks. After 1969, Cobbers could gain student teaching experiences in foreign countries through a program developed by the Moorhead State education department. And in 1973, classics professor Olin Storvick led five Cobbers on the first of many archeological digs at Caesarea Maritima, Israel.[46]

Stave Church at Skogfjorden, the Norwegian Language Camp.

Meanwhile, language villages developed rapidly. Initially a financial embarrassment because land and buildings exceeded cost estimates and fundraising did not produce anticipated sums, the program eventually took off and became self-sustaining. In December 1965, the board of language camp development advisors announced that the language camp complex would be located on the 800 acre Turtle River Lake site ten miles northeast of Bemidji. When ground was broken for Norwegian Village, the first permanent site and the first stage of the complex, acting Dean Dovre noted appropriately that "it represents a milestone." Indeed. When completed, Skogfjorden served not only summer campers but provided a year-round place for collegian and faculty retreats, language miniweeks and snow sports. The $650,000 project attracted support from fifteen foundations and corporations, including a $150,000 grant from the Bush Foundation, and various other individuals and fraternal organizations. What President Knutson called "a marvelous facility" was dedicated in September 1970. A year later, Odell Bjerkness replaced Vernon Mauritsen as director; until August 1989 he presided over the program's continued expansion. In Summer 1975 there were thirty sessions for campers between the ages of 8 and 18 who came for one, two and four-week sessions at French, German, Norwegian, Russian, Spanish or Swedish camps. The previous year, 1,600 attended from thirty-eight states. Some earned high school credit through intensive four-week sessions. Enthusiasm for the experience brought nearly one-half back the next season, and a few enrolled for seven consecutive summers.[47]

James Hofrenning

At this time, Concordia pioneered in ecumenism and two significant forms of educational outreach. Communiversity, "a university of the community for continuing education," originated in 1964 as a faith-in-life seminar. Under the direction of its first coordinator, Dr. James Hofrenning, it expanded to offer courses in theology, congregational leadership, personal and family life, humanities, sciences and regionalism. An interfaith committee comprised of

Protestants, Catholics and Jews assisted in curricular design. Grants, gifts from area churches and registrants provided financial support. Then in 1969 the American Lutheran Church selected the college as its site for an innovative scheme of service to the community. Directed initially by Rev. Wayne Stumme, CHARIS—Ecumenical Center for Church and Community—developed a strong curriculum of graduate theological education taught by thirty-five professors drawn from Concordia and neighboring institutions as well as scholars serving parishes. In 1974, more than 300 clergy and religious from ten denominations studied at twenty-three centers located in the four-state area of North and South Dakota, Minnesota and Wisconsin.[48]

The library grew along with the expansion of other physical facilities and programs. By 1966, the collection had about doubled in the decade since completion of the new building. It now totalled 95,000 volumes and 20,000 pamphlets, augmented by the approximately 600 periodicals received annually. A decade later, holdings—increasing at 1,000 books per month—exceeded 190,000 volumes. In 1973, hours were extended to midnight and a new electronic book monitoring system had been added to reduce losses (which had totalled $4,400 the previous year). When hours were reduced because of staff shortages, collegian protests and petitions again lengthened them to midnight except for Friday (10:30 p.m.) and

Library reading room, a place for socializing and study.

Saturday (5:00 p.m.). At the same time, the library committee struggled to reduce noise, a perennial problem for the academically inclined caused by the socially minded. Although the committee asserted "that students have a right to expect a quiet atmosphere in the library, conducive to study," their pleas did not induce silence.[49]

Limits to Growth

Growth was not continuous in the decade. Straitened financial circumstances, an enrollment decline, uncertain future registrations and a high percentage of tenured faculty necessitated cuts and changes in the tenure system. Consequently, President Knutson postponed tenure decisions and pressed for eliminating staff. Paul Dovre, recently appointed academic dean, inherited this task in Fall 1971. His letter to the faculty explained. Compensation could be strengthened and the leaves program reinstituted if the student-faculty ratio was increased over the next two years from the then-current 14.8:1 to 16.5:1. This eliminated ten positions, affecting six people, in the first year. Subsequently, additional cuts were made. The institution promised to assist those released in what, unfortunately, turned out to be a declining academic market.[50]

The recently completed curriculum reform, which introduced the course plan and required fewer teachers, facilitated this contraction. An intensive study by Walther

Prausnitz, the director of liberal arts studies, and detailed consultation with the chairs preceded the decision. In a related action, a hotly debated tenure quota system was adopted in 1973. This plan placed a ratio on promotions and a ceiling on tenure at the departmental and college levels. An appeal to flexibility justified these changes. The college wanted freedom to reduce staff quickly if financial exigency required; at the same time, it desired to maintain contact with the graduate schools by attracting the fresh ideas of newly minted doctorates.[51]

In retrospect, the Knutson success story continued until his retirement in 1975. Despite expanding enrollments, physical plant and programs, Knutson's last years were nonetheless troubled by the student protests affecting many campuses. Although these were never sufficient to prevent expansion, they did generate anxiety in the mind of Knutson and others that the constituency might be alienated, growth undermined and the soul of a Christian college destroyed.

Chapter 15

The Turbulent Sixties
and an Anxious President

A Stormy Decade

The emergence of the counterculture, the unpopular Vietnam War and the rise of campus protest made the 1960s a difficult period for the conservative President Knutson. He viewed student rebellion as a manifestation of the secularism which directly threatened his conception of a Christian college. Although politically oriented dissent at Concordia was mild compared to that of Berkeley, Columbia and other elite universities, it did not seem mild to a president inclined to see vital principles threatened by this youthful challenge to authority.

Nationwide student protest is difficult to characterize because it was not a single movement and it changed over time. Numbers expanded or contracted in response to national politics and specific campus issues. Because protests were so dramatic, the media exaggerated the degree of radicalism. Radicals who viewed dissent as a means

Painted car and beanie-clad Cobbers reflected some new issues of the decade.

for building a movement to change American society were a tiny minority within a minority; depending on national events and the institution in question, radicals comprised only 3 to 12 percent of the student body. At their height in response to the Cambodian bombing in May 1970, demonstrations occurred on only about one-half of American campuses. In 1969 only 28 percent of the college population had taken part in a demonstration of any kind in the preceding four years. The percentage at Concordia was much smaller. Moreover, many of the traditional collegiate customs—weakened somewhat or altered to reflect the time—continued at Concordia and elsewhere. Athletics, Greek societies, the newspaper, student government, other extracurriculars and even academics remained important for the majority.[1]

Rebellion accelerated several nascent trends: the discontinuance of *in loco parentis* (parietal rules), increased student representation in college governance and elimination of general education course requirements to maximize choice. These trends mirrored changes in American society and Lutheranism. Families became more permissive as they became more affluent. Liberal organizations like AAUP and ACLU asserted

A civil rights march demonstrated for racial equality.

that collegians were more likely to mature as citizens if they had adult rights and responsibilities. The Supreme Court, which held in 1957 that students were entitled to the same substantive and procedural rights as other citizens, supported the drive for greater freedom from institutional restrictions.[2]

The attitudes of the ALC constituency similarly changed as the church increasingly became part of mainstream American denominationalism. Although most Lutherans retained a conservative theological position which emphasized an historic, traditional system of beliefs—knowledge of a personal and caring God, a biblical and gospel orientation, faith in Jesus Christ—important differences between youth and adults on social issues became apparent at this time. Youth were more open to oppressed peoples and more likely to urge social action. This generational difference fostered controversy and calls for change at Concordia and her sister institutions.[3]

Given the trends of the day, President Knutson often felt like a voice crying in the wilderness and he often tired of his struggle. Although a note of self-pity sometimes appears in personal correspondence, Knutson was not without humor about his role. He once wrote, "I try not to take myself so seriously that I think I'm John the Baptist." The president was not as isolated as he feared. The constituency expected him to take the stands he did. And even when students did not agree they sometimes respected his courage. Jim Nestingen ('67), a former *Concordian* editor, wrote, "I couldn't help but admire a man who would stand up in front of all those students and say exactly what he thought." A 1972 graduate voiced similar praise many years after her graduation. Writing about the J. Paul Nesse statue of the president that stands in the Knutson

Center, *Forum* reporter Cathy Mauk said that viewing the statue proved wrong her assumptions as a student. "Instead of seeing a hard-headed Norwegian, I saw a very human man who well knows the tragedies and injustices of life. ... Instead of seeing a rigid authoritarian, I saw a man with an ear cocked to listen." Mauk now believed that Knutson loved even the troublemakers.[4]

However much President Knutson may have loved the rebels, he clearly perceived the threat they posed to his patriarchal conception of a Christian college. "An institution is something like a family," he wrote, "and no family fulfills its function unless there is a father at the head of it and certain customs, traditions, rules and mores that make for unity and order. ..." In keeping with this family metaphor, Knutson conceived of the church college as custodian and protector. He maintained that commitment to the Christian view of life contained in scriptures and to the ideal of liberal studies made Lutheran colleges the "custodian of the teachings, culture, and traditions of the church." As custodians, they contributed to the great ideological struggle against encroaching secularism and thereby were the "church's most effective witness today." To accomplish their role as custodians, the colleges must also be protectors. They must shield students from worldly influences so they might develop Christian maturity and become faithful servants of the church.[5]

President Knutson greatly feared cultural trends that undermined piety in church and school. The growing secularization of American culture generated intense pressures toward "non-affirming colleges" only nominally connected with their founding churches. Determined to resist this drift, the president upheld *in loco parentis* as a way to maintain Christian morality, welcomed the outpouring of God's spirit on campus and worked for the spiritual renewal of the Lutheran church.

Despite this evangelical emphasis and the anxiety of several professors who detected anti-intellectual tendencies in the president's policies, Concordia essentially remained a "free Christian college" and did not become a "defender of the faith" institution. Although the school fostered Lutheran ecclesiastical ties and theological traditions, collegians and professors generally were not coerced into a narrow Lutheran orthodoxy. With some notable exceptions in the religion department, the president's pietism did not lead him to tamper with academic program; and whether they sympathized or not with the president's pietistic crusades, the faculty promoted academic quality. Like Luther College and her other sisters, Concordia remained in the tradition of Christian humanism, devoted to thoughtful reflection about both Christianity and the liberal arts.[6]

Despite presidential anxiety about the turbulent 1960s, Concordia prospered. The ideals of the college as a family and a caring Christian community mitigated the impact of dissent. Administrators and professors met regularly with collegians to resolve differences and to expand student participation in college governance despite opposition of a president who preferred clear lines of authority. While alarmed by the implications of rebellion, President Knutson recognized that the rebels—often highly vocal and visible as members of the *Concordian* and Student Association—were after all only a tiny minority. Fortunately for Knutson, the tempest did not last long. By 1971, the president reported that the school was calm and that the students were the happiest they had been for some time.[7]

A Fun Protest

The explosive cultural issues of the Sixties moved campus activities in nontraditional directions that both frightened and bewildered many college authorities and parents. These new directions did not entirely displace customary collegiate activities at Concordia, however. Indeed, the most broadly based—and the most fun—demonstration combined elements of both the new and old. In October 1966, Cobbers marched to protest renaming Old Main Bogstad Hall in honor of the president responsible for its construction. They sold more than 1,000 buttons labeled "Old Main Shall Remain." More than 500 gathered on the shores of Prexy's Pond to rename it "Bogstad's Bog." Student Association President Dan Lee ('67) proclaimed "that the building ... shall remain Old Main in the hearts, minds and affections of all assembled here." He closed in parody of Martin Luther: "Here we stand. We cannot and will not recant. We can do no other. Old Main Shall Remain." Three faculty spouses—Mardy

This sign appeared in protest against renaming Old Main.

Dovre, Marcella Gulsvig and Ann Lee—sang a song they had composed especially for the ceremony. Pastor Carl Lee dedicated the bog to the ministry of love and pleasure. Following the rally, participants—blowing trumpets—marched seven times around the building to prove that its walls would not fall. They then sang "We Shall Overcome" and "Give Me That Old Time Religion." The students won their fight. In February 1967 President Knutson announced that he would propose restoring the name at the next board of regents meeting.[8]

The Civil Rights Revolution

Campus protests of the decade began as a byproduct of the civil rights movement. The civil rights revolution affected Concordia in many ways. Although hampered by geographical location, ethnic background and Lutheran affiliation, the college succeeded in its new effort to recruit minorities. By Spring 1968, two Native Americans and twenty-six African-Americans were enrolled. A committee on minority students organized by Dean Dovre had achieved an Afro-American club, a black admissions and teaching assistant, a black instructor, a seminar on black heritage, a modified faculty advisor and tutorial system for minorities and a student scholarship committee for nonwhite students. As discussed elsewhere, exchange programs were established in 1965 with Virginia Union, an urban black school, and in 1969 with Ft. Lewis College, an institution with substantial Indian enrollment.[9]

To further enhance intercultural education on campus, an intensive program with four scholars-in-residence and a weeklong race relations institute were scheduled for 1967–1968 and repeated the following year. Black plays—*Beware of the Young, Gifted and Black*, written and produced by the Afro-American organization, and *Slow Dance on the Killing Ground*, produced as part of the Concordia-Virginia Union theatre exchange—were performed in 1969–1970. Virginia Union drama professor William Kramer, who much appreciated the opportunity offered by the exchange, reported that blacks had been impressed by Concordia and had to revise many preconceived ideas; Cobbers did likewise, to the mutual benefit of both.[10]

A weekly *Concordian* column, "The Other Side," appeared in 1970–1971. That spring an African-American religious service was performed in chapel; it received a rave review—"one of the most stirring services of the month, if not the entire semester." The following January, a weeklong program entitled "Focus: Human Relations" explored cultural pluralism. In February black history month observances attempted to involve the entire community. In Fall 1973 a weekly intercultural affairs film festival at times drew audiences of over one hundred. Curriculum changed as well;

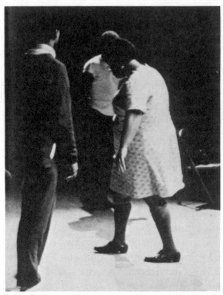

Beware of the Young, Gifted and Black, a student production.

history added black and Indian courses in 1969 and 1974 respectively and in 1972 sociology offered "Ethnic Minority and Social Differences." In response to the suggestion by Eric Fontaine ('74), the first black elected Student Association president, the college invited black Congressman Andrew Young to speak at the 1974 spring commencement. Young's stirring address received a standing ovation.[11]

Congressman Andrew Young (second from right) addressed the 1974 graduates.

Heightened racial consciousness led the college at last to give attention to Native Americans, a long-neglected minority from the region that offered a natural recruiting pool. Dorothy Still Smoking ('73) articulated the formidable cultural differences in a 1971 letter to the *Concordian.* "As Indian students at Concordia we hope to find some part of us here," she wrote. "We feel Concordia should offer more for the Indian student in the line of more Indian-authored books, more magazines, and most of all, *more* Indian students." Concordia and other Minnesota schools tried. Recently hired Indian recruiters at Concordia, Saint Olaf, Macalester and Saint Scholastica increased Indian enrollment from sixty to 150 during 1972. At Concordia, Carole Ann Hart, and then Dominick Sillitti, advised Native Americans. Indian emphasis weeks in 1972 scheduled nationally known speakers Vine

President Joseph L. Knutson, 1951–1975

Deloria, Jr., and Dennis Banks of the American Indian Movement. The first Tri-College Indian Week, held in 1973, was devoted to the theme of music and art.[12]

More minority students unfortunately increased racial tensions despite efforts at campus-wide human relations education. Strains—particularly in regard to interracial dating—were present from the beginning, but the minority student committee had defused problems and thus avoided major incidents. A cultural exchange center, located in the basement of Old Main, enabled blacks to satisfy social needs left unmet in an all-white environment. Nonetheless, when numbers of blacks increased to seventy-five in Fall 1973, hostility became overt. Threatening and obscene phone calls were made to black males and females. Student Association President Fontaine said it was unfortunate that some on a Christian campus "should feel a need to threaten and inflict harm on us, simply because we are different, simply because we are black." The blacks read a statement in chapel requesting that the threats and insults cease before anyone was harmed. The administration held special meetings, seeking ways to ease tension.[13]

President Knutson published a community letter calling for harmony. In November, the *Concordian* devoted a special issue to the crisis. Letters expressed "shock, shame and disgust" for racist expressions and exhorted members of the community not to tolerate racist slurs. Intercultural Affairs Director Gloria Hawkins urged respect and understanding as a way to ease tension. Other articles were informational, attempting to control troublesome rumors—which may have fueled the crisis—about financial aid, discrimination in the music department and the need for the intercultural center. To mitigate tensions, a human relations workshop followed in January. One hundred eighty administrators, faculty and students participated. The workshop recommended human relations instruction for freshmen, continuing education on race issues and hiring more minority personnel.[14]

Changing Parietal Rules

Attempts to dismantle *in loco parentis* caused considerable controversy. On the one hand, President Knutson asserted that he had made a commitment to parents and constituents "that Concordia is going to be carried on in a certain fashion." He felt "badly that some students don't realize what Concordia is all about" and pleaded with them "to keep Concordia oriented in the person and work of Christ as the college charter demands." On the other hand, collegians demanded more freedom from the rules they considered oppressive. Faculty were divided. Conservatives supported the president, arguing that institutional uniqueness required the administration to proceed cautiously on all matters affecting social policy and student participation in governance. Liberals believed in reducing paternalism and enlarging involvement. At the time, many in the college community were sympathetic to change. According to a survey conducted by psychology professor Gertrude Donat on student, faculty and city attitudes about Vietnam, free speech and press, criticism of the government, female rights, long hair/beards and revolution, faculty and students were similarly liberal in contrast to the Fargo-Moorhead community. This liberalism surfaced in demands for social dancing, elimination of women's hours, smoking for women and open dormitories.[15]

Cobbers had agitated for permission to dance since 1963. In that year's special election, 835 favored dancing—either on or off campus—while 486 opposed. In 1965 the student-faculty forum recommended another poll of faculty and students and, depending on results, a possible Student Association request to the regents. Apparently many collegiate organizations were sponsoring dances off-campus despite the ban. This demonstrated that many Cobbers now came from homes where dancing was accepted. The survey, administered by the sociology department, reflected these changed midwestern Lutheran attitudes: 90 percent of both faculty and students did not consider dancing a moral issue, 72.2 percent of the students and 61.5 percent of the faculty favored on-campus dancing, and 90.7 percent of the students but only 46.2 percent of the faculty favored off-campus dancing.[16]

Meanwhile Knutson stood firm. In a chapel talk subsequently mailed to the constituency, the president said that the controversy might be detrimental. For him, the issue was worldliness—whatever dimmed the eye of faith and weakened the fellowship of Christ. The dancing ban was one of those rules that made a Christian college distinctive. Knutson's stand drew considerable support from constituents. For them as for the president, no dancing symbolized a Christian lifestyle; their letters testified that they sent children to Concordia because it was distinctive. As one pastor stated in praising Knutson for his opposition to dancing, "may God give you grace to stand firm against all kinds of worldliness in our church schools that they may worthy to be called Christian. ..." This view was reiterated by the Moorhead Pastors Association, who petitioned the board not to change the policy. Given the president's position, pastoral opposition and constituent attitudes, the regents upheld the ban on social dancing in May 1966.[17]

Although the president won this battle, there were already signs that he would soon lose the war. Campus organizations continued to sponsor dances off-campus. Other Lutheran colleges dropped their prohibitions. That Knutson no longer had the support of his presidential brethren is suggested by a letter that Saint Olaf President Sidney Rand sent to a regent and to Knutson. In a veiled criticism of Knutson's stand, Rand refused to make one issue the litmus test for a Christian institution. With or without social dancing, Lutheran colleges were faithful witnesses of the gospel, he insisted.[18]

The Student Association again studied the issue in Spring 1968. The sociology department conducted another survey and the alumni office polled its members. On the basis of this information, the Student Association hoped that a new policy might be adopted. When a poll of parents revealed that they favored a change in policy by a ratio of two to one, the game was up. The president could no longer appeal to parental support. The regents dropped the ban in January 1969, making Concordia the last Lutheran institution to surrender. To secure presidential assent, the Student Association promised not to schedule dances during Lent, the Christmas concert and homecoming. Knutson unhappily accepted the decision; he did not think dancing a good pastime for collegians and he feared that the degrading influence of rock bands would change the complexion of church colleges. Nonetheless, he knew resistance was futile when other Lutheran institutions permitted dancing. As he wrote one critic of the innovation, "It is impossible for us at Concordia to keep a style of Christian living that is radically different from that which our young people experience in the local parish."[19]

Although one troublesome question had been settled, there were many others that strained relations. Women's hours and legalization of women smoking were framed in September 1968 as a matter of women's rights. In a *Concordian* editorial, Wendy Ward ('70) charged that these discriminatory rules reduced "the Concordia coed to the rank of second class citizen." Therefore they should be eliminated or "applied to both men and women." The following month, a women's rights action committee was founded. On October 31, many Cobbers participated in a torchlight demonstration for social equality. Two weeks later, Dean Dorothy Olsen said no to any rule revisions unless a majority supported change. Conducted in December, the poll indicated that 85 percent of on-campus women favored an extension of hours. The next month, women's hours were extended to 2:00 a.m. on weekends and to midnight during the week.[20]

Ward was pleased, but not satisfied. She urged continued pressure to permit smoking and to eliminate the different hours for seniors and freshmen. Agitation persisted. In November 1970, the president approved midnight hours Sunday through Thursday for all women; 2:00 a.m. hours on Friday and Saturday for freshmen; and no weekend hours for others. Finally in September 1972 the student affairs committee recommended to the president that all curfews be dropped. This policy was approved on trial basis for one semester in January 1973. There was no return. After five years of discussion, women's hours had been set aside. Meanwhile, women asserted their right to smoke. Again Ward led the way. "Concordia women ... are being denied their right to make what is a personal decision," she editorialized in January 1968. Most important to her, "they are also being denied acceptance of the responsibility entailed in making such a decision." Two years later, Cobber coeds had won this right. While the regents made this concession, they enunciated a new policy that discouraged smoking for everyone because of the health hazard; the board still prohibited on-campus tobacco sales.[21]

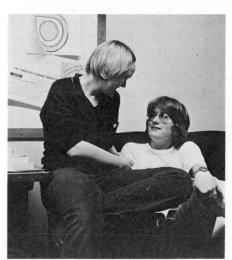

The Women's Center evolved from 1960s issues.

Women's rights advocates soon raised questions about other campus practices. A 1970 *Concordian* editorial charged that the college discriminated against women; hiring and promotion, pay and the male domination of the administrative hierarchy were cited as proof. Others in the administration and the ALC shared these concerns. To deal with these issues, President Knutson in October 1972 established a college-wide equal opportunity commission to examine existing personnel policies. Concordia sought to avoid discrimination because of age, race, sex or marital status. The next month, a women's awareness association was formed by twenty women. By Fall 1973, the association met monthly; sponsored panels, speakers and community service; and aimed to promote individuality, freedom of choice and development of potential. In seeking to avoid stereotyping of women and men in society, the association questioned the practice of selecting a homecoming queen. Perhaps association influence accounts for abandoning the practice in 1974 in favor of a ceremony honoring six outstanding seniors—three women and three men. As homecoming chairman Ken Fitzer ('75) explained, the coronation activities had been altered "in order to remove the sexist ideals which have hung over the event for many years." Two indignant Cobber males protested this change of "a forty-eight-year-old tradition without at least token consultation of the student body."[22] After a time, elements of old and new were combined; the campus now elects a homecoming king and queen.

In this atmosphere of heightened feminist consciousness, it is not surprising that the annual AKX-Mondamin bridal show was modified to the bridal and fashion show in Spring 1970 before it quietly disappeared. In their letters to the *Concordian* in Fall 1971, professors Carol Falk and Reidar Thomte debated whether a Nietzsche quotation displayed on the philosophy department bulletin board demeaned women and could be posted without a disclaimer. A 1974 ALC report documented discrimination against women at ALC colleges. The report called for full support and compliance with federal regulations for employment, uniform rules in men's and women's dormitories and career counseling for women that included all available options. Through courses, the library and workshops, ALC schools should "raise their awareness level concerning women in society." The women's awareness association and socially conscious *Concordian* editorialists served as the community conscience when the campus fell short of these standards.[23]

With victories achieved for dancing, smoking and open hours, Cobbers now requested interdorm visitation. Already in February 1970, Carol Knapp ('72) complained that "most progressive prisons are more lenient in their restrictions on visitation of inmates than Concordia . ..." At the time, visitation was limited to Sunday open house, scheduled twice monthly from 2:00 to 6:00 p.m. Doors were kept open; nonparticipating residents received permission to lock their doors. President Knutson again took a strong stand in opposition; he even proposed organizing ALC pastors to block open dormitories at other Lutheran institutions. For Knutson the moral question was simple and clearly defined, "approved bedroom visitation is just plain immorality."[24]

As had been the case previously, these presidential pronouncements did not deter Cobbers. In October 1972 the student senate considered a proposal to extend open house to four periods of visitation totaling eighteen hours per weekend. Knutson responded with a letter to Student Association President Mark Halaas ('73) and Vice President Larry Van Hunnik ('73), informing them he would not compromise. Moreover, in view of the clear stand taken by administration "this agitation for inter-dorm visitation is out of order and amounts to a clear case of insubordination." In a more conciliatory tone, the president indicated that he would not block an attempt to bring the case to the student affairs committee or to the board of regents. When the Student Association appeared before the regents, the board backed the president but acknowledged that the proposal had been stated with clarity, conviction and responsibility. As a propitiatory gesture, the regents established a standing student affairs committee to improve communication.[25]

After two more years of student agitation, in March 1974 President Knutson expanded intervisitation slightly when he approved new hours of 1:00 to 5:00 p.m. every Saturday and Sunday for all dormitories. Implementation was delayed when five of eight dormitories rejected some of the new regulations controlling visits. These included mandatory sign in and out, escorts, prohibitions against locking or closing doors and floor supervision. The next fall, the sign-in system was dropped and students were permitted to close but not lock doors during visits. That spring, Saturday hours shifted to evenings from 8:00 to midnight on an experimental basis for the duration of the semester. This preoccupation with rules reflected a longstanding concern of the president and the institution for the moral development of Cobbers.[26]

Other Issues of the Sixties

Cultural concerns of the decade shaped Cobbers' discussions of the Peace Corps, legalization of drugs, the counterculture, homosexuality, birth control, environmental issues, world hunger and the Vietnam war. Of these, the war and the consequent antiwar movement were the most impor-

tant for campus rebels. By Fall 1966, an opposition had appeared; students and faculty from Concordia, Moorhead State and North Dakota State formed the Fargo-Moorhead Committee for Peace in Vietnam. The group supported de-escalation and negotiation; it hoped to influence policy and public opinion by means of forums, discussions and speakers. The following October, protesters were prevented from distributing literature questioning United States policy during a speech on Vietnam by Army Chief of Staff General Harold K. Johnson. The *Concordian* protested their expulsion from the Memorial Auditorium as an infringement on freedom of expression. Two weeks later, forty Concordia collegians and professors joined others in a downtown Fargo-Moorhead demonstration held in conjunction with a national antiwar march in Washington, D.C. In October 1968, a silent vigil for peace was

Chief of Staff General Harold K. Johnson provoked protest.

staged by Eighth Street east of Old Main. In April 1969 a two-evening Vietnam symposium attracted large audiences. In addition to sponsoring this event, the recently founded January 19th Movement—named after Castro's organization—published a newsletter, *Impetus*, and set up a draft information table in the Commons. To foster a Vietnam dialogue, they observed the national Vietnam War Moratorium Day, which included class talk-ins, distribution of literature, black armbands and marching.[27]

Concordian articles suggest that antiwar protest peaked during 1969–1970. Mark Bratlie ('70) turned in his draft card, provoking considerable debate. Cobbers joined in a tri-college antiwar picket during a Milton Young appreciation dinner held at the Fargo Civic Auditorium. Student Association presidents at ALC institutions signed a

> "I believe that one of the reasons for the deep divisions in this nation, about Vietnam is that many Americans have lost confidence in what their government has told them about our policy." (Richard Nixon Nov. 3, 1969)

IMPETUS

newsletter of
JANUARY 19 MOVEMENT

COBBERS READY NOVEMBER
PEACE OFFENSIVE

An antiwar newsletter publicized the peace movement.

resolution supporting the Vietnam Moratorium Day which January 19th organized on campus. The year of protest culminated with the walkout of more than 100 persons at commencement to protest ROTC commissionings. One irate critic suggested that

Knutson fire the ten professors and deny diplomas to the sixty seniors who participated. The incident greatly irritated the president but he did not consider such extreme action. Indeed, an explanation of the protest had been inserted in the bulletin and the protesters had been given permission to leave as a matter of conscience. Although an estimated one-half of the audience had given a standing ovation to the commissioning, in October Knutson announced that the practice would no longer be part of the commencement ceremony. Essentially this was the movement's last gasp. With the change in draft laws and Nixon's Vietnamization policy, protest quickly faded. At the 1971 commencement a few seniors and faculty wore white armbands as an antiwar gesture. And in January 1974 Cobbers raised $460 for Vietnamese children as part of a program sponsored by the Yale Divinity School.[28]

The Ward twins, Concordian editors, challenged the community.

Administrative problems with rebellion culminated in a widely publicized clash with the *Concordian*. When Chris and Wendy Ward, sophomore twin children of home economics professor Jean Ward, became editor and managing editor in March 1968 the paper immediately manifested a radicalism shocking to a conservative community. Their policy was symbolized by a picture of the twins burning a copy of the *Concordian* with the caption, "Chris and Wendy prepare for a blazing future in the newspaper business, beginning with a scorched paper policy." The Wards reported critically on campus, local and national issues and aimed to provoke questioning of current policies. The quality of the Ward-edited paper was recognized with an all-American rating from the Associate Collegiate Press. The Wards' successor, Roger Gruss ('70), continued their editorial stance. Student Association President Don Gaetz ('71) approved. When all are happy with the *Concordian* opinions, he wrote in a September 1969 letter, "then the student press will have lost its legitimacy as a free agent for dialogue and discourse."[29]

Tensions between newspaper and administration culminated in December 1970 when presidential edict closed the *Concordian*. Editor Omar Olson ('71) printed an advertisement by the Abortion Referral Service in New York City. When Olson refused to withdraw the advertisement from future editions Knutson, supported by board of regents chairperson Carrol Malvey, dismissed the editor and suspended publication until a new agreement could be reached which harmonized the paper's purpose with college ideals. He gave three reasons for his action. Abortion advertisements were illegal under Minnesota law. Standards of decency had been violated because it appeared that drugs and sex

> **PREGNANT? NEED HELP?**
>
> PREGNANT? NEED HELP? Abortions are now legal in New York City up to 24 weeks. The Abortion Referral Service will provide a quick and inexpensive end to your pregnancy. We are a member of the National Organization to Legalize Abortion. CALL 1 - 215 - 878-5800 for totally confidential information. There are no shots or pills to terminate a pregnancy. These medications are intended to induce a late period only. A good medical test is your best 1st action to insure your chance for choice. Get a test immediately. Our pregnancy counseling service will provide totally confidential alternatives to your pregnancy. We have a long list of those we have already assisted should you wish to verify this service. COPY OUR NUMBER FOR FUTURE REFERENCE 1 - 215 - 878-5800.

The abortion advertisement that closed the Concordian.

preoccupied Cobbers. The advertisement violated institutional goals; it circumvented on-campus counseling which someone in trouble should have.[30]

Defending himself from the public criticism that followed, Knutson maintained that freedom of discussion had not been denied. First, academic freedom should be a two-way street; i.e., both sides of issues should be heard. An advertisement did not intelligently discuss the problem; nor did its prohibition end proper and tasteful discussion of the question. Second, suspension was temporary; publication would resume when the student affairs committee had established new guidelines and appointed another editor. Third, Knutson charged recent editors with having a false notion of freedom of the press. A single individual could never be the standard for truth and propriety. An editor must always consider social norms if dependent on subscriptions and advertising. Thus the abortion advertisement irresponsibly abused freedom by violating community canons.[31]

The constituency supported President Knutson's stand in the crisis. In the first month, he received hundreds of letters and telegrams with only a dozen criticizing his decision. Evidencing the pervasive anxiety which student rebellion triggered in American society, many expressed pleasure that at least one president still existed who upheld authority. Others praised his stand against abortion, agreed that the editor had been irresponsible and applauded his rejection of religious liberalism. Even collegian letters commended Knutson for upholding Christian standards of decency. Interestingly, only seven faculty wrote in support. At least a few others believed that Knutson had overreacted; as longtime philosophy professor Reidar Thomte pointedly commented over coffee, "You don't need a cannon to kill a canary!" Similarly, other critics disliked Knutson's heavy-handed regimentation. In particular, students emphasized freedom—the right to discuss issues of drugs, abortion and sex which were parts of their world.[32]

Although emotions ran high on campus for several days, college committees followed established procedures and resolved the crisis. The appeal board accepted Knutson's suspension of the paper but sustained Olson's appeal because dismissal procedures outlined in the student rights document had not been followed. The board repeated the president's request to the student affairs committee to draw up guidelines. In March 1971, the committee agreed on a statement acceptable to the president. The college owns the paper and the president is publisher; it is published for the campus community and it should help the institution realize its goals. Publication then resumed under new editor Lynn Bruer ('72).[33]

Discontent of the 1960s vanished rather quickly, but it did influence academic life in various ways. The pass-fail course option, more relevant subject matter and more cooperative joint-inquiry styles of learning appeared at Concordia and elsewhere. Introduced in September 1966, pass-fail allowed Cobbers to experiment with two electives in areas outside their majors without harming their grade point averages. In February 1969, the English department announced an independent study alternative for two introductory courses. During the following academic year, this option was extended to twenty randomly selected freshmen who studied with eight professors from the departments of physics, philosophy, psychology, religion, political science and English. Hopes that this experiment might evolve into a plan for achieving the baccalaureate entirely through independent study were dashed by the financial constraints of the 1970s. In March 1973, Cobbers were permitted to earn the equivalent of at least four courses through credit by examination. By mid-decade, grade inflation—seemingly another byproduct of the permissiveness of the Sixties—was under study by the academic regulations and procedures committee. At that time the national average grade had become B instead of C; to avoid debasing the currency of academe, the committee hoped increased awareness would stop spiraling inflation.[34]

More effective faculty course evaluation is another product of the decade's participatory concerns. In 1967 the Student Association cabinet recommended publishing a booklet. Besides assisting Cobbers in registration, they hoped it might improve instructional quality. The student senate defeated the proposal. Not to be dissuaded, the *Concordian* experimented briefly with a course evaluation column in 1968. It did not survive for the same reasons the bill was defeated. Both provoked negative faculty reactions by making sensitive information entirely too public in a very small community. Nonetheless, under Dean Dovre's leadership the faculty senate passed a teacher evaluation system in November 1974. Its purpose was primarily developmental; it helped teachers improve instruction. Judgment was not entirely absent, however, as the information gathered was also used in determining tenure and promotion.[35]

Traditional Collegiate Culture

Despite the turbulence of the Sixties, much traditional collegiate culture persisted. Paradoxically, this period of rebellion was also a time of campus religious renewal. President Knutson, a Haugean by upbringing and temperament, welcomed this warmly. In the face of pervasive secularization, he believed that the church needed rebirth. Historically, awakenings had begun in the colleges. "Dare we pray," Knutson asked, "that the church today may be renewed through a spiritual awakening in our church colleges."[36]

No wonder the president was pleased when signs of what Pastor Art Grimstad called "a visitation by the Spirit of God" appeared at Concordia in 1967. It began with a prayer group of twenty-seven Cobbers. Blessed with support from a friendly administration and advised by Grimstad, the awakening blossomed. It multiplied into a dozen teams annually; these carried their message two weekends each month to churches within a 300 mile radius. They sponsored prayer services, ministry to the aged and alcoholic, Bible studies, the Pat Boone Family Show in 1971 and the Richard and Patti Roberts concert in 1972.

Dr. Abdul Haqq addressed the 1972 New Horizons Conference.

Their annual New Horizons Conference, first held in 1969, renewed spiritual emphasis week. Summer teams toured the corporate territory. Two became fulltime ministries. The New Pace II, led by Walther Kallestad ('71) and renamed the Earthrise Singers, visited ALC churches nationwide. The Kingsmen traveled in the United States and Europe. This success and administration support provoked controversy in the student senate. By formal action in November 1969 on a bill introduced by William Hoverson ('70), the senate encouraged the development office to make clear to the constituency that outreach team theology did not necessarily represent all members of the Concordia community. The office should therefore support similar programs portraying the religious views of other collegians.[37]

Because of his commitment to evangelism, Knutson objected in the mid-1960s to a danger he perceived at ALC student conferences and Luther League conventions. He feared that too much intellectual sophistication and social concern threatened to stifle preaching the gospel. Knutson believed that "a real inspirational evangelical challenge"

The Sunshine Folk, an outreach team.

should be issued at all these meetings. Similarly, by 1974 Knutson refused to defend the National Council of Churches and the World Council of Churches because they had made a gospel of social action and had thus become enemies of evangelical Christianity.[38]

His evangelical concerns led Knutson to serve on the executive committee of a small group who launched a church renewal movement within the ALC in 1969. Knutson gave the keynote address at a Minneapolis meeting held for one hundred pastors in January 1970. Desiring "a fellowship of concerned evangelicals who are not anti-church," Knutson and the other leaders objected to "creeping liberalism," the belated dose of the social gospel infecting the Lutheran church and the critical study of the Bible, which had become excessive to the point of undermining biblical authority for many pastors. Instead, individual witness and the role of Christian as soul-winner should be emphasized. The movement attracted the interest of the ALC, LCA and LC-MS evangelism directors; it hoped to schedule several area conferences. Knutson received twenty-nine letters, almost all favorable; only two criticized his participation. One shared his desire for an evangelical emphasis but feared that the rhetoric of the 1920s—"creeping liberalism," "modernism," "social gospel," "critical study of the Bible"—would alienate younger people. Instead the movement should work to unite the church by an evangelical emphasis that did not destroy the social gospel. At this time, Lutheran theologians and social action boards—mindful of the criticism that Lutherans had been guilty of social quietism—began to redefine the public role of the church. The ALC moved in this direction as well, limiting the impact of the church renewal effort.[39]

Given the president's Haugean background, he eagerly acted on the suggestion made by O.I. Hertsgaard—an alumnus and former professor—that Concordia would be the logical place for observing the 200th anniversary of Hans Nielsen Hauge's birth. To commemorate the day, the college invited Dr. Fridtjov Birkeli, Bishop of Oslo and Primate of the Church of Norway, to give two addresses during homecoming week. An audience of more than 1,500 gathered in the Memorial Auditorium on a Thursday evening for the bishop's address, in which he called Hauge the most influential individual of the last four centuries on Norwegian spiritual life.[40]

College Pastor Carl Lee led campus worship and religious activity. Lee based his ministry on the concept of family, an idea with a long Concordia tradition. As he stated in the 1967 *Cobber*: "Here is a family—an academic and worshipping and caring community— ... And it's out of this kind of relationship and experience we share with each other here that moves us into a deeper understanding of what it is to be related to God." For Lee, faith was more relationship than assent to doctrine. If people do not experience "friendship and love ... we can't really understand much about a God whose very nature is love." Through its program of religious activities, the college accepted religious diversity, fostered ecumenism and yet affirmed a strong relationship with the ALC. Mirroring the growing youthful indifference to the institutional church, voluntary chapel attendance declined despite efforts to encourage regular participation; a 1968 survey found that only one in five Cobbers attended more than three times a week.[41]

A freshman recorded her impressions of campus religion shortly after arrival in September 1966. Although she had feared being assaulted with a pietistic emphasis on sin and repentance, she was relieved to find religion "quietly surrounding me and being a normal part of my college life." Moreover, daily chapel was "refreshing," "relaxing" and "a pleasant break in class and study routine." Perhaps religion remained this comfortable for many, but it did not entirely escape the cultural anxieties of the Sixties, as evidenced by the quote from Malcolm Boyd's *Are You Running With Me, Jesus?* reprinted in the 1970 *Cobber*:

I'm crying and shouting inside tonite, Lord
And I'm feeling completely alone
All the roots I thought I had are gone—
Everything in my life is in an upheaval.
I'm amazed that I can still maintain any composure
When I'm feeling like this.[42]

Similarly, intellectual life reflected the decade's cultural concerns. Speakers ranged from liberal to conservative. Several addressed civil rights and race—Andrew Young (1967), Vincent Harding (1968), Dr. William Wilson (1968), Jesse Jackson (1969), Stokely Carmichael (1973), Dick Gregory (1974) and Robert Williams (1974). Among liberal politicians who appeared were Senator Walter Mondale (1966), former Kennedy press secretary Pierre Salinger (1967), New Dealer Leon Keyserling (1968) and Hubert Humphrey (1968). In addition many notables addressed C-400, including Abigail Van Buren (1970), Charles M. Schulz (1972), Archbishop Fulton J. Sheen (1973), Catherine Marshall (1973), Paul Harvey (1974) and former astronaut Jim Irwin (1974).[43]

At times a speaker's ideology offended constituents of the opposite persuasion. In 1970 someone objected to conservative Walter Judd and in 1973 another resented socialist Stokely Carmichael. In response, Knutson articulated his conception of academic freedom. The conservative Judd was brought to balance the many liberals who had appeared recently. The president believed

Rev. Jesse Jackson

that most colleges and universities practiced a false concept of academic freedom; according to Knutson, "a college is hardly a free marketplace of ideas when only one side of the question is presented." The president defended Carmichael's appearance on the grounds that one cannot deny someone the right to speak because he is socialist; instead capitalism must demonstrate its superiority in the free marketplace of ideas.[44]

Cobbers manifested interest in literary and political issues. *Afterthought*—a monthly publishing poetry, short stories, essays, commentary and book reviews—appeared in 1966. *Young Guardian*, a conservative political magazine, came off the press in September 1968. The next fall, *Amabatis*—a new literary publication—replaced *Afterthought*. Campus political discussions echoed those of a divided country. The meaning of the 1968 Chicago Democratic Convention was briefly debated. For Chris Ward ('70), the convention ushered in the "politics of frustration." The established political system had defeated Eugene McCarthy, who symbolized the hope of change for collegians; thus "the future course of American politics for these young activists is bleak." Stephen G. Tweed ('71), coeditor of the *Young Guardian*, disagreed. He argued that many youth supported the Republican Party and were not liberal, secular idealists. After that brief exchange, the election disappeared from the *Concordian*. The 1972 election provoked some debate for and against Nixon. Apparently no mock election was held; therefore the political preferences of the student body cannot be determined. One year later, the Student Association council of commissioners headed by President Fontaine unanimously voted to write each Minnesota congressman urging the impeachment of President Nixon. An editorialist argued that Nixon should be removed in order to rebuild the presidency and the country.[45]

"Student power," an oft-expressed slogan of the decade, was also heard at Concordia and contributed to enhanced student representation in college governance. As used by Wendy Ward in a 1967 article and by Student Association President Jim Parke ('68) in a January 1968 state-of-the-campus address, student power meant that they should take personal responsibility for the decisions that affect their lives. Both noted the paradox embodied in the ideal of the Christian liberal arts; the ideal stressed freedom of inquiry while it imposed restrictive social rules. We have seen that President Knutson staunchly defended *in loco parentis* and opposed student participation in college governance. Nevertheless the ideals of family and Christian community committed the college to open dialogue; therefore collegian demands were heard sympathetically by most administrators who willingly made changes.[46]

Vice President Paul Dovre best expressed this openness when he enunciated his ideal of collegiality in an address to new freshmen in September 1969. He invited them to become involved in community life. This meant assuming responsibility for participation in the decision-making process while remaining "faithful to the norms, decisions and procedures of this community." Students, faculty and administration all had a common interest in the college. Dovre believed that bringing together people with diverse responsibilities and interests ensured more informed decisions. He also recognized that compromise was necessary and that not all factions would be satisfied with the outcome. This has proved true. Nonetheless, Student Association leaders appreciated Dovre's stand and recognized his commitment with the association's collegiality award in January 1970.[47]

President Knutson's tough rhetoric notwithstanding, collegians earlier had not been entirely excluded from decision-making. The Student Association sponsored a retreat for the three estates each September to discuss mutual problems. Beginning in January 1968, a series of informal discussions over coffee were held to improve communications with faculty. This tradition of participation, implementation of Dovre's collegiality ideal and the decade's rhetoric of student power combined at this time to expand greatly the collegian role in governance. The 1968 *Cobber* stated enthusiastically that the integration of the three estates had successfully begun. Parallel committee structures and a student affairs committee had been established. The next fall, the regents created a counterpart to the student affairs committee. At the same time, revision of the college constitution by a Dovre-chaired committee added four student members to the faculty senate, three to the long-range planning committee and representatives to all other committees. The student rights and responsibilities document, approved in Fall 1969, took a step toward due process. Two years later, the college established a student intern program, a proposal directly influenced by recent experience, as President Knutson made explicit: "In these days of student-college confrontations, we believe the internship offers a positive means to ameliorate the tensions that divide a college community." It familiarized leaders with institutional purpose and operations and cultivated leadership skills.[48]

Collegiate social life continued in familiar channels. A freshman, recording her initial impressions in 1966, had been immediately impressed by the friendliness of the place. With everyone so "outgoing and helpful," she had found a warm and caring community. Bleak House, a coffeehouse opened by students in March 1966 in a former residence located just north of the president's home on Eighth Street, reflected the culture of the decade. Open weekend evenings, it offered music, formal discussion of social issues and a relaxed atmosphere for informal meetings between students and staff. When it closed in 1969, Student Productions considered opening a replacement in the experimental theatre.[49]

Victorious Dorothy Johnson and partner in a go-cart race.

Societies, a more traditional form of collegiate culture, remained active. In September 1967, Kappa Gamma Phi and Kappa Theta Phi sponsored the first Mardi Gras in Jake Christiansen Stadium; besides a snake dance, side and talent shows, dunking stool and fireworks, it featured a faculty go-cart race. In January 1972, AKX-Mondamin sponsored the first dance marathon. As in the past, initiation remained a problem. Despite periodic attempts at control, hazing at times became excessive. In Spring 1972, the administration suspended initiation until a task force drew up new guidelines. For the more service-minded, opportunities for community work were created. Circle K, a youth auxiliary of Kiwanis International, was organized in November 1971. It assisted disadvantaged youth. The following year, Dean Morris Lanning originated a volunteer service program. It had a highly successful first year as 100 volunteers helped with hospitals, day care, the YMCA and juvenile detention centers.[50]

Many participated in the traditional extracurricular activities of music, debate, theatre, campus publications and intercollegiate athletics. These attained several notable achievements. In 1974 the choir enjoyed another successful Norway tour; despite the Norwegian tradition of no applause in a church building, audiences often applauded.

Nurse Kathy Benson joined the 1975 European Band Tour.

The Concordia Symphonic Band toured Europe the following summer on the fortieth anniversary of its first trip. It was well received by almost 10,000 concert-goers and praised by critics as "professional in quality." Coached by Allwin Monson, Vicki Welch and Don Gaetz won national college oratory championships in 1965 and 1968 respectively. With completion of the humanities building in 1969, the theatre program achieved the facilities for expanded offerings and a more serious cultural effort. That effort began immediately when the Summer Circle Theatre Company enrolled thirty in a workshop which performed William Hanley's *Slow Dance on the Killing Ground* and *The Boys from Syracuse* based on Shakespeare's *Comedy of Errors* with a score by Rodgers and Hart. As theatre director Clair Haugen had explained several years before, theatre had an integral place in a Christian liberal arts college because it explored the crux of Christian thought by dramatizing what humans are and what they ought to be.[51]

Significantly, equal opportunity became available for women athletes as expanded intercollegiate competition in tennis, track, basketball, badminton and field hockey debuted during the 1970–1971 academic year. The football team won an MIAC championship in Coach JimChristopherson's first season and then were runners-up in the NAIA Championship Bowl. Intramurals still offered a

The 1971 Women's Basketball Team, equal opportunity in athletics.

special physical outlet for youthful energy. Besides the familiar football, basketball and volleyball, the Tae Kwon Do karate club was organized in 1974 with Dominick Sillitti as advisor and instructor. Briefly in 1974, "streaking" offered an alternative sport. Attired only in socks, shoes and ski masks, streakers raced through the Normandy, Park Region, Brown, East Complex and even Jake Christiansen Stadium during a football game.[52]

End of the Knutson Era

In February 1974 President Knutson announced that he would retire after one more year. His early announcement allowed time for naming a successor. The selection process began almost immediately. Advertisements placed in *The Lutheran Standard* and *The Chronicle Higher Education* attracted 125 applicants. Summer work reduced the field to twenty-five. By December the search had narrowed to three candidates, one of whom withdrew. After on-campus interviews with Erno Dahl, academic dean of Wittenburg University in Ohio, and Dean Paul Dovre, the latter was appointed.[53]

As president, Knutson compiled a remarkable record. Sixteen structures were erected at the cost of more than $16 million. Constituting more than one-half the physical plant of twenty-eight major buildings, these included Memorial Auditorium (1952), Ylvisaker Library (1956), Park Region (1956), Cobber Commons (1960), Livedalen and Normandy (1962), Hvidsten (1963), Administration (1964), Hoyum (1965), Jake Christiansen Stadium (1966), Science (1967), East (1968), Humanities (1969), library addition (1971), Knutson Center and swimming pool (1975). Berg (1953), Academy (1953), Bishop Whipple (1954) and Old Main (1974) were remodeled for the expenditure of another $2 million. Endowment increased $1.5 million and deferred gifts $2 million; current operating budget expanded from $800,000 (1951–1952) to $9 million (1974–1975). Enrollment grew from 890 (1951) to 2,482 (1973–1974).[54]

Growth clearly characterized the Knutson presidency. At the same time, tributes praised Knutson for maintaining Christian integrity. Regent Norman Lorentzsen commended Knutson for being "the most outstanding president of any of our church colleges; ... stable, proven, and yet on target to the ultimate objectives." The executive director of the Minnesota Private College Council noted that Knutson's "assertions of Christian objectives have been

President Knutson Enjoys Prexys Pond

Knutson's sense of humor helped him survive the turbulent Sixties.

emphatic—even evangelistic. Yet there is little indication that your faculty and staff have felt their freedom was inhibited." Indeed, Knutson was praised by his staff for running an open and honest administration. He showed confidence in the people he appointed and allowed them to achieve institutional goals in their own way.[55]

President Knutson's leadership represented the institution in such a way that it generated confidence in him and the college. The *Forum* credited his emphasis on a Christian liberal arts education, rather than a narrow Lutheranism, for broadening Concordia's constituency to include Catholics and other Protestants and for his success as a champion fundraiser. This testifies to Knutson's remarkable political gifts; a man who repeatedly emphasized Lutheran identity in order to maintain the college as a faithful servant of the church is commended for attracting the support of other denominations. It also demonstrates his ability as an academic leader. He took a keen interest in academic affairs and supported those policies that strengthened the institution. A better credentialed and more professional faculty had been recruited. Academic freedom had been established. Notwithstanding several faculty members who would disagree, the goal of a "free Christian college," outlined in *Blueprint I*, had been substantially achieved.[56]

At Knutson's final commencement in 1975, the faculty recognized the retiring president's substantial contributions to academic life by awarding him an honorary degree, Doctor of Humane Letters, *honoris causa*. As the citation read by former Dean Carl Bailey stated, "No one has known better how to combine and practice the foundation of Christian conviction with the principle of liberal education."[57]

At times Knutson grew weary of the presidential burden. The tragic death of his younger son in May 1974 was a terrible blow. Nonetheless, years later he recalled his presidency fondly. Moreover, he expressed faith in the future. The school had a fine physical plant and good financial foundation; as he said, "it will be an institution that some people will still want to attend because of the high academic standards and the nature of the college community."[58]

Prexy and Beatrice retired to a Moorhead home given to the institution by longtime faculty member J.H. Hjelmstad. Prexy kept busy serving as interim minister in neighboring parishes until a pastor surplus ended that activity. The couple enjoyed reading, Concordia functions and their summer lake cottage. They deeply appreciated community efforts, orchestrated by Howard Binford, to have the newly elected Reagan administration nominate Knutson as ambassador to Norway. Despite a *Forum* endorsement and more than 300 letters on his behalf, the attempt did not succeed; the presidential couple were allowed to enjoy their quiet retirement.[59]

PART IV

President Paul J. Dovre, 1975–

Continuing Mission, Enhancing Quality and Maintaining Accessibility

"I urge us to avoid two pitfalls: to assume that academic life and the Christian faith can be artfully separated in some fashion or ... to assume that there is some dogmatic formula by which the relationship can be defined once and for all. One strength of the Lutheran tradition is that we have taken those issues seriously, recognizing that through lively discussion insights could be discovered and refined without being dogmatized. ... So let us proceed with these initiatives and discussions as an expression of our commitment to religious faith and life, but with healthy tolerance for divergency of views."

— *Paul J. Dovre (1976)*

"I ask you to be leaders of a college related church. Without a nurturing church, colleges will be left to their own resources and historically, that's not been for the best. We need each other if we are to fulfill Christ's mission for all of us."

— *Paul J. Dovre (1977)*

"Achieving this end of individual growth through community demands significant interaction between the individual and the community. It requires, first of all, a community or environment that fosters growth through acceptance and expectation. Secondly, it requires that individuals—faculty, students, staff—call each other to excellence by creating and renewing challenges for each other and for themselves. And finally, it requires that individual members provide the support necessary for others to accept and pursue challenges and to become increasingly the authors of their own challenges."

— *Blueprint III (1983)*

"We believe that Concordia College exists as a college of the Lutheran church to glorify God through teaching and learning. Faculty are called to excellent teaching and to the pursuit of truth through scholarship. ... As scholars in this community, we affirm that there is no part of the natural, historical, political or social world we need hesitate to examine. ... We also recognize an obligation as scholars in a college of the Lutheran Church to pursue and encourage dialogue about the relationships between our discipline and Christian faith. ... We reaffirm our commitment to the liberal arts as an education that can prepare students for productive, meaningful lives in the home, the community and the world."

          — An Agenda for Concordia's Academic Life (1984)

Chapter 16

A Managerial and Mission-Minded President

The New President

Paul J. Dovre was elected the eighth president of Concordia on December 14, 1974, after a search process of almost eight months involving a search committee comprised of regents and the chairpersons of advisory subcommittees of administrators, alumni, faculty and students. On that Saturday afternoon when the balloting had been completed and the regents had cast a unanimous ballot for Dovre, board chair Carrol Malvey attempted to call the victor but received only a busy signal. Even presidential aspirants may have teen-agers who tie up the phone at inopportune times. Malvey drove the few blocks from Frida Nilsen Lounge to the Dovre home to deliver the good news.[1]

A Minnesota native, Dovre graduated from Canby High School and Concordia. A Rockefeller Fellowship (1959–1960) supported a year's study at Luther Theological Seminary in between receiving an M.A. and a Ph.D. in speech communication from Northwestern University. Upon completing his doctorate in 1963, Dovre's "deep appreciation of the Concordia community ... [and] the liberal arts" brought him back to his alma mater. Although narrowly defeated in his campaign for student body president during his undergraduate days, Dovre became a winner after his return. A highly regarded teacher and debate coach, his teams were the first from the college to compete in national tournaments. In 1964 he was elected governor of the upper midwest province of Pi Kappa Delta, a national forensics fraternity, and in 1968 he co-edited an anthology of argumentation theory, *Readings in Argumentation*. At Concordia he rose rapidly through the ranks: associate dean (1967), acting vice president for academic affairs (1968), executive vice president (1969), vice president for academic affairs (1971) and, at forty, the presidency.[2]

Dovre's appointment was well received in Fargo-Moorhead. A *Forum* editorial praised the regents for their wise choice and suggested that the new president's commitment to the Christian liberal arts assured continued success for Concordia. Naturally President Knutson was pleased. He long had been impressed with Dovre's financial acumen, administrative knowledge and managerial skill. As Knutson stated in a letter of recommendation: "I think so much of Paul Dovre that I hope no other institution is ever able to get him away from Concordia." Nor did the prospect of a lay successor trouble Knutson. A precedent existed; the first two principals had not been clergy. What counted was Dovre's "commitment to the Lord and His church and ... his personal character and integrity."[3]

Knutson's confidence was not misplaced; Dovre the layman eagerly and capably assumed a pastoral role for the community. He became an active member of the campus ministry team and articulated clearly an expectation of continued service to Christ in church and society.

That the new first lady, Mardeth Dovre, proved as gracious as the former also fostered good will. Her life did not change dramatically when she moved into "the Big

House," as the presidential residence has been humorously dubbed. As a neighborhood resident since 1963, a church and community volunteer and a parttime business teacher at Fargo South High School, she knew the community and the Lutheran church.

Mardeth and Paul Dovre greet wellwishers at inaugural reception.

Moreover, as the spouse of a professor and dean she understood the world of academic protocol. A warm, vivacious hostess and enthusiastic booster, Mardy Dovre's anxiety about entertaining famous visitors disappeared immediately when she met her first, the Norwegian anthropologist Thor Heyerdahl. Upon arrival for a reception at the president's home, Heyerdahl's first words were: "Hello, Mrs. Dovre, I'm pleased to meet you. Can you tell me where the bathroom is?"[4]

An unknown to the constituency, the new president astutely assured continuity with the previous administration by promising to build on the firm foundation that Knutson had laid. Speaking upon the occasion of his appointment in December, Dovre pledged his talents of leadership and administration to "the Christ whose advent we now celebrate and who is the Lord of this college;" to the constituency he vowed "constancy with the mission;" to faculty and staff he promised "my support for your ministries;" and to students he assured "quality education and a caring, listening community." In order "to fulfill these dimensions of my servanthood," Dovre solicited "support and understanding" and "continuing care for and commitment to the purpose of this college." Appropriately, he closed with the college motto, *"Soli Deo Gloria*—To God alone the glory."[5]

Months later, in his first interview after taking office, the new president reiterated his traditionalism as he articulated the challenges he perceived—maintaining purpose, quality and support. He formulated the problem and solution in a manner similar to that of his predecessor. Concordia would continue to be a liberal arts college of the church committed to God's work. If the college remained true to its mission and maintained quality, then support in the forms of students and dollars would naturally follow.[6]

Once in office, the new president moved quickly to take charge. During the summer, he directed planning for setting the priorities of his administration and for presenting his administrative agenda at the fall regents' retreat. These activities anticipated what became a more formal relationship with a more tightly organized board of regents. Nine staff, five faculty and four students attended the retreat. In addition, regents received notebooks containing material on administrative plans, and participated in a seminar on the function of the board conducted by educational consultant Chuck

Nelson. Among the priorities presented were emphases on increased communication with the constituencies and long-range financial planning. Loren Anderson played key roles in both initiatives. To become better acquainted with constituents, Dovre planned extensive travel; he therefore appointed Anderson presidential assistant. Anderson also

assumed responsibility for financial planning and worked with Vice President for Development Edward Ellenson in studying the feasibility of a major fund drive.[7]

Another indication of the new president's vision came in his inaugural address, "Look to the Rock," delivered Sunday, October 12, in Memorial Auditorium. Speaking on the text, Isaiah 51:1-2: "... you who seek the Lord, look to the rock from which you were hewn ..." Dovre invited the audience to reflect on principles that had shaped the college— the gospel, Lutheran theology, quality liberal arts education and nurturing community. True to precedents established by his predecessors, Dovre envisioned the

President Dovre addresses a convocation.

college as based on the premise of the gospel. Enabled by God's spirit, the community carried out its mission by offering liberal arts education for Christian service and leadership. It drew on the resources of Lutheran theology to supply dependable values and a legitimate lifestyle for a secular age, and relied on the word and sacrament to maintain itself. The Concordia community as conceived by Dovre was more than the sum of its parts; it was a nurturing fellowship between college, constituency and church. Possessed with a strong sense of shared commitment to the gospel and bound by the Holy Spirit, the community could debate issues and policies without shattering the binding tie.[8]

Events quickly tested President Dovre's communal vision. During March 1976, a petition signed by 1,445 collegians objected to an on-campus housing shortage, and during April thirty blacks boycotted classes for a week charging racial prejudice.

The president addressed these issues in a chapel talk

1976 black student strike protested campus prejudice and racism.

entitled "The Reconciling Community." Dovre frankly acknowledged the tensions; people who had been ignored, betrayed and discriminated against understandably developed feelings of anger, bitterness and hopelessness. To reconcile these differences, Dovre urged Cobbers to be agents of reconciliation through a ministry to individuals by saying words of repentance, affirmation and forgiveness. He also pointed to the community as an instrument of reconciliation. But for the community to reconcile, members must express communal values of caring, loving and healing through individual ministries, and they must respect the integrity of communal procedures. The president pledged that "I shall preside over a community that honors its processes and that is at the same time open to changing and improving itself when necessary." He bluntly warned, however, that decisions would not be made "by headline or press conference, by intimidation or coercion."[9]

Following the presidential principle of resolving differences through established procedures, collegians in both cases met with administrators. They agreed that the sessions on housing were productive; the racial crisis was less easily resolved. The strikers nevertheless returned to classes as talks addressing their concerns continued. In reporting to the faculty senate and the board of regents, Dovre reiterated that he would not be pressured or intimidated. Thus he cast himself in the Knutson mold of standing firm in the face of student rebellion. At the same time, the president emphasized that the community had the unity and resilience to solve the problems at hand.[10]

The Administrative Team

During his first eighteen months in office, President Dovre had proven to be an articulate, energetic and decisive leader. He articulated a vision of institutional mission consistent with that of his predecessors Knutson and Brown. He energetically set an administrative agenda and decisively dealt with his first crisis. Dovre displayed similar qualities when appointing his administrative team.

Continuity proved as important in designating administrators as it had in articulating mission. Three retained their positions: Vice President for Business Affairs William Smaby, who delayed retirement one year at the president's request to ease the transition; Vice President for Development Edward Ellenson; and Dean of Admissions James Hausmann. Three assumed new titles and corresponding duties: Morris Lanning, dean of students; David Benson, director of college relations; and Loren Anderson, director of financial planning and executive assistant to the president.[11]

David Benson

The president's most important appointment was his own replacement as vice president for academic affairs and dean of the college. After an extensive search process involving input from administrators, faculty and collegians, he named Gerald E. Hartdagen, a Northwestern Ph.D. in American colonial history, a Danforth Fellow and the author of several historical publications. Hartdagen possessed extensive university-wide committee experience at Indiana University-Purdue University in Indianapolis; he came with strong recommendations for straightforwardness, capacity for good working relationships and ability as an industrious leader. Although Hartdagen proved an efficient administrator and spurred some younger professors to greater scholarly productivity, he generally was not effective. What passed as straightforward in an urban university seemed abrasive to a small college faculty suspicious of an outsider in the dean's office. His brusque military manner alienated even those who might have agreed with him on academic issues. Many were therefore pleased when he resigned at the end of his four-year term to assume the deanship of Wilkes College in Pennsylvania.[12]

David Gring, designated Hartdagen's successor in 1979, proved a happier choice. Promoted from the assistant deanship he had accepted three years previously, Gring enjoyed strong faculty support. When he left a decade later to take the presidency of Roanoke College in Virginia, Gring retained his popularity, a testimony to his ready smile and winsome personality. A Phi Beta Kappa from Franklin and Marshall College with a Ph.D. in zoology-genetics from Indiana University, Gring possessed more than public relations gifts. Upon his departure, President Dovre praised Gring for his "steadiness, fairness and great depth." As the president explained, "This depth is not only of subject matter (through study and understanding), but also the depth of his commitment to values, to education and to people with whom he works." Gring's administrative talent received national recognition in 1986 when he was selected to attend the prestigious Institute for Educational Management at Harvard and was funded by joint fellowships: a Bush Summer Grant and the J.C.K. Preus Leadership Award from the American Lutheran Church.[13]

Gerald Hartdagen

As vice president for academic affairs, Gring was assisted successively by two able associate deans: Olin Storvick, longtime professor of classics with a passion for archeology who appropriately resembles Zeus, and Linda Johnson, a Macalester Phi Beta Kappa with a Ph.D. in East Asian Studies from Stanford University who is the first woman appointed associate academic dean at Concordia. Together this trio stoutly affirmed the liberal arts in the face of professorial, parental and collegial pressures toward vocational majors. When Gring departed and Johnson returned to the classroom in 1989, H. Robert Homann—professor and chairperson of chemistry, director of Principia, and former associate dean from 1969 to 1976—and Storvick were appointed interim vice president for academic affairs and associate dean respectively. After thorough searches lasting several months, Homann was selected as vice president in January 1990; and Virginia Coombs, assistant to the president of Susquehanna University, was appointed associate dean in May.[14]

As Academic Vice President David Gring looks on, Associate Dean Olin Storvick passes a corncob to his successor, Linda Johnson.

President Dovre also made major appointments in business affairs and development. Donald E. Helland succeeded William Smaby. A Minneapolis native and former Lutheran pastor who had served parishes in Wisconsin and Michigan, Helland came from a similar position in California. His experience and skill provided creative

Academic affairs leaders, Associate Dean Virginia Coombs and Vice President H. Robert Homann.

solutions to pressing problems and strengthened the institution financially. When Helland died suddenly of a heart attack in June 1982, Controller Bob Foss replaced him until February 1983, when Clyde Allen, Minnesota commissioner of revenue, assumed the vice presidency.[15]

Development similarly witnessed a succession of appointees. Edward Ellenson, Loren Anderson, David Benson and Jerry M.

Anderson have occupied the vice presidency. Currently Loren Anderson is executive vice president with responsibility for planning and advancement programs and Benson is associate vice president for development.[16]

The Dovre administrative team represented a new generation with a new vision. Mostly alumni who had grown up in post-depression America and who had been nurtured by the Knutson administration, they looked optimistically to the future, set ambitious goals for themselves and the institution, and innovated accordingly. They envisioned Concordia not in comparison to any other Lutheran college, but out of their own sense of the school's unique strengths and possibilities. Following President Dovre's lead, they cultivated a more positive self-concept worthy of the strong institution they had inherited.[17]

Clyde Allen

The Managerial Ethos

President Dovre has brought a managerial philosophy and strong management skills to the task of administration. Although Dovre gives his vice presidents considerable latitude to run their own divisions, he is a hands-on administrator who wants to be closely involved. He fosters rational discourse and careful planning, seeking to consult concerned parties and avoid crisis or surprise decisions; insists on establishing and following procedures; believes in regular evaluations for administrators as well as faculty; and stresses that staffing and budgeting must be monitored by comparative studies with other ELCA institutions and a national sample of liberal arts colleges. In keeping with a collegial managerial style, all vice presidents are on an equal basis, often work together on special projects and are encouraged to adopt a broad view of the institution. The president's council—comprised of the five vice presidents, the associate vice president for development and the presidential assistant—meets weekly and, after gathering information from those affected, makes administrative decisions. The president prides himself on running an open administration. He frequently stresses the important role of debate in college life, pointing to the range of views represented by visiting speakers and the lively exchanges on academic program, tenure policy, student life policies and other issues. Although President Dovre believes the quality of senate argumentation could be improved, he detects signs of an increasing communal willingness to discuss differences.[18]

Consistent with his managerial approach, Dovre has perpetuated the planning tradition that originated in the development initiatives of the 1950s. A *Blueprint for Concordia College* (1962) was followed by *Blueprint II* (1974), *Financial Blueprint* (1977) and *Blueprint III* (1983). As this is written, *Blueprint IV* is in preparation. Each document has appeared after college-wide discussions over a period of several months examined such issues as mission, societal changes, the liberal arts and community. The process has built community and has enhanced commitment to mission; the ensuing document has given direction for the next decade. For President Dovre planning is a theological imperative. Through planning, the institution adapts the enduring elements of its mission to the constantly changing social circumstances. Theology leads the college to conceptualize its mission as ministry and itself as a community of expectation called "to new challenges of excellence."[19]

Relations with the federal government have influenced the structure and policies of the Dovre administration. As the president freely admits, public support remains significant for Concordia. Like most presidents, Dovre wants to maintain autonomy of purpose and operation. Although he does not quarrel with necessary accountability for the funds received, he shares with his presidential brethren the hope that compliance procedures might be simplified. Complicating the desire for institutional autonomy is the fact that not all encroachment has derived from federal spending. A significant share, widely accepted as beneficent, has stemmed from the civil rights revolution of the 1960s. Yet college compliance with legislation for occupational safety, environment, the handicapped, affirmative action and Title IX directives providing equal athletics for men and women, has required expanded bureaucracy to monitor funds, programs and requirements. College officials thereby have been left with less discretion and their authority has diminished at the same time their numbers have increased.[20]

The Dovre administration has resisted federal encroachment when it has threatened the mission of a church-related institution. Affirmative action is a case in point. Not a government contractor and therefore not compelled, the college in 1977 chose not to use affirmative action terminology which prohibits discrimination on the basis of religion. Committed to inclusive hiring practices, however, it identifies itself as an "equal opportunity employer" which permits the exercise of a preference for Lutherans demanded by the institutional charter. This stand was threatened in 1989 when a new Minnesota law required schools to submit affirmative action programs if they wanted state funding. The college submitted a plan but again reserved the right to exercise religious discretion in hiring. The Minnesota Department of Human Rights rejected this proposal. Fortunately for Concordia's traditional policies, the law was changed after significant lobbying by the Minnesota Private College Council. Concordia can still receive state funds but need not submit to affirmative action. A basis for a distinctive religious identity, affirmed by most other church-related colleges, was preserved for the moment and much additional bureaucratic paperwork avoided.[21]

Throughout his presidency, Dovre has maintained good relations with the board of

The Board of Regents has developed the managerial skills required for governing a more complex college.

regents. The board has adapted to the president's managerial ethos by revising the committee structure to involve all members in resolving increasingly complicated issues. Careful planning enables administrators to communicate proposals well in advance of the date for decision. Regents have time to reflect, react and fine-tune initiatives before registering their approval. The growing complexity of administration demands that board committees engage in specialized study of issues and meet more frequently than in the past. Students participate on committees, often address the entire board and generally enjoy a good working relationship with the regents. A conscious effort is made continuously to strengthen the board through orientation and selection of new members. Following the principle of balance, regents are chosen to represent different geographic, occupational and educational backgrounds. Church ties remain important and are reflected in the three bishops, four representatives from the Women of the Evangelical Lutheran Church in America, four pastors and the requirement that the board be predominantly Lutheran. Of the twenty-six members, sixteen must be affiliated with the ELCA and only three may be non-Lutheran.[22]

Articulating Mission

As did President Knutson, Dovre has conceptualized his presidential role in relation to Lutheran theology and institutional mission. To sustain mission as a vital force, Dovre frequently has emphasized the need for the rigor and discipline of theological reflection; the recruitment of students, faculty and administrators who can realize institutional goals; and constant nurture of community through reaffirming continuity with the past, renewing close ties with the traditional constituency and evoking God's Spirit. Dovre, like Knutson, has recognized that these efforts run counter to the "spirit of the age." In American society of the late twentieth century, he often has noted, "values are increasingly self-indulgent, and religious and moral practices are increasingly privatistic." Nor are there any quick fixes to "the brokenness around us and the confusion of values that results." For a church college mission must therefore be expressed in the daily task of attempting to reconcile the spirit of the age to the spirit of Christ. This reconciliation must be done competently by taking academic quality seriously; it must be done faithfully by taking the gospel seriously; and it must be done holistically so that gospel, daily

President Paul J. Dovre, 1975 --

life and learning are of a single piece.[23]

President Dovre models the Christian liberal arts in an annual ritual of addresses to the fall matriculation convocation and faculty banquet or workshop—events which are exercises in community-building. To introduce new citizens to the academic community and to remind others of their communal obligation, his speeches draw on the Western liberal arts tradition, scripture, individual Christian witness, world events and significant current books by Allan Bloom, Robert Bellah and others. The president's theological understanding undergirds these addresses. He affirms that Lutheran confessionalism compels colleges to examine the intersections of faith and culture and to ask ethical questions. His audiences are therefore urged to avoid two pitfalls: "to assume that academic life and the Christian faith can be artfully separated in some fashion or . . . to assume that there is some dogmatic formula by which the relationship can be defined once and for all." The Lutheran academy thus ought to be marked by freedom, tolerance, seriousness of purpose and lively discussion.[24]

The academy should also be joined by worship, according to Dovre, for two fundamental reasons. First, because "where people gather together around God's word in prayer ... a miracle happens—oneness in Christ, where differences can exist and be respected while we remain one in the spirit." Second, daily chapel expresses tangibly that Concordia operates "under the auspices of the Gospel." Dovre believes that gospel-centered institutions offer a meaningful vision to a secular age and "a culture in decline, a society without a core of values." Accordingly, the president plays an active role in campus ministry. He meets weekly with the college pastors and often assumes the pastoral role himself.[25]

President Dovre clearly perceives that achieving his communal vision depends upon attracting the right kind of people. Just as the college has initiatives to increase the percentage of women and minorities, it seeks to maintain the strong percentage of Lutherans which ranks highest among its sister institutions. Required by the bylaws as a general rule for employment, the hiring of Lutherans is rooted in concern about loss of "critical mass." Research sponsored by the Lutheran Church of America (LCA)—a denomination where "laicization" of schools had progressed much further than at Concordia—indicated the potential danger to mission posed by indifferent students and non-Lutheran faculty. According to the findings of Richard Solberg and Merton Strommen, strength of commitment to campus religious programs varied among groups. LCA clergy, synod board members, administrators and trustees gave strong support. Non-Lutheran faculty showed the least enthusiasm in contrast to Lutheran professors, who exhibited more intense commitment. The presence of significant numbers who are religiously indifferent might threaten institutional Christian witness, Solberg and Strommen warned. To ensure an adequate pool for replacing the large number of professors scheduled to retire by 2005, Concordia joined in the new data link program which identifies Lutheran college alumni pursuing graduate study.[26]

Given President Dovre's commitment to community and tradition, it is appropriate that expressions of ethnicity reappeared after Norwegian-ness apparently had been buried in the 1950s. This growing interest in "roots" had a twofold cause: a new awareness of unmelted ethnic diversity in the United States and a diminished pressure to conform to Yankee values. Hence many of the third generation felt free to mine the cultural richness of their ethnic heritage. Concordia mirrored this trend. In October 1975 Prime Minister Trygve Bratteli appeared at one of several events commemorating the 150th anniversary of the first Norwegian emigration to America. A

Scandinavian studies minor was approved in 1977. Crown Princess Sonja visited in November 1978 for a brief campus tour and a banquet in her honor. On this occasion, Paul J. Christiansen received St. Olav's Medal, awarded for dissemination of knowledge about Norway and for the advancement of relations between emigrants and their homeland. That same year a visiting scholar of Scandinavian studies, Ellen H. Johnson—professor emeritus of art at Oberlin—lectured on Edvard Munch, Ernst Josephson and Carl Frederik Hill.[27]

Then in October 1982 King Olav V made his third visit. Addressing a capacity crowd of 3,000 at a special convocation in his honor, King Olav recalled that in 1939

King Olav V marches with President Dovre.

he had urged the college to keep its windows open to Norway. The king was pleased to note that his hopes had been fulfilled; "the windows of Concordia College out to society around you, to Norway and to the world at large seem wide open indeed." The campus warmed to the royal visit; as a Norwegian student who had come to Minnesota to meet her King said, "In Norway everyone loves him. He's just like a grandpa."[28]

In keeping with his commitment to Concordia traditions, President Dovre has emphasized Concordia's ties to the American Lutheran Church. Historically church relations with Concordia have been supportive, persuasive and decentralized, according to J.L. Rendahl. Ownership and control were confined to a segment of the denomination, congregations of the corporate territory; the ALC Division of College and University Services exercised some centralized direction. Church and college were mutually helpful; the former provided annual appropriations, congregational support and educational leadership; the latter offered education that produced pastors, missionaries, parish workers and other professionals who served society and congregation in a variety of capacities. In addition the college furnished chapel broadcasts, special events for church youth, CHARIS and Communiversity and a fulltime director of church relations who gave assistance to congregations in the corporate territory. President Dovre has reaffirmed this relationship, characterizing it as substantive in contrast to the looser arrangement of the LCA. Because of the many ties, ALC colleges have seen themselves as integral members of the church body and therefore have understood the educational enterprise as rooted in the gospel. Clearly President Dovre treasured this tradition and he worked to perpetuate it when the new Lutheran Church was formed.[29]

Concordia affirmed close church ties in several actions. The regents endorsed church investment policy in South Africa; as a matter of Christian concern for world problems, the board did not invest in those companies which in their judgment contributed to apartheid. In 1978 Concordia became the first affiliated college to host a national ALC convention. Dovre proudly characterized this event as a great experience for both college and church because "it was a tangible expression of relationship."

The weeklong meeting attracted more than 2,000 delegates, visitors and guests. It discussed South African investment, nuclear weapons, the equal rights amendment, the Nestle boycott, racism, the future of the family farm and the tax revolt. It heard Vice President Walter Mondale address the issues of morality and politics, human rights, peace and nuclear weapons.[30]

Concordia hosted the convention for a second time in 1984. This historic gathering approved guidelines for the pending merger of Lutheran church bodies; it reaffirmed ALC opposition to overt destabilization of Nicaragua and military aid to El Salvador and other governments that did not uphold human rights; and it heard Bishop David Preus urge negotiated arms reduction in order to move beyond the waste of resources.[31]

As a member of the commission for planning the new Lutheran Church, Dovre worked to perpetuate the substantive ALC church-college relationship in the new body. Unfortunately from Dovre's point of view, formation of the Evangelical Lutheran Church in America followed the looser LCA pattern in creating a diminished role for the national church in the nurture of its colleges. Advent of the ELCA was therefore greeted with a sense of foreboding among college leaders. Fortunately from the perspective of midwestern colleges, the regional ownership plan was preserved, allowing these colleges to retain the association they cherished. Because this traditional tie had been preserved, President Dovre hoped that the ELCA would allow Concordia to be the kind of college it always had been—one that prepared people to serve God in the world.[32]

Bishop David Preus speaks to a national ALC convention at Concordia.

A Successful President and College

President Dovre's leadership of Concordia has been assessed positively by the board of regents. In Fall 1979 they conducted a formal evaluation, extending over a period of three months. Besides a lengthy self-evaluation, personal interviews and questionnaires were directed toward students, faculty, administrators, state and national higher education officials, alumni, constituents and regents. The results were outstanding; there was little or no criticism and the corporation has since reelected him to his second and third six-year terms.[33]

Similarly, faculty and staff have assessed Dovre's performance positively. They consider him a skilled manager with an ambitious, clearly defined academic and religious agenda: He wants to make Concordia the premier college of the Evangelical Lutheran Church in America. His example and leadership in committing resources toward this goal have improved academic quality and faculty competence. Although his style is very different from President Knutson's, Dovre's conception of the Christian college is similar. Thus reassured, constituents have continued their faithful support, considerably easing the presidential transition and enabling Dovre to build on the firm foundation established by his predecessor.[34]

Of course approval is not total. Several believe that the president's religious stance has hurt the college academically by inhibiting discussion and inquiry. Some fear they may be judged adversely for their nonconformity to an implied orthodoxy. Others fret that family feeling disappears with expansion of the managerial ethos. As tasks become more specialized and as the people who exercise them become more professional in outlook, communal sense is weakened.[35]

Along with a myriad of other causes, bureaucratization with the specialization of functions necessary to manage a multi-million dollar budget and plant may at times undermine the family cohesiveness the president works so hard to promote. To counteract what may be an inevitable trend, the managerial process has been kept more participatory than at most institutions. Gregarious administrators participate in the broader life of the community and suggest that the ideals of family and Christian community foster a cooperative spirit which offsets deadening bureaucratization. And the president, ever alert to erosion of community, repeatedly admonishes faculty and staff to cultivate the communal rituals. "We dare not take for granted the habits of the heart," he warns. "In our teaching and serving we must affirm and celebrate such values as civic responsibility and religious discipleship."[36]

Despite criticisms, president and college clearly have been successful. Moreover, this personal and institutional success have been recognized nationally and internationally. Dovre in 1979 was awarded Knight, First Class, of the Royal Norwegian Order of St. Olav. The ALC National Convention in 1982 named him to the seventy-member Commission for a New Lutheran Church. He has served as president of the Lutheran Education Conference of North America and the Minnesota Private College Fund. Dovre's peers in 1986 placed him among the one hundred outstanding presidents. The following year, he was elected chairman of the Council of College Presidents of the Evangelical Lutheran Church in America. In 1990 he was one of thirty-three ELCA delegates to the Lutheran World Assembly which met in Curitiba, Brazil.[37]

National recognition for the institution came when the November 1982 issue of *Changing Times* listed Concordia as one of fifty public and private colleges with high academic standards and below-average prices. From 1986 through 1988 *Changing Times* annually included the college among forty-six of the nation's best low-priced high-quality schools. Additional distinction came in 1985 when Concordia was again cited in two national publications—*U.S. News and World Report* and the *New York Times* book, *Best Buys in Education*. Concordia has also been listed among the 300 included in the 1988 and 1990 editions of *Petersen's Competitive Colleges* and in the 1990 first edition of *The Barron's 300: Best Buys in College Education.*[38]

At the end of his first decade in office, President Dovre took stock of the considerable accomplishments of his administrative team and charted the institutional course for the future. The ambitious and visionary physical plant agenda set out by the Knutson administration thirty years before had been completed. Old Main and Grose Hall had been remodeled. The Science Center, housing the biology and home economics departments, had opened in 1980. The prestigious $3.4-million Olin Foundation grant had funded the art-communication facility to be completed in 1986. Off campus, the Norwegian Language Village had been essentially finished and the German Village begun. Founders Fund I had exceeded its $10.75 million goal by $1.3 million in 1981 and Founders Fund II soon would surpass its target. Looking to the future, Dovre reaffirmed the basic premises that had served so well in the past. Concordia should adhere to its religious-academic mission and should define and achieve new dimensions of quality. To attain these goals, a larger endowment was needed for recruiting and retaining a high quality faculty, reducing the student-faculty ratio and keeping the college affordable for its traditional regional constituency.[39]

Although the dean of the college ordinarily exercises academic leadership, President Dovre has forcefully articulated academic mission on ceremonial occasions. A particularly striking instance was his 1980 homecoming sermon—"Our Father's World"—delivered on the day of the Science Hall dedication. Addressing the often thorny problem of science and religion, Dovre emphasized that for Lutherans *who* created the world is more important than *how* the creation occurred. Because Lutherans have been a culture-affirming church called to discover the truth of God's creation, they were not likely to make the mistake of some Christians who have attempted to direct science according to a misplaced biblical literalism. For Lutherans, the Genesis 1 affirmation that this is God's world provides a secure foundation from which academics can inquire how the world works without fearing what their inquiry reveals.[40]

Professors Lester Meyer and Elinor Torstveit echoed these ideas in their *Lutheran Standard* articles three years later.[41] This characteristic Lutheran attitude toward the freedom of scientific inquiry and biblical interpretation has enabled Lutheran colleges to avoid the extremes of secularism and fundamentalism. They are academically strong without sacrificing religious belief; at the same time, they have not adopted a doctrinaire, defender of the faith attitude that may restrict academic freedom, inquiry and quality.

Dovre's seriousness about presidential tasks has not diminished his capacity for humor. Indeed, this capacity has grown proportionally with length of tenure and degree of success. The homecoming show regularly has fun at Dovre's expense. This plays well with Cobbers, old and young. As one remarked upon hearing the president's solo on a vacuum cleaner, "He's such a

President Dovre costumed for the homecoming variety show.

good sport!" Similarly, Dovre has earned good will by other antics: careening through the homecoming crowd on his archaic bicycle, "The Clipper"; appearing as Crocodile Dundee at fall freshmen orientation; and being pied at the dance marathon. In a chapel talk at the height of the annual spring rite of sun worship, he even expressed concern for the bikini-clad maidens lying near the treacherous waters of Prexy's Pond.[42]

Concordia certainly has prospered under President Dovre's leadership. Yet for the president humor, academic leadership, efficient management, successful fundraising and new buildings are secondary to maintaining the Christian faithfulness of the institution. Like his presidential predecessors, Dovre knows that material success is not enough; the college must always keep foremost the purpose of the founders: *Soli Deo Gloria*—"To God alone the glory."

Chapter 17

Maintaining Enrollments, Facilities and Funding

The Business of Attracting Collegians

Paul Dovre became president at a time of economic difficulty for the American nation. Stagflation—a combination of high inflation and economic stagnation—persisted throughout the remainder of the 1970s, limiting President Jimmy Carter to one term and ushering Ronald Reagan into the White House. Stagflation posed a challenge for Concordia as well. How could the institution maintain accessibility by holding the line on fee increases and by lessening the cost difference with state schools? How could students afford to pay the proportionately higher costs of private education? How could private colleges influence economy-minded governments to fund the financial assistance necessary to sustain enrollments? Where would the college find the funds to remodel and build needed facilities?

The Dovre administration met this challenge. As in the past, enrollments were the key to financial health because tuition still accounted for approximately 80 percent of institutional income. If numbers were sustained, then facilities could be used efficiently and bills paid. Statistics indicate Concordia's success. During President Dovre's first year, a record 2,570 enrolled. Registrations thereafter peaked at 2,667 in Fall 1978. Careful budget planning accommodated a gradual decline that bottomed out at 2,464 in 1984. Enrollment again increased incrementally until by Fall 1989 a record 2,884 attended, 500 more than had been projected a decade before.[1]

This success in maintaining numbers has been part of the continued popularization of higher education and rising levels of educational attainment fueled by federal spending that had been underway since the end of World War II. In 1945, forty-five of 100 graduated from high school and only sixteen entered college. By 1980, seventy-five of 100 received secondary school diplomas and forty-five continued at a higher level. That year more than 12 million attended higher schools, subsidized annually by more than $5 billion in federal grants and loans. Notwithstanding the shrinkage of federal aid in the 1980s, offset somewhat by state aid, 64 percent of Minnesota high school juniors in 1988 planned to complete college.[2] Demography, changing attitudes and public policy thus combined to help Concordia maintain its enrollment in the economically troubled 1970s and beyond.

Generally pleased that enrollment increased, administrators were unhappy about an accompanying decrease in the proportion of Lutherans. The percentage had remained above 80 percent during the 1970s but declined steadily throughout the next decade, reaching 69 percent in 1988. This has been attributed partially to new programs like ACCORD (for older students returning to school), the German Institute and nursing which boosted enrollment by attracting non-Lutherans, and to a higher percentage not reporting their religious affiliation. Comforted by this explanation and by having the highest percentage of all ELCA schools, officials still felt compelled to reassure regents that the decline was not taken lightly. At issue were institutional mission and ties to the church. Accordingly, a specially formed committee developed initiatives for strengthening bonds with congregations and educating the constituency on the value of Christian higher education. Although Concordia prided itself on its openness to everyone regardless of religious, racial or cultural background, it made explicit "that the college, within the context of its mission as an institution of the Evangelical Lutheran Church in America, does make a concerted effort to recruit Lutheran students."[3]

Concordia has remained committed to recruitment of minorities, but has not done as well as it would like. Minority enrollments declined in the late 1970s, and even these reduced numbers proved difficult to sustain in the following decade. Decreasing African-American enrollment reflected a trend among northern schools, as well as a 22 percent decline in blacks attending ALC colleges in 1982. Revitalized after 1986, Indian recruitment yielded more than twenty collegians by 1989. Due to the growing number of Native Americans and Asians, minority enrollment increased from twenty-seven (1978–1979) to fifty-seven (1988–1989), from 1 to almost 2 percent of the student body.[4]

Other sociological characteristics of the student body have remained almost unchanged. Minnesotans in 1988 still comprised almost 64 percent; another 15 percent were North Dakotans, and almost 12 percent were Montana, South Dakota and Wisconsin natives. The other 9 percent came from thirty-four states and seventeen foreign countries. The percentage of men and women has remained at approximately 41 and 59 respectively. Academic quality has stayed almost constant. High school record is the single most important factor considered in admission, contingent on satisfactory character references and standardized test scores. Consequently, more than one-half rank in the top 20 percent of their high school classes. On the average they score in the 80th percentile of the ACT. Currently, nearly one-half are first generation collegians; 73 percent come from communities of less than 7,999. Several elements have shaped their decision to attend. Ninety-five percent identify friendliness and the helpfulness of people on campus as a major factor. Other reasons are academic

Vice President
James Hausmann

reputation, Christian college and family encouragement. About one-half are related to former Cobbers.[5]

In the face of adverse economic conditions and a declining number of high school seniors, recruiting success has required constant attention to marketing and commitment of increased resources to the admissions office. By 1976 the staff had been increased from three to seven admissions counselors who traveled throughout the Upper Midwest. Research findings, which indicated that church colleges with a strong sense of identity and mission would continue to grow, sustained the morale of recruiters and confirmed the beliefs of a mission-minded president. Moreover, the institution now advertised itself as "a good college that costs less," a slogan validated by recently received recognition from several national publications.[6]

The recruiting effort benefited from the strong leadership of Vice President for Admissions James Hausmann, a man who believed in the quality of his product. In a 1980 address to the Lutheran Educational Conference of North America, Hausmann called for a campaign to improve the image of the liberal arts. Colleges had talked too much about skills and not enough about attitudes,

Hausmann charged. Research demonstrated that liberal arts colleges furthered attitude development in ways not true of other institutions. These attitudes of tolerance, receptivity to ideas, confidence and understanding of self in relation to others were as marketable as skills, Hausmann maintained.[7]

To halt the enrollment slide of the early 1980s, the college again overhauled admissions. Additions to staff and budget improved productivity. More sophisticated marketing techniques, some of which reflected Hausmann's emphasis on attitudes, were also adopted. *The Record* became exclusively a newsletter for prospective students. In 1984 it began advertising "the Concordia Equation—A Complete Person = Intellectual Growth + Career Preparation + Personal Development + Spiritual Maturity + Recreational Expression." To better market this new statement of its traditional holistic Christian emphasis on educating mind, body and spirit, three twelve-minute videos were produced. The videos—a campus tour, "The Spirit of Concordia" (a collegian perspective on everything from campus living and music to relations with professors and athletics) and "The Concordia Equation"—tried to answer most questions asked by prospective Cobbers and their parents.[8]

Besides new marketing techniques, the college relied on traditional congregational ties and time-tested recruiting methods. Because congregations had formed the backbone for solicitation throughout most of the institution's history, the declining percentage of Lutherans naturally aroused alarm about the possible weakening of these bonds. To counteract this possible trend, the admissions office emphasized active recruitment of church youth. Hence the continued importance of such annual events as Church Youth Day, Christian Scholars Day and Lutheran College Nights. Following the time-honored principle that "they will never be happy down on the farm, once they have seen Concordia," the college designed events to bring as many as possible to Moorhead. Church Youth Day represented the revival in 1976 of the former Luther League Day; it annually attracted between 1,500 and 2,200 youth throughout the 1980s. Christian Scholars Day, created in 1979, each year has drawn an additional 250 of the best and brightest.[9]

Friends and Family Weekends were other events designed to attract people. The former existed for a brief time in the early 1980s; it awarded meal cards, pool passes and football tickets to visiting friends. The change in name from Parents to

Family Weekend attracts large numbers.

Family Weekend reflected a shift to including the extended family. Attendance expanded accordingly; in 1988 1,100 enjoyed activities including a brunch, slide program, ice cream social, football game and "brat burn," a variety show and all-campus worship.[10]

Admissions has utilized alumni more systematically than ever before. In 1975 alumni admissions representatives were named and assigned these tasks: answer questions from interested local students, assist counselors traveling in their areas, provide names of prospective Cobbers, and serve as local resources for friends of the college. This effort was not misplaced. When freshmen were surveyed a decade later,

68 percent identified alumni as significant in their decision. Moreover, Cobber kids now became consequential; the institution publicized their numbers and created Homecoming for the Alumni Kid, a special event as part of the autumn celebration, to encourage their attendance. In 1987, 379 Cobber kids enrolled, including 109 for the first time. Homecoming for the Alumni Kid attracted eighty-four.[11]

Financial aid also has served in the admissions effort. The faculty scholars program, initiated in 1984, in 1990 awarded thirty $15,000 four-year scholarships to outstanding freshmen who ranked in the top 5 percent of their classes or in the top 10 percent of a national entrance examination. Introduced in 1985, thirty-four $5,000 four-year performing arts scholarships are distributed annually among thirty music, two forensic and two theatre freshmen.[12]

Besides these special awards to recruit talented individuals, rising costs have dictated continued emphasis on general assistance for everyone. Comprehensive fees rose from $3,250 (1975–1976) to $10,650 (1990–1991), an increase of 228 percent. Concordia still pursued its traditional strategy of keeping its ranking for costs among the lower third of the regional private colleges. At the same time it devoted a larger share of its resources to financial aid. For 1975–1976 the institution distributed $3.2 million in assistance, approximately 63 percent funded from government sources. As government funding decreased for 1981–1982, the college responded by committing an additional $1.75 million for aid. By 1988–1989, the financial aid budget totaled almost $14.6 million; toward this amount distributed as grants, loans and salaries, the college contributed 33 percent, the federal government 41 percent and Minnesota 22 percent. The state and federal subsidy thus amounted to more than $9 million.[13]

Whether or not expanded assistance has lessened the parental sacrifice for their children's education is difficult to say. Theoretically aid increases helped to offset higher costs for Cobbers; individual payments rose 228 percent during the Dovre era while the total assistance distributed grew 349 percent. As determined by the objective analysis of detailed financial aid statements processed by the College Scholarship Service, by 1985 nearly 80 percent qualified for aid and by 1988 more than 65 percent held parttime jobs. Given this evidence of financial need, continued government subsidies have been regarded by administrators as fundamental for institutional survival.[14]

Difficult economic conditions have created uncertainties about levels of public funding, which in turn has generated anxiety among parents, collegians and admissions staff. School officials therefore have watched public policy closely and have acted to secure advantageous legislation. They welcomed a 1976 Supreme Court decision, upholding the expenditure of state tax revenue on annual grants for nonreligious education at church-related colleges. Thus encouraged, they have lobbied state and federal lawmakers to secure funding for private education. President Dovre has been recognized as an effective lobbyist at both the state and national levels. Collegians also have contributed to the effort. In Spring 1981 the Student Association organized the most successful letter-writing campaign in Minnesota; 688 letters were sent to the legislature and 411 to Congress.[15]

Expanding and Beautifying the Campus

President Dovre brought to fruition the bold twenty-year development plan laid down by the Knutson administration in the 1950s. High inflation delayed completion by one decade. Despite the unfavorable economic climate of the mid-1970s, Concordia responded to the challenge of raising funds for constructing new buildings while remodeling older facilities and advancing campus beautification.

At the same time, admissions successes caused growing pains. To ease the housing crunch of 1975, the school rented the Cobber Motel—located on Eighth Street opposite the athletic field—and a block of rooms from Ramada Inn. In 1987 Cobbers still complained about lack of space. The library was crowded and noisy. The dormitories lacked study rooms. Post office boxes were shared and parking spaces were in short supply. Even the grounds themselves had become cramped, compelling the administration to be on the lookout for available adjacent property.[16]

Regardless of expansion, Concordia strove to be a good neighbor and generally enjoyed harmonious relations with the city government and with the neighborhood. Advance planning enabled the acquisition of property from willing sellers at market prices. The majority of the council and planning commission were pleased with the effort to develop off-street parking by providing attractively designed parking lots. Neighborhood concerns sometimes surfaced, primarily due to the changing character of the entire area along Eighth Street between the city center and Eventide Nursing Home on Fourteenth Avenue South. To avoid possible strained relations, vice presidents called personally on the neighbors and school officials ensured that projects improved acquired properties. These efforts generally succeeded. One acquisition did irreparable damage, however, leaving a void forever in Cobber hearts (and stomachs). To make way for a new building on the corner of Eighth Street and Twelfth Avenue, the Tastee Freez—a popular spot for collegians since 1954—closed on May 15, 1988.[17]

The Tastee Freez sustained several student generations.

Overcrowding prompted the first construction of the Dovre era. The college built a thirty-three unit apartment complex housing 126 Cobbers; financed by the Minnesota State Bonding Agency, it cost $520,000. The facility offered attractive flexibility during uncertain economic times. The apartments provided an alternative to the standard room and, because they could easily be converted into commercial rental property, avoided the prospect of an empty dormitory if enrollment dropped. Named Bogstad Manor for the former president, the building opened Fall 1976 on the site of recently razed North Hall, past home of Nathaniel the ghost. The long-awaited science addition, completed in Fall 1980, housed the biology and home economics departments, which had been located in temporary facilities since 1947 and 1938 respectively.[18]

Double-digit inflation had deferred an art building, another long-desired part of the campus plan. A $2.75 million Olin Foundation grant, the largest and most prestigious in Concordia's history, made it possible to proceed. When plans projected higher costs, the foundation graciously increased its award to $3.4 million. Designed in an architectural style congruent with surrounding structures and constructed of familiar buff brick, the Olin Art and Communications Center is connected by a skyway with the Frances Frazier Comstock Theatre; it opened for classes in Fall 1986.[19]

Although the Olin Center completed the development plan adopted early in the Knutson administration, the appearance of new needs assured continued construction. Of course Cobbers still wanted a larger centralized union, but existing dispersed facilities and other priorities worked against fulfilling their long-expressed desires. In December 1987 the college proceeded with plans for another dormitory, an office building and a maintenance center. Bogstad East, similar in design to the adjacent

The Olin building, new home for the art and communications departments.

Bogstad Manor, opened in Fall 1988; for parking, five houses were razed in a neighboring block to the west.[20]

The $300,000 purchase of the Beltline Health Club in south Moorhead eased somewhat the demand for recreational space. Renamed the Cobber Club, its nine racquetball courts, two weight rooms, mirrored aerobics and dance studio, sauna, whirlpool and social gathering area became available for open recreation and physical education classes in November 1987. Shuttle service provided transportation to the site two miles south of campus. Shortly thereafter plans went forward for remodeling the field house and construction of a new sports and fitness center. Originally scheduled for completion by the centennial celebration in Fall 1991, the $5 million center was delayed until after the celebration and until funds were available.[21]

The new maintenance and office buildings were completed and opened in Fall 1989. After a struggle with the neighborhood over whether the maintenance edifice would indeed create an "obnoxious industrial zone," the Moorhead City Council allowed construction on the corner of Seventh Avenue and Sixth Street. The Outreach Center, located on the site of the lamented former Tastee Freez, housed offices dealing with the outside community— Leadership Center, Cultural Events, Language Villages, World Discovery Program (including May Seminars), CHARIS and the ELCA Northwestern Minnesota Synod and Regional Center for Mission.[22]

New construction was not the only task facing the Dovre administration. De-

The Cobber Club offers weight and other exercise rooms.

ferred maintenance, energy conservation and federal legislation mandating handicap accessibility dictated additional millions for remodeling. Although much of the physical plant was new with relatively low maintenance overhead, many of the older buildings now required extensive and expensive work. Spiraling energy costs, induced by the OPEC oil embargo of 1973, contributed to the urgency. Energy conservation measures were undertaken including adjusted heating-cooling standards, improved energy control systems, insulation, caulking and window replacement. By 1988 these efforts had yielded a monetary savings of $1.6 million. The Rehabilitation Act (1973), which required handicapped accessible programs and facilities as a prerequisite to federal funding, also spurred remodeling. The list, scale and succession of major projects is impressive: Old Main (1977), $500,000; Grose and Academy Halls (1978), $350,000; Brown Hall (1982), $1.5 million; Fjelstad Hall(1984),

The Outreach Center houses programs that extend beyond Concordia.

$600,000; dining hall renovation (1987), $490,000; Bishop Whipple Hall(1989), $1.2 million. Besides fostering accessibility and energy conservation, these projects jointly promoted campus beautification and preserved historically significant buildings.[23]

Beautification, a goal long pursued by Presidents Brown and Knutson through their interest in campus plans prepared by architects, remained an important objective of the Dovre administration. Like his predecessors, Dovre followed a unified plan and carried on what Knutson had begun—turning the grounds into a park. Arden Toso, hired in April 1959 as the first full-time groundskeeper, expressed an aesthetic philosophy the presidents shared: "Kids need beauty too!"[24]

Architect E.A. Sövik first articulated the concept of an academic circle in his campus plan of the mid-1950s. Accordingly, the library—a place of study—and the centrum—a place of worship—are located in the center surrounded in concentric fashion by the academic buildings; the service facilities of dormitories, bookstore and maintenance; and the parking lots. The concept excluded automobiles from the central area. An elaboration by Sövik two decades later set forth plazas and courtyards graced by sculpture as aesthetic principles for developing the spaces between buildings.[25]

These ideas fostered the acquisition of sculpture, mosaics and murals. In Sum-

Groundskeeper Arden Toso

mer 1979 two works by Minnesota artists were purchased through a gift from the estate of Clarence H. (Chris) Berg ('64). Raymond Jacobson's "Arvegods"became the center of the Founders Court between Academy Hall and Old Main. The twelve-foot copper forms suggested a male and female complement, supportive companions symbolizing the timeless union of caring and vitality reflected in the past and present of Concordia. Paul T. Granlund's "The Founders," an eight-and-one-half foot bronze of four figures and geometric shapes placed in the library, presented timeless and universal forms because founding is a continuous process, as is the realization by succeeding genera-

tions of their freedom, understanding and commitment. After 1986 a sculpture of machined and anodized aluminum, "Squares in Symmetry" by Merlin Rostad ('35), highlighted the courtyard in front of the Frances Frazier Comstock Theatre. It has been retitled "Group Portrait of Lutherans" by a mischievous wag.[26]

Several other works adorn building interiors. Cyrus Running murals are located in the library, Lorentzsen Hall and the Science Center. The Lorentzsen mural (1965) surveys the purpose and promise of Concordia through a pioneer family, influential Christian educators of the re-

The Founders Court, graced by "Arvegods," and Professor Roger Spilde.

gion, C-400 Club founders and two beanie-wearing freshmen who look to the past and the future of the college. The Ylvisaker Library mural (1966) represents the ages of humankind through a lively panorama of work and play activities. Bronze sculptural portraits of significant individuals—C.M. Running, Joseph L. Knutson, Ed Fuglestad, Jack Spier, King Olav and Martin Luther—have been created by J. Paul Nesse ('73). Reflecting the tradition of modern classicism pioneered by Auguste Rodin, Nesse's works symbolize the religious, ethnic and personal strands that have formed the institution. Mosaics by David Hetland ('69) are located in Grant Commons

and Ylvisaker Library. "All Things Made Whole," commissioned for the 1978 ALC national convention, expresses the biblical wholeness theme through brokenness, reconciliation and rebirth. "Inquiry," commissioned for the library's twenty-fifth anniversary observance, intertwines the symbols of all disciplines with a quotation from the philosopher C.S. Peirce: "The irritation of doubt causes a struggle to attain a state of belief."[27]

The $1.2 million centennial mall and parking lot project, begun during Summer 1990 as a culmination of the Sövik plan, proposed constructing a 100 foot bell tower capped by a six-foot cross as the focus of the mall and a newly designed main entrance to the college. To achieve the beauty promised by this design, thirty-nine trees and two old frame

"Squares in Symmetry" with sculptor Merlin Rostand.

structures were removed. Leveling the "temporary" war-surplus biology building and replacing it with a natural amphitheatre waggishly dubbed "the cliffs of Dovre" did not provoke protest. Dismantling the Art Annex (former home economics house) in

The Cyrus Running mural in Lorentzsen Hall states the college mission.

1986 aroused opposition by the Student Association which wanted the space for offices. Similarly, tree removal three years later provoked a negative *Concordian* editorial and slogans like "Tree Killer!" chalked on the steps of the administration building. Many professors and collegians argued that the money should have been spent on something useful like a classroom or union building. Nonetheless, after considerable debate and consultation with the neighborhood and campus community, the project went forward. For the first time in its history, as E.A. Sövik has noted, Concordia could afford to spend money primarily for beauty. At last the old Seventh Street strip, which had long complicated design, could be used in an aesthetic way. By placing a religious symbol at the heart of campus, the institution expressed its commitment to mission and affirmed that life with only incidental beauty is not sufficient. For the architect, as for others at the school, beauty ultimately is an avenue to the transcendent.[28]

The firm foundation on which the centennial tower is grounded.

In addition to creating the new, old architectural treasures were preserved. Two notable landmarks—the English cottage-style president's home and the neoclassical Old Main—are now listed on the National Register of Historic Places. Prexy's Pond,

The Bell Tower signifies that the college is centered on religion.

long remembered by alumni as an idyllic spot, had in reality become a source of bad odors and unsanitary water. Both problems were corrected in 1979 by dredging accumulated muck from the pond and installing a storm sewer which placed the stream underground.[29]

This care for historic preservation, artistic appreciation and campus beautification is much valued by most who work at the school. Although sometimes the subject of humor, these efforts are a visible expression of the Christian liberal arts tradition and enhance significantly the quality of college life.

A New Development Strategy

As it had since early in the Knutson presidency, the development office played a crucial role; it sought the funds needed for maintaining the physical plant and for enhancing endowment so that the college might remain accessible to the youth of its regional constituency.

The office was restructured with the appointment of David Benson as director of college relations in 1975 and Rev. Donald Rice as director of church relations in 1980. Both aimed at fostering close relations with the constituency; Rice had the special task of strengthening ties with ELCA congregations in the region. The ALC sanctioned this effort by its colleges at its 1980 convention; others in the church shared the concern sometimes heard at Concordia about the declining percentage of Lutherans at its schools. Both church and college desired an enhanced sense of congregational ownership. Donald Rice has contributed significantly to this effort. He travels the corporate territory preaching, appearing at meetings and conventions, and coordinating corporation activities. He works through Project CORD—Coordinated Outreach for Recruitment and Development—initiated in 1980. Shortly thereafter, the CORD Matching Scholarship Program was instituted. By Fall 1989, congregations had contributed $548,989, which had been matched by the college. During 1988–1989, 211 congregations gave $110,069 to 391 Cobbers. In exchange for enhanced financial and enrollment support, the office of church relations provided services for local congregations—computer workshops, archival conferences, videotapes of campus events, a speaker's bureau and theological education through cooperation with CHARIS.[30]

The growth of gift income indicates that the development office benefited from strong leadership, restructuring and the new strategy of capital fund drives. Gifts for Dovre's first year (1975–1976), totaled almost $2.3 million. By 1989 donations had grown to $6.6 million, a rise of 29 percent over the previous year and almost triple what it had been thirteen years before. An increase in the size and number of major gifts largely accounts for this growth. The prestigious $3.4 million Olin Foundation grant in 1984 marked a major breakthrough in fundraising. Not only did the award make possible the construction of a badly needed facility for the programs of art and communications which served a large number of students, it represented significant national recognition. Foundation officials were impressed that Concordia had constructed a science center without government assistance in 1980, an effort that capped an impressive twenty-five-year record of physical plant expansion and quality service to its region.[31]

Major fund drives generated this dramatic increase in gift income. When Dovre became president he immediately began promoting the idea of a capital campaign, a shocking departure from the Knutson tradition. The administration had to convince a skeptical board about the compatibility with C-400, the use of professional consultants and the necessity for the tenfold increase in funds requested. Their case rested on the need to build two multimillion dollar buildings without federal funding and the desire to accelerate institutional progress by increasing annual gifts, which had leveled off in the $1- to $2-million dollar range. Dovre and Vice President for Development Edward Ellenson and his successor Loren Anderson, aided by professional consultants, planned the campaign between 1975 and 1978. Undaunted when the leadership phase fell significantly short of its goal, a confident yet naive administration recommended going ahead. Led by Norman Jones, who headed the campaign, and board chair Norman Lorentzsen, the regents approved.[32]

C-400 has played an integral role in three capital fund drives.

Administered by Vice President for Development Loren Anderson and publicly announced as a three-year effort in late January 1978, Founders Fund I aimed to raise $10.75 million—$5 million for academic facilities, $3.75 million for annual support and $2 million for endowment—from the four state region of the Dakotas, Montana and Minnesota. This marked the first comprehensive effort among constituents for endowment funds since the historic 1926 campaign. Two capital fund drives in the 1940s yielded dollars for repaying the Fjelstad debt, constructing Brown Hall and building the auditorium-field house. Founders Fund I followed the principle of "inside out"; faculty and staff were solicited successfully with participation and contributions far exceeding the averages for similar campaigns. When the drive concluded in 1981, it had surpassed its goal by $1 million and the science hall built by its income had already opened.[33]

Vice President Loren Anderson

Encouraged by this success that fostered a more positive image of Concordia's strengths and revealed an untapped potential, the development staff rested only two years before launching the even more ambitious Founders Fund II. *Blueprint III*, Concordia's long-range plan for the '80s, identified economic stability as the major challenge. The new three-year drive (1984–1986) therefore sought $21.5 million, with two-thirds distributed to endowment and the remainder to operating expenses. When the canvass concluded in April 1986, almost $26.4 million had been pledged, far exceeding the original goal. In addition, the college had benefited from other advancement efforts. Besides the Olin grant, $250,000 had been awarded by the National Endowment for the Humanities for developing humanities academic programs, and $1.6 million had been raised for construction of the German village at the Bemidji site.[34]

Feasibility studies for a possible centennial fund drive quickly followed the completion of Founders Fund II. Donald Campbell and Co., a Chicago-based consulting firm, conducted sixty in-depth interviews with Concordia supporters. Next came thirty small-group meetings with college employees, parents, alumni and friends. On the basis of these findings, the regents in April 1988 set an initial goal of $46.5 million and approved implementation of the leadership phase to be concluded in Fall 1989. Built on the principles of "from inside out" and "from top down," officials again targeted Concordia staff and big contributors. Both succeeded; when publicly announced in October 1989, $25 million had already been committed, including 90 percent employee participation to raise $2 million and a $5 million gift from Earl and Dorothy Olson of Willmar. The Olson gift is the largest ever received by Concordia and one of the largest private donations made to any college in the Upper Midwest.[35]

Earl and Dorothy Olson, presenters of the largest individual gift to the college.

Endowment, scholarships and physical improvements have been major objectives in the centennial campaign. Endowment income represented the key to maintaining the quality and accessibility of Concordia's academic program. To improve quality, the institution intended to lower the student-faculty ratio to 15.5:1 and to improve real wages for faculty and staff. To maintain accessibility, tuition should be moderated and financial aid increased. To achieve these goals, the college attempted to shift the allocation of its income resources by reducing the tuition share from 80 to 70 percent, and increasing the endowment portion from 2 to 10 percent. The Dovre administration and the development office have been quite successful in moving toward these goals. Endowment grew from less than $2 million in 1977 to more than $19.2 million by April 1989. Happiness with this dramatic increase was tempered by the reality that a college of Concordia's size and quality should have an endowment of more than twice this amount.[36]

Reliance on major fundraising campaigns represented a departure from the slow-but-steady approach undertaken by the Knutson administration. Knutson's direction had been dictated by a bad experience with professional fundraisers in resurrecting the collapsed field house and by the historical lesson of the Brown presidency. The

President Paul J. Dovre, 1975 --

seemingly constant fundraising efforts of the 1940s had alienated the constituency. This necessitated President Knutson's change of direction. How is it that the Dovre administration could succeed with three nearly consecutive major campaigns undertaken within a span of thirteen years, an approach abandoned by President Knutson because it had failed with President Brown? Several factors account for recent success. The region's economy has matured since the 1940s; businessmen, professionals and farmers are better able financially to respond positively to the Dovre drives. Alumni have increased in number, financial capacity and willingness to support the college. Knutson's slow-but-steady approach built up a loyal constituency of friends and alumni who have provided the essential foundation for the victories of the Dovre years.

Capital fund campaigns shaped the politics for naming buildings, endowed chairs and other entities. The board approved guidelines in April 1977 setting a $50,000 minimum for sub-units and a $500,000 minimum for endowed chairs, authorized the president to negotiate with prospects but reserved final authority for the regents, and recommended extreme caution in naming after college personnel because of the certainty of hurt feelings. Although limits have since been raised, the principle remains unaltered. Following these guidelines, several structures were renamed in the 1980s for major donors: Frances Frazier Comstock Theatre, Rudy and Ruby Erickson Men's Residence Hall, Jessie Fern Hallet Women's Residence Hall, Ivers Hall and Lorentzsen Hall.[37]

The continued growth of C-400 was fundamental to all three campaigns. Club projects were closely coordinated with financial needs. In 1975 Vice President for Business Affairs William Smaby recommended repaying a $500,000 debt before undertaking extensive projects generating additional longterm debt. He therefore requested a modest C-400 project including funds for debt retirement, scholarships and renovation. The club responded positively to Smaby's request; in 1976 they announced Project 7, a two-year, $700,000 drive to remodel Grose Hall and retire institutional debt. For Project 8, undertaken in 1978, the organization sought 2,000 new memberships over a three-year period in support of Founders Fund I. At the time, C-400 already had 5,000 members. Project 9, a two-year drive to raise $1 million, surpassed its goal in 1983. The funds were used for student financial aid to replace the Reagan administration cuts in government assistance. In Project 10, which supported Founders Fund II, total membership passed 10,000 and the club raised $2.7 million, exceeding its goal of $2.5 million. As in the past, the organization promptly announced a new undertaking. "Keeping Faith with the Heartland," Project 11, sought 1,800 new and renewed memberships over three years to fund 450 annual scholarships valued at from $500 to $2,000 for incoming freshmen from rural areas. Completed successfully in 1989, the drive secured 1,908 members. Project 12 began immediately; it supported the centennial fund drive with a three-year goal of $2.5 million. Meanwhile, the C-400 Business Division sought $500,000 for that campaign.[38]

In addition to being a wonderful financial resource for Concordia, C-400 has added significantly to the culture of college and community. Authors, athletes, entertainers, journalists, politicians or alumni have appeared at least four times a year. Speakers have ranged from baseball immortal Hank Aaron (1979) to newsman Ed Bradley (1979), from Governor Rudy Perpich (1986) to actress Liv Ullman (1985), from singer Karen Armstrong ('63) in 1987 to former Saint Olaf College President and Ambassador to Norway Sidney Rand ('38) in 1984.[39]

The annual alumni fund raises unrestricted dollars for current use. Instituted during the Knutson administration, in 1956 the fund yielded $29,199 from contributions by

28.6 percent of the 5,606 alumni. By 1975, 10.2 percent of 15,306 alumni gave $234,317. Through the class challenge program initiated in 1980, amounts rose; the drive secured $1.1 million from 40 percent of the alumni in 1988.[40]

The Dovre administration has met successfully its enrollment and financial challenges. To utilize efficiently its physical plant and staff during the economically troubled 1970s, Concordia sought an enrollment between 2,400 and 2,600. Ranging from a low of 2,464 (1984) to a high of 2,884 (1989), the college has exceeded 2,600 seven times during the Dovre years. Enrollment equilibrium has translated into financial stability. Not only were announced targets exceeded in two major fund drives and a third confidently launched, but the institution won its annual battle of a balanced operating budget as well. The budget grew from almost $9.8 million in 1975–1976 to more than $23.9 million in 1987–1988.[41]

Between his arrival in 1976 and his untimely death in 1982, Vice President for Business Affairs Donald Helland introduced several bold financial strategies. He built

Vice President
Donald Helland

more sophisticated systems of managing the budget and the endowment fund. He creatively financed the biology building with longterm low-interest tax-deferred bonds while investing the debt service fund at high interest. Most important, he began the decade-long process of creating an operating reserve fund equal to 10 percent of the annual budget. For successive years the college achieved an annual contribution to reserve of $200,000. The benefits of the fund have been many; it has eliminated short-term borrowing, increased financial flexibility, protected the college from economic slumps and provided significant shortterm investment income in times of high interest. At the same time the institution has repositioned long-term debt; debt reserves should exceed indebtedness by 1992.[42]

Although not rich, Concordia is thus in a strong financial position to begin its second century. Enrollment has been stable, fund drives successful, and budgets balanced. These successes provide a solid foundation for confronting the reduction of college-age population that continues into the 1990s. Moreover, the designs to cope with this decline are working: "a bold development strategy," "an aggressive admissions policy" and the decision to charge less than comparable private colleges. Aggressive recruiting is attracting a higher percentage of the shrinking number of secondary school graduates. Lower tuition, in accord with the economic capabilities of regional students, has maintained accessibility. Bold development, combined with the nearing completion of the physical plant, has made available a larger amount and a higher percentage of gift income for endowment and current operations.[43]

Chapter 18

Preserving the Liberal Arts

Academic Mission

The 1970s and 1980s were not propitious for higher education or the liberal arts. Considerable national discussion ensued about the deterioration of quality, lack of coherence and irrelevance of the liberal arts to the vocational interests of the public. The National Assessment of Educational Progress found an overall decline in performance of American seventeen-year-olds in most subjects during these two decades. Similarly, the International Evaluation of Educational Achievement discovered in the early 1980s that the performance of American school children lagged behind that of other industrial nations. Ernest Boyer's study of incoming freshmen revealed a predominance of vocational concerns: Between 85 and 90 percent wanted preparation for a specific occupation, a better job or a more satisfying career; only 37 percent sought to clarify values or beliefs; merely 27 percent endeavored to become more thoughtful and responsible citizens.[1]

Drawing on this and other evidence, some critics like Allan Bloom and E.D. Hirsch, Jr., argued that schools and colleges were not producing an educated citizenry because graduates lacked the requisite broad knowledge and commitment to humane values. Others like historian Helen Horowitz noted the dominance of a "grim professionalism"; many collegians were preoccupied only with "making the grade" and their basic philosophy seemed to be "study, work and get rich." Still others, such as sociologist Robert Bellah and his collaborators who published *Habits of the Heart: Individualism and Commitment in American Life* (1985), documented the individualistic self-seeking among middle-class Americans; they deplored this trend toward privatism and called for a revived "public virtue" and commitment to public affairs. Faced with this barrage of criticism, educational institutions wondered whether they had not gone too far in dissolving admission and graduation requirements in response to the demands for freedom heard during the 1960s. Certainly course offerings were multitudinous, as noted by two aptly titled Carnegie Commission studies: *Any Person, Any Study* (1971) and *Three Thousand Faces* (1980).[2]

Despite this unfavorable cultural climate, Concordia retained, redefined and reaffirmed its traditional commitments to liberal arts education. President Dovre and Vice President for Academic Affairs David Gring often affirmed on public occasions the enduring institutional commitment to mission, quality and liberal learning. They repeatedly urged a continual dialogue about purpose among faculty and a constant restatement of what it meant to be a church-related liberal arts college. Accordingly, admissions literature assured prospective Cobbers that they would become liberally educated persons who were knowledgeable, ethically minded, responsible and productive citizens. And the ongoing community-wide dialogue about academic mission produced *Blueprint III: A Long-Range Plan for Concordia College* (1983) and a companion volume, *An Agenda for Concordia's Academic Life: A Curriculum Plan for Concordia College* (1984).

In articulating the theological foundations of academic mission, both documents mirrored the national movement by most denominations to reaffirm church-related higher education and to stimulate faculty to integrate faith and learning. Among Lutherans, the LCA and ALC redefined church and college relations during the 1970s. Historically and structurally diverse, the LCA experienced problems in developing unity of purpose and program. Nonetheless, the LCA convention agreed that Lutheran colleges should foster intellectual growth, Christian life and learning, and service to church and society. The ALC in contrast maintained that colleges were integral to the church; they are the "church in mission" in higher education and have a redemptive and reconciling role in addition to their investigative and creative function.[3]

The American bicentennial celebration in 1976 and ALC-LCA cooperation enhanced efforts at redefinition. Cooperation was evidenced by frequent meetings of deans and other staff; experience in joint ownership and cooperation in support of colleges; and the creation of a network of twenty-nine colleges and universities as part of the projected new Lutheran church. The bicentennial led Lutherans to reflect upon the United States' religious heritage and upon the Reformation roots of Lutheran theology and education. One product of this reflection, Richard Solberg's *Lutheran Higher Education in North America* (1985), was sponsored by the Lutheran Educational Conference of North America (LECNA). Launched while Paul Dovre was president of the conference, he chaired the project. Solberg's book subsequently became the subject of a faculty workshop at Concordia. Thus it should not surprise that college documents have reflected similar theological understandings.[4]

Planning documents are a Concordia tradition.

A product of two years' discussion between 1980 and 1982, *Blueprint III* articulated new theological and theoretical definitions of what it meant to be a church-related liberal arts college. Appropriately, theological interpretation followed that of the recent ALC statement: Concordia was an institutional ministry of the church. As implied by Luther's doctrine of the priesthood of all believers, ministry was understood as the vocation of all Christians who minister by diligently practicing the vocations to which they have been called. Therefore at Concordia inquiry and learning were worthy vocations in their own right preparing Cobbers for other ministries in the world. As members of an inquiring community, all faculty and students were called to the scholarly pursuit of truth, creativity and responsible criticism. As responsible Christian critics, graduates should seek creative alternatives to the idolatrous tendencies of the dominant American culture and should see careers as part of a sum of activities calling them to the Christian service that gave meaning to life. In addition to these theological understandings and as a way to strengthen commitment to the liberal arts, the community discussed the "theorizing with values" model proposed by philosopher Gregg Muilenburg. The model suggested that theory construction and evaluation were the way all academics practice their disciplines. Because all disciplinary knowledge issued from a context of cultural and disciplinary governing beliefs, the concept offered a way to understand how Christian belief informs scholarly activity and how scholarship shapes Christian commitments. Thus theorizing with values provided a framework for defining and clarifying the central role of values, including religious commitments, in a liberal arts education.[5]

An Agenda for Concordia's Academic Life, authored by a ten-member academic commission appointed by the faculty senate and chaired by Dean Gring, originated from the blueprint process. *Blueprint III* urged a comprehensive review of the curriculum with attention to issues of global interdependence, prejudice and technology. It advocated strengthening the core, reinforcing critical skills, enhancing the understanding of values inherent in the liberal arts and developing an academic environment and curricular structure that encouraged scholarship, improved communication between faculty and students and promoted liberal arts practices.[6]

The ensuing academic agenda consisted of two parts. The first outlined the goals for student and faculty academic life including expectations for modeling the scholarly and Christian life; the second summarized curricular revisions. The goals were grounded appropriately in a theological understanding of Concordia's mission already articulated in *Blueprint III* and the ALC statement on college-church relations. Expressed in the familiar rhetoric of religious commitment and academic excellence, most of the goals and the modest reforms derived from them were not new or remarkable. What was novel was the way *Agenda* set forth an expectation of active scholarship on the part of professors and collegians as a prerequisite for Concordia becoming a superior undergraduate institution. In order to graduate liberally educated persons, they must be taught by faculty who were intellectually vital. To have vitality, one must practice scholarship.[7]

How could this new understanding of academic mission be achieved? Implicit in *Agenda* was the notion of academic community as a process of discussion about religious and scholarly goals. For this community to work effectively as a mode of liberal education, it must be comprised of the right elements. Accordingly, Concordia gave attention to faculty recruitment and development, intellectual milieu and academic program.

Agencies of Liberal Arts Education

Dean Gring frequently cited faculty as the most vital agency for fulfilling academic mission and for providing a coherent undergraduate experience. In terms of their qualifications, faculty were by now better able to fulfill these scholarly expectations. The percentage of completed doctorates increased markedly from 49 percent in 1977 to 62 percent a decade later. To fulfill Concordia's academic aspirations, the dean set a target of 75 percent to be achieved within five years.[8]

Better qualifications and better institutional support led to growing regional, national and international recognition of faculty achievement. A few individuals may serve as an illustration of others too numerous to discuss. When Paul J. Christiansen retired from directing the choir in 1986, he had attained an international reputation. As President Knutson once said in a moment of exasperation at faculty carping about the director's exalted status, "Paul Christiansen is the first professor at Concordia to achieve anything of quality that people will pay money to hear!" Determined and demanding, Christiansen's choral ideal was that of his father, F. Melius: to achieve a standard comparable to that of a professional symphony. Although Christiansen

Paul J. Christiansen achieved distinction in choral music.

usually ignored reviews, he cherished those from concerts in Washington, D.C., and Vienna which indicated that youthful amateurs sometimes attained a professional level. Christiansen applied equally high standards to himself: "As a musician, I'm a student constantly refining my art. ... A musician never reaches what he dreams." Constant striving after these high ideals enabled this would-be concert pianist and self-confessed poor singer to achieve distinction as a choral director and composer.[9]

Another who attained international recognition was professor of history Hiram Drache, author of several books on regional history and agriculture. A man of great energy who combined for many years the occupations of scholar, teacher and farmer, Drache explained simply, "I'd rather farm than play golf. Farming helps me work off the nervous energy that builds up when I'm teaching." His first book, *The Day of the Bonanza*, appeared in 1964 and examined the large-scale commercial farmers who opened up the Red River Valley in the 1870s. By 1970, when he published *The Challenge of the Prairie* on the life of the early pioneers in the valley, his first had sold 12,000 copies, making it a best-seller for local history. He has subsequently published five more volumes on agriculture and the region. His publications have led to invitations to

Historian Hiram Drache

lecture in the United States, Canada, Australia and Europe.[10]

Although not as well known as Christiansen or Drache, others achieved notable recognition while modeling the liberal arts for generations of undergraduates. Olin Storvick's archeological work since 1973 at Caesarea Maritima in 1988 became part of the traveling Smithsonian Institution exhibit, "King Herod's Dream: Caesarea on the Sea." When the Twin Cities Alumni Association sponsored a private tour of the exhibition at the Minnesota Science Museum it hoped fifty might come; the association was pleasantly overwhelmed when 680 attended Storvick's presentation. A genuinely modest man who says "archeology is a disease" and admits he "is a terminal case," Storvick always credits the quality of collegians and colleagues with making Concordia a special place.[11]

Professor Daryl Ostercamp

Another who personifies the liberal arts with his range of interests and scholarly productivity is professor of chemistry Daryl Ostercamp. Winner of a Fulbright professorship to Iraq in 1964 and a National Science Fellow at the University of East Anglia in 1969, Ostercamp has published sixteen articles in the *Journal of Organic Chemistry* and *Journal of the American Chemical Society* and has involved two dozen students in research projects. As a result of teaching in Saudi Arabia (1977–1980), he helped found the Middle Eastern Lectureship at the college to present the Palestinian side of the conflict with Israel.[12]

Long recognized as a great teacher, an innovative administrator and an indefatigable researcher, Walther Prausnitz assumed another fulltime job in the 1970s when he published *Capsules: A Review of Higher Education Research*, which abstracted about 3,500 books and articles annually. By 1976 the journal had 1,200 subscribers in forty-nine states, all Canadian provinces, Mexico and Puerto Rico. In 1982 Joan Buckley, professor of English, was selected the first recipient of the Lily B. Gyldenvand Endowed Professorship of Communications. She and other female professors have come a long way from the day in 1958 when a shocked President Knutson had ushered her from his office for suggesting that she continue

Dr. Marilyn Guy

teaching in the final months of her pregnancy. A Phi Beta Kappa and winner of three National Endowment for the Humanities (NEH) Fellowships, Buckley firmly believes in doing research. She has authored an article on her doctoral thesis which was a critical study of Martha Ostenso's novels about the Norwegian immigrant experience, coedited two volumes on the popular Norwegian-American comic strip *Han Ola og Han Per* and given a hundred talks on the experience of immigrant women.[13]

In 1986 Marilyn Guy, chairperson of the education department, became president-elect of the Association of Independent Liberal Arts Colleges and Teacher Education. During her three-year term, Guy promoted teacher education programs in colleges with a strong liberal arts emphasis. She also served on accreditation teams for the National Council for Accreditation of Teacher Education. Two years later, Gerald Heuer, professor of mathematics, was chosen coach of the American team in the International Math Olympiad. His team of twenty-four, selected from a field of over 400,000 who entered national math competition, finished fifth in 1989 behind China, Romania, USSR and East Germany.[14]

Conductor J. Robert Hanson

In 1989 two others were honored by professional associations for their contributions. J. Robert Hanson, nearing the end of his sixteen-year tenure as conductor of the Fargo-Moorhead Symphony, was named the Music Educator of the Year by the Minnesota Music Educators Association for his meritorious service to music education. Laurence Falk, a charter member and past president, received the Sociologists of Minnesota's Award for Distinguished Service.[15]

Two others were honored with collections of scholarly essays. On Reidar Thomte's seventy-third birthday, a gathering of close friends and associates presented him with a volume written by eight of his former students. According to one, Thomte's life bears witness to an ideal community of liberal arts where first-rate minds can examine every value in light of

Jesus's claims. In 1987 the Professor Harding C. Noblitt Scholarship was created by alumni who, inspired by his teaching, pursued careers as professors, lawyers, authors and political scientists. That fall several former students spoke to the Faith, Reason and World Affairs Conference on the United States Constitution and planned to publish their addresses in Noblitt's honor. The jovial, energetic political activist and former DFL congressional candidate retired in August 1990 after more than forty years of teaching political science at the college.[16]

Academic policies were created to foster the necessary community to sustain these individuals in their work and to encourage others to do likewise. As the college enters the 1990s, recruitment poses a great challenge. With almost two-thirds of the present faculty scheduled to retire by 2005, replacement appears difficult especially in light of concerns about the deteriorating quality and lack of religious commitment among graduate students. Nonetheless, Dean Gring expressed optimism as he surveyed this situation in 1989. He believed that increased demand would improve the quality of applicants as faculty once more encouraged the best and the brightest to prepare for college teaching. In addition, Gring viewed recruiting as a tremendous opportunity to improve academic quality. Consequently, the college worked harder and spent more money, but the many new bright lights who came and strengthened several departments justified the effort.[17]

Following national trends, the college attempted to recruit minorities and women. It enjoyed more success in the latter than the former; the proportion of female faculty rose to 36 percent by 1989. Minorities comprised 3 percent of the professorate, comparable to the proportion at other Lutheran and regional institutions; hiring was restricted by limited supply and lack of minority population in Fargo-Moorhead.[18]

This concern with finding suitable replacements contrasted with the fears expressed only two decades earlier about stagnation brought on by excessive stability. To avoid being "tenured-in" at that time of financial instability, a tenure quota of not more than two-thirds both institutionally and departmentally had been adopted in 1973. Discontent grew thereafter as younger faculty faced dismissal due to the quota and faculty hired between 1970 and 1973 objected to being held in the temporary status of tenure-eligible nonprobationary (TENP). After prolonged discussion, the quota was redefined in 1982 as a guideline that may be excused in those instances where the college believed that it had the right person. This was sufficient to give hope to the non-tenured. At the same time, those in the TENP category were awarded tenure. Morale improved considerably.[19]

Meanwhile, the college aggressively fostered professional development. In 1974 it implemented systematic evaluation. In Spring 1976 sabbaticals replaced an earlier leaves program and promised double-barrelled intellectual stimulation. Tenured faculty were awarded one-semester or one-year leaves for professional study; their replacements brought new ideas and renewed contact with the graduate schools. A decade later, the Bush Scholars program supported joint faculty-collegian research into questions of values, society or disciplinary importance. Bush scholars unanimously praised the educational benefits of student research and pondered how to replicate this experience for larger numbers in the classroom. The Student Lecture Series, initiated in 1987, recognized outstanding collegiate researchers and offered them the opportunity to present their work publicly.[20]

In addition to these development efforts, the college benefited from the strong instructional assessment program that has been in place since the early 1970s. Director of Liberal Arts Studies Walther Prausnitz surveys graduates annually and alumni three and ten years after graduation. Other assessment data has come from regular core course evaluations and from accreditation studies. Institutional assessment, combined with systematic professional development and institutional planning symbolized by the blueprint process, was a key to ensuring academic quality.[21]

The artist and lecture series contributed to the academic milieu. The artist series annually scheduled nationally known performers in music, dance and theatre. A few remained in residence from a day to a week, conducting master classes for musicians or working with performing groups. The lecture series featured faculty and outside speakers recruited by the committee or by individual departments. As in the past, poor attendance provoked lament. Accordingly, the search continued for ways to increase participation.[22]

"Beyond '76," the well-publicized college-sponsored American bicentennial observance, focused on ways and means of shaping the third century and aimed at cultivating civic awareness and political responsibility among collegians. Because it was an election year, a prominent politician was recruited to speak. Shirley Chisholm, the first black woman in Congress and first to seek a major-party presidential nomination, spoke on "The Democratic Process." President Dovre placed the series in a theological context. He called "Beyond '76" "a welcome theme for an academic community bent on shaping a better world in God's behalf." A Lutheran liberal arts college was an excellent place for examination of the past and preparation for the future. He affirmed that if Americans willed it, the bicentennial could be a time of reexamination, goal-setting and recommitment.[23]

President Dovre called "Beyond '76" a success that he hoped would be duplicated in future programming. His hopes were not realized for several years, but in Fall 1982 the college sponsored the Conference on National Security and Nuclear Arms. Three keynote speakers and several panel discussions presented a wide variety of perspectives. Although the speakers assumed war is an inevitable outcome and ignored the paramount role of women in peacemaking throughout the ages, according to a perceptive critique by senior Becky Ellenson ('83), the conference was well-attended and served as a starting point for education on a crucial subject. It also served as a model of things to come. Two years later the senate approved President Dovre's proposal to create a college task force on cultural events programming. The committee's

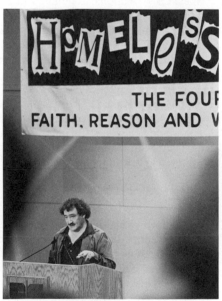

The Faith, Reason and World Affairs Symposium on homelessness heard activist Mitch Snyder.

report, presented in April 1985 by presidential assistant Esther Allen, recommended that a cultural events committee replace the existing lecture and fine arts committees and that a permanent director be appointed. Thus began the Concordia Cultural Events program directed by Lowell Larson. It had the advantages of better publicity, greater funding from endowment and better coordination from a permanent director. With all this, attendance improved.[24]

"Faith, Reason and World Affairs," an annual symposium series modeled on the earlier national security conference, has become the flagship of the new effort. Funded by an endowment from Dorothy and Stanley Kresge, the series explores significant contemporary issues in the context of the Christian faith. The first, "Food, Farming and the Future," was held September 15–17, 1985. It featured national speakers Orville Freeman, Frances Moore Lappé, Garrett Hardin and Ron Sider. It viewed problems from local, national and international perspectives. The conference has been held each fall since. The third, "The Constitution of the U.S.: Facing the Third Century," presented ten speakers at nine events attended by more than 4,000 people. In 1988 "Homeless in America" attracted an audience of 7,767 and received an Outstanding Service Award from the Mental Health Association for "thought–provoking public education."[25]

Besides this significant public service aspect, the symposia provide a cultural events focus at the beginning of each academic year. Events are incorporated into many classes, and therefore many Cobbers attend what they would not otherwise. By integrating cultural programs into academic work both benefit; classwork is related to the affairs of the world and collegians discover that public speakers are relevant to their formal academic training.

Speakers of national reputation in many fields have come to campus on other occasions as well. These have ranged from Abba Eban, the former foreign minister of Israel, to Jeanne Kirkpatrick, former ambassador to the United Nations and member of the Reagan Cabinet, and from Scandinavian immigration specialist Ingrid Semmingsen to feminist biblical scholar Elisabeth Schussler-Fiorenza. During the same period FM Communiversity scheduled many outstanding speakers for its opening convocation: an authority on death, Elisabeth Kubler-Ross (1975); Gray Panther activist Maggie Kuhn (1979); Illinois Congressman Paul Simon (1983); and Bernice King, the youngest child of Dr. Martin Luther King, Jr. (1986).[26]

All provided a wonderful cultural resource for classes and for the Fargo–Moorhead area. They were therefore a significant element in campus intellectual life and contributed to fulfilling the academic mission of a church-related liberal arts college.

Academic and Outreach Programs

As do faculty and milieu, academic programs further academic mission. During the Dovre years attempts have been made to strengthen academic quality, the liberal arts and vocational offerings. In reviewing his decade as dean on the eve of his departure, David Gring maintained that academic quality had improved. Students were now pushed harder than they once were; he believed that the academically talented should be challenged even more. To achieve his goals, Gring encouraged honors work and initiated the Bush Scholars program, with its emphasis on joint faculty-student research. He believed that community support for higher scholarly expectations developed by the process of writing and approving of *An Agenda for Concordia's Academic Life* had made these initiatives possible.[27]

Agenda's modest program aimed at strengthening the liberal arts and academic quality. The most important programmatic change was the creation of a required freshman course—Principia: Foundational Study of the Liberal Arts. Principia was designed to provide a common intellectual experience, emphasize value–reflective inquiry, and introduce liberal arts skills and habits of mind. These goals were to be accomplished through the study of classical texts and great thinkers that comprised the intellectual heritage and served as models of inquiry. By developing the skills of careful reading of original materials, reflective thought and argumentative writing, Principia supported discourse objectives.[28]

Equally significant were proposals for across-the-curriculum requirements: verbal competence, a writing/speaking component in all courses; computer instruction, a call for each student and professor learning to use computers as creative instruments although skill levels depended on one's major; and inclusive education, a requirement that ethnic, global and women's studies perspectives should be evident in all relevant courses. *Agenda* reforms plugged a hole in core distribution. Cobbers were now required to take courses in all five areas, including at least one semester of foreign language. *Agenda* also fostered review of all present core courses and all departmental majors and minors according to the new standards stated in the goals for student and faculty academic life.[29]

When the *Agenda* proposals were submitted to the faculty senate they provoked a prolonged and thorough debate which revealed the community's predilection for consensus decision-making. Principia and the foreign language requirement attracted fire. Nonetheless, the proposals passed the senate in April 1984. The jury is still out on whether the reforms achieved their desired effect. Some benefits accrued immediately. A $250,000 NEH grant matched on a three-to-one basis established a $1 million endowment for the humanities. Income supported Principia, humanities faculty development, the writing program and library acquisitions. Survey data reveal that writing and speaking have come to play a significantly more important role in the curriculum.[30]

The economics and business computer laboratory indicates the growing importance of computers.

Nonetheless, complaints still surface. Often collegians have an aversion to required courses. They dislike the language requirement for being too much, while many professors dislike it for being too little. Faculty grievances about Principia are diverse: The course has not attained their hopes as a common intellectual experience; it has not worked as a development tool because too many temporary instructors have been used; it has neglected classical texts, according to unhappy humanities professors; and it has not been sufficiently multidisciplinary to satisfy natural and social scientists.

Two existing honors programs contributed to Dean Gring's academic agenda. CREDO, meaning "I believe," had been established in 1975 for high-ability, highly motivated students who were admitted upon invitation by the dean. It is a nine-course, four-year program based on the theme,"the making of the modern mind." The initial three-year sequence emphasizes the way societies and values have evolved over the centuries; a senior seminar examines the disciplinary values of individual majors. Departmental honors had existed since the mid-1950s. They fell into disuse during the 1970s when the demand for college teachers declined. Nonetheless Dean Gring, believing that exceptional Cobbers ought to be challenged, encouraged departments to adopt or expand honors work. At this writing it is too early to determine whether his promptings will have their desired effect.[31]

Computers, the most important recent academic technological innovation, are much in evidence. A computer science major was first offered in September 1977 in cooperation with the Tri-College University. By Fall 1983, majors were no longer the only computer users. Ten new IBM personal computers were installed in the library for student use. Five terminals and one printer were added to the mainframe VAX 750, and nine IBM personal computers were placed in other locations. Thereafter, to achieve the *Agenda* goal of computer literacy, the college committed substantial funds annually for additional computer equipment and software. Susan Gammill, instructor in mathematics and computer science, was appointed coordinator for academic computing services. Besides enhancing mainframe capacity and acquiring additional personal computers, new teaching laboratories were created in 1987 in Ivers Science and in the economics–business administration department of Old Main.[32]

Even the humanities joined the technological revolution. Discourse taught word processing. The art department opened a computer laboratory for graphic design and layout in Fall 1989, culminating three years' planning by David Boggs, who already was urging expansion by adding a color monitor, a larger screen and added software with more typefaces. By 1990, the college had made available individual purchase plans, achieved a ratio of one personal computer for every forty students, and embarked on putting a machine into each professor's office.[33]

The library participated in the technological revolution as well. Its collection expanded from 210,000 (1975) to 275,000 books (1989), plus fifty newspaper and 1,500 serials subscriptions. This overflowing collection in 1990 necessitated expansion into the top two floors of the library addition constructed in 1971. Librarians eagerly acquired new technology. Concordia was among the first one hundred schools in the United States to purchase a book detector after the device had been on the market only one year. Placed at the exit, the detector reduced thefts markedly. Head Librarian Verlyn Anderson called computerization, the on-line catalog, the Tri-College University, Minnetex and other cooperative ventures a godsend. Computers quickly performed the previously time-consuming and arduous library chores of filing and searching.[34]

Cooperation offset soaring costs and provided access to much larger collections than a small college could formerly afford. The TCU consortium alone made available nearly one million volumes and 7,500 serials which are delivered via a twice-daily shuttle between libraries. Any of more than three million volumes in fifty regional college and university libraries can be located by the on-line catalog and can be used through interlibrary loan.[35]

Although services were modern, the perennial student complaints were still heard. Hours were too short and noise too great. The ubiquitous Sony Walkman, another technological marvel of the new age played at distracting volume levels, added to the hubbub. The academically minded coped by retreating to the solitude of second-and third-floor stacks, while the socially inclined encamped on the first floor and in the "fish bowl," (the former reading room now occupied by personal computers).[36]

President Paul J. Dovre, 1975 –

Academic programs were expanded and retooled to meet the vocational desires of this generation of career-minded collegians. In 1975 the catalog advertised majors in thirty-three areas, with minors available in most. By 1989, partly through more careful counting and adding specialized variations to existing programs, the college listed fifty-one majors. Twenty teaching majors, ten teaching licensures and an undetermined number of minors were also offered. In 1975 music, biology, elementary education and business administration were the majors most frequently chosen by graduating seniors; by 1988, business was by far the most popular followed by biology and communications. Education still claimed 20 percent of the graduates annually. By stating that vocational preparation was a major reason for attending college and by prominently displaying professional and pre-professional courses of study, the catalog frankly addressed vocational concerns foremost in the minds of most Cobbers. Nor need the undecided be uneasy; the school provided career information, testing and counseling to assist vocational choice. Advisers then gave the necessary direction.[37]

Because of the many business majors, it became an administrative priority to strengthen that department. A special effort was made to improve communication with the business community. Toward that end, retired Fargo businessman P. James Onstad was named executive-in-residence in 1986. His duties were to serve as a liaison between the department and businesses, assist in promoting and executing department programs and advise the faculty. Similarly, a council of business advisers—comprised of local and regional executives in addition to departmental members—was formed the following year. Both sides benefited; business had the chance to influence education and thereby Concordia gained practical experience.[38]

Professor Susan Johnson demonstrates for nursing students.

Health professions were another burgeoning area of the 1980s. By 1984 the college offered professional preparation in medical technology, hospital administration, healthcare financial management and long-term administration; it also provided pre-professional education for dentistry, medicine, veterinary medicine, optometry, nursing, chiropractic, physical and occupational therapy, and food and nutrition. Health profession majors supplemented their formal academic training with actual work experience. The placement rate in professional schools of more than twice the national average was cited as evidence of program quality. Between 1981 and 1989, 125 Cobbers were placed in medical schools; in 1983 the placement rate in dentistry and optometry reached 90 percent. After an absence of more than two decades, nursing reappeared. In 1978 Dean Hartdagen worked out an agreement with Mary College in Bismarck which allowed up to five Cobbers to transfer to that nursing program for their junior and senior years. Then in 1985 a bachelor's degree in nursing was offered in cooperation with North Dakota State University and St. Luke's Hospitals. Dr. Lois Nelson, who served as project director during the planning year, was named chairperson.[39]

Health professions and cooperative education attract many Cobbers.

The Tri-College University and practical work experience are advertised as important elements in Concordia's academic program. Cooperative education, a program whereby juniors and seniors earned a maximum of two credits for an approved work experience, returned to Concordia in 1974 after an absence of several years; the former five-year business administration program had disappeared during the Vietnam draft. Directed by E. Daniel McKenna, cooperative education enrolled twenty-eight that first year. When it celebrated its tenth anniversary, placements had expanded to 290 and more than 30 percent of the graduates had participated. Similarly, TCU expanded opportunities for Cobbers. Besides the baccalaureate degree in nursing, the consortium recognized minors earned through the course exchange and jointly conducted economic education and environmental studies centers. Chinese and Japanese were first offered in Fall 1986. Others regularly have taken engineering, ROTC and special education.[40]

Concordia outreach programs, serving Fargo-Moorhead and the region, exemplify Christian academic community in service to others. CHARIS and Communiversity continue to flourish under the leadership of Arland Jacobson who replaced James Hofrenning as director in 1983. When Communiversity celebrated its twenty-fifth anniversary in 1990 almost 20,000 people had registered for nearly 650 courses taught by more than 900 instructors. This cornerstone of continuing education has served as a model for similar programs in other locations. Founded in 1970, CHARIS initially enrolled ninety-five clergy from eleven church bodies in seven theological courses. During the next decade, more than 1,500 clergy, professionals and laity from more than twenty-five church bodies registered

Author Garrison Keillor spoke to Communiversity Convocation on its twenty-fifth anniversary.

for 160 courses. In 1979, 4,862 people participated in CHARIS-sponsored events including Communiversity. That the program spawned imitators, including the Shalom Center at Augustana, additionally testified to its success. Under the direction of James Hofrenning in cooperation with the ALC and several denominational bodies, the first annual Summer Conference on Theology and Ministry was held in 1977. Other Hofrenning-initiated programs included a Lay Theological Conference, the FM Lay Academy, occasional seminars for laity and a Ministry for Youth.[41]

The Concordia Leadership Center, established in 1987, was directed by professor of speech John Burtis, funded by the West Central Minnesota Initiative Fund of Fergus Falls and operated in conjunction with the Reflective Leadership Center at the Hubert H. Humphrey Institute of Public Affairs at the University of Minnesota. The office has offered workshops, networking opportunities and leadership resources for individuals in the region. Even Cobbers might benefit through the Leadership Encounter Series, a series of Saturday morning workshops initiated in Fall 1989 to teach student leaders.[42]

Through all its agencies of outreach, Concordia College adds considerably to the culture of the Red River Valley. Two other services are a significant cultural resource. The annual Northlight Writers Conference, founded and directed by English professor W. Scott Olsen, was termed "wonderful" by many of the 135 participants who gathered for the third such event held in February 1990. KCCM, the first outstate station established by Minnesota Public Radio and housed at Concordia since 1971, broadcasts "Concordia Today"—a thirty-minute daily program of chapel and music—and twenty-four hours daily of excellent classical music and public affairs programming for the region.[43]

Multicultural Education

Multicultural education, already a significant part of Concordia's academic program when *Agenda* urged attention to gender, global interdependence and ethnic studies, grew in importance as the institution moved toward its second century. As reflected by expanding programs and breadth of concerns, the college indeed had moved a long way from ethnic ghetto toward global community.

The Women's Center, descendant of the earlier Women's Awareness Association, advertised itself in 1976 as a place rather than an organization; thus it provided "a safe place for women who feel a need for help, comfort or support from other women." The center additionally offered workshops, lectures and materials on women's issues and careers. It sponsored an appearance in 1978 by Marilyn Preus, local feminist and church woman, who spoke on "Feminism and Biblical Tradition." Preus defined feminism as "a radical social critique which ... for Christians ... is a contemporary reformation."[44]

The *Concordian* occasionally has expressed feminist views. A 1980 editorial documented the male domination at Concordia; the Student Association, President's Council and thirteen of twenty-four academic departments were exclusively male. There were only thirty-two women (21.9 percent) among a faculty of 146. Two years later an editorialist urged the hiring of a female pastor and counselor because there were some matters women wanted to discuss only with other women. This issue was raised again in 1985.[45]

Administrators were not insensitive to feminist concerns. A sexual harassment policy, adopted in November 1985 in the hope that it would foster wider awareness, established public guidelines for detecting harassment and making complaints. A concerted effort was made to recruit women. Between 1983 and 1989, 51 percent of the persons placed in tenure-eligible positions were women. Consequently their numbers increased to sixty-nine, 36 percent of the faculty in 1989. Women became steadily more visible in the administration: longtime Associate Director of Development Rosalie Lier (1969–1987), Assistant Placement Director Sylvia Lell (1975), Director of Communications Louise Nettleton (1978), Associate Dean of Students Barbara Eiden-Molinaro (1979), Auxiliary Services Director Jane Grant Shambaugh (1979), Presidential Assistant Esther Allen (1984), Controller Linda Brown (1985), Associate Dean Linda Johnson (1985) succeeded by Virginia Coombs (1990), Director of Continuing Education Michele McRae (1986) and Concordia Language Village Director Christine Schulze (1989).[46]

Barbara Eiden-Molinaro

To provide a network of resources for female students, a women's awareness weekend was scheduled in 1986. Sixteen alumnae shared experiences; Joyce Monson Tsongas ('63), president of trial consultants Tsongas and Associates, delivered the keynote address. The conference was again held in 1988. Meanwhile, women's studies steadily advanced in the curriculum encouraged by the *Agenda* requirement and by recently employed female professors.[47]

Concordia similarly has been committed to attaining the ELCA goal of inclusiveness by fostering the education of ethnic minorities. An office of intercultural affairs, recently renamed "multicultural affairs" to reflect a greater emphasis on pluralism, has been headed by Walter McDuffy since 1983. The office provides specialized assistance to minority students and

Christine Schulze

Walter McDuffy

plans activities to promote better understanding among various cultures. Despite this institutional commitment and aggressive recruiting, the number of African-American students has decreased from its peak of seventy-five (1973) to only nine (1989). Many reasons account for this drop. Although the college experienced its share of racial tension culminating in a black student strike in 1976, these problems did not lead to an exodus of African-Americans from Concordia. Instead the numbers eroded through graduation. This decline made it even more difficult to attract newcomers to an all-white campus in an all-white community. The occurrence of ugly racial incidents at many predominantly white universities in recent years has aroused fears among potential recruits about the lack of a support group on a possibly hostile campus. For this and other reasons, there has been a shift within the black community to a greater emphasis on attending colleges closer to home or the historic black colleges.

President Paul J. Dovre, 1975 –

Consequently, the college decided in 1986 to shift its recruiting emphasis and renew its efforts among Native Americans, the largest minority in its region. By 1989, minority numbers had increased to fifty-seven with Indians and Asians as the largest groups; eighty-five international students from seventeen different countries were also enrolled.[48]

Throughout the 1970s, human relations days were a primary vehicle of multicultural education. Initially classes were canceled to schedule special lectures, discussions and events promoting a greater awareness of the contributions and lifestyles of various racial, cultural and economic groups. Unfortunately, most Cobbers viewed the day as a vacation. In 1978 the day was reorganized; scheduled classes focused on human relations appropriate to each department in hopes that more collegians would benefit. These hopes were ill-founded, and human relations day soon faded. Black history week, sponsored by the office of multicultural affairs, continues to be observed, however. Even that event often provokes snide racist remarks or else is completely ignored by an apathetic white majority.[49]

Actress Cassiete West commemorated Martin Luther King's birthday.

Although charges of racism persisted in the late 1970s, they largely faded with the dwindling of African-American enrollment in the 1980s. Black students of the new decade admit initial cultural shock in encountering an environment with little diversity, but say they feel accepted. Their limited number notwithstanding, they have provided significant cultural education, as in 1983, when Karen Cherry ('83) and Cassiete West ('84) initiated and produced Ntzoke Shange's *For Colored Girls Who Have Considered Suicide/When the Rainbow is Enuf* in commemoration of King's birthday.[50]

Native American recruiting has waxed, waned and waxed again. In 1975–1976 when Minnesota private colleges together enrolled 174 Indians, seventy-four of them in their first year, eight attended Concordia. For the preceding five years numbers had fluctuated between ten and fifteen, most of whom came from the Dakotas. Two Native Americans had worked as counselors and recruiters but neither increased enrollment. The college provided supportive services for the marginally qualified. Academic loads were reduced for the first year; courses were scheduled for which students had background; and their teachers were alerted. Gillian Hennesy, newly hired as Indian counselor in January 1977, bluntly assessed the situation at that time. She desired an active Indian program or none. As it then existed, it benefited neither Indians nor whites. Because of the dwindling numbers, she advised unhappy collegians to transfer to schools where there were more Indians and better programs. At that time only four were enrolled and the program almost disappeared. Nonetheless Indian awareness weeks continued intermittently, either sponsored by Concordia or by the Tri-College University.[51]

In 1987 Warner Huss began his work as Native American representative. Despite competition from other educational and military recruiters and the financial barrier of private school costs, twenty-three were enrolled by Fall 1988 and fourteen had

Warner Huss talks with students Calvin Walks Over Ice and Romee Trottier.

graduated by Spring 1990. Although these collegians occasionally have encountered racist remarks on campus, they generally have liked Concordia. The Indian Awareness Club, comprised of 50 percent non-Indian members, provides a forum for discussion of racial incidents and problems of cultural adjustment and offers educational programs for the white majority in public schools and at the college. In 1990 the McKnight Foundation granted $269,400 to Concordia for increasing the numbers of Native American students and staff and for designing the Native American lecturer-in-residence program, which will bring ten notables to spend separate one-week residences on campus each semester.[52]

In addition to women's and minorities education, the college expanded an already strong international studies program. In 1977 Lester Meyer began teaching a two-semester sequence in Biblical Hebrew. The following year, a three-year, $45,000 grant from the Fargo-based Alex Stern Family Foundation funded a program in Judaic studies. Visiting Jewish scholars served as resource persons and offered courses for interested students and faculty. The faculty senate approved an interdisciplinary Scandinavian studies minor; Joan Buckley and Verlyn Anderson started negotiations for an exchange with Hamar Teachers College, located in Fargo's sister city of Hamar, Norway. The first students went in 1982 and the exchange is now operating success-fully. In addition, the library offers assistance on Norwegian genealogy, and librarian Anderson has taken groups to Norway for the Red River Valley Heritage Society.[53]

Language villages grew phenomenally, earning Concordia a national reputation for language study. The two-week Winter Abroad Program in the Soviet Union began in 1976. In 1984 plans were announced for a Chinese village, the first of its kind in the nation, sponsored by a fund established by longtime history professor Herman Larsen in memory of his wife, Ruth. When a Japanese village was established in 1988, Minnesota Governor Rudy Perpich commented, "We are very fortunate to have in

President Paul J. Dovre, 1975 –

Minnesota such a program. ..." That same year, gifts totaling more than $1 million from the Rockefeller, Harrison and Fish families, all of whom had children in the program, made it possible to begin construction on the $2 million French Language Village at the Turtle River site near Bemidji. Following the pattern for authenticity established by the Norwegian and German facilities, architecture would be in the Bretagne style of the French west coast.[54]

When Odell Bjerkness, director since 1971, and Alvin Traaseth, coordinator since 1972, resigned in Spring 1989, they could point to sustained and remarkable expansion. Enrollment had grown from 1,180 (1972) to 4,263 (1988), with another 2,300 attending weekend mini-camps during the school

The German Institute offers total immersion language study.

year. Fulltime employees had increased from two to forty-one, villages from five to ten, and the budget from $275,000 to more than $3.6 million. Permanent villages had been established for Norwegian, German and French. No wonder Charles Kuralt called the language villages one of the most innovative language programs in the country in a cover story on "CBS News Sunday Morning" in July 1987. An August 1990 story in *Time* provided additional national recognition.[55]

Institute students work with German language materials.

The Institute of German Studies, another indication of Concordia's leadership in language study, opened in Fall 1983 at *Schwarzwald Haus.* A total immersion experience for college credit, the Institute features German library materials, instruction and daily conversation. When the program was reviewed in 1986, the evaluation team was impressed with evidence of language fluency, but expressed reservations about communal values. They recommended improvement in these areas: increased numbers of sophomores and juniors from Moorhead; better integration of faculty and program with the college; and strengthened community through more attention to counseling, student services and religious life. Once these suggestions were implemented, then feasibility studies would begin for an Institute of French Studies.[56]

Overseas study opportunities similarly expanded. By 1988, approximately one-third of the graduates had participated in May Seminars. Others had experienced more extended study in programs ranging from the summertime Caesarea Maritima archeological expedition to practicums in several countries conducted by the foreign language departments and various exchanges with Hong Kong, Norway and Tanzania. Study options had become sufficiently numerous and significant by October 1986 that the senate established an overseas study task force. As a result of their report a World Discovery Program—headed by political science professor Peter Hovde—was created to monitor, enhance and expand opportunities for study abroad. Meanwhile, a three-year development project in global studies—also directed by Hovde and funded by the Consortium for Advancement of Private Higher Education—provided a solid foundation for further expansion. The project defined global studies as "the interdisciplinary and value-reflective teaching and research about problems global in nature," conducted two workshops and funded global studies projects undertaken by forty faculty.[57]

Achieving Academic Mission

Concordia had an impressive array of programs and personnel—but were these sufficient to attain the lofty goals of the institutional academic mission? Despite perennial professorial complaints about increasingly ill-prepared students and about a "happy Cobber" ethos that discourages serious academic work, evidence suggests considerable achievement. Indeed, the North Central Review Report in 1983 identified mission as a distinctive strength. The report characterized faculty as "solid professionals" and the governance as effective. The report concluded that given the strength of institutional planning, the strong commitment of dedicated personnel and students and the presence of talented leadership, Concordia would continue to accomplish its academic purpose.[58]

Collegians also gave evidence of adopting academic goals. An educational consultant who visited the campus in 1975 observed, "The dimension of Concordia which

David Hetland's "Inquiry" challenges all who enter Ylvisaker Library.

impresses me most is the mutual respect which faculty and students have for one another." Speaking at the 1988 Honors Convocation on "The Irritation of Doubt," senior Stephanie J. Moen took her title from the C.S. Peirce quotation adorning the Hetland mosaic in the library. For her, the quote challenged Cobbers both to attain a state of belief and to maintain the irritation of doubt as a motive for learning throughout their lives. Moen expressed gratitude both for the opportunity to learn and to develop a style of learning; Concordia through its curriculum and activities had demanded fulfillment for her inquiring mind.

Even critics revealed a commitment to academic mission when they identified ways in which the institution fell short. A 1988 editorial, written in the spirit of improving teaching, listed six shortcomings of professors. In two features for the 1989 annual, collegians even pointed out ways in which their own foibles obstructed academic mission. "Study Habits Are Not Always So Productive" discussed the widely practiced fine art of procrastination brought on by an enhanced interest in social life. "Lectures Can Be Enriching" named those professors who offered cake and cookies as the lure for always-hungry Cobbers. [59]

Senior Stephanie Moen addresses the 1988 honors convocation.

Moreover, much evidence suggested that attending college made considerable difference in graduates. A Carnegie Commission Report issued in the 1970s identified a widening gap between those who attended and those who did not. Attenders acquired new knowledge, skills and attitudes; they used printed media more often, were more aware of world events and more conscious of how society works; they were more open-minded, less authoritarian and more inclined to support civil liberties. Research by Herbert S. Hyman and Charles R. Wright in the 1980s found a correlation between levels of schooling and the amount of general and specific information that a person possessed; more schooling also fostered more humane values about civil liberties, due process of law, freedom of information and equal opportunity. Despite charges by elitist critics about the shortcomings of American education, evidence suggested outcomes that were valuable to individual graduates and to society at large. [60]

Similarly, instructional assessment revealed that Cobbers changed significantly during their college years. Their communication skills improved and their appreciation for religious and cultural diversity increased. Alumni surveyed ten years after graduation displayed a comparable esteem for diversity. They emphasized the importance of developing personal values and were sensitive to how moral beliefs shape contemporary issues and one's own actions. They were also strongly attached to Concordia; 84 percent had visited in the decade since their commencement and 70 percent would enroll again if they could start over. [61]

On the basis of accreditation evaluators, personal testimony and institutional assessment surveys, the college thus can be assured that many Cobbers were sent forth with an education and a commitment to influence the world on God's behalf.

Chapter 19

Nurturing Christian Community

A Caring Place

In his 1987 annual report Vice President for Student Affairs Morris Lanning wrote, "As a college of the church, Concordia strives to care for its students as God would have us do." For Lanning, that meant living in a Christian community committed to educating the whole person; his office enhanced "the spiritual, intellectual, physical, social and emotional growth in students that will help them achieve the fullest development of personality and life." This demanded that Cobbers be challenged and yet nurtured by Christian care and support.[1]

The 1988 *Cobber* concurred with these official views: "Concordia is unique because of the feeling of community" and its goal of "shaping ... the complete person." Taking the Concordia hymn as its text for defining the institution, the 1983 *Cobber* maintained that the school is a place to grow on the firm foundation of the Christian faith surrounded by dedicated people.[2]

*Vice President
Morris Lanning*

The clubs, activities and beanies encountered by newcomers during orientation week each fall are designed to foster Christian community. According to Dean Lanning, "the C on the beanies stands for community." In describing the games played as a club activity, 1989 orientation chair Max Richter ('90) clearly stated their purpose: "Playfair meets our need for community-building. And community is a total feeling that Concordia possesses." The point is not lost on incoming freshmen. As one described her feelings in 1989, "I really did feel a sense of community during Playfair. It was almost as though we were becoming a great big family."[3]

Orientation clubs watch an attempted shopping cart jump of Prexy's Pond.

Exactly! The more than forty clubs for freshmen and transfers annually serve as family while activities furnish information, fun and a chance to meet new friends. Fun is much in evidence and administrators willingly participate. Over the

340   President Paul J. Dovre, 1975 –

years, Dovre and Lanning have appeared at the opening meeting in Memorial Auditorium as the Blues Brothers, Crocodile Dundee and Rambo, and the Joker and Batman. Upperclassmen are not to be outdone. In 1979 Orientation Club "51," a group of nine seniors led by Student Association President Dan Hofrenning ('80), outfitted themselves in scuba gear for their historic plunge into recently renovated Prexy's Pond. Later in the week, Chi Delt Society President Scott Larson ('82) failed in his attempt to jump the pond in a shopping cart.[4]

Concordia as Christian community seeks to promote godly living through an educational process of encouraging some behaviors and restricting others. No longer so numerous or stringent compared to the heyday of *in loco parentis*, college regulations are still affirmed by administrators and still resented by some undergraduates. What the former regard as necessary limits for communal life, the latter view as an unwarranted restriction on individual freedom. Freshmen and sophomores must live in residence halls; alcohol, drugs and gambling are forbidden; alcohol use off campus and smoking are discouraged; birth control devices are not distributed; and intervisitation in each dormitory is limited to specified times subject to approval of the dean of students.[5] Of all regulations, the last has been the most irritating to many Cobbers.

For almost two decades, Student Association presidents often have been elected on platforms that feature expanding intervisitation. Armed with periodic survey results showing that majorities of varying amounts are dissatisfied and want hours increased, they have presented their case to administrators and regents who have given them respectful hearings. Tactics have ranged from the confrontational by President Woody Fuller T ('78) to the "unantagonistic open discussion" by President Hemchand Gossai ('79). The student argument affirms their right to a balance between privacy and relationship. They reject any appeal to theology because dwelling on justification and sanctification stresses evil, lack of trust and sin. They insist that a reasonable opportunity to communicate with the opposite sex would lead to better awareness and understanding, not promiscuity. In defending its policy, the administration states the need for preserving privacy, promoting academic study on weeknights and cultivating a sense of moral responsibility. For all their effort on this issue, student leaders have been rewarded on various occasions with incremental expansions of hours from eight (1976) to the present twenty-eight weekly for the underclass dormitories. Although these hours are the fewest among ELCA colleges, Concordia offers more liberal options to upperclass students than most of its sister institutions. These range from the on-campus Bogstad apartments, where visitation hours total forty-nine per week, to off-campus living for 40 percent of the student body where they may establish their own visitation patterns.[6]

Birth control has been another issue on which Cobbers sometimes have agitated. In keeping with its educational and religious mission, the college provides birth control and pregnancy counseling upon request but does not dispense birth control devices, asserting premarital chastity as an ideal worth encouraging for reasons of health and morality. If they desire birth control assistance, Cobbers are referred elsewhere or can simply walk across Eighth Street to Foster's Pharmacy or Twelfth Avenue to Moorhead South Clinic. Naturally, some find these policies unnecessarily archaic, restrictive and expensive.[7]

Other healthful life styles based on Christian values are promoted. In the face of alcoholism and the omnipresence of alcohol in American society, the college has encouraged an alternative life style. As it always has been, alcohol use is prohibited on campus. Toward this end, the administration steadfastly opposes personal refrigerators in the dormitories. As part of an institutional alcohol education effort, the chemical awareness and responsibility committee (CARes) has conducted "coolers" featuring nonalcoholic beverages, as well as alcohol and wellness weeks. In 1984 the

The CARes committee promotes healthful living.

committee established peer health educators who foster health and well being by offering confidential non-diagnostic information and referral services. That same year a lifestyle improvement program began. LIMP, as one wag has called the program, schedules a wide variety of exercise activities for all collegians and college personnel. The Cobber Club, a recently purchased health club in south Moorhead, has become an important instrument for promoting healthful living. Used by more than 60 percent of the students during 1988–1989, it received nearly 36,000 visits. Cobber Cooler South operates as a health-awareness refreshment center and serves nonalcoholic drinks at club social activities. The smoking policy established in Fall 1988 returned to the practice of almost a half century before. Smoking is again restricted to specified campus areas.[8]

Thus the rules of the founders have been validated. Use of alcohol and tobacco, often opposed by Norwegian-American pietists only on moral grounds, is now discouraged primarily in the name of healthful living.

In keeping with the personal concern characteristic of a Christian community, counseling services have been expanded. Appropriately, campus pastor Carl Lee also serves as director of counseling and carries a fulltime counseling load. His office has had a working relationship with a psychiatric consultant for two decades and is now connected with the Fargo Clinic's Neuroscience Clinic in order to provide more immediate professional assistance. An educational counseling center (ECC) established in 1977 has offered career, academic and personal counseling to "help students become more aware of their interests, goals, and abilities; explore educational and vocational options; and decide which choices are best for them." As a means towards these goals, ECC sponsored twenty personal life seminars during Fall 1989. These ranged from a week on study skills to managing homesickness and writing research papers.[9]

By 1985, twenty-one people on the student affairs staff did some counseling; twelve had professional training. In addition, 200 students were trained as peer counselors. All these services are used by Cobbers; almost one-fourth utilized ECC in 1987–1988. Academic counselors had worked with 208 students, helping them improve their performance. Peer health educators met with nearly 500 on a wide range of personal concerns.[10]

Dormitories, another important part of the non-classroom environment, offered many opportunities for educating whole persons. Professionally trained directors, assisted by student staff, plan numerous social-educational programs to promote community and social growth among approximately 60 percent the student body. The housing office assists others in finding appropriate off-campus accommodations. Even the food service is considered part of the educational environment. Aware of strong student preferences, the cafeteria furnishes a variety of choices and services. Concerned about the social aspects of eating, it schedules an all-college dinner almost monthly. The dinner is served smorgasbord-style with decorations and entertainment by campus organizations.[11]

President Paul J. Dovre, 1975 –

A Christian Milieu

Concordia as a Christian community continues to be characterized by extensive religious activities and a lively Christian atmosphere. Periodically community members present their image of what this atmosphere ought to be. A graphic symbol created by David Hetland in 1979 utilizes the letters CC over MM in the pattern of a butterfly, a traditional symbol of resurrection; its cloverleaf symmetry suggests the unity and balance of life in Christ. Quickly employed on stationery and in nearly all publications, the symbol was adopted as the floor plan for different levels of the Normandy remodeling in 1987, reinforcing its hold on campus imagination.[12]

In a 1980 chapel talk, philosopher Thomas Christenson expressed his vision of the need for questions in a Christian academy. Unfortunately, Christians hear only rhetorical questions in church. These answers disguised as queries are only occasions for affirmation, itself quite meaningless for lack of an opportunity to say no. Instead, utilizing biblical models such as Psalm 77 for raising serious doubts, the church college ought to be a place for honest questioning within the life of faith. It ought to be a place where we admit our confusion and probe the depth of our ignorance.[13]

Similarly, Professor Olin Storvick followed the Danforth Commission typology in characterizing Concordia as a "free Christian college" in which freedom of inquiry provides the context for taking seriously questions of faith.

Concordia College's butterfly logo.

Storvick even suggested that when an institution stops raising questions about its religious mission, it has probably lost its sense of mission.[14]

Artist, philosopher and classicist thus set high standards for religious atmosphere and life only partially met by Concordia as a Christian community. Nonetheless, the community has shared many questions, much discussion, ample activity and the hope of becoming better.

The Centrum has provided an appropriate worship setting for a Christian community whose graduates are educated for service in the world. Designed by campus architect E.A. Sövik, the building reflects his rejection of the otherworldly monumentalism of traditional church architecture and his belief that Christian structures should serve the community. Instead of holy places, they ought to be multipurpose spaces where the church can carry out Jesus's message of ministering to the daily life and needs of people. Although life is contingent, through the Christian message the church supplies the comfort of permanence in a world of change. For this reason beauty should be present, because it is a mystery that can move people to a sense of wonder and open portals to the transcendent. Appropriately, therefore, the Centrum's Holtkamp Organ was dedicated in 1976 by a beautiful program of organ and voice performed by the husband-wife team of Donald Sutherland and alumna Phyllis Bryn-Julson. No wonder campus pastors Carl Lee and Ernie Mancini in the same year praised the Centrum as a setting for chapel. They shared architect Sövik's view that worship should not be an

Chapel is held daily in the Centrum, a multipurpose space designed for community service.

isolated part of life; Lee especially appreciated the Centrum's warmth and light which conveyed a closer feeling of togetherness.[15] After Lee's years at the foot of the mountain in the cavernous field house, his feelings are understandable.

The campus pastor remains central to campus religious life and the institutional ideology of the Concordia family. Workload became so great that the position expanded to a team ministry. Lowell Almen came as halftime associate pastor in 1969; after he departed, Ernie Mancini became the first fulltime associate pastor in 1975. Pastor Lynn Ronsberg served as interim pastor upon Mancini's departure in 1983 until Pastor Phil Holtan was called in 1984. With the help of the religion (renamed "campus ministry") commission, the pastors "are responsible for fostering and encouraging the development of a worshipping, learning, ministering, and witnessing community of faith within the context of the academic community." They have shared the burden of expanded counseling services, headed by Lee. Their joint ministry has personified active caring. The family feeling generated by this "loving team" was evidenced in the appreciation night for Ernie Mancini upon his departure in 1983. The evening took the form of a love feast and roast in Memorial Auditorium before moving to the Centrum for an ice cream social. During the roast, President Dovre ironically ad-

*Alumni Director
Ernie Mancini*

monished Mancini for his retiring and shy personality; he advised him to be more assertive and outgoing in his next position. While the crowd flanked the sidewalks as it had for the visit of the Norwegian King, Cobbers waving Italian flags escorted Ernie and his spouse Diane to the Centrum, followed by their gift of a canoe and motor.[16]

In February 1986 Pastor Lee was honored for twenty-five years of service. "Carl Lee Day" was proclaimed in chapel, a trip for two to Hawaii was awarded, and

President Dovre gave a special tribute to the dean of ALC and LCA campus pastors. Dovre credited Lee for bringing uncommon stability and attributed his longevity to an effectiveness in living and preaching the gospel. Lee ascribed his staying power to the support of God and family: "Knowing that campus ministry has caring support of ministry partners, presidents, students and staff helps ease the load; it seems together we carry the burden." Lee gave special credit to Presidents Dovre and Knutson: "Both Joe and Paul have given a strong sense of priority to campus ministry as being the heart and center of Concordia and they have been so supportive and involved." Reflecting on his career as a counselor, Lee noted many similarities between needs of present-day students and those in 1961; nonetheless he believed stress was greater, as evidenced by more eating disorders, anxiety and depression. Family instability and desire for a good job with consequent pressure for high academic achievement were contributing factors. While sympathetic to the call for academic excellence, Lee feared that by overemphasizing academics some Cobbers might miss many benefits of a liberal arts education. To ease stress, Lee urged enhancing the supportive family aspects of the Concordia community.[17]

Pastors Phil Holtan and Carl Lee minister to the campus community.

The pastors coordinate participation in a myriad of activities. Worship is still "viewed as the center of life and work." Although chapel attendance ebbs and flows from year to year, it has been complemented by the large crowds—ranging between 400 and 1,000—who regularly participate in Wednesday night communions. Indeed, collegians from other Lutheran institutions are often amazed at the high level of participation and activities at Concordia.

For religious programming, the pastors are assisted by the Student Association campus ministries commission. Desiring to nurture Cobbers in building "bridges of faith to God and to the community," the commission annually coordinates many activities—chapels, midweek communions, Bible studies, tabernacles, retreats, residence hall devotions, clown ministry and community service. No wonder the 1983 *Cobber* could report that "a certain spirituality pervades every aspect of Concordia life."[18]

Wednesday night communion, a well-attended experiential service.

To meet spiritual needs, midweek communions involve Cobbers in the service and employ a variety of worship forms—traditional, candlelight, joyous temple band and nontraditional clowning. This popular experiential service is unique among ELCA colleges and reaches the greatest proportion of the student body. It expresses the hospitality and the "tight-boundedness" of the Concordia communal spirit; visitors often remark that they sense "a warm supporting community." Besides its primary task of appearing at Wednesday night communion, the temple band—formed in 1975 as musicians of the temple who spread the word of God to people through contemporary Christian music—often performs at fall orientation services of celebration, tabernacles, family weekends, church youth days and Christian scholar days.[19]

Ideally, devotional life nurtures Christian service. In the past, this often took the form of sponsoring missionaries and mission work; today it is expressed somewhat differently. Since 1975, Bread and Cheese has studied world hunger; the annual Lenten offering has aided a number of overseas self-help projects. In 1982, a typical year, Cobbers raised $6,000 and distributed it to Operation Bootstrap, directed by alumnus Rev. David Simonson, for building a school in Tanzania; to a project for establishing fish farms to restore the traditional livelihood to Hong Kong fishermen; and to Somalia camps for helping refugees become self-supporting. Thanksgiving ingatherings support others in need. In a unique cooperative effort with Moorhead's First Congregational Church, the $4,000 raised in 1979 sponsored a Laotian family of five. Four years later, the thanksgiving offering supported Vietnamese refugees. In 1989 the $1,071 gathered was divided equally between the Dorothy Day House and Churches United for the Homeless. In addition, Cobbers have continued their longstanding ministry to the neighboring White Earth reservation; during 1989–1990 they also aided Native American children in Fargo schools.[20]

A Cobber volunteer visits a friend in a local nursing home.

The recent growth of volunteer services is remarkable. During 1986–1987, about 150 volunteers helped as big brothers-big sisters and in nursing homes, hospitals and the Dorothy Day House. The next year more than 600 aided others, including 100 who worked in homeless shelters. In 1990 a coordinator was appointed, and the program restructured and renamed. Sources for Service (SOS) promotes "service learning" by engaging collegians in meaningful tasks and by helping them integrate these with their studies and career aspirations.[21]

Conservative evangelicals remain a significant presence among the student body. Their biblical literalism and conservative cultural beliefs occasionally lead to complaints about the historical-critical study of the Bible undertaken in required religion courses and public condemnation of rock music, homosexuality, abortion and extramarital sex. These attitudes sometimes lead to *Concordian* debates with other collegians.[22]

Although outreach team membership has recently declined from approximately 200 to 125, team activity remains important for these Cobbers. Outreach members meet weekly for Bible study, traveling teams visit churches within 200 miles and fellowship teams minister to groups in the Fargo-Moorhead area. The annual New

Horizons Conference disappeared during the 1980s. Faith Haven Retreats, attended by more than 100 each fall and winter, focus on a particular aspect of Christian life. Spirit Song Promotions for a time brought Christian artists to campus. Thus in April 1987 Debbie Boone shared her Christian music with a crowd of about 800 much as her father, evangelist Pat Boone, had years before. Tabernacles, which schedule various groups to share God's word through song, skits or personal testimony, are particularly favored by outreach team members. As one observer described them, the small area in which they are held "makes these gatherings more intimate and increases the feelings of excitement and love for Christ."[23]

Political Attitudes and Activities

In recent years Cobbers have displayed less interest in politics and political issues than in Christian activity and service. To be sure, the "campus radical" still occasionally appears in the *Concordian*. Mark Hinton's "Marksism" column in Fall 1980, for example, insisted that too much energy, talent and intelligence were wasted fighting the local rules instead of addressing the important world issues. In another, the columnist discussed the compatibility of socialism and Christianity in opposition to the then-popular argument by fundamentalists that American Christianity and capitalism were parts of a unified system ordained by God. In 1987 eight Cobbers protested an appearance by a CIA recruiter. Allowed in the Centrum if they did not disrupt, the group silently held signs saying "CIA Oppresses" and "Concordia + CIA = Morality." *Concordian* columnist Max Gulias ('91) argued in 1989 that the workers' rejection of communist regimes did not necessarily mean the triumph of capitalism in Eastern Europe. During the next semester Gulias joined Peter Engen ('93) in reviving the socialist club for the purpose of political discussion.[24]

If radical politics were almost nonexistent, mainstream politics are more evident. The Student Association sometimes has conducted "political awareness weeks" to involve Cobbers with the issues of the real world. The number and frequency of these have varied with election years and the political interests of SA officers. In November 1979 Republican presidential hopefuls George Bush and John Connally both spoke at a testimonial dinner for congressional candidate Arlan Stangeland. After his speech, Bush answered questions from a gathering of 150 collegians. Governor Al Quie met with local and area groups to discuss issues when Moorhead became "Capital for a Day." The following fall, Student Association sponsored an awareness day featuring a debate between congressional candidates Gene Wenstrom and Arlan Stangeland. Awareness weeks have been held only intermittently thereafter. Spanish week in November 1986 featured an address by the area representative of Amnesty International and a panel on Nicaragua. STAND (Students to Advocate Nuclear Disarmament) sponsored Nuclear Know More Week in 1988 to shape Cobber views on the arms race. The second annual Nobel Peace Prize Forum, held at Augsburg College in February 1990, attracted 175 Concordia students and staff.[25]

Minnesota Public Interest Research Group (MPIRG), active from 1972 to 1984 when it disbanded for lack of funds, promoted recycling and energy conservation. Recycling barrels for paper and aluminum cans appeared in Fall 1976. A 1979 summer study by Cobbers proposed a labor-intensive, minimal-mechanization recycling unit for Fargo-Moorhead. That same year MPIRG opened a small natural foods shop in the Cobber Bookstore and established an energy task force to influence college policy.

STEM (Students Toward Energy Management) aimed at lowering fuel costs to help reduce the rise in tuition rates. That spring MPIRG supported the Nestle boycott to prevent marketing baby formula in developing countries where a correlation existed between bottle-feeding and infant mortality. A year later, newspaper collection boxes were placed on every floor of Erickson-Hallet Halls. Red River Rehabilitation and Recycling collected and resold the papers. After MPIRG disbanded, recycling lapsed until Spring 1990 when students Rick Adkins ('90) and Kirk Johnson ('91), with administrative blessing, again initiated a campus-wide project for office paper and aluminum cans.[26]

Cobbers have exhibited fluctuating enthusiasm for national elections. The campaign of 1980 sparked more interest than usual. The *Concordian* carried several articles on candidates and platforms. One criticized the Republicans for reversing their stand of forty years and withdrawing endorsement of the Equal Rights Amendment. Another supported Reagan and the GOP platform. Others praised independent candidate John Anderson and the achievements of the Carter administration. The former two-to-one margin enjoyed by Republicans had not quite disappeared by 1980, but preferences based on party affiliation had changed. According to a poll conducted by a political science class of 414 randomly selected Cobbers, 35 percent would vote for John Anderson, 30 percent for Ronald Reagan and 23 percent for President Jimmy Carter. In party affiliation, 45 percent were still Republican, only 26 percent Democrat and 22 percent independent. Anderson drew support equally from all groups. Preferences almost returned to the normal two-to-one margin in 1984. According to the Student Association political and legislative affairs committee poll of 104 Cobbers, 61.6 percent favored President Reagan while only 36.6 percent supported Democrat Walter Mondale. Matters shifted again in 1988. The political affairs commission poll of 255 Cobbers revealed that 40.3 percent favored Democrat Michael Dukakis and 39.2 percent supported Republican George Bush. An unusually high 19.2 percent were undecided.[27]

The Expanding Extracurriculum

That Cobbers did not exhibit much interest in politics should not surprise. Students of the 1980s much resembled those of the 1950s; they were silent and career-minded. A higher percentage worked than formerly. With work and pursuit of academic achievement as the means to a good job, Cobbers had little time, energy or interest in political causes. Extracurricular—now called co-curricular—activities, however, were still valued for careerist reasons.

Student Association remains the hub for extracurricular life because many activities depend on it for funding and personnel. Cobbers are significantly involved in college governance. They assume important leadership positions in planning for fall orientation, homecoming, family weekend and other events. They hold voting membership on most standing committees of the faculty senate. They serve on many ad hoc committees, subcommittees, task forces and faculty evaluation committees. Collegians learn quickly that their political effectiveness depends upon establishing rapport with the administration and the board of regents. Channels exist for this purpose. Administrators and the regents are accessible. Summer student interns, chosen for their leadership ability and campus responsibilities, work with the administration on mutual concerns, learn how the college functions and develop leadership skills. The annual student-faculty retreat offers another opportunity for dialogue. At the same time, leaders attempt to serve their constituency and combat the perennial problem of student apathy. A student concerns board, formed in 1989 to enhance involvement, distributed a questionnaire which identified these as major concerns: housing, computer lab hours, financial aid, increased recreational space, a student forum on the centennial and a campus-wide attendance policy.[28] Clearly, these collegians are focused on matters of daily life; they are not out to change the world.

Organizations proliferated and membership expanded after 1976. This paralleled a national revival of Greek fraternities and sororities, a trend attributed by many observers to the lack of national issues compelling to youthful imaginations. Paradoxically, societies—long a mainstay of campus life at Concordia—declined from five to three brother-sister organizations: AKX-Mondamin, AES-LDS and Chi Zete-Chi Delt. AKX, the oldest sister society, faced extinction in 1979 with only two actives; it revived with thirteen pledges. Throughout the next decade, societies persisted in providing social events for their members until finally convinced by administrators in 1987 to construct new mission statements. The college wants them active throughout the year and not just during pledge season. Thus encouraged, they are attempting to increase community service and counteract the poor reputations acquired as a consequence of past hazing. As part of the new image, AKX-Mondamin in 1989 sponsored the second annual intersociety charity Christmas Ball to raise funds for Toys for Tots. The void created by the fading of societies has been filled by more than 150 organizations representing a wide spectrum of academic, social, dramatic, religious and athletic interests. These afford many opportunities for group involvement and leadership.[29]

The *Concordian* still offers valuable experience for aspiring journalists and sometimes serves as the collegiate conscience. Marla Temanson's 1989 editorial noted with not a little nostalgia that the *Concordian* was not the paper that it had been twenty years before when editors wrote thoughtful criticisms of college policy, local politics and national events. In contrast, she suggested, today's editorials are aimed at apathetic students rather than the restrictive rules. The editor offered to make the *Concordian* the voice of the student body, if collegians would only let the paper know what their views were. In her editorial on the fiftieth anniversary of the beginning of World War II in Europe, which most Cobbers and Americans ignored as isolationists had done a half century before, Temanson ('90) urged collegians to take seriously the institutional mission and become "thoughtful and informed about our world." After all, "the Christian life doesn't mean isolating ourselves in our comfortable campus."[30]

As they have been since the 1960s, editors are sensitive to any sign of administration censorship and are quick to wrap themselves in the mantle of the free press. It is noteworthy that alleged censorship has not prevented their rather frequent criticisms of the college, its regulations or its leaders. Desiring to be more than a bulletin board or public relations sheet, the *Concordian* has sought to promote the debate that should characterize an academic community. Over the years, faculty columns often have been attempted. "Beyond College 101" appeared in 1985, featuring faculty discussions of weekly topics. David Moewes opened with an essay on South Africa, "Are Economic Sanctions Wise Foreign Policy?" Jorge Roman-Lagunas's "The U.S. Role in Latin America" appeared the next week; then the feature quietly died, apparently from lack of material.[31]

Another effort, "Speaking Out," had a similar fate in 1982 but a more interesting history. This feature appeared as a consequence of *The Extra Mile*, a sharply critical underground newspaper published by nine seniors just before commencement in Spring 1982. The publication was much criticized by collegians and administrators alike because it appeared too late to permit dialogue on the issues raised. Hence, when school opened in the fall, the paper's editor urged that constructive discussion now take place. "Speaking Out" was an effort in that direction. President Dovre initiated the series with a column on the values of Concordia as a Christian community. Dovre's column provoked sharp response. Contrary to the president's views, several Cobbers maintained that Concordia was neither a contented nor homogeneous community based upon traditional values. They insisted that *The Extra Mile* was a legitimate avenue of expressing student concerns because the traditional means of the *Concordian* and Student Association were restricted by the administration and by student leaders who were not responsible to their constituents. Although "Speaking Out" soon disappeared and the lively exchange stimulated by *The Extra Mile* quickly faded, the feeling lingered among some collegians that the Concordia community handles criticism poorly. This attitude has not inhibited collegiate complaints or attempts to change institutional practices, however.[32]

Besides the *Concordian*, other opportunities for expression exist. A succession of literary magazines has appeared, each claiming to be the first at the college. *Lodestar*, featuring short stories, poems and graphics, was published in April 1978. It quickly went the way of earlier soon-forgotten efforts. *Afterwork*, first published in 1987, survives. It prints creative work—poetry, short stories and art—and the editors critique rejections, about three-fourths of the submissions, in order to provide feedback for

Professor Rusty Casselton assists an announcer in the KORD studio.

aspiring writers. *New Voices*, sponsored by the English department and edited by Professor Scott Olsen, appeared in 1988 for the purpose of publishing collegiate nonfiction work.[33]

With growing popularity of the communications major after its creation in 1975, other creative outlets soon appeared. The radio club organized in March 1979 restored a student-operated station. KORD—a closed-circuit broadcasting system initially located in the Fjelstad basement and later moved to the Olin Building—debuted in October 1980, featuring music, special events and live coverage of sports. By 1988 a KORD staff of sixty broadcast daily, dreamed of becoming an FM station and contributed to noise pollution each orientation week by blasting-out "spinning live" from the "beanie tent" for new frosh and unwilling professorial listeners. "Concordia Magazine," a student produced weekly TV program in a thirty minute talk show format, began in 1985. Featuring on-location segments, entertainment, news, sports and interviews, the show is broadcast in the Centrum every Friday afternoon and semiweekly over the Fargo-Moorhead community access cable television channels.[34]

An extensive theatre program, professionally directed by Jim and Helen Cermak, enriches college cultural life while annually teaching the craft to more than 250 Cobbers. Four faculty-directed plays, including a musical, comprise the main bill;

advanced students design scenery, lighting, sound and costumes, and manage business affairs. Experimental and readers theatre and student-produced plays in the laboratory program provide other opportunities. Developed by Clair Haugen in 1985, experimen-

tal theatre presents more challenging innovative works. For the summer dinner theatre held from 1980 to 1982 cast members served the meal and presented cabaret acts prior to the play. In January 1987 the department was honored to perform Helen Cermak's *The Wind Is a Color* for the American College Festival in Minneapolis.[35]

Concordia Magazine, a student-produced TV program.

During the 1980s, Director Fred Sternhagen shaped debate and forensics into high-ranked national programs. In 1987 the forensics team—competing in oral interpretation, extemporaneous speaking and oratory—won an overall second-place ranking in the Pi Kappa Delta National Forensic Tournament, with seven students achieving superior ratings. In Spring 1988, eight placed eighth overall in the American Forensic Association's National Individual Events Tournament. For the first time two debate teams qualified for the National Debate Tournament; individual teams had competed in 1967, 1968, 1973 and 1987. At this event, Concordia ranked thirteenth overall among seventy-two teams. The Courtney Ward ('89)-Joseph Schmitt ('89) team placed among the top twenty-five. Success continued during 1988–1989. Concordia was one of only eight schools invited to the prestigious Kentucky Thoroughbred Round Robin Debate Tournament. At the National Individual Events Tournament, Concordia finished fifth among 113 schools. Cort Sylvester ('89) won a national championship in impromptu speaking, joining Jill Strickler ('82) and Bart Coleman ('83) who had won national championships in 1982 and 1983 respectively. At the Pi Kappa Delta National Tournament, Concordia finished second among more than ninety schools competing in speech and debate. As Director Sternhagen commented, "Forensics is the ultimate liberal arts experience. Students deal with complicated subject material. They have to use sophisticated thinking skills and confront complex value questions, and in the end they have to create and share something of their own."[36]

Debate champions Cort Sylvester, Courtney Ward, Joseph Schmitt and Bob Groven.

Music involves more than 20 percent of the student body in one of nine musical organizations every Monday through Friday from 4:00 to 6:00 p.m.; nearly 400 Cobbers take weekly lessons. The department prides itself that non-music collegians can study as music majors do. Approximately ten faculty and fifty student recitals are scheduled annually. Choir, band and orchestra do annual national or regional concert tours; periodically they journey to Europe. Directed by J. Robert Hanson, the orchestra enjoyed its first European success in Spring 1986. It gave concerts for enthusiastic crowds in nine cities in England and Central Europe. As one Cobber commented, "It was a great experience for us to be appreciated so much by European audiences."[37]

The Concordia orchestra at Innsbruck, Austria.

When Paul J. Christiansen retired in 1986, René Clausen became director of the Concordia Choir. At homecoming that fall, a Christiansen reunion choir of 550 alumni honored the director and his spouse Eleanor for their half century at Concordia. Filling risers extending the width of the auditorium, the alumni sang four well-known anthems from the Christiansen era and perhaps surprised themselves that they so quickly became a unified whole under such familiar direction. It is difficult to replace a legendary figure, but young Clausen is making his own mark. Formerly director of choral activities at West Texas State, Clausen has established a reputation in the Midwest and Southwest for his choral work and conducting. He earned his baccalaureate from Saint Olaf and a master's of musical performance from the University of Illinois where he is completing his doctorate. In Spring 1990 he enjoyed a successful first European tour with stops in England, Denmark, Sweden and Norway.[38]

Choir Director
René Clausen

In Fall 1976, Armin Pipho succeeded the retiring Irv Christenson as athletic director. An Iowa native and Luther College graduate with a Ph.D. from the University of Oregon, Pipho came from a similar position at California State College-Stanislaus and carried on the Concordia tradition of maximum participation. The college offered a four-point program of intercollegiate sports, intramurals, professional course instruction and recreation designed to make sports an important part of every person's life in the present and future. Intercollegiate competition featured the student athlete. Hence the department noted with pride that it had more participants than either Moorhead State or North Dakota State and that it had a higher graduation rate. Almost 500 try out annually; 98.2 percent graduated of the 453 who completed four years of competition between 1981 and 1989. Meanwhile, intramurals expanded, reflecting the department's belief that everyone who wants to compete should be given the opportunity. New sports were added for a similar reason; as Pipho explained, new additions "support the college's philosophy of providing students with as much

President Paul J. Dovre, 1975 –

quality and opportunity as possible."[39]

To offer maximum opportunity, the college developed or acquired new facilities. The addition of the $172,000 all-weather synthetic polyform surface track in 1983 made Concordia the host for many high school meets. The purchase of the Beltline Health Club in 1987 eased somewhat the overcrowded recreational facilities. The department in 1990 eagerly looked forward to several major renovations. The remodeled field house included a wood basketball floor, an enlarged storage area and eight new faculty offices; a softball diamond and six new tennis courts were placed behind East Complex; and the proposed Sports and Fitness Center, to be constructed early in the college's second century, is to include an indoor running track, four basketball courts, and room for tennis and volleyball courts.[40]

Concordia not only features broad participation; teams have also won in many sports. Jim Christopherson surpassed the success of his illustrious predecessor, Jake Christiansen. By 1990, Christopherson had the most wins in school history with a 153-57-5 won-lost-tied record; he had won nine conference titles, including four in a row between 1978 and 1981, bracketed by two national championships. Christopherson had been named MIAC coach of the year five times and NAIA Division II coach of the year once. Even when the coach accomplished the unusual, like back-to-back losing seasons in 1983 and 1984, his teams featured their trademark strong defense and were competitive, losing several close games. Christopherson-coached teams were led by numerous outstanding players who earned All-American honors: Barry Bennet (1977), Allen Holm (1978), Bob Beliveau (1978), Dave Klug (1979), Ralph Halvorson (1980), Mark Heysse (1980), Dave Rosengren (1981), Jim Klug (1981), Doug McMillan (1982), Roger Lindahl (1983), Jim Southwick (1986), Terry Storm (1988) and Terry Horan (1988). Of these, the most outstanding was Barry Bennett, one of the best defensive tackles in the country and the first Cobber to win an individual national wrestling title, which he successfully defended twice. He played in the East-West Shrine game and the North-South Senior Bowl before being drafted in the third round by the New Orleans Saints. He played ten years in the National Football League with the Saints and the New York Jets. Dave Klug went on the play linebacker with the Kansas City Chiefs before injuries shortened his career. Terry Horan set many records as a wide receiver with 173 receptions for 2,901 yards and 33 touchdowns; he holds the conference mark for yards gained.[41]

Barry Bennett, All-American defensive tackle.

When Edwin "Sonny" Gulsvig resigned as basketball coach in March 1978, he had led Cobber cagers for twenty-three seasons and had been named NAIA District 13 coach of the year in 1975. Pipho expressed appreciation for the man and his long service: "His energy, his enthusiasm and his concern for students are invaluable asssets to our department and our program." John Eidsness, Yankton College instructor and basketball coach, succeeded Gulsvig. Eidsness initiated a fast break offense, renamed his team the "Running Cobbers"

and sought ways to enhance home crowd enthusiasm. His teams won back-to-back conference championships in 1982 and 1983, the first in fifty-one years. For the first, Eidsness was named MIAC and NAIA District 13 coach of the year; for the second, he repeated as MIAC coach of the year.[42]

The 1982 MIAC championship team.

Many other men's teams competed in conference play. Besides cross country, track, golf and wrestling, a varsity soccer team began intercollegiate competition in Fall 1986 and joined the conference the next season. First-year coach Steve Baumgartner guided the hockey team to the MIAC championship in 1987 and was named coach of the year. Led by All-American Mike Hassman, Baumgartner's 1989–1990 pucksters earned a third-place finish and a play-off berth. When the baseball team won their second MIAC title in 1985, Donald "Bucky" Burgau, in his seventh year, was named MIAC and NCAA III Midwest Region coach of the year.[43]

Women's basketball has enjoyed spectacular success under three talented coaches. In 1979 Collette Folstad won her 100th game, captured a second straight Minnesota small college championship and earned nomination for the national women's small college coach of the year. In 1982, second-year coach Marc Langseth led the Lady Cobbers to a national title. Duane Siverson succeeded Langseth in 1984 and continued the success by winning four MIAC titles, taking teams to postseason play each season, placing second in the NCAA Division III national tournament in 1987 and then winning the national championship in

1988 NCAA III national championship trophy proudly displayed by senior team members.

1988. That season he was named Converse Coach of the Year for Division III Women's Basketball. Siverson's teams have been the finest at Concordia in recent years; they

President Paul J. Dovre, 1975 –

feature the fast break, a full-court pressing defense and alternating units to maintain the pressure and the pace. These coaches were helped by talented players, a number of whom were named All-Americans: Coral Beske (1978), Sue Ekberg (1981, 1982), Mary Beth Stephan (1982), Nancy Halda (1982), Paula Langseth (1982), Jodie Bock (1983, 1984), Jessica Beachy (1987, 1988), Mary Lee Legried (1988), Jillayn Quaschnick (1989), Patty Kubow (1989) and Michelle Thykeson (1990). Beachy was named NCAA Division III player of the year in 1988 and Quaschnick was one of five finalists for the honor the next season.[44]

*Player of the Year
Jessica Beachy*

Women compete in tennis, golf, track and cross country. Gymnastics disappeared; soccer replaced field hockey in Fall 1982. The softball team began intercollegiate competition in Spring 1987. In Fall 1988 the volleyball team under coach Kathy James completed its most successful season by finishing 11-0 in conference play and third in the MIAC tournament for a second place conference finish. Success in national competition earned All-American honors for two tracksters in 1990. Chris Fredrick ('91) finished sixth in the 1,500 meter run at the NCAA III national indoor meet and Kris Kuehl ('92) won a national discus title.[45]

In addition to opportunities for viewing or participating in athletic, musical and theatrical events, many other entertainments exist in bewildering variety, quickly appearing, disappearing or reappearing. The weeklong Winter Carnival endured longer than most; first held in 1942, it lasted as an annual event into the 1980s. Toga-clad picketeers demanded rites of spring in 1979; they received a ten-day gala that included films, a tabernacle, a Gene Cotton concert and a formal dance. The small but enthusiastic turn-out may explain why the event did not long survive. Student Productions sponsored concerts into the late 1980s. Among the most successful were the Mission Mountain Wood Band concert in April 1980, which drew 2,000 people to Jake Christiansen Stadium for music and a pre-concert barbecue. In 1983 the Oak Ridge Boys played to a fervent field house crowd of 6,500. The Dove Boat, featuring all-college dinners, dancing, live entertainment and movies, appeared annually in the mid-1980s before being replaced by "Go-Hawaiian" in March 1986. Dance marathons have been annual February events since 1976. In 1984 this twenty-four hour affair on the theme "A Life Enhanced Because We Danced" raised $12,000 for Alcohol Outreach, Inc. and Hospice of the Red River Valley. It featured a "wellness" approach with warm-ups, aerobics, Christian rock and nutritious foods during breaks. Casino nights have been held each fall since 1977. The range of events sponsored by the Student Association can be seen from the activities of the campus entertainment commission (formerly Student Productions). In 1987 the commission sponsored seventeen events including dances, concerts, comedy nights, cabarets, cinema, casino night and a game show, "Blizzard of Bucks."[46]

If this plethora of happenings does not entertain, the more hardy and energetic each fall spend the midsemester biking across Minnesota or perhaps canoeing in the Boundary Waters. In February they might ski in Yellowstone. From 1978 to 1981 they could participate in the Nordic Ski Classic, *Skogfjorden Rennet*, held in January at the language village near Bemidji, to which other Minnesota private colleges were invited. Jazzercise, reflecting the national craze, appeared in 1982. Aerobics continue at the

Cobber Health Club. If these are too strenuous for dedicated couch potatoes, then TV lounges are available. Each day hundreds religiously watch their favorite soap operas. For passively viewing television or a class, the necessary pop, candy or popcorn can be obtained at the Korn Krib located in the Knutson Student Life Center.[47]

Communal Ties, Achievements and Celebrations

Commencement ends student life, but it does not sever all connections with Concordia. Alumni take positions in many walks of life, but occupational preferences have shifted since 1975. In 1976, 28 percent were placed in teaching positions, 25 percent in business, 7.2 percent in health care and 6 percent in social or Christian service, while 20.4 percent continued their education. A decade later, only 15 percent taught while 40 percent joined businesses. The proportions for other occupations did not change. To assist in finding business jobs, Placement Director Philip Hanson in 1984 formed Volunteers in Placement, a network of alumni. By 1987, more than 300 volunteers nationwide served as liaisons between seniors and businesses in their area, alerted the office of openings, arranged interviews and served as hosts for interviewees. Partly as a result of this network, 1986 graduates within one year of commencement had spread out to thirty-one states and five foreign countries.[48]

Paul Erickson, leader of the Greenland ski expedition.

Alumni distinguished themselves in many different careers and sometimes in unusual ways. Paul Erickson ('74) led the 1980 Minnesota Ski Expedition Across Greenland, only the third successful crossing of the world's largest island, and the 1982 Ski Across Lapland Expedition, the first American group to complete this journey. During Summer 1982, Deborah Asp ('84) was a crew member for the Atlantic crossing of the Viking ship, Hjemkomst, fulfilling the dream of her late father, Robert Asp ('52), who built the vessel. Guy Doud ('75) was named Minnesota Teacher of the Year in 1985 and National Teacher of the Year in 1986. George Robert Hanson ('80) won first place in May 1986 in the prestigious fifth International Conductors Competition sponsored by Hungarian Television in Budapest.[49]

Deborah Asp, Hjemkomst crew member.

As evidenced by annual alumni achievement awards, others have distinguished themselves in more prosaic but equally significant ways. Norman Lorentzsen ('41), a man of rock-ribbed integrity, set high standards of leadership in business and civic affairs. He served as chief executive officer of Burlington Northern, Inc., fifth largest transportation company in the United States; president of St. Paul's Chamber of Commerce; and chair of the Concordia Board of Regents. In recognition of his eighteen years as a regent and his contributions to Founders Fund I and II, the administration building was named for him in 1988. Rev. David Simonson ('51) has conducted an amazing ministry to Tanzania where he heads Operation Bootstrap, a self-help program which by 1987 had funded construction of 700 schools to

The Norman Lorentzsen family and the renamed administration building.

promote universal primary education. Former chemistry professor and regent Richard Green ('61) became a senior management development specialist with Honeywell Inc. in Minneapolis. Paul Peterson ('62) established himself as one of the leading national authorities on the politics of cities, schools and public policy with numerous articles and books. Connie Farden Friesen ('67), an attorney with a New York law firm, achieved eminence as "one of the most knowledgeable and sophisticated banking lawyers practicing in New York."[50]

In church, business, academe, law, banking, teaching and the arts, these dedicated Christians served in the world with distinction. Their lives represent the success of the Concordia mission carried out in the lives of other graduates. Loanne Brager Thrane ('55), state director for United States Senator Rudy Boschwitz, summed up what being "sent forth" meant when she said, "[it means] being equipped to live a thoughtful life and assuming responsibility and exercising stewardship in the use of money and time, whether on the job or in church and community."[51]

Appropriately, the committee planning the centennial celebration scheduled for 1991–1992 adopted "Sent Forth" as its theme. The logo designed by David Hetland incorporated these

The Centennial logo depicts the college mission.

The annual Christmas concert, an expression of Christian community.

elements: Old Main represents the historic, academic and spiritual dimensions of the place; a dove—symbolizing peace, promise and Holy Spirit—breaks out of a rectangle to signify being sent forth into the world; the world with its earth and sky represents God the creator; and the cross signifies Christ, who is above all and encompasses all. Concordia thus embarked on its second century by calling to mind the values which had guided its first.[52]

Alumni embody the Concordia mission in the world. They remain bound by many ties to their alma mater, however. They are tied by the Concordia memorabilia purchased at the Cobber Bookstore. This can be substantial; during 1988–1989 the store sold about $300,000 worth of clothing. More significant are the communal celebrations which affirm the values of the Christian community. Commencement and related activities annually celebrate the values of Christian home and college. Nurtured by family, church and college, graduates are sent forth in a dignified manner to serve the world. Each fall the homecoming celebration welcomes back almost 5,000 alumni for the week-end of class reunions, parade, game, variety show and worship. More than 200 students are involved in planning the weeklong activities which include Frosh Frolics, Fantastic Feats for Fools, fireworks, C-400 banquet and dance. The 1989 theme, "Together We Celebrate," embraced alumni, established the spirit of unity among current Cobbers and affirmed the values of Christian community represented by the college and its constituency.[53]

At Christmas, the annual concert of five performances in the field house and in Minneapolis features nearly 300 musicians and has attracted as many as 30,000 people from distances of up to 2,000 miles. The mural—designed by David Hetland, one of the late Cy Running's last students—underscores the narrative and songs through lighting arranged by Theatre Director Jim Cermak. The Christmas Concert

President Paul J. Dovre, 1975 –

symbolizes the Christian community of Concordia. It draws together the college and its constituency in celebration of a central event of its Christian faith; it involves the time, talents and teaching of many professors and students who dedicate themselves to this annual celebration. The concert is thus a parable of the Concordia community and mission. *Soli Deo Gloria*—"To God Alone the Glory." On this firm foundation, the community has been built; on this firm foundation the community carries on its educational vocation; on this firm foundation the college serves the world through the lives of its graduates.[54]

Epilogue

Beyond 1991

Continuity and change are the stuff of history. Concordia College has changed greatly in its first century. Materially it has expanded beyond the most visionary dreams of its founders. The institution began as a Christian academy with only three professors, twelve pupils, one building and two city blocks situated outside a frontier town. Today it is a fully-accredited comprehensive college offering numerous programs with about 185 fulltime and forty-nine parttime faculty, more than 2,900 students and more than thirty major buildings located on 120 acres in the heart of residential Moorhead. The Norwegian-American Lutheran institution has evolved from its roots in regional ethnic ghettoes to a a school marked by greater diversity and more ties to national and global communities. The "little Norways" have disappeared. Collegians are no longer exclusively local or Lutheran. They now come from more than forty states, fifteen nations and approximately thirty different religions and denominations.[1]

Yet continuity is as impressive as change. Community, Lutheran identity and service to society are still valued as evidenced by communal ceremonies. The Concordia community began the last academic year of its first century in Fall 1990 as it had opened each fall term since J.N. Brown occupied the presidential office in Old Main and the faculty gathered in North (now Frida Nilsen) Lounge of Fjelstad Hall. President Paul Dovre strolled from his office in Lorentzsen Hall along newly-laid sidewalks past the partially-erected centennial bell tower. Perhaps he mused about unmet construction deadlines, which left the red-and-buff-brick walks in the new mall uncompleted for the opening of school, and what he would say to those gathered in the Centrum.

The annual community-building observance of a two-day faculty workshop opened with devotions followed by introductions of newcomers, an address by an outside speaker, small-group discussions of a draft of *Blueprint IV* and an evening banquet. For devotions the community sang hymns—"Joyful, Joyful We Adore Thee," "O Day Full of Grace" and "Now Thank We All Our God"—prayed and heard Scripture readings. Assuming his pastoral role, President Dovre urged his listeners to emulate their collegiate forebears, "to stand aside and hear the word of God." That evening emeriti, staff, professors, spouses and friends gathered for a festive meal and a presidential speech entitled "Credo and Community." A communion service, an address by Academic Dean H. Robert Homann, and meetings of advisers, departments and committees constituted the agenda for the second day.

Historical themes of change within continuity were evident as well in the draft of *Blueprint IV.* The editors identified three defining qualities of the Concordia tradition that informed the future they wished to create: constancy in mission and program, a close and harmonious relationship with the constituency and a tradition of conservatism and innovation. As the document's title suggests, planning itself was a tradition of almost four decades duration. Familiar topics were combined with new motifs in the latest *Blueprint*: first, reaffirmation of mission, academic program and an emphasis on community building; second, living out actively all areas of mission and program; third, responding to the call to be global citizens and leaders; and, fourth, cultural diversity.[2]

The document affirmed continuity with the past by upholding the now-classic one-sentence mission statement from *Blueprint I*—"The purpose of Concordia College is to influence the affairs of the world by sending into society thoughtful and informed men and women dedicated to the Christian life." To be sure, the declaration was again scrutinized to determine what it might mean for the decade ahead. For the 1990s, this interpretation was proposed: It called the community to "1) Equip students with capacities for action, 2) Empower them with a vision of freedom in the Gospel, and 3) Excite them with a commitment to service."[3]

As had the previous reports, *Blueprint IV* assessed the changing world into which graduates were sent forth. Changes in the physical, economic, family, religious and educational environments were briefly reviewed and the growing diversity in populations and institutions, the marked increase in global interaction and the acceleration in the rate of change were noted as the primary characteristics of society. To meet the challenge of educating Cobbers for a changing global society, the goals of a Lutheran liberal arts education were reaffirmed with admixtures of feminism, environmentalism and hopes for a new educational paradigm of wholeness.

Community—rooted in theological understanding—continues to be asserted as the hallmark of the college. The draft document proposed that Concordia be viewed as a covenant-based community in which "God's love ... calls ... [members] to an active living of its values in commitment to one another."[4] Inclusiveness, caring and loyalty were set forth as desirable communal qualities. Global, ethnic and racial diversity were also affirmed even though they challenge a communal cohesion formerly based on religious and ethnic homogeneity. Nonetheless the document argued that a covenant-based commitment to love, inclusiveness and reconciliation would be adequate to maintain cohesion in diversity. Similarly, the college confidently expected to recruit a more diverse staff, declaring that "the complexities and diversities of the 1990s enable us to recognize more strongly what ... we share in common": a calling to serve the college mission.[5]

As it has throughout its history, Concordia College educates collegians from a region of modest individual incomes. *Blueprint IV* therefore asserted that the goals of access and quality would provide the framework for the resource planning of the nineties as the college sought to maintain a stable enrollment of between 2,600 and 2,750 students. At the same time, the college should maintain its historic relationship to the church by strengthening its ties to the recently formed Evangelical Lutheran Church in America.

Not all these formulations were greeted with unanimity by the community. Searching questions were raised. Was the mission statement too narrow and authoritarian? Had the tension between diversity and community been recognized and addressed adequately? Was covenant an appropriate theological formulation? Had the religious dimensions of mission been overemphasized to the exclusion of the intellectual? Did the action-orientation of the document slight the contemplative role of the liberal arts college? In the face of these and other questions, President Dovre called for further discussion by the community and stressed the importance of participation by all individuals in that communal process.

These questions and the ongoing dialogue should not surprise for the Concordia community has changed greatly from the days when the ideology of Christian education viewed the Christian college as an extension of the Christian home and a patriarchal president assisted by a predominantly male faculty enforced *in loco parentis* on a student body comprised mostly of white Lutherans aged eighteen to twenty-two. The president retains final authority on all recommendations to the board of regents, but those recommendations are derived from a participatory process informed by many other administrators, professors and collegians. Several Cobbers are older as the ACCORD program has enrolled approximately one hundred non-traditional students. Other Collegians, now joined by some parents, continue in their questioning of parietal rules. The faculty has changed as well. There are more female professors, working mothers, single parents of both sexes and faculty with professional spouses. All seek to grow professionally while maintaining that elusive balance between their professional and personal lives. In recognition of these changes, infant day care began on campus in Fall 1990. Meanwhile, the longstanding use of family as a metaphor for community is debated. On the one hand, some feminists argued that families have been less than hospitable places for women, and that by blurring lines between home and job the metaphor made it more difficult to analyze how the work environment can become more responsive to real family needs.[6] On the other hand, several sought to rehabilitate the term by emphasizing the positive family values of caring nurture as desirable attributes worth retaining at the school.

However resolved, the questions raised during the *Blueprint IV* discussions and the annual faculty workshop observance suggest important characteristics of Concordia College. While there is disagreement, all sides of the debate agree that maintaining strong community is necessary for the institution to carry out successfully its mission to church and world. Concordia counts on the loyalty and commitment to mission of all elements of the community—administrators, staff, professors, collegians and constituency. It seeks to define precisely its conception of mission through a communal process of discussion and debate. Of course, it is unlikely that institutional mission can ever be precisely defined. Indeed, it could be argued that some ambiguity is an essential quality of mission statements because it allows room for individual interpretation and commitment. Nonetheless, discussion develops the communal bond and provides sufficient understanding for the community and its members to carry out the educational mission of Concordia College. That understanding and the loyalty of its constituency will be essential for continued institutional success as the college enters its second century.

Notes

Abbreviations

BDM	Board of Directors, Minutes
BRM	Board of Regents, Minutes
BTM	Board of Trustees, Minutes
CA	*Concordia Alumnus*
CAN	*Concordia Alumni News*
Cat	*Catalog*
CB	*Concordia Banner*
Cob	*Cobber*
Con	*Concordian*
CQR	*Concordia College Quarterly Review*
Crst	*Crescent*
FF	*The Forum of Fargo-Moorhead*
FM	Faculty Minutes
FSM	Faculty Senate Minutes
HBG	*Howard Binford's Guide*
LCH	*Lutheran Church Herald*
LH	*Lutheran Herald*
LS	*Lutheran Standard*
MDN	*Moorhead Daily News*
MI	*Moorhead Independent*
MWN	*Moorhead Weekly News*
Sct	*Scout*
TR	*The Record*
VL	*Valley Lutheran*

Preface

[1] Quoted in Arthur Huseboe and R. Lynwood Oyos, "Blindly into the Impossible: Augustana College," *From Idea to Institution: Higher Education in South Dakota*, ed. Herbert Hoover, *et. al.* (Vermillion, 1989), 151.

[2] Paul K. Conkin, *Gone With the Ivy: A Biography of Vanderbilt University* (Knoxville, 1985), 737.

[3] For this insight, I am indebted to Larry J. Zimmerman and Patricia M. Peterson, "Epilogue," *From Idea to Institution,* 220. Also see, Robert Redfield, *The Little Community: Viewpoints for the Study of a Human Whole* (Chicago, 1955), 4-5, 79-80, 146, 156-157 and *Peasant Society and Culture:An Anthropological Approach to Civilization* (Chicago, 1956), 70, 86-87.

Prologue

[1] Ingrid Semmingsen, *Norway to America: A History of the Migration,* trans. Einar Haugen (Minneapolis, 1978), 100-109; Theodore C. Blegen, *Norwegian Migration to America: The American Transition* (Northfield, 1940), 464-468; Carlton C. Qualey and Jon A. Gjerde, "The Norwegians," *They Chose Minnesota: A Survey of the State's Ethnic Groups,* ed. June Drenning Holmquist (St. Paul, 1981), 220; Jon Gjerde, *From Peasants to Farmers: The Migration from Balestrand Norway to the Upper Middlewest* (New York, 1985), 3.

[2] Odd S. Lovoll, *The Promise of America: A History of the Norwegian- American People* (Minneapolis, 1984), 8-16; Blegan, *Norwegian Migration to America,* 466-468; Gjerde, 20.

[3] Lovoll, 11-13, 18; Qualey and Gjerde, 221.

[4] Qualey and Gjerde, 220-222; Gjerde, 4-9.

[5] Qualey and Gjerde, 220, 228; Lovoll, 82-83.

[6] Lovoll, 84-85, 92-93; Blegen, *Norwegian Migration to America,* 504-507; Elwyn B. Robinson, *History of North Dakota* (Lincoln, 1966), 130, 290.

[7] Lovoll, 107, 153; Qualey and Gjerde, 230; Harris E. Kaasa, "Epilogue," *Letters of Longing,*

ed. Frida R. Nilsen (Minneapolis, 1970), 129, 134; Gjerde, 166-167.

[8]Gjerde, 9-11, 201-201, 222.

[9] Robinson, 283, 290; Quoted in Qualey and Gjerde, 235; *MDN,* 21 January 1893.

[10]Lovoll, 121, 129-131; Qualey and Gjerde, 236-237; Jon Wefald, *A Voice of Protest: Norwegians in American Politics* (Northfield, 1971), 4.

[11]Sydney E. Ahlstrom, *A Religious History of the American People* (New Haven, 1972), 761; Winthrop S. Hudson, *Religion in America* (New York, 1965), 260; Semmingsen, 82-83, 134-135; Verlyn Anderson, "History and Acculturation of the English Language Hymnals of the Norwegian-American Lutheran Churches, 1879-1958" (Ph.D. diss., University of Minnesota, 1972), 31-35.

[12]Carl H. Chrislock, *From Fjord to Freeway: 100 Years of Augsburg College* (Minneapolis, 1969), 2; Lovoll, 55-56, 60, 101; Duane Bodell Lindberg, "Men of the Cloth and the Social-Cultural Fabric of the Norwegian Ethnic Community in North Dakota" (Ph.D. diss., University of Minnesota, 1975), 277.

[13]Lovoll, 59, 98; Anderson, 50; Lindberg, 277.

[14]Lovoll, 100-102; Lindberg, 104, 277.

[15]Lovoll, 98, 113-114; Anderson, 58.

[16]Frederick Rudolph, *The American College and University: A History* (New York, 1965), 47-49, 54.

[17]Robinson, 298-299; Theodore C. Blegan, *Minnesota: A History of the State* (Minneapolis, 1963), 416.

[18]Richard W. Solberg, *Lutheran Higher Education in North America* (Minneapolis, 1985), 227-228; E. Clifford Nelson, *The Lutheran Church Among Norwegian Americans* (Minneapolis, 1960), II, 116-117; Lovoll, 110; "The Lutheran, An Educating Church," *CB,* 1(March 1897), 5-6; W.P. Rognlie, "Culture and the Lutheran Church," *CB,* 2(June 1898), 4-5.

[19]Solberg, 15-19, 228; Nelson, *Lutheran Church,* II, 119.

[20]Solberg, 277-278; Rudolph, 314, 320-322; Rosalind Rosenberg, *Beyond Separate Spheres: The Intellectual Roots of Modern Feminism* (New Haven, 1982), 44; Roberta A. Frankfort, *Collegiate Women: Domesticity and Career in Turn-of-the-Century America* (New York, 1977), 90-94, 99-100.

Chapter 1

[1]Rasmus Bogstad, *Early History of Concordia College* (n.p., n.d.), 3-6; G.H. Gerberding, *Reminiscent Reflections of a Youthful Octogenarian* (Minneapolis, 1928), 188-189.

[2]Gerberding, 184; *MDN,* 8 and 16 April, 5 and 11 May 1891.

[3]*MDN,* 8 May and 9 June 1891; Clarence A. Glasrud, *The Moorhead Normal School* (Moorhead, 1987), 3, 29-30; *CAN,* 14(Summer 1976), 32-33.

[4]Erling Nicolai Rolfsrud, *Cobber Chronicle: An Informal History of Concordia College* (Moorhead, 1976), 11-12; Hiram M. Drache, *The Challenge of the Prairie: Life and Times of the Red River Pioneers* (Fargo, 1970), 280-283; Glasrud, 21.

[5]*Con,* 31 October 1925; John R. Borchert, "Network of Urban Centers," *Minnesota in a Century of Change: The State and Its People Since 1900,* ed. Clifford E. Clark, Jr. (St Paul, 1989), 57-62.

[6]Bogstad, *Early History,* 14-15, 19; *MDN,* 13 June and 7 July 1891; Oscar I. Hertsgaard Interview, n.d. (unless otherwise indicated, all interviews, Concordia College Archives, Moorhead).

[7]*Cat,* 1891-1892, 24-25, 1937, 37; *Kaldsbrev* to I.F. Grose, August 1891; (unless otherwise indicated, all presidential correspondence, Presidents' Papers, Concordia Archives); *MDN,* 13 June 1891.

[8]Joseph Shaw, *History of St. Olaf College, 1874-1974* (Northfield, 1974), 148; Hertsgaard Interview; Grose to H.T. Ytterboe, 29 August and 7 September 1891, 10 March 1892, Ytterboe Papers, (unless otherwise indicated, St. Olaf College Archives, Northfield); Grose to O.G. Felland, 11 September 1891, Ole G. Felland Papers, Box 4 (unless otherwise indicated, Norwegian American Historical Association Archives, Northfield).

[9]*Sct,* 1919-1920, 138, 142.

[10]*MDN,* 31 August 1891; *Sct,* 1919-1920, 139-141; Todd W. Nichol, "The American Lutheran Church: An Historical Study of Its Confession of Faith According to its Constituting Documents" (Th.D. diss., Berkeley Graduate Theological Union, 1988), 72-77.

[11]Rolfsrud, *Cobber Chronicle,* 19-20; Gerberding, 185.

[12]Grose to Ytterboe, 24 October 1891, Ytterboe Papers; Bogstad, *Early History,* 30-31; *MDN,*

4, 6, 9 and 16 January 1892; *MWN,* 14 January 1892.

[13]Grose to Ytterboe, 7 September 1891, Ytterboe Papers; Lars Christianson to R.R. Bogstad and J.O. Hougen to Bogstad, 28 October 1891.

[14]Grose to Felland, 5 November 1891, Felland Papers; Grose to Ytterboe, 19 September 1891, Ytterboe Papers; Chrislock, 57, 61; James S. Hamre, *Georg Sverdrup: Educator, Theologian, Churchman* (Northfield, 1986), 108- 109, 118-120; *MDN*, 31 October and 2 November 1892.

[15]Grose to Felland, 9 January 1892, Felland Papers.

[16]Grose to Felland, 9 January and 12 February l892; Felland Papers; Grose to Ytterboe, 24 October 1891, 1 February and 10 March 1892, Ytterboe Papers; *MDN*, 19, 20, 23 and February 1892.

[17]Rudolph, 26-27, 87-92; Glasrud, 24-25.

[18]*MDN, 27 April, 24 June, 2 and 23 November 1892, 21 January 1893; Glasrud, 32.*

[19]Hertsgaard Interview; *Cat,* 1891-1892, 19-20, 1892-1893, 24, 1893-1894, 24, 1900-1901, 15.

[20]*CA,* 1(February 1955); Report of Principal Aaker in Northwestern Lutheran College Association (hereafter NWLCA), Annual Reports, 1894 and 1896 (unless otherwise indicated, all board, association and corporation documents, Governing Bodies Papers, Concordia Archives).

[21]Bogstad, *Early History,* 113; O.T. Holty, "Letter," *VL* (May 1958), 5.

[22]*Cat,* 1891-1892, 14, 1892-1893, 27-28, 1893-1894, 17, 24-25; Aaker Report in NWLCA, Annual Report, 1894.

[23]*Cat,* 1891-1892, 20, 1892-1893, 25, 1894-1895, 33; *MDN*, 26 October 1892, 9 March 1893 and 19 February 1900.

[24]Rasmus Bogstad, *Concordia College, Moorhead, Minnesota Through Fifty Years* (n.p., n.d), 177-179.

[25]*Cat,* 1891-1892, 19.

[26]*Cat,* l893-1894, 24, 1895-1896, 26, 29; *MDN,* 27 October 1899; O.T. Holty, "Letter"; "$1000 Plumbing Job," *CB,* 3(September 1899), 12-13; Drache, 46-47.

[27]*Cat,* 1891-1892, 2, 23, 1900-1901, 21; Drache, 316.

[28]*Cat,* 1891-1892, 13, 22, 1892-1893, 15-16, 1893-1894, 15, and 1894-1895, 25; I.F. Grose, "Administrative Problems of Concordia College at the Time of Its Establishment," *LH* (August 1931), 970, 987.

[29]*MDN,* 1 and 6 October 1891; *Cat,* 1891-1892, 17-18; *CA,* 1(February 1955).

[30]*VL* (May 1958); *MDN,* 13 June 1896, 13 June 1901 and 12 June 1902.

[31]*CB,* 2(September 1898), 1; *Cat,* 1900-1901, 19.

[32]Grose to Felland, 22 May and 7 September 1893, Felland Papers; Shaw, 148; *MDN*, 24 June and 12 July 1893, 25 July 1895, 29 June and 2 July 1896.

[33]J.L. Rendahl to Richard W. Solberg, 31 December 1982, Information on Concordia College for LECNA History Project, 1983-1984 (unless otherwise indicated, Concordia Archives).

Chapter 2

[1]NWLCA, Annual Report, 1897; J.P. Hertsgaard, *Early Community History:Kindred, North Dakota, 1870-1900* (Northfield, 1948), 22; Bogstad, *Early History,* 67-69.

[2]Drache, 296, 302, 306.

[3]Timothy L. Smith, *Uncommon Schools: Christian Colleges and Social Idealism in Midwestern America, 1829-1950* (Indianapolis, 1978), 36; *MDN,* 1 November 1901.

[4]Shaw, 17; *CB,* 1(June 1896), 7-8; *Cat,* 1901-1902, 7; Ness Report in NWLCA, Annual Report, 1895.

[5]Hertsgaard, 22; *CB,* 1(September 1896), 8, 2(September 1898), 4-5 and 3(September 1899), 1.

[6]*CB,* 1(September 1896), 2; *Cat,* 1894-1895, 16, 1900-1901, 11; Barbara Miller Solomon, *In the Company of Educated Women: A History of Women and Higher Education in America* (New Haven, 1985), 85-87.

[7]*Cat,* 1895-1896, 17, 1897-1898, 19, 1911-1912, 46-47.

[8]*Cat,* 1894-1895, 15-16, 1900-1901, 9, 1901-1902, 8-9, 1911-1912, 45.

[9]*CB,* 1(December 1896), 5-6; *MDN*, 11 January 1897.

[10]*MDN,* 27 September 1894, 15 April 1895, 9 April, 5 and 28 May 1897, 13 February 1900.

[11]Lawrence A. Cremin, *American Education,*

vol. III: *The Metropolitan Experience, 1876-1980* (New York, 1988), 3-4, 116; William Ringenberg, *The Christian College: A History of Protestant Higher Education in America* (Grand Rapids, 1984), 102.

[12]*MDN*, 25 February and 17 May 1895, 25 February 1896, 19 May 1897, 24 February 1899 and 28 February 1900.

[13]Mohn quoted in Shaw, 240; Gerberding, 158, 162.

[14]Drache, 39, 297, 308.

[15]*MDN*, 17 March 1894 and 18 March 1896; Semmingsen, 148-150; John Washness to A. Tollefson, 15 October 1896, Tollefson Papers, Norwegian American Historical Association Archives.

[16]*MI*, 18 March and 27 May 1898, 23 March and 10 August 1900; *MDN*, 12 February, 16 and 27 March, 6 April, 7 June and 16 August 1900.

[17]*MDN*, 18 April, 26 June and 11 December 1900, 15, 16 and 27 February 1901; R.H. Aaker to E.N. Rolfsrud, 9 October 1964, (unless otherwise indicated, all Rolfsrud correspondence in Rolfsrud Papers, Concordia Archives).

[18]*MDN*, 17 July and 13 November 1897; Rolfsrud, *Cobber Chronicle*, 38-39.

[19]*MDN*, 27 November 1897.

[20]Treasurer's and Ness Reports in NWLCA, Annual Reports, 1896-1902.

[21]NWLCA, Annual Reports, 1894-1896 and 1901.

[22]Aaker Report in NWLCA, Annual Reports, 1898-1902; *CB*, 6(July 1901), 4; *MDN*, 22 March 1897, 19 July 1899, 1 April 1901 and 19 November 1900.

[23]Bogstad, *Early History*, 102, 105-108.

[24]Ness Report in NWLCA, Annual Reports, 1899 and 1901; NWLCA, Annual Report, 1901.

[25]*CB*, 6(December 1901), 20-21 and 7(December 1902), 7-8.

[26]Aaker to Rev. G.A. Larsen, 30 March and 23 April 1902; Bogstad to Ness, 1 April 1902.

[27]BDM, 23 April 1902; Ness Report in NWLCA, Annual Report, 1902.

[28]Aaker Report in NWLCA, Annual Report, 1902.

[29]Aaker Report in NWLCA Annual Report, 1902; Ness Report in NWLCA, Annual Reports, 1903 and 1904.

[30]NWLCA, Annual Report, 1902.

[31]Bogstad, *Early History*, 72-73; Ness and Christianson to Bogstad and Christianson to Bogstad, 26 June 1902.

[32]*CB*, 7(December 1902), 6-7.

Chapter 3

[1]Cremin, 242-247, 555-556.

[2]Christianson to Bogstad, 9 April 1903; BTM, 28 June 1906; *MDN*, 10 October 1941; *CB*, 7(December 1902), 6; Hertsgaard Interview.

[3]Valborg C. Bogstad, "The Bogstad Family's Trip" in *Concordia College*, by Bogstad, 158-159, 163-167.

[4]James S. Hamre, "Humanism and the Lutheran Tradition: A Case Study," *Journal of Church and State*, 27(Spring 1985), 289-291. For a discussion of the ideals informing higher education, see Laurence R. Veysey, *The Emergence of the American University* (Chicago, 1970).

[5]Bogstad, *Early History*, 100-101; Bogstad to Martin Lyberg, 9 August 1907.

[6]*Cat*, 1902-1903, 1.

[7]Bogstad and Ness Reports in NWLCA, Annual Reports, 1906 and 1909.

[8]Bogstad Report in NWLCA, Annual Reports, 1906 and 1907.

[9]Solomon, 101; Bryce E. Nelson, *Good Schools: The Seattle Public School System, 1901-1930* (Seattle, 1988), 69-73.

[10]*CB*, 7(December 1902), 7; *Cat*, 1903-1904, 32; Bogstad Report in NWLCA, Annual Reports, 1908 and 1909; BTM, 16 July 1908; Harriet Wanberg to Rolfsrud, 17 February 1965.

[11][Bogstad?],"Points That Ought to Be Considered About Prof. J.P. Hertsgaard," Personnel Records, 1909ff, Concordia Archives; J.P. Hertsgaard to J.N. Kildahl, 17 December 1908, Kildahl Papers (unless otherwise indicated, St. Olaf Archives); BDM, 5 August 1909.

[12]S.O. Kolstoe to O.I. Hertsgaard, 21 December 1964, Rolfsrud Papers; O.I. Hertsgaard to Rolfsrud, 14 December 1965; *CB*, 7(December 1902), 7; *MDN*, 23 December 1903.

13 Bogstad Report in NWLCA, Annual Report, 1906; *Cat,* 1904-1905, 18, and 1905-1906, 12; Mrs. Ness to Rolfsrud, 21 September 1964; *MI,* 25 September 1908.

14 *Cat,* 1906-1907, 15; Bogstad to J.N. Kildahl, 23 February 1903, Kildahl Papers; *MI,* 26 February 1909; *MDN,* 15 June 1904.

15 *Cat,* 1903-1904, 31; Bogstad Report in NWLCA, Annual Report, 1904; Ness Report in NWLCA, Annual Report, 1909; *MI,* 4 May 1906, 25 September 1908 and 18 June 1909.

16 Bogstad Report in NWLCA, Annual Report, 1904; NWLCA, Annual Report, 1909; BDM, 14 December 1910; Mrs. Ness to Rolfsrud, 21 September 1964; *MDN,* 16 February 1903; *MI,* 18 May 1906, 30 April, 12 and 19 November 1909.

17 *Cat,* 1906-1907, 7, 11; Bogstad Report in NWLCA, Annual Report, 1906; *MI,* 5 July 1907 and 19 June 1908.

18 *Cat,* 1907-1908, 23; Bogstad Report in NWLCA, Annual Report, 1908.

19 *Cat,* 1907-1908, 27 and 1905-1906, 24.

20 Bogstad and Ness Reports in NWLCA, Annual Report, 1905; *Cat,* 1904-1905, 23.

21 *MDN,* 10 October 1941; *CA,* 7(May 1960), 3; Bogstad Report in NWLCA, Annual Report, 1909; Bogstad, *Early History,* 117-118; *MI,* 25 September 1908; Ness Report in NWLCA, Annual Report, 1905.

22 Bogstad Report in NWLCA, Annual Reports, 1903-1905; BTM, 16 March 1904; Peter L. Peterson, *A Place Called Dana: The Centennial History of Trinity Seminary and Dana College* (Blair, 1984), 37.

23 *Cat,* 1903-1904, 33 and 1908-1909, 13; Ness Report in NWLCA, Annual Report, 1904; *MI,* 20 July 1906 and 10 January 1908; *MDN,* 2 March 1906.

24 Ness Report in NWLCA, Annual Reports, 1904 and 1906; Report of The Building Committee in NWLCA, Annual Report, 1907; *MDN,* 29 March 1906.

25 *MI,* 15 June 1906; Mrs. Ness to Rolfsrud, 21 September 1964; Rolfsrud, *Cobber Chronicle,* 48-50.

26 Ness Report in NWLCA, Annual Report, 1907; Rolfsrud, *Cobber Chronicle,* 49-50.

27 *MI,* 25 May and 5 October 1906, 16 August 1907 and 5 August 1910.

28 Bogstad to Board of Trustees, 8 July 1909; Bogstad Report in NWLCA, Annual Reports, 1907-1908; Bogstad, *Early History,* 120-122; BTM, 16 July 1908; BDM, 8 December 1909; Ness Report in NWLCA, Annual Report, 1908.

29 Treasurer's Report in NWLCA, Annual Report, 1906; Ness Report in NWLCA, Annual Reports, 1903, 1905 and 1909.

30 *MDN,* 14 November 1902; Ness Report in NWLCA, Annual Reports, 1903 and 1909; Bogstad Report in NWLCA, Annual Report, 1909; *Cat,* 1903-1904, 33 and 1908-1909, 13.

31 BTM, 29 June 1905 and 27 June 1907; Bogstad Report in NWLCA, Report, 1905; O.I. Hertsgaard to Rolfsrud, 23 November 1964.

32 BTM, 30 July 1907; Bogstad to J.N. Kildahl, 23 November 1903.

33 BTM, 24 June and 6 July 1909; Bogstad, *Early History,* 122-123; Bogstad to Ness, 8 July 1909.

34 NWLCA, Special Joint Meeting Minutes, 5 August 1909; Edward Engerud to Bogstad, 14 September 1909.

35 Bogstad to C.G. Dosland·(n.d.); H.S. Hilleboe to Bogstad, 13 September 1909; Bogstad to H.S. Hilleboe, 16 September 1909; Revocation, 28 September 1909; BTM, 17 September 1909.

36 Bogstad, *Early History,* 125-138; L.H. Scheck to Bogstad, 7 June 1909; Secretary's Report and Bogstad, Letter of Resignation, 30 June 1910 in NWLCA, Annual Report, 1910; *LH,* 17 June 1947; *MI,* 1 July 1910.

Chapter 4

1 Ness Report in NWLCA, Annual Report, 1910; Ness to J.A. Aasgaard and Letter of Call, 19 April 1911.

2 *Sct,* 1923, 17; *FF,* 25 January 1917 and 6 April 1952.

3 *FF,* 6 April 1952; T. Braaten to Rolfsrud, 30 July 1964; 1920s Oral History, 1984, Tuesday 1B (Side A); *An Orphan's Saga: The Autobiography of Carl Robert Narveson* (privately printed, 1982), 275; Rolfsrud, *Cobber Chronicle,* 93.

4 *FF,* 31 October 1911; *MI,* 6 and 13 June 1913; Aasgaard Report in NWLCA, Annual Report, 1912.

[5]Qualey and Gjerde, 239; Lindberg, 121-124; Aasgaard Report in NWLCA, Annual Reports, 1913-1915; *Con,* 26 May 1950; *TR,* 42(October 1938), 4.

[6]John L. Shover, *First Majority—Last Minority: The Transforming of Rural Life in America* (DeKalb, 1980), 44.

[7]Minneapolis *Tribune,* 6 June 1954 in Aasgaard Biographical File (unless otherwise indicated, Evangelical Lutheran Church in America Region 3 Archives, Luther Northwestern Theological Seminary, St. Paul); Ness Report in BTM, 9 March 1911.

[8]Aasgaard and Ness Reports in NWLCA, Annual Reports, 1912, 1913 and 1915; Aasgaard to Kildahl, 9 August 1912, Kildahl Papers.

[9]*FF,* 3 July, 10 and 18 September, 7 October 1914, 13 September 1915 and 10 January 1916; Rolfsrud, *Cobber Chronicle,* 52, 65, 67.

[10]Ness and Aasgaard Reports in NWLCA, Annual Reports, 1913 and 1914.

[11]BDM, 7 February 1911 and BTM, 9 March 1911; Shurson Report in NWLCA, Annual Report, 1911.

[12]Ness and Aasgaard Reports in NWLCA, Annual Reports, 1913-1914.

[13]Ness and Aasgaard Reports in NWLCA, Annual Reports, 1913 and 1915.

[14]*Cat,* 1915-1916, 18-19.

[15]*MDN,* 24 January 1917; *FF,* 24 January 1917.

[16]*MDN,* 31 January 1917, 10 October 1941; *FF,* 31 January and 2 February 1917; Marie Hanson Interview, 1984.

[17]BDM, 10 April 1917; *FF,* 11 April 1917.

[18] Hanson Interview, 1984; Fernanda Urberg Malmin Interview, 1985.

[19]J.L. Rendahl, "Landmark Decisions," Board of Regents Address, 1983, Concordia Archives; Urberg Malmin Interview; Rolfsrud, *Cobber Chronicle,* 71.

[20]Ness Report in NWLCA, Annual Report, 1914.

[21]Drache, 285-286, 291-292; *FF,* 7 October, 3 and 6 November 1915.

[22]*MDN,* 26 December 1916; *FF,* 8 March, 16 and 23 December 1916.

[23]*Cat,* 1911-1912, 12.

[24]*Crst* (January 1912), 16 and (April 1914), 183-184.

[25]*Crst* (March 1915), 126, 128.

[26]*Crst* (October 1916), 17, (February 1915), 101-102, (May 1915), 161-162.

[27]Daniel J. Singal, "Towards a Definition of American Modernism," *American Quarterly,* 39(Spring 1987), 19-20.

[28]Wilson quoted in William DeVane, *Higher Education in Twentieth-Century America* (Cambridge, 1965), 18-19.

[29]*Crst* (October 1914), 6-7.

[30]*Crst* (December 1914), 56-57, (October 1916), 1-5, (November 1916), 47, (April-May 1912), 24.

[31]L.A. Vigness to Aasgaard, 9 January 1918, Vigness Papers (unless otherwise indicated, St. Olaf Archives); *Crst* (November 1909), 12, (October 1912), 15, (October 1913), 24, (October 1916), 12; Rudolph, 375-377.

[32]*Crst* (December 1911), 8-9, (April-May 1912), 23, (February 1915), 101; *FF,* 9 March 1916.

[33]Denise E. Johnson, "The History of the Concordia College Band, 1891-1966" (Master's Thesis, University of Minnesota, 1984), 48, 50, 56, 59, 197.

[34]*Cat,* 1908-1909, 15; *Crst,* (April 1917), 228-229.

[35]*Crst* (April 1916), 206.

[36]Helen Horowitz, *Campus Life: Undergraduate Cultures From the End of the 18th Century to the Present* (New York, 1987), 151.

[37]*Crst* (March 1911), 10, (April 1913), 147-149, (April 1914), 155, (October 1914), 4-5.

[38]*Crst* (December 1909), 14, (February 1914), 112 and (January 1916), 100; Cremin, 336-337; *FF,* 30 November 1915.

[39]*Crst* (November 1910), 5, (February 1911), 4, (April 1911), 16-17.

[40]*Crst* (April 1911), 16-17, (March 1913), 127-128, (February 1914), 5-6, (November 1915), 27-28, (January 1917), 111-112, (May 1918), 216. On socialism in North Dakota and its rural Norwegian roots, see Robinson, 329.

[41]Robinson, 354-357; *Crst* (November 1914), 36, (January 1915), 70-71, (April 1915), 133, 135, (March 1916), 160-161.

[42]Robinson, 357-367; Blegen, *Minnesota,* 471, 473; *Crst* (April 1917), 224-225 and (May 1917), 270-271; *FF,* 6 April 1917.

[43]David Kennedy, *Over Here: The First World*

War and American Society (New York, 1980), 45-46, 106, 118-119, 143, 152-154.

[44]*Crst* (October 1917), 18 and (November 1917), 57; *MWN*, 20 September 1917; *LCH*, 10 and 24 August 1917, 97 and 136.

[45]*MWN*, 1 November 1917 and 7 February 1918; *Crst* (November 1917), 61-62, (December 1917), 109, (January 1918), 141, 149-151, (October 1918), 15.

[46]*FF*, 6 June 1918 and 15 October 1917; Qualey and Gjerde, 240.

[47]Carol S. Gruber, *Mars and Minerva: World War I and the Uses of Higher Learning in America* (Baton Rouge, 1975), 213-214, 216, 219, 228-230.

[48]Rolfsrud, *Cobber Chronicle,* 80-81; *Crst* (January 1919), 16; Ledger Book 2, 1905-1927, 1557 in Business Office Papers, Concordia Archives.

[49]*FF*, 9 October 1918; *MWN*, 6 February 1919; Rolfsrud, *Cobber Chronicle,* 81-82.

[50]*Crst* (October 1917), 17-18, (February-March 1918), 214, (November 1918), 4, (October 1918), 22.

[51]*Crst* (November 1917), 55, (April 1918), 264; Gruber, 82.

[52]Robert H. Ferrell, *Woodrow Wilson and World War I, 1917-1921* (New York, 1985), 201; *MWN*, 5 June 1919; *Crst* (December 1919), 19-21, (January 1919), 33-34, (February 1920), 12-13.

[53]Gruber, 95, 99; *Crst* (December 1917), 103-105, (November 1918), 10; *MWN*, 6 February 1919.

Chapter 5

[1]Brochure in Concordia College Papers, Box 1, Norwegian American Historical Association Archives.

[2]Solberg, 288; Nelson, *Lutheran Church,* II, 245; J.A. Aasgaard to L.W. Boe, 25 June 1919, Boe Papers (unless otherwise indicated, St. Olaf Archives); BTM, 8 April and 23 December 1919; *TR,* 23(June 1919), 1; *LCH*, 3 June 1919, 338-339.

[3]BTM, 6 August 1921 and 25 January 1922; Aasgaard Report in BDM, 19 December 1922; H.C. Nordlie to Rolfsrud, n.d..

[4]*Con,* 3 February and 9 June 1922; 1920s Oral History, 1984, Wednesday 1A (Side A); *FF*, 25 October 1925.

[5]Aasgaard Reports in BDM, 16 December 1919 and 21 December 1920; Ferrell, 193.

[6]Solberg, 282; *Sct*, 1923, 159-160.

[7]Aasgaard to Boe, 10 May 1923 and Boe to Aasgaard, 15 May 1923, Boe Papers.

[8]*Cat*, 1925-1926, 8-10; J.L. Rendahl to Richard Solberg, 31 December 1982, Information on Concordia College for LECNA History Project, 1983-1984.

[9]BDM and BTM, 30 December 1925; 1920s Oral History, 1984, Tuesday 1B (Side B).

[10]*Con,* 31 March and 19 May 1922; Nichol, 183-187, 476-477.

[11]1930s Oral History, Session I, 22 July 1985 and Alfreda Torgerson Interview, 1982

[12]*Cat*, 1924-1925, 23-27, 34-35, 1920-1921, 30-31.

[13]*Cat*, 1916-1917, 20-21, 30, 1920-1921, 24, 32, 1923-1924, 35; "Sociology" in Teachers' Reports, Registrar's Office; Joan Grace Zimmerman, "College Culture in the Midwest, 1890-1930" (Ph.D. diss., University of Virginia, 1978), 225.

[14]Aasgaard Report in BDM, 16 December 1919.

[15]David Levine, *The American College and the Culture of Aspiration, 1915-1940* (Ithaca, 1986), 24, 38.

[16]Aasgaard Reports in BTM, 23 December 1919 and 29 December 1920; Aasgaard Report in BDM, 21 December 1920.

[17]Aasgaard Reports in BDM, 19 December 1922, 27 November 1923 and 12 December 1924.

[18]*Cat*, 1917-1918, 13, 1920-1921, 11 and 1923-1924, 11-12; *Sct*, 1926, 118; Orval E. Stettan to Aasgaard, 15 July 1925; *MWN*, 31 January 1918.

[19]*Crst* (May 1918), 221 and (January 1920), 7; *Sct*, 1919-1920, 83; *Con*, 3 February 1922 and 21 April 1925.

[20]1920s Oral History, 1984, Monday 1B-Side B and 3B (Side A); Narveson Interview, 1981.

[21]Aasgaard Report in BTM, 16 December 1924; *MWN*, 11 September 1919; Rolfsrud, *Cobber Chronicle,* 87-90.

[22]Aasgaard Reports in BTM, 16 December 1924, 20 December 1924, 13 March 1923 and BDM, 25 June 1925; *FF*, 18 April 1918; *MWN*, 31 March 1923.

[23]BTM, 20 December 1922; *Cat*, 1924-1925, 17.

[24]Board of Education, Minutes (1917-1925), 115, 125, 206 (unless otherwise indicated, ELCA Region 3 Archives, Luther Northwestern Theological Seminary, St. Paul); Aasgaard Report in BTM, 29 December 1920.

[25]Board of Education, Minutes (1917-1925), 272, 277; Report of the Norwegian Lutheran Church of America, 1923, 165.

[26]Board of Education, Minutes (1917-1925), 312; Report of the Norwegian Lutheran Church of America, 1925, 54, 245; BTM, 1 July 1925; Aasgaard Report in BDM, 25 June 1925.

[27]Aasgaard Report in BDM, 16 December 1919; *Con,* 14 October 1921; Urberg Malmin Interview.

[28]Rudolph, 369-370; *Crst* (October 1920), 23-24, 33-34; *Sct*, 1923, 115.

[29]*Sct,* 1926, 119; *Con*, 19 October and 16 November 1923.

[30]Frederick Lewis Allen, *Only Yesterday: An Informal History of the Nineteen-Twenties* (New York, 1931).

[31]*Clay County Herald* (Hawley), 11 February 1921; 1920s Oral History, 1984, Monday 1B (Side A).

[32]*Cat*, 1916-1917, 4-7, 1920-1921, 10-11; 1920s Oral History, 1984, Tuesday 1B (Side A); Aasgaard Report in BTM, 20 December 1922.

[33]*Crst* (February-March 1918), 202 and (April 1919), 23; *Con*, 2 June 1924 and 2 March 1925.

[34]*Crst* (April 1919), 20; *An Orphan's Saga*, 77-78; 1930s Oral History, Session I, 22 July 1985.

[35]Zimmerman, 12-13, 43.

[36]*Crst* (May 1919), 8-9, (May 1920), 15-16; *Sct*, 1923, 68.

[37]Rolfsrud, *Cobber Chronicle*, 86.

[38]*Crst* (January 1918), 17-18; Torgerson Interview; *CAN*, 19(Winter 1980), 8-9.

[39]Aasgaard Reports in BDM, 12 December 1924 and BTM, 16 December 1924; *Sct*, 1926, 125; *Cat*, 1918-1919, 13 and 1922-1923, 11, 14; *MDN*, 19 April 1923; *MWN*, 20 March 1919.

[40]Aasgaard Report in BDM, 19 December 1922;

Sct, 1926, 97.

[41]*Con*, 23 March 1921; Helen L. Horowitz, *Alma Mater: Design and Experience in Women's Colleges from their 19th Century Beginnings to the 1930s* (New York, 1984), 156-157.

[42]*Con*, 23 March 1921, 2 June 1924 and 1 June 1925; *Cat*, 1921-1922, 13- 14; Rolfsrud, *Cobber Chronicle*, 86, 92, 189-193.

[43]Rolfsrud, *Cobber Chronicle*, 87, 207-208; *Con*, 6 June 1923.

[44]*Con*, 6 June 1923, 19 May and 20 October 1922; *Sct*, 1923, 156; Horowitz, *Alma Mater*, 159, 162.

[45]Rolfsrud, *Cobber Chronicle*, 9l.

[46]*Con*, 13 May 1921.

[47]*Sct*, 1919-1920, 89 and 1926, 124; *Con*, 1 June 1925; Rolfsrud, *Cobber Chronicle*, 90-93.

[48]*Con*, 23 February and 9 March 1921; *Crst* (April 1920), 18.

[49]*Crst* (April 1918), 265-266 and (April 1919), 17-18; *Con*, 22 April 1921; *Sct,* 1923, 31-40.

[50]*Con*, 3 March 1922; *Crst* (March 1919), 10-12, (December 1919), 21-24, (May 1920), 44-47, (March 1920), 44.

[51]*Crst* (February 1919), 3-9 and (January 1920), 25-26.

[52]*Crst* (March 1919), 10, (December 1912), 53; *Con*, 3 March 1922.

[53]Aasgaard Report BDM, 25 June 1925 and 12 December 1924; *Crst* (May 1920), 8-9; *Cat*, 1924-1925, 9.

[54]BTM, 29-30 June 1911.

[55]Aasgaard Report and J.N. Brown to Lars Christianson in BDM, 25 June and 1 July 1925; *MDN*, 13 June 1925.

[56]*MDN*, 9-10 August 1925; *MWN*, 24 January 1925.

Chapter 6

[1]J.N. Brown to C.L. Kjerstad, 7 October 1925; L.W. Boe to J.A. Aasgaard, 18 June 1923, Boe Papers; J.L. Rendahl Interview, 1987; Lindberg, 101, 235.

[2]*FF*, 9 December 1966; *TR*, 44(October 1940), 3; *Cob*, 1939, 18; Brown to Magnus Nodtvedt, 15 September 1927.

[3]Brown to Gould Wickey, 18 January 1927; *MDN*, 19 March 1928 and 14 January 1929;

Gould Wickey, *Lutheran Cooperation Through Lutheran Higher Education: A Documentary History of the NationalLutheran Educational Conference, 1910-1967* (Washington, D. C., 1967), 10-11, 181.

[4]Erling N. Rolfsrud, *Tiger-Lily Years* (Alexandria, 1975), 8; Conkin, 295; Roland Lincoln Guyotte III, "Liberal Education and the American Dream:Public Attitudes and the Emergence of Mass Higher Education, 1920-1952" (Ph.D. diss., Northwestern University, 1980), 35-36.

[5]Nichol, 187-189, 208-209, 222-224, 263-264. On modernism, see W.S. Hudson, *Religion in America* (New York, 1965), 275-276.

[6]Nelson, *Lutheran Church,* II, 283, 283n, 284-285, 285n; George M. Marsden, *Fundamentalism and American Culture: The Shaping of Twentieth- Century Evangelicalism* (New York, 1980), 164, 169-170, 194-195.

[7]*Con,* 19 September 1929; Brown to P.A. Lee, 16 April 1926; Brown to Mrs. G.J. Hegg, 25 January 1927; Brown to G.L. Harmrast, 25 August 1927; Brown to Carl M. Weswig, 27 October 1927.

[8]Brown to Byron C. Nelson, 22 September 1927 and 27 July 1932; Brown to M.E. Waldeland, 11 February 1932; Brown to H.L. Fevold, 23 December 1927; *Con,* 21 April 1950.

[9]William L. Harwood, "The Ku Klux Klan in Grand Forks, North Dakota," *South Dakota History,* 1(Fall 1971), 302, 305, 314; Blegen, *Minnesota,* 482; *FF,* 20 September 1925; *North Dakota American,* 14 November 1925.

[10]Brown to *North Dakota American,* 20 February 1926 and to Samuel Miller, 20 and 27 February 1926.

[11]Lovoll, 195-196; *MDN,* 12 April 1924, 16, 23 and 30 May, 18 June, 19 September and 5 October 1925; *Con,* 31 October 1925.

[12]Brown to J.G. Holland, 17 October 1925; *Con,* 20 December 1927 and 16 January 1931; Brown to R.R. Syrdal, 3 April 1926; 1920s Oral History, 1984, Monday 2B (Side A) and Monday 3B (Side B).

[13]Brown to Victor L. Peterson, 11 September 1925; Brown to Mrs. S.S. Wegge, 4 October 1928.

[14]Lovoll, 208-212; Semmingsen, 142, 153, 156-157; Nelson, *Lutheran Church,* II, 251, 254.

[15]*Con,* 26 September and 31 October 1925; Brown, "The Christian College," Presidents' Papers.

[16]Brown to L.J. Hauge, 16 August 1926 and to Oscar L. Olson, 22 December 1926.

[17]Brown to Deane Wiley, 4 October 1926; Brown to A.M. Rovelstad, 19 November and 16 December 1926; Brown to W.M. Sandstrom, 16 February 1927; Brown to Lancelot A. Gorden, 24 June 1926.

[18]Brown to H.L. Fevold, 23 December 1927; Brown to C.M. Weswig, 16 September 1925; Brown to J.O. Silseth, 20 February 1926.

[19]Brown Report in BDM and BTM, 29 December 1926 and 28 December 1927; *Con,* 19 January 1928.

[20]*Con,* 26 September 1925, 20 May 1927, 7 December 1928; Brown to Pres. Gould Wickey, 28 April 1927; Brown Report in BTM, 1 December 1925 and 21 April 1927; BDM and BTM, 25 January 1928.

[21]John S. Brubacher and Willis Rudy, *Higher Education in Transition: A History of American Colleges and Universities, 1636-1976* (3rd ed.; New York, 1976), 332-344.

[22]*MDN,* 9 January 1926; *Con,* 29 September 1927.

[23]Rolfsrud, *Cobber Chronicle,* 93; *Cat,* 1927-1928, 93; *Sct,* 1929, 102.

[24]Guyotte, 37-38, 46; Brubacher and Rudy, 269-272.

[25]Brown to P.M. Glasoe, 17 October 1925; *Con,* 16 January 1931; Brown to Liberal Arts College Movement, 13 March 1931.

[26]Brown to H.M. Dale, 25 January 1926; *Con,* 5 May 1927.

[27]Brown to Concordia Student Forum, 15 November 1926; Brown to Gould Wickey, 22 December 1926; Brubacher and Rudy, 367-368.

[28]Brown's Report to the Board of Education, Norwegian Lutheran Church of America, Presidents' Papers; BDM and BTM, 25 January 1928; *Con,* 3 February 1928; Brubacher and Rudy, 410.

[29]Brown to J.W. Johnson, 20 September 1926; Brown to T.J. Gronningren, 30 January 1926; Brown to Mrs. E.A. Tannas, 19 October 1926.

[30]*Con,* 28 November 1925 and 18 January 1926.

[31]Brown to Andrew Thorson, 4 September 1925; Levine, 114, 117, 119; Brown to Miss Ruth Liljegren, 13 August 1926; *Con,* 31 January

1927.

[32]Brown to J.G. Rugland, 1 October 1927 and to J. Jorgen Thompson, 13 February 1926.

[33]Brown to P.M. Glasoe, 17 October 1925; Brown Report in BDM and BDM, 29 December 1926; Levine, 138-139; Brown to R.R. Syrdal, 6 September 1927; Brown to P. Rasmussen, 1 August 1927; *MDN,* 4 December 1928, 1 March 1929.

[34]Sinclair quoted in Rudolph, 168; Brown to M.C. Johnshoy, 17 February 1926.

[35]"Church Appropriations, 1925-1929," Miscellaneous Financial Statements, President's Office Correspondence; Brown to R.R. Syrdal, 6 September 1927; Brown to H.O. Shurson, 22 September and 8 December 1925; Brown to Paul G. Schmidt, 11 February 1926.

[36]Brown Report in BDM and BTM, 30 December 1925 and in BTM, 1 December 1925.

[37]*MDN,* 2 December 1925, 22 January, 3, 10 and 24 February, 18 March 1926; Brown to A.J. Bergsaker, 18 November 1937; Brown to George Henricksen, 25 September 1926; Concordia College Papers, Box 1, Norwegian American Historical Association; Brown Report, BTM, 1 December 1925; *Con,* 5 February 1926.

[38]Dan Weigle to Brown, March 1926; "The Story of Concordia College:Education, Religion, Business" (pamphlet), 3, 8-9, Concordia College Papers, Box 1, Norwegian American Historical Association Archives; *Con,* 4 May 1926.

[39]*MDN,* 15 February, 1, 5 and 7 May and 3 June 1926, 24 August 1927; *Con,* 25 May 1926; Brown to R.B. MacLean, 10 July 1926; Brown to J.H. Dahl, 23 April 1926; Brown to P.L. Hjelmstad, 16 April 1926; Brown to George P. Holmes, 3 May 1926; Brown to R.A. Nestos, 12 May 1926.

[40]L.W. Boe to J.A. Aasgaard, 28 October 1925, Boe Papers; H.O. Shurson to Brown, 28 September 1928; Brown to G.A. Larson, 11 February 1926; O.R. Svore to Brown, 22 November 1928; Brown to Ole Tuneberg, 26 November 1926; Robinson, 537.

[41]Rolfsrud, *Cobber Chronicle,* 96; Brown Report in BDM and BTM, 29 December 1926; Brown to David Stoeve, 8 March 1927; Brown to Harold Smith, 16 November 1927; *Con,* 9 November 1928.

[42]*Con,* 6 April 1927; Brown to David Stoeve, 21

March 1927; *TR*, 31(September 1926), 4.

[43]Merrill E. Jarchow, *Private Liberal Arts Colleges in Minnesota: Their History and Contributions* (St. Paul, 1973), 48; Brown to Olaf Hagen, 2 October 1928.

Chapter 7

[1]Donald R. McCoy, *Coming of Age: The United States During the 1920s and 1930s* (New York, 1973), 176-179.

[2]Levine, 185-186; Solberg, 299.

[3]*LH*, 23 May 1933, 475 and 29 May 1934, 503-505.

[4]*MDN,* 31 October 1931; Brown to Leonard Kolden, 22 December 1931; Brown to O.M. Norlie, 28 July 1933.

[5]*MDN,* 19 January, 9 April and 5 June 1931, 17 April 1933, 25 February 1938, 5 January 1939, 3 May 1941, 12 June and 18 October 1940; 1930s Oral History, Session III, 23 July 1985.

[6]Brown to J.M. Erickson, 21 October 1933; Brown to E.O. Ulring, 28 May 1938; Brown to Mrs. E.H. Gilbertson, 28 June 1933; Brown to T.F. Gullixson, 16 September 1933; Brown to Ferdinand Palladeau, 27 September 1933.

[7]Brown to P.O. Sathre, 5 October 1932; Brown to Caroline Evingson, 12 November 1932; Brown to J.E. Engstad, 15 April 1930; Brown to Joseph Stump, 28 March 1930.

[8]Brown to R. Malmin, 30 November 1931; Brown, "Address" and "Lutheran Evangelism" (n.d.), Speeches and Addresses, 1925-1955, Presidents' Papers.

[9]Brown to Gordon A. Reigher, 7 December 1933; *Beloit Daily*, 10 September 1915 in J.N. Brown Biographical File, ELCA Region 3 Archives.

[10]*Con,* 7 November 1930 and 28 April 1933.

[11]Nelson, *Lutheran Church*, II, 304-308, 314-315.

[12]*Con,* 15 January 1932 and 11 January 1935; Brown to David Stoeve, 27 November 1931; Brown to J.C.K. Preus, 8 and 16 December 1931; Brown to N.J. Gould Wickey, 19 December 1931; Brown Report in Corporation Minutes, 11 June 1938.

[13]Brown to S.G. Hauge, 18 and 24 August 1933; Brown to A.E. Hanson, 29 May 1937; Brown to C.M. Granskou, 16 May 1938; Brown to

J.C.K. Preus, 25 May 1938.

[14]Brown to A.E. Hanson, 23 December 1932; Brown to L.W. Boe, 3 December 1938; Brown to G.P. Homnes, 8 February 1933; Brown to Senator G.D. McCubrey, 3 April 1933; Brown to Hon. Paul Kvale, 12 May 1933; C.A. Glasrud, *Moorhead State Teachers College (1921-1957)* (Moorhead, 1990), 33.

[15]Brown to Gov. Floyd B. Olson, 1 March 1934; Brown to G.B. Nord, 3 November 1934; Brown to Robert Hovland, 6 November 1934.

[16]Brown to J.C.K. Preus, 2 January and 1 July 1932; Brown to A.E. Hanson, 29 January 1932; Board of Education, Minutes, 1931-1933, 115-116, 120-122, ELCA Region 3 Archives.

[17]Board of Education, Minutes, 1934-1941, 163, 176-177, 183.

[18]Brown to R.A. Nestos, 12 November 1930; J.A. Fjelstad to Brown, 5 May 1931; Brown to J.A. Fjelstad, 7 May 1931.

[19]Brown to Leonard Kinsell, 24 October 1930; Brown to Pastors, 26 June 1930; *MDN*, 5 December 1929 and 21 February 1930; *Con*, 10 October 1930, 16 January 1931, 1 February and 29 May 1933, 19 January 1934; *Cat*, 1938, 21.

[20]Brown to G.S. Hauge, 30 September and 23 October 1936; Brown to L.B. Hanna, 15 May 1934; Brown to Gould Wickey, 4 March 1940; *Con*, 22 January 1937.

[21]1930s Oral History, Session III, 23 July 1985; *Cat* 1931, 19- 20; Brown to Morris Fredericks, 21 July 1938.

[22]Brown to Gustav Andreen, 26 February 1934; Brown to John Nystul, 2 March 1933; Brown to J.C.K. Preus, 29 December 1933.

[23]Brown to P.O. Holland, 29 October 1931; Brown to Colleagues, 8 February 1933.

[24]Brown to A.E. Hanson, 5 January 1933; Brown to Anna Jordahl, 21 February 1933; Annual Treasurer's Report, 1932-1933 and 1933-1934; Brown to Miss Ellingson, 10 January 1935; Brown to Gustav Andreen, 26 February 1934.

[25]Rolfsrud, *Cobber Chronicle*, 99, 104-106; Hazel Mohle to Rolfsrud, 15 July 1964; *MDN*, 29 December 1933; *LH*, 14 November 1933, 1042-1043; *Cat*, 1929-1930, 16 and 1933-1934, 16.

[26]J.L. Rendahl Interview, 1987; Joseph L. Knutson Interview, 1988; *TR*, 49(October 1945), 10; Rolfsrud, *Cobber Chronicle*, 106.

[27]*Con*, 11 January 1935; Brown to O.J. Johnson, 7 November 1936; *MDN*, 29 July 1938; North Central Association of Colleges and Secondary Schools Report, 1935-1936 (unless otherwise indicated, Concordia Archives).

[28]North Central Association of Colleges and Secondary Schools Report, 1935-1936.

[29]Thomas Burgess, "Concordia: Liberal Arts College," *TR*, 44 (June 1940), 3, 6; Peter Anderson, *A Liberal Arts Education*, Pamphlet, 13 May 1936, Frida Nilsen, "A Christian Power Station," *TR*, 41(August 1937) and Carl Ylvisaker, "Spiritual Life at Concordia," *TR*, 41(December 1937) in Concordia College Papers, Box 1, Norwegian American Historical Association Archives.

[30]Brown to Mrs. E.H. Gilbertson, 9 January 1930; *Con*, 16 December 1937, 19 May 1938 and 23 March 1939.

[31]*Cob*, 1932, 110; *Con*, 28 September 1934 and 29 April 1943; Concordia College Papers, Box 1, Norwegian American Historical Association Archives.

[32]*Con*, 18 May 1939; *MDN*, 29 March, 5 and 9 June 1939.

[33]Brown to O.H. Pannkoke, 28 January 1936; Brown to J.C.K. Preus, 26 March and 13 July 1931, 20 February 1932.

[34]*Cat*, 1933, 23 and 1938, 22-24.

[35]Brown to Walter J. Swenson, 28 June 1932; *Cat*, 1933, 26-27; Brown to John C. Acheson, 2 April 1934; Brown to A.J. Gravdal, 9 January 1930; Brown to Elsie Fossum, 13 July 1931; *Con*, 10 October 1930, 6 November 1941 and 7 April 1933; Rolfsrud, *Cobber Chronicle*, 100.

[36]Levine, 188; Brown to Mrs. Herman I. Muus, 22 September 1931; Brown to O.J. Johnson, 7 April 1933.

[37]Brown to Clara Holey, 4 November 1931; Clara Holey to Brown, 24 May 1932; Brown to Palmer Halverson, 24 February 1932; Brown to Harold Johnson, 5 May 1933.

[38]Erling Nicolai Rolfsrud, *With the Wind At My Back: Recollections and Reflections* (Farwell, 1988), 55-57; Brown to F.S. Hallanger, 27 September 1937; Brown to Norris W. Stoa, 18 January 1936; Rolfsrud, *Cobber Chronicle*, 100.

[39]Levine, 195-196, 201; Brown to Harold Benjamin, 15 December 1933; Brown Report in Corporation Minutes, 11 June 1938.

[40]*Con,* 27 May 1939 and 23 May 1941; Brown to Charlotte Horneland, 26 February 1935; Brown to Mrs. Oscar Kjorlie, 6 January 1931; 1930s Oral History, Session II, 23 July 1985; Brown to waiters and waitresses, n.d.

[41]Solomon, 142; Levine, 210; Figures compiled from *Cat,* 1929-1942 and 1942, 110.

[42]North Central Association of Colleges and Secondary Schools Report, 1935-1936; *Con,* 9 November 1939; *LH,* 4 November 1941, 1184.

[43]Rolfsrud, *Cobber Chronicle,* 99-100; Brown to Vivian Hanore, 17 August 1932; *Con,* 20 September 1935, 30 September 1937, 18 March 1938; Brown to Kenneth Flugstad, 22 June 1934.

[44]Gretchen Urnes Beito, *Coya Come Home: A Congresswoman's Journey* (Los Angeles, 1990), 48-49.

[45]Solomon, 173, 176; *Cat,* 1929-1930, 105 and 1942, 111.

[46]*Perspective,* 5(Spring 1966), 3; Mattie Ostby Dale Interview, 1990; 1920s Oral History, 1984, Tuesday 2A (Side A); Brown to Sigurd Mundhjeld, 7 May 1937; Brown to B.M. Branford, 20 May 1930; *Cat,* 1940, 13.

[47]North Central Association of Colleges and Secondary Schools Report, 1935-1936; Horowitz, *Campus Life,* 111; *Cat,* 1931, 6-7, 16, 1935, 6, 16.

[48]*Cat,* 1936, 34 and 1939, 40.

[49]Rolfsrud, *Cobber Chronicle,* 99; *Con,* 29 May 1933.

[50]Brown to Mr. Dean, 28 May 1935 and to Merrill Distad, 7 May 1935; Kenneth Bradley Orr, "The Impact of the Depression Years, 1929-1939, on Faculty in American Colleges and Universities," (Ph.D. diss., University of Michigan, 1978), 174, 179, 190-194; Richard Polenberg, *One Nation Divisible: Class, Race, and Ethnicity in the United States Since 1938* (New York, 1980), 18.

[51]*Cat,* 1931, 8-11 and 1940, 9-13.

[52]North Central Association of Colleges and Secondary Schools Report, 1935-1936; Brown to E. Helte, 16 November 1937; G.L. Schoberg Interview, 1985; *MDN,* 22 April 1937 and 10 October 1941; *Con,* 19 September 1930, 13 March 1931, 4 March 1932, 10 January 1936.

[53]*Con,* 13 February 1931 and 4 November 1932.

[54]*Studies in Lutheran Higher Education: Trends and Issues Affecting Lutheran Higher Education, The Report of a Committee Representing The Higher Educational Institutions of the American Lutheran Conference* (Minneapolis, 1933), 7, 15-16, 18, 22-25.

[55]Diane Ravitch, *The Troubled Crusade: American Education, 1945-1980* (New York, 1983), 51-54; *Studies in Lutheran Higher Education,* 27-41, 60.

[56]*Studies in Lutheran Higher Education,* 69-74.

[57]*Con,* 24 November 1933, 19 October 1934 and 13 March 1936; *Cat,* 1935, 3 and 1937, 12.

[58]*Cat,* 1925-1926, 29-30 and 1937, 42-43.

[59]*Cat,* 1927-1928, 53-54, 1937, 42-43; Solomon, 102; Levine, 99.

[60]*Cat,* 1925-1926, 55-56 and 1938, 48-85; Brown to A.E. Rolfson, 26 July 1926.

[61]*Cat,* 1928-1929, 62-63, 1934, 50, 1938, 53-54, 81, 1939, 68 and 1940, 57; *Con,* 13 April 1928; *CA,* 5(April 1958), 4; *FM,* 12 February 1941.

[62]*Con,* 18 March and 15 September 1938, 23 May 1940; Johnson, 110; Brown to N.J. Gould Wickey, 11 October 1926; Brown to S.G. Hauge, 9 August 1938; Brown Report in Corporation Minutes, 11 June 1938.

[63]*Con,* 19 January 1934, 17 September 1937, 31 October, 1 February 1940 and 6 March 1941; *Cat,* 1937, 55.

[64]*Con,* 20 December 1927, 18 March 1932, 19 February 1942, 24 February and 3 March 1938; Brown to Frida Nilsen, 20 August 1931; *Cat,* 1936, 18 and 1940, 18; North Central Association of Colleges and Secondary Schools Report, 1935-1936.

[65]*Con,* 24 February and 3 March 1938; Brown to Supt. Ira L. Plummer, 28 June 1932.

[66]BTM and BDM, 25 January 1928; *Con,* 13 May 1932 and 29 May 1933.

[67]Brown to L.W. Boe, 6 March 1934; Brown to J.A. Aasgaard, 13 April and 5 May 1934; Brown to Verne Giere, 29 February 1936; North Central Association of Colleges and Secondary Schools Report, 1935-1936.

[68]Brown to C.G. Dosland, 22 June 1934; Brown to I.T. Aastad, 10 March 1937; Brown to Harold M. Tolo, 9 October 1937.

[69]Brown to S.G. Hauge, 16 May 1938; Brown to John Nystul, 20 May 1938; Brown to C.G. Dosland, 28 May 1938.

[70]Brown to I.T. Aastad, 23 April 1937; 1920s Oral History, 1984, Thursday 1A (Side A).

[71]Brown to F. Melius Christiansen, 20 November 1936; Brown to Gunnar Malmin, 5 May 1937; Brown to Carl Thompson, 8 June 1937; Brown to L.M. Larsen, 2 July 1938.

[72]1930s Oral History, Session IV and V, 24 July 1985; Rolfsrud, *Cobber Chronicle*, 193.

[73]*Con,* 7 May 1937; *CAN*, 16(Autumn 1977), 15-16; Paul J. Christiansen Interview, 1983.

[74]Brown to Paul A. Rasmussen, 27 April 1936.

[75]Brown to Verne Giere, 29 February 1936; *Con*, 2 November 1939.

[76]*TR*, 40(October 1936), 7; *Con*, 24 April 1936; Brown to Carl Olsen, 2 January 1937; Brown to C.G. Dosland, 18 November 1936; Brown to Paul A. Rasmussen, 11 January 1937.

[77]*TR*, 41(October 1937), 4; *MDN*, 10 October 1941; *Con*, 1 June 1936; 1930s Oral History, Session VI, 25 July 1985.

[78]Brown to L.W. Boe, 16 July 1938; *Con*, 16 July 1938.

[79]Brown to L.W. Boe, 18 April 1940, Boe Papers.

[80]Brown to *Cob*, 1941 and to L.W. Boe, 16 March 1942, Boe Papers; *Con*, 12 March 1942.

[81]*Con*, 21 January 1944, 6 April and 12 October 1945.

[82]Brown to Judith Johnson, 16 August 1938; 1920s Oral History, 1984, Thursday 1A (Side A); *MDN*, 25 May 1932; Brown to C.M. Granskou, 5 November 1951, Granskou Papers (unless otherwise indicated, St. Olaf Archives); *Minneapolis Star*, 9 August 1962.

[83]*Cob*, 1941, 2-3; Jarchow, 105; *Con*, 31 October 1940.

Chapter 8

[1]*Con*, 22 September 1933.

[2]*Con*, 29 September 1927, 20 September 1935 and 2 October 1936; FM, 15 March 1935; Frida Nilsen to Cobber-to-be, 19 August 1935 in Helen Mickelson Papers, Concordia Archives; Frida Nilsen, *Eyes of Understanding: A Biography* (Minneapolis, 1947), 25.

[3]*Con*, 6 November 1936, 19 October 1934, 29 May 1933, 18 May 1939.

[4]*MDN*, 9 May 1936, 5 October 1939; *Con*, 27 October 1928, 15 April 1943.

[5]*MDN*, 17 November 1937 and 28 January 1941; *Con*, 13 January and 13 October 1938, 25 April 1940; H.W. Case to Rolfsrud, 2 August 1965.

[6]*Cat*, 1925, 19 and 1943, 35; *Con*, 1 December 1938; 1930s Oral History, Session I, 22 July 1985; E. Clifford Nelson, *et. al.*, ed., *The Lutherans in North America* (Rev. ed.; Philadelphia, 1980), 356, 460.

[7]Brown to E. Kristensen, 22 March 1932; Brown to E.G. Lockhart, 20 May 1926; Brown to S.G. Hauge, 2 January 1930; Brown to Mr. and Mrs. A. Swensrud, 1 April 1926.

[8]*Con*, 1 February 1929, 30 January 1931 and 23 April 1937; Brown to Peter Malvey, 20 June 1930; Brown to J.S. Halverson, 11 April 1933; Brown to David Stoeve, 2 May 1933.

[9]*Con*, 24 February, 3, 10, 17, 24, and 31 March, 28 April, 6 and 14 May, 6 June 1938.

[10]*Con*, 5 June 1928, 17 April 1931 and 29 May 1933; *Cob*, 1939, 24-25.

[11]*Con*, 10 October 1930 and 14 October 1937.

[12]1920s Oral History, 1984, Thursday 2B (Side B); *Con*, 16 November 1934, 8 February 1935, 23 October 1936, 11 May 1939 and 25 February 1944.

[13]North Central Association of Colleges and Secondary Schools Report, 1935-1936; Rolfsrud, *With the Wind*, 55.

[14]*MDN*, 19 and 20 October 1934.

[15]Nelson, ed, *Lutherans*, 458; Ringenberg, 126; 1920s Oral History, 1984, Wednesday 3A (side B); *Con*, 16 March 1928, 7 April 1933, 16 February 1939 and 23 May 1941.

[16]1920s Oral History, 1984, Wednesday 3A (Side B); *Con*, 2 December 1932 and 9 December 1937.

[17]*Con*, 23 November 1938, 13 March 1931, 5 October 1934; *Cob*, 1932, 140-144; Beito, 44.

[18]*Con,* 16 April 1937 and 23 March 1934; *Cob*, 1937, 130.

[19]Nelson, *Lutheran Church*, II, 260; 1920s Oral History, 1984, Wednesday 3A (side B); *Con*, 4 December 1931, 8 February 1935, 10 February and 20 October 1938, 26 September

1940; *Cob*, 1932, 146.

[20]1930s Oral History, Sessions II and IV, 23 and 25 July 1985; Shaw, 314.

[21]*Con*, 9 and 23 March 1934; 1930s Oral History, Session VI, 25 July 1985; Brown to Rev. R.M. Fjelstad, 14 March 1934.

[22]*Con*, 14 and 21 February 1936.

[23]Nelson, ed., *Lutherans*, 279, 355-356, 466.

[24]*Con*, 12 April 1929, 30 October 1931, 26 October 1935 and 8 December 1938.

[25]Horowitz, *Campus Life*, 118-119; *Cob*, 1935, 26-31; *Con*, 26 October 1929.

[26]*Con*, 4 April 1940; North Central Association of Colleges and Secondary Schools Report, 1935-1936.

[27]*Cob*, 1932, 107-109.

[28]*Con*, 31 October 1936.

[29]*Cob*, 1941, 65.

[30]*Cob*, 1932, 122-132; *Con*, 24 February 1933, 5 December 1930, 21 January 1977 and 13 October 1978.

[31]*Con*, 6 November 1936, 13 October 1938, 11 April and 17 October 1940, 1 May 1941.

[32]1920s Oral History, 1984, Wednesday 2B (Side B); *Cob*, 1935, 114, 119 and 1937, 99, 107.

[33]*Con*, 22 April 1927, 8 December 1933, 13 April 1934, 5 February 1937 and 31 October 1941; *Cob*, 1932, 149-150, 155 and 1935, 155; 1930s Oral History, Session II, 23 July 1985.

[34]*Con*, 22 April 1927, 18 September 1936, 24 May 1935 and 27 April 1939; 1930s Oral History Session VI, 25 July 1985.

[35]*MDN*, 1 February, 8 and 26 June 1933, 27 April and 22 June 1935; *LH*, 27 August 1935, 843-844; Johnson, 126, 130; 1930s Oral History, Session VI, 25 July 1985.

[36]Rolfsrud, *Cobber Chronicle,* 183-184; *MDN*, 3, 12, 29 August 1935.

[37]*Cob*, 1932, 163; *Con*, 16 April 1937; Johnson, 143, 148.

[38]*Con*, 9 March 1926; Brown Report to Board, 29 December 1926.

[39]"Concordia and Athletics," *TR*, 40(April 1936).

[40]*Sct*, 1929, 197, 199; *Cob*, 1932, 184-212; *Con*, 10 April 1930, 24 March 1933, 21 September 1934, 27 April 1939 and 8 May 1941.

[41]*Con,* 13 March 1930; Rolfsrud, *Cobber Chronicle,* 217.

[42]*Con*, 20 November 1931; Rolfsrud, *Cobber Chronicle,* 206, 209-211.

[43]Rudolph, 388; *Con*, 16 January 1931; *Cob*, 1939, 146.

[44]*Con*, 22 April 1927 and 30 October 1931; *Cob*, 1932, 214-215.

[45]Carl Bailey Interview, 1985; *Con*, 6 May 1938.

[46]Nilsen, *Eyes of Understanding*, 44, 47, 73; *MDN*, 16 May 1936.

[47]*Con*, 1 March 1935 and 26 September 1940.

[48]*Con,* 7 March 1940 and 6 May 1949; 1920s Oral History, 1984, Wednesday 2A (Side A).

[49]Gladys Hoversten Adams to Rolfsrud, 9 October 1964; 1920s Oral History, 1984, Monday 4B (Side A); *Con*, 19 December 1930 and 23 May 1941.

[50]1930s Oral History, Session VI, 25 July 1985; 1920s Oral History, 1984, Wednesday 3A (Side A).

[51]Nelson, ed., *Lutherans*, 417; Urberg-Malmin Interview; *Con,* 13 November 1925.

[52]*Con*, 22 April and 8 December 1927, 16 February 1928 and 21 November 1929.

[53]1920s Oral History, 1984, Wednesday 3A (Side A); *Con,* 13 March 1936.

[54]*Con*, 4 December 1936, 1 February 1940 and 22 January 1942.

[55]*Con*, 23 April 1937 and 11 May 1939; *TR*, 42(December 1938), 2-3; Program of Faculty Studies, 1940-1941, FM; Glasrud, *MSTC*, 118-119.

[56]*Con*, 4 May 1926 and 15 May 1931.

[57]*Con*, 27 October 1928, 7 October 1932, 9 and 23 October 1936, 24 and 31 October, 7 November 1940.

[58]*Con*, 30 September 1937 and 1 February 1935.

[59]*Con,* 11 January, 1 and 8 February 1935.

[60]*Con*, 15 March 1935, 17 November 1938, 19 January 1939.

[61]*Con*, 16 January 1931, 28 April, 24 November and 8 December 1933, 19 January, 13 and 27 April, 25 May 1934; *MDN* 6 and 12 January 1934; Glasrud, *MSTC*, 234.

[62]*MDN*, 12 April 1935; *Con*, 1 and 8 February 1935, 17 April 1936, 9 and 16 April 1937.

[63]Nelson, ed., *Lutherans*, 473-474; John E. Haynes, "Reformers, Radicals and Conservatives," *Minnesota*, ed. Clark, 380-383; *Con*, 13 January and 18 March 1938.

[64]*Con*, 22 September, 6 October and 1 December 1938.

[65]*FF*, 30 May 1948 and 22 May 1960; *TR*, 52(February 1948).

[66]Thomas Christenson, "Persons of Influence: Frida Nilsen," *CAN*, 16(Winter 1977), 12; Margaret Nordlie Interview, 1985; 1930s Oral History, Session IV, 24 July 1985.

[67]1920s Oral History, 1984, Tuesday 3A.

[68]*Con*, 8 December 1927; C.M. Granskou to Brown, 18 April 1945, Granskou Papers; 1930s Oral History, Session IV, 24 July 1985; *Cob*, 1939, 81.

[69]*Cob*, 1948, 5; 1930s Oral History, Session IV, 14 July 1985; Nordlie Interview; *MDN*, 5 November 1930.

[70]Allwin Monson Interview, 1982; 1920s Oral History, 1984, Tuesday 3A (Side B).

[71]Thomas Christenson, "Persons of Influence: Professor Charles H. Skalet," *CAN*, 14(Summer 1976), 9.

[72]*Cob*, 1946, 16; *Con*, 13 November 1925, 1 March 1929 and 23 April 1965; *FF*, 10 June 1966; *LH*, 20 January 1931, 75; *MDN*, 6 September and 1 December 1927, 28 June 1928, 20 February 1929, 18 February 1931, 5 March 1934 and 18 March 1935.

[73]Johnson, 99, 106-107, 113; Karl Holvik Interview, 17 August 1983; 1920s Oral History, 1984, Tuesday 3A (Side B); *Con*, 18 November 1949.

[74]Thomas Christenson, "Persons of Influence: Heglund Nikolai Grunfor," *CAN*, 15(Spring 1977), 10.

Chapter 9

[1]William M. Tuttle, Jr., "Higher Education and the Federal Government:The Lean Years, 1940-1942," *Teachers College Record*, 71(December 1969), 304, 306-307; *MDN*, 9 January 1942.

[2]*MDN*, 9 and 22 January 1942, 9 October 1941; Brown to L.W. Boe, 9 January 1942, Boe Papers; FM, 16 December 1941.

[3]Peterson, 89; Figures compiled from *Cat*, 1930-1946 and 1953.

[4]FM, 20 November 1942; Geoffrey Perrett, *Days of Sadness, Years of Triumph: The American People, 1939-1945* (New York, 1974), 216-225.

[5]*MDN*, 17 January 1942; *Con,* 9 October 1942; Peter Anderson to Alvin Stenberg, 14 August 1942, Academic Deans' Papers (unless otherwise indicated, Concordia Archives); Anderson to Winston Wolpert, 21 September 1942 and to Orville Erickson, 24 September 1942.

[6]*Con*, 15 January 1942; Committee on Relations to the Armed Forces (February 1945) and *Campus News Nibbles*, 1 (July 1945), Rolfsrud Papers.

[7]Miscellaneous Financial Statements, Presidents' Papers; *MDN*, 3 March 1944; Board of Education Minutes, 1934-1941, 272, 276; *Con*, 11 March 1943; Brown to J.J. Thompson, 12 May 1943 and to Dr. J.A. Aasgaard *et. al.*, 18 May 1943, Granskou Papers.

[8]Brown to L.W. Boe, 2 October 1942, Boe Papers; *Con*, 14 March 1940; Sigurd Mundhjeld to Harold W. Knutson, 14 January 1944 (unless otherwise indicated, Mundhjeld Papers, Concordia Archives).

[9]*Con*, 1 October 1942, 18 February 1943 and 1 December 1944; *Cat*, 1943, 17-18.

[10]*Con*, 3 March 1944 and 2 November 1945; NLCA, Annual Report, 1944-1945.

[11]Brown to L.W. Boe, 21 September 1942, Boe Papers; *Con*, 1 October 1943 and 17 November 1944; *LH*, 24 November 1942, 1255.

[12]Mundhjeld to H. Knutson, 18 October 1943.

[13]*Con*, 26 September 1940 and 1 October 1942, 1 October 1943; *MDN*, 3 March 1941, 25 September 1942 and 15 December 1943.

[14]FM, 16 December 1941 and 11 December 1942; *MDN*, 23 January 1942 and 23 April 1943; *LH*, 19 May 1942, 543.

[15]*MDN*, 1 February 1944; *Con*, 26 February 1942 and 21 January 1943.

[16]*Con,* 12 March 1942 and 6 May 1943; *Cob*, 1943, 64; *MDN*, 15 December 1943.

[17]Brown to J.J. Thompson, 3 and 11 February 1943; J.J. Thompson to Brown, 8 February 1943, Granskou Papers; *Con*, 11 and 25 February, 4 March 1943; *MDN*, 8 February 1943.

[18]Glasrud, *MSTC*, 288; *Con*, 1 April and 6 May 1943; FM, 14 May 1943; George Howell to Mae Anderson, 30 May 1943 (unless otherwise indicated, World War II

Correspondence, Concordia Archives);
MDN, 31 July 1943.

[19]Nelson, ed., *Lutherans,* 473-474; *MDN*, 1 June
1943.

[20]*MDN*, 21 September 1942; *Con*, 22 October
1942.

[21]*Con*, 22 October 1942, 20 May and 16 December 1943, 11 February 1944; *MDN*, 13 May
and 6 December 1943.

[22]*Con*, 1 October 1942; *MDN*, 29 April 1942, 2
February 1943.

[23]*Con*, 12 and 26 February, 5 March, 16 April
and 9 October 1942; *MDN*, 15 May and 11
April 1942.

[24]*MDN*, 10 and 20 March 1944; *Con*, 18 March
1943; Richard Polenberg, *War and Society:
The United States, 1941-1945* (Philadelphia,
1972), 132-133.

[25]*Con*, 8 April 1943.

[26]*Con*, 3 March 1944, 11 March 1943 and 12 October 1945.

[27]Clarence Tweet to Sigurd Mundhjeld, 27 January 1945, Presidents' Papers.

[28]*Con,* 12 and 26 February, 15 October 1942.

[29]*Con*, 17 March, 6, 13 and 20 October 1944, 23
May 1945.

[30]Norman Jeglum to Mae Anderson, 16 June
1942.

[31]Milton Lindell to Mae Anderson, 27 October
1944; Waldo Lyden to Mae Anderson, 27
June 1944.

[32]Lyden to Anderson, 27 June 1944; Norman Lorentzsen to Mae Anderson, 19 January 1945.

[33]*Campus News Nibbles,* 1 (February 1945),
Rolfsrud Papers; FM, 28 September and 12
October 1945

[34]*Con*, 20 May 1943; *MDN*, 9 November 1940, 7
January 1944, 11 June and 26 September
1942, 1 June 1943.

[35]Thomas Christenson, "Persons of Influence:
Nels Mugaas," *CAN*, 15(Autumn 1976), 9;
Con, 31 March 1944.

[36]*TR*, 46(December 1942), 2; Cyrus Running Interview, 1976.

Chapter 10

[1]Ravitch, 12-16; Jarchow, 141-143.

[2]Ravitch, 15-16; Solberg, 305.

[3]Roy A. Harrisville to C.M. Granskou, 31 Au-
gust and 26 October 1945, Granskou Papers;
MDN, 15 September and 18 October 1945, 6
September 1946.

[4]*MDN*, 6 August and 30 October 1946.

[5]J.L. Rendahl, "The History of Concordia," Address to New Faculty, 7 September 1985,
Concordia Archives; J.L. Rendahl Interview,
1984; *Con*, 2 October 1981.

[6]Brown to C.M. Granskou, 2 February 1951,
Granskou Papers.

[7]*Campus News Nibbles*, 1(March 1945), Rolfsrud Papers; *Cat*, 1945 and 1948, 8; Brown to
Colleagues, 6 February 1945, Business Office Papers.

[8]John Olson, Correspondence (1944-1952) and
Maintenance Rules and Regulations (1946),
Business Office Papers; Carl Narveson Inter-
view, 1985.

[9]Narveson Interview; *An Orphan's Saga*, 264.

[10]1920s Oral History, 1984, Thursday 1A (Side
A); Irvin Christenson Interview, 1989 and
J.L. Rendahl Interview, 1987.

[11]Raymond Farden Interview, 1989.

[12]*The Concordia Volunteer Committee Review*,
15 September 1948, Concordia College Pa-
pers Norwegian American Historical
Association Archives; Concordia Volunteer
Committee, Bulletins, 1947-1948, Concordia
Archives.

[13]1920s Oral History, 1984, Thursday 1A (Side
A); Executive Session, BDM, 28 November
1947; *Con*, 29 October 1948; *MDN*, 28 October 1948.

[14]Brown to Granskou, 7 and 12 July 1947, Granskou Papers; By-Laws of the Concordia
College Corporation in BDM, 25 October
1948.

[15]*Con*, 29 October 1948, 1 April 1949; Peter Anderson to Johannes Knudsen, 12 October
1949, Academic Deans' Papers; *Cat*, 1951, 9;
Farden Interview.

[16]*FF*, 24 August 1945.

[17]*FF*, 24 August 1945 and 30 June 1948; *MDN*,
8 March 1946; Rolfsrud, *Cobber Chronicle*,
116.

[18]*FF*, 19 June 1947; *MDN*, 19 April, 4 and 26
September 1947; *Con*, 4 October 1946.

[19]Clarence Tweet to Sigurd Mundhjeld, 27 January 1945 and Brown Report to BD, 16
October 1946, President's Office Correspon-

dence; Brown Report in BDM, 15 June 1950; *MDN*, 8 July 1950; *Con*, 20 January and 12 May 1950, 20 April 1951; *TR*, 54(September 1950).

[20] *Con*, 14 February and 17 October 1947, 18 May 1951.

[21] *MDN*, 27 October 1949.

[22] *MDN*, 8 March 1946; *FF*, 31 December 1946; Brown Report to Corporation, 27 October 1949, President's Office Correspondence.

[23] Brown to Henry O. Raaen, 29 April 1948, J.C.K. Preus to Brown, 16 October 1950 and Miscellaneous Financial Statements, President's Office Correspondence; Solberg, 306.

[24] *An Orphan's Saga*, 267-268; figures compiled from *Cat*, 1945-1952; *Con*, 27 April 1951.

[25] Peter Anderson to Allwin Monson, 31 July 1947 and to Honorable Harold Hagen, 23 June 1949, Academic Deans' Papers; enrollment percentages compiled from *LH*, 15 October 1946, 925, 12 October 1948, 971 and 11 October 1949, 980; *MDN*, 23 October 1947 and 10 September 1950; *FF*, 19 June 1947 and 30 June 1948; *Con*, 18 April and 14 February 1947, 14 October 1949.

[26] Sigurd Mundhjeld to Harold Knudson, 31 July 1947, President's Office Correspondence.

[27] O.E. Ellickson to Members of the Board, 1 October 1951, Ellickson Correspondence, Business Office Papers.

[28] Brown to Lovella Aasen, 9 December 1946 and "Salary," Board Meeting, 16 October 1946, President's Office Correspondence.

[29] Byron Murray, *Climate Architects: The Story of Moorhead and Its Chamber of Commerce, 1927-1977* (Moorhead, 1977), 17; *MDN*, 12 August 1948; Peter Anderson to Olaf Torstveit, 20 July 1949, Academic Deans' Papers; *An Orphan's Saga*, 231; *Con*, 24 October 1947; Brown Report in BDM, 13 February 1951.

[30] Brown to L.W. Boe, 2 November 1942, Boe Papers; Brown Report to BD, 16 October 1946 and Sigurd Mundhjeld to BD, 15 January 1947 in President's Office Correspondence; Executive Committee in BDM, 27 February 1948; H.M. Dale to A.L. Eliason, 23 December 1946, President's Office Correspondence.

[31] Brown to Bernhard Christensen, 3 January 1944, Christensen Papers, Section 25, Box 7, Augsburg College Archives, Minneapolis; Sigund Mundhjeld to Harold Knudson, 31 July 1947, President's Office Correspon-

dence; BDM, 17 October 1950; Brown to C.M. Granskou, 2 December 1950, Granskou Papers; Orr, 194, 199-201.

[32] Peter Anderson to Allwin Monson, 7 August 1947 and Brown to Monson, n.d., Academic Deans' Papers; Monson Interview; Ivan Larson Interview, 1985; Brown to Harding Noblitt, 29 April 1949 and Peter Anderson to Harding Noblitt, 23 September 1949, Noblitt Papers (unless otherwise indicated, in Noblitt's possession); Harding Noblitt Interview, 1989; *Cat*, 1942, 59, 67- 68, 78-79, 90-91 and 1947, 77-78.

[33] *MDN*, 31 January 1947; Sigurd Mundhjeld to Mae R. Anderson, 9 August 1946 and to Clara, Julia and Martha Brennun, 5-6 August 1946, President's Office Correspondence; Boulay, Anderson, Waldo and Co. to J.N. Brown and to H.M. Dale, 6 August 1946, President's Office Correspondence.

[34] *MDN*, 31 January 1947, 28 February and 28 June 1948, 24 October, 8 November and 31 December 1949, 29 September, 9 October and 18 May 1950.

[35] FM, 28 February 1947 and 9 September 1949; *TR*, 52(September 1948); Annual Report of Faculty Activities Committee, 1950-1951, John A. Olson, Faculty Material (1950-1952), Business Office Papers.

[36] *MDN*, 16 April 1945, 20 September 1947, 29 March 1948, 7 April 1950.

[37] Brown to Allwin Monson, n.d. and Peter Anderson to Allwin Monson, 27 June 1947, Academic Deans' Papers; *An Orphan's Saga*, 269.

[38] *An Orphan's Saga*, 269; Allwin Monson to Peter Anderson, 1, 23 and 28 July 1947 and Peter Anderson to Allwin Monson, 19 July 1947, Academic Deans' Papers.

[39] FM, 2 December 1949; Faculty Executive Committee Minutes, 1 November 1950; Noblitt Interview; Christenson Interview.

[40] Figures compiled from *Cat*, 1945, 9-13, 1950, 9-17.

[41] *Con*, 12 January 1951 and 1 February 1946.

[42] Solomon, 189-191, 194, 196, 198; figures compiled from *Cat*, 1946-1953; Brown Report in BDM, 13 February 1951.

[43] *Cat*, 1945, 20, 1950, 25 and 1951, 32, 75-139.

[44] *MDN*, 1 March and 30 June 1948; *Con*, 27 October 1950 and 27 April 1951.

[45] *Cat*, 1943, 71, 1947, 76-77, 1945, 48-49, 100,

1946, 77; *Con*, 16 January 1948, 9 November 1945, 11 October 1946, 24 March 1950.

[46]*Cat*, 1945, 48-49; Peter Anderson to I.B. Hauge, 9 August 1950, Academic Deans' Papers; *LH*, 3 April 1951, 349; BDM, 13 February 1951; Pearl Bjork Interview, 1984; G.D. Robbins to Pearl Bjork, n.d. and F.R. Adams to Peter Anderson, 5 March 1951, Academic Deans' Papers; *LH*, 6 March 1951, 248; *An Orphan's Saga*, 266.

[47]*Con*, 16 February 1951 and 10 November 1950.

[48]*Con*, 25 February and 4 March 1949, 17 March 1950, 12 January 1951.

[49]*MDN*, 8 September 1950.

[50]*MDN*, 17 February 1951; *Cat*, 1946 and 1950; *Con*, 22 September 1950; *Cob* 1946, 110, 1949, 171; *TR*, 50(February 1946).

[51]Brown Report to BD, 16 October 1946, President's Office Correspondence; *Con*, 4 October, 1 and 8 November, 13 December 1946, 5 December 1947, 12 November 1948, 25 February 1949; *MDN*, 30 October and 13 December 1950.

[52]*Con*, 12 April 1946, 10 March 1950, 29 March 1951, 24 October 1947; *LH*, 14 January 1947, 50 and 25 January 1949, 96; *MDN*, 9 December 1950.

[53]Enrollment data compiled from *Cat*, 1946-1952.

[54]Brown Report to BD, 16 October 1946, President's Office Correspondence; Peter Anderson to J.R. Lavik, 15 July 1949, Academic Deans' Papers; Solberg, 309; *Con*, 8 November 1946 and 14 January 1949; *Cat*, 1949, 130.

[55]*Cat*, 1945, 24-25, 1950, 29; Brown to Doris Pederson, 3 September 1948, President's Office Correspondence.

[56]*Cat*, 1946, 112 and 1951, 159; *TR*, 54(October 1950), 10-11; *LH*, 1 June 1948, 1.

[57]*Con*, 26 April and 17 May 1946, 28 February 1947, 12 and 19 November, 10 December 1948, 8 and 29 April 1949, 24 March 1950.

[58]*Con*, 15 March and 22 November 1946.

[59]Myrtle Rendahl Interview, 1985; *Con*, 11 and 19 March 1949.

[60]*Con*, 5 April and 15 November 1946.

[61]*MDN*, 5 November 1945, 1 May 1946 and 29 April 1949.

[62]*MDN*, 28 May 1949 and 17 February 1951; Brown to Peter Anderson, 9 July 1949, Academic Deans' Papers; Johnson, 158; *Con*, 3 November 1950.

[63]Johnson, 158; *Con*, 8 November 1946.

[64]*Cob*, 1949, 60-62.

[65]*Cob*, 1947, n.p.; *Con*, 1 June 1948, 24 March 1950.

[66]*Con*, 31 March, 28 April 1950.

[67]*Con*, 23 April 1948, 29 April 1949, 26 May and 27 October 1950; *Cob*, 1949, 71-83.

[68]*Con*, 5 March 1942; Brown to James S. Lombard, 5 June 1945, President's Office Correspondence.

[69]*Con*, 1 March 1946.

[70]Polenberg, *War and Society*, 214; Robinson, 469-470.

[71]*Con*, 15 and 22 November, 20 December 1946 and 17 January 1947.

[72]*Con*, 11, 18 and 25 October, 1 November, 6 December 1946, 7 and 14 February 1947.

[73]*Con*, 15 March, 22 November, 6 and 13 December 1946, 31 January, 7 February, 28 March, 31 October 1947 and 27 February 1948.

[74]*Con*, 5 May and 8 December 1950, 12 January 1951.

[75]*LH*, 13 December 1949, 1221; *MDN*, 1 December 1949, 3 May, 24 October, 30 November and 19 December 1950; *Con*, 20 April 1951.

[76]*Cob*, 1951, 5; *LH*, 29 May 1951, 553; BDM, 13 February 1951; Selmer Berge, "Report of the President of the Board of Directors," *TR*, 54 (October 1950), 21-22.

[77]BDM, 26 June and 16 October 1951; Brown to C.M. Granskou, 20 July, 4 October, 5 November 1951, 2 February and 19 September 1952, Granskou Papers; J.N. Brown Biographical File, ELCA Region 3 Archives.

[78]Carrol E. Malvey Interview, 1990; Elinor Torstveit Interview, 1990; *FF*, 12 December 1966; Brown to Rolfsrud, 3 June 1964.

Chapter 11

[1]Knutson Interview, 1986; *Con*, 20 September 1963; Letter of Call to Joseph L. Knutson, 23 April 1951; BDM, 13 February 1951; Corporation Minutes, 17 April 1951.

[2]Knutson Interviews, 1985 and 1986; Peter Anderson to Bertha Okland, 28 April 1951, Academic Deans' Papers.

[3]Knutson Interview, 1985; *FF*, 22 August 1951.

[4]Knutson Interview, 1985; Knutson to Thomas Pederson, 28 January 1966.

[5]Knutson Interview, 1987; Knutson to Concordia Teachers, 7 September 1951.

[6]Christenson Interview; Noblitt Interview; *FF*, 22 August 1951; Knutson Interviews, 1985 and 1986; "Dr. Joseph L. Knutson," *HBG*, 13(December 1980), 21-23.

[7]Knutson to Pastors, 20 July 1951.

[8]Ronald Lora, *Conservative Minds in America* (Chicago, 1971), 10-17.

[9]*MDN*, 13 October 1951; J.L. Knutson, "The Superscription of Concordia," *LH*, 13 November 1951, 1076-1077 and 20 November 1951, 1104-1106.

[10]Knutson, "Superscription," 1104-1105.

[11]Knutson, "Superscription," 1106.

[12]Knutson Interviews, 1987 and 1988; *FF*, 22 August 1951; Knutson to S.R. Torgeson, 9 October 1951; Jarchow, 218.

[13]Howard G. Johnshoy to Oscar H. Kjorlie, 7 March 1951, Presidents' Papers; J.N. Brown to Knutson, 27 April 1951; Johnshoy to Knutson, 20 July 1951 and 13 January 1952; Knutson to Johnshoy, 22 January 1952; Knutson to C.M. Granskou, 16 September 1966; Stuart M. Folland to Knutson, 7 March 1966; *CAN*, 6(Spring 1968), 12.

[14]Knutson Interviews, 1985 and 1986; Noblitt Interview, 1989; *FF*, 16 April and 1 and 2 June 1951, 18 February and 5 May 1952, 5 September 1954; *Con*, 28 September 1951, 25 January, 25 April, 17 October and 21 November 1952; Brown to Knutson, 5 July 1951.

[15]Knutson Report, Corporation Minutes, 21 October 1952; Knutson, "A New Chapter," January 1953, Presidents' Papers.

[16]Knutson Report, Corporation Minutes, 21 October 1951; *Con*, 6 and 13 February 1953.

[17]Knutson Report, Corporation Minutes, 21 October 1952; Knutson Interview, 1986.

[18]Knutson Interview, 1986; Knutson to Elmer B. Siebrecht, 12 April 1952; Knutson to Dorothy Johnson, 6 February 1954.

[19]Knutson to Irving Nelson, 18 August 1951; Knutson to Pastors, 11 September 1952; Knutson to Faculty, 3 July 1952; Knutson to Friends of Concordia, 28 April and 28 May 1952; Knutson to Friends in Christ, 28 January 1954.

[20]Knutson to Pastors, 8 December 1953 and 1 November 1954; Knutson to R.L. Mortvedt, 5 November 1953; Knutson to Concordia Employees, 18 December 1951.

[21]Knutson Interview, 1986; Knutson to Odean Monson, 22 July 1952; J.L. Rendahl to Friends, May 1953, Presidents' Papers.

[22]Knutson to Friends, 19 February 1952; Knutson to Pastors, 11 September 1952; *Con*, 25 April and 16 May 1952, 27 March 1953; Knutson to Employers, 10 September 1952; Knutson to Faculty, 16 January 1953.

[23]Knutson Interview, 1986; Knutson to R.E. Morton, 23 February 1954.

[24]Knutson Interview, 1986; Carl Bailey Interview, 1985; William Smaby Interview, 1986.

[25]Smaby Interview; Knutson Interviews, 1985 and 1986; J.L. Rendahl Interview, 1984; BDM, 25 March 1952.

[26]Smaby Interview; Knutson to William Smaby, 12 April 1952; W.A. Smaby to Knutson, 27 May 1952.

[27]J.L. Rendahl Interview, 1984.

[28]J.L. Rendahl Interview, 1984.

[29]*Con,* 14 November 1958; Corporation Minutes, 9 October 1958; Noblitt Interview; Knutson to Carl Bailey, 2 April 1971; Bailey Interview, 1985; Knutson Interview, 1986; *CAN*, 9(Summer 1971), 4-5 and 26(Spring 1988), 8; Olin Storvick Interview, 1990; Manning M. Patillo, Jr. and Donald M. Mackenzie, *Eight Hundred Colleges Face the Future: A Preliminary Report of the Danforth Commission on Church Colleges and Universities* (St. Louis, 1965), 68-70.

[30]Dorothy H. Olsen Interview, 1990.

[31]*FF*, 8 April 1973; *Con*, 23 February 1973.

[32]*Con*, 13 December 1963 and 18 November 1988; Olsen Interviews, 1985 and 1990.

[33]Olsen to Knutson, 14 July 1953; Knutson to Olsen, 17 July 1953; Olsen Interview, 1985.

[34]Knutson Interview, 1986; Bailey Interview, 1985.

[35]Ringenberg, 121-122, 215, 218.

[36]*Con*, 28 September, 5 and 12 October, 9 and 16 November 1951, 9 May and 11 December

1952, 12 February and 24 September 1954; *Cob*, 1953, 7 and 1955, 2, 5.

[37]*Con*, 18 January and 2 May 1952, 22 May 1953, 14 May 1954; *Cob*, 1953, 5, 7 and 1954, 22-23.

[38]*Cat*, 1953-1955, 18-19; [Knutson?] Letter to Parents, n.d. [1952?].

[39]*Con*, 26 October, 16 November and 14 December 1951; Knutson Interview, 1986; *CAN*, 17(Summer 1979), 32.

[40]*Con*, 5 October 1951, 13 and 20 February, 6 March and 2 October 1953, 26 February, 12 November and 10 December 1954.

[41]Knutson to Concordia Students, 10 March 1952; *Con*, 2 November 1951, 7 March, 3 October and 12 December 1952, 6 February and 17 April 1953.

[42]*Cob*, 1952, 119-122, 151; *Cat*, 1953-1955, 113.

[43]Knutson to Torgeson, 9 October 1951; *Con*, 16 November, 7 and 14 December 1951, 2 May 1952 and 9 January 1953.

[44]*Con*, 21 March, 4 April, 2 May and 12 December 1952, 16 January, 13 and 20 March, 18 September, 20 November 1953.

[45]*Con*, 15 January, 19 and 26 February, 24 September 1954; FM, 2 December 1949; Administration Committee Minutes, 9 February 1951.

[46]Ravitch, 112; *Con*, 19 October 1951, 11 January, 29 February, 3, 10, 24 and 31 October 1952, 27 February, 5 November and 11 December 1953, 12 and 26 February 1954.

[47]*Con*, 19 and 26 October, 2 November 1951, 15 February 1952.

[48]*Con*, 16 and 30 October 1953, 19 February, 30 April, 22 and 29 October, 10 and 17 December 1954; Paul Dovre to Carroll Engelhardt, 3 January 1990.

[49]*Cob*, 1952, 150; *Con*, 27 March and 17 April 1953.

[50]BDM, 20 October 1952; *Con*, 24 October and 21 November 1952, 27 February, 27 March, 1, 8, 15, and 22 May 1953, 12 and 26 March, 10 December 1954.

[51]*Con*, 27 February and 23 October 1953, 2 May 1952.

[52]Rolfsrud, *Cobber Chronicle*, 166; *Con*, 10 April and 25 September 1953, 26 February 1954.

[53]*Con*, 28 September and 12 October 1951, 15

October 1954; Knutson Interview, 1986.

[54]Alice T. Polikowsky Interview, 1990; Knutson to Pastors, 1 November 1954; Knutson Interview, 1986.

Chapter 12

[1]J.L. Rendahl Interview, 1984; *Con*, 20 September 1963.

[2]DeVane, 18-21; Ravitch, 12-19.

[3]D. Jerome Tweton, "The Business of Agriculture," and David Nass, "The Rural Experience," *Minnesota*, ed. Clark, 263 and 147-148.

[4]*Con*, 11 and 18 May 1956, 4 December 1959, 20 September 1963; Knutson to Leslie Bingum, 12 January 1960 and Knutson to Parents, 12 July 1955.

[5]*Cat*, 1960-1962, 113; *Cob*, 1955, 29; *Con*, 13 January 1956, 12 December 1958, 18 September 1953, 5 November 1954, 18 November 1955, 10 October 1958, 21 October 1960, 23 March and 5 October 1962; Irv Christiansen to Knutson, n.d. [1957?].

[6]*CAN*, 18(Spring 1980), 18-19, 18(Summer 1980), 6, 27(Winter 1987), 20.

[7]*Con*, 12 October and 30 November 1951, 4 April 1952, 23 September and 4 March 1960, 2 October 1981; Knutson to Pastors, 19 September 1956; Knutson to Sidney Rand, 15 October 1957; *CAN*, 18(Summer 1980), 5; *Perspective,* 2(March 1963), 2; *CQR*, 1(June 1955), 2.

[8]*Con,* 16 October 1953, 7 October 1955, 30 September 1960 and 24 September 1965; *CA*, 5(February 1958), 2.

[9]Jarchow, 146; Ringenberg, 210.

[10]*Cat*, 1953-1955, 133 and 1960-1962, 136-137.

[11]American Council of Education Questionaire (1960), Presidents' Papers; BRM, 19 October 1960; Report of Concordia College to the Board of College Education of the American Lutheran Church [1965?], Academic Deans' Papers; *Con*, 12 March 1965; Knutson to Willmar Thorkelson, 26 November 1957.

[12]Peter Anderson to James W. Hampton, 26 June 1951, Academic Deans' Papers; *Cat*, 1960-1962, 24; *Con*, 25 October and 8 November 1963, 23 April 1965, 17 and 24 September 1965; Elizabeth Hassenstab Interview, 1985.

[13]Anderson to Hampton, 26 June 1951, Academic Deans' Papers; *Con*, 11 January 1963,

21 February 1964 and 26 February 1965; *Cat*, 1960-1962, 28 and 1964, 28-32; *TR*, 60(March 1956); *CAN*, 18(Summer 1980), 5; DeVane, 131; Ringenberg, 211.

[14]Leigh D. Jordahl and Harris E. Kaasa, *Stability and Change: Luther College in Its Second Century* (Decorah, 1986), vi-vii; Chrislock, 222-223; National Education Association, Study of College and University Practices and Policies in Instructional Staff Administration (May 1954), American Council of Education Questionnaire (1960) and Undated Document [1965?], Presidents' Papers.

[15]Knutson to Robert Berens, 12 April 1957 and to F.R. Brehmer, 28 September 1957; *Con*, 17 October 1958; Knutson Interview, 1986; Knutson to Mrs. Thomas Gabby, 25 March 1964; Bailey Interview, 1987; Bruce Larson to Martin Lutter, 4 February 1964, Lutter Papers (unless otherwise indicated, Concordia Archives).

[16]Knutson to Concordia Faculty, 19 March 1956; Knutson to Eric Fietz, 19 February 1957 and Eric Fietz to Faculty, 25 February 1957 in Faculty Executive Committee Minutes, 1956-1958; Storvick Interview, 1990.

[17]Bailey Interview, 1985; *Con*, 17 February 1961.

[18]Martin Lutter to Dr. and Mrs. Joseph L. Knutson, 16 April 1975, Lutter Papers.

[19]Knutson to Wendell Weed, 22 August 1956 and to Rand, 16 September 1960; Carl Bailey, "Salary and Rank," November 1955 in Faculty Executive Committee Minutes, 1952-1955; BRM, 18 May 1960.

[20]Harding Noblitt to William Smaby, 4 April 1961, Noblitt Papers; Plan for Summer Employment of Concordia (1960), Presidents' Papers.

[21]BDM, 2 May 1957 and 20 October 1953; BRM, 14 December 1964; Noblitt Interview; Faculty Travel (n.d.), Presidents' Papers.

[22]Bailey to Knutson, 21 January [1957?]; Proposed Policies on Staff Appointment, Tenure, Contract, Promotion and Academic Freedom (February 1961), Presidents' Papers.

[23]Proposed Policies on Staff Appointment . . . (February 1961); Knutson to Edgar Carlson, 2 March 1960.

[24]Proposed Policies on Staff Appointment . . . and Academic Freedom (February 1961); Carl Bailey, "Academic Freedom," *Greater Works*, 6(July 1966), 2-7.

[25]Brubacher and Rudy, 320-329; Mark Noll, "Introduction: Christian Colleges, Christian World Views, and An Invitation to Research," in Ringenberg, *The Christian College*, 36; Ringenberg, 216.

[26]Faculty Executive Committee Minutes, 27 September 1956 and 29 November 1959; Bailey to Knutson and Smaby, 3 October 1957; Knutson to Director of Internal Revenue, 25 July 1962 and 7 May 1963; *Con*, 1 November 1957.

[27]Roger Haugen, "Who is That Man?" *LH*, 26 July 1960, 3-4; *Con*, 14 May 1954, 8 February 1957, 10 October 1958, 3 April 1959, 10 February and 10 October 1961; 21 September 1962 and 7 February 1964.

[28]*Con*, 8 November 1963; Al Anderson to "Brain Pickers," n.d., Academic Deans' Papers.

[29]*Cob*, 1956, 30; Julia Brennun Interview, 1982.

[30]Bailey Interview, 1987; *Con*, 18 January 1952, 8 January 1954 and 26 February 1960.

[31]*Con*, 24 October 1952, 11 November 1955 and 25 October 1957; Knutson to Cordelia Skeim, 22 June 1957.

[32]*Cob*, 1958, 16; Anderson to Hampton, 26 June 1951, Academic Deans' Papers; *Cat*, 1989-1991, 165.

[33]Solberg, 315-317.

[34]Solberg, 311; J.L. Rendahl to Richard W. Solberg, 9 September 1983, Information on Concordia College for LECNA History Project, 1983-1984.

[35]Knutson to Rand, 16 September 1960.

[36]*CQR*, 1(June 1955), 2; *FF*, 19 January 1958.

[37]Jarchow, 144-148; J.M. McDaniel, Jr. to Knutson, 24 June 1957; *Con*, 16 December 1955.

[38]Knutson Interview, 1986; Knutson to Philip Smaby, 19 December 1952; Knutson to Rand, 17 June 1957, 25 January and 27 October 1960; Rand to Knutson, 9 October 1959.

[39]Knutson Interviews, 1985 and 1986; Knutson to Weed, 22 August 1956; Knutson to Jacob Stolee, 21 October 1957; Knutson to Rand, 1 February 1957 and 5 November 1958; *CQR*, 4(October 1958), 1.

[40]*Con*, 18 October and 8 November 1957; Jarchow, 219; Knutson to Martin Ackermann, 4 February 1960; Smaby Interview; Knutson Interview, 1986.

[41]*CA*, 3(May 1956), 1; *CAN*, 2(November 1963), 3; *Con*, 5 April 1963; Knutson to Acker-

mann, 4 February 1960; Knutson to Whom it May Concern, 12 July 1961; Knutson to Milton Wilson, 11 September 1967.

[42]*A Blueprint for Concordia College* (Moorhead, 1962), 3-4; Pattillo and Mackenzie, 68-70.

[43]*Con*, 19 February 1960; Knutson to Martin Ackermann, 4 February 1960; Knutson to Rand, 16 September 1960; Tom Gonser Minutes, 3-5 January, 17-18 February and 8-9 June 1961; Bailey Interview, 1985.

[44]Rolfsrud, *Cobber Chronicle,* 126-129; Smaby Interview; *Con,* 18 October 1957; Knutson to Rand, 25 January 1960.

[45]*Con,* 10 February 1961, 19 and 26 April 1963; *CAN,* 2(November 1963), 7.

[46]Solberg, 308; Ravitch, 229.

[47]Wickey quoted in Solberg, 309; Knutson to Harold Hagen, 22 May 1952; Knutson to Archer Nelson, 14 February 1963; Knutson to Edward J. Thye, 10 March 1958; Knutson Interview, 1986; Knutson to Odin Langen, 14 January 1969 and 22 January 1970.

[48]Jarchow, 146-147, 222; Knutson to Edith Green, 10 March 1962; *Con,* 2 October 1959; J.L. Rendahl Interview, 1984.

[49]Knutson Interview, 1986.

[50]Knutson to O.V. Ellingson, 9 May 1973; Knutson to Mrs. Rodger Jensen, 17 April 1968; *Cob*, 1958, 17; *Cat*, 1953-1955, 122 and 1960-1962, 119-120.

[51]BDM, 30 March 1954; Knutson to Rand, 9 May 1957; Knutson to Moorhead City Council, 2 April 1954; *FF*, 18 November 1954.

[52]Bailey Interview, 1985; Carl R. Narveson, "The Library Situation at Concordia College" (mimeograph, n.d. [1954?]), Presidents' Papers; Knutson to David Berge, 28 December 1954; E.A. Sovik Interview, 1990; *CQR*, 1(June 1955), 3.

[53]*Cob*, 1956, 9; *Con*, 18 March and 18 November 1955, 20 January 1956.

[54]BDM, 30 March 1954; Smaby Interview; *Con,* 3 December 1954 and 19 October 1956.

[55]*Con*, 14 November 1958, 29 April 1955, 15 March 1957, 21 November 1958, 3 April 1959 and 26 February 1960; Knutson to Ed Sovik, 26 April 1958; Knutson to Rand, 20 May 1958 and 20 January 1960.

[56]Knutson to Rand, 25 January 1960; Jarchow, 219; *Con*, 22 September 1961, 12 December 1962, 8 February 1963, 10 September 1965

and 1 September 1967; Rolfsrud, *Cobber Chronicle*, 132-135.

[57]*Cob*, 1962, 14, 44 and 1963, 12-13.

[58]*Cob*, 1964, 31; Knutson to T.E. Tatum, 18 December 1959; Knutson to Paul Guenzel, 13 February 1960; Knutson to C.E. Ronning, 24 February 1960; *Con*, 8 February and 11 October 1963.

[59]Rolfsrud, *Cobber Chronicle*, 135.

Chapter 13

[1]Solberg, 310.

[2]Solberg, 309-310.

[3]Knutson Chapel Talks, 1 and 13 May 1957 (unless otherwise indicated, Presidents' Papers); Knutson, "When is a College Christian?" *Concordian*, 18 October 1957; Knutson to Sidney Rand, 9 May 1957.

[4]Knutson Chapel Talks, 2 April 1955, 17 April 1956 and 30 April 1957; Knutson to Donald C. Spencer, 6 November 1956; Knutson to Lawrence M. Stavig, 30 April 1956.

[5]Knutson to Odean Monson, 16 March 1956; Knutson to M.L. Mahmquist, 12 October 1951; Knutson to Rand, 2 August and 4 September 1957.

[6]*Cat*, 1953-1955, 18-19, 1955-1957, 26, 1960-1962, 34, 1966, 37; Knutson to Concordia Faculty and Staff, 13 September 1962; Knutson to Orville Sunde, 31 March 1962.

[7]Cheryl Urdahl, "Cobber Women Examined," 7 April 1961, Concordia Archives; *Con*, 15 November 1963.

[8]Knutson Interview, 1986; Jim Hoxeng, *et. al.,* "The Blue Paper" (Mimeographed, December 1960), Concordia Archives.

[9]Knutson to Rand, 16 September 1960.

[10]*Con*, 3 November 1961, 12 January 1962, 17 May 1963, 24 April 1964, 26 March 1965.

[11]*Cat*, 1955-1957, 8; J.L. Knutson, "The Purpose of Concordia College," *TR*, 61(July 1957), 4; Ringenberg, 123.

[12]Faculty Executive Committee Minutes, 17 November 1953 and 8 April 1954.

[13]Carl Bailey, "Natural Sciences," *Christian Faith and the Liberal Arts*, ed. Harold H. Ditmanson, *et. al.* (Minneapolis, 1960), iii-iv, 211-223.

[14]Carl Bailey, "What is a Liberal Arts College?"

TR, 58(September 1954) and 61(July 1957); *FF*, 30 May 1965; "Objectives of the College," 5 December 1958, Presidents' Papers; *Cat*, 1960-1962, 6.

[15]*CA*, 5(April 1958), 4; Noblitt Interview; Prausnitz Interview; Walther Prausnitz to Engelhardt, 2 October 1989.

[16]Farden Interview; Noblitt Interview.

[17]*Cat*, 1953-1955, 20-34.

[18]*Cat*, 1958-1960, 13-18, 98; *Con*, 22 November 1957, 7 October and 4 November 1960, 5 October and 9 November 1962, 1 March 1963; *TR*, 67(March 1963), 3.

[19]*Cat*, 1953-1955, 91, 104, 1957-1959, 59-60, 89, 87.

[20]*FSM*, 24 March and 4 April 1952; Noblitt Interview; Bailey Interview, 1987.

[21]*FF*, 15 February 1953; *Con*, 13 May 1955, 22 September 1961, 15 May 1953, 19 March 1954, 11 January 1957 and 1 April 1960; Knutson Interview, 1986.

[22]*Con*, 26 October 1951, 25 May 1955, and 17 April 1959; Corporation Minutes, 21 October 1952, Presidents' Papers; Knutson Interview, 1986; *CA*, 6(April 1959), 3 and *CAN*, 19(Spring 1981), 14; Polikowsky Interview.

[23]*FSM*, 18 November 1955; *Con*, 9 December 1955, 21 September 1956 and 5 February 1960; *Cat*, 1957-1959, 45-47.

[24]*Con*, 13 February, 20 March, 13 November 1959, 14 April 1961, 18 January 1963; Ravitch, 231.

[25]*Con*, 1 March 1957 and 24 May 1963; *LH*, 6 October 1959, 4-5; *CQR*, 3(March 1957), 1.

[26]*TR*, 68(April and December 1964); *CAN*, 5 February 1967), 5; *Con*, 15 May and 23 October 1953.

[27]*Cat*, 1962, 119, 1964, 129 and 1965, 129.

[28]*Con*, 18 February 1955, 24 September 1954, 27 April and 24 July 1956; Christiansen Interview, 1983; Knutson to Ed Neese, 19 March 1954; Prausnitz Interview; *CAN*, 17(Summer 1979), 32-34.

[29]*Con*, 13 February 1953, 2 October, 20 November and 18 December 1959, 15 January 1960, 3 May 1963, 28 February 1964.

[30]*Cat*, 1957-1959, 118; Anderson to Hampton, 26 June 1951, Academic Deans' Papers; Carl Bailey to Engelhardt, 8 November 1989; American Council of Education Questionnaire (1960), Presidents' Papers; *Con*, 17

January 1958, 7 October 1960, 9 February and 2 March 1962, 16 March 1956 and 26 March 1965; Brubacher and Rudy, 283.

[31]*Con*, 29 October 1954, 3 October 1958, 7 December 1962, 8 February 1963, 26 March 1965; *Cat*, 1957-1959, 14.

[32]*Con*, 9 May 1958, 6 March 1959 and 12 October 1962; *Cat*, 1957-1959, 35.

[33]*Con*, 23 and 30 September 1960, 30 August 1965; Carl Bailey to Don Spencer, 15 December 1958, Presidents' Papers; Prausnitz Interview; *CQR*, 6(October 1960), 2; Harding Noblitt to Carl Bailey, 31 July 1961 and Bailey to Noblitt, 3 August 1961, Academic Deans' Papers.

[34]*Con*, 1 November 1963 and 9 April 1965; Bailey to Engelhardt, 8 November 1989.

[35]Knutson to Melvin Voxland, 15 March 1957; Knutson to Eunice C. Roberts, 14 June 1960 and 4 January 1961.

[36]*Con*, 28 September 1951 and 12 December 1962; Susan Goplen, "The Women's Movement and the American Lutheran Church" (Independent Study Project, Concordia College, 1988), 3-4, 11-12.

[37]*TR*, 58(March 1954) and 59(March 1955); *CA*, 8(September 1960), 5; *CAN*, 4(Fall 1965), 18.

[38]*Con*, 8 February 1957, 30 November 1956.

[39]*Con*, 6 March and 4 December 1959, 23 September 1960 and 19 October 1962.

[40]*Cob*, 1963, 3-4.

[41]*Con*, 7 and 12 December 1962.

[42]*CA*, 6(September 1958), 2; *Con*, 4 March and 23 September 1960, 13 January, 2 February and 24 March 1961.

[43]*Con*, 7 March 1958, 23 October and 13 November 1959, 19 April 1963, 11 November 1955, 24 February and 9 March 1956, 24 February 1961; *Cob*, 1955, 30-31, 1956, 26-27, 1957, 84-85, 1961, 160-161, 1962, 154; Dovre to Engelhardt, 3 January 1990.

[44]*Con*, 7 March 1952, 8 February 1957, 6 March and 13 November 1959, 8 February 1963, 22 October 1965; *Cat*, 1960-1962, 113-115.

[45]*Con*, 27 February 1953, 18 February 1955, 20 February 1959 and 8 December 1962.

[46]*Con*, 24 February 1961, 7 December 1956, 31 October 1958, 4 November 1960; Knutson to J. Donald Rice, 13 January 1965.

[47]*Cobber*, 1960, 21.

[48]*Con*, 2 March, 21 September, 26 October, 2 and 12 November 1956, 11 November and 5 February 1960, 6 November 1959, 1 November 1963 and 23 October 1964.

[49]*Con*, 22 April 1955, 16 November and 14 December 1956, 11 January 1957, 28 February 1958, 24 April and 13 November 1959.

[50]Bailey to Engelhardt, 8 November 1989; Richard Werth Interview, 1990; *Con*, 9 January, 20 February and 13 March 1959, 30 October 1964, 25 February 1955 and 20 April 1956.

[51]*Con*, 10 November 1961, 18 October 1963, 10 and 17 January, 7 February 1964 and 12 November 1965.

[52]*Con*, 22 March 1957, 29 April and 2 December 1960, 14 February 1964, 12 March and 12 November 1965.

[53]Knutson to Jack Eichhorst, 17 April 1964; *Cob*, 1964, 30; *Con*, 16 May 1958 and 10 April 1964.

[54]*Cob*, 1955, 30-31 and 1962, 20-27; *Con*, 15 December 1961, 12 March and 10 September 1965; *Cat*, 1960-1962, 112-113 and 1964, 122-124; Knutson to Bailey, 14 April 1959.

[55]Carl Lee Interview, 1990; Knutson to Carl Lee, 13 January 1961; Lee to Knutson, 6 March 1961; Knutson to H.M. Blegen, 2 March 1962; *Con*, 22 September 1961 and 6 March 1964.

[56]*Con*, 2 April 1965.

[57]*Con*, 7 November 1958, 3 April 1959 and 22 March 1963; *Cob*, 1964, 63; Rolfsrud, *Cobber Chronicle*, 227.

[58]*Con*, 4 December 1964; *Cob*, 1966, 17, 20-21.

[59]Knutson to Mrs. Karsten Baalson, 29 September 1965; Knutson to James Brooks, 14 November 1967; *Con*, 8 February 1967.

[60]*Con*, 15 March and 20 December 1957.

[61]*Cat*, 1960-1962, 112.

[62]*Con*, 23 September 1955, 12 April 1957, 12 February 1965; *FF*, 13 March 1958.

[63]*Con*, 1 October 1954, 4 February 1955, 19 May 1961 and 30 August 1965.

[64]*CAN*, 18(Autumn 1979), 18; *Con*, 12 November 1954, 19 October 1956, 20 November 1959, 15 and 22 February 1957, 3 October 1958, 2 February 1968.

[65]*Con*, 6 March 1959, and 11 November 1960, 6

[66]November 1964.

[66]*Con*, 4 May 1956 and 22 April 1960.

[67]*Con*, 23 September 1955, 25 October and 15 November 1957, 23 September 1960, 19 May and 20 October 1961, 25 October 1963; *Cob*, 1961, 116-117.

[68]*Con*, 30 October 1959, 10 February 1956, 18 April 1958, 5 May 1961, 2 April 1965; *Cob*, 1955, 110-111.

[69]*Cat*, 1960-1962, 116; *Con*, 6 March 1953, 29 April 1955, 19 March 1965 and 31 March 1967.

[70]*Cat*, 1960-1962, 115-116; *Cob*, 1955, 93; *Con*, 28 February 1958.

[71]Rolfsrud, *Cobber Chronicle*, 196-198; Knutson to Senator Edward J. Thye, 10 March 1958; Knutson to W.L. Thorkelson, 7 March 1958; *Con*, 12 December 1952, 17 December 1954, 9 December 1955, 19 December 1958 and 16 January 1959.

[72]*Cat*, 1960-1962, 117; *MDN*, 3 March 1956.

[73]*Cat*, 1960-1962, 117; *Con*, 13 January and 21 October 1955, 2 March 1956, *Cob*, 1956, 96.

[74]*Con*, 10 October 1955, 30 October, 13 November and 11 December 1964.

[75]Christenson Interview; *Cob*, 1956, 102-108; *Con*, 27 February 1953, 2 and 30 April 1954, 25 February and 9 December 1955, 21 February and 2 May 1958, 20 March 1959.

[76]*Cob*, 1957, 111, 1959, 102, 122, 1966, 130-131; *Cat*, 1966, 131; *Con*, 28 September 1956, 8 and 22 April 1960.

[77]*Cat*, 1960-1962, 117; *Cob*, 1952, 92-94; *Con*, 20 March 1953 and 24 Janurary 1958.

[78]Rolfsrud, *Cobber Chronicle*, 166; *Cat*, 1960-1962, 115; *Con*, 9 November 1956, 15 February 1957, 3 March 1961 and 22 March 1963.

[79]Dorothy Johnson Interview, 1973; *CAN*, 20(Autumn 1981), 18 and 20(Winter 1981), 4-5; Hassenstab Interview.

[80]*Con*, 16 December 1955, 11 January and 15 February 1957, 10 January, 14 March 1958, 27 February 1959, 19 February and 7 October 1960, 17 May 1963.

[81]*Con*, 25 October 1963 and 3 October 1958.

Chapter 14

[1]Knutson to Room Reservation Clerk, 4 Septem-

ber 1970; *CAN*, 26(Spring 1988), 8; Mrs. Darwin Zahrbock to Knutson, 7 August 1967; J.L. Knutson, "Let's Demonstrate for the Farmer!" *LS*, 8 August 1967, 6-7.

[2]Paul Dovre to Department Chairmen, 26 September 1972; Carl Bailey to Faculty, 10 June 1966, Academic Deans' Papers; *Con*, 5 April 1967.

[3]*CAN*, 7(Winter 1968), 12; Administrative Council Minutes, 11 May 1970; *Con*, 8 November 1968.

[4]*CAN*, 8(Fall 1969), 14; *Con*, 6 September 1968, 11 April and 12 September 1969.

[5]*Con*, 8 September 1972; Paul Dovre to Loren J. Anderson, 26 February 1967, Academic Deans' Papers.

[6]*CAN*, 7(Fall 1968), 15; *Cat*, 1967, 22-23; *Con*, 24 January 1969 and 10 November 1972.

[7]Brubacher and Rudy, 331, 346.

[8]BRM, 4 May 1973; FSM, 7 December 1970; *Con*, 12 January 1973 and 24 January 1975.

[9]*CAN*, 5(August 1966), 9; Faculty Executive Committee Minutes, 11 October 1968; BRM, 30 April 1971; *Blueprint II* (Moorhead, 1974), 4, 9, 10- 11.

[10]O.W. Snarr to Knutson, 19 November 1953; *Con*, 27 September 1957, 17 March 1961, 27 January 1967.

[11]*Con*, 23 February 1968, 11 April and 10 October 1969, 5 February and 13 November 1970, 8 October 1971; Knutson Interview, 1986.

[12]*Con*, 3 November 1967; *Alone* (Concordia Admissions Brochure, [1966-1968?]; *Cat*, 1971, 6.

[13]Rolfsrud to Knutson, 10 February 1964; Joe D. Bjordal to Rolfsrud, 21 February 1975, Rolfsrud Papers.

[14]*Con*, 23 September 1966, 7 and 28 September 1973; *Blueprint II*, 34-38; *CAN*, 7(Fall 1968), 14 and 9(Fall 1970), 16; *Cat*, 1971, 184-185.

[15]President's Report, 1969-1970, in Annual Reports to North Dakota District, Presidents' Papers; Knutson to Pastors and Parents, 18 October 1974.

[16]*Con*, 20 October 1967, 10 October 1969, 4 September 1970, 28 September 1973, 27 September 1974; *Cat*, 1966, 24-36, 1972, 32-33; *CAN*, 5(December 1966), 11.

[17]Carl Bailey to Arthur Grimstad, 15 December 1967, Academic Deans' Papers; Knutson to

B.J. Kemper, 4 April 1967; J.L. Rendahl to Richard W. Solberg, 9 September 1983, Information on Concordia College for LECNA History Project, 1983-1984; *Con*, 19 November 1971 and 16 February 1973; *CAN*, 5(December 1966), 16 and 12(Fall 1973), 2; Solberg, 320.

[18]Brubacher and Rudy, 383; Solberg, 335-336; Jarchow, 147, 222.

[19]Solberg, 337-338.

[20]Smaby Interview; *Con*, 16 October 1964, 28 January and 21 October 1966.

[21]Bailey Interview, 1985; *Con*, 1 March 1963, 4 December 1964, 22 January and 3 September 1965.

[22]*Con*, 27 October 1967 and 25 February 1966; Rolfsrud, *Cobber Chronicle*, 233.

[23]Horowitz, *Alma Mater*, xix; *Con*, 15 October 1965, 3 February and 15 March 1967; Rolfsrud, *Cobber Chronicle*, 232.

[24]*Con*, 30 November 1966, 27 October and 8 December 1967, 26 September 1969; *Cat*, 1989-1991, 13; Rolfsrud, *Cobber Chronicle*, 232-233.

[25]*Con*, 12 December 1969, 20 February 1970 and 1 October 1971; *CAN*, 8(Fall 1969), 28.

[26]*Con*, 8 September 1972 and 8 March 1974; Curtiss Danielson Interview, 1985.

[27]*Con*, 24 January 1969, 11 September 1970 and 21 January 1972.

[28]*Con*, 15 September 1972, 26 October 1973 and 4 April 1975; Rolfsrud, *Cobber Chronicle*, 233-234.

[29]Solberg, 321; Knutson to Norman Fintel, 13 March 1970; Knutson to Raymond M. Olson, 22 November 1966.

[30]Figures supplied by Dee Ann Krugler, Secretary to President and Academic Dean; *CAN*, 7(Winter 1968), 18; Christenson Interview; *Con*, 9 October 1959.

[31]*CAN*, 6(Summer 1968), 5, 16(Winter 1977), 10-11, 26(Winter 1987), 18- 19.

[32]*CAN*, 7(Summer 1969), 5, 15(Spring 1977), 2 and 19(Summer 1981), 5-7; *Con*, 17 April 1964; 1930s Oral History, Session IV, 24 July 1985; Afton Fuglestad Nellermoe Interview, 1990.

[33]*Perspective*, 2(October 1962), 5; Cyrus Running Interview, 1976; *CAN*, 16(Spring 1978), 40.

[34]Running Interview; Thomas Christenson, "Christmas Past," *CAN*, 18(Winter 1979), 10.

[35]*CAN*, 12(Summer 1974), 3 and 16(Spring 1978), 10-11; Thompsons Tribute Dinner Program, 30 March 1974, Concordia Archives.

[36]"The Improvement of Teaching at Concordia College," Teaching Seminar File, 1972, Academic Deans' Papers.

[37]Knutson Interview, 1986; Nelson, *Lutheran Church*, II, 270-271; Solberg, 332; Ringenberg, 199; Jordahl and Kaasa, 23-46; Chrislock, 213- 214, 222-223.

[38]Bailey to Knutson, 24 October 1957; Knutson to Rev. E.O. Stenson, 30 January 1957; Knutson to A.N. Rogness, 19 February 1959.

[39]Knutson to A.N. Rogness, 31 August 1972; Knutson to Herman A. Larsen, 4 March 1963; Knutson to Kent Knutson, 21 November 1968; Knutson to Marc Borg, 17 June 1970; Knutson to Roy A. Harrisville, 27 February 1967; Knutson to Rev. J. Glad, 23 January 1970; Knutson to L.J. Alderink, 29 August 1972.

[40]*CAN*, 7(Spring 1969), 2-3.

[41]Jarchow, 220-221; *Con*, 12 September 1969, 24 April and ll September 1970; *Curriculum Reform for Concordia College* (Moorhead, 1970), iv-vi, 4- 11.

[42]*Cat*, 1971, 15-18.

[43]Ravitch, 69, 225.

[44]*Con*, 11 March 1966 and 3 March 1972; *Cat*, 1973, 74-75; Linda Stoen Interview, 1989.

[45]*Con*, 26 February and 10 December 1965, 27 September 1968, Rolfsrud, *Cobber Chronicle,* 254-255.

[46]*Cat*, 1971, 23-25; *Con*, 27 January 1967, 10 January and 26 September 1969 and 23 March 1973.

[47]Knutson Interview, 1986; BRM, 1 May 1974; *Con*, 3 December 1965, 6 September 1968, 14 March 1969, 4 September 1970, 3 September 1971; Rolfsrud, *Cobber Chronicle,* 252-253.

[48]*CAN*, 18(Spring 1980), 10-12, 34-35; Rolfsrud, *Cobber Chronicle,* 257- 258.

[49]*Cat*, 1966, 145 and 1974, 156; *Con*, 7 April 1967, 14 September 1973, 6 September 1974 and 17 January 1975.

[50]Brubacher and Rudy, 384; Knutson to Paul Dovre, 9 February 1971; Dovre to the Faculty, 14 October 1971, Academic Deans'

Papers; Knutson to Chloe I. Elmgren, 28 March 1972; *Con*, 15 October 1971.

[51]BRM, 4 May 1973.

Chapter 15

[1]Ravitch, 222-224; Horowitz, *Campus Life*, 233-234, 252-253.

[2]Ravitch, 225-226; Jarchow, 152; Brubacher and Rudy, 351-352.

[3]Merton P. Strommen, *et. al., A Study of Generations* (Minneapolis, 1972), 100-110, 258-260, 294; Jordahl and Kaasa, 40.

[4]Knutson to Carl Narveson, 28 November 1967 and 27 November 1968; Knutson to Norman D. Fintel, 11 February 1971; Jim Nestingen to Knutson, 1 October 1967; *FF*, 3 August 1986.

[5]Knutson to Fintel, 3 January 1969 and 13 March 1970; Knutson to Raymond Olson, 24 March 1966; Knutson to J. Elmo Agrimson, 20 February 1967; Knutson, "Just How is it with Concordia?" *CAN*, 10(Fall 1971), 2-3; President's Report, 1965-1966, 1967-1968 and 1969-1970, Annual Reports.

[6]Pattillo and Mackenzie, 65-70; Jordahl and Kaasa, v.

[7]*Blueprint II*, 18, 48-50, 58; Knutson Interview, 1986; Knutson to Paul Dovre, 9 February 1971.

[8]*Cob*, 1967, 32; *Con*, 19 October 1966 and 22 February 1967.

[9]Knutson to Rev. Harry H. Fullilove, 9 April 1968; Paul Dovre to Albert E. Finholt, 4 November 1968, Academic Deans' Papers; *Con*, 16 February 1968; "Integration and Fair Employment Practices," 18 March 1970, Presidents' Papers.

[10]*Con*, 22 September 1967, *Cob*, 1969, 99 and 1970, 93-94; William Kramer to Knutson, 25 November 1969.

[11]*Con*, 6 November 1970, 1 October 1971, 7 January, 4 February and 17 November 1972, 12 October 1973, 22 February 1974; Knutson to Andrew Young, 12 November 1973.

[12]*Con*, 1 October 1971, 7 January, 7 April and 8 September 1972, 30 March 1973 and 4 October 1974.

[13]Knutson to Narveson, 27 November 1968; *Con*, 20 September 1968, 12 September 1969 and 26 October 1973.

[14]*Con*, 26 October and 23 November 1973, 24 January 1974.

[15]*Con*, 29 March 1974, 24 April 1970; Faculty Executive Committee Minutes, 10 February 1969, Noblitt Papers.

[16]*Con*, 11 January 1963, 29 October 1965, 4 February and 18 March 1966; "A Report from the Student Association on Social Dancing at Concordia College," 13 December 1968, Presidents' Papers.

[17]J.L. Knutson, "Concerning Dancing and What Not at Concordia," 15 March 1966, Rolfsrud Papers; Knutson Social Dancing File, 1961-1975; Nils Klungtvedt to Knutson, 7 February 1966; Moorhead Pastors Association to Board of Regents, 25 March 1966, Presidents' Papers.

[18]Sidney Rand to Ralph L. Okland, 4 March 1966.

[19]"A Report from the Student Association on Social Dancing at Concordia College"; *Con*, 31 January 1969; Knutson to Fintel, 11 February 1971; Knutson Interview, 1986; Knutson to James Belgum, 18 March 1969.

[20]*Con*, 20 September, 4 October, 8 and 15 November, 13 December 1968 and 10 January 1969.

[21]*Con*, 12 January 1968, 23 January and 20 November 1970, 15 September 1972 and 26 January 1973.

[22]*Con*, 9 October 1970, 6 October and 17 November 1972, 12 October 1973, 6 and 13 September 1974.

[23]*Cob*, 1970, 86; *Con*, 29 October, 5 and 12 November 1971; 6 September and 1 November 1974; Susan Goplen, "The Women's Movement and the American Lutheran Church: The Impact of Feminism on the ALC, 1961-1975" (Independent Study Project, Concordia College, 1988), 50.

[24]*Con*, 20 February and 6 March 1970; Knutson to Fintel, 21 March 1972; Knutson to Kent Knutson, 11 April 1972.

[25]*Con*, 6 and 27 October 1972; Knutson to Mark Halaas and Larry Van Hunnik, 12 October 1972; BRM, 17 October 1972.

[26]*Con*, 8 and 22 March, 11 October 1974, 21 March 1975; BRM, 28 February 1974.

[27]*Con*, 21 October 1966, 13 and 27 October 1967, 4 October 1968, 11 April, 5 September and 10 October 1969.

[28]*Con*, 19 and 26 September, 3 October 1969, 2

and 16 October 1970, 23 April 1971, 18 January 1974; *CAN*, 8(Summer 1970), 14; Myron Erickson to Knutson, 10 June 1970; Knutson to Erickson, 10 June 1970.

[29]*Con*, 15 March and 6 September 1968, 19 September 1969; *Cob*, 1969, 120.

[30]*Con*, 4 December 1970; Knutson to Concordia Student Body, Faculty and Administration, 7 December 1970; BRM, 10 December 1970.

[31]Knutson, "Suspension of the *Concordian*," n.d. [December 1970?], Presidents' Papers.

[32]Knutson *Concordian* File, 1970-1971; Knutson to Elizabeth Alin, 4 January 1971; Rodger Tveiten to Knutson, 20 December 1970; Merton G. Fish to Knutson, 11 December 1970; Sieghard Krueger to Knutson, 10 December 1970.

[33]Knutson to Concerned Friends, 12 March 1971; *CAN*, 9(December 1971), 11.

[34]Brubacher and Rudy, 278-286; *Cat*, 1967, 16; *Con*, 3 September 1966, 14 February and 25 April 1969, 30 January 1970, 16 March 1973 and 4 April 1975.

[35]*Con*, 17 and 22 March 1967, 9 February 1968, 17 January 1975.

[36]President's Report, 1969-1970, Annual Reports.

[37]Rolfsrud, *Cobber Chronicle*, 247-248; Knutson to Norval R. Wigtil, 21 November 1969; Arthur Grimstad to Rolfsrud, 4 December 1974, Rolfsrud Papers; *Con*, 21 November 1969, 26 March 1971, 13 October 1972 and 1 November 1974.

[38]Knutson to Fintel, 19 March 1965; Knutson to Joe Rutherford, 28 August 1974.

[39]Art Grimstad to ALC, LCA and LC-MS Pastors, 5 December 1969 and J.L. Knutson, "For the Renewal of the Church," September 1969, Presidents' Papers; Knutson to Rev. O.M. Grimsby, 24 April 1970; Julian Erickson to Knutson, *et. al.*, 28 December 1969; Nelson, ed., *Lutherans,* 526.

[40]O.I. Hertsgaard to Knutson, 16 February 1971; *FF*, 1 October 1971.

[41]*Cob*, 1967, 82; *Con*, 25 October 1968; *Blueprint II*, 28-31, 38.

[42]*Con*, 9 September 1966; *Cob*, 1970, 30.

[43]*Con*, 2 December 1966, 7 April and 8 December 1967, 26 September 1969, 20 March 1970, 14 April 1972, 14 and 28 September 1973, 18 January, 22 February, 6 and 27 Sep-

tember 1974; *Cob*, 1968, 34-35.

[44]Knutson to John Xavier, 16 June 1970; Knutson to A.O. Barstad, 30 May 1973.

[45]*Con*, 13 October 1967, 6, 13 and 20 September 1968, 26 September 1969, 3 November 1972 and 16 November 1973.

[46]Brubacher and Rudy, 375-376; *Con*, 10 November 1967, 19 January 1968.

[47]*Con*, 5 September 1969 and 30 January 1970.

[48]*Con*, 29 September 1967, 2 February, 11 October and 6 December 1968, 7 and 21 March, 19 September and 31 October 1969; *Cob*, 1968, 78; Knutson to General Electric Foundation, 31 March 1971.

[49]*Con*, 4 March and 9 September 1966, 8 February and 22 March 1967, 26 September 1969.

[50]*Con*, 15 September 1967, 12 November 1971, 21 April, 8 September, 10 and 21 January 1972, 23 March 1973.

[51]*CAN*, 6(Summer 1968), 7, 7(Summer 1969), 9, 13(Autumn 1974), 7 and 14(Autumn 1975), 24-25; *FF*, 4 May 1969; *Con*, 10 May 1962.

[52]*Cob*, 1969, 81 and 1971, 224-225; *Con*, 15 March and 4 October 1974.

[53]*Con*, 15 February, 8 November, 6 and 13 December 1974.

[54]Accomplishments of Knutson Years, 1951-1975 (mimeograph, n.d.), Presidents' Papers; *Cat*, 1974, 156.

[55]Norman Lorentzsen to Knutson, 6 March 1974; Edgar Carlson to Knutson, 20 February 1974; *CAN*, 13(Autumn 1974), 4-6.

[56]*FF*, 22 December 1974.

[57]*CAN*, 13(Summer 1975), 5; Bailey Interview, 1987.

[58]Knutson to Kemper, 27 September 1973 and 1974; Knutson Interview, 1985 and 1986.

[59]Knutson Interview, 1985; *Con*, 16 February 1973; Knutson to C.M. Granskou, 18 April 1975; *FF*, 23 January 1981.

Chapter 16

[1]BRM, 1 May and 14 December 1974.

[2]*Con*, 3 May 1957, 20 March 1959, 20 September 1963, 4 September 1964, 6 September 1968 and 17 January 1975.

[3]*FF*, 22 December 1974; J.L. Knutson to Bernadine Thoennes, 17 December 1968 and to Melvin R. Knudson, 17 September 1974; President's Report, 1974- 1975, Annual Reports File, Presidents' Papers.

[4]Louise Nettleton, "First Lady," *CAN*, 24(Winter 1985), 5.

[5]*CAN*, 13(Spring 1975), 13.

[6]*CAN*, 13(Summer 1975), 14-15.

[7]BRM, 23 July and 18-19 September 1975; *CAN*, 14(Autumn 1975), 15-16.

[8]*CAN*, 14(Winter 1975), 20-25.

[9]*CAN*, 14(Summer 1976), 14-15.

[10]FSM, 13 April 1976; BRM, 30 April 1976.

[11]*CAN*, 14(Autumn 1975), 6-7.

[12]*CAN*, 13(Summer 1975), 5; BRM, 2 May 1975; Paul Dovre to Lloyd Svendsbye, 14 May 1975, Academic Deans' Papers; *Con*, 27 April 1979.

[13]BRM, 7 December 1979; Bruce C. Swaffield, "Pursuing the Dream," *The Roanoke College Magazine*, (Summer 1989), 8-11.

[14]*Con*, 5 September 1980 and 15 September 1989; *CAN*, 24(Autumn 1985), 16.

[15]*CAN*, 14(Spring 1976), 4; BRM, 22 June and 4 December 1982.

[16]BRM, 29 April 1977, 25 April 1980, 20 June 1984 and 15 May 1985; *CAN*, 26(Autumn 1987), 30.

[17]Dovre to Engelhardt, 15 May 1990; Paul Dovre Interview, 1990.

[18]BRM, 25 April 1980, 25 April and 6 December 1986, 28 April 1978; David Gring Interview, 1989; Loren Anderson Interview, 1990; James Hausmann Interview, 1990; Clyde Allen Interview, 1990; Dovre Interview; Dovre to Engelhardt, 15 May 1990.

[19]*CAN*, 15(Winter 1976), 14-15; *Con*, 4 September 1981; BRM, 20 September 1982; *Blueprint III: A Long-Range Plan for Concordia College* (Moorhead, 1983), 4-6.

[20]*CAN*, 15(Autumn 1976), 23; J. Victor Hahn, ed., *Lutheran Higher Education in the 1980s: Heritage and Challenge* (Washington, D.C., 1980), 51; Ravitch, 305, 311, 318.

[21]BRM, 10 December 1977, 10 December 1983, 28 April, 13 June and 14-16 September 1989; Dovre to Engelhardt, 15 May 1990.

[22]Malvey Interview; *Con*, 8 December 1989; *CAN*, 25(Winter 1986), 14-15; Norman Lorentzsen Interview, 1990.

[23]*Cob*, 1979, 134; BRM, 28 April 1979; *CAN*, 28(Autumn 1989), 5; *Con*, 5 October 1984.

[24]Paul J. Dovre, "What is Lutheran About Church Colleges?" *LS*, 3 February 1976, 8-9; Dovre, Faculty Banquet Address, 23 August 1976; Dovre, "The Road to Freedom," Convocation Address, 1986; Dovre, "The Marks of Community," Convocation Address, 3 September 1987; Dovre, "The Academic Culture," Faculty Banquet Address, 27 August 1987.

[25]*Cob*, 1980, 254; *CAN*, 18(Autumn 1979), 29 and 23(Spring 1985), 9; Lee Interview.

[26]BRM, 26 April 1984; Richard Solberg and Merton P. Strommen, *How Church-Related Are Church-Related Colleges?* (New York, 1980), 57, 62; *CAN*, 26(Winter 1987), 22; Dovre to Engelhardt, 15 May 1990.

[27]Qualey and Gjerde, 242; *CAN*, 14(Winter 1975), 5 and 18(Autumn 1979), 20; *Cob*, 1979, 80, 82.

[28]*TR*, 86(October 1982).

[29]J.L. Rendahl to Richard Solberg, 6 June 1983, LECNA History Project Materials, 1983-1984, Concordia College Archives; Paul Dovre, "Colleges in the New Church," *CAN*, 23(Autumn 1984), 22.

[30]BRM, 18 September 1980; *Con*, 13 and 27 October 1978; *CAN*, 18(Autumn 1979), 20.

[31]*Cob*, 1985, 60.

[32]Dovre to Engelhardt, 15 May 1990; Dovre, Address to ELCA Council of College Presidents, 2 February 1988; Dovre, "Colleges in the New Church," 22-23; Dovre, "Concordia: College of the Church," *CAN*, 26(Autumn 1987), 8- 9.

[33]BRM, 28 April 1978 and 22 September 1979; *Con*, 18 January 1980.

[34]Gring Interview; Noblitt Interview; Farden Interview; Prausnitz Interview.

[35]Farden Interview; Prausnitz Interview.

[36]Dovre to Engelhardt, 15 May 1990; Don Dale Interview, 1990; Dovre, "Habits of the Heart," Faculty Banquet Address, 22 August 1985.

[37]*Con*, 2 November 1979, 8 October 1982 and 16 February 1990; *CAN*, 25(Winter 1986), 9 and 25(Spring 1987), 22; Dovre to Engelhardt, 15 May 1990.

[38]*Con*, 19 November 1982, 13 December 1985 and 21 April 1990; *CAN*, 24(Winter 1985),

19, 26(Spring 1988), 23 and 28(Winter 1989), 18; *Intercom*, 22 May 1990.

[39]*CAN*, 24(Winter 1985), 4-5; Gring Interview.

[40]*CAN*, 19(Winter 1980), 14.

[41]*LS*, 16 September 1983, 4-8.

[42]*Cob*, 1980, 254.

Chapter 17

[1]*Cat*, 1979-1981, 32 and 1987-1989, 147.

[2]Ravitch, 324; Cremin, III, 555; Clarke Chambers, "Educating for the Future," *Minnesota*, ed. Clark, 479.

[3]*CAN*, 25(Autumn 1986), 15; BRM, 4 October and 8 December 1984, 26 April 1985 and 3 December 1988; *Cat*, 1989-1991, 32.

[4]Hausmann Interview; Nicholas R. Ellig, "The Composition of Concordia's Student Population," *Blueprint IV Resource Papers* (Moorhead, 1989), 54; BRM, 4 December 1982; *Con*, 21 September 1979.

[5]*CAN*, 24(Autumn 1985), 10-12, 25(Winter 1986), 22; *Cat*, 1989-1991, 32, 164; Ellig, 54-55.

[6]*CAN*, 13(Spring 1975), 3, 15(Autumn 1976), 25, 15(Summer 1977), 9, 16(Autumn 1977), 26.

[7]James Hausmann, "Admissions and the Liberal Arts," *Lutheran Higher Education in the 1980s*, 61.

[8]BRM, 18 September 1986; *TR*, 88(March 1984) and 93(September 1989); *Con*, 18 October 1985.

[9]*CAN*, 26(Autumn 1987), 16, *Con*, 17 September 1976 and 11 November 1983.

[10]*CAN*, 26(Winter 1987), 11; *Con*, 11 September 1981; *Cob*, 1989, 153.

[11]*CAN*, 13(Summer 1975), 17, 24(Spring 1986), 8-9 and 26(Winter 1987), 14, 17.

[12]*TR*, 93(December 1989), 2; *CAN*, 24(Autumn 1985), 12.

[13]*Cat*, 1975-1976, 25, 29-33; *Con*, 15 October 1976; *CAN*, 15(Autumn 1976), 26, 21(Autumn 1982), 23, 28(Autumn 1989), 13.

[14]*CAN*, 24(Autumn 1985), 10 and 27(Autumn 1988), 6.

[15]*CAN*, 15(Autumn 1976), 4; BRM, 10 February 1976, 22 September 1979, 25 April 1980 and 24 April 1981; *Con*, 6 and 27 March, 3 April

1981.

[16]*Cob*, 1988, 228; BRM, 23 July 1975.

[17]BRM, 31 December 1986, 16 October 1987 and 13 June 1988; Morris Lanning Interview, 1990; *Cob*, 1988, 229.

[18]BRM, 24 October 1975; *CAN*, 14(Winter 1975), 6; *Con*, 10 October 1980.

[19]BRM, 27 March 1985; *CAN*, 22(Spring 1984), 4-5; *Con*, 6 September 1985; *Cob*, 1985, 161.

[20]BRM, 31 December 1986 and 5 December 1987.

[21]BRM, 16 September 1987; *CAN*, 26(Winter 1987), 2; *Con*, 22 September 1989.

[22]*Con*, 9 September 1988 and 8 September 1989.

[23]*CAN*, 14(Summer 1976), 30, 23(Autumn 1984), 7, 27(Autumn 1988), 6; *Con*, 7 October 1977, 21 April and 1 September 1978, 18 January 1980 and 10 February 1984; BRM, 10 April 1987 and 13 June 1988.

[24]*CAN*, 27(Spring 1989), 9.

[25]Sovik Interview; *Blueprint II*, 97; "Campus Concept Plan," Long Range Planning Committee Minutes.

[26]*Cob*, 1980, 15; *CAN*, 25(Winter 1986), 2.

[27]*CAN*, 14(Summer 1976), 26-27, 16(Spring 1978), 40, 23(Winter 1984), 2 and 25(Winter 1986), 8-9; *Cob*, 1979, 53 and 1982, 45.

[28]*Cob*, 1982, 17, 1986, 82; *Con*, 22 September 1989 and 9 March 1990; Sovik Interview.

[29]*HBG*, 17(May 1985), 4; *Cob*, 1980, 9.

[30]*CAN*, 19(Summer 1981), 15, 26(Autumn 1987), 14 and 28 (Autumn 1989), 7; *Con*, 5 December 1980.

[31]*CAN*, 15(Autumn 1976) 27 and 28(Autumn 1989), 7; *TR*, 88(April 1984), 6.

[32]Loren Anderson Interview.

[33]BRM, 6 December 1976; *Con*, 14 January 1976 and 3 February 1978; *CAN*, 16(Spring 1978), 2, 22.

[34]Loren Anderson Interview; *CAN*, 22(Winter 1983), 14-15, 25(Autumn 1986), 3, 10.

[35]*CAN*, 26(Winter 1987), 18; BRM, 22 April 1988 and 14-16 September 1989; *Con*, 6 October 1989.

[36]*Con*, 23 September 1988; *CAN*, 27(Autumn 1988), 6 and 28(Autumn 1989), 16; BRM, 8 December 1984.

[37]BRM, 29 April 1977, 25 April 1980 and 20 September 1982; *Con*, 14 October 1988.

[38]BRM, 18 September 1975; *CAN*, 15(Autumn 1976), 27, 16(Spring 1978), 19- 20, 22(Autumn 1983), 36, 25(Autumn 1986), 14, 20, 28(Autumn 1989), 7; "Update: Centennial Fund," *CAN*, 28(Winter 1989), 8; *Con*, 4 September 1981, *TR*, 90(November 1986).

[39]*Con*, 9 March and 12 October 1979, 10 February 1984, 17 January 1986; *Cob*, 1985, 91 and 1987, 236.

[40]*CAN*, 14(Winter 1975), 19 and 27(Autumn 1988), 7.

[41]*CAN*, 15(Autumn 1976), 26 and 27(Autumn 1988), 5, 15.

[42]Loren Anderson Interview; *CAN*, 18(Autumn 1979), 22-23 and 27(Autumn 1988), 5.

[43]*Blueprint III*, 45-49.

Chapter 18

[1]Cremin, III, 661-662; Ernest L. Boyer, *College: The Undergraduate Experience in America* (New York, 1987), 2-6, 12, 90, 102.

[2]Cremin, III, 563, 664, 674-675; Horowitz, *Campus Life*, 263, 268, 288; Ravitch, 226.

[3]Ringenberg, 199; Solberg, 341-343.

[4]Solberg, 347-348.

[5]*Blueprint III*, 7, 19-22, 26-28.

[6]*Blueprint III*, 29-31; *Con*, 27 January 1984.

[7]*An Agenda for Concordia's Academic Life: A Curriculum Plan for Concordia College* (Moorhead, 1984), 6, 8-17; *CAN*, 26(Autumn 1987), 10.

[8]David Gring, "A College of Distinction in Service to Students," *Teaching at Concordia*, 12(1988-1989), 1-4; BRM, 24 April 1987.

[9]Christiansen Interview, 1985; *Con*, 7 December 1979 and 25 April 1986; *CAN*, 24(Spring 1986), 5-6.

[10]*Perspective*, 4(Winter 1964); *CAN*, 9(Winter 1970), 8; *Con*, 11 December 1981.

[11]*CAN*, 27(Spring 1989), 6 and 27(Winter 1988), 20; *TR*, 87(July 1983).

[12]*Con*, 19 October 1979; *TR*, 87(July 1983) and 88(January 1984).

[13]*CAN*, 15(Winter 1976), 20; *TR*, 86(October 1982).

[14]*CAN*, 24(Spring 1986), 19; *Con*, 8 September 1989.

[15]*Con*, 3 November and 1 December 1989.

[16]*CAN*, 14(Winter 1975), 18 and 26(Winter 1987), 21; *FF*, 22 April 1990.

[17]Gring Interview.

[18]Ravitch, 291-292; H. Robert Homann, "Challenges of Recruitment of Faculty," *Blueprint IV*, 2-3.

[19]*Con*, 15 September 1978, 28 March 1980 and 30 November 1984; BRM, 23 April 1982.

[20]*CAN*, 15(Autumn 1976), 24; *Cob*, 1989, 36-37; "Teaching and Scholarship:A Panel Discussion of Experience of Bush Scholars," *Teaching at Concordia*, 5-10.

[21]*CAN*, 27(Autumn 1988), 8-9.

[22]*Cat*, 1979-1981, 18.

[23]Paul Dovre to Ab Hermann, 2 September 1976 and to Harding Noblitt, 15 December 1976, Noblitt Papers; *Con*, 3 September and 12 November 1976; *CAN*, 14(Spring 1976), 2.

[24]*Con*, 24 September 1982; *Cob*, 1983, 46; FSM, 17 September 1984 and 22 April 1985; *CAN*, 25(Autumn 1986), 2.

[25]*Cob*, 1986, 46 and 1989, 20; *CAN*, 26(Winter 1987), 12-13.

[26]*Con*, 21 April 1978, 7 November 1980 and 1 November 1985; *CAN*, 26(Spring 1988), 9-11 and 14(Spring 1975), 5; *Con*, 2 February 1979, 4 February 1983 and 31 January 1986.

[27]Gring Interview.

[28]*Agenda for Concordia's Academic Life*, 23-24; *CAN*, 24(Autumn 1985), 8.

[29]*Agenda for Concordia's Academic Life*, 34-39.

[30]*Con*, 11 November 1983, 27 January and 17 February 1984, 17 January 1986; Prausnitz Interview; Gring Interview; Barbara Olive, "Writing and Speaking in Academic Program," *Blueprint IV*, 26.

[31]*Cat*, 1975-1976, 19, 1989-1991, 28-29; *CAN*, 14(Spring 1976), 16-17.

[32]*CAN*, 15(Spring 1977), 4; *Con*, 9 September 1983; *TR*, 91(October 1987).

[33]*Con*, 29 September 1989; Susan Gammill, "Computers in the Academic Program," *Blueprint IV*, 31-32.

[34]*Cat*, 1975-1976, 152, and 1989-1991, 12; *Con*, 28 January 1977, 9 October 1981 and 13 October 1989; Verlyn Anderson Interview, 1985.

[35]*Cat*, 1989-1991, 28; Verlyn Anderson, "The Library and Ancillary Services," *Blueprint IV*, 35.

[36]*Cob*, 1988, 16.

[37]*Cat*, 1975-1976, 5 and 1989-1991, 21; *Con*, 7 October 1977; Office of Registrar, Distribution of Majors and Minors For Concordia Graduating Classes of 1975 and 1988.

[38]*CAN*, 25(Winter 1986), 22 and 25(Spring 1987), 24.

[39]*TR*, 88(April 1984), 3 and 93(November 1989), 2; *CAN*, 16(Spring 1978), 7 and 24(Autumn 1985), 9; *Con*, 4 October 1985.

[40]*Cat*, 1975-1976, 19 and 1989-1991, 28; *Con*, 11 March 1977; *CAN*, 24(Autumn 1985), 9; *TR*, 90(September 1986).

[41]*The F/M Communiversity, 1965-1990*, 7, 17; *CAN*, 16(Summer 1977), 24-25 and 18(Spring 1980), 35-36.

[42]*Con*, 3 November 1989.

[43]*Con*, 9 February 1990; *CAN*, 19(Winter 1981), 16.

[44]*Con*, 10 September 1976, 15 September and 6 October 1978.

[45]*Con*, 3 October 1980, 10 October 1982 and 18 January 1985.

[46]*Con*, 5 November 1982; *Cat*, 1989-1991, 166-172; Polly Fassinger, "Women's Studies' Impact on the Academic Life of Concordia College," *Blueprint IV*, 15; Dee Ann Krugler to Engelhardt, 24 May 1991.

[47]*CAN*, 25(Autumn 1986), 13.

[48]*Cat*, 1975-1976, 148 and 1978-1980, 104-105; Walter McDuffy Interview, 1990; *CAN*, 28(Autumn 1989), 11.

[49]*Con*, 4 February and 17 September 1976, 4 February and 16 September 1977, 10 and 17 February, 22 September 1978.

[50]*Con*, 8 February 1985; *Cob*, 1983, 112.

[51]Minnesota Private College Research Foundation Indian Research Education Project, Minutes, 11 and 21 November 1975, Academic Deans' Papers; *Con*, 21 January and 1 April 1977, 21 April 1978, 21 February 1986; *Cob*, 1985, 111.

[52]Warner Huss Interview, 1990; *Con*, 30 September 1988 and 6 April 1990.

[53]*Con*, 1 April 1977 and 27 January 1978; *CAN*, 16(Spring 1978), 5; *CAN*, 16(Autumn 1977), 25; Verlyn Anderson Interview; *Cob,* 1983, 130.

[54]*CAN*, 13(Summer 1975), 5, 15(Autumn 1976), 6 and 26(Spring 1988), 23-24.

[55]*CAN*, 27(Spring 1989), 24; *Cob*, 1988, 27.

[56]*TR*, 86(December 1982); *Con*, 22 October 1982; BRM, 18 September 1986.

[57]*Cob*, 1989, 32; *Cat*, 1989-1991, 30; FSM, 6 October 1986; *CAN*, 27(Autumn 1988), 8 and 27(Winter 1988), 5-7.

[58]BRM, 10 December 1983.

[59]*CAN*, 14(Autumn 1975), 17 and 27(Autumn 1988), 17; *Con*, 28 October 1988; *Cob*, 1989, 10, 16.

[60]Brubacher and Rudy, 263; Cremin, 662-664, 672-673.

[61]Prausnitz to Engelhardt, 21 June 1990; Prausnitz, "Liberal Arts Education: Perspective of Students and Graduates," *Blueprint IV*, 52.

Chapter 19

[1]*CAN*, 26(Autumn 1987), 12-13 and 24(Autumn 1985), 10-11; *Blueprint III*, 37.

[2]*Cob*, 1983, 4 and 1988, 2.

[3]*Con*, 8 September 1989.

[4]*Cob*, 1979, 25, 1980, 9 and 1989, 12; *Con*, 8 September 1989.

[5]*Cob*, 1976, 1; *Cat*, 1975-1976, 149; *Con*, 16 February 1990.

[6]*Con*, 10, 17 and 24 September, 1 October 1976, 7 October and 2 December 1977, 29 September 1978, 30 January 1981, 11 April and 5 December 1986; *Cob*, 1979, 38; *Cat*, 1989-1991, 49; Paul Dovre to Parents, 28 October 1986; Lanning Interview.

[7]Lanning Interview; *Con*, 27 January 1978 and 21 February 1986.

[8]Residence Hall Handbook, 1989-1990, 7; Lanning Interview; *Con,* 11 Janaury 1980, 11 December 1981, 10 February and 28 September 1984, 30 September and 9 December 1988; *CAN*, 27(Autumn 1988), 9-10 and 28(Autumn 1989), 10.

[9]Lee Interview; *Con*, 26 September 1980 and 8 September 1989; *CAN*, 16(Autumn 1977), 7.

[10]*CAN*, 27(Autumn 1988), 10; BRM, 7 December 1985.

[11]Residential Life Student Staff Handbook, 1989-1990, 8; Lanning Interview; *CAN*, 24(Autumn 1985), 11 and 26(Autumn 1987), 12; *Cat*, 1978-1980, 96.

[12]*Cob*, 1980, 2.

[13]*CAN*, 18(Spring 1980), 37-38.

[14]*CAN*, 27(Spring 1989), 15.

[15]E.A. Sovik, *Architecture for Worship* (Minneapolis, 1973), 9-10, 18-21, 37-39, 61-64, 68, 70; *Con*, 3 December 1976; *CAN*, 14(Spring 1976), 18-19.

[16]*CAN*, 24(Autumn 1985), 7; *Con*, 22 April 1977 and 13 January 1984; *Cob*, 1979, 129 and 1983, 160.

[17]*Con*, 7 February 1986; *Cob*, 1986, 152; *CAN*, 24(Winter 1985), 7.

[18]*Cat*, 1975-1976, 148-149; BRM, 3 December 1988; *Con*, 17 November and 1 December 1989; *Cob*, 1983, 52, 1988, 64, 1989, 197.

[19]Lee Interview; Carl Lee and Philip Holton, "Worship and Community," *Blueprint IV*, 59; *Cob*, 1988, 212 and 1989, 202.

[20]*CAN*, 14(Autumn 1975), 18; *Cob*, 1983, 161; *TR*, 84(March 1980) and 86(March 1982); *Con*, 18 November 1983 and 1 December 1989; *Intercom*, 19 December 1989.

[21]*CAN*, 25(Spring 1987), 5-7, 27(Autumn 1988), 11, 28(Autumn 1989), 10 and 28(Spring 1990), 20.

[22]For examples of religious controversy, see *Con*, 10 and 17 November 1989.

[23]*TR*, 91(December 1987); *Cob*, 1987, 71, 1988, 65, 1989, 193; *Con*, 19 January 1990.

[24]*Con*, 14 November and 5 December 1980, 8 December 1989 and 16 March 1990; *Cob*, 1987, 243.

[25]*Con*, 9 November 1979 and 23 February 1990; *Cob*, 1980, 38-39, 56, 1981, 33, 1987, 235, 1988, 252.

[26]*Con*, 17 September and 8 October 1976, 14 April and 22 September 1978, 20 April, 31 August and 30 November 1979, 25 January and 14 November 1980, 6 February 1981, 29 January 1982, 20 January 1984 and 23 February 1990.

[27]*Con*, 5, 19 and 26 September, 3, 24 and 31 October 1980, 2 November 1984 and 4 November 1988.

[28]*Cat*, 1979-1981, 17; *Cob*, 1987, 85; *CAN*, 14(Autumn 1975), 4; *Con*, 15 September and 3 November 1989.

[29]*Cat*, 1975-1976, 141-142, 1976-1977, 153 and 1978-1980, 97; *CAN*, 15(Autumn 1976), 25; *Cob*, 1979, 149, 1980, 65, 1988, 70; *Con*, 23 September 1977, 13 October, 17 November and 1 December 1989.

[30]*Con*, 8 and 22 September 1989.

[31]*Con*, 8 and 15 November 1985.

[32]*Con*, 3, 10 and 17 September 1982, 4 March 1983.

[33]*Con*, 21 April 1978 and 9 March 1990; *Cob*, 1989, 84.

[34]*Con*, 30 March and 19 October 1979; *Cob*, 1985, 67 and 1988, 48.

[35]*Cat*, 1975-1976, 144; *Cob*, 1983, 120; *Con*, 11 October 1985; *TR*, 85(June 1981) and 86(June 1982); *CAN*, 26(Autumn 1987), 6.

[36]*Cat*, 1975-1976, 144; *CAN*, 26(Autumn 1987), 6, 26(Spring 1988), 26, 27(Winter 1988), 20 and 27(Spring 1989), 12-13.

[37]*TR*, 87(March 1983); *CAN*, 24(Winter 1985), 21, 25(Autumn 1986), 5.

[38]*CAN*, 25(Autumn 1986), 32 and 25(Winter 1986), 7; *Con*, 13 October 1989.

[39]*CAN*, 14(Summer 1976), 5 and 24(Spring 1986), 21; *Cat*, 1975-1976, 144-145 and 1979-1981, 18; *TR*, 93(December 1989), 1.

[40]*TR*, 87(December 1983); *Con*, 27 April 1990.

[41]*Cob*, 1979, 37, 1980, 101, 1984, 201, 1985, 80 and 1987, 142; *Con*, 12 January 1979, 20 November 1981, 6 and 13 October 1989; *CAN*, 15(Summer 1977), 31, 16(Spring 1978), 12-15, 25(Winter 1986), 9 and 27(Winter 1988), 24; *TR*, 86(April 1982).

[42]*Con*, 10 and 17 March 1978; *CAN*, 16(Winter 1977), 44; *Cob*, 1979, 131, 133; *TR*, 86(April 1982) and 87(July 1983).

[43]*Cob*, 1987, 148; *CAN*, 24(Winter 1985), 24 and 25(Spring 1987), 20 and 28(Spring 1990), 24-25.

[44]*Cob*, 1979, 166, 1980, 116 and 1984, 215; *TR*, 86(April 1982); *CAN*, 24(Spring 1986), 20, 25(Spring 1987), 20, 26(Spring 1988), 20-21 and 28(Spring 1990), 24.

[45]*Cob*, 1983, 86; *CAN*, 24(Spring 1986), 21, 27(Winter 1988), 24 and 28(Spring 1990), 24; *FF*, 27 May 1990.

[46]*Cob*, 1979, 110 and 157, 1980, 76, 1983, 101, 1984, 44 and 62, 1986, 138, 1988, 37 and 218, 1989, 155; *Con*, 15 November 1985.

[47]*Cob*, 1979, 59, 1985, 109, 1986, 136, 1987, 30-31 and 1989, 133; *Con*, 2 December 1977, 19 January 1979, 16 January 1981 and 1 December 1989.

[48]*CAN*, 18(Autumn 1979), 24 and 26(Autumn 1987), 13; *Con*, 3 February 1984; *TR*, 91(February 1987); *Cat*, 1989-1991, 27.

[49]*Cob*, 1981, 156, 1983, 20 and 25; *Con*, 5 September 1980 and 12 February 1982; *CAN*, 25(Autumn 1986), 12-13.

[50]*CAN*, 23(Autumn 1984), 38, 25(Autumn 1986), 20-21, 25(Spring 1987), 14, 26(Autumn 1987), 36 and 27(Winter 1988), 2.

[51]*CAN*, 27(Spring 1989), 5.

[52]*CAN*, 27(Spring 1989), 36.

[53]*Con*, 29 September and 1 December 1989.

[54]*Cob*, 1980, 42; *TR*, 87(December 1983).

Epilogue

[1]*Catalog*, 1989-1991, 9-10.

[2]*Blueprint IV* (Draft Copy, August 1990), 2-4.

[3]Ibid., 5-6.

[4]Ibid., 22.

[5]Ibid., 36.

[6]Jean Gumper, *et. al.*, "How Faculty See Themselves," and Polly Fassinger, "Inclusive Education," *Blueprint IV*, 11 and 19.

Picture Credits

The majority of photographs and illustrations were provided by Concordia College Archives and the Office of Communications. Individuals who supplied additional photographs are listed below.

Borge, John   294, 295(top), 297(bottom), 298(top), 303, 305, 312, 314(top), 315(bottom), 316, 317(top), 324(top), 327, 331, 332, 336, 337, 339, 344(top), 345, 346, 350, 351(top), 352, 354, 357(top)

Fenton, Kelly   309

Hanson, Art   302, 335, 351(top)

Hanson, Russ   85(bottom)

Hetland, David   343, 353, 357(bottom)

Johnson, Michael   295(bottom), 313(bottom)

Lee, Ron   340(bottom)

Mathre, Stevie   314(bottom), 318

Miller, Nathan   329, 342, 356(bottom)

Thykeson, Michelle   313(top)

Index

A

E

F

G

J

I

K

L

N

412

V

W

Y

Z